EAST SUSSEX CORONERS' RECORDS

1688–1838

EAST SUSSEX CORONERS' RECORDS

1688–1838

Edited by

R F Hunnisett

SUSSEX RECORD SOCIETY
VOLUME 89

Issued to members of the Society for the year 2005

Published in 2005 by
Sussex Record Society
Barbican House
Lewes
East Sussex
BN7 1YE

ISBN 085445 068 8

Printed by Hobbs the Printers Ltd., Totton, Hampshire.

SUSSEX RECORD SOCIETY

VOLUMES ISSUED BY THE SOCIETY

Vol. 1 *Marriage Licences at Lewes, 1586-1642*

Vol. 2 *Sussex Fines, 1190-1248*

Vol. 3 *Post Mortem Inquisitions, 1558-1583*

Vol. 4 *Ecclesiastical Returns for East Sussex, 1603; Sussex Poll Book, 1705; Sussex MSS in the Harleian MSS; Bishop Praty's Register, 1438-1445.*

Vol. 5 *West Sussex Protestation Returns, 1641-1642*

Vol. 6 *Marriage Licences at Lewes, 1670-1732*

* Vol. 7 *Sussex Fines, 1249-1307*

* Vol. 8 *Bishop Rede's Register, 1397-1415 (Pt.1)*

Vol. 9 *Marriage Licences at Chichester 1575-1730*

* Vol. 10 *Subsidy Rolls, 1296, 1327 and 1332*

* Vol. 11 *Bishop Rede's Register, 1397-1415* (Pt. I)

* Vol. 12 *Marriage Licences at Chichester* (peculiars), 1579-1730

* Vol. 13 *Cuckfield Parish Register, 1598-1699*

Vol. 14 *Post Mortem Inquisitions, 1485-1649*

Vol. 15 *Bolney Parish Register, 1541-1812*

Vol. 16 *Star Chamber Proceedings, 1500-1558*

Vol. 17 *Ardingly Parish Register, 1558-1812*

Vol. 18 *Angmering Parish Register, 1562-1687*

Vol. 19 *Sussex Manors and Advowsons, etc., 1509-1833*, A-L

Vol. 20 *Sussex Manors and Advowsons, etc., 1509-1833*, M-Z

Vol. 21 *Horsham Parish Register, 1541-1635*

Vol. 22 *Cowfold Parish Register, 1558-1812*

Vol. 23 *Sussex Fines, 1308-1509*

Vol. 24 *East Grinstead Parish Register, 1558-1661*

Vol. 25 *Marriage Licences at Lewes, 1771-1837*, A-L

Vol. 26 *Marriage Licences at Lewes, 1772-1837*, M-Z

Vol. 27 *Preston Manor Court Rolls, 1562-1702*

Vol. 28 *Sussex Apprentices and Masters, 1710-1752*

Vol. 29 *Abstracts of Documents relating to the Dobell family*, 16th-18th cents.

Vol. 30 *Glynde Parish Register, 1558-1812*

Vol. 31 *Thirteen Custumals of the Sussex Manors of the Bishop of Chichester, c.1256-1374*

Vol. 32 *Sussex Marriage Licences at Chichester, 1731-1774*

Vol. 33 *Sussex Inquisitions (from Bodleian Library), 1541-1616*

Vol. 34 *The Book of John Rowe, Steward to Lord Bergavenny, 1622*

Vol. 35 *Marriage Licences at Chichester, 1775-1800*, with Index covering Licences, 1731-1800

Vol. 36 *Sussex Chantry Records, 1535-1652*

Vol. 37 *Hastings Rape Records, 1387-1474*

Vol. 38 *Chartulary of Lewes Priory* (Pt. I), 11th-14th cents.

Vol. 39 *The Buckhurst Terrier, 1597-1598*

Vol. 40 *Chartulary of Lewes Priory* (Pt. II), 12th-14th cents.

Vol. 41 *Transcripts of Sussex Wills up to 1560*, Vol.1 Albourne - Chichester

Vol. 42 *Transcripts of Sussex Wills up to 1560*, Vol.2 Chiddingly - Horsham

Vol. 43 *Transcripts of Sussex Wills up to 1560*, Vol.3 Horsted Keynes - Pyecombe

Vol. 44 *Records of the Barony and Honour of the Rape of Lewes, 1265-1466*

Vol. 45 *Transcripts of Sussex Wills up to 1560*, Vol.4 Racton - Yapton
Vol. 46 *Chichester Cathedral Chartulary*, 13th-16th cents.
Vol. 47 *Survey of Robertsbridge Manor, 1567-1570*
* Vol. 48 *The Town Book of Lewes, 1542-1701*
Vol. 49 *Churchwardens' Presentments*, (Pt. I), Archdeaconry of Chichester, 1621-1628, 1664-1670
Vol. 50 *Churchwardens' Presentments*, (Pt. II), Archdeaconry of Lewes, 1674-1677
Vol. 51 *Record of Deputations of Gamekeepers, 1781-1928*
* Jubilee Volume *Sussex Views from the Burrell Collection*
Vol. 52 *Chapter Acts, Chichester, 1472-1544* (The White Act Book)
Vol. 53 *The Manor of Etchingham cum Salehurst, 1597-1865*
Vol. 54 *Quarter Sessions Order Book, 1642-1649*
Vol. 55 *Ministers' Accounts of the Manor of Petworth, 1347-1353*
Vol. 56 *Lay Subsidy Rolls, 1524-1525*
Vol. 57 *Custumals of Sussex Manors of the Archbishop of Canterbury, 1285-1330*
Vol. 58 *Chapter Acts, Chichester, 1545-1642*
Vol. 59 *Chartulary of Boxgrove Priory*, 12th-14th cents.
Vol. 60 *Custumals of the Manors of Laughton, Willingdon and Goring, 1292-1338*
Vol. 61 *A Catalogue of Sussex Estate and Tithe Award Maps* (Pt. I), 1606-1884
* Vol. 62 *Minutes of the Common Council of the City of Chichester, 1783-1826*
Vol. 63 *The Book of Bartholomew Bolney*, 15th cent.
Vol. 64 *Rye Shipping Records, 1566-1590*
* Vol. 65 *Cellarers' Rolls of Battle Abbey, 1275-1513*
Vol. 66 *A Catalogue of Sussex Maps*, (Pt. II) 1597-1958
Vol. 67 *Estate Surveys of the Fitzalan Earls of Arundel*, 14th cent.
Vol. 68 *The Journal of Giles Moore of Horsted Keynes, 1655-1679*
Vol. 69 *The Town Book of Lewes, 1702-1837*
Vol. 70 *The Town Book of Lewes, 1837-1901*
* Vol. 71 *Accounts of the Roberts Family of Boarzell, 1568-1582*
Vol. 72 *Printed Maps of Sussex, 1575-1900*
* Vol. 73 *Correspondence of the Dukes of Richmond and Newcastle, 1724-1750*
Vol. 74 *Sussex Coroners' Inquests, 1485-1558*
* Vol. 75 *The Religious Census of Sussex, 1851*
* Vol. 76 *The Fuller Letters, 1728-1755*
* Vol. 77 East Sussex Land Tax, 1785
* Vol. 78 *Chichester Diocesan Surveys, 1686 and 1724*
* Vol. 79 *Saint Richard of Chichester*
* Vol. 80 *The Ashdown Forest Dispute, 1876-1882*
* Vol. 81 *Sussex Schools in the 18th century*
* Vol. 82 *West Sussex Land Tax, 1785*
* Vol. 83 *Mid Sussex Poor Law Records, 1601-1835*
* Vol.84 *Sussex in the 1st World War*
* Vol. 85 *Sussex Depicted: Views and Descriptions 1600-1800*
* Vol. 86 *Sussex Shore to Flanders Fields: E. Heron–Allen's Journal of the Great War*
* Vol. 87 *East Sussex Parliamentary Deposited Plans, 1799-1970*
* Vol. 88 *Sussex Cricket in the 18th century*
* Vol. 89 *East Sussex Coroners' Records, 1688-1838*

Volumes marked with an asterisk can be obtained from the Hon. Secretary, Sussex Record Society, Barbican House, Lewes, East Sussex, BN7 1YE.

Volumes 1-68 are available on microfiche from Messrs. Chadwyck-Healey Ltd., The Quorum, Barnwell Road, Cambridge, CB5 8SW.

CONTENTS

ACKNOWLEDGEMENTS

This volume consists of records preserved in the National Archives and the East and West Sussex Record Offices. They are published by permission of the Keeper of Public Records and the two county archivists. I have received valued assistance fom the staff of those three repositories, the Centre for Kentish Studies and the Brighton History Centre; especially from Philip Bye, William Spencer who checked the entry 'Army regiments and corps' in the subject index, and Christopher Whittick who introduced me to a number of records at Lewes and three early inquests at Kew (printed here as nos 470–472) none of which could have been discovered from the available finding aids. I am grateful to my colleagues on the council of the Sussex Record Society for their support and in particular to Peter Wilkinson, the honorary secretary.

In the 1980s Joan Herdman identified and transcribed nearly all the coroners' bills which are on the East Sussex quarter sessions rolls and form the greater part of the first three sections of my text. I have presented their contents in a different order and have added the distances travelled and the expenses claimed, but the accuracy of her transcription and the clarity of her handwriting eased my labours on the original documents.

My final thanks are to my wife, Janet Stevenson, who has been involved in every stage of this work and has been primarily responsible for coaxing the computer to convert it into camera-ready copy for the printer.

January 2005 R F Hunnisett

ABBREVIATIONS

ACC	ESRO: Accessions
AMS 5622	ESRO: Additional Manuscripts: Documents from the Offices of Raper and Fovargue of Battle, Solicitors
AMS 6445/1	ESRO: Additional Manuscripts: Printed Poll-Book for the Election of Thomas William Wheeler as Coroner for the Eastern Division, 12–14 Oct. 1809
ASSI 36	TNA: PRO: Assizes: Home, Norfolk and South-Eastern Circuits: Depositions
ASSI 94	TNA: PRO: Assizes: Norfolk and Home Circuits: Indictments Files 1689–1850
Baines	J M Baines, *Historic Hastings*, 2nd edn (Hastings, 1963)
Brent	C Brent, *Georgian Lewes 1714–1830* (Lewes, 1993)
C 202	TNA: PRO: Chancery: Petty Bag Office: Writ Files
Collier	*Correspondence of Mr. John Collier (deceased) and his family 1716–1780*, ed. C L Sayer, 2 vols (London, 1907)
DAP	ESRO: Archive of Messrs Dawes, Son and Prentice of Rye, Solicitors
Ep. II/16	WSRO: Archdeaconry of Lewes: Parish Register Transcripts
Ep. V/10	WSRO: Deanery of South Malling: Parish Register Transcripts
ESRO	East Sussex Record Office
E Sx Land Tax	*East Sussex Land Tax 1785*, ed. R Davey (SRS, LXXVII, 1991)
FRE	ESRO: Archive of the Frewen Family of Brickwall in Northiam
Fuller Letters	*The Fuller Letters 1728–1755: Guns, Slaves and Finance*, ed. D Crossley and R Saville (SRS, LXXVI, 1991)
Horsfield	T W Horsfield, *The History, Antiquities, and Topography of the County of Sussex*, 2 vols (Lewes, 1835)
KB 11	TNA: PRO: Court of King's Bench: Crown Side: Out-Counties Indictments Files
KB 29	TNA: PRO: Court of King's Bench: Crown Side: Controlment Rolls and other Memoranda Rolls of the Clerk of the Crown
Med. Coroner	R F Hunnisett, *The Medieval Coroner* (Cambridge, 1961)
ODNB	*Oxford Dictionary of National Biography*, ed. H C G Matthew and B Harrison, 60 vols (Oxford, 2004)
P142/1	Centre for Kentish Studies: East Farleigh Parish Records: Incumbent: Registers
P216/1	Centre for Kentish Studies: Lamberhurst Parish Records: Incumbent: Registers
PAB	ESRO: Paine and Brettell Manuscripts
PAR	Apart from the two listed immediately below, every document cited with a reference beginning PAR is an ESRO parish register. Unless otherwise stated, the register is of the place where the death occurred. As an example, PAR 253/1 is ESRO: Parish of Brede: Incumbent: Registers; and subnumbers identify the particular register.
PAR 236/2/4	ESRO: Parish of Battle: Incumbent: Papers relating to Registers: Clerk's Rough Register Book
PAR 367/26/1	ESRO: Parish of Hastings St Clement: Miscellaneous: Town Clerk
Par.	Every document cited with a reference beginning Par. is a WSRO parish register. Unless otherwise stated, the register is of the place where the death occurred. As an example, Par. 100/1 is WSRO:

	Parish of Henfield: Incumbent: Registers; and subnumbers identify the particular register.
PEV	ESRO: Pevensey Corporation Records
Pigot's Directory	*Pigot & Co's Royal National and Commercial Directory and Topography of the Counties of Kent Surrey Sussex* (London, 1839, facsimile edn 1993)
PRO	Public Record Office
PRO 30/26	TNA: PRO: Public Record Office: Gifts and Deposits: Miscellaneous
PROB 11	TNA: PRO: Prerogative Court of Canterbury and Related Probate Jurisdictions: Will Registers
QAF 2/1/E	ESRO: Quarter Sessions: Treasurers' Accounts and Bonds: County Stock Account Books
QCC/E	ESRO: Quarter Sessions: Clerk of the Peace: Case Papers
QM/EW	ESRO: Quarter Sessions: Minute Books
QO/EW	ESRO: Quarter Sessions: Order Books
QR/E	ESRO: Quarter Sessions: Sessions Rolls
QR/W	WSRO: Quarter Sessions: Sessions Rolls
RAF 1/3	ESRO: Archive of Raper and Fovargue of Battle, Solicitors: Client Account Ledgers
RAF 1/4	ESRO: Archive of Raper and Fovargue of Battle, Solicitors: Day Books
SAC	*Sussex Archaeological Collections* (1848–)
Salzmann	L F Salzmann, *The History of the Parish of Hailsham, the Abbey of Otham and the Priory of Michelham* (Lewes, 1901)
SAS	ESRO: Sussex Archaeological Society
SAY	ESRO: Sayer MSS
SC 2	TNA: PRO: Special Collections: Court Rolls
SCM	*Sussex County Magazine* (1926–1956)
SHE 2/2	ESRO: Archive of Charles Sheppard and Sons of Battle, Solicitors: Coronership of the Rye District of East Sussex and Predecessor Jurisdictions: Returns to the Home Office and Parliament and Associated Papers 1834–1844
SNQ	*Sussex Notes and Queries* (1926–1971)
SRS	Sussex Record Society
SWA	*The Sussex Weekly Advertiser: or Lewes Journal*
Swinson	*A Register of the Regiments and Corps of the British Army*, ed. A Swinson (London, 1972)
Sx Inqs 1485–1558	*Sussex Coroners' Inquests 1485–1558*, ed. R F Hunnisett (SRS, LXXIV, 1985)
Sx Inqs 1558–1603	*Sussex Coroners' Inquests 1558–1603*, ed. R F Hunnisett (Kew, 1996)
Sx Inqs 1603–1688	*Sussex Coroners' Inquests 1603–1688*, ed. R F Hunnisett (Kew, 1998)
TNA	The National Archives
Turner's Diary	*The Diary of Thomas Turner 1754–1765*, ed. D Vaisey (East Hoathly, 1994)
VCH Sx	*The Victoria History of the County of Sussex* (London, 1905–)
WAM	*Wiltshire Archaeological and Natural History Magazine* (1854–)
Wilts Bills	*Wiltshire Coroners' Bills 1752–1796*, ed. R F Hunnisett (Wiltshire Record Society, XXXVI, 1981)
WSRO	West Sussex Record Office

INTRODUCTION

The text of this volume is in three parts. The first consists of all the extant East Sussex coroners' bills (**1–308**).[1] They are followed by the surviving inquests[2] of the period 1688 to 1838 (**309–468**), some with associated records such as depositions, and four much earlier ones which have recently come to light (**469–472**). Finally, an appendix contains a series of documents concerning the prosecution of Thomas William Wheeler, a county coroner, for offences committed in the course of his duties (**473–549**).

In the middle ages, despite their busy official lives, coroners were unpaid and it was a punishable offence for them to take fees of any kind or to refuse to perform their duties without remuneration.[3] In 1487 they were allowed by statute to receive 13s 4d for holding any inquest which returned a verdict of murder or manslaughter, the money to be paid from the goods and chattels of the homicide or, if he had none, from any amercements imposed upon the township for his escape.[4] The purpose of that statute was to improve the adminstration of criminal justice, not to reward coroners, and it remained illegal for them to receive payment for holding inquests into suicides, deaths by misadventure and natural deaths.[5] That remained the position until 24 June 1752 when they became entitled to receive £1 for every inquest held in a place which contributed to the county rate and 9d a mile for travelling from their usual place of residence to the inquest venue, except that the total payment for an inquest held on anyone dying in gaol was limited to £1. They could still additionally receive the 13s 4d for homicide inquests. The new fees were to be paid out of the county rate by order of the justices of the peace at quarter sessions.[6] To substantiate their claims the coroners had to submit regular bills. The bills contain either lists or summaries of the inquests for which the coroners were claiming and they were subsequently filed on the quarter sessions rolls. There is an almost complete series of East Sussex bills from 1752 to 1830. No later ones have been preserved, probably to reduce the size of the ever-expanding quarter sessions rolls, although they continued to be presented at quarter sessions until 1 April 1889 when the payment of coroners was transferred from quarter sessions to the newly established county councils by the Local Government Act of 1888.[7] However, there are versions of the Hastings rape bills of 1830 to 1838 in solicitors' ledgers (**290–299**), the last of which provides the terminal date of this volume.

1 Throughout the volume figures in bold type refer to entries as numbered in the text. For convenience East and West Sussex are frequently used in this introduction instead of the more correct eastern and western divisions of Sussex.

2 'Inquest' has three meanings in this introduction: an inquiry held by a coroner; the formal record of that inquiry; and the entry relating to it in a bill. It should be clear from the context which one is intended in each case.

3 *Med. Coroner*, 118–122.

4 3 Henry VII c 2.

5 *Med. Coroner*, 122; *Reports of Cases from the time of King Henry VIII*, ed. J H Baker, I (Selden Soc., CXX, 2003), p 111.

6 Statute 25 George II c 29.

7 51 & 52 Victoria c 41 ss 3, 5.

The starting date, 1688, is the year when the previous edition of Sussex inquests ends. With those calendared here, all the East Sussex inquests held between 1194 and 1838 that are known to survive are now in print, apart from those held after 1688 in the Cinque Ports confederation, there being too many Rye, Winchelsea, Hastings, Pevensey and Seaford inquests to be included.[1] An exception has been made for one Seaford inquest (**468**) with which Thomas William Wheeler professed to have been involved as county coroner in 1815 (**185**). In the same bill he claimed payment for other inquests held at Seaford, but his bills of that time were shown to contain many false claims. For a very brief period, in 1836, the coroner of Hastings rape held a few inquests in Hastings and Rye, lawfully as will be explained later. They are entered on his bills (**295, 296**). The officials of the Cinque Ports did not normally compile bills comparable to those of the coroners elsewhere, although some payments of expenses involved in holding inquests have been found for Hastings, Winchelsea and Pevensey.[2] The special nature of the Cinque Ports coronerships and their records warrants detailed investigation on another occasion. Otherwise this volume presents all the known records of or relating to inquests which were compiled by or for the East Sussex coroners from 1688 to 1838, including those which they held in West Sussex. It is unlikely that any more coroners' bills will come to light but almost inevitable that a few other inquests will be discovered in unexpected places.

It is a characteristic of official records that they tend to be formulaic and to omit much human detail. That is true even of those which are as inherently appealing as coroners' inquests. One of the reasons for including the documents relating to the case against Thomas William Wheeler — in addition to their intrinsic interest, the importance of the various questions raised and the implicit warning that records should always be treated with healthy scepticism — is that they show in graphic detail what an inquest could mean for relatives, friends and neighbours of the deceased and for local officials. Further details of inquests can often be found in parish registers, diaries and journals, and particularly in reports in local newspapers. Material from those sources has been used only to solve problems presented by the text, but references have been given to relevant extracts from the *Sussex Weekly Advertiser* as printed in the *Sussex County Magazine*.

This volume contains far too many deaths for them to be discussed or analysed here, as was possible for those of earlier centuries, but two notorious cases are worth mentioning. One is the murder of his wife Celia by John William Holloway, sometimes referred to as Brighton's first trunk murder (**399**).[3] The other is the alleged poisoning in 1826 of Benjamin Russell by his wife Hannah, which constituted not merely murder but also petty treason (**434**). It was the last case of petty treason to be tried in Sussex before its abolition as a separate offence in 1828 when it was subsumed under murder.[4] As well as the usual information about the types of sudden and unnatural death and the social and economic conditions under which they occurred, the records printed here provide evidence of new developments. One is the growth of the seaside towns of Brighton and,

1 R F Hunnisett, 'Sussex Coroners in the Middle Ages', I, *SAC*, XCV, 42–58; *Sx Inqs 1485–1558*; *Sx Inqs 1558–1603*; *Sx Inqs 1603–1688*.

2 e.g. PAR 367/26/1/1, pp 27, 96 (Hastings); DAP Box 235/8 (Bill Ledger 1799–1811), pp 131–135 (Winchelsea); RAF 1/3/8, ff 78, 132 (Pevensey).

3 W H Johnson, *Brighton's First Trunk Murderer, 1831* (Eastbourne, 1995). Cf. *The Brighton Murder: an authentic and faithful history of the atrocious murder of Celia Holloway* ..., ed. C Hindley (Brighton, 1875).

4 Statute 9 George IV c 31 s 2.

to a lesser extent, Eastbourne, and the increasingly cosmopolitan nature of Brighton. Another is the greater importance of the medical profession and of the coroners' use of surgeons at inquests. Also new is the number of deaths of or caused by the military, the inevitable consequence of there being large numbers of regular soldiers and militia stationed along the Channel coast and just inland ready to counter any invasion during the Revolutionary and Napoleonic wars. Not unconnected are the deaths from explosions in gunpowder works. It is hoped that those and many other interests are adequately served by the indexes, particularly the index of subjects. This introduction is limited to explaining the coroners' place in local affairs and the administrative background to the records they produced.

The Coroners and their Areas of Jurisdiction

In theory the two Sussex county coroners were elected for the whole county, but it had become recognized as early as the thirteenth century that one of them should normally operate in the three western rapes and the other in the three eastern ones (in only Lewes and Pevensey rapes after 1455).[1] The East Sussex county coroners regularly officiated at inquests in places, such as East Grinstead and Cuckfield, which are in Pevensey and Lewes rapes and were therefore at that time in the administrative division of East Sussex but are now in the county of West Sussex. After 1688 their jurisdiction also extended, at least intermittently, into that part of Bramber rape which was part of the archdeaconry of Lewes. Throughout the period of this volume they accordingly held inquests in the parishes of Albourne, Upper Beeding, Edburton, Henfield, Ifield, Kingston by Sea, Shermanbury, New and Old Shoreham, Southwick and Woodmancote, but not Cowfold. Freeholders of those places were among the electors of the East Sussex coroners.[2] Despite that, there seems always to have been some uncertainty about the division between the two county coroners' jurisdictions. At the Michaelmas quarter sessions of 1771 the JPs, uniquely, disallowed the fees claimed by the East Sussex county coroner for inquests which he had held at New Shoreham and Shermanbury, but there is no record of his having been paid for them from the West Sussex rate (**30**). Much later, in the first draft of the case against Thomas William Wheeler (**510**), compiled in 1817, it was stated that the West Sussex coroner's district was the three western rapes, 'or as nearly so as may be', and that of the eastern coroner Lewes and Pevensey rapes, 'each district running through the county from the sea to its northern boundary'; but in a revised draft (**511**) one coroner was said ordinarily to act for that part of the county west of the Shoreham river, containing Chichester, Arundel and Bramber rapes and a small part of Lewes rape, and the other to act for the rest of Lewes rape and Pevensey rape. The compilers of the drafts seem otherwise to have had good local knowledge. Given the confusion, it is unsurprising that West Sussex coroners held inquests in the archdeaconry of Lewes parishes listed above, at least occasionally. A detailed study of the West Sussex bills and inquests would be necessary to establish which county coroner acted more frequently there or if there were periods when one rather than the other was more likely to be summoned. A spot check of a few of the West Sussex bills has revealed only three such inquests, all held in Upper Beeding, two by William Johnson in the year to Michaelmas 1784 and the other by John Luttman Ellis in 1816.[3]

1 R F Hunnisett, 'Sussex Coroners in the Middle Ages', III, *SAC*, XCVIII, 44–45; *Sx Inqs 1485–1558*, xxvii–xxix.
2 e.g. AMS 6445/1.
3 QR/W 567, no 24; QR/W 703, no 85, 9th inquest.

It is as yet unknown when or if the Bramber rape parishes of the archdeaconry of Lewes were formally assigned to the jurisdiction of the East Sussex coroner. None of the few surviving medieval inquests is from that area,[1] but there are four from between 1485 and 1558. Two were held by West Sussex county coroners, at Edburton and Old Shoreham, and the others by East Sussex coroners, at Cowfold and, again, at Edburton, the only ones they held outside the eastern rapes.[2] In the reign of Elizabeth I the coroner of the bishop of Chichester held six inquests at Henfield between 1576 and 1598.[3] Before that, the West Sussex coroner had held one there in 1566 and another at Ifield in 1559, and later the newly-established Bramber rape coroner held others at ?Old Shoreham in 1579, Ifield in 1582, New Shoreham in 1592 and Henfield in 1603.[4] From 1603 to 1639 all the known Bramber rape inquests were held by the coroners of that rape, but the eleven surviving from then until 1688, of which only five were from the archdeaconry of Lewes parishes, were held by the county coroners of East Sussex.[5] The fact that Lewes and Bramber rapes had often previously shared a coroner probably accounts for the East Sussex coroners being given, or assuming, both rapes as part of their jurisdiction in the later seventeenth century, after the rapes ceased to have their own franchisal coroners. When the Bramber rape part of the East Sussex coroner's district became limited to the archdeaconry of Lewes parishes is so far unknown, but it must have been between 1672 and 1752. That is one of several questions posed by the records printed here which it is hoped may be resolved by users of this book.

Each of the two county coroners was expected to act in the other's district in the event of illness or other incapacity and during vacancies. Indeed, a legal opinion to that effect given during the Wheeler proceedings went so far as to state that no temporary or deputy coroner, or even a coroner of a liberty, could act for a county coroner despite the long journeys involved in holding inquests in the other part of the county (**513**). The use of deputies had been a punishable offence since the thirteenth century,[6] although the records printed here show that franchisal coroners frequently used them, as did at least two county coroners, William and Thomas William Wheeler (**487**); but when West Sussex coroners were ill or before a coroner had been elected for the western division the East Sussex county coroners were invariably called upon and so can be found holding inquests in Bramber, Chichester, Easebourne, Hardham, Kirdford, Northchapel, Petworth, Sompting, Storrington, West Tarring, Warnham and Worthing. The two they held at Horsham (**315**, **340**) must have been for the same reasons unless they were in Horsham on business at the county gaol. In the 1760s Francis Wheeler submitted two bills containing such inquests to the West Sussex quarter sessions (**21**, **23**), but thereafter the expenses were claimed in the coroners' normal bills and paid from the East Sussex rate (**110**, **157–159**, **190**).

The western coroners similarly acted in the east, and John Luttman Ellis submitted two bills to the Lewes quarter sessions: one for inquests held in 1809, between the coronerships of William and Thomas William Wheeler, and the other for those held in 1817, during Thomas William Wheeler's imprisonment (**163**, **193**). Both were paid out

1 *SAC*, XCV, 45–58; **469**.
2 *Sx Inqs 1485–1558*, nos 34, 86, 226, 236.
3 *Sx Inqs 1558–1603*, nos 169, 232, 256, 436, 502, 508.
4 *Sx Inqs 1558–1603*, nos 4, 36, 223, 288, 438, 578.
5 *Sx Inqs 1603–1688*, xix.
6 *Med. Coroner*, 190–191.

of the East Sussex rate. However, he was paid by West Sussex at Easter 1817, on his normal bill for that division, for two undated inquests held at Upper Beeding,[1] which, as explained above, was normally within the jurisdiction of the East Sussex coroner. The second of them was on the body of John Payne who was buried at Upper Beeding on 18 February 1817[2] and so must have been taken while Wheeler was in prison but just before Ellis began to compile the bill which was paid in East Sussex. In 1831, beyond the period from which bills survive, Ellis held inquests at Heathfield and Preston (**398**, **399**) for reasons unknown. Richard Holmes, an earlier West Sussex coroner, had held five in East Sussex in 1764 — three, at Henfield, New Shoreham and Upper Beeding, during the last months of Thomas Attree's coronership when he was probably too ill to attend to his duties, and the other two, at Upper Beeding and South Malling, after Attree's death but before the election of his successor — and successfully claimed for them in his regular bill at the West Sussex quarter sessions (**18**). He was also paid from the West Sussex rate for two inquests entered in his bill for the year to Michaelmas 1785.[3] They are undated, but one was held at Upper Beeding on an unknown man who was certainly the 'unknown blackamore' buried there on 18 November 1784,[4] shortly before the death of Francis Wheeler, the East Sussex coroner, and the other was at Edburton on Richard Trusler who was buried on 23 February 1785,[5] the day before Wheeler's successor was elected. It is likely that the West Sussex coroners' bills contain other occasional inquests taken in the east, but it is striking that of those noted above which were paid for from the West Sussex rate all but the South Malling one were held in the Bramber rape part of the archdeaconry of Lewes. Perhaps the West Sussex JPs were unwilling to pay for their coroners' journeys far into the eastern division or the coroners were reluctant to travel that far. The employment of deputy coroners in East Sussex, of necessity or from choice, may well have occurred more frequently than can now be discovered.

The periods of office of the county coroners of East Sussex between 1688 and 1838 can be established with some confidence. Their names were recorded at the assizes, which were held at least twice a year; from 1752 the dates of virtually all their inquests are known; and most of their elections are recorded. The first of them, Alexander Luxford, had been coroner since 1669 and remained in office until his death in 1710.[6] On 18 November of that year a writ issued for the election of a coroner in his place and John Michell was duly elected on 30 November.[7] Michell's last surviving inquest is of 30 May 1734 (**327**), but he continued to attend assizes until 2 August 1735.[8] He was replaced by Thomas Attree some time between that date and the following assizes of 22 March 1736 which Attree attended as coroner.[9] Attree held his last inquest on 12 March 1764 and was buried at Barcombe on 13 May.[10] Richard Holmes, the West Sussex county coroner, had held two inquests in January and another on 4 April which Attree would normally have taken, presumably because he was too ill to perform his duties, and two more on 17 and 23 June (**18**). It was not until 27 June that a writ issued for the election of a new

1 QR/W 703, no 85.
2 Par. 16/1/5/1.
3 QR/W 571, no 19.
4 Par. 16/1/1/2.
5 Ep. V/10/2A.
6 *Sx Inqs 1603–1688*, xxxv; C 202/97, no 4.
7 C 202/97, no 4.
8 ASSI 94/585.
9 ASSI 94/595.
10 Ep. II/16/9A.

coroner and on 4 July Francis Wheeler was elected unopposed, Attree's son William having abandoned his candidature despite a promising beginning.[1] Wheeler also remained in office until his death, at the age of 54, holding his last inquest on 22 December 1784 (**63**). He was buried at All Saints, Lewes, on 2 January 1785, and the writ for a successor issued on 19 January.[2] This time there was a contest and Francis Wheeler's son William was elected on 24 February, defeating William Attree by 511 votes to 217.[3] The first inquest in William Wheeler's bills is dated 10 February (**64**), which means either that he acted as coroner before his election or that he claimed for an inquest which had been taken, unlawfully, by a temporary coroner.[4] William Wheeler continued to hold inquests until 14 August 1809 (**162**). Two days later he suddenly died at the same age, 54, as his father, was the subject of an inquest (**163**) taken by the West Sussex coroner, John Luttman Ellis, and was buried at All Saints, Lewes, on 18 August, a writ for a new coroner issuing on 6 September.[5] Again there was a contest, Thomas William Wheeler, son of Francis Wheeler's youngest son Charles, defeating Christopher Kell of Lewes by 481 votes to 353 on 14 October, when only just 21 years old.[6] Technically he remained in office until removed by a writ of 2 August 1817 (**543**) but, as will be explained in more detail later, he held no inquest after 11 December 1816 (**192**, **476**) because he was in gaol. His successor was George Gwynne who had considered standing for election in 1809 but had stood down in favour of Wheeler.[7] Kell having declined to stand again, Gwynne was elected unopposed on 14 August 1817[8] on a writ of 4 August (**544**) and officiated at inquests from 18 August 1817 (**194**) until 10 February 1829 (**216**). The last county coroner in this volume, Francis Harding Gell, also elected unopposed,[9] held his first inquest on 12 February 1829 (**217**) and died in office shortly before 18 November 1864 when a writ for a new coroner issued, upon which Lewis Greene Fullager was elected on 7 December.[10] Gell presented bills at quarter sessions until Michaelmas 1864 and a final bill was paid to his executors at Epiphany 1865. Fullager's bills were submitted from Easter 1865 until Epiphany 1880, the last two by John Edward Fullager as his deputy. Further payments were made to county coroners by order of the JPs until Easter 1889 after which they were no longer responsible for them: to Wynne Edwin Baxter from Easter 1880 to Epiphany 1888 and to A W Rawlinson for Baxter's last bill at Easter 1888; and then to George Edward Hillman, who had been in office since 18 November 1887, from Easter 1888.[11] After 1710, with the exception of Attree who lived at Newick (**1**), all the county coroners from 1688 to 1838 lived at Lewes (strictly Cliffe in the case of the Wheelers), although Thomas William Wheeler moved to

1 C 202/152/2; Brent, 71–72.
2 PAR 410/1/1/5; C 202/173/13.
3 C 202/173/13; Brent, 72. William Wheeler, the son of Francis and Mary Wheeler, was born on 7 September and baptized at All Saints, Lewes, on 20 September 1754: PAR 410/1/1/5.
4 That 10 February was the correct date of the inquest is confirmed by the burial of the deceased, Mary Horscroft, at Chalvington on 12 February: PAR 291/1/1/2.
5 *SWA*, 21 Aug. 1809; PAR 410/1/1/5; C 202/197/16.
6 AMS 6445/1; C 202/197/16. Thomas William Wheeler, son of Charles Wheeler, was baptized at St Michael's, Lewes, on 15 August 1788 and Charles at All Saints on 1 December 1763: PAR 414/1/1/3; PAR 410/1/1/5.
7 *SWA*, 17 Mar. 1817.
8 *SWA*, 4 Aug. 1817, 18 Aug. 1817.
9 Brent, 72.
10 C 202/254/9.
11 QO/EW 59–92; QAF 2/1/E11–14.

Brighton in August 1814, towards the end of his period of office (**183**).[1] That those in office after 1752 lived permanently in those places is proved by their claiming no travelling expenses for inquests held in them.

By 1688 there were no liberties within Lewes rape which had their own coroners and, outside the two corporate members of the Cinque Ports — Pevensey, whose lowy included Westham and part of Hailsham as well as Pevensey itself,[2] and Seaford — only one certain one in Pevensey rape, namely Rotherfield hundred. The Lords Abergavenny had had coroners there from at least 1614[3] and three inquests were taken by Richard Taylor, as coroner of the hundred, in 1696, 1712 and 1721 (**445–447**). The coronership must have been discontinued some time between 1721 and 1752 because there are no bills for the hundred, the county coroners making regular claims for holding inquests at Rotherfield and Frant, its only parishes, after 1752. An inquest (**448**) at Hailsham in 1714 was said to have been taken by Anthony Trumble as coroner of Dill hundred, but Dill is not known to have had special coroners either earlier or later. His description proves that he must have acted in place of the county coroner in that part of Hailsham which lay outside the lowy of Pevensey, perhaps because he lived at Hailsham.[4] Trumble held another similarly isolated inquest (**449**), in 1723, when he was described as coroner of Guestling hundred in Hastings rape. Between those two dates he was certainly the Hastings rape coroner (**413, 414**) and it is probable that he sometimes called himself the coroner of the hundred in which he was sitting, as some seventeenth-century coroners did in West Sussex.[5] If he was Hastings rape coroner in 1714 he was acting illegally in officiating outside the rape even if the county coroner could not attend (**513**). Another phantom jurisdiction in Hastings rape made a fleeting appearance, in 1763, when Joseph Acton held an inquest (**452**) as deputy coroner of Goldspur hundred for that term only. It is not stated exactly where the venue was and the situation is further clouded by the jurors being said to be ‘of the said hundred of Gostrow’. In fact, five of the jurors sat on other inquests at Iden and Playden (**347, 426**) and the witnesses were of Peasmarsh, all three places being in Goldspur hundred. The inquest is preserved with a run of others held by coroners of Gostrow hundred, including two by Acton (**453, 454**), and it is therefore probable that, although the death occurred at Tillingham Level in Goldspur hundred, the body was taken to John Woodhams's house, which was almost certainly at Udimore in Gostrow hundred (cf. **451**), where the inquest was held. All other Goldspur hundred inquests were taken by the coroner of Hastings rape, in whose jurisdiction both Goldspur and Guestling hundreds were included in a return made by the clerk of the peace to Whitehall in 1832.[6]

Even without those complications, the Hastings rape jurisdictions present problems. Apart from the Cinque Port of Hastings and the ancient towns of Rye and Winchelsea, whose chief officers were ex officio coroners,[7] there could be as many as six coroners: one each for the hundreds of Battle, Bexhill, Gostrow, Foxearle and Robertsbridge, and

1 ASSI 94/513 (Michell); PAR 410/1/1/5, 2 Jan. 1785 (Francis Wheeler); *SWA*, 21 Aug. 1809 (William Wheeler); Ep. II/16/71 (Thomas William Wheeler); ASSI 94/1993 (Gwynne); ASSI 94/2072 (Gell); Brent, 71–72.

2 *VCH Sx*, II, 226.

3 *Sx Inqs 1603–1688*, xiv, xxxvi, xliii.

4 Salzmann, 118, 146, 256.

5 *Sx Inqs 1603–1688*, xiv.

6 SHE 2/2/1.

7 *Sx Inqs 1603–1688*, xiv, xxxviii, xxxix.

another for the rest of the rape, all appointed by the lords of the particular liberties. The return of 1832 listed the most recent appointments in all six liberties, although without naming the coroners.[1] There had been five appointments in 1830: for Battle hundred by Sir Godfrey Webster, bt, on 13 November; for Bexhill hundred by the earl of Plymouth and Foxearle hundred by William Doun Gillen, both on 17 November; for Gostrow hundred by the earl of Burlington on 18 November; and for the rest of Hastings rape, comprising Baldslow, Guestling, Goldspur, Hawksborough, Henhurst, Netherfield, Staple and Shoyswell hundreds, by the earl of Chichester on 23 November. It is almost certain that what happened was that Thomas Charles Bellingham was appointed to all five jurisdictions as he was serving in all of them in 1835.[2] The 1832 return has a note in pencil that Edward Allfrey had appointed a coroner for Robertsbridge hundred on 15 December 1822.[3] That may also have been Bellingham, although Charles Martin was coroner there by 1832.[4]

The lords of the honor of Hastings had appointed a coroner for the rape almost continuously since 1455, as they continued to do during the period of this volume.[5] There are few records of appointments and by 1688 the rape and other liberty coroners were no longer entered on the assize files. It is therefore not until 1752 that one can be fairly sure of the exact sequence of the Hastings rape coroners. John Purfield had been coroner of the rape since at least December 1666[6] and was still in office in January 1689 (**410**). He was buried at Battle on 1 May 1695[7] and may well have died in office and been succeeded by his son George[8] who held an inquest in January 1697 (**411**). George was buried at Battle on 1 January 1703, having probably also died in office.[9] Whether or not Samuel Brewer was his immediate successor, he was holding inquests by December 1707 (**412**). Anthony Trumble was the rape coroner by May 1715 (**413**) and may well have been in January 1714 when he took the Dill hundred inquest discussed above (**448**). By March 1716 John Collier had replaced him (**415**), but Trumble was back in office by January 1717 (**414**) and it is almost certain that it was as coroner of the rape that he held the Guestling hundred inquest of February 1723 already mentioned (**449**). He died on 1 September 1733, aged 63,[10] and may have been succeeded, either then or earlier, by Robert Chambers who is known from only one inquest, held in October 1735 (**416**). With George Tilden the succession becomes clearer. He was appointed in 1737,[11] remained in office until his death in 1765, holding his last inquest on 13 March (**228A**), and was buried at Battle on 7 June.[12] He was succeeded by his son John, then aged 23,[13] who on 22 November 1797 formally changed his name to John Tilden Sampson[14]

1 SHE 2/2/1.
2 Horsfield, I, 87.
3 SHE 2/2/1.
4 SHE 2/2/2.
5 *SAC*, XCVIII, 47, 69; *Sx Inqs 1558–1603*, xx, xxii; *Sx Inqs 1603–1688*, xvii, xxxv, xliii.
6 *Sx Inqs 1603–1688*, xxxv.
7 PAR 236/1/1/2.
8 George son of John Purfield had been baptized at Battle on 1 January 1669: PAR 236/1/1/2.
9 PAR 236/1/1/2.
10 Salzmann, 118.
11 SHE 2/1/8.
12 PAR 236/1/1/2.
13 John son of George and Mary Tilden was baptized at Battle on 4 December 1741: PAR 236/1/1/2.
14 *An Index to Changes of Name under authority of Act of Parliament or Royal Licence ... 1760 to 1901*, ed. W P W Phillimore and E A Fry (London, 1905), 316.

although, for consistency, he is referred to as John Tilden throughout this introduction. He also died in office, at the age of 68, having held inquests from 8 July 1765 to 19 May 1810 (**228B–272**), and was buried at Battle on 14 June 1810.[1] His successor was William Thorpe, who held his first inquest on 19 June 1810 and his last on 21 January 1819 (**273**, **279**). Thomas Barton was acting by 18 March 1819 (**308**). His final inquest was at Westfield on 19 October 1830 although his last bill has another held at Crowhurst on 24 December (**290**), but it is struck through and repeated as the first entry on Thomas Charles Bellingham's first bill (**291**). Bellingham, who had been appointed Hastings rape coroner on 23 November,[2] remained in office until his death. His final inquest, the last to be recorded in the extant bills, was held at Mountfield on 3 April 1838 and he died two days later, aged 41, of water on the brain at 4 Vere Street, St Marylebone, in the presence of Burrell Hayley of Brightling, later a long-serving rector of Catsfield.[3] Payment of Bellingham's last two bills was made to Charles Arnold, a witness to his will, on 9 May and 5 July (**298**, **299**). The new coroner was Nathaniel Polhill Kell whose bills were presented from Midsummer 1838 to Midsummer 1865. Payment of the last one was made to his executors and Charles Sheppard, his successor, who thereafter submitted his own bills until Easter 1889.[4] The Purfields lived at Battle and Brewer may well have been the man who was buried at Battle on 25 February 1729.[5] Collier lived at the Mansion (now Old Hastings House) in Hastings, Trumble at Hailsham and Chambers probably at Burwash;[6] but from 1737 to 1838, except for Thorpe who lived at Hastings,[7] the coroners of Hastings rape all lived at Battle as is confirmed by their claiming no travelling expenses for inquests held there.

The records printed here seem to show the smaller coronerships appearing and disappearing kaleidoscopically. The Battle coronership is known to have existed from at least 1255 and throughout the middle ages belonged to the abbots.[8] Their successors in the liberty continued to appoint coroners.[9] Nevertheless, the first Battle inquest known after 1688 (**413**) was held, in 1715, by the coroner of Hastings rape. There follows a long period for which there is no evidence, including the years 1752–1765 when George Tilden returned bills as Hastings rape coroner. It is inconceivable that there were no inquests in Battle hundred during that time. If Tilden had held them he would have claimed payment for them, as he did for Bexhill inquests. Battle must therefore have had its own coroner then, and possibly well before 1752. Inquests from 1766 to 1780 held at Battle and Whatlington, the Battle hundred parishes, are in three bills (**300–302**) presented by Charles Nairn as coroner of Battle and Robertsbridge hundreds. He lived at Battle, as the bills prove. Between 1789 and 1808 inquests in those parishes were entered on the bills of John Tilden, the Hastings rape coroner, but notes on the bills show that £1 for the first inquest (**247**), held on 3 February 1789, was paid to Mr Nairn, presumably Charles Nairn, and that the same almost certainly happened with the fourth (**252**), held on

1 PAR 236/2/4.
2 SHE 2/2/1.
3 Office for National Statistics: General Register Office: Marylebone Registration District: Register of Deaths; J Foster, *Alumni Oxonienses: the menbers of the University of Oxford 1715–1886* (Oxford, 1891), II, 634.
4 QO/EW 55–92; QAF 2/1/E12–14.
5 PAR 236/1/1/2.
6 Baines, 64; Salzmann, 118, 146, 256; *VCH Sx*, IX, 197.
7 Baines, 29.
8 *SAC*, XCVIII, 45–46, 69.
9 *Sx Inqs 1485–1558*, xxxii–xxxiii; *Sx Inqs 1558–1603*, xx, xxii; *Sx Inqs 1603–1688*, xxxv, xliii.

22 March 1792. Nairn must still have been acting as Battle coroner, or deputy coroner, on those occasions, but there is no similar note against the two Battle inquests of 1791 (**251**) or any of the later ones in Tilden's Hastings rape bills. However, two of the original inquests, of 1799 and 1803, survive (**458**, **459**) and in them Tilden is called coroner of Battle hundred. Further inquests held between 1812 and 1817 appear on two bills (**307**, **308**) presented by Thomas Barton as coroner of Battle, Robertsbridge and Gostrow hundreds. Thereafter they are all again on the Hastings rape bills, first those of Thomas Barton (beginning with the last part of bill **308**, which he began as coroner of his hundreds and completed as coroner of the rape) and then those of Thomas Charles Bellingham. It therefore seems that from the 1790s the coroners of Hastings rape and of the hundred of Battle were usually the same person, the exception being Barton's tenure of the Battle office while William Thorpe was coroner of the rape, probably because Thorpe was exceptional in living at Hastings rather than Battle. It was presumably Bellingham who was appointed coroner of Battle hundred on 13 November 1830, ten days before his appointment for the rape.[1]

A similar pattern emerges for the liberty of Gostrow hundred, formerly more commonly known as the liberty or manor of Brede. It had had its own coroner at least as early as 1545 and several are known in the seventeenth century, the last in 1680.[2] The next piece of evidence is provided by an inquest of 1743 (**450**) which was held at Brede by Robert Lovelace Chambers as deputy coroner of Gostrow hundred for that term only. It is not known for whom he was acting, but in November 1751 George Worge, who lived at Starr's Green (later Rose Green) in Battle,[3] was coroner of the hundred and had a deputy, Henry Dodson (**451**). Worge was almost certainly coroner as early as January 1748 when he was consulted by Richard Patrick, who was deputising for George Tilden, the Hastings rape coroner, then suffering from gout, about a death resulting from the wreck of the *Amsterdam* off Bulverhythe, an event with which John Collier, the former Hastings rape coroner, was also concerned.[4] Worge was possibly still in office at his death in 1765, aged 63. There are no inquests for Brede or Udimore, the two parishes of the hundred, on George Tilden's bills for Hastings rape but, as already noted, in 1763 Joseph Acton held one in either Gostrow or Goldspur hundred as deputy coroner (**452**). Acton, who lived at Hastings,[5] claimed fees for holding six inquests as Gostrow hundred coroner between 11 August 1768 and 3 February 1779 (**303–305**), although the first of them was actually taken by Charles Nairn as deputy coroner for that turn only (**455**), the second, on 19 April 1770, by John Tilden (the Hastings rape coroner) as Acton's deputy for that turn (**457**) and the last, on 3 February 1779, by Charles Bristow, likewise as Acton's deputy (**462**). It was to Bristow that payment of Acton's final bill was made (**305**). It appears that, like Battle, Gostrow had its own coroners from well before 1752 until at least 1780. There are five Brede and Udimore inquests held between 1788 and 1792 on John Tilden's Hastings rape bills. In December 1794 Tilden issued a jury summons as coroner of the rape for an inquest to be held before him at Brede, but in the event it was taken by Walter Acton, one of Joseph Acton's sons,[6] as coroner of Gostrow

1 SHE 2/2/1.

2 *Sx Inqs 1485–1558*, xxxi; *Sx Inqs 1558–1603*, xx, xxii; *Sx Inqs 1603–1688*, xxxv, xliii.

3 *Collier*, II, 192.

4 Baines, 368; J L André, 'Battle Church', *SAC*, XLII, 233–234.

5 Baines, 65.

6 Walter son of Joseph and Elizabeth Acton was baptized at All Saints, Hastings, on 6 December 1767: PAR 361/1/1/4. That he was the coroner is proved by his signature on **464–466** being identical to that

hundred (**464**), in which capacity he held two further Brede inquests in 1796 (**465**, **466**). None of the three is on a bill. John Tilden took a number of Brede and Udimore inquests between 1801 and 1809 which are all entered on his bills as the coroner of the rape, but there follow five, from 1811 to 1817, held by Thomas Barton as Gostrow hundred coroner (**307**, **308**). Again there is a striking similarity with Battle, although there is a Brede inquest of 1815 on one of the bills of William Thorpe, the Hastings rape coroner (**276**). There may have been a good reason why Barton could not take it. From 1819 all the Gostrow inquests were entered on the rape coroners' bills. It must have been Thomas Charles Bellingham who was appointed coroner of the hundred on 18 November 1830, five days before he was appointed coroner of the rape.[1]

The first two recorded coroners of the liberty of Bexhill were acting from 1578 to 1600, but none is known for the seventeenth century or the first half of the eighteenth.[2] From 1754 to 1772 there are Bexhill inquests on the bills of the Hastings rape coroners, but Joseph Acton held one in 1775 and five more in 1781 and 1782 which are on his bills as coroner of Bexhill and Gostrow hundreds (**305**, **306**). Thereafter there are many Bexhill inquests on the Hastings rape bills, including two held by John Tilden and one by Thomas Barton of which the originals survive (**460**, **461**, **467**) and in which they are called coroners of Bexhill hundred. Two Bexhill inquests of 1810 are noted in a solicitors' ledger immediately after Tilden's last bill as Hastings rape coroner, but they are marked with a cross and are not entered in any bill as submitted (**273**). Perhaps it was thought that a separate Bexhill hundred coroner should have been appointed and would claim for them, but they are not on Thomas Barton's bill as coroner of various hundreds (**307**) and all the other Bexhill inquests of 1810–1818 are on William Thorpe's Hastings rape bills. Once again, it must have been the last Hastings rape coroner whose bills survive, Thomas Charles Bellingham, who was appointed coroner of Bexhill hundred on 17 November 1830.[3]

The other two liberties are more shadowy and never had coroners of their own before the eighteenth century. Robertsbridge hundred consisted of Robertsbridge itself, Sedlescombe and Westfield. There is just one, Westfield, inquest on George Tilden's Hastings rape bills (**225**), which may indicate that the hundred had its own coroner before 1765, but the first person known to have acted as coroner of the hundred is Charles Nairn who held inquests there from 1766 to 1775 (**300–302**). Stephen Swatland, who had received payment of Nairn's last bill, was deputy coroner of the hundred for that turn only on 2 April 1782 (**463**), but the inquest which he then arranged survives neither in the original nor on a bill. The only other person called coroner of Robertsbridge hundred before 1830 was Thomas Barton who held inquests there in 1815 and 1816 and his surviving bills (**307**, **308**) suggest that he was in office in Battle, Gostrow and Robertsbridge hundreds from 1811 until 1817, although William Thorpe claimed for a Westfield inquest in 1814 (**276**) as he had for two held at Robertsbridge in 1810 (**273**). At all other times the Robertsbridge hundred inquests were entered on the Hastings rape coroners' bills, except for one of 1806 held at Robertsbridge turnpike (**268**) which is noted in a solicitors' day book but was omitted from the corresponding ledger and from

made as witness to the marriage of his brother John at East Farleigh, Kent, on 7 July 1798: P142/1/4, p 48. John had been baptized at All Saints, Hastings, on 27 September 1775: PAR 361/1/1/4.

1 SHE 2/2/1.

2 *Sx Inqs 1558–1603*, xx; *Sx Inqs 1603–1688*, xiv.

3 SHE 2/2/1.

the bill presented by the coroner of the rape, perhaps because it was taken by the hundred coroner or a deputy. A Sedlescombe inquest of 1827 was entered on the bill of Thomas Barton, the Hastings rape coroner, but was stated elsewhere to have been held by Thomas Charles Bellingham (**286**) who could therefore have been the coroner appointed to the hundred on 15 December 1822.[1] However, in both 1832 and 1835 Bellingham was coroner for the whole of Hastings rape except for Robertsbridge hundred whose coroner was Charles Martin of Battle,[2] although Bellingham's Hastings rape bills contain four Westfield inquests of 1836 and 1837 (**295**, **296**).

No Foxearle hundred coroner is known with certainty to have acted as such. Thomas Barton held an inquest (**431**) at Wartling on 18 March 1819 as Hastings rape coroner, although it identifies Wartling as being in Foxearle hundred and the jurors were of the hundred. It is entered in a bill (**308**) whose earlier inquests, in 1816 and 1817, were taken by Barton as coroner of Battle, Gostrow and Robertsbridge hundreds, but he must have held those of early 1819 as coroner of the rape as two of the four were at Northiam and Burwash which are not in any of the hundreds with their own coroners. All other Foxearle inquests — at Wartling, Herstmonceux and Ashburnham — are on the rape bills, including several of 1752–1765 and 1811–1816. However, an Ashburnham inquest of 1827, although on the rape coroner's bill, was, like the Sedlescombe inquest of the same year, said to have been taken by Bellingham (**286**). Perhaps Bellingham was by then Foxearle hundred coroner and was reappointed on 17 November 1830.[3]

Bellingham's involvement in Robertsbridge and Foxearle hundreds in 1827 is known only from the chance survival of a return to Whitehall.[4] There is normally just the evidence of the bills, from which there would have been no suspicion that Thomas Barton had not held the two inquests. Similarly, but for the existence of earlier versions of some of the Hastings rape bills among the Raper and Fovargue archives it would not be known that Charles Nairn was paid for two Battle inquests which are on John Tilden's bills (**247**, **252**). Such instances may not have been exceptional and the relationship between the coronership of the rape and those of the hundreds may have been even more involved than outlined above. The use of deputies could also have been much more common.

It is not surprising that the coroner of the rape sometimes held or was concerned with an inquest in one of the smaller liberties, even during a time when it had a separate coroner of its own; but, if one ignores the Gostrow/Goldspur hundred case, the hundred coroners seem never to have acted outside their own areas. It was strictly unlawful for the Hastings rape coroner to act for the county coroner (**513**) and there is only one known instance of his probably having done so, at the Dill hundred inquest discussed above (**448**). By contrast, on the rare occasions when the coroner of the rape was unavailable the county coroner was called upon. In 1806 William Wheeler held an inquest at Hollington because John Tilden was ill (**150**) and on 13 June 1810 Thomas William Wheeler held one at Gardner Street in Herstmonceux because Tilden was dead (**166**). It must have been illness or some other incapacity which caused the county coroners to act at Playden in 1766 and Herstmonceux in 1826 (**22**, **211**).

1 SHE 2/2/1.
2 SHE 2/2/2; Horsfield, I, 87.
3 SHE 2/2/1.
4 SHE 2/2/8.

The Cinque Ports guarded their privileges vigorously and it would normally have been unthinkable for an inquest to have been taken in any part of the confederation by anyone other than one of its own officials. However, a brief, exceptional period was introduced by the Municipal Corporations Act of 1835, which inadvertently removed the right of the Cinque Ports to have their own coroners.[1] The previous position was restored by statute in 1836,[2] but before it came into force Thomas Charles Bellingham held two inquests at Hastings and two at Rye in 1836 as coroner of Hastings rape for which he claimed in his bills (**295**, **296**). No other Hastings inquests are recorded on the rape bills apart from those taken in the parish of St Mary in the Castle and in St Leonards, which were outside the liberty of the Cinque Ports, and one said to have been at Bulverhythe in 1805 (**267**). Bulverhythe was a non-corporate member of the Cinque Ports and it is therefore probable that the inquest jury met just outside, especially as the death had occurred at Bexhill. There are a few similar claims for inquests at Rye, three made by John Tilden between 1776 and 1782 (**236**, **237**, **242**), four by Thomas Barton between 1819 and 1825 (**280**, **282–284**) and one by Bellingham in December 1836 (**296**). It is virtually certain, however, that they were held not in Rye itself but outside, in either Rye Foreign or Playden. In 1777 Tilden claimed for an inquest at Playden for which an earlier version of the bill has Rye (**238**) and the venue of one of Barton's inquests is given as Rye in the final bill but as Playden earlier (**283**). Another Barton inquest was said to have been taken at Rye but the body was found in Rye Foreign (**280**). Those two coroners clearly used Rye to mean the Rye area and there is no evidence that they ever challenged the privileges of the Cinque Ports. There is also no suggestion that any county or Hastings rape coroner ever acted in either Pevensey or Winchelsea, but Thomas William Wheeler claimed for inquests held at Seaford on 9 March 1815 on the bodies of three sailors who had drowned as a result of the wreck of the *York* (**185**). It is possible that Wheeler held the inquests near Seaford but not within the liberty. Alternatively, he might have heard of the wreck and fatalities but did not hold the inquests. Such false entries would not have been unique in his later bills: it was not long afterwards that the investigation into his peculation began. However, his having officiated in Seaford may be supported by his statement in the same bill that he had been sent for by the bailiff and coroner of Seaford to hold an inquest there on Solomon Young who had been murdered by Joseph Stephens. He did not expressly claim to have held it, only that he 'went through the business', adding that, when he met the bailiff and jury, the bailiff had asked that the proceedings should be recorded in his (the bailiff's) name only. Wheeler further alleged that he had been unable to return home until very late at night and asked if the JPs might authorize payment of expenses to him. The JPs must either have disbelieved Wheeler's story or known that he should not have been involved with any deaths occurring within the Cinque Ports confederation and he received no allowance of any kind. The original inquest survives and makes no mention of Wheeler's participation (**468**). Perhaps the Seaford authorities had made a belated defence of their rights after Wheeler's usurpation of them on 9 March. The inquest on Young was held on 20 March and Wheeler made no attempt to pretend that he was concerned with later investigations concerning the deaths of other sailors from the *York* who were also drowned (**185**).

1 5 & 6 William IV c 76 ss 62–64. Cf. *The Records of Rye Corporation*, ed. R F Dell (Lewes, 1962), 15.
2 6 & 7 William IV c 105 s 10.

There were too many coroners, county and franchisal, in East Sussex between 1688 and 1838 for it to be practicable to present even the shortest of biographies of them here, but four general features must be mentioned. First, the election of successive Wheelers as county coroners and the appointment of Purfields and Tildens in Hastings rape and Actons in Gostrow hundred continued a tradition of Sussex families providing coroners which began in the fourteenth century with two Thomas Pelhams and continued in the early modern period with the Roots and Playfairs.[1] In addition, George Worge was John Collier's son-in-law[2] and Thomas Barton and Thomas Charles Bellingham were brothers-in-law.[3] A second similarity with earlier centuries was the number of men who held more than one coronership, either simultaneously or at different times.[4] As well as those Hastings rape coroners who were also coroners of hundreds, Charles Nairn served as coroner of Battle and Robertsbridge hundreds and deputy coroner of Gostrow hundred, Joseph Acton as coroner of Gostrow and Boxhill hundreds and, more unexpectedly, John Collier and William Thorpe as coroners of Hastings rape and mayors and coroners of Hastings.[5] Thirdly, from 1688 onwards it was normal for the East Sussex county and franchisal coroners, like most of those elsewhere, to be solicitors or attorneys-at-law.[6] The coronerships were often, in effect, attached to particular firms of solicitors, such as the Battle practice to which the Tildens, Thomas Barton and Bellingham belonged.[7] That practice held the Hastings rape coronership from at least 1765 until 1838, except for the years 1810 to 1819, although even then Barton was coroner of Battle, Robertsbridge and Foxearle hundreds. Francis Harding Gell, who was a partner in the Lewes firm of Gell and Fullager, was succeeded as county coroner by Lewis Greene Fullager.[8] None of the coroners had medical qualifications, unlike many in Wiltshire in the second half of the eighteenth century.[9]

Finally, like their predecessors, the Sussex coroners held various other offices and carried out a number of other administrative duties, often while coroners. To give a few examples of the activities of the county coroners: in 1803–1804 William Wheeler raised a company at Cliffe for the South Pevensey Volunteers to help counter the military threat from France and a few years later he was serving as clerk to the trustees for rebuilding All Saints' church, Lewes, and repairing its tower;[10] at least twice, on 17 October 1823 and 14 July 1825, George Gwynne received fees at the Lewes quarter sessions on the conviction of vagrants;[11] and Francis Harding Gell was town clerk of Seaford and clerk to the Uckfield and Hailsham magistrates.[12] The franchisal coroners were equally busy.

1 L F Salzman, 'The Persistent Coroner', *SNQ*, XIII, 54–55; *SAC*, XCVIII, 58, 60; *Sx Inqs 1485–1558*, xxiii–xxiv; *Sx Inqs 1558–1603*, xx.

2 *Fuller Letters*, no 82; *Collier*, II, 192.

3 PROB 11/1896, f 104v (manuscript foliation). Bellingham married Lucy Barton at Battle on 12 January 1824: PAR 236/1/3/1.

4 Cf. *Sx Inqs 1558–1603*, xx–xxvii; *Sx Inqs 1603–1688*, xv–xix, xxxv–xxxvii.

5 Baines, 29, 63.

6 e.g. E H W Dunkin, 'A Calendar of the Deeds and other Documents in the possession of the Sussex Archaeological Society', *SAC*, XXXIX, 187 (Attree); *SWA*, 21 Aug. 1809 (William Wheeler); *SWA*, 17 Mar. 1817 (Thomas William Wheeler); Brent, 196 (Gwynne and Gell); Baines, 62 (Collier); PAR 236/1/1/2 (George Tilden: burial at Battle 7 June 1765); *Fuller Letters*, no 82 (Worge).

7 RAF 1/3/1–10; AMS 5622/1/4.

8 *Pigot's Directory*, 261; C 202/254/9.

9 *Wilts Bills*, xlviii–l.

10 Brent, 78–79; QR/E 714, no 102.

11 QO/EW 46, 47.

12 *Pigot's Directory*, 261.

Many served as stewards of manors, John Purfield, for example, being steward of the manor of Crowham in Westfield.[1] Anthony Trumble was under-sheriff of Sussex and acted as Lord Pelham's deputy at the Exchequer;[2] George Worge was Sir Thomas Webster's steward and on 19 July 1750, during his period of office as town clerk, he was elected a freeman of Pevensey;[3] Joseph Acton was town clerk of both Hastings and Pevensey;[4] Thomas Barton town clerk of Pevensey and clerk to the magistrates at Battle;[5] John Tilden clerk of the subdivision meetings and of petty sessions in Hastings rape, in which capacity he was given duties in the execution of supplementary militia, army and navy acts;[6] William Thorpe mayor of Hastings, although he did not complete his year, being removed from office because of bankruptcy;[7] and Thomas Charles Bellingham under-sheriff.[8] The busiest of them all was John Collier. He was town clerk of Hastings from 1706 to 1749 except for the five years when he served as mayor and ex officio coroner. His other offices included solicitor of the Cinque Ports, surveyor-general of the riding officers of the customs of Kent, usher and cryer of King's Bench, judge advocate and principal deputy of the duke of Newcastle as vice admiral of the Sussex coast, steward of several manors and agent for the Sussex estates of Henry Pelham, the prime minister. Also, as one of the barons of the Cinque Ports, he supported the queen's canopy at the coronation of George II.[9]

The Records: Bills

The county coroners' bills are printed first (**1–219**), followed by those of the Hastings rape coroners (**220–299**), both in chronological order, and finally the few bills presented by coroners of hundreds of which three are for Battle and Robertsbridge (**300–302**), four for Gostrow and Bexhill (**303–306**) and two for Battle, Robertsbridge and Gostrow hundreds (**307**, **308**) the second of which ends with four inquests held by the same coroner, Thomas Barton, as coroner of Hastings rape.

All but two (**14**, **224**) of the coroners' bills end with the total of the individual sums claimed for each inquest. Exceptionally, to bill **193** is added: 'I declare this to be a true and just account: J L Ellis, coroner'.[10] The addition may have resulted from the fact that Ellis, a West Sussex coroner, had been acting in the east during the proceedings against Thomas William Wheeler and that, as will be shown below, the bill is unique for its date in claiming for expenses incurred in holding inquests a long distance from Ellis's home at Petworth. Most of the bills contain signed or initialled notes of their having been examined and that they had been allowed by the chairman of quarter sessions. Other frequent notes state that the order had been 'made out' or 'entered', meaning respectively that the order to the treasurer to pay the bill had been written and that it had been entered

1 PAB 188.
2 Salzmann, 146.
3 *Fuller Letters*, nos 82, 393; PEV 385.
4 Baines, 65; PEV 547; PEV 559.
5 PEV 68; QO/EW 43, Midsummer 1817.
6 QR/E 674, no 71; QR/E 678, no 111; QR/E 703, no 181; QO/EW 26, 15 Apr. 1779; QO/EW 32, 6 Oct. 1797; QO/EW 33, 17 Jan. 1799.
7 Baines, 29.
8 QO/EW 52, 5 Apr. 1832.
9 Baines, 62–64, 377; *Collier*, I, vii.
10 The passages quoted in this paragraph will not be found in the text entries cited but only in the original bills.

in the quarter sessions minute or order book. Among the more expansive notes are: 'Let the treasurer of the eastern division of the county of Sussex pay the above bill: G L Newnham, chairman. Made out' (**121**); 'To the treasurer of the eastern division of the county of Sussex. I do allow the above account: G L Newnham, chairman. Lewes, 5 April 1799. Easter Quarter Sessions. Made out' (**120**); 'Examined and approved: Francis Newbery. Allowed: Pelham, chairman. Made out' (**263**); and 'I have perused this bill and I believe that the charges are proper and correct: E J Curteis. Allowed Epiphany sessions 1810: T Partington, chairman. Order made out: T S' (**271**). Normally there is much less, such as 'allowed' (**22**) or 'allowed by the court' (**32**). Occasionally one or two words are in Latin, for example 'In court allocatur: William Kempe' (**87**) or 'Allowed per curiam: William Kempe, chairman. Made out: J H. Entered' (**58**). Except in the earliest bills, there is almost always the date of the sessions, given in the form of either feast and year or day, month and year, or both.

The examination of the bills seems not to have been over rigorous. They contain very few arithmetical errors and those are of a minor nature. A claim for one inquest was too large by 3d (**24**) and another by 6d (**204**) and the bill totals were correspondingly inflated. In another bill (**194**) 6s 9d too much was charged for one inquest and 2s 3d too little for another with the result that the total claimed was 4s 6d too large. One total was 10s too high, the result of faulty addition (**31**). None of those four errors was spotted and corrected by the examiner and the incorrect claims were therefore allowed and paid. Even when £1 1s was charged for each inquest in John Tilden's last bill (**272**) the bill was allowed. It is more understandable that the examiners did not realize that some hundred coroners' inquests were included in two bills, especially as the bills were presented at well separated sessions and the payments were made to different people. The first inquest in Charles Nairn's second bill (**301**) had been in his first (**300**) and the other two were repeated in his third (**302**). The second bill therefore contains nothing which was not included and allowed in the others. The other coroner to have inquests paid for twice was Joseph Acton. One of his bills (**304**) contains only two and they were repeated in the next (**305**) and allowed in both. By contrast, a Crowhurst inquest entered at the end of Thomas Barton's last bill as Hastings rape coroner (**290**) was struck through and repeated as the first entry of Thomas Charles Bellingham's first bill (**291**) in which it was allowed.

The examiners were equally lax about the mileages claimed in the bills. On 27 March 1833 Thomas Charles Bellingham held one inquest at Salehurst and another at Burwash. He charged only £1 for the first and £1 and 10s 6d for 14 miles for the second (**293**). He presumably went on from Salehurst to Burwash before returning home because he normally charged 5s 3d or 6s for the 7 or 8 miles to Salehurst and 6s 9d or 7s 6d for the 9 or 10 miles to Burwash, as he did for other inquests in the same bill. In all other cases when coroners held two or more inquests on the same day but at different places, as they frequently did, they invariably claimed for the full distance from their homes to each of the venues despite the unlikelihood of their always going back home between inquests. Thus on 17 December 1818 George Gwynne held inquests at Bevendean, East Hoathly and West Firle and successfully claimed mileage allowances as though he had travelled to all three places from Lewes (**195**) as did William Wheeler on 16 August 1808 for inquests at Brighton and Worthing (**158**). The fact that the examiners never queried the practice may be because it was strictly in accordance with the letter, if not the spirit, of the 1752 statute. More surprisingly, although coroners sometimes claimed for only one journey when they held two or more inquests on the same day and at the same place, especially when the deaths all arose from the same event (e.g. **284**, 6 inquests at Pett, 5 of them related), on many more occasions they charged full mileages for every inquest. For example, on 2 October 1805 William Wheeler took five inquests at Eastbourne on people who had drowned when a boat capsized and his charge for a journey of 18 miles for each was allowed (**146**). On only one occasion did the examiner challenge such entries, when, in one bill (**116**), William Wheeler claimed five sums of 10s 6d for travelling 14 miles to hold inquests at New Shoreham on 13 January 1798 on five men who had accidentally drowned and two sums of 7s 6d for travelling 10 miles to hold inquests at Hove on 23 February into two other accidental drownings. The court allowed only one journey for each day and so deducted £2 9s 6d from the total claim. By contrast, when Thomas William Wheeler claimed for three separate journeys from Brighton to Eastbourne on 11 December 1815, three more men having accidentally drowned, it was not the number but the length of the journeys that was challenged, as was the 24 miles to East Dean for another inquest because the shortest route was only 15 miles by the coast. The notes made against the relevant entries are much altered, but the result was that the bill total was reduced by 12s 9d (**188**). That was the only time when mileages were queried. In less than a year much more serious accusations were to be levied against Wheeler and there may already have been concerns about his trustworthiness. In some of the above cases a single inquest may have been held on two or more bodies although presented as several inquests in the bills. Other bills contain a single entry for two or more deaths when only one inquest must have been held, as can be proved for one entry as the full inquest on two bodies survives (**265, 459**). Nevertheless claims were made in that case, and in another with two bodies (**205**), for two inquests and one journey; in one with three bodies, for three inquests and one journey (**264**); and in one with seven bodies, for seven inquests and one journey (**164**). Not even the last claim, made by Thomas William Wheeler, was questioned. By contrast, Thomas Barton claimed for only one inquest when he sat on two bodies and for one inquest and one journey for sitting on three (**307, 308**).

There were two other types of adjustment made to a few bills as a result of their examination. On 9 September 1765 Francis Wheeler held an inquest at St Pancras, Chichester, the West Sussex coroner being ill. The £2 10s which he claimed for it in his usual bill was disallowed and he was instructed to apply for the money in West Sussex which he successfully did (**21**). More controversially, when, a few years later, the same coroner held inquests at New Shoreham and Shermanbury, the sums claimed for them were also disallowed, an error in the subtraction resulting in the total being reduced by an extra shilling (**30**). Both New Shoreham and Shermanbury were in that part of Bramber rape in which the East Sussex coroners regularly acted and on no other occasion was their right to do so questioned. It is not surprising that Wheeler was not paid for the two inquests from the West Sussex rate.

The other adjustments were made to adjourned inquests, but in only one bill. When an inquest was adjourned from one day to another it was usual for the coroner to claim a single fee of £1 for the inquest but mileage payments for two full journeys from his home to the venue. That had never previously been challenged and was not again, but in 1819 the claims for the second journeys for each of the ten adjourned inquests which George Gwynne made in one of his early bills (**196**) were all disallowed and the bill total was accordingly reduced by £7 5s 6d, which should strictly have been £7 4s 6d, the examiner not having noticed that a shilling too much had been claimed, probably carelessly, for another inquest. Why Gwynne was singled out for such harsh treatment in just that one bill is unknown, especially as no objection was made to his claiming for two journeys in a similar case in his next bill (**197**). In 1829, when Francis Harding Gell held an inquest at Brighton which was adjourned to a later day, he charged for two inquests but only one journey and he did the same in the next year for adjourned inquests at Hove and Newhaven (**218, 219**). Occasionally single inquest fees and journeys were claimed for inquests which extended over more than one day (**152, 183**), even when they were in West Sussex (**157**), and in one case, of petty treason, it would never have been known from either the bill entry or the full inquest that there had been an adjournment (**236, 423**).[1] When Thomas William Wheeler held an inquest at Petworth on 2 and 3 July 1816, he charged for one inquest and one journey but asked the JPs if they would make any addition to the sum (**190**). That they did not may have been in part because they disapproved of spending East Sussex money on West Sussex business, but also perhaps because word of Wheeler's sharp practices was already circulating. The same considerations may partly account for their refusal of his request for remuneration for attending an inquest at Seaford the year before (**185**).

When a bill had been examined and allowed, an order was made by the quarter sessions for the treasurer to pay the coroner. In some counties the order took the form of a voucher, signed by the clerk of the peace, requiring the treasurer to pay the coroner the sum allowed.[2] It is uncertain if that was the practice in East Sussex but no voucher survives. The order was often entered in the quarter sessions minute book and almost always in the quarter sessions order book. The payment was recorded in the treasurer's account book from February 1761, the year when the first book was begun. If one ignores Thomas William Wheeler's disputed bills, orders for the payment of only four bills (**9, 194, 219, 278**) were omitted from the order books and payment for the last three was entered in the account books. Only for the first is there no supplementary record: the account books had not yet begun and there is nothing in the minute book. Receipt of the money was in at least some cases entered in the ledger of the firm of solicitors to which the coroner belonged. Payment was made either to the coroner himself or to his representative, usually a colleague or, if the coroner had died, to his heir, executor or successor. The county coroners seem normally to have received their payments in person, but after their deaths Thomas Attree's last bill (**18**) was paid to William his son and executor, Francis Wheeler's almost certainly to William his son and successor (**63**) and William Wheeler's to his personal representatives (**162**). Uniquely, George Tilden's last bill as Hastings rape coroner was continued by John his son and successor who was naturally paid for all its inquests (**228**). Although John Tilden was often paid for his bills in person (e.g. **265–267**),[3] payment of five of them (**259, 268–271**) was received by Thomas Barton, his colleague, who is expressly recorded as passing the payment for one of them (**268**) on to Tilden. Barton was very probably one of the personal representatives to whom Tilden's last bill was paid after his death (**272**). On eight occasions payment of Barton's bills was made to Thomas Charles Bellingham, his colleague and successor, the last time after Barton's death (**283–290**). Bellingham usually received payment of his bills in person (e.g. **291–295**).[4] His last two bills were paid to Charles Arnold, one of the witnesses to his will (**298, 299**). Various people were paid on behalf of coroners of hundreds during their periods of office: a Mr Farnes, probably Thomas Farnes, a Lewes solicitor, and Stephen Swatland, later a deputy coroner, for Charles Nairn (**300, 302**) and

1 Cf. *SCM*, XIII, 500.
2 e.g. *Wilts Bills*, xxxii–xxxiii.
3 See the RAF 1/3/4 references in those entries.
4 See the RAF 1/3/10 references in those entries.

Mr Jackson and Charles Bristow, another deputy coroner, for Joseph Acton (**304**, **305**). Jackson must have been Henry Jackson who held lands in Brede and Udimore, the parishes of Acton's Gostrow hundred jurisdiction, and was a son-in-law of John Collier, the earlier Hastings rape coroner (**304**).[1] The Raper and Fovargue ledgers often specify that the payments were received in cash (e.g. **260–263**)[2] and that was probably normal.

The entries in the minute, order and account books contain a few minor copying errors: the sum paid or ordered to be paid may occasionally be slightly incorrect in one of them (e.g. **54**, **100**);[3] the coroner is sometimes assigned a wrong jurisdiction, usually a coroner of a liberty being called a county coroner;[4] and the order for the payment of bill **209** was erroneously entered in the order book (but not the account book) as payable to Thomas Barton, Hastings rape coroner, instead of to George Gwynne, the county coroner.[5] Nevertheless their existence makes it possible to be confident that, with two exceptions, all the bills presented between 1752 and 1830 survive as do ledger entries of all the Hastings rape bills from then until 1838. Confidence is enhanced when the entries give the date of the sessions at which the previous bill had been submitted despite there being some errors. The errors are often explicable by the first inquest of the bill having been taken some months after the submission of the former bill: for example, an order book[6] has an entry ordering payment for taking inquests (entered in bill **264**) since the last Easter sessions; in fact the previous bill (**263**) had been presented at Epiphany, but the first inquest in **264** was not taken until April. One bill which has not survived was presented by Francis Wheeler to the Midsummer sessions of 1777 when an order was made for £14 5s 3d to be paid to him. Not only the bill but the whole quarter sessions roll on which it would have been filed is lost (**39**). In 1818 William Thorpe submitted a bill for inquests held between 13 February 1817 and 8 July 1818 and its total of £23 4s was allowed at the Midsummer sessions. Attached to the bill is a note containing the sum of £7 4s to which was added 5s, making £7 9s. Thorpe was paid the £23 4s with an additional 5s in July and the £7 9s in August (**278**). The latter sum was for inquests, but no details of them survive. They must have been held between 8 and 23 July when the first inquest of his next bill was taken (**279**).

It follows that, incredible as it may seem, coroners made no claims for payment for inquests held during the sometimes lengthy periods for which there are no bills or no inquests in extant bills. There are relatively few such gaps in the county coroners' inquests: they are never of more than four months and are confined to the earlier years when fewer inquests were held. Only one surviving inquest (**361**) held by a county coroner between 1752 and 1830 is not entered on a bill. It was taken by William Wheeler in 1795 and should have been in bill **107**. That Wheeler made a claim for returning it to the clerk of assize (**108**) proves that it was omitted in error. He was usually keen to ensure that he obtained all the money to which he was entitled, on three occasions claiming in later bills for inquests omitted from earlier ones (**101**, **110**, **159**). There were nevertheless a number of deaths not in the bills into which the county coroners should

1 *East Sussex Land Tax 1785*, ed. R Davey (SRS, LXXVII, 1991), 27, 205; Baines, 377.

2 See the RAF 1/3/3 and 4 references in those entries.

3 For **54**, QO/EW 27 has £10 1s 3d (the bill total plus 5s) but QAF 2/1/E2 has £10 1s 6d; and for **100**, QO/EW 31 has £7 2s 3d (the bill total plus 5s) but QAF 2/1/E3 has £7 4s 3d.

4 John Tilden was often called a county coroner in QO/EW 23 and 24, as was Charles Nairn in QO/EW 23, 17 Jan. 1771 and Joseph Acton in QO/EW 24, 8 Oct. 1772.

5 QO/EW 48; QAF 2/1/E9.

6 QO/EW 35.

have held inquests, such as that of Thomas Butler at Brighton in 1782 for which Alexander Watson was indicted and tried at the assizes.[1] With just a few exceptions (e.g. **22**, **296**) inquests were entered in the bills in strict chronological order, although occasionally an adjourned session at a later date appears immediately after the first session (e.g. **212**, where it created a larger disorder) and a claim for returning an inquest to the clerk of assize is entered immediately after the inquest (e.g. **260**). The gaps between some Hastings rape bills and also between inquests within them were more frequent and much longer. For example, no inquest is recorded before 28 December 1753 or between June 1755 and July 1756, October 1757 and November 1758, October 1779 and September 1780, November 1769 and November 1771 or November 1783 and September 1784, each of the last two gaps occurring within single bills (**232**, **244**). That might just represent the rape coroners' more relaxed attitude towards the bureaucratic element of their work, as evidenced by their irregular submission of their bills, because, while it is true that their district was smaller and less populous than that of their county colleagues, it is difficult to believe that they held, or should have held, no inquests for such lengthy periods. No original inquest survives which should have been in any of their bills and is not. Perhaps the rape coroners were summoned to fewer borderline cases, but the parish registers contain many burials of persons whose deaths should have occasioned inquests. To give just one example, the Battle register records the burial, in one grave, on 5 December 1764 of two men who had been killed by an explosion at Sedlescombe gunpowder mill, two other victims having been buried at Sedlescombe.[2] The Hastings rape bills of that period contain other Sedlescombe inquests but not one for those deaths. It is difficult to deduce much from the few bills of hundred coroners, but one of Joseph Acton's extant inquests (**452**) is not on a bill and Walter Acton never submitted a bill although three of his inquests survive (**464–466**).

The coroners could submit their bills at the Epiphany, Easter, Midsummer or Michaelmas quarter sessions which were held at Lewes roughly every three months. The frequency with which they did so varied markedly. Even the county coroners were erratic. Thomas Attree and Francis Wheeler presented theirs after three, six, nine or twelve months, whereas William and Thomas William Wheeler never waited more than three months. The financial problems he experienced during his last years as coroner suggest that Thomas William Wheeler may always have been anxious to be reimbursed at the earliest possible date. George Gwynne's first bill covered a whole year but all his others and those of Francis Harding Gell were presented every six months, probably because of the great increase in the number of inquests which they held. The Hastings rape coroners claimed payment less frequently, after anything from three to thirty months, three or six months being abnormal. The bills of the coroners of hundreds contain inquests held over much longer periods, more than eleven years in one (**302**). In 1837 it was ordered by statute that coroners should make their claims within four months of holding an inquest,[3] which meant that thereafter bills had to be submitted at every session and the last three Hastings rape bills were (**297–299**). The new regulation may also account for the previous bill (**296**) being divided into two, the second part covering roughly three months.

1 ASSI 94/1235.
2 PAR 236/1/1/2.
3 1 Victoria c 68.

The amount of detail about the inquests provided in the bills varies considerably. Thomas Attree, the first county coroner to present bills, merely included the date and place of the inquest, the name of the deceased and the barest inquest verdict, such as 'accident' or 'murder', although just occasionally he added some further information, for example 'by a fall from a horse' or 'felo de se, hanged'. For most of the inquests in two of the earlier of Francis Wheeler's bills (**25**, **26**) not even the brief verdict is included, but otherwise the three Wheelers' bills are among the most informative, except for inquests held in the House of Correction for which there is never a verdict in the bills of any county coroner. The last two, George Gwynne and Francis Harding Gell, presented their bills in list form, with date, place and name of deceased, sometimes in ruled columns (e.g. **294**), and no verdict, their brevity doubtless dictated by the larger number of inquests each contains. The first Hastings rape bills, those of George Tilden, also omitted verdicts, but all the other franchisal coroners gave at least a brief summary of the deaths.

Whatever else may or may not have been in the bills, until 1837 they all contain the sums allowed since 1752,[1] namely £1 for holding each inquest and 9d a mile for travelling to the venue which were the equivalent of £103 22p and £3 87p a mile in 2002 money.[2] One early bill (**24**) omitted all the mileages but not the sums for the journeys. Two other early ones (**14**, **224**) do not have a bill total. In most bills the £1 for the inquest and the sum claimed for the journey are entered separately, but in the later county coroners' bills, which are more succinct, the two amounts are added together. There is one exceptional bill in which £1 1s was claimed for each inquest and that amount was paid without being queried. It was the last bill of John Tilden, the Hastings rape coroner, and was paid to his personal representatives after his death. It is strange that in the version of the bill in a Raper and Fovargue ledger all the inquest charges were nevertheless changed from £1 1s to £1 (**272**). Between 1752 and 1837 the pound had lost roughly half of its value, falling from the 2002 equivalent of £103 22p to £53, and in 1837 the inquest fee was increased to £1 6s 8d, although less for that reason than because of the extra duties introduced by the same statute.[3] The first inquest in the extant bills for which the higher fee was claimed was held on 18 July 1837 (**296**). Travelling expenses remained unchanged, although by 1837 9d a mile represented £1 99p, not £3 87p; but, during the proceedings against Thomas William Wheeler, Serjeant Samuel Shepherd had given it as his opinion that coroners should be paid 9d a mile for travelling both to and from an inquest, which was the practice in some counties such as Middlesex and Kent, although he accepted that elsewhere payment was made for the outward journey only (**508**). Certainly no Sussex coroner, not even Wheeler, had ever attempted to claim for returning home, nor did any after 1817. The county coroners never claimed travelling expenses for inquests held in the places where they lived, but coroners who lived in Battle occasionally claimed for one or two miles (e.g. **252**, **283**), presumably when the venue was in a remote part of the parish. In some instances (e.g. **271**) when an inquest was held in a place other than that in which the coroner lived, he specified that it was in the 'further part' of the parish in order to justify his claim for a longer journey than normal. The fact that the 1752 statute did not allow travelling expenses for inquests held in gaol was irrelevant for East Sussex coroners during the period of their surviving bills because the county gaol was at Horsham until the 1830s[4] and, although they could have held

1 By the statute 25 George II c 29.
2 2002 values in this paragraph are from the Economic History website (www.eh.net).
3 1 Victoria c 68.
4 *VCH Sx*, VI (2), 134.

inquests there, they never did so. Houses of Correction probably did not qualify as gaols under the statute, although the East Sussex evidence is ambiguous. Thomas Attree, who lived at Newick, held no inquests in the House of Correction. Thereafter the county coroners held many there, but as they normally lived at either Lewes or Cliffe they could have claimed nothing for travelling because the House of Correction was at Cliffe until 1793 and then in North Street, Lewes.[1] Thomas William Wheeler charged only £1 for the first inquest he held there after his move to Brighton (**184**), but 6s for the 8-mile journey for all subsequent ones (**187–189**) which was always allowed.

The bills contain several other kinds of claims. One was for the reimbursement of the coroners for 5s which they had paid the clerk of assize for returning an inquest to him at the assizes. The first such claim was made by Francis Wheeler in 1774 (**35**) and the county coroners made 22 more, one for 10s for two inquests (**112**), between 1781 and 1808. The only others were made by John Tilden for returning four Hastings rape inquests in 1799, 1803 and 1807. For one of the four, which was held on two bodies, Tilden claimed and was allowed 10s (**265**, **459**). All the inquests recorded in the bills as being returned to the clerk of assize survive except for one of 1781 (**50**). Their verdicts were either murder or manslaughter, although not all resulted in a trial at assizes. Nine other inquests of the years 1774 to 1808 delivered to the assizes by coroners survive for which no claims were made (**350**, **356**, **422**, **423**, **425–428**, **460**), but one of them (**350**) was into a natural death and six were held in Hastings rape earlier than 1799. Perhaps John Tilden, who held all six, was unaware of the possibility of claiming reimbursement until the last years of the practice. It may have been started by the county coroners without any legal basis but only questioned and discontinued after more than thirty years. That is something which warrants further research. It would also be interesting to discover if any such payments were made to coroners in other counties. Certainly Wiltshire coroners did not receive them.[2]

Also unknown in Wiltshire, and possibly elsewhere, was an additional 5s often paid to the county and franchisal coroners of East Sussex between 1761 and 1823 over and above the sums claimed and allowed in their bills. It was paid only erratically until 1775, but regularly thereafter: on the county coroners' bills at Midsummer 1761 (**14**), Epiphany 1771 to Epiphany 1773 (**29–32**), and Epiphany 1775 to Epiphany 1823 (**36–190**, **193–203**), excluding two of Thomas William Wheeler's disputed bills (**191**, **192**); on the Hastings rape bills at Midsummer 1761 (**225**), Epiphany 1766 and Easter 1767 (**228**, **229**) and Epiphany 1772 to Epiphany 1822 (**232–281**); and on the hundred coroners' bills from Epiphany 1771 to Midsummer 1819 (**301–308**). Francis Wheeler presented two bills (**21**, **23**) to the West Sussex quarter sessions, at Easter 1766 and Easter 1767, for inquests which he had held in that half of the county. He was paid the amount claimed in the first, but the court ordered an extra 5s to be added to the second.[3] John Luttman Ellis, the West Sussex county coroner, was also paid the additional 5s on the two bills (**163**, **193**) which he presented to the East Sussex quarter sessions. In most cases the addition of the extra 5s is known because that is the amount by which the sum ordered to be paid as recorded in the quarter sessions order book, and entered as being paid in the treasurer's account book, exceeded the total claimed by the coroner. Twice the additional 5s was included in

1 Brent, 70–71.
2 *Wilts Bills*.
3 QM/EW 10; QO/EW 23, p 40.

the former but not the latter[1] and five times in the latter but not the former.[2] On eight occasions (**115**, **130**, **137**, **140**, **150**, **160**, **177**, **278**) the addition of the 5s was made on the bill itself, sometimes specifically stated as being by order of the court, meaning quarter sessions. When receipt of payment was recorded against the Hastings rape bills in the Raper and Fovargue ledgers the additional 5s was never included (**232–272**). The authorization of the payment of the 5s and the reason for its discontinuance have yet to be discovered. An extra 8s was added to one of George Gwynne's bills without any explanation, but, when he was paid, the additional sum was recorded separately in both the quarter sessions order book and the treasurer's account book. It was nothing to do with his duties as coroner but was for his fees on the conviction of a vagrant (**208**).

Before 1837 the only claims in the bills for the coroners' payments to others were for those made to the clerks of assize. Modest expenses incurred in holding inquests were sometimes paid by the town or parish but they were purely local arrangements which were not entered on the coroners' bills: as, for example, when Lewes paid £1 6s in 1741 for the expenses of the coroner and jury.[3] The bill containing the inquests held by John Luttman Ellis, the West Sussex coroner, while acting in place of the imprisoned Thomas William Wheeler (**193**) is exceptional in that he claimed and was allowed expenses for being out all night on eight occasions, for two nights on two others, and once for the hire of a horse and gig. The long journeys entailed must have persuaded the JPs to bend the rules in his case. It is interesting that when Ellis presented an earlier bill for inquests held between the coronerships of William and Thomas William Wheeler he made no such claims (**163**). There was a major development in 1836, although one which had no immediate effect on their bills, when coroners were given the power by statute to summon medical witnesses either to give evidence or to perform post-mortem examinations unless the death had occurred in a hospital, infirmary or lunatic asylum. The medical practitioners were entitled to fees of £1 1s for giving evidence or £2 2s for also performing a post mortem, payment to be made, on the coroner's order, by the churchwardens and overseers of the place where the inquest was held out of the parish funds for the relief of the poor.[4] A year later that Act was repealed and coroners were henceforth to pay the medical witnesses their fees at the end of the inquest and to claim reimbursement at quarter sessions from the county rate. The 1837 Act also required the justices of the peace at the next quarter sessions to draw up a schedule of any other 'fees, allowances and disbursements' that might lawfully be paid by the coroners in holding inquests and which could similarly be claimed by them at quarter sessions. Presumably as recompense for the more onerous nature of their duties, the coroners were to be paid 6s 8d for every inquest over and above the other fees to which they were entitled.[5]

A schedule was accordingly drawn up at the quarter sessions held at Lewes on 16 October 1837 which was to remain in force until fourteen days after the following Easter. The expenses authorized were: to the messenger for the coroner, for any distance not exceeding 5 miles 2s 6d and for any distance above 5 miles a maximum of 6d a mile, viz 3d a mile for going and returning, at the discretion of the coroner; to the constable, for

1 For **32** (QO/EW 24; QAF 2/1/E1); and **189** (QO/EW 42; QAF 2/1/E7).

2 For **175**, **186**, **188** (QO/EW 40–42; QAF 2/1/E7); **234** (QO/EW 24; QAF 2/1/E1); and **239** (QO/EW 26; QAF 2/1/E2).

3 QR/E 454.

4 6 & 7 William IV c 89.

5 1 Victoria c 68.

summoning the jury, including the charge of summoning witnesses from the immediate neighbourhood and his attendance during the inquest 5s; to the constable, for summoning witnesses attending under a summons issued from the coroner — if they reside within 4 miles to be included in the above charges, if beyond that distance 3d a mile for going and returning; for the use of a room to deposit the body of a pauper or stranger where necessary, for each day and night 2s; to each juryman upon an inquest the holding of which does not exceed 5 hours 1s, if longer 2s, and the same allowances for every day of adjournment; to the witnesses, if residing within 4 miles the like allowances, if beyond that distance 3d a mile for going and returning in addition; and for a room to hold the inquest, if at an inn 5s per day, and so for every adjourned day the inquest is held.[1] No change was made at the Easter sessions of 4 April 1838.[2]

Although the schedule was not compiled until 16 October 1837, it was applied retroactively from the passing of the statute on 15 July. The first Hastings rape inquest after that date was held on 18 July and the coroner's extra 6s 8d and expenses for the constable, 12 jurymen and two witnesses were claimed. The bill submitted to the quarter sessions does not survive, but the expenses for that and subsequent inquests, which sometimes included payments to a surgeon as well as to the constable, jurymen and witnesses, were pinned to a later page in the Raper and Fovargue ledger with the total added to the ledger version of the bill (**296**). The magnitude of the changes is illustrated by the claims for the inquests to 10 June being totalled separately and the sum being included in the final total for the bill, although one further inquest was held, on 29 June, before the new fees became payable; and by the note in the quarter sessions order book that the account included sums due to the coroner under 1 Victoria c 68 with a specific mention of payments to medical witnesses.[3] The final three Hastings rape bills (**297–299**) contain claims for expenses for every inquest but omit to whom they had been paid. The details may have been in the bills as presented, but more probably were in vouchers which by the statute the coroners were to submit to substantiate their claims. No such vouchers survive which is not surprising given that the bills to which they were subsidiary were not preserved.

There remains the question from what material the bills were compiled. It will be reserved for the next section, after a consideration of the compilation of the full inquests.

The Records: Inquests

The extant bills record 3,620 inquests: 2,678 held by county coroners between 1752 and 1830, 898 by Hastings rape coroners between 1752 and 1838 and 44 by coroners of hundreds from 1752 to 1830. For the same periods only 79 full inquests are known to survive: 53 held by county coroners, 11 by Hastings rape coroners and 15 by coroners of hundreds. Five of the 79 (**361**, **452**, **464–466**) are not on any bill, although there is a claim for returning the first of them to the clerk of assize (**108**). The four others were held by Gostrow hundred coroners. For the whole period of this volume there are a mere 142 inquests: 100 from the body of the county (**309–409**), 21 from Hastings rape (**410–437**) and 21 from the hundreds (**445–467**), if one accepts the jurisdictions assigned to the coroners in them. The survival rate of inquests had declined rapidly from the middle of

1 SHE 2/5/1.
2 SHE 2/5/2.
3 QO/EW 55, 16 Oct. 1837.

the seventeenth century when the inquests of the Home Circuit, and of Sussex in particular, ceased to be returned regularly into the court of King's Bench and preserved on its files.[1] That situation was even more marked after 1688. Although the King's Bench files continued for many years to overflow with inquests from other circuits, they contain very few from the Home Circuit of which only three (**311–313**), from 1690 and 1691, are from East Sussex. A fourth inquest, of 1689, is recorded as having been returned into King's Bench but the file in which it should have been preserved is missing (**410**). The assize indictments files contain 128 inquests. The remaining eleven, all but one of which were held by coroners of hundreds, are in the East Sussex Record Office. The exception (**415**) was held by the coroner of Hastings rape and originally belonged in an assize indictments file which strayed from official custody and became dispersed, although the Essex part of it has since been restored to the parent series in the National Archives.[2]

The three inquests now with the records of King's Bench were almost certainly delivered into that court either by or for the coroner, not via the assizes: it would have been strange if the clerk of assize had forwarded just those three. As described above, the inquests now on the assize files and the single stray were returned to the clerk of assize by the coroners. The ten others owe their survival to the misdemeanours perpetrated by Joseph Acton, not as coroner but as town clerk of Hastings. After his death his son John was ordered in 1799 'to deliver the records belonging to the corporation which were purloined by his father during the time of his town clerkship'.[3] In an excess of zeal John Acton must have returned not only Hastings borough records but also the ten Gostrow hundred inquests, at which Robert Lovelace Chambers, Joseph Acton himself, Charles Nairn, Charles Bristow and Walter Acton had officiated, and a jury summons issued by George Worge as coroner of Gostrow hundred (**451**), with none of which Hastings had any concern. Walter Acton's last inquest was held in 1796 which suggests that Joseph was not the only member of the Acton family who regarded official documents as his personal possessions. After 1799 the ten inquests and the jury summons were in the borough's custody until the year 2000 when they were transferred from the Hastings Museum and Art Gallery to the East Sussex Record Office.

The fact that the majority of the extant inquests were returned to the clerk of assize explains the imbalance in the verdicts. They are heavily biased towards homicide of various kinds, especially infanticide. There are 124 homicide inquests. Of the 18 others, 9 are deaths by misadventure (**311**, **312**, **450**, **452–455**, **462**, **466**), 6 natural deaths (**337**, **340**, **350**, **415**, **457**, **465**), 2 suicides (**313**, **464**) and one a stillbirth (**377**). They comprise the eleven held locally, the three on King's Bench files and four on assize files. Three of the four on assize files — the stillbirth and two natural deaths — and the natural death on the strayed assize file were undoubtedly returned to the clerk of assize because there was a suspicion of murder: in three cases the grand jury presented murder indictments on which there were trials, but in the fourth it rejected a bill of indictment.

When inquests do not survive but are known to have been held because they are represented in the bills, associated records are printed among the extant inquests as separate items, in their correct geographical and chronological positions. There are

1 *Sx Inqs 1603–1688*, xii–xiii.
2 As ASSI 94/344.
3 Baines, 65–66.

15 such items and two others which have no entries on the bills. The two exceptions relate to a Gostrow hundred inquest of 1751, just before the first bills and well before the earliest Gostrow bill, and a Robertsbridge hundred inquest of 1782 (**451**, **463**); of the other 15, one (**390**) concerns an entry on a county coroner's bill and the rest have entries on Hastings rape bills. Three are outline inquests (**432**, **438**, **439**), three are indictments at assizes (**390**, **424**, **434**), four jury summonses issued by coroners (**433**, **444**, **451**, **463**), two coroners' warrants for conveying suspects to gaol (**430**, **436**), one a coroner's burial warrant (**435**), one a coroner's summons of a medical witness (**441**), two letters to coroners concerning inquests (**440**, **443**) and one a report of a death to the coroner (**442**). The three indictments are on the assize indictments files and all the other documents are now in the East Sussex Record Office. The Gostrow hundred jury summons is among the records rescued by John Acton and all the others except for the Robertsbridge hundred jury summons are in the archive of Charles Sheppard and Sons of Battle, solicitors, where they were kept as precedents, some being copies or summaries of returns made by the Hastings rape coroners under orders of Parliament.

As previously, the earlier inquests printed here were signed by the coroner, but beginning with that of 1734 (**327**) most had the coroner's seal appended as well as his signature. That practice was in its turn changed some time between January 1778, the date of the last extant East Sussex inquest to be signed and sealed by the coroner alone (**350**), and August 1781, after which all inquests, beginning with **351**, were signed and sealed by the coroner and every juror, although illiterate jurors made their marks instead of signing (e.g. **355**). The change may well have taken place in 1779 as it did in Kent and probably in most other counties.[1] Until 1733 coroners' inquests had normally been written in Latin, but on 25 March of that year Latin was replaced by English for all courts.[2] Inquest **327**, again, is the first in this volume to have been written in English as were all subsequent ones, but whatever the language the inquests as submitted to superior courts were always written on parchment and retained the style and wording that had evolved over the preceding centuries and which give their contents an unreal uniformity. What lay behind the rigidity of the formal inquests can occasionally be discovered from two other sources: the depositions of witnesses which have occasionally survived and the few extant drafts of the inquests. All known depositions are printed here, four with county coroners' inquests (**391**, **392**, **394**, **404**) and five with inquests of hundreds (**450**, **452**, **464**, **465**, **467**). The first four and the last one were returned to the clerk of assize with their inquests and are especially detailed, showing what a wealth of information had to be reduced to the bare bones of the formal inquest. The other four are preserved in the East Sussex Record Office with their inquests.

There are only two known drafts of extant formal inquests: one (**413**) is in the East Sussex Record Office with the papers of John Collier, the successor of Anthony Trumble who held the inquest in 1715 as Hastings rape coroner; and the other (**417**), of 1741, was returned, obviously by mistake, to the clerk of assize by George Tilden, another Hastings rape coroner, with the formal version. Both drafts are written on paper and contain the signatures or marks of the coroner and jurors, long before they began to appear on formal inquests. In each case both draft and formal inquest are printed in the text in full calendar form to illustrate the many differences between them. It is therefore unnecessary to give

1 ASSI 94/1178; ASSI 94/1184: Kent files containing the last inquest without and the first with jurors' signatures and seals.

2 By the statute 4 George II c 26.

every detail of their variation here, but it is interesting that in the formal inquest of 1741 Tilden is called county coroner whereas in the draft, which he wrote himself, he is correctly called coroner of Hastings rape. Both inquests were adjourned, but that information is recorded only in the drafts. The narratives vary considerably and are much more discursive in the drafts. Indeed, in the 1715 draft the narrative is given as the deposition of named witnesses with just the final sentence as the jury's verdict. Neither draft contains the fact that the homicide had no possessions which is the last sentence in the versions sent to the higher court. Because returns were made in a very small minority of cases, it is probable that only those few inquests were formally engrossed in the standardized form which had become recognized as acceptable to the courts. It is surprising that so few drafts have survived. Other than the two just described, the only East Sussex drafts are those of Gostrow hundred inquests preserved as a result of Joseph Acton's retaining them extra-officially, but there are two copies of one of them (**454**), a corrected draft and a fair copy draft. Their rarity means that much local colour and drama as well as more mundane detail have been lost.

The variations between the draft and formal versions of the inquests are similar to those between the latter and the related entries on the coroners' bills. The drafts must have been based on a number of subsidiary documents: jury summonses and panels, notes made during the sittings and, as already shown, depositions of witnesses. The bill entries must have been compiled either from the same documents or, in most cases more probably, from the draft inquests themselves. Three of the Gostrow hundred draft inquests (**453**, **455**, **457**) contain a note of the miles travelled and the fee to be claimed, which was obviously added in readiness for the compilation of the bills. One of them (**455**) also notes the receipt of the money by the coroner. In twelve instances (e.g. **185**, **378**) the bills state that the inquests were adjourned from one day to another whereas the corresponding formal records returned to the clerk of assize give only one date. It was, of course, more important for the adjournments to be in the bills because of the payments involved. Similarly, to justify their mileage claims coroners were often more specific in their bills about the places where the inquests were held than was thought necessary for the formal returns. Thus one bill has Fairlight church but the inquest just Fairlight (**260**, **429**). Other examples are Cooden and Bexhill (**267**, **460**), Burwash Down and Burwash (**235**, **422**), Sewers Bridge in Hooe and Hooe (**227**, **420**), Southbourne and Eastbourne (**212**, **391**) and Handcross in Slaugham and Slaugham (**54**, **352**). Occasionally, however, it is the inquest which has the greater detail about the venue. In two bills it is given as Bexhill while in the inquests it is the Bell Inn at Bexhill (**269**, **284**, **461**, **467**). More interesting are the differences in the narrative sections which show how the two documents often chose different parts of the underlying sources. Three men are said in the bills to have been killed in boxing-matches, but there is no mention of boxing in the inquests (**78**, **89**, **111**, **357**, **358**, **363**); and in another case only in the bill is it stated that the deceased had agreed to the fight in which he was killed (**145**, **371**). According to one bill a homicide was a private in the East Kent regiment of militia but the inquest calls him a soldier, late of St Clement's, Hastings (**258**, **428**); in another bill the two deceased are called gunners of the Royal Artillery but have no descriptions in the inquest (**265**, **459**); and in a third a homicide is unnamed but called a seaman belonging to a revenue cutter at New Shoreham whereas the inquest names him but merely describes him as a mariner (**111**, **364**).

John Tilden's bill which begins with an inquest of 10 March 1766 (**229**) — his first bill if one ignores his continuation of his father's last bill (**228**) — was entered in a Raper and Fovargue ledger before being submitted to quarter sessions, as were all Hastings rape bills from that time until early 1838 except for those of William Thorpe between 1810 and 1819, Thorpe not belonging to the same firm of solicitors. Indeed, as already noted, the bills of the last eight years are known only from the ledger versions. Additionally, many of the bill entries from 11 January 1792 (**251**) to 12 October 1825 (**284**), again with the exception of Thorpe's period of office, can be found entered separately in their correct chronological positions in the Raper and Fovargue day books. The fact that not every inquest was entered in the day books, and for some years very few of them were, means that the bills could not have been compiled from them. Nevertheless, all differences of substance between the day book entries and those in the bills submitted to quarter sessions have been noted below the text of each bill as have material differences between the bills as entered in the ledgers and as presented. It would be tedious to rehearse most of the variations here. They are of two kinds: inevitable copying errors and changes introduced to produce a more polished text. Some of the errors prove that the bills submitted to the JPs were not copied, or not copied solely, from the ledgers. Sometimes the venue is defined more exactly in the former than in the latter: Seacox Heath in Etchingham and Bardown in Ticehurst instead of just Etchingham and Ticehurst (**237**, **253**). In other cases it is the ledger version which is more explicit, with the farthest part of Beckley and Mountfield Park as against Beckley and Mountfield (**244**, **253**). There are similar differences in the names of persons on whom inquests were held: William Peck and Samuel Beeding in the formal bills, William Pack and Samuel Beeching in the ledgers (**249**, **252**): the parish registers show that the submitted bill was correct in the first case and the ledger in the second. The narrative parts of the entries also vary, with sometimes the ledger and sometimes the final bill having the greater detail. To give just two examples among many, in only the ledger version of one case is it said that a man was found dead at Westfield and his body was removed to Brede where the inquest was held (**252**), but the ledger version of another omits the fact that the deceased had been killed by his wife (**236**). Finally, whereas the total amounts claimed in the bills presented are almost always correct, there are often errors in the ledgers (e.g. **244**, **246**, **266**), although when £1 1s was successfully claimed for every inquest in one bill that sum had been changed to £1 in the ledger where there was also an error in calculation (**272**). Such variations prove that the two versions must have been compiled independently of each other, as were bills and inquests, and that is confirmed by the occasional omission of an entry from the ledger but not from the bill proper (e.g. **246**). From 1819, however, the ledger versions and the final bills were almost identical, but there were still many differences between the day book entries and the bills (**280–284**).

Some Wiltshire coroners of the late eighteenth century wrote their own bills.[1] The East Sussex bills were all written by men experienced in engrossing formal documents. No detailed study of the handwriting has been undertaken, but a spot check of a few bills which contain notes made by the coroners shows that the notes were in the same handwriting as the bills themselves (e.g. **185**, **190**, **193**). It might have been thought that, as the coroners were all busy lawyers and had ready access to clerks in their practices, the clerks would normally have compiled their bills. It is virtually certain that the formal bills of the Hastings rape coroners which survive in duplicate (and some of their entries in triplicate) were written by the same men who made the corresponding entries in their firm's day books and ledgers. Other coroners, both county and franchisal, may have had

1 R F Hunnisett, 'Eighteenth-Century Coroners and their Clerks', *WAM*, LXXVI, 126.

a similar system or some of them may have kept draft bills on separate sheets of paper as one Wiltshire coroner did on at least one occasion.[1] Like the Wiltshire coroners,[2] those of East Sussex sometimes wrote the draft inquests (e.g. **417**), and sometimes the attendant depositions as well (e.g. **464**, **465**), but the inquests returned to the clerk of assize are consistent in appearance as well as wording over long periods. They must have been engrossed by scriveners who specialized in producing documents in a form which was acceptable to the higher courts. Before 1779 there was no need for the formal record to be drawn up at the inquest because it had merely to be signed, or signed and sealed, by the coroner. Presumably that was done later, only if and when it was needed at the assizes. After 1779 formal inquests must have been drawn up immediately after homicide verdicts had been returned in order for the jurors to sign and seal them. That may account for the adjournment of some inquests, as happened in Wiltshire where one inquest in a murder case was adjourned for eight days in 1790 'chiefly to have [the inquest] engrossed and then subscribed with the jurors' hands and seals as now directed and required by the assize judges', although also to take further depositions.[3] Perhaps such formal inquests were written only when a homicide verdict was given or expected, which may account for the occasional return of non-homicide inquests to the assizes and the absence of the vast majority of them. Until 1779 it was probably considered unnecessary for clerks to attend inquests, but thereafter they drew up the formal document at the venue for signature and sealing before the jurors dispersed. At least outside the smaller franchises, they were probably also employed to take down depositions as they were delivered because the deponents had to sign them or make their marks. The depositions, particularly the later, longer ones, read as though they were answers to questions and the clerks must have written them down as they were spoken. They were certainly written in a different hand to that of the coroners (e.g. **391**, **392**).

The foregoing discussion of the compilation of coroners' records prompts one obvious question: what trust can be placed in their contents? A similar study of medieval coroners' records led to a melancholy conclusion: that 'it has long been realized that medieval chronicles must be approached with caution, but at least historians can usually recognize and allow for the chronicler's bias. The reliability of many official records seems to be no greater, and from their haphazard mixture of fact, fiction and error the complete truth can rarely be distilled.'[4] Whether or not that judgment is equally true of the eighteenth and early nineteenth centuries can be determined only after a consideration of the case of Thomas William Wheeler.

The Case of Thomas William Wheeler

On 17 October 1816 James Cranbourne Strode, a Sussex JP who was shortly to become sheriff of the county, wrote to William Balcombe Langridge, the clerk of the peace, questioning the legality of Wheeler's charging the family of a woman on whom he had held an inquest at Frant £4 3s as expenses which they had paid (**477**). In reply Langridge informed Strode that he had presented his letter to the quarter sessions with Wheeler's bill (**191**) in which he had claimed the full amount allowed by statute for the Frant inquest

1 *WAM*, LXXVI, 125–128.
2 *Wilts Bills*, xl.
3 *Wilts Bills*, nos 1689, 1692.
4 R F Hunnisett, 'The Reliability of Inquisitions as Historical Evidence', in *The Study of Medieval Records: essays in honour of Kathleen Major*, ed. D A Bullough and R L Storey (Oxford, 1971), 227.

and that Wheeler had been severely censured and the bill disallowed. He asked Strode to make an investigation into the matter (**478**). The investigation revealed that Wheeler had travelled from Brighton to Frant in a post-chaise with two ladies and a child and that he had been paid the consequent £4 3s expenses — but, at Wheeler's insistence, not in the presence of the jury — and also the 'customary' 6s for refreshments (**479**). Wheeler's behaviour seems not to have surprised the magistrates who suspected that it was not an isolated case and also disapproved of his demeanour in court (**510**, **511**). Not long before, they had reduced the amount claimed in one of his bills because he had not taken the most direct route to inquest venues (**188**) and had refused to pay him extra money for a Petworth inquest which had been adjourned (**190**) or anything for travelling to Seaford for an inquest in which, in the event, he did not participate (**185**). On 18 October, the day on which they learned of Strode's letter (**518**), they ordered Langridge to inquire about Wheeler's conduct in all the inquests he had taken since Midsummer 1816 when his previous bill (**190**) had been presented. Langridge therefore wrote to the overseers of the poor in all the parishes in which, according to his bill, Wheeler had held inquests since Midsummer, asking them if the inquests had been taken by Wheeler in person and, if not, the name of the deputy, if any money had been demanded or taken by Wheeler or a deputy, and if anything had been paid for a deodand (**480**). The returns by the overseers revealed so many and such serious offences that the inquiry was extended to cover the previous quarter, from Easter to Midsummer (e.g. **496**).

The replies to Langridge are printed in the appendix (**479–504**). The story that they tell is one of consistent extortion by the coroner. His most frequent practice was to demand money from relatives of the deceased, however poor (e.g. **504**), or, if they were quite unable to pay, from the parish officers (e.g. **499**) whom he also charged for refreshments. Only rarely was payment refused (e.g. **485**). Another of Wheeler's demands, usually successful, was for money for deodands even when there was considerable doubt as to whether they had caused the deaths (e.g. **488**). Some of the inquests were found to have been held by deputies who lived near the inquest venues and it was revealed that Wheeler had been using them for much longer than the period under investigation. One East Grinstead man had been in the habit of deputizing in the East Grinstead area not only for Thomas William Wheeler but also for his predecessor, William Wheeler (**487**). The use of deputies had never been mentioned in the bills of either coroner in which they always claimed the full mileage allowances as though they had travelled personally from their homes to the venues. On one occasion Thomas William Wheeler asked for no money beyond 6s for refreshments, but took the fowling-piece with which the deceased had shot himself (**494**). On another he refused to authorize the burial of the deceased until one of the churchwardens had paid him £2 which he assured him was customary (**502**). Most serious of all were the two deaths for which Wheeler claimed inquest and travelling fees in his bill but on which neither he nor a deputy held an inquest. One was a sudden death at Brighton resulting from a fit and no inquest was held because friends and relations thought it unnecessary (**493**). The other deceased was not an unchristened infant, as Wheeler alleged in his bill, but a child aged five or six who had been baptized. Wheeler had been sent for but attended neither in person nor by deputy, saying that it was unnecessary as a doctor had been with the child when it choked on a plum-stone (**497**). Some of the replies give details of payments of 1s to each juror and, less often, of small amounts to the headborough or constable (e.g. **499**), but that seems to have been regarded as an acceptable tradition as does the provision of refreshments.

The offences reported to Langridge were to form the basis of two indictments against Wheeler, but in the meantime he had presented a final bill (**192**) containing claims for eleven inquests taken between 9 November and 21 December 1816. No payment was made, but annotations on the bill show that five of the last six inquests had been taken by deputies, one by a Mr Barrow and four by a Mr Billingham and that it was suspected that others might have been taken by men named Hargraves and Brown (**476**). The last one that Wheeler could have held in person was at Wivelsfield on 11 December because by 17 April 1817 he had been in the county gaol for debt for over four months (**534**). How long before his committal to gaol he had been in financial difficulties is unknown. He had moved from Lewes to Brighton only two years before (**164**, **183**), perhaps leaving creditors behind. More probably he found the social life of Regency Brighton difficult to resist. By 1816 he was still only in his late twenties but he had a family to support: he had married Sarah Mockett of West Firle, aged 20, on 8 February 1813[1] and had two young children (**534**). Whatever its causes, his financial embarrassment must have been what led him into peculation.

When the extent of Wheeler's offences became clear the main aim of the magistrates was to secure his removal from office as quickly as possible which it was found could best be achieved by prosecuting him. Langridge, as clerk of the peace, was kept very busy in the following months preparing the case. There had been no precedent for that in Sussex, although a remarkably similar case involving a Somerset coroner was discovered and taken into consideration (**538**). In the early part of 1817 Langridge was occupied with obtaining opinions from law officers and others and with drawing up the charges, business which produced a considerable number of documents (**505–529**). Ultimately the grand jury presented two indictments at the Horsham assizes of 24 March. One (**530**) charged him with demanding and receiving money on seven occasions — for taking inquests, for travelling to hold inquests (including the one at Frant which had initiated the proceedings) and for giving permission for a body to be buried — whereas in none of the cases was a fee due. The other (**531**) charged him with claiming fees for holding two inquests and for travelling to the venues when no such inquests were held. Wheeler pleaded not guilty to both indictments and was remanded in gaol until the next assizes unless in the meantime he entered into a recognizance in £100 with two sureties in £50 each. It was highly unlikely that he would have been able to raise the necessary money in any event, but it was rendered irrelevant by his also being detained in custody at the suit of Edward Cobby Sharpin for a debt of £31 13s 4d and on an attachment for contempt of court for non-payment of £1859 11s 5d (**530**, **531**).

On 17 April Wheeler wrote to George Shiffner, MP, begging him to intercede for him with the quarter sessions to allow his last two bills as coroner, or such part of them as should be considered due, to relieve his wife, children and mother since he had no relations to give them any assistance (**534**). His plea was ultimately successful and on 6 August he was paid £32 12s 3d for inquests held from 22 July to 11 December 1816,[2] proof that he had not held the later ones in his final bill in person. The amount paid was considerably less than the £46 5s which Wheeler had claimed in his last two bills, but in

1 Ep. II/16/71; *Calendar of Sussex Marriage Licences ... 1772–1837, M–Z*, ed. E H W Dunkin and E W D Penfold (SRS, XXVI, 1919), 460.

2 QAF 2/1/E8, ff 21v–22. The corresponding order incorrectly gives the date of the last inquest as 11 July 1817: QO/EW 43.

the circumstances he could consider that he had been treated with compassion and he expressed his gratitude to the JPs (**542**).

Meanwhile, attempts were made to secure the appointment of an additional or temporary coroner for East Sussex during Wheeler's imprisonment and while he remained in office, it being unlawful for the coroner of Hastings rape to act outside his own jurisdiction and the other county coroner living many miles away (**510**, **511**, **513**, **533**, **535**). The advice was that no coroner could lawfully appoint or authorize a deputy to act for him, that no one could appoint an extra or temporary coroner while the elected coroner remained in office and that the county coroner of the western division would therefore have to act in the east, however expensive and inconvenient that might be (**513**). It was only after that advice, given on 4 February 1817, that John Luttman Ellis, the West Sussex coroner, began regularly to take inquests in Lewes and Pevensey rapes and to claim for them in East Sussex. It certainly proved to be expensive and inconvenient. He was often away from home for one night, sometimes for two, and for one inquest he hired a horse and gig, the consequent expenses for which he claimed amounting to more than half the sum of his inquest and mileage fees (**193**). It is tempting to wonder if news got through to Wheeler of what could be obtained legally.

Throughout the time during which Ellis held East Sussex inquests moves had been under way to secure Wheeler's removal from office. One possibility suggested was for JPs in quarter sessions to be given the power to remove coroners for malversation of office, as Wheeler's offences were collectively defined, or for incapacity, but they were dismissed by the attorney general on the grounds that the law officers would never approve and that the Lord Chancellor had the power to remove coroners for malversation (**533**, **535**, **536**). On 9 June the earl of Chichester, joint Postmaster General and formerly a Sussex MP (**533**), told Langridge that JPs out of sessions could not stop proceedings already entered but that he would agree to the withdrawal of the prosecution if Wheeler resigned (**539**). Langridge therefore encouraged Wheeler to petition to be allowed to resign. Wheeler's petition was delivered to him on 13 July and the JPs in quarter sessions accepted his resignation on 18 July (**546**, **547**). As a result of that, on 2 August a writ at last issued for the sheriff to remove Wheeler from office because he was so impoverished as to have no prospect of being discharged from gaol and therefore of being able to perform his duties (**543**). The next day Ellis held his last East Sussex inquest (**193**) and on 4 August a writ for the election of a new coroner issued on which George Gwynne was elected on 14 August (**544**).[1] The sheriff who executed the writs was James Cranbourne Strode. He must have derived considerable satisfaction from completing the process which he had initiated almost a year before. John Woodward, a magistrate, had less happy thoughts. It was reported that the gist of the remarks he made at Gwynne's election was:

> At such a moment as this I cannot forget that I voted for the late coroner. Humanity teaches me to draw a veil over the name of a fallen fellow creature; it is permitted as to recollect and to allude to his errors only as lights and beacons to warn others from those rocks on which he was shipwrecked — extravagance and inattention to business.[2]

A few days after Wheeler's position as county coroner was terminated his case was resumed at the Lewes assizes of 9 August. Having already pleaded not guilty to both

1 *SWA*, 18 Aug. 1817.
2 *SWA*, 18 Aug. 1817.

indictments, he was tried, acquitted and discharged (**545**) although he remained in Horsham gaol for debt.[1] The trial was presumably a formality, the result of something akin to plea-bargaining, Wheeler's acquittal being obtained in exchange for his resignation.

The Wheeler case provides much of incidental interest. There was the opinion, which must have come as a surprise to the East Sussex authorities, that it was perfectly legal, and the practice in some counties, for coroners to charge for the journey both to and from the inquest venue, although the East Sussex coroners continued to charge for only the first. Secondly, Wheeler's taking relatively small amounts of money for refreshments and to pay the jurors and sometimes the headborough or constable for their service was clearly not regarded as more than a venial offence, if an offence at all. It did not feature in the indictments or in the correspondence leading up to their compilation, having probably become a tradition unofficially but harmoniously agreed between coroner and parish and therefore not previously questioned or even concealed. Deputy coroners may also have been employed regularly and openly. It would have been impossible to have disguised their use and coroners might not have appreciated the impropriety of claiming travelling expenses as if they had attended in person. It was by pure chance that the inquiries into Thomas William Wheeler's activities disclosed that William Wheeler had also employed deputies and his predecessors may well have done the same, as the franchisal coroners certainly did. It may have been a deputy who officiated at the first inquest in William Wheeler's bills which was held a fortnight before his election (**64**).[2] Wheeler would not have risked jeopardising his election by holding it himself. Again, it is probably significant that Thomas William Wheeler was not charged in the indictments with using deputies.

No suggestion was ever made that any other East Sussex coroner had committed any of the more serious offences of which Wheeler seems to have made a habit and it is highly unlikely that any of his successors would have risked doing so. Even a thorough study of all the inquests recorded in the bills against the burials of the deceased in the parish registers might be insufficient to identify any other bogus inquests. However, a considerable number of burials were looked for during the preparation of this volume in order to confirm the reading of names, only a few of which have been noted in the text, and it is encouraging that the vast majority were found, the rest probably being in registers of places other than those where the inquests were held. William Wheeler's sudden death inspired the following eulogy:

> His integrity was proverbial. His temper, abroad and at home, even, cheerful and endearing. His manners fascinating and elegant; and he was, in every sense of the words, a well-bred man. Possessed of rich, convivial powers, his sallies of pleasantry and merriment were ever chaste and unoffending. His conversation was always discriminating, candid and improving. It is a pleasure to speak of a man where no one can say this is flattery. The town of Lewes, the county of Sussex and all who knew Mr Wheeler will, placing their hands on their breasts, say 'We never saw so undeviatingly good and amiable a man, one so beloved in life and lamented in death'.[3]

1 *SWA*, 4 Aug. 1817.
2 C 202/173/13.
3 *SWA*, 21 Aug. 1809.

That may well be an example of *de mortuis nil nisi bonum*, but it is almost certainly closer to the sentiments inspired by the majority of East Sussex coroners than by Thomas William Wheeler.

Editorial Note

The bills, which form the first part of the text, are presented there uniformly. The information in each of their inquests is given in the order: date of inquest; inquest venue; name of deceased; narrative or simple verdict, if any; number of miles travelled; and sum claimed. Every bill ends with the total claim and the quarter sessions at which it was allowed. Such treatment does not distort the essential nature of the originals and is essential to keep the printed version within reasonable bounds, but it suggests that they have a greater uniformity than is the case. For example, the name of the deceased is often given only in the narrative and when no inquest venue is specified it has been assumed to have been the place where the death occurred. Most narratives are succinct and it was therefore felt justifiable to use the original words to preserve the flavour of the documents, but without any repetition. Thus 'he died by the visitation of God' has been replaced by 'he died a natural death' and the occasional 'murthered' will be found instead of 'murdered'. In the majority of bills the claim for £1 for holding an inquest is recorded separately from the sum claimed for the journey, but here they have been added together. The text of each bill is followed by its brief archival reference. Where necessary, any general points about a bill are printed immediately below it within square brackets. Comments about individual inquests are in numbered notes. They contain such matters as variations between different versions; references to surviving inquests, parish registers, the *Sussex County Magazine* and a few other printed books and journals; and corrections and editorial comments.

The use of entry notes means that very few additions have been made in the body of the text and they relate to omissions in the manuscripts. When an omission could be confidently supplied, as when the number of miles travelled is omitted but the sum claimed is not, the missing words or figures are provided in roman type within square brackets. Dates of inquests are most commonly omitted. They have been supplied in six circumstances: when there is a surviving inquest which is dated; when the preceding and following entries have the same date; when the preceding and following entries have immediately adjacent dates; when no mileage was claimed and the previous inquest was at the same place (or mileage was claimed but not for the previous inquest); when the order for the payment of the bill was made on the date of the preceding entry (e.g. **96**); and when the date is given later in the bill because the mileage was disallowed (e.g. **116**). When ditto marks are used in the bill to indicate the same date, that date is given without square brackets. In the majority of other cases the omitted date was probably the same as that of the preceding entry, but 'date omitted' has been printed in italic within square brackets which is the convention adopted for the few other editorial comments, such as 'place omitted', made in the body of the text. The entries relating to payments to the clerk of assize are also sometimes undated. When they are dated the date is usually the first day of the assizes, but occasionally a day or two later (e.g. **74**, **90**). The undated ones have therefore been given the first day within square brackets with a query, for example '[?23 Mar.] 1774'. That has been done even when the previous entry has a slightly later date (e.g. **80**).

Similar, but far fewer, insertions, comments and entry notes will be found in the inquests in the second part of the text which are printed exactly as in previous volumes. No person, place or matter of substance has been excluded, only repetition and common form, but the exact wording of the originals is not adhered to as closely as for the bills, 'he died by the visitation of God', for example, being rendered 'he died a natural death'. Vernacular words in the pre-1733 Latin inquests have been retained in their manuscript spellings and printed in inverted commas, but only very unusual words in the later English inquests have been so treated. When inquests came to be written in English a few traditional renderings of Latin words were replaced by slightly different ones: for example, 'immediately died' by 'instantly died' and 'four neighbouring townships' by 'four next adjoining vills'. Here, for consistency, the earlier usage has been retained. Each inquest's reference is printed immediately after it and nearly every one is followed by a passage in square brackets. Such passages are usually accounts of the delivery of the inquest into King's Bench or assizes and of later proceedings in the case, but when draft inquests or depositions have survived they come first. Unless there is evidence to the contrary it has been assumed that the inquests were delivered to the clerk on the first day of the assizes. The sources are listed at the end of the square-bracketed material in the order: cross-references to other entries in the volume, in bold type; references to other documents, in alpha-numerical order; and printed works, in alphabetical order.

Throughout the volume document references are in the abbreviated forms used in the repositories in which they are housed and, unless they occur only once, printed books and journals are also severely abbreviated. Full documentary and bibliographical details will be found in the list of abbreviations against the abbreviated forms which are in alpha-numerical order. Where possible, references to manuscripts which are printed or cited in the text or introduction end with the relevant page, folio or membrane numbers. However, four of the Raper and Fovargue ledgers are foliated eccentrically and inconsistently and have inconsistent internal references.[1] Uniformity has been imposed here by citing each folio by the number on it, whether it is on the recto or verso, and treating that number as applying to that folio and not also to an adjacent page. Many of the records used lack any internal numeration. All the King's Bench files, most of the assize indictments files and many of the later quarter sessions rolls have no membrane numbers and references are therefore merely to the files or rolls.[2] As the assize files are not large, particular items can readily be found in them, but the quarter sessions rolls present a greater challenge. The King's Bench files are daunting in the extreme — unwieldy and enormous — but at least they are cited only occasionally. There is no great problem with books, such as quarter sessions order books, treasurers' account books and Raper and Fovargue day books, which are unpaginated and unfoliated but whose contents are in chronological order.

In both the bills and the inquests all place names have been modernized, although it is rarely that the manuscript form differs from the modern one and then only slightly. Forenames have been given in their most common modern spellings, Harriet being used throughout whereas Harriot and Harriett also appear in the manuscripts. Surnames, however, have been kept in their manuscript spellings in the text, but in the index of persons they have been brought together under the most common modern form. That means that the coroners normally found in the records with the spelling John Purfeild and

1 RAF 1/3/2; RAF 1/3/5; RAF 1/3/7; RAF 1/3/8.

2 e.g. ASSI 94/1478; KB 11/14, Mich. 2 William and Mary; QR/E 778.

John Michell are indexed under Purfield and Mitchell. With so many people in the index it is inevitable that there are a large number of homonyms. It would have been unhelpful and wasteful of space to have indexed them all separately. An asterisk following a forename indicates that all the following entry numbers refer to different people of that name. Where there is no asterisk the numbers all refer to the same person. The index of places follows the pattern of earlier volumes of inquests except that obsolete forms have not been included. Towns and ancient parishes have their own entries. So have other substantial settlements; they are defined in terms of their towns or parishes from which there are cross-references to them. Lesser but named features, such as fields and woods, are indexed as subentries under their towns or parishes. It may be assumed that a place is in Sussex unless it is followed by the name of another county — always an historic, not a modern, county — and there are cross-references from those out-counties to the places within them. The volume contains too many deaths for it to be possible to have indexed them in detail as was done for earlier centuries. With that exception, it is hoped that the subject index includes all matters which users of the book might expect to find.

COUNTY CORONERS' BILLS

Bills of Thomas Attree

1 28 July 1752. New Shoreham. Thomas Butler of New Shoreham: accident. 20 miles. £1 15s.
11 Dec. 1752. Newick Green. John Marten of Barcombe: accident. 1 mile. £1 0s 9d.
1 Jan. 1753. Hodore in Hartfield. Edward Leany of Hodore, lunatic. 13 miles. £1 9s 9d.
Total £4 5s 6d; allowed at Epiphany sessions 1753. [QR/E 495, no 26]

[In bills **1–12** nearly all Attree's journeys are said to be from Newick (two, in **6**, from his house there). In **13** and **14** that is stated for the first entry only and in **15–18** not at all.]

2 28 Jan. 1753. Streat. Nathaniel Hosmar of Streat: accident. 5 miles. £1 3s 9d.
5 Feb. 1753. Mr Hills's house, Woodmancote. Peter Hills of Woodmancote: natural death. 15 miles. £1 11s 3d.
3 Mar. 1753. Cliffe. John Bexell of Cliffe, felo de se. 7 miles. £1 5s 3d.
10 Mar. 1753. Newick Green. John Cripps of Lewes: accidentally drowned. 1 mile. £1 0s 9d.
1 May 1753. William Pocock's house, Ifield. William Burtenshaw, infant: drowned by accident in Ifield. 24 miles. £1 18s.
Total £6 19s; allowed at Easter sessions 1753. [QR/E 496, no 73]

3 7 May 1753. Laughton, near the Dicker. Susannah Lidlow, lunatic. 9 miles. £1 6s 9d.
11 May 1753. Fletching. John Read, lunatic: hanged himself. 2 miles. £1 1s 6d.
27 June 1753. Near Broad Street, Fletching. Robert Jarret: accident. 3 miles. £1 2s 3d.
7 July 1753. Framfield. Henry Stone: accident. 7 miles. £1 5s 3d.
26 July 1753. Little Horsted. George Taylor: accident. 6 miles. £1 4s 6d.
1 Aug. 1753. Withyham. Mary Groombridge, idiot: accident. 12 miles. £1 9s.
20 Sept. 1753. New Shoreham. George Grover, lunatic: hanged himself. 18 miles. £1 13s 6d.
Total £9 2s 9d; allowed at Michaelmas sessions 1753. [QR/E 498, no 134]

4 18 Oct. 1753. Ripe. Mary Looker, lunatic: hanged herself. 12 miles. £1 9s.
31 Jan. 1754. Pyecombe. Elizabeth Poiney: natural. 13 miles. £1 9s 9d.
15 Feb. 1754. Bolney. Edward Dartnell, lunatic: hanged. 14 miles. £1 10s 6d.
19 June 1754. Hartfield. Thomas Turner: accident. 14 miles. £1 10s 6d.
24 Aug. 1754. Folkington. Edward Cardin, lunatic: drowned. 19 miles. £1 14s 3d.
Total £7 14s; allowed at Michaelmas sessions 1754. [QR/E 502, no 112]

5 20 Dec. 1754. Rottingdean. Richard Cowper, gent.: accident, by a fall from a horse. 13 miles. £1 9s 9d.
6 Feb. 1755. Chailey. Virtue Adams: accidentally drowned. 1 mile. £1 0s 9d.
15 Feb. 1755. Imberhorne in East Grinstead. Morris Sayers: by a fall from a horse. 14 miles. £1 10s 6d.

10 Mar. 1755. Beddingham. Catherine Taylor: natural. 10 miles. £1 7s 6d.
31 Mar. 1755. Portslade. John Vallance: manslaughter. 17 miles. £1 12s 9d.[1]
Total £7 1s 3d; allowed at Easter sessions 1755. [QR/E 504, no 62]

1 Cf. **341**.

6 12 May 1755. Grubbs in Hurstpierpoint. Mrs Ann Lindfield, lunatic: hanged herself. 11 miles. £1 8s 3d.
22 May 1755. Uckfield. John Vine, infant: accident, by a cart. 6 miles. £1 4s 6d.
6 Sept. 1755. Brighton. William Robertson: accident, drowned. 14 miles. £1 10s 6d.
15 Sept. 1755. Edburton. Thomas Slaughter, infant: accident. 17 miles. £1 12s 9d.
Total £5 16s; allowed at Michaelmas sessions 1755. [QR/E 506, no 120]

7 26 Nov. 1755. East Grinstead. John Comber of East Grinstead. 13 miles. £1 9s 9d.
16 Dec. 1755. South Malling. Joseph Austen of South Malling. 8 miles. £1 6s.
12 June 1756. Hangleton. Mary Hollingdale, lunatic: hanged herself. 16 miles. £1 12s.
16 June 1756. Ansty Cross. John Nye, lunatic: hanged himself. 9 miles. £1 6s 9d.
Total £5 14s 6d; allowed at Michaelmas sessions 1756. [QR/E 510, no 141]

8 14 Oct. 1756. Telscombe. [*blank*] Hodge of Telscombe. 14 miles. £1 10s 6d.
15 Oct. 1756. Eastbourne. John Michel, lunatic: hanged himself. 24 miles. £1 18s.
16 Nov. 1756. East Grinstead. William, an unknown person, non compos: hanged himself. 13 miles. £1 9s 9d.
17 Feb. 1757. [*Place omitted.*] William Reynolds: drowned in Lewes river. 8 miles. £1 6s.
25 Apr. 1757. Wivelsfield. Thomas Jenner, lunatic: hanged himself. 5 miles. £1 3s 9d.
6 June 1757. West Hoathly. Benjamin Ellis, infant, aged about 3: drowned. 12 miles. £1 9s.
20 June 1757. Chiddingly. Robert Hollibone: natural death. 12 miles. £1 9s.
Total £10 6s; allowed at Midsummer sessions 1757. [QR/E 513, no 93]

9 3 Oct. 1757. New Shoreham. William White, lunatic: drowned. 16 miles. £1 12s.
19 Nov. 1757. Lewes. William Kenward: accident. 8 miles. £1 6s.
21 Dec. 1757. Balcombe. John Mills, lunatic. 11 miles. £1 8s 3d.
30 Dec. 1757. Ringmer. Thomas Crunden: accidentally drowned. 8 miles. £1 6s.
7 Jan. 1758. Hurstpierpoint. Peter Wood: accidentally drowned. 11 miles. £1 8s 3d.
23 Jan. 1758. Iford. Thomas Frier: accident. 10 miles. £1 7s 6d.
31 Jan. 1758. Rotherfield. Mary Roger: perished with cold. 11 miles. £1 8s 3d.
Total £9 16s 3d; allowed at Easter sessions 1758. [QR/E 516, no 49]

10 20 May 1758. Forest Row. Elizabeth Jarret: accidentally drowned. 10 miles. £1 7s 6d.
3 June 1758. Cliffe. Thomas Gallop: accidentally drowned in Lewes river. 8 miles. £1 6s.
27 June 1758. Eastbourne. Samuel Tourl: killed by a fall from a house. 24 miles. £1 18s.
9 Sept. 1758. Laughton. James Shoesmith: apoplectic fit. 10 miles. £1 7s 6d.
18 Sept. 1758. Portslade. Mr John Friend, lunatic: throat cut. 16 miles. £1 12s.
28 Oct. 1758. East Grinstead. Henry Meers: accident, by a fall. 13 miles. £1 9s 9d.

3 Nov. 1758. Poynings. Frances Baker: accidentally killed in a mill. 13 miles. £1 9s 9d.
1 Dec. 1758. Fletching. John Edwards, lunatic: hanged himself. 3 miles. £1 2s 3d.
Total £11 12s 9d; allowed at Epiphany sessions 1759. [QR/E 519, no 19]

11 15 Mar. 1759. Lindfield. Sarah Roser: accident. 5 miles. £1 3s 9d.
19 Mar. 1759. West Dean. Mr Edward Stanford: accident. 19 miles. £1 14s 3d.
16 Apr. 1759. Waldron. John Goodman, lunatic: hanged. 11 miles. £1 8s 3d.
26 Apr. 1759. [*Place omitted.*] John Honey: accidentally drowned in Lewes river. 8 miles. £1 6s.
30 May 1759. Brighton. Robert Howell: killed by John May. 15 miles. £1 11s 3d.[1]
23 June 1759. Rotherfield. Mary Moon: accidentally drowned. 12 miles. £1 9s.
17 July 1759. [*Place omitted.*] Thomas Mills: accidentally drowned in Lewes river. 8 miles. £1 6s.
23 July 1759. East Chiltington. Robert Day, lunatic: hanged himself. 4 miles. £1 3s.
1 Aug. 1759. Hartfield. Richard Finch: killed by William Mayor. 11 miles. £1 8s 3d.[2]
3 Aug. 1759. Wapsbourne. William Wheeler: by the kick of a horse. 3 miles. £1 2s 3d.
13 Aug. 1759. Cliffe. Mary Gatland, lunatic: cut her throat. 8 miles. £1 6s.
21 Aug. 1759. Portslade. James Davison: by a fall from a horse. 17 miles. £1 12s 9d.
10 Sept. 1759. Chiddingly. Richard Cussins, felo de se: drowned. 12 miles. £1 9s.
28 Sept. 1759. Edburton. Isaac Marchant: accident. 16 miles. £1 12s.
Total £19 11s 9d; allowed at Michaelmas sessions 1759. [QR/E 522, no 98]

1 Cf. **342**.
2 Cf. **343**.

12 23 Oct. 1759. South Malling. Robert Bentlett: accident. 5 miles. £1 3s 9d.
30 Oct. 1759. Horsted Keynes. George Virgoe: drowned by accident. 10 miles. £1 7s 6d.
[*Date omitted.*] Horsted Keynes. John Brett: accident, drowned. 10 miles. £1 7s 6d.
18 Dec. 1759. Buxted. John Chripps: accident, drowned. 6 miles. £1 4s 6d.
4 Jan. 1760. Southbourne. John French, lunatic: hanged himself. 26 miles. £1 19s 6d.
16 Jan. 1760. East Grinstead. Thomas Peacham: accident. 12 miles. £1 9s.
25 Jan. 1760. Frant. Robert Smith, lunatic: hanged himself. 21 miles. £1 15s 9d.
4 Feb. 1760. East Grinstead. Richard Bestam: accident, by a cart. 11 miles. £1 8s 3d.
Total £11 15s 9d; allowed at Easter sessions 1760. [QR/E 524, no 44]

13 29 Apr. 1760. Lindfield. Isaac Harman: accident. 6 miles. £1 4s 6d.
6 May 1760. Chalvington. Elizabeth Clarke, lunatic: drowned. 15 miles. £1 11s 3d.
26 May 1760. Maresfield. Ann Relf: naturally. 5 miles. £1 3s 9d.
4 June 1760. Worth. Elizabeth Sherlock, lunatic: drowned. 15 miles. £1 11s 3d.
5 July 1760. Glynde. John Driver: accident. 11 miles. £1 8s 3d.
11 Aug. 1760. Lewes. Mary Lee: accident. 8 miles. £1 6s.
1 Sept. 1760. South Malling. John Standen: accident. 8 miles. £1 6s.
10 Oct. 1760. Upper Beeding. Mr Charles Bridger: naturally. 18 miles. £1 13s 6d.
31 Oct. 1760. Brighton. Elizabeth Coby: accident. 15 miles. £1 11s 3d.
Total £12 15s 9d; allowed at Epiphany sessions 1761. [QR/E 527, no 13]

14 24 Jan. 1761. Lamberhurst. John Braban, lunatic: hanged himself. 22 miles. £1 16s 6d.

23 Feb. 1761. Buxted. Unknown woman:[1] natural death. 7 miles. £1 5s 3d.
25 Mar. 1761. Chailey. John Snell: natural death. 2 miles. £1 1s 6d.
23 Apr. 1761. Lewes. Samuel Milner: accidentally drowned. 8 miles. £1 6s.
25 May 1761. Wadhurst. John Clarke: accidentally drowned. 20 miles. £1 15s.
4 June 1761. Laughton. Edward Weaver: accidentally drowned. 14 miles. £1 10s 6d.
10 June 1761. Near Saddlescombe. Richard Jordan: accidentally drowned. 15 miles. £1 11s 3d.
6 July 1761. South Malling. William Postle: accidentally drowned. 7 miles. £1 5s 3d.
[Total £11 11s 3d]; allowed at Midsummer sessions 1761. [QR/E 529, no 76]

1 *Travelling woman* in PAR 286/1/1/2.

15 6 Aug. 1761. Brighton. Thomas Griffen: accidentally drowned. 15 miles. £1 11s 3d.
8 Oct. 1761. Danehill. Stephen Athrell: killed. 5 miles. £1 3s 9d.
19 Oct. 1761. Gravetye Furnace. Thomas Todmans: natural death. 13 miles. £1 9s 9d.
30 Dec. 1761. East Grinstead. John Payne: drowned. 13 miles. £1 9s 9d.
24 Jan. 1762. Brighton. Mr Elgate,[1] lunatic: cut his throat. 15 miles. £1 11s 3d.
3 May 1762. Rotherfield. Thomas Luck, felo de se: hanged. 15 miles. £1 11s 3d.
11 June 1762. Ovingdean. Jonas Guest: accident. 13 miles. £1 9s 9d.
Total £10 6s 9d; allowed at Midsummer sessions 1762. [QR/E 533, no 71]

1 *Captain Dighton Elgate* in PAR 255/1/1/4.

16 23 July 1762. Wannock. James Richardson: accidentally killed. 19 miles. £1 14s 3d.
16 Aug. 1762. Fletching. Thomas Maynard, lunatic: hanged. 5 miles. £1 3s 9d.
15 Nov. 1762. Alciston. Thomas Bateup: perished in the cold. 15 miles. £1 11s 3d.
6 Dec. 1762. Rodmell. Sarah Wood, lunatic: hanged. 12 miles. £1 9s.
24 Dec. 1762. Worth. John Humphery: accident. 13 miles. £1 9s 9d.
15 Jan. 1763. Worth. Richard King: natural death. 13 miles. £1 9s 9d.
24 Jan. 1763. Wadhurst. Joseph Huggens, lunatic: hanged. 20 miles. £1 15s.
1 Feb. 1763. Wadhurst. Sarah Walliss, lunatic: hanged. 20 miles. £1 15s.
9 Mar. 1763. Uckfield. Thomas Marten, lunatic: hanged. 6 miles. £1 4s 6d.
12 Mar. 1763. East Grinstead. John Combridge: accident. 13 miles. £1 9s 9d.
31 Mar. 1763. Keymer. John White, lunatic: hanged. 9 miles. £1 6s 9d.
Total £16 8s 9d; allowed at Easter sessions 1763. [QR/E 536, no 47]

17 18 Apr. 1763. West Hoathly. Edward Wood, lunatic: cut his throat. 13 miles. £1 9s 9d.
18 Apr. 1763. East Grinstead. Daniel Constable: accidentally drowned. 10 miles. £1 7s 6d.
30 Apr. 1763. Hurstpierpoint. Unknown male infant: murder. 10 miles. £1 7s 6d.
30 Apr. 1763. Hurstpierpoint. Mary Scrase, felo de se: hanged. 10 miles. £1 7s 6d.
4 June 1763. Eastbourne. Mary Smith: accidental death. 24 miles. £1 18s.[1]
4 July 1763. Hurstpierpoint. Thomas Davey, lunatic: hanged. 11 miles. £1 8s 3d.
11 July 1763. Cliffe. Sarah Young's male bastard child: murder. 8 miles. £1 6s.[2]
24 Aug. 1763. East Blatchington. John Shirlock: accidental death. 15 miles. £1 11s 3d.
12 Sept. 1763. Ringmer. John Walket: accidental drowning. 10 miles. £1 7s 6d.
21 Sept. 1763. Rodmell. William Roswell: accidental drowning. 12 miles. £1 9s.
Total £14 12s 3d; allowed at Michaelmas sessions 1763. [QR/E 538, no 86]

1 Cf. **344**.
2 Cf. **345**.

18 28 Nov. 1763. East Grinstead. John Burnet: accidentally killed by a wagon-wheel. 13 miles. £1 9s 9d.
28 Dec. 1763. Barcombe. William Hards: natural death. 4 miles. £1 3s.
14 Jan. 1764. East Hoathly. William Lidlow: natural death. 9 miles. £1 6s 9d.[1]
1 Feb. 1764. [*Place omitted.*] Mr John Slatter: accidentally, by a fall from his horse. 5 miles. £1 3s 9d.
12 Mar. 1764. Piddinghoe. Ann Page, lunatic: hanged herself. 14 miles. £1 10s 6d.
Total £6 13s 9d; allowed at Easter sessions 1765.[2] [QR/E 544, no 62]

[Richard Holmes, the West Sussex coroner, had a bill allowed at the West Sussex sessions of Michaelmas 1764. Five of its 24 inquests would normally have been held by the East Sussex coroner:
26 Jan. 1764. Henfield. W Banks.[3] 15 miles. £1 11s 3d.
30 Jan. 1764. New Shoreham. W Rusbridge.[4] 14 miles. £1 10s 6d.
4 Apr. 1764. Upper Beeding. J Newman.[5] 12 miles. £1 9s.
17 June 1764. Upper Beeding. W Hills.[6] 12 miles. £1 9s.
23 June 1764. South Malling. H Holder.[7] 28 miles. £2 1s. QR/W 488, no 15.]

1 Cf. *Turner's Diary*, 284.
2 Payment was made after Thomas Attree's death to William, his son and executor: QM/EW 10; QAF 2/1/E1.
3 *William Banks, travelling pedlar* in PAR 100/1/1/1.
4 *William Rusbridge* in Par. 170/1/1/4.
5 *John Newnham* in Par. 16/1/1/2.
6 *William Hills* in Par. 16/1/1/2.
7 *Henry Holder* in PAR 419/1/1/1.

Bills of Francis Wheeler

19 19 July 1764. Hurstpierpoint. Thomas Simmons: hanged himself. 12 miles. £1 9s.
20 July 1764. Mayfield. Thomas Turner: killed by a fall from a wagon. 17 miles. £1 12s 9d.
24 July 1764. Brighton. John Taylor: fell over the cliff and killed himself. 8 miles. £1 6s.
16 Aug. 1764. Hurstpierpoint. John Davey: murdered by his wife. 13 miles. £1 9s 9d.[1]
Total £5 17s 6d; allowed at Michaelmas sessions 1764. [QR/E 542, no 95]

[All Wheeler's journeys were from Cliffe but that is never stated in his bills.]

1 Cf. **346**.

20 10 Nov. 1764. East Hoathly. Matthew Lewer: found dead in a wood. 8 miles. £1 6s.[1]
5 Dec. 1764. Ringmer. Edward Peters: killed by a fall from a wagon. 3 miles. £1 2s 3d.
1 Jan. 1765. Rotherfield. Samuel Taylor: fell into the fire and was burned to death. 16 miles. £1 12s.
4 Mar. 1765. Shiprods in Henfield. William Hoad: hanged himself. 18 miles. £1 13s 6d.

18 Mar. 1765. Ringmer. Robert Ransley: dropped on the highway and died suddenly. 3 miles. £1 2s 3d.
23 Mar. 1765. Henfield. Henry Paine: hanged himself. 18 miles. £1 13s 6d.
Total £8 9s 6d; allowed at Easter sessions 1765. [QR/E 544, no 64]

1 Cf. *Turner's Diary*, 307–308.

21 30 Apr. 1765. Piddinghoe. Francis Divall: drowned. 6 miles. £1 4s 6d.
14 May 1765. Frant. Richard Eldridge: killed by falling from his horse. 26 miles. £1 19s 6d.
25 May 1765. Rottingdean. John Tuppen: drowned. 6 miles. £1 4s 6d.
4 June 1765. Chailey. John Dobson: dislocated his neck. 8 miles. £1 6s.
8 June 1765. Wadhurst. Henry Stiles: killed in a marl-pit. 23 miles. £1 17s 3d.
11 June 1765. Horsted Keynes. George Langridge: drowned. 14 miles. £1 10s 6d.
8 July 1765. Mayfield. George Roberts: killed in a marl-pit. 19 miles. £1 14s 3d.
1 Aug. 1765. Newhaven. Gabriel Burroughs jun.: drowned. 8 miles. £1 6s.
4 Sept. 1765. Brighton. George Patching: killed in a chalk-pit. 8 miles. £1 6s.
8 Sept. 1765. Brighton. Richard Carver: found dead. 8 miles. £1 6s.
9 Sept. 1765. St Pancras, Chichester. New-born infant: found murdered. 40 miles. £2 10s.
10 Oct. 1765. Southwick. Thomas Howard: killed by falling into a coal-pen. 12 miles. £1 9s.
Total £18 13s 6d. The £2 10s for the inquest of 9 Sept. was deducted, to be applied for in West Sussex, leaving £16 3s 6d which was allowed at Michaelmas sessions 1765. [QR/E 546, no 111]

[On 7 Jan. 1766 Wheeler sent the following bill to Mr Scutt, attorney-at-law, at Midhurst for submission to the West Sussex quarter sessions:
9 Sept. 1765. St Pancras, Chichester. New-born infant: found murdered. 40 miles. £2 10s.
8 Nov. 1765. Sompting. New-born infant. 18 miles. £1 13s 6d.
Total £4 3s 6d; allowed at Easter sessions 1766. QR/W 494, no 15.
The 2 inquests were taken by Wheeler during the illness of the West Sussex coroner, Richard Holmes, whose final bill was allowed at the Petworth sessions of Michaelmas 1766 after his death and paid to Elizabeth, his widow and executrix: QM/EW 10.]

22 18 Nov. 1765. Eastbourne. Sarah Bridger: hanged herself. 17 miles. £1 12s 9d.
1 Jan. 1766. Lindfield. William Hamlin: found dead. 12 miles. £1 9s.
7 Mar. 1766. Lindfield. Sarah Watford: fell into a well. 12 miles. £1 9s.
13 Apr. 1766. Portslade. Christopher Knight: found dead in a barn. 12 miles. £1 9s.
17 Apr. 1766. Newhaven. Thomas Nye: drowned. 8 miles. £1 6s.
23 Apr. 1766. Cliffe. John Philcox: died suddenly in a fit. £1.
23 Apr. 1766. Hailsham. Frances Taylor: killed by a cart. 14 miles. £1 10s 6d.
24 Apr. 1766. Playden. New-born infant: murdered. 40 miles. £2 10s.[1]
9 May 1766. The Dicker. Elizabeth Pele: bled to death at the Dicker fair. 11 miles. £1 8s 3d.
31 May 1766. Buxted. Stephen Taylor: drowned. 10 miles. £1 7s 6d.
4 May 1766. Ditchling. Thomas Howell: killed by a wagon. 8 miles. £1 6s.
12 June 1766. Little Horsted. William Cooper: hanged himself. 6 miles. £1 4s 6d.
15 June 1766. South Malling. Samuel Henty: found drowned in the river. £1.
21 June 1766. Keymer. Unknown man: found dead. 9 miles. £1 6s 9d.

Total £19 19s 3d; allowed at Midsummer sessions 1766. [QR/E 549, no 83]

1 Cf. **347**.

23 14 Aug. 1766. Mayfield. John Dine: found dead in a wood. 17 miles. £1 12s 9d.
2 Sept. 1766. Fletching. William Wood: killed by a wagon. 10 miles. £1 7s 6d.
3 Oct. 1766. Broyle. James Chamberlin: found dead. 3 miles. £1 2s 3d.
8 Dec. 1766. Cuckfield. Elizabeth Mitchell: fell into a well. 14 miles. £1 10s 6d.
30 Dec. 1766. Mayfield. John Fry: found dead. 16 miles. £1 12s.
23 Jan. 1767. Slaugham. Richard Putland: hanged himself. 18 miles. £1 13s 6d.
3 Feb. 1767. Brighton. Samuel Bartholomew: killed in a mill. 8 miles. £1 6s.
13 Apr. 1767. Newhaven. Thomas Alderton jun.: drowned. 8 miles. £1 6s.
25 Apr. 1767. Blackham Common, Withyham. Robert Bartlet: hanged himself. 23 miles. £1 17s 3d.
Total £13 7s 9d; allowed at Easter sessions 1767. [QR/E 552, no 67]

[Wheeler also submitted the following bill to the West Sussex quarter sessions:
9 Sept. 1766. Easebourne. Thomas Enticknap. 40 miles. £2 10s.
23 Sept. 1766. West Tarring. George Birchell. 20 miles. £1 15s.
16 Oct. 1766. Kirdford. Unknown man: found dead. 42 miles. £2 11s 6d.
23 Oct. 1766. West Tarring. Hannah Fisher. 20 miles. £1 15s.
Total £8 11s 6d; allowed at Easter sessions 1767. QR/W 498, no 20.]

24 14 May 1767. Rodmell. John Grover, gent. [4 miles.] £1 3s.
30 May 1767. Brighton. John Wood: killed on board a ship. [8 miles.] £1 6s.
8 July 1767. Rottingdean. Stephen Boys: drowned. [7 miles.] £1 5s 3d.
9 July 1767. Albourne. John Miles: found dead in the highway. [12 miles.] £1 9s.
11 July 1767. Brighton. William Stevens: found drowned. [8 miles.] £1 6s.
30 July 1767. Isfield. Thomas Ford: killed by a fall from a wagon. [6 miles.] £1 4s 6d.
3 Aug. 1767. Waldron. William Henly: killed digging gravel. [12 miles.] £1 9s.
9 Aug. 1767. East Dean. James Simpson: drowned. [14 miles.] £1 10s 9d.[1]
23 Sept. 1767. Worth. John Parsons: choked. [23 miles.] £1 17s 3d.
7 Oct. 1767. Rottingdean. John Gillham: drowned. [7 miles.] £1 5s 3d.
8 Oct. 1767. Rottingdean. William Bradford: drowned. [7 miles.] £1 5s 3d.
Total £15 1s 3d; allowed at Michaelmas sessions 1767. [QR/E 554, no 122]

1 Recte *£1 10s 6d*. The extra 3d was included in the bill total and allowed.

25 17 Oct. 1767. Lamberhurst. John Hilder. 30 miles. £2 2s 6d.
3 Jan. 1768. Hurstpierpoint. William Vinall. 12 miles. £1 9s.
9 Jan. 1768. East Grinstead. Unknown woman:[1] found dead. 19 miles. £1 14s 3d.
13 Jan. 1768. [*Place omitted*.] Francis Hoey: drowned in Lewes river. £1.
4 Feb. 1768. Lindfield. William Elsey. 15 miles. £1 11s 3d.
8 Apr. 1768. Telscombe. Joseph Mayner.[2] 7 miles. £1 5s 3d.
22 Apr. 1768. West Firle. Richard Reed. 5 miles. £1 3s 9d.
12 May 1768. East Grinstead. James Lucas. 20 miles. £1 15s.
21 May 1768. Henfield. Mary Soper. 16 miles. £1 12s.
14 June 1768. Brighton. Martha Martin. 8 miles. £1 6s.
11 July 1768. Wivelsfield. Joseph Farncomb. 12 miles. £1 9s.
[11 July] 1768. Cliffe. William Taylor. £1.2
12 July 1768. Hartfield. William Read. 22 miles. £1 16s 6d.

Total £19 4s 6d; allowed at Midsummer sessions 1768. [QR/E 557, no 109]

1 *A traveller* in Par. 348/1/1/2.
2 *Joseph Maynard, a stranger, found dead upon Bannings ground* in PAR 491/1/1/1.

26 16 July 1768. Blackham in Withyham. William Peerless. 23 miles. £1 17s 3d.
15 Aug. 1768. South Malling. Mary Wisdom. £1.
[*Date omitted.*] Alciston. John Hudson. 8 miles. £1 6s.
29 Aug. 1768. Brighton. William Denby. 8 miles. £1 6s.
27 Sept. 1768. Buxted Bridge. Thomas Batchelor. 11 miles. £1 8s 3d.
8 Oct. 1768. Cliffe. John Johnson. £1.
14 Oct. 1768. Framfield. Richard Brand. 10 miles. £1 7s 6d.
20 Oct. 1768. Uckfield. Mary Marten. 8 miles. £1 6s.
21 Oct. 1768. All Saints, Lewes. William Groves. £1.
[21 Oct.] 1768. New Shoreham. Albinas Pelham. 14 miles. £1 10s 6d.
22 Oct. 1768. South Heighton. John Blundell.[1] 8 miles. £1 6s.
2 Nov. 1768. Wilmington. William Wickens. 13 miles. £1 9s 9d.
19 Nov. 1768. All Saints, Lewes. William Novis. £1.
[*Date omitted.*] West Firle. Samuel Collingham. 5 miles. £1 3s 9d.
12 Dec. 1768. Glynde. Stephen Balcomb. 3 miles. £1 2s 3d.
Total £19 3s 3d; allowed at Epiphany sessions 1769. [QR/E 559, no 25]

1 *John Blunden, accidentally drowned at Stockferry, buried at Bishopstone*: PAR 374/1/1/2, f 7.

27 1 Feb. 1769. Brighton. Matthew Kent: killed by a fall of the cliff. 8 miles. £1 6s.
3 Feb. 1769. Streat Green. John Pierce: found dead. 7 miles. £1 5s 3d.
[*Date omitted.*] Hailsham. Thomas Delves: drowned. 12 miles. £1 9s.
25 Feb. 1769. Staplefield Common, Cuckfield. Elizabeth Mitchell: hanged herself. 17 miles. £1 12s 9d.
6 Mar. 1769. Fletching. Mr William Shaw: shot. 10 miles. £1 7s 6d.
11 Mar. 1769. Frant. Thomas Welfare: found dead. 22 miles. £1 16s 6d.
22 Mar. 1769. Near Groombridge. Elizabeth Streatfield: cut her throat. 21 miles. £1 15s 9d.
27 Mar. 1769. [Cliffe] House of Correction. Francis Juniper. £1.
8 Apr. 1769. Barcombe. Charles Evans: drowned. 5 miles. £1 3s 9d.
21 Apr. 1769. Piddinghoe. Joseph Jackson: killed by a cart. 6 miles. £1 4s 6d.
10 May 1769. Newhaven. John Dean: killed by falling from the mast of a ship. 8 miles. £1 6s.
13 May 1769. Newhaven. John Phillips: shot. 8 miles. £1 6s.[1]
19 May 1769. Hurstpierpoint. Joseph Osborn: killed by a fall from his horse. 12 miles. £1 9s.
23 May 1769. Newhaven. John Greentree: drowned. 8 miles. £1 6s.
25 May 1769. Chiddingly. Edward Elphick: hanged himself. 9 miles. £1 6s 9d.
7 June 1769. Withyham. Elizabeth Everest: hanged herself. 23 miles. £1 17s 3d.
12 June 1769. Cuckfield. John Daniel: hanged himself. 12 miles. £1 9s.
27 June 1769. South Malling. John Floyd: drowned in the river. £1.
Total £25 1s; allowed at Midsummer sessions 1769. [QR/E 561, no 90]

1 Cf. **348**.

28 18 July 1769. Arlington. Thomas French: hanged himself. 12 miles. £1 9s.

7 Aug. 1769. Newhaven. George Corbridge: drowned. 8 miles. £1 6s.
9 Aug. 1769. Newhaven. Thomas Newberry: drowned. 8 miles. £1 6s.
15 Aug. 1769. Streat. William Martten: killed in a chalk-pit. 6 miles. £1 4s 6d.
30 Sept. 1769. East Grinstead. Mary Wellfare: killed by falling out of a cart. 17 miles. £1 12s 9d.
18 Oct. 1769. Newhaven. William Marshall: killed by a stone falling on him. 8 miles. £1 6s.
19 Oct. 1769. Folkington. William Trangmer: hanged himself. 12 miles. £1 9s.
8 Dec. 1769. [Cliffe] House of Correction. Ann Miles: natural death. £1.
11 Dec. 1769. East Grinstead. Nicholas Botley: hanged himself. 22 miles. £1 16s 6d.
Total £12 9s 9d; allowed at Epiphany sessions 1770. [QR/E 563, no 23]

29 15 Jan. 1770. Rotherfield. George Weller: killed by a hayrick falling on him. 16 miles. £1 12s.
8 Feb. 1770. Ditchling. Richard Fryer: hanged himself. 8 miles. £1 6s.
23 Feb. 1770. East Grinstead. New-born infant: found dead. 22 miles. £1 16s 6d.
13 Mar. 1770. Brighton. John Upton: fell into a well and was drowned. 8 miles. £1 6s.
28 Mar. 1770. West Firle. Thomas Collingham: poisoned himself. 5 miles. £1 3s 9d.
15 June 1770. Arlington. Edward Wenham: hanged himself. 13 miles. £1 9s 9d.
24 July 1770. Henfield. Thomas Russell: natural death. 16 miles. £1 12s.
27 July 1770. Bishopstone. Thomas West: drowned in a well. 8 miles. £1 6s.
28 July 1770. Brighton. Edward Stiles: drowned in a well. 8 miles. £1 6s.
20 Aug. 1770. Brighton. Revd William Gwyn: found dead. 8 miles. £1 6s.
15 Sept. 1770. Chailey. James Child: killed falling from a carriage. 8 miles. £1 6s.
5 Oct. 1770. Clayton. Mary Waller: killed by a cart. 10 miles. £1 7s 6d.
15 Oct. 1770. Withyham. Ralph Swetman: hanged himself. 20 miles. £1 15s.
10 Nov. 1770. Cuckfield. Francis Mitchel: suffocated in a well. 12 miles. £1 9s.
[10 Nov.] 1770. Cuckfield. William Thomas: suffocated in a well. £1.
26 Nov. 1770. Chiddingly. Unknown man: found drowned. 10 miles. £1 7s 6d.
15 Dec. 1770. Framfield. Robert Diggins: found dead. 9 miles. £1 6s 9d.
24 Dec. 1770. Fletching. Joseph Parsons: drowned. 10 miles. £1 7s 6d.
Total £25 3s 3d; allowed at Epiphany sessions 1771. [QR/E 567, no 20]

30 24 Jan. 1771. Bolney. Richard Nye: found dead in a field. 19 miles. £1 14s 3d.
30 Jan. 1771. East Grinstead. James Saunders: hanged himself. 21 miles. £1 15s 9d.
5 Feb. 1771. Rottingdean. Revd Mr Weston: fell over the cliff. 7 miles. £1 5s 3d.
11 Feb. 1771. New Shoreham Ferry. Mr Butcher: drowned. 14 miles. £1 10s 6d.
[*Date omitted*. Cliffe] House of Correction. Thomas Avery alias Allfrey. £1.
23 Mar. 1771. Mayfield. John West: found dead. 17 miles. £1 12s 9d.
26 Mar. 1771. Newhaven. Richard Bellamy: died by the inclemency of the weather. 8 miles. £1 6s.
3 Apr. 1771. Eastbourne. William Boswell: hanged himself. 17 miles. £1 12s 9d.
8 May 1771. Clayton. Hannah Jenner: hanged herself. 10 miles. £1 7s 6d.
20 May 1771. Ringmer. Edward Smart: killed by a fall of chalk. 3 miles. £1 2s 3d.
27 June 1771. Hamsey. Thomas Freeman: drowned. 3 miles. £1 2s 3d.
29 June 1771. Shermanbury. Sarah Duney: drowned. 18 miles. £1 13s 6d.
2 July 1771. [*Place omitted*.] Thomas Alcorn: killed by falling from a load of hay. £1.
9 July 1771. Brighton. Unknown man:[1] killed by a mill-sweep. 8 miles. £1 6s.

29 July 1771. Horsted Keynes. Mary Bristow: supposed to be murdered but died a natural death. 16 miles. £1 12s.
17 Aug. 1771. [*Place omitted.*] William Tooth: killed by a fall from his horse. £1.
28 Aug. 1771. Hurstpierpoint. Mary Michell: hanged herself. 12 miles. £1 9s.
10 Sept. 1771. Whitemans Green, Cuckfield. Edward Scrase: drowned. 15 miles. £1 11s 3d.
19 Sept. 1771. East Grinstead. Edward Geer: killed by falling from a bank. 21 miles. £1 15s 9d.
24 Sept. 1771. Laughton. Thomas Wickerson: killed by falling from a load of chalk. 8 miles. £1 6s.
Total £28 2s 9d. The £1 10s 6d and £1 13s 6d for the inquests of 11 Feb. and 29 June were deducted, leaving £24 17s 9d[2] which was allowed at Michaelmas sessions 1771.[3]
[QR/E 570, no 24]

1 *David* [blank] in PAR 255/1/1/4.
2 Recte *£24 18s 9d.* £24 17s 9d was paid with an additional 5s: QO/EW 24, p 67; QAF 2/1/E1.
3 There is no record of the payment by order of the West Sussex quarter sessions of the sums deducted: QO/EW 24.

31 19 Oct. 1771. Frant. Thomas Gates: drowned. 23 miles. £1 17s 3d.
23 Oct. 1771. Rotherfield. Thomas Bassett: found dead in his chair. 18 miles. £1 13s 6d.
30 Oct. 1771. Buxted. William Day: drowned. 10 miles. £1 7s 6d.
5 Nov. 1771. Rotherfield. Mary Ovenden: drowned. 20 miles. £1 15s.
30 Nov. 1771. Lewes. William Longley: killed by falling from a ladder. £1.
24 Dec. 1771. Laughton. Martha Rippington: drowned. 8 miles. £1 6s.
4 Feb. 1772. Lindfield. Henry Weston: found dead in a ditch. 12 miles. £1 9s.
18 Feb. 1772. Hamsey. Thomas Nicholls: killed by a wall falling on him. 2 miles. £1 1s 6d.
19 Feb. 1772. New Shoreham. John Peak:[1] drowned. 14 miles. £1 10s 6d.
8 Mar. 1772. Ringmer. Thomas Smith: found dead in a field. 3 miles. £1 2s 3d.
25 Mar. 1772. Oldlands in Buxted. Benjamin Harris: drowned. 13 miles. £1 9s 9d.
31 Mar. 1772. Newhaven. John M'Guire: drowned. 8 miles. £1 6s.
10 Apr. 1772. Waldron. Richard Savage: drowned. 12 miles. £1 9s.
Total £18 17s 3d;[2] allowed at Easter sessions 1772. [QR/E 572, no 20]

1 *John Pike, soldier* in Par. 170/1/1/4.
2 Recte *£18 7s 3d.* The full £18 17s 3d was paid with an extra 5s: QO/EW 24, p 170; QAF 2/1/E1.

32 26 May 1772. [*Place omitted.*] Henry Woodward: killed by a fall from his horse. £1.
27 June 1772. Newhaven. Alexander Elliot: drowned. 8 miles. £1 6s.
29 June 1772. Brighton. George Curley: drowned. 8 miles. £1 6s.
4 Aug. 1772. Slaugham. John Wells: drowned. 20 miles. £1 15s.
8 Aug. 1772. Barcombe. Sarah Hoadley: drowned. 4 miles. £1 3s.
7 Sept. 1772. Beddingham. Thomas Davis: being delirious, drowned himself. 4 miles. £1 3s.
16 Oct. 1772. Eastbourne. Charles Coleman: hanged himself. 17 miles. £1 12s 9d.
13 Nov. 1772. East Grinstead. Unknown man:[1] found dead. 16 miles. £1 12s.

18 Nov. 1772. Chiddingly. Richard Guy: killed by falling out of a wagon. 10 miles. £1 7s 6d.
16 Dec. 1772. Wellingham. Edward Saxby: found dead. 2 miles. £1 1s 6d.
Total £13 6s 9d; allowed at Epiphany sessions 1773. [QR/E 575, no 36]

1 *Unknown traveller* in Par. 348/1/1/2.

33 22 Jan. 1773. Twineham. William Turner: found dead. 18 miles. £1 13s 6d.
30 Jan. 1773. Rodmell. Thomas Pace: found dead. 4 miles. £1 3s.
3 Feb. 1773. Beddingham. Ann Hide: hanged herself. 5 miles. £1 3s 9d.
12 Feb. 1773. Hove. James Saunders: shot. 10 miles. £1 7s 6d.
18 Feb. 1773. Rotherfield. Thomas Harwood: killed in a gravel-pit by a fall of the gravel. 18 miles. £1 13s 6d.
18 Feb. 1773. Cliffe House of Correction. Elizabeth Haylor. £1.
23 Feb. 1773. Cliffe House of Correction. Elizabeth Jordan. £1.
5 Mar. 1773. Withyham. John Maynard: found dead. 18 miles. £1 13s 6d.
14 Mar. 1773. New Shoreham. John Grimes: found dead. 14 miles. £1 10s 6d.
9 Apr. 1773. Berwick. Richard Richards: found dead. 9 miles. £1 6s 9d
Total £13 12s; allowed at Easter sessions 1773. [QR/E 576, no 34]

34 28 Apr. 1773. Rodmell. Robert Saxby: threw himself into a draw-well. 4 miles. £1 3s.
29 Apr. 1773. Arlington. John Page: drowned. 10 miles. £1 7s 6d.
22 May 1773. Wivelsfield. John Johnson: hanged himself. 11 miles. £1 8s 3d.
29 May 1773. Brighton. Thomas Marshall: found dead. 8 miles. £1 6s.
10 July 1773. Patcham. Ann Moppet: killed by a wagon. 7 miles. £1 5s 3d.
29 July 1773. New Shoreham. William Stoneham: drowned. 14 miles. £1 10s 6d.
27 Aug. 1773. Hurstpierpoint. Jane Dunton: drowned. 12 miles. £1 9s.
2 Oct. 1773. Slaugham. Elizabeth Miles: found dead. 21 miles. £1 15s 9d.
14 Oct. 1773. Chailey. John Jennings: drowned. 7 miles. £1 5s 3d.
25 Oct. 1773. Brighton. Mary Sergeant: hanged herself. 8 miles. £1 6s.
2 Nov. 1773. East Grinstead. Stephen Flemming: hanged himself. 21 miles. £1 15s 9d.
12 Nov. 1773. Ifield. William Charman: drowned. 24 miles. £1 18s.
13 Nov. 1773. Rottingdean. Joseph [*blank*],[1] servant to Major Digby: killed by the cliff falling on him. £1.
13 Nov. 1773. Rottingdean. David Dunbar: killed by the cliff falling on him. 7 miles. £1 5s 3d.
15 Nov. 1773. Mayfield. John Gilbert: died suddenly. 17 miles. £1 12s 9d.
5 Dec. 1773. Bishopstone. James Hollebone: hanged himself. 8 miles. £1 6s.
13 Dec. 1773. Ardingly. Edward Tingley: found dead. 15 miles. £1 11s 3d.
24 Dec. 1773. Newhaven. James Stevens: drowned. 8 miles. £1 6s.
24 Dec. 1773. Rodmell. William Davis: killed by the tackle of a windmill. 4 miles. £1 3s.
28 Dec. 1773. Lewes. John Bristow: killed by a timber-tree falling on him. £1.
31 Dec. 1773. Folkington. John Thorneycroft: found dead. 12 miles. £1 9s.
6 Jan. 1774. Southover. John Croucher jun.: shot. £1.
7 Jan. 1774. Poynings. Unknown man:[2] found dead. 12 miles. £1 9s.
12 Jan. 1774. Hove. Unknown man: found dead. 10 miles. £1 7s 6d.
Total £33; allowed at Epiphany sessions 1774. [QR/E 579, no 23]

1 *Job Cowin* in PAR 466/1/1/2.
2 *A poor man found dead upon the Hill* in Par. 451/1/1/2; he was probably identified afterwards as Richard Harding from Henfield whose name is written on the next line and appears to have been inserted later.

35 17 Jan. 1774. Newhaven. William Vinall: killed by a fall from his horse. 8 miles. £1 6s.
26 Jan. 1774. Worth. William Franks: killed by falling from the top of a barn. 20 miles. £1 15s.
1 Mar. 1774. Buxted. Hannah Wilmshurst: found dead. 12 miles. £1 9s.
7 Mar. 1774. Barcombe. Thomas Markwick: killed by the kick of a horse. 5 miles. £1 3s 9d.
[7 Mar.] 1774. Chelwood. John Crowhurst: shot. 14 miles. £1 10s 6d.[1]
[?21 Mar.] 1774. Paid the clerk of assize on returning this inquisition 5s.[1]
30 Mar. 1774. New Shoreham. Richard Mugridge: killed by falling from the mainmast of a ship. 14 miles. £1 10s 6d.
2 Apr. 1774. Brighton. Alexander Cook: shot himself. 8 miles. £1 6s.
29 Apr. 1774. Rottingdean. George Lamport: hanged himself. 8 miles. £1 6s.
5 May 1774. Brighton. Henry Smithers: cut his throat. 8 miles. £1 6s.
4 June 1774. West Firle. Richard Pike: drowned. 5 miles. £1 3s 9d.
27 June 1774. Barcombe. Richard Parsons: killed by a wagon. 5 miles. £1 3s 9d.
30 June 1774. Ditchling. Elizabeth Hockham: drowned. 8 miles. £1 6s.
Total £16 11s 3d; allowed at Midsummer sessions 1774. [QR/E 581, no 29]

1 Cf. **349**.

36 26 July 1774. East Grinstead. Elizabeth Cooper: drowned herself. 21 miles. £1 15s 9d.
11 Aug. 1774. East Grinstead. Ann Ferminger: drowned herself. 21 miles. £1 15s 9d.
29 Aug. 1774. Arlington. John Smith: died suddenly. 11 miles. £1 8s 3d.
5 Sept. 1774. Brighton. Martha Upton: killed by a wagon going over her. 8 miles. £1 6s.
6 Sept. 1774. [Cliffe] House of Correction. Samuel Easton. £1.
26 Sept. 1774. Lewes. William Wilkinson: hanged himself. £1.
2 Oct. 1774. Beddingham. Richard Tuppen: hanged himself. 5 miles. £1 3s 9d.
3 Oct. 1774. Eastbourne. Thomas Mitchell: hanged himself. 17 miles. £1 12s 9d.
31 Dec. 1774. Brighton. Richard Hollands: killed by his horse falling. 8 miles. £1 6s.
4 Jan. 1775. Frant. Hannah Clifton: drowned. 20 miles. £1 15s.
Total £14 3s 3d; allowed at Epiphany sessions 1775. [QR/E 583, no 30]

37 15 Jan. 1775. Woodmancote. Elizabeth Leffen: hanged herself. 14 miles. £1 10s 6d.
5 Feb. 1775. Newhaven. John Kitchener: drowned. 8 miles. £1 6s.
24 Feb. 1775. Worth. James Chantler: cut his throat. 20 miles. £1 15s.
10 Mar. 1775. Rodmell. Ann Teeling, infant: scalded to death by falling into a keeler of hot beer. 4 miles. £1 3s.
11 Apr. 1775. Friston. Charles Triger: killed in falling into a well. 13 miles. £1 9s 9d.
17 Apr. 1775. Beddingham. Samuel Banks: cut his throat. 4 miles. £1 3s.
21 Apr. 1775. Cliffe Hill. Sarah Chapman: killed on the side of the hill. £1.
15 June 1775. Frant. George Gabriel:[1] cut his throat. 22 miles. £1 16s 6d.

17 June 1775. Lamberhurst. George Gabriel:[2] drowned by falling into the water in a fit. 30 miles. £2 2s 6d.
Total £13 6s 3d; allowed at Midsummer sessions 1775. [QR/E 585, no 38]

1 Buried at Frant 17 June: PAR 344/1/1/3.
2 Buried at Lamberhurst 18 June: P216/1/2.

38 8 Aug. 1775. Wivelsfield. Mary Penfold: drowned in a pit of water. 11 miles. £1 8s 3d.
10 Aug. 1775. East Grinstead. Sarah Everest: drowned in a dipping-hole. 18 miles. £1 13s 6d.
16 Aug. 1775. Newhaven. Hugh Colley: drowned. 8 miles. £1 6s.
13 Sept. 1775. Brighton. James Bishop: found dead in a hayloft. 8 miles. £1 6s.
20 Sept. 1775. ?Old Shoreham. Thomas Boniface: drowned. 14 miles. £1 10s 6d.
22 Sept. 1775. ?Old Shoreham. James Boniface: drowned. 14 miles. £1 10s 6d.
2 Oct. 1775. Malling Hill, near Southerham. Samuel Harmer: killed by a fall on the side of the hill. £1.
14 Oct. 1775. [*Place omitted.*] John Robinson: drowned by falling out of a barge. £1.
19 Oct. 1775. Hellingly. John Pike: hanged himself in a wood. 12 miles. £1 9s.
21 Oct. 1775. Brighton. Francis Penfold: drowned. 8 miles. £1 6s.
21 Oct. 1775. Brighton. Thomas Clear: drowned. 8 miles. £1 6s.
22 Oct. 1775. Newhaven. John Saunders: drowned. 8 miles. £1 6s.
[*Date omitted.*] Newhaven. Unknown man: drowned. 8 miles. £1 6s.
[*Date omitted.*] Newhaven. Robert Finch: drowned. 8 miles. £1 6s.
24 Nov. 1775. Mayfield. Mary Moon: found dead on the highway. 14 miles. £1 10s 6d.
6 Dec. 1775. Newhaven. Elizabeth Cook: drowned herself. 8 miles. £1 6s.
20 Dec. 1775. Wych Cross. William Francis: killed by a wagon going over him. 15 miles. £1 11s 3d.
9 Jan. 1776. Uckfield. Ann Day: burned to death by falling into the fire in a fit. 8 miles. £1 6s.
Total £24 7s 6d; allowed at Epiphany sessions 1776. [QR/E 587, no 28]

39 29 Jan. 1776. Hamsey. John Burton: perished in the snow. 2 miles. £1 1s 6d.
30 Jan. 1776. South Heighton. Mary Coppard: perished in the snow. 6 miles. £1 4s 6d.
2 Feb. 1776. Cliffe House of Correction. Israel Neeves. £1.
4 Feb. 1776. Lullington. John Banister: perished in the snow. 12 miles. £1 9s.
19 Feb. 1776. Chailey. Thomas Gurr: hanged himself. 8 miles. £1 6s.
27 Feb. 1776. Beddingham. William Friar: killed by the floor of a granary falling on him. 4 miles. £1 3s.
4 Apr. 1776. Buxted. John Berwick: natural death. 11 miles. £1 8s 3d.
9 June 1776. East Dean. Henry Willard: killed by a boat oversetting in getting it afloat. 14 miles. £1 10s 6d.
29 June 1776. New Shoreham. John Phillips:[1] drowned. 14 miles. £1 10s 6d.
1 July 1776. Lewes. Thomas Tippen: killed by a chaise. £1.
8 July 1776. Hailsham. John Gower: hanged himself. 12 miles. £1 9s.
18 July 1776. Fletching. John Simmons: found dead. 11 miles. £1 8s 3d.
19 July 1776. Hurstpierpoint. Richard White. 12 miles. £1 9s.
29 July 1776. Framfield. Thomas Fenner jun.: drowned. 10 miles. £1 7s 6d.
1 Aug. 1776. Cliffe. Sarah Mitchell: drowned. £1.

16 Aug. 1776. Brighton. Unknown man:[2] drowned. 8 miles. £1 6s.
9 Sept. 1776. East Grinstead. Thomas Ferminger: fell from a horse in a fit. 21 miles. £1 15s 9d.
Total £22 8s 9d; allowed at Michaelmas sessions 1776. [QR/E 590, no 26]

[By an order made at Midsummer sessions 1777 £14 5s 3d was paid to Francis Wheeler for inquests held by him: QO/EW 25; QAF 2/1/E1. Wheeler's bill would have been in the quarter sessions roll of Midsummer 1777 which does not survive. Among the inquests which it should have contained was that on Charles Emers of Lewes who was drowned in the river below Newhaven Ferry on 29 June 1777 while fishing from a boat: *SCM*, X, 551, where 28 is an error for 30 June (cf. *SWA*, 30 June 1777). He was buried at South Malling as Charles Emery: PAR 419/1/1/1.]

1 *John Phillips, mariner* in Par. 170/1/1/4.
2 *A sojourner* in PAR 255/1/1/4.

40 21 July 1777. Hailsham. Mildred Cuckney: drowned herself. 14 miles. £1 10s 6d.
25 July 1777. Wadhurst. John Streater: cut his throat. 23 miles. £1 17s 3d.
28 July 1777. Ringmer. Thomas Brown: found dead. 4 miles. £1 3s.
29 July 1777. Brighton. Samuel Burton: found dead. 8 miles. £1 6s.
4 Sept. 1777. Bolney. John French: killed by some plank falling on him. 18 miles. £1 13s 6d.
3 Oct. 1777. Brighton. Joseph Hide: died of excessive drinking. 8 miles. £1 6s.
10 Oct. 1777. East Grinstead. Emmy Charlwood: drowned. 21 miles. £1 15s 9d.
18 Nov. 1777. Jevington. John Langham: shot. 15 miles. £1 11s 3d.
29 Nov. 1777. Brighton. John Greentree: fell over the cliff. 8 miles. £1 6s.
4 Dec. 1777. Horsted Keynes. John Pattenden: found dead. 16 miles. £1 12s.
31 Jan. 1778. Worth. John Saunders. 25 miles. £1 18s 9d.[1]
25 Feb. 1778. Lindfield. Thomas Carewood: died of excessive drinking. 12 miles. £1 9s.
13 Mar. 1778. Keymer. William Watford: hanged himself. 10 miles. £1 7s 6d.
15 Apr. 1778. Rodmell. John Steel: drowned. 4 miles. £1 3s.
10 June 1778. Ringmer. Thomas Guy jun.: drowned. 4 miles. £1 3s.
14 July 1778. Stanmer. Edward Wilding: killed by a wall falling on him. 4 miles. £1 3s.
Total £23 5s 6d; allowed at Midsummer sessions 1778. [QR/E 596, no 17]

1 Cf. **350**.

41 30 July 1778. Ringmer. Joseph Colvill: drowned. 3 miles. £1 2s 3d.
3 Aug. 1778. Balcombe. Mary Illman: drowned herself in a well. 16 miles. £1 12s.
6 Aug. 1778. East Grinstead. Elizabeth Bodle: found dead. 21 miles. £1 15s 9d.
18 Aug. 1778. Brighton. Daniel Wain: drowned. 8 miles. £1 6s.
24 Aug. 1778. Brighton. William Butler: drowned. 8 miles. £1 6s.
7 Oct. 1778. Worth. James Pilbeam: strangled himself. 22 miles. £1 16s 6d.
17 Oct. 1778. Brighton. Ann Miles: burnt to death. 8 miles. £1 6s.
[*Date omitted.*] Barcombe. John Pomfrey: found dead. 6 miles. £1 4s 6d.
22 Oct. 1778. Brighton. John Aylesbury: drowned. 8 miles. £1 6s.
10 Dec. 1778. Framfield. Mary Middleton: found dead. 11 miles. £1 8s 3d.
14 Jan. 1779. Cliffe House of Correction. Thomas Hasseck. £1.
Total £15 3s 3d; allowed at Epiphany sessions 1779. [QR/E 598, no 20]

42 17 Feb. 1779. Rotherfield. Mary Verrall: drowned herself. 18 miles. £1 13s 6d.
2 Mar. 1779. New Shoreham. David Foster: drowned himself. 14 miles. £1 10s 6d.
5 Mar. 1779. Willingdon. John Pomfrey: killed by a sandstone falling on him. 16 miles. £1 12s.
6 Mar. 1779. East Grinstead. William Luck: hanged himself. 21 miles. £1 15s 9d.
18 Mar. 1779. Upper Beeding. William Gadsby: hanged himself. 18 miles. £1 13s 6d.
14 Apr. 1779. Waldron. Nicholas Martin: drowned himself. 12 miles. £1 9s.
Total £9 14s 3d; allowed at Easter sessions 1779. [QR/E 599, no 17]

43 8 May 1779. Lewes. Thomas Tasker, postmaster: hanged himself. £1.
14 May 1779. Rotherfield. Mary Godley: found dead. 18 miles. £1 13s 6d.
17 May 1779. Brighton. John Baker: drowned. 8 miles. £1 6s.
18 May 1779. Lewes. Elizabeth Stevenson, infant: killed herself by eating poison. £1.
22 May 1779. Hailsham. John Taylor: thrown from a horse and killed. 12 miles. £1 9s.
27 May 1779. Glynde. Mary Elliott: hanged herself. 3 miles. £1 2s 3d.
2 June 1779. Cliffe House of Correction. Priscilla Lynes. £1.
6 June 1779. Framfield. Richard Gatland: hanged himself. 11 miles. £1 8s 3d.
7 June 1779. Chelwood Gate. William Russell: cut his throat. 15 miles. £1 11s 3d.
14 June 1779. Brighton. Mary Dean: fell down stairs and dislocated her neck. 8 miles. £1 6s.
18 June 1779. Henfield. Charles Cheat: died of excessive drinking. 17 miles. £1 12s 9d.
26 June 1779. Rotherfield. Elizabeth Wickens: cut her throat. 18 miles. £1 13s 6d.
Total £16 2s 6d; allowed at Midsummer sessions 1779. [QR/E 600, no 63]

44 19 July 1779. Balsdean Bottom. John Madgwich: found dead. £1.
20 July 1779. Hartfield. Ann May: hanged herself. 18 miles. £1 13s 6d.
1 Aug. 1779. Hailsham. Henry Smith jun.: killed by a wagon. 12 miles. £1 9s.
30 Aug. 1779. New Shoreham. Cornish Hasselgrove: drowned. 14 miles. £1 10s 6d.
2 Sept. 1779. Rottingdean. John Thomas: drowned. 7 miles. £1 5s 3d.
3 Sept. 1779. Maresfield. Joseph Holford: killed by the kick of a horse. 10 miles. £1 7s 6d.
19 Sept. 1779. Chalvington. William Sicklemore: killed by a fall from a load of faggots. 11 miles. £1 8s 3d.
22 Sept. 1779. Hellingly. John Richardson jun.: drowned. 13 miles. £1 9s 9d.
Total £11 3s 9d; allowed at Michaelmas sessions 1779. [QR/E 601, no 21]

45 18 Oct. 1779. Chiddingly. Edward Russell: found dead. 11 miles. £1 8s 3d.
11 Nov. 1779. Alfriston. Jesse Hollands: found dead. 10 miles. £1 7s 6d.
14 Nov. 1779. Twineham. John Bonniface: hanged himself. 18 miles. £1 13s 6d.
18 Nov. 1779. Shortgate. Timothy Farley: hanged himself. 6 miles. £1 4s 6d.
8 Dec. 1779. Wych Cross. John Brett: fell into Wych Cross pond and was drowned. 16 miles. £1 12s.[1]
21 Dec. 1779. Wellingham. Susannah Howell: drowned. 2 miles. £1 1s 6d.
31 Dec. 1779. Lamberhurst. Ann Blinks: hanged herself. 30 miles. £2 2s 6d.
1 Jan. 1780. Halland Park. Unknown man: found in the park. 8 miles. £1 6s.
10 Jan. 1780. Henfield. John White: fell from a load of straw and was killed. 17 miles. £1 12s 9d.
Total £13 8s 6d; allowed at Epiphany sessions 1780. [QR/E 602, no 19]

1 Cf. *SCM*, XI, 85.

46 9 Feb. 1780. Brighton. Piercy Cheesman: fell from the wall at the Battery Gate and was killed. 8 miles. £1 6s.
14 Feb. 1780. Winterbourne near Lewes. George Ellis: shot. £1.
23 Feb. 1780. Fletching. Henry Pomfrey: killed by the fall of a bough of a tree. 11 miles. £1 8s 3d.
1 Mar. 1780. Rotherfield. John Bastin:[1] died of excessive drinking. 18 miles. £1 13s 6d.
30 Mar. 1780. Worth. Anthony Harland. 21 miles. £1 15s 9d.
Total £7 3s 6d; allowed at Easter sessions 1780. [QR/E 603, no 10]

1 *John Basting otherwise Gin and Bitters* in PAR 465/1/1/9.

47 29 Apr. 1780. Worth. James Tullett: drowned at Blackwater Brook. 24 miles. £1 18s.
7 June 1780. Brighton. William Guildford: drowned. 8 miles. £1 6s.
15 Aug. 1780. Brighton. Luke Lester: killed by a kick from a horse. 8 miles. £1 6s.
29 Aug. 1780. East Grinstead. Richard Edwards: drowned himself in a pond. 22 miles. £1 16s 6d.
1 Sept. 1780. Newhaven. James Brooker: drowned. 8 miles. £1 6s.
[*Date omitted.*] Newhaven. Edward Tasker: drowned. 8 miles. £1 6s.
18 Sept. 1780. Sea Houses, Eastbourne. Richard Rast: killed by lightning. 18 miles. £1 13s 6d.
[*Date omitted.*] Sea Houses, Eastbourne. John Gouldsmith: killed by lightning. 18 miles. £1 13s 6d.
25 Sept. 1780. West Firle. Richard Clarke, infant: drowned. 5 miles. £1 3s 9d.
5 Oct. 1780. Rotherfield. Elizabeth Sawers: died in a fit. 19 miles. £1 14s 3d.
Total £15 3s 6d; allowed at Michaelmas sessions 1780. [QR/E 605, no 44]

48 23 Nov. 1780. Falmer Street. Thomas Belton: killed by the overturning of a cart. 4 miles. £1 3s.
18 Dec. 1780. Hurstpierpoint. Ann Steel: killed by a wagon. 12 miles. £1 9s.
4 Jan. 1781. Bevendean. John Read: hanged himself. 7 miles. £1 5s 3d.
13 Jan. 1781. Mayfield. Elias Baldock: found dead. 18 miles. £1 13s 6d.
19 Feb. 1781. Kingston by Sea. Thomas Stammer: shot. 12 miles. £1 9s.
24 Feb. 1781. Ripe. Unknown man:[1] found dead. 11 miles. £1 8s 3d.
1 Mar. 1781. Newhaven. Edward Tielhen: fell over the cliff and was killed. 8 miles. £1 6s.
11 Mar. 1781. Old Shoreham. John Steer: fell down a hill and was killed. 14 miles. £1 10s 6d.
14 Mar. 1781. Wadhurst. John Baldwin: hanged himself. 23 miles. £1 17s 3d.
18 Mar. 1781. Tarring Neville. Samuel Moore: died of excessive drinking. 6 miles. £1 4s 6d.
29 Mar. 1781. New Shoreham. Richard Lashmer: found dead. 14 miles. £1 10s 6d.
6 Apr. 1781. Wilmington. Thomas Holloway: died at Wilmington in consequence of a wound received on the head at the Dicker. 13 miles. £1 9s 9d.[2]
8 Apr. 1781. Lamberhurst. Richard Latter: hanged himself. 30 miles. £2 2s 6d.
18 Apr. 1781. South Malling. William Cuckney: drowned. £1.

Total £20 9s; allowed at Easter sessions 1781. [QR/E 607, no 29]

1 *Unknown traveller* in PAR 462/1/1/3.
2 Cf. **50**, **351**.

49 29 Apr. 1781. Hailsham. Rebecca Harrison: reported to have been killed by drinking some medicine usually applied to horses' heels. 12 miles. £1 9s.
9 May 1781. Beddingham. Unknown woman:[1] found dead in an ox-lodge. 4 miles. £1 3s.
23 May 1781. Eastbourne. Samuel Elphick: killed by a fall of chalk. 18 miles. £1 13s 6d.
8 June 1781. Frant. Samuel Baker: drowned himself. 23 miles. £1 17s 3d.
11 June 1781. Hailsham. New-born infant: killed by a person or persons unknown. 12 miles. £1 9s.[2]
15 June 1781. Lamberhurst. Richard Prickett: drowned. 30 miles. £2 2s 6d.
21 June 1781. Clayton. Ann Browne: hanged herself. 10 miles. £1 7s 6d.
9 July 1781. Alciston. James Wood: hanged himself. 8 miles. £1 6s.
Total £12 7s 9d; allowed at Midsummer sessions 1781. [QR/E 608, no 41]

1 *Travelling woman* in PAR 238/1/1/1.
2 Cf. **50**. The inquest does not survive.

50 14 July 1781. St John sub Castro, Lewes. John Clark: found dead. £1.
19 July 1781. Ardingly. John Gallard: killed by a team of oxen running away with a plough. 18 miles. £1 13s 6d.
6 Aug. 1781. Withyham. Tasker Knight: fell into a well and was killed. 20 miles. £1 15s.
10 Aug. 1781. Paid the clerk of assize on returning the inquisition taken on Thomas Holloway who was killed by Robert Hitchcock 5s.[1]
[10 Aug.] 1781. Paid him on returning the inquisition taken on a new-born infant at 2Hailsham 5s.[2]
29 Aug. 1781. Broyle. Thomas Watson: hanged himself. 4 miles. £1 3s.
20 Sept. 1781. Edburton. John Pollard: fell down in a fit and died. 13 miles. £1 9s 9d.
Total £7 11s 3d; allowed at Michaelmas sessions 1781. [QR/E 609, no 39]

1 Cf. **48**, **351**.
2 Cf. **49**. The inquest does not survive.

51 5 Oct. 1781. West Hoathly. Nathaniel Langford: hanged himself. 20 miles. £1 15s.
10 Oct. 1781. Worth. Mark Brooker: fell down dead. 25 miles. £1 18s 9d.
13 Nov. 1781. Brighton. Joseph Martin, infant: killed by a wagon going over him. 8 miles. £1 6s.
13 Dec. 1781. East Grinstead Common. Thomas Buckland, a soldier in the South Hants Militia: died of excessive drinking. 22 miles. £1 16s 6d.
11 Jan. 1782. Wadhurst. George Swift: found dead. 23 miles. £1 17s 3d.
Total £8 13s 6d; allowed at Epiphany sessions 1782. [QR/E 610, no 40]

52 31 Jan. 1782. Chiddingly. Thomas Durrant: found dead. 10 miles. £1 7s 6d.
22 Feb. 1782. Maresfield. Nicholas Langford: found dead in a field. 10 miles. £1 7s 6d.
9 Mar. 1782. Brighton. Friend Tree: hanged himself. 8 miles. £1 6s.
22 Mar. 1782. Brighton. Joseph Holdsworth: found dead. 8 miles. £1 6s.

5 Apr. 1782. Brighton. William Moore: drowned. 8 miles. £1 6s.
[*Date omitted.*] Brighton. Cornelius Washer jun.: drowned. 8 miles. £1 6s.
Total £7 19s; allowed at Easter sessions 1782. [QR/E 611, no 32]

53 20 May 1782. Eastbourne. Joseph Earle: killed by a capstan-bar. 19 miles. £1 14s 3d.
30 June 1782. Hellingly. Mary Hickmer: fell into a pond. 12 miles. £1 9s.
3 July 1782. East Hoathly. Mary Burfield: fell into a pond. 9 miles. £1 6s 9d.
Total £4 10s; allowed at Midsummer sessions 1782. [QR/E 612, no 50]

54 29 July 1782. Ripe. Mary Pannett, widow: fell down a flight of stairs and was killed. 10 miles. £1 7s 6d.
5 Aug. 1782. Brighton. Joseph Dean: found dead in a boat. 8 miles. £1 6s.
26 Aug. 1782. Fletching. Joseph Diplock: hanged himself. 13 miles. £1 9s 9d.
28 Aug. 1782. West Firle. Valentine Birch: drowned. 5 miles. £1 3s 9d.
7 Sept. 1782. Chailey. Thomas Eagars: killed by a timber-carriage going over him. 8 miles. £1 6s.
16 Sept. 1782. Chiddingly. Ann Newnham Pont: drowned. 12 miles. £1 9s.
28 Sept. 1782. Handcross in Slaugham. Jonathan Godfrey: shot. 19 miles. £1 14s 3d.[1]
Total £9 16s 3d; allowed at Michaelmas sessions 1782. [QR/E 613, no 28]

1 Cf. **56**, **352**; *SCM*, XI, 370.

55 19 Oct. 1782. Lewes. Charles Carpenter: fell down and expired on School Hill. £1.
3 Nov. 1782. Hurstpierpoint. George Langridge: drowned. 12 miles. £1 9s.
19 Dec. 1782. Shermanbury. Nicholas Matthews: died in a fit. 18 miles. £1 13s 6d.
15 Jan. 1783. Old Shoreham. Thomas Freeman: drowned in Shoreham river. 14 miles. £1 10s 6d.
Total £5 13s; allowed at Epiphany sessions 1783. [QR/E 614, no 42]

56 5 Feb. 1783. Henfield. John Muzzell: drowned. 18 miles. £1 13s 6d.
19 Feb. 1783. Henfield. Edmund Cherryman: drowned. 18 miles. £1 13s 6d.
8 Mar. 1783. Hartfield. Robert Farnes: drowned. 22 miles. £1 16s 6d.
17 Mar. 1783. Paid the clerk of assize on returning the inquisition on Jonathan Godfrey who was killed by Thomas Rogers 5s.[1]
17 Apr. 1783. Friston. William Batchelor: killed by a fall from a horse. 14 miles. £1 10s 6d.
21 Apr. 1783. Brighton. Mary Piper: cut her throat. 8 miles. £1 6s.
Total £8 5s; allowed at Easter sessions 1783. [QR/E 615, no 34]

1 Cf. **54**, **352**; *SCM*, XI, 370.

57 23 May 1783. Rottingdean. Thomas Noakes: shot. 7 miles. £1 5s 3d.[1]
14 July 1783. Poynings. Thomas Marchant: drowned. 10 miles. £1 7s 6d.
[*Date omitted.*] Poynings. William Parsons: drowned. 10 miles. £1 7s 6d.
Total £4 0s 3d; allowed at Midsummer sessions 1783. [QR/E 616, no 32]

1 Cf. **58**, **353**.

58 13 Aug. 1783. Spital Mill. William Jenner: killed by lightning in the mill. £1.

15 Aug. 1783. Paid the clerk of assize on returning the inquisition on Thomas Noakes who was shot at Rottingdean 5s.[1]
19 Aug. 1783. Southover. John Balcombe: fell down dead. £1.
1 Sept. 1783. Rottingdean. John Pope: fell over the cliff and was killed. 7 miles. £1 5s 3d.
8 Sept. 1783. Berwick. John Ranger: found dead in his house. 9 miles. £1 6s 9d.
[*Date omitted.*] The Battery, Brighton. William Kidds: shot. 8 miles. £1 6s.
16 Sept. 1783. Framfield. Richard Wickham: killed by a wagon. 11 miles. £1 8s 3d.
19 Sept. 1783. Withyham. John Akehurst: drowned. 20 miles. £1 15s.
1 Oct. 1783. Newick. Thomas Bull: killed by a fall from his horse. 9 miles. £1 6s 9d.
Total £10 13s; allowed at Michaelmas sessions 1783. [QR/E 617, no 43]

1 Cf. **57**, **353**.

59 24 Nov. 1783. Stockferry. Mr William Saxby: drowned. 6 miles. £1 4s 6d.
24 Dec. 1783. Hailsham. Edward Fryer: found dead. 14 miles. £1 10s 6d.
27 Dec. 1783. Uckfield. James Gold: drowned. 8 miles. £1 6s.
[*Date omitted.*] Alfriston. Thomas Shelley: killed by his horse falling. 10 miles. £1 7s 6d.
1 Jan. 1784. Southwick. Richard Cook: found dead. 12 miles. £1 9s.
7 Jan. 1784. Hailsham. John Walker: shot. 14 miles. £1 10s 6d.
Total £8 8s; allowed at Epiphany sessions 1784. [QR/E 618, no 46]

60 3 Feb. 1784. Portslade. Hannah Kent: died through the inclemency of the weather. 12 miles. £1 9s.
13 Feb. 1784. Brighton. David Hannsom: rode over the cliff between Rottingdean and Brighton and was killed. 8 miles. £1 6s.[1]
12 Mar. 1784. Framfield. William Cornwall: died through the inclemency of the weather. 11 miles. £1 8s 3d.
12 Mar. 1784. Henfield. Thomas Holden: died through the inclemency of the weather. 16 miles. £1 12s.
25 Mar. 1784. Lindfield. Anthony Harland, infant: fell into a mill-pond and was drowned. 12 miles. £1 9s.
25 Mar. 1784. Ardingly. William Wale: killed by part of a haystack falling on him. 16 miles. £1 12s.
Total £8 16s 3d; allowed at Easter sessions 1784. [QR/E 619, no 50]

1 Cf. *SCM*, XI, 636.

61 26 Apr. 1784. East Dean. Thomas Standley: drowned. 14 miles. £1 10s 6d.
1 May 1784. Rodmell. Abraham Marshall: killed by a fall from his horse. 4 miles. £1 3s.
11 May 1784. New Shoreham. Sarah Moses: drowned herself. 14 miles. £1 10s 6d.
19 May 1784. Worth. Richard Chapman: hanged himself. 23 miles. £1 17s 3d.
23 May 1784. Iford. George Picknal: killed by a fall from his horse. 2 miles. £1 1s 6d.
11 June 1784. Ditchling. Richard Tester: killed by a wagon. 8 miles. £1 6s.
15 June 1784. Cliffe House of Correction. William King. £1.
4 July 1784. Arlington. Ann Bray: drowned. 10 miles. £1 7s 6d.
15 July 1784. Streat. Elizabeth Hampsher: drowned. 7 miles. £1 5s 3d.
Total £12 1s 6d; allowed at Midsummer sessions 1784. [QR/E 620, no 36]

62 21 July 1784. Newhaven. James Moore: drowned. 8 miles. £1 6s.
2 Aug. 1784. Ifield. John Smith: killed by a wagon. 24 miles. £1 18s.
9 Aug. 1784. Hove. John Greentree: drowned. 10 miles. £1 7s 6d.
14 Aug. 1784. Brighton. John Nevill: fell into a mash-tun and was scalded to death. 8 miles. £1 6s.
11 Sept. 1784. Newick. John Pierce: fell into a cistern and received a mortal wound of which he instantly died. 8 miles. £1 6s.
13 Sept. 1784. Henfield. Abel Muzzell: drowned. 18 miles. £1 13s 6d.
29 Sept. 1784. Arlington. Sarah Mepham: found dead. 11 miles. £1 8s 3d.
Total £10 5s 3d; allowed at Michaelmas sessions 1784. [QR/E 621, no 41]

63 9 Oct. 1784. Rodmell. Nicholas Earle: drowned himself. 4 miles. £1 3s.
13 Nov. 1784. Chiddingly. Richard Guy: died by excessive drinking. 10 miles. £1 7s 6d.
3 Dec. 1784. Westout in Lewes. Unknown man:[1] found dead in New Field. £1.
6 Dec. 1784. Bolney. Rachel Horley: fell into a pond and was drowned. 18 miles. £1 13s 6d.
13 Dec. 1784. Alciston. Richard Kennard: hanged himself. 8 miles. £1 6s.
[*Date omitted.*] Berwick. William Creasy: found dead in the snow. 9 miles. £1 6s 9d.
22 Dec. 1784. [Cliffe] House of Correction. John Tooth. £1.
Total £8 16s 9d; allowed at Epiphany sessions 1785.[2] [QR/E 622, no 50]

1 *A vagrant, name unknown* in PAR 411/1/1/1.
2 Payment was made after Francis Wheeler's death, presumably to William his son and successor: Brent, 72.

Bills of William Wheeler

64 10 Feb. 1785. Chalvington. Mary Horscroft: threw herself into a pond and was drowned. 10 miles. £1 7s 6d.
4 Mar. 1785. [Cliffe] House of Correction. John Flexon. £1.
10 Mar. 1785. Brighton. James Curtis, infant: his clothes caught fire and he was burned to death. 8 miles. £1 6s.
14 Mar. 1785. Ringmer. Unknown man: found dead. 3 miles. £1 2s 3d.
15 Mar. 1785. [Cliffe] House of Correction. John Camps. £1.
31 Mar. 1785. Buxted. William Isted: found dead in bed. 12 miles. £1 9s.
Total £7 4s 9d; allowed at Easter sessions 1785. [QR/E 623, no 44]

[All Wheeler's journeys were from Cliffe but that is never stated in his bills.]

65 2 May 1785. New Shoreham. John Wicks: hanged himself. 14 miles. £1 10s 6d.
4 May 1785. Cliffe. Harriet Fowle: died suddenly. £1.
23 May 1785. Hailsham. James Divall: killed by his horse falling. 14 miles. £1 10s 6d.
25 June 1785. [Cliffe] House of Correction. Sarah Cashel. £1.
1 July 1785. Horsted Keynes. Philip Tyehurst: drowned. 14 miles. £1 10s 6d.
Total £6 11s 6d; allowed at Midsummer sessions 1785. [QR/E 624, no 50]

66 5 Aug. 1785. Brighton. Thomas Wilson: drowned. 8 miles. £1 6s.
15 Aug. 1785. Newhaven. James White: drowned. 8 miles. £1 6s.

16 Aug. 1785. Near Landport. Richard Fry: drowned. £1.
14 Sept. 1785. [Cliffe] House of Correction. Samuel Frost. £1.
28 Sept. 1785. Withyham. George Adams: killed by a fall from a horse. 22 miles. £1 16s 6d.
5 Oct. 1785. Barcombe. John Grainger, infant: burned to death. 6 miles. £1 4s 6d.
Total £7 13s; allowed at Michaelmas sessions 1785. [QR/E 625, no 28]

67 14 Oct. 1785. Alciston. Walter Brook: killed by his horse falling with him. 8 miles. £1 6s.
10 Nov. 1785. Near Southerham Corner. Delph Hollebone: drowned herself. £1.
18 Nov. 1785. Brighton. Hannah Tuppen: found dead. 8 miles. £1 6s.
6 Dec. 1785. Westmeston. Thomas Godden: found dead. 8 miles. £1 6s.
8 Jan. 1786. Brook Street, Cuckfield. Henry Isted: found dead. 16 miles. £1 12s.
Total £6 10s; allowed at Epiphany sessions 1786. [QR/E 626, no 76]

68 9 Feb. 1786. Barcombe. Thomas Crofts: died of excessive drinking and by the inclemency of the weather. 5 miles. £1 3s 9d.
8 Mar. 1786. Preston. Mary Gosley: found dead in the snow. 8 miles. £1 6s.
13 Mar. 1786. [Cliffe] House of Correction. James Hopkins. £1.
29 Mar. 1786. Lindfield. William Elliott: hanged himself. 12 miles. £1 9s.
Total £4 18s 9d; allowed at Easter sessions 1786. [QR/E 627, no 79]

69 2 June 1786. East Dean. Ann Michell, infant: fell into a tub of water and was drowned. 15 miles. £1 11s 3d.
6 June 1786. Rotherfield. William Upton: died of excessive drinking. 15 miles. £1 11s 3d.
10 June 1786. South Malling. John Stanford: killed by a fall of chalk in Malling Pit. £1.
[10 June] 1786. Frant. Benjamin Gower: hanged himself. 21 miles. £1 15s 9d.
11 June 1786. Albourne. William Mockford: died in a fit in a field. 13 miles. £1 9s 9d.
9 July 1786. Hailsham. William Head: killed by a fall from his horse. 14 miles. £1 10s 6d.
Total £8 18s 6d; allowed at Midsummer sessions 1786. [QR/E 628, no 37]

70 12 Aug 1786. Plumpton. Joseph Babcock: killed by a cart. 6 miles. £1 4s 6d.
18 Aug. 1786. Lamberhurst. Elizabeth Burr: drowned. 30 miles. £2 2s 6d.
22 Aug. 1786. Old Shoreham. Edward Moon: hanged himself. 14 miles. £1 10s 6d.
4 Oct. 1786. Cliffe. William Saunders: died of excessive drinking. £1.
6 Oct. 1786. Lamberhurst. John Dodd: hanged himself. 30 miles. £2 2s 6d.
Total £8; allowed at Michaelmas sessions 1786. [QR/E 629, no 52]

71 10 Oct. 1786. New Shoreham. Benjamin Ashman: drowned. 14 miles. £1 10s 6d.
[*Date omitted.*] New Shoreham. Michael Tiltstone:[1] drowned. 14 miles. £1 10s 6d.
[*Date omitted.*] New Shoreham. Unknown boy:[2] drowned. 14 miles. £1 10s 6d.
[*Date omitted.*] New Shoreham. Joseph Morris: drowned. 14 miles. £1 10s 6d.
12 Oct. 1786. Southwick. John Young: drowned. 12 miles. £1 9s.
[*Date omitted.*] Kingston by Sea. Unknown person: drowned. 13 miles. £1 9s 9d.
[*Date omitted.*] Kingston by Sea. Unknown person: drowned. 13 miles. £1 9s 9d.
20 Oct. 1786. Brighton. Isaac Greenfield jun.: killed by his horse falling with him. 8 miles. £1 6s.

28 Oct. 1786. Newhaven. Alice Alderton: hanged herself. 8 miles. £1 6s.
29 Nov. 1786. West Firle. Charity Stephens, widow: found dead. 5 miles. £1 3s 9d.
5 Dec. 1786. Tarring Neville. Edmund Baker: drowned. 6 miles. £1 4s 6d.
12 Dec. 1786. Cliffe. Thomas Elliker: drowned. £1.
Total £16 10s 9d; allowed at Epiphany sessions 1787. [QR/E 630, no 55]

1 *Tilstone* in Par. 170/1/1/5; *Tillstone* in Ep. II/16/178A.
2 *A sailor-boy, name unknown* in Par. 170/1/1/5.

72 14 Jan. 1787. Southwick. William Kent, infant: killed by a horse. 12 miles. £1 9s.[1]
[*Date omitted.*] Edburton. Thomas Cripps: found dead. 13 miles. £1 9s 9d.
3 Feb. 1787. Lewes Castle. Joseph Hall: died of excessive drinking. £1.
20 Feb. 1787. Maresfield. Patrick Owen: found dead. 12 miles. £1 9s.
1 Apr. 1787. Twineham. Ann Henley: drowned. 18 miles. £1 13s 6d.
3 Apr. 1787. Clayton. Thomas Payne: hanged himself. 10 miles. £1 7s 6d.
Total £8 8s 9d; allowed at Easter sessions 1787. [QR/E 631, no 46]

1 Cf. *SCM*, V, 809.

73 18 June 1787. Preston. Henry Bonner: killed by Philip Jenden. 8 miles. £1 6s.[1]
8 July 1787. Henfield. Thomas Lucock:[2] killed by a cart. 17 miles. £1 12s 9d.
11 July 1787. Frant. James Ashby: drowned. 25 miles. £1 18s 9d.
12 July 1787. East Grinstead. Charles Streater: killed by a cart. 20 miles. £1 15s.
Total £6 12s 6d; allowed at Midsummer sessions 1787. [QR/E 632, no 47]

1 Cf. **74**, **354**; *SCM*, VIII, 697–698; *SCM*, XVIII, 22, 54–55.
2 *Thomas Wilcock* in Par. 100//1/1/1.

74 26 July 1787. Brighton. William Hart: fell over the cliff and was killed. 8 miles. £1 6s.[1]
4 Aug. 1787. Brighton. John Newland: rode a horse into the sea and was drowned. 8 miles. £1 6s.
5 Aug. 1787. Henfield. Catherine Hill: killed in a sand-pit. 17 miles. £1 12s 9d.
6[2] Aug. 1787. Paid the clerk of assize on returning the inquisition taken on Henry Bonner who was killed by Philip Jenden 5s.[3]
9 Aug. 1787. Worth. John Hill: fell into a pit and was drowned. 23 miles. £1 17s 3d.
13 Aug. 1787. Brighton. Robert Tribe: went into the sea to bathe and was drowned. 8 miles. £1 6s.
12 Sept. 1787. Frant. Barnaby Goldsmith: cut his throat. 22 miles. £1 16s 6d.
Total £9 9s 6d; allowed at Michaelmas sessions 1787. [QR/E 633, no 42]

1 Cf. *SCM*, XII, 782; *SCM*, XIX, 9.
2 ?Recte *4*: cf. ASSI 94/1290.
3 Cf. **73**, **354**; *SCM*, VIII, 697–698; *SCM*, XVIII, 22, 54–55.

75 19 Oct. 1787. Cuckfield. Jane Tasker: drowned. 16 miles. £1 12s
30 Oct. 1787. Hartfield. Edward Walter: cut his throat. 20 miles. £1 15s.
19 Nov. 1787. Lewes. John Read: hanged himself. £1.
8 Dec. 1787. West Firle. Mary Stephens: killed by her husband George. 5 miles. £1 3s 9d.[1]
30 Dec. 1787. Hailsham. [*blank*] Durrant: died of bruises received falling into a ditch. 13 miles. £1 9s 9d.

Total £7 0s 6d; allowed at Epiphany sessions 1788. [QR/E 634, no 60]

1 Cf. **76**, **355**.

76 1 Feb. 1788. Brighton. Elizabeth Pelling: burnt by her clothes taking fire. 8 miles. £1 6s.
4 Feb. 1788. Old Shoreham. George Morley: killed in a mill. 14 miles. £1 10s 6d.
13 Feb. 1788. Piddinghoe. William Jenner: shot. 6 miles. £1 4s 6d.
8 Mar. 1788. Lewes. Henry Postlethwaite: died in consequence of excessive drinking. £1.
17 Mar. 1788. Rotherfield. Charity Hoadley: threw herself into a well and was drowned. 18 miles. £1 13s 6d.
24 Mar. 1788. Paid the clerk of assize on returning the inquisition taken on Mary Stephens 5s.[1]
Total £6 19s 6d; allowed at Easter sessions 1788. [QR/E 635, no 37]

1 Cf. **75**, **355**.

77 6 Apr. 1788. Framfield. John Weaver: died of excessive drinking. 10 miles. £1 7s 6d.
9 May 1788. Telscombe. Thomas Trill: kicked by a horse and killed. 6 miles. £1 4s 6d.
[*Date omitted.*] Chiddingly. Fanny Guy: drowned. 12 miles. £1 9s.
16 May 1788. Bolney. James Fillery: drowned. 18 miles. £1 13s 6d.
22 May 1788. East Grinstead. Ann Underwood: drowned. 20 miles. £1 15s.
[*Date omitted.*] East Grinstead. John Chapman: shot. 20 miles. £1 15s.
3 June 1788. Lindfield. Thomas West: hanged himself. 14 miles. £1 10s 6d.
13 June 1788. Waldron. Samuel Pattenden: killed by a fall of sand in a sand-pit. 12 miles. £1 9s.
[*Date omitted.*] Waldron. John Harmar: killed by a fall of sand in a sand-pit. 12 miles. £1 9s.
7 July 1788. Brighton. Charity Venner: threw herself into the sea and was drowned. 8 miles. £1 6s.[1]
9 July 1788. Newhaven. Edward West: drowned. 8 miles. £1 6s.
Total £16 5s; allowed at Midsummer sessions 1788. [QR/E 636, no 45]

1 Cf. *SCM*, XIV, 260; *SCM*, XX, 181.

78 7 Aug. 1788. Brighton. Richard Earle: killed in a boxing-match. 8 miles. £1 6s.[1]
4 Sept. 1788. Brighton. Elizabeth Kensley: hanged herself. 8 miles. £1 6s.
5 Sept. 1788. Clayton. John Hammond: fell out of a cart and was killed. 12 miles. £1 9s.
4 Oct. 1788. Ringmer. Unknown woman:[2] found dead. 3 miles. £1 2s 3d.
Total £5 3s 3d; allowed at Michaelmas sessions 1788. [QR/E 637, no 36]

1 Cf. **80**, **357**.
2 *Mary Apted, traveller* in PAR 461/1/1/9.

79 11 Oct. 1788. Eastbourne. Jane Chapman, widow: found dead. 18 miles. £1 13s 6d.
20 Oct. 1788. Horsted Keynes. John Mitchell: found dead. 14 miles. £1 10s 6d.
7 Nov. 1788. Mayfield. Thomas Foster: dragged by a horse and killed. 17 miles. £1 12s 9d.

7 Dec. 1788. Brighton. Ann Tree: supposed to have poisoned herself. 8 miles. £1 6s.
Total £6 2s 9d; allowed at Epiphany sessions 1789. [QR/E 638, no 48]

80 30 Mar. 1789. Uckfield. Lucy Verrall: fell into a dung hole and was suffocated. 8 miles. £1 6s.
[?23 Mar.] 1789. Paid the clerk of assize on returning the inquisition taken on Richard Earle who was killed in a boxing match with Thomas Tine 5s.[1]
2 Apr. 1789. Westmeston. Infant son of John Hoadley: fell into a pond and was drowned. 8 miles. £1 6s.
14 Apr. 1789. New Shoreham. Peter White: found dead in a lane. 14 miles. £1 10s 6d.
17 Apr. 1789. Twineham. Thomas Starley: hanged himself. 18 miles. £1 13s 6d.
Total £6 1s; allowed at Easter sessions 1789. [QR/E 639, no 37]

1 Cf. **78, 357**.

81 25 Apr. 1789. Rodmell. Thomas Hollands: hanged himself. 4 miles. £1 3s.
20 May 1789. Uckfield. Richard Morris: fell from a building and was killed. 8 miles. £1 6s.
27 May 1789. East Grinstead. Henry Edwards: drowned. 20 miles. £1 15s.
3 June 1789. Cuckfield. Francis Jones: fell from behind a chaise and was killed. 18 miles. £1 13s 6d.
10 July 1789. Hurstpierpoint. Mary Ingram: found dead. 12 miles. £1 9s.
Total £7 6s 6d; allowed at Easter[1] sessions 1789. [QR/E 640, no 69]

1 Recte *Midsummer*.

82 29 July 1789. [*Place omitted*.] Richard Phillips: drowned himself in Lewes river. £1.[1]
5 Aug. 1789. Cuckfield. Thomas Haselgrove: hanged himself. 14 miles. £1 10s 6d.
7 Aug. 1789. Beddingham. Henry Haywood: drowned. 4 miles. £1 3s.
17 Aug.[2] 1789. Brighton. The Chevalier de Maupeou:[3] shot himself. 8 miles. £1 6s.
20 Aug.[2] 1789. Newhaven. Edward Waterman:[4] fell from his horse in a fit. 8 miles. £1 6s.
Total £6 5s 6d; allowed at Michaelmas sessions 1789. [QR/E 641, no 37]

1 Cf. *SCM*, XV, 191.
2 Recte *Sept.*
3 *Chevalier de Maupau, maître des Requêtes, son of Monsieur de Maupau, chancellor of the kingdom of France, died 15 Sept., buried 30 Sept.* in PAR 255/1/1/5.
4 Not in PAR 426/1/1/5.

83 12 Oct. 1789. Framfield. Man: fell down stairs and was killed. 9 miles. £1 6s 9d.
26 Oct. 1789. Ditchling. Elizabeth Hubbard: found dead. 8 miles. £1 6s.
Total £2 12s 9d; allowed at Epiphany sessions 1790. [QR/E 642, no 63]

84 21 Jan. 1790. Brighton. William Hazelgrove: burnt to death. 8 miles. £1 6s.
9 Feb. 1790. Wadhurst. William David: hanged himself. 23 miles. £1 17s 3d.
15 Feb. 1790. Tarring Neville. Henry Parker: fell into the river and was drowned. 6 miles. £1 4s 6d.
11 Mar. 1790. Brighton. Richard Reeder: killed by a cart. 8 miles. £1 6s.

13 Mar. 1790. Southease. Mr Griffiths: fell into the river and was drowned. 4 miles. £1 3s.
25 Mar. 1790. Eastbourne. Mary Verrall: hanged herself. 18 miles. £1 13s 6d.
11 Apr. 1790. Framfield. Bet Stephens: burnt to death. 9 miles. £1 6s 9d.
11 Apr. 1790. Hurstpierpoint. John Simmonds: found dead. 12 miles. £1 9s.
14 Apr. 1790. Brighton. Speed Jasper: drowned. 8 miles. £1 6s.
Total £12 12s; allowed at Easter sessions 1790. [QR/E 643, no 67]

85 17 May 1790. Laughton. James Funnell: found dead. 8 miles. £1 6s.
24 May 1790. Withyham. William Sewtus: killed by lightning. 20 miles. £1 15s.
29 June 1790. Lewes. William Emmery: drowned. £1.
Total £4 1s; allowed at Midsummer sessions 1790. [QR/E 644, no 65]

86 17 July 1790. Cuckfield. George Rowland: killed by a cart. 16 miles. £1 12s.
22 July 1790. South Malling. James Pankhurst: killed by a wagon. £1.
6 Aug. 1790. Newhaven Harbour. Summey Carter: fell out of a boat and was drowned. 8 miles. £1 6s.
3 Sept. 1790. Framfield. Charles Relfe: killed by a wagon. 10 miles. £1 7s 6d.
Total £5 5s 6d; allowed at Michaelmas sessions 1790. [QR/E 645, no 54]

87 9 Oct. 1790. Frant. Felicia Budgen: found dead. 24 miles. £1 18s.
18 Oct. 1790. Hurstpierpoint. William Foster: hanged himself. 12 miles. £1 9s.
1 Nov. 1790. Newhaven. Peter Dunham: drowned. 8 miles. £1 6s.
29 Nov. 1790. Henfield. Edward Hayler: died by excessive drinking. 17 miles. £1 12s 9d.
24 Dec. 1790. Chiddingly. Richard Holman: hanged himself. 12 miles. £1 9s.
6 Jan. 1791. Newick. James Haffenden: found dead. 9 miles. £1 6s 9d.
Total £9 1s 6d; allowed at Epiphany sessions 1791. [QR/E 646, no 67]

88 3 Feb. 1791. Newtimber. William Mitchell: fell into a pond and was drowned. 13 miles. £1 9s 9d.
28 Feb. 1791. Hurstpierpoint. John Mitchell: died through the inclemency of the weather. 14 miles. £1 10s 6d.
4 Mar. 1791. Cuckfield. John Rice: fell from a wagon and was killed. 17 miles. £1 12s 9d.
29 Mar. 1791. Frant. Isaac Cheesman: fell from a ladder and was killed. 26 miles. £1 19s 6d.
12 Apr. 1791. East Hoathly. Sarah Penfold: hanged herself. 8 miles. £1 6s.
17 Apr. 1791. Park Corner, Rotherfield. James Sales, infant: drowned. 21 miles. £1 15s 9d.
19 Apr. 1791. Brighton. Robert Cotterel: run over by a wagon and killed. 8 miles. £1 6s.
Total £11 0s 3d; allowed at Easter sessions 1791. [QR/E 647, no 83]

89 1 June 1791. Wadhurst. Elizabeth Mercer: drowned. 23 miles. £1 17s 3d.
[*Date omitted.*] Wadhurst. Thomas Mercer: drowned. 23 miles. £1 17s 3d.
17 June 1791. Wivelsfield. Henry Farncomb: killed in a boxing-match. 12 miles. £1 9s.[1]
Total £5 3s 6d; allowed at Midsummer sessions 1791. [QR/E 648, no 32]

1 Cf. **90**, **358**; *SCM*, XVII, 143.

90 15[1] Aug. 1791. Paid the clerk of assize on returning the inquisition taken on Henry Farncomb who was killed in a battle with Stephen Thompson at Wivelsfield 5s.[2]
12 Sept. 1791. Cuckfield. John Whitchurch, infant: fell into a well and was drowned. 14 miles. £1 10s 6d.
2 Oct. 1791. Hartfield. John Spencer: killed by a wagon. 22 miles. £1 16s 6d.
Total £3 12s; allowed at Michaelmas sessions 1791. [QR/E 649, no 51]

1 ?Recte *13*: cf. ASSI 94/1351.
2 Cf. **89**, **358**; *SCM*, XVII, 143.

91 11 Oct. 1791. Brighton. William Edwards: shot himself. 8 miles. £1 6s.[1]
12 Oct. 1791. Uckfield. Matthew Lewer: fell from a scaffold and was killed. 8 miles. £1 6s.
8 Nov. 1791. Buxted. New-born infant: murdered. 12 miles. £1 9s.[2]
11 Nov. 1791. Cuckfield. Elizabeth Anscombe: cut her throat. 14 miles. £1 10s 6d.
14 Nov. 1791. Alfriston. William Borrer: fell into a ditch and was drowned. 10 miles. £1 7s 6d.
15 Nov. 1791. Worth. Benjamin Wing: died of excessive drinking. 20 miles. £1 15s.
5 Dec. 1791. Worth. John Geer: died by the inclemency of the weather. 26 miles. £1 19s 6d.
11 Dec. 1791. Near Isfield Lock. Thomas Baker: fell into the river and was drowned. 7 miles. £1 5s 3d.
14 Dec. 1791. [Cliffe] House of Correction. William Gates. £1.
26 Dec. 1791. Waldron. Ann Midmer, a new-born child: reported to have been murdered but died a natural death. 14 miles. £1 10s 6d.
27 Dec. 1791. Hailsham. Phyllis Miller, infant: died in consequence of taking a quantity of laudanum. 14 miles. £1 10s 6d.
29 Dec. 1791. Worth. Mary Lashmer: found dead. 21 miles. £1 15s 9d.
4 Jan. 1792. Brighton. William Hobden: found dead. 8 miles. £1 6s.
Total £19 1s 6d; allowed at Epiphany sessions 1792. [QR/E 650, no 98]

1 Cf. *SCM*, XVII, 296.
2 Cf. **92**, **359**.

92 21 Jan. 1792. New Shoreham. Robert Grover: found dead in his boat. 14 miles. £1 10s 6d.
25 Jan. 1792. Little Horsted. Thomas Rose: fell into a pond and was drowned. 6 miles. £1 4s 6d.
29 Jan. 1792. Iford. James[1] Trigger, infant: killed by a tree falling on her. 4 miles. £1 3s.
30 Jan. 1792. Ringmer. John Buckman: hanged himself. 3 miles. £1 2s 3d.
15 Feb. 1792. Newhaven. Hans Peters: fell into the river and was drowned. 8 miles. £1 6s.
27 Feb. 1792. East Grinstead. William Hoath: died by the inclemency of the weather. 21 miles. £1 15s 9d.
7 Mar. 1792. Horsted Keynes. Elizabeth Isted: found dead. 16 miles. £1 12s.
[?7 Mar.] 1792.[2] Lewes. Samuel Grover: found dead in his house. £1.

19 Mar. 1792. Paid the clerk of assize upon returning the inquisition taken on a new-born infant that was murdered at Buxted 5s.[3]
5 Apr. 1792. Ringmer. John Pentecost: died by having taken a quantity of arsenic in some gin and water. 3 miles. £1 2s 3d.
17 Apr. 1792. Plumpton. John Herriott: hanged himself. 6 miles. £1 4s 6d.[4]
Total £13 5s 9d; allowed at Easter sessions 1792. [QR/E 651, no 81]

1 *Jane* in PAR 403/1/1/2.
2 Grover was buried in St John sub Castro on 8 Mar.: PAR 412/1/1/5.
3 Cf. **91**, **359**.
4 Cf. *SCM*, XXII, 28.

93 30 Apr. 1792. Balcombe. Edmund Pentecost: drowned. 18 miles. £1 13s 6d.
11 June 1792. Bolney. Ann Sanders: drowned herself. 18 miles. £1 13s 6d.
16 June 1792. Barcombe. Edward Evans: found dead. 6 miles. £1 4s 6d.
21 June 1792. Lewes. Thomas Marten: cut his throat. £1.
Total £5 11s 6d; allowed at Midsummer sessions 1792. [QR/E 652, no 93]

94 20 July 1792. Framfield. Richard Vaughan: killed by a wagon. 10 miles. £1 7s 6d.
[*Date omitted.*] Cliffe. John Gouldsmith: fell into the river and was drowned. £1.
14 Aug. 1792. East Grinstead. Thomas Philcox: drowned. 20 miles. £1 15s.
29 Aug. 1792. East Grinstead. Edward Muggeridge: killed by a wagon. 18 miles. £1 13s 6d.
4 Sept. 1792. Litlington. Sarah Cox: drowned. 10 miles. £1 7s 6d.
Total £7 3s 6d; allowed at Michaelmas sessions 1792. [QR/E 653, no 92]

95 13 Oct. 1792. Rottingdean. James Moor: drowned. 6 miles. £1 4s 6d.
[*Date omitted.*] Rottingdean. Francis Hards: drowned. 6 miles. £1 4s 6d.
[*Date omitted.*] Rottingdean. Richard Knight: drowned. 6 miles. £1 4s 6d.
[*Date omitted.*] Rottingdean. Joseph Holden: drowned. 6 miles. £1 4s 6d.
15 Oct. 1792. Ringmer. John Nicholls: died of a wound he received with a prong. 3 miles. £1 2s 3d.
14 Nov. 1792. Ringmer. Martha Fletcher: fell down in a fit and expired. 3 miles. £1 2s 3d.
20 Nov. 1792. Rotherfield. Sarah Wickens: found dead. 18 miles. £1 13s 6d.
22 Nov. 1792. East Grinstead. Thomas Nelthorpe: killed by the overturning of a chaise. 20 miles. £1 15s.
10 Dec. 1792. Worth. Thomas Jeale: hanged himself. 25 miles. £1 18s 9d.
17 Dec. 1792. [Cliffe] House of Correction. Sophia Clark. £1.
26 Dec. 1792. Horsted Keynes. Richard Tamplin: fell down in a fit and expired. 16 miles. £1 12s.
5 Jan. 1793. Wivelsfield. William King: found dead. 13 miles. £1 9s 9d.
Total £16 11s 6d; allowed at Epiphany sessions 1793. [QR/E 654, no 86]

96 4 Feb. 1793. Cliffe. George King: killed by a fall. £1.
5 Feb. 1793. Maresfield. Richard Wright: found dead. 12 miles. £1 9s.
15 Feb. 1793. Hailsham. New-born female child: suspected to have been murdered but died a natural death. 12 miles. £1 9s.
16 Feb. 1793. Portslade. Mary Tuppen: threw herself into a well and was drowned. 12 miles. £1 9s.

11 Apr. 1793. Newhaven. Thomas Holliday: drowned. 8 miles. £1 6s.[1]
[11 Apr.] 1793.[2] Newhaven. Peter Mockford: drowned. 8 miles. £1 6s.[1]
Total £7 19s; allowed at Easter sessions 1793. [QR/E 655, no 54]

1 Cf. *SCM*, XXII, 316; *SCM*, XXIII, 100.
2 The order for the payment of this bill was made on 11 Apr.: QO/EW 31.

97 13 Apr. 1793. Cuckfield. James Brooker: hanged himself. 14 miles. £1 10s 6d.
9 May 1793. Newhaven. Henry Lower: drowned. 8 miles. £1 6s.[1]
18 May 1793. Chiddingly. William Lewer: drowned. 10 miles. £1 7s 6d.
22 May 1793. Handcross. Unknown woman: died of excessive drinking. 20 miles. £1 15s.[2]
18 July 1793. Bolney. Mary Renville: hanged herself. 19 miles. £1 14s 3d.
Total £7 13s 3d; allowed at Midsummer sessions 1793. [QR/E 656, no 38]

1 Cf. *SCM*, XXII, 316; *SCM*, XXIII, 100.
2 Cf. *SCM*, XXIII, 272.

98 17 Aug. 1793. Brighton. John Tutt jun.: drowned. 8 miles. £1 6s.
19 Aug. 1793. East Hoathly. Samuel Fuller: drowned. 8 miles. £1 6s.
[*Date omitted.*] East Hoathly. Samuel Huben: drowned. 8 miles. £1 6s.
18 Sept. 1793. Chiddingly. Richard Marshall: drowned himself. 9 miles. £1 6s 9d.
20 Sept. 1793. Church Hill, Brighton. Thomas Stoner: fell down in a fit and suddenly expired. 8 miles. £1 6s.
8 Oct. 1793. Brighton. Richard Carpenter: drowned himself. 8 miles. £1 6s.
Total £7 16s 9d; allowed at Michaelmas sessions 1793. [QR/E 657, no 59]

99 12 Oct. 1793. Kingston by Sea. Charles Geere: fell from his horse and was killed. 12 miles. £1 9s.
[*Date omitted.*] Rottingdean. John Pritchard: drowned. 7 miles. £1 5s 3d.
18 Oct. 1793. Westout in Lewes. Peter Mockford: killed by a horse running against him and beating him to the ground. £1.
23 Oct. 1793. Lewes. Edward Shrimpton: fell down in a fit and died suddenly. £1.
2 Nov. 1793. Brighton. Moses Martin, infant: killed by a wagon. 8 miles. £1 6s.
14 Nov. 1793. Mayfield. Unknown man: died of excessive drinking. 17 miles. £1 12s 9d.
[*Date omitted.*] Fletching. Thomas Huggett: found dead. 10 miles. £1 7s 6d.
28 Nov. 1793. Barley Banks in St John sub Castro, Lewes, near Offham. Richard Hollands: hanged himself. 2 miles. £1 1s 6d.
7 Dec. 1793. Wilmington. William Crowhurst: hanged himself. 12 miles. £1 9s.
11 Dec. 1793. Patcham. Standing Crosskeys: killed by a large quantity of chalk falling on him. 7 miles. £1 5s 3d.
30 Dec. 1793. New Shoreham. Richard Blair: shot. 14 miles. £1 10s 6d.[1]
1 Jan. 1794. Isfield. William Weston jun.: shot. 6 miles. £1 4s 6d.
Total £15 11s 3d; allowed at Epiphany sessions 1794. [QR/E 658, no 56]

1 Cf. **100**, **360**.

100 3 Mar. 1794. Alciston. John Coates sen.: fell into a ditch and was suffocated. 8 miles. £1 6s.
18 Mar. 1794. Newick. William Pulman: found dead. 10 miles. £1 7s 6d.

22 Mar. 1794. Eastbourne. Margaret Gibbs: cut her throat. 18 miles. £1 13s 6d.
24 Mar. 1794. Paid the clerk of assize on returning the inquisition taken on Richard Blair who was shot at sea and died at New Shoreham 5s.[1]
31 Mar. 1794. Cliffe. Richard Ditch: fell from the top of the mast of a sloop and was killed. £1.
8 Apr. 1794. Patcham. Thomas Carter: drowned. 7 miles. £1 5s 3d.
Total £6 17s 3d; allowed at Easter sessions 1794. [QR/E 659, no 40]

1 Cf. **99**, **360**.

101 Omitted from the last bill. 30 Jan. 1794. Isfield. Charles Comber: hanged himself. 6 miles. £1 4s 6d.
10 May 1794. Tarring Neville. James Rowland: fell down in a fit and suddenly expired. 6 miles. £1 4s 6d.
19 May 1794. Lindfield. Hannah Brown: hanged herself. 12 miles. £1 9s.
5 June 1794. All Saints, Lewes. John Ellis, infant: fell into the river and was drowned. £1.
14 June 1794. Berwick. Sion Gouldsmith, infant: killed by a cart. 9 miles. £1 6s 9d.
4 July 1794. Hove. William Balsam, a private in the Dorsetshire Regiment of Militia: drowned. 10 miles. £1 7s 6d.
Total £7 12s 3d; allowed at Midsummer sessions 1794. [QR/E 660, no 73]

102 12 Aug. 1794. Hurstpierpoint. James Parker: fell into a pond and was drowned. 13 miles. £1 9s 9d.
1 Sept. 1794. Hove. John Holmes, a quartermaster belonging to the Lancashire Light Dragoons: killed by his horse falling with him. 10 miles. £1 7s 6d.
4 Sept. 1794. Newhaven. Joseph Townsend: killed by the overturning of a cart. 8 miles. £1 6s.
11 Sept. 1794. Hove. George Best: threw himself into a well and was drowned. 10 miles. £1 7s 6d.
6 Oct. 1794. Hurstpierpoint. William Morley: hanged himself. 12 miles. £1 9s.
Total £6 19s 9d; allowed at Michaelmas sessions 1794. [QR/E 661, no 31]

103 23 Oct. 1794. Eastbourne. Richard Morris: killed by a large quantity of chalk falling on him. [18 miles.] £1 13s 6d.
6 Nov. 1794. Portslade. Thomas Tippen, a private belonging to the Sussex Regiment of Militia: died of excessive drinking. 10 miles. £1 7s 6d.[1]
17 Nov. 1794. Lewes House of Correction. William Pearce. £1.
1 Dec. 1794. Barcombe. Richard Elphick: found hanging. 6 miles. £1 4s 6d.
4 Dec. 1794. Newhaven. Richard Winter: fell into the river and was drowned. 8 miles. £1 6s.
23 Dec. 1794. Maresfield. Thomas Ridley: fell from a hay-mow and was killed. 13 miles. £1 9s 9d.
26 Dec. 1794. Fletching. Sarah Sawyers: killed by a fall. 12 miles. £1 9s.
27 Dec. 1794. Westmeston. Elizabeth White, infant: burnt to death by her clothes catching fire. 8 miles. £1 6s.
31 Dec. 1794. Newhaven. Robert Woolett: fell into the river and was drowned. 8 miles. £1 6s.
5 Jan. 1795. Slaugham. Robert Harding: found dead. 19 miles. £1 14s 3d.

13 Jan. 1795. Lewes House of Correction. William Carey. £1.
Total £14 16s 6d; allowed at Epiphany sessions 1795. [QR/E 662, no 48]

1 Cf. *SCM*, XXIV, 514.

104 28 Jan. 1795. Framfield. Mary Divall: found dead. 10 miles. £1 7s 6d.
5 Feb. 1795. Brighton. John Evans, a soldier in the 5th Battalion of the Royal Regiment of Artillery: went into the sea to swim and was drowned. 8 miles. £1 6s.
18 Feb. 1795. Southease. James Collins: fell into a ditch and was drowned. 6 miles. £1 4s 6d.
16 Mar. 1795. East Grinstead. Martha Weston: fell from her horse and was killed. 21 miles. £1 15s 9d.
Total £5 13s 9d; allowed at Easter sessions 1795. [QR/E 663, no 43]

105 20 Apr. 1795. Framfield. Mary Seamour, infant: fell into a pond and was drowned. 11 miles. £1 8s 3d.
24 Apr. 1795. South Malling. Thomas Hillman: fell into the river and was drowned. £1.
25 Apr. 1795. Brighton. William Peckham: went into the sea to bathe and was drowned. 8 miles. £1 6s.
30 Apr. 1795. Brighton. John Erridge: was overset in a boat and was drowned. 8 miles. £1 6s.
30 May 1795. Buxted. Richard Batchelor, infant: fell into a pond and was drowned. 10 miles. £1 7s 6d.
7 June 1795. Newick. Thomas Osborne: went into a pond to bathe and was drowned. 8 miles. £1 6s.
25 June 1795. Frant. Thomas Allcorn: killed unloading a piece of timber. 21 miles. £1 15s 9d.
29 June 1795. Newick. William Stone: hanged himself. 8 miles. £1 6s.
Total £10 15s 6d; allowed at Midsummer sessions 1795. [QR/E 664, no 63]

106 19 Aug. 1795. Little Horsted. Thomas Muddle: went into a pond to wash himself and was drowned. 6 miles. £1 4s 6d.
21 Aug. 1795. Barcombe. Ann Jenner: hanged herself. 5 miles. £1 3s 9d.
25 Aug. 1795. Brighton. John Thompson, ensign and surgeon's mate in the West Essex Militia: went into the sea to bathe and was drowned. 8 miles. £1 6s.
27 Aug. 1795. Denton. Thomas Bartlett: killed by the kick of a horse. 8 miles. £1 6s.
28 Aug. 1795. Brighton. Samuel Mockford: went into the sea to bathe and was drowned. 8 miles. £1 6s.
Total £6 6s 3d; allowed at Michaelmas sessions 1795. [QR/E 665, no 52]

107 10 Oct. 1795. Brighton. John Riley: drowned. 8 miles. £1 6s.
14 Oct. 1795. Brighton. Thomas Willard: found dead. 8 miles. £1 6s.
26 Oct. 1795. Poynings. Barbara Marshall: killed by a wall falling on her. 12 miles. £1 9s.
30 Oct. 1795. Portslade. Unknown man:[1] drowned. 12 miles. £1 9s.
1 Nov. 1795. Balcombe. William Snelling: killed by a fall from a horse. 18 miles. £1 13s 6d.
19 Nov. 1795. Henfield. William Vinall: killed by a blow from the cog of a wheel in a mill. 16 miles. £1 12s.

8 Dec. 1795. Westout in Lewes. William Humphrey: killed by a wagon. £1.
16 Dec. 1795. Brighton. Ambrose Smith: found dead. 8 miles. £1 6s.
31 Dec. 1795. Arlington. Mary Bodle: cut her throat. 10 miles. £1 7s 6d.
Total £12 9s; allowed at Epiphany sessions 1796. [QR/E 666, no 67]

[This bill should have contained the inquest on John Bridger Norton held at Southwick on 17 Oct. Cf. **108**, **361**.]

1 Probably William Bundy of Bosham, drowned, who was buried at Portslade on 3 Nov.: PAR 449/1/1/2. Cf. *SCM*, XXV, 522.

108 12 Feb. 1796. Brighton. Edmund Borman: killed by a piece of timber falling on him. 8 miles. £1 6s.
29 Feb. 1796. Ringmer. John Wakelyn: killed by a fall from his horse. 3 miles. £1 2s 3d.
14 Mar. 1796. Paid the clerk of assize on returning the inquisition on John Bridger Norton, esq. 5s.[1]
5 Apr. 1796. East Dean. Richard Peirce: hanged himself. 15 miles. £1 11s 3d.
Total £4 4s 6d; allowed at Easter sessions 1796. [QR/E 667, no 51]

1 Cf. **361**; not entered in **107**.

109 21 Apr. 1796. New Shoreham Harbour. John March: attempting to walk across the harbour, was drowned. 14 miles. £1 10s 6d.
7 May 1796. West Hoathly. William Upton: hanged himself. 20 miles. £1 15s.[1]
19 May 1796. Brighton. Elizabeth Hedgely: murdered by some person or persons unknown. 8 miles. £1 6s.[2]
28 May 1796. Brighton. John Russell: killed by a wagon going over him. 8 miles. £1 6s.
2 June 1796. Brighton. William Edward Matthews: died of excessive drinking. 8 miles. £1 6s.
11 June 1796. Mayfield. James Weston, infant: killed by a piece of timber falling on him. 18 miles. £1 13s 6d.
18 June 1796. New Shoreham. Samuel Wood, a private in the Huntingdonshire Militia: went into the river to swim and was drowned. 14 miles. £1 10s 6d.
7 July 1796. Near Lewes Bridge. Dived Chapman:[3] fell into the river and was drowned. £1.
Total £11 7s 6d; allowed at Midsummer sessions 1796. [QR/E 668, no 55]

1 Cf. *SCM*, XXVI, 235–236.
2 Cf. **110**, **362**; *SCM*, XXVI, 237.
3 Buried at All Saints, Lewes as Divan Chapman, aged 11: PAR 410/1/1/5.

110 Omitted from an earlier bill. [?25 Feb. 1788.] Bramber. New-born infant: found dead. 16 miles. £1 12s.[1]
22 July 1796. Paid the clerk of assize on returning the inquisition on Elizabeth Hedgeley, murdered at Brighton, 5s.[2]
25 July 1796. Brighton. Simon Cook: going into the sea to bathe, was drowned. 8 miles. £1 6s.
2 Aug. 1796. West Firle. John Hayler: killed by a fall. 6 miles. £1 4s 6d.
9 Aug. 1796. Lewes Race Hill. Julian Thomas Bernard, clerk: was run against by a carriage. £1.

19 Aug. 1796. East Grinstead. John Reeves: hanged himself. 21 miles. £1 15s 9d.
27 Aug. 1796. Cliffe. Jane Marshall: fell into the river and was drowned. £1.
19 Sept. 1796. Brighton. William Hoad: going into the sea to bathe, was drowned. 8 miles. £1 6s.
20 Sept. 1796. Barcombe. John King: fell off a barley-mow and fractured his skull. 5 miles. £1 3s 9d.
Total £10 13s; allowed at Michaelmas sessions 1796. [QR/E 669, no 44]

1 Possibly **356**.
2 Cf. **109**, **362**; *SCM*, XXVI, 237.

111 8 Oct. 1796. Withyham. Christopher Chrippes: found dead. 18 miles. £1 13s 6d.
11 Oct. 1796. Arlington. John Stevens: accidentally killed by the vanes or sweeps of a mill. 12 miles. £1 9s.
15 Oct. 1796. Lewes. Thomas Pockney, late of Piddinghoe, labourer: accidentally killed by a wagon going over him at Hamsey. £1.
7 Nov. 1796. Falmer. Richard Criss: feloniously killed by Joseph Sayers in a boxing-match. 4 miles. £1 3s.[1]
19 Nov. 1796. Patcham. Daniel Scales: feloniously killed by a seaman belonging to a revenue cutter at New Shoreham. 7 miles. £1 5s 3d.[2]
2 Dec. 1796. Upton's Mill, Framfield. John Newnham, miller: forced by the spur-wheel of the mill against the nut and killed. 10 miles. £1 7s 6d.
31 Dec. 1796. Wadhurst. Richard Latter: drowned in a pond. 25 miles. £1 18s 9d.
4 Jan. 1797. Brighton. Lucy Measor, infant: it having been suspected that she was murdered, but there was no evidence of the fact. 8 miles. £1 6s.
Total £11 3s; allowed at Epiphany sessions 1797. [QR/E 670, no 88]

1 Cf. **112**, **363**.
2 Cf. **112**, **364**; *SCM*, XXI, 226.

112 2 Mar. 1797. Alfriston. John Penfold: hanged himself. 10 miles. £1 7s 6d.
3 Mar. 1797. Piddinghoe. James Hughes Waterman: killed by a wagon going over him. 8 miles. £1 6s.
4 Mar. 1797. Barcombe. Mary wife of William Towner: cut her throat. 6 miles. £1 4s 6d.
13 Mar. 1797. Paid the clerk of assize on returning inquisitions of manslaughter taken in Nov. last on Richard Criss and Daniel Scales 10s.[1]
28 Mar. 1797. Hammerwood Lodge, East Grinstead. Abraham Stenning: hanged himself. 21 miles. £1 15s 9d.
10 Apr. 1797. Newhaven. William Primmer: died suddenly. 8 miles. £1 6s.
[*Date omitted.*] Beddingham. Richard Gates: fell down in a fit and expired. 5 miles. £1 3s 9d.
15 Apr. 1797. Worth. Robert Matthews: found dead in a hovel. 24 miles. £1 18s.
Total £10 11s 6d; allowed at Easter sessions 1797. [QR/E 671, no 43]

1 Cf. **111**, **363**, **364**; *SCM*, XXI, 226.

113 20 May 1797. Hangleton. Ann wife of Charles Carter: being lunatic, hanged herself. 10 miles. £1 7s 6d.
30 May 1797. East Dean. James Williams, a private belonging to the South Hampshire Militia: accidentally drowned. 15 miles. £1 11s 3d.

5 July 1797. Near Lewes Bridge. Robert Spice: being lunatic, threw himself into the Ouse and was drowned. £1.
Total £3 18s 9d; allowed at Midsummer sessions 1797. [QR/E 672, no 110]

114 18 July 1797. New Shoreham. Lieutenant Richard Fowler: shot and stabbed himself in a fit of lunacy. 14 miles. £1 10s 6d.
24 July 1797. Near Lewes Bridge. James McTaggart, a gunner and driver in the Royal Artillery: fell into the river and was drowned. £1.
27 July 1797. South Malling. John Billingham, a private in the Northamptonshire Militia: went into the Ouse to bathe and was drowned. £1.
31 July 1797. Alfriston. Caroline Newman, infant: killed by a cart. 10 miles. £1 7s 6d.
19 Aug. 1797. Hamsey. Barney Lanham: found dead. 4 miles. £1 3s.
3 Sept. 1797. Hove. James Howell: found dead. 10 miles. £1 7s 6d.
16 Sept. 1797. Newhaven Harbour. James Bartlett: accidentally drowned by a boat sinking with a heavy sea. 8 miles. £1 6s.
21 Sept. 1797. Brighton. John Lang, a private in the Lanark and Dunbarton Fencible Cavalry: washed off the rocks and drowned near Rottingdean. 8 miles. £1 6s.
[21 Sept.] 1797. Brighton. Joseph Barrow: went into the sea to bathe and was drowned. 8 miles. £1 6s.
21 Sept. 1797. Brighton. William Biggs: went into the sea to bathe and was drowned. 8 miles. £1 6s.
Total £12 12s 6d; allowed at Michaelmas sessions 1797. [QR/E 673, no 34]

115 14 Oct. 1797. Lewes House of Correction. Unknown man. £1.
16 Oct. 1797. Ringmer. William Cruttenden: killed by the overturning of a chaise-cart. 3 miles. £1 2s 3d.
28 Oct. 1797. Eastbourne. Thomas Mantle: in gathering samphire, fell from the cliff at Beachy Head and was killed. 17 miles. £1 12s 9d.
15 Nov. 1797. Jevington. Ann Putland: found dead. 14 miles. £1 10s 6d.[1]
6 Dec. 1797. [Lewes] House of Correction. Samuel Jordan: hanged himself. £1.[2]
3 Jan. 1798. Cuckfield. Roger Hickton, a private in the Derbyshire Militia: died of excessive drinking. 14 miles. £1 10s 6d.[3]
9 Jan. 1798. Piddinghoe. Unknown negro man: found dead. 7 miles. £1 5s 3d.
Total £9 1s 3d; allowed at Epiphany sessions 1798 when 5s was added by order of the court, making £9 6s 3d. [QR/E 674, no 69]

1 Cf. *SCM*, XXVII, 552.
2 Cf. *SCM*, XXVII, 599.
3 Cf. *SCM*, XXVIII, 38.

116 13 Jan. 1798. New Shoreham. George Fincle: accidentally drowned. 14 miles. £1 10s 6d.
[13 Jan.] 1798. New Shoreham. Thomas Virgoe: accidentally drowned. 14 miles. £1 10s 6d.
[13 Jan.] 1798. New Shoreham. James Phillips: accidentally drowned. 14 miles. £1 10s 6d.
[13 Jan.] 1798. New Shoreham. Thomas Guy: accidentally drowned. 14 miles. £1 10s 6d.

[13 Jan.] 1798. New Shoreham. William Clarke: accidentally drowned. 14 miles. £1 10s 6d.
15 Jan. 1798. Lewes House of Correction. Hannah Broon alias Brown, vagrant. £1.
24 Jan. 1798. Southerham in South Malling. James Hope jun.: dragged by a colt and killed. £1.
1 Feb. 1798. New Shoreham. Thomas Miles: accidentally drowned. 14 miles. £1 10s 6d.
23 Feb. 1798. Hove. Unknown man:[1] accidentally drowned. 10 miles. £1 7s 6d.
[23 Feb.] 1798. Hove. Young unknown man:[1] accidentally drowned. 10 miles. £1 7s 6d.
23 Mar. 1798. Twineham. Nicholas Wood: found dead. 16 miles. £1 12s.
12 Apr. 1798. Eastbourne. Lewis Thomas, a private in the Monmouth and Brecon Militia: accidentally drowned. 17 miles. £1 12s 9d.
Total £17 2s 9d, from which were deducted £2 2s for four of the inquests of 13 Jan. and 7s 6d for one of those of 23 Feb. (the court allowing only one journey on each day), leaving £14 13s 3d which was allowed at Easter sessions 1798. [QR/E 675, no 88]

1 *John Court and Anthony Chapman, mariners, found dead on the beach near Hove* in PAR 386/1/1/3. Cf. *SCM*, XXVIII, 95.

117 21 Apr. 1798. Lewes Barracks. Richard Masters, a grenadier belonging to the South Hants Militia: accidentally fell into one of the privies and was suffocated. £1.
13 May 1798. Telscombe. Judith Sturt: fell from the shafts of a wagon and was killed. 6 miles. £1 4s 6d.[1]
14 May 1798. Rotherfield. James Roberts: killed by the sweeps of a mill. 18 miles. £1 13s 6d.
18 May 1798. [*Place omitted.*] Alexander Fairbairn, a private in the Royal Lanark and Dunbarton Regiment of Fencible Cavalry: died of a fever a few days after receiving a punishment by the sentence of a court martial. 17 miles. £1 12s 9d.
21 May 1798. Newhaven. Richard Brady: accidentally drowned. 8 miles. £1 6s.
22 May 1798. Westmeston. Henry Elliott. Journey to take an inquisition which was adjourned to the next day that a surgeon might examine the body. 6 miles. 4s 6d.
23 May 1798. Westmeston. Henry Elliott. Journey to finish taking the inquisition. Died of excessive drinking. 6 miles. £1 4s 6d.
24 May 1798. Danehill. Stephen Wood: fell into the Ouse at Gold Bridge Lock and was drowned. 13 miles. £1 9s 9d.
26 May 1798. East Grinstead. Joseph Parker: killed by a wagon. 18 miles. £1 13s 6d.
8 June 1798. Preston. Richard Scrase: fell into a well and was drowned. 8 miles. £1 6s.
Total £12 15s; allowed at Midsummer sessions 1798. [QR/E 676, no 44]

1 Cf. *SCM*, XXVIII, 244.

118 31 July 1798. Bolney. Norah Tulley: fell into a pond and was drowned. 18 miles. £1 13s 6d.
4 Aug. 1798. Hurstpierpoint. John Juniper: found dead. 11 miles. £1 8s 3d.
9 Aug. 1798. South Heighton. Robert Pagden: found dead. 7 miles. £1 5s 3d.
16 Aug. 1798. Lewes. Thomas Tompsett: found dead in a stable. £1.
20 Aug. 1798. Arlington. Stephen Hayler: drowned. 12 miles. £1 9s.[1]
14 Sept. 1798. Rotherfield. John Lockyer: shot by the accidental discharge of his fowling-piece. 19 miles. £1 14s 3d.

15 Sept. 1798. East Blatchington. Thomas Powles, a private in the Monmouth and Brecon Militia: drowned. 10 miles. £1 7s 6d.
22 Sept. 1798. Newhaven. William Pope: murdered by John Hanning. 8 miles. £1 6s.[2]
24 Sept. 1798. Lewes House of Correction. John Hanning: hanged himself. £1.
Total £12 3s 9d; allowed at Michaelmas sessions 1798. [QR/E 677, no 88]

1 Cf. *SCM*, XXVIII, 430.
2 Cf. **120**, **365**.

119 12 Oct. 1798. Lewes House of Correction. Margaret Smith. £1.
18 Oct. 1798. Newhaven. Henry Elwood: in a fit of lunacy hanged himself. 8 miles. £1 6s.
20 Oct. 1798. East Grinstead. John Ingleton: found dead in a barn. 24 miles. £1 18s.
31 Oct. 1798. Henfield. William Woolgar: killed by a large quantity of sand falling on him in a sand-pit. 16 miles. £1 12s.
23 Nov. 1798. Chiddingly. William Alchorn: in a fit of lunacy cut his throat. 10 miles. £1 7s 6d.
5 Dec. 1798. Mayfield. Samuel Moon: in a fit of lunacy hanged himself. 16 miles. £1 12s.
6 Dec. 1798. Henfield. Samuel Shoulder: found dead. 16 miles. £1 12s.
Total £10 7s 6d; allowed at Epiphany sessions 1799. [QR/E 678, no 108]

120 26 Jan. 1799. Henfield. Edward Hoare: accidentally fell into a pond and there died. 16 miles. £1 12s.
29 Jan. 1799. Rottingdean. George Lindsay. Journey for the purpose of taking an inquest but it was necessarily deferred for want of material witnesses. 7 miles. 5s 3d.
30 Jan. 1799. Rottingdean. George Lindsay: accidentally fell over the cliff and was killed. 7 miles. £1 5s 3d.
4 Feb. 1799. Alciston. Benjamin Hudson, infant: burnt by its clothes accidentally taking fire. 8 miles. £1 6s.
[4 Feb.] 1799. Laughton. Thomas Fuller: died through the inclemency of the weather. 6 miles. £1 4s 6d.
5 Feb. 1799. Lewes House of Correction. John Sweatman, prisoner: died of a fever. £1.
23 Feb. 1799. Near Langney Fort, Willingdon. Thomas Timmis, a private in the Derbyshire Militia: accidentally drowned. 20 miles. £1 15s.
19 Mar. 1799. Lewes House of Correction. David Dowden, prisoner: natural death. £1.
26 Mar. 1799. Wadhurst. Ann Campeny: accidentally fell into a pond and was drowned. 24 miles. £1 18s.
[?25 Mar.] 1799. Paid the clerk of assize on returning the inquisition taken on view of the body of William Pope who was murdered at Newhaven 5s.[1]
Total £11 11s; allowed at Easter sessions 1799. [QR/E 679, no 59]

1 Cf. **118**, **365**.

121 20 Apr. 1799. Newhaven. Thomas Lee, pilot: accidentally drowned by the oversetting of a boat. 8 miles. £1 6s.
[20 Apr.] 1799. Newhaven. William Huggett: accidentally drowned by the oversetting of a boat. £1.
29 Apr. 1799. Preston. Grace Stammer: being lunatic, poisoned herself. 8 miles. £1 6s.

14 May 1799. Brighton. George Parris, a private in the Hampshire Fencible Light Dragoons: died of excessive drinking. 8 miles. £1 6s.
15 May 1799. Ringmer. Robert Smith jun.: killed by a large quantity of chalk falling on him in Bridgwick chalk-pit. 3 miles. £1 2s 3d.
17 May 1799. Worth. John Waklen: being lunatic, hanged himself. 25 miles. £1 18s 9d.
3 June 1799. West Hoathly. Thomas Anscombe: found dead in a wood. 20 miles. £1 15s.
10 June 1799. East Grinstead. Joseph Dean: went into a pond to bathe and was drowned. 20 miles. £1 15s.
11 June 1799. Cuckfield. Joseph Thomas: fell into a pond and was drowned. 14 miles. £1 10s 6d.
12 June 1799. New Shoreham. William Evans, a private belonging to the Royal Denbighshire Militia: going into the river to bathe, was drowned. 14 miles. £1 10s 6d.[1]
21 June 1799. Henfield. William Chandler: accidentally thrown out of a chaise cart and killed. 16 miles. £1 12s.
17 July 1799. West Hoathly. Joseph Brown: being lunatic, hanged himself. 18 miles. £1 13s 6d.
Total £17 15s 6d; allowed at Midsummer sessions 1799. [QR/E 680, no 55]

1 Cf. *SCM*, XXIX, 293.

122 7 Aug. 1799. Henfield. John Taylor: feloniously poisoned and murdered himself. 16 miles. £1 12s.
10 Aug. 1799. Brighton. Thomas Coates: fell down in a fit and died suddenly. 8 miles. £1 6s.
13 Aug. 1799. Worth. John Brooker: accidentally fell into a sand-pit and was killed. 24 miles. £1 18s.
22 Aug. 1799. Rotherfield. Peter Izzard: accidentally fell down and was killed by a wagon going over him. 16 miles. £1 12s.
5 Sept. 1799. Cuckfield. Elizabeth French, widow: upon her removal, under an order of 2 of the JPs for the town and hundred of Tenterden in Kent, from Tenterden to Cuckfield, died a natural death upon the road. 14 miles. £1 10s 6d.
30 Sept. 1799. Uckfield Bridge. John Curtis: accidentally carried by the current in a great flood into the river and, remaining in the water suspended by a bush for several hours, died in consequence thereof. 8 miles. £1 6s.
30 Sept. 1799. Uckfield Bridge. William Wood: accidentally carried by the current in a great flood into the river and was drowned. £1.
10 Oct. 1799. New Shoreham Harbour. George Miller, a seaman belonging to HM's sloop *The Hound*: accidentally drowned in the harbour. 14 miles. £1 10s 6d.
Total £11 15s; allowed at Michaelmas sessions 1799. [QR/E 681, no 23]

123 12 Oct. 1799. Hartfield. Mary Page: found dead. 18 miles. £1 13s 6d.
14 Oct. 1799. Cliffe. Betty wife of Edward Ewen: died of excessive drinking. £1.
26 Oct. 1799. Eastbourne. Elizabeth wife of John Graves, an armourer in the Westminster Militia: being intoxicated, accidentally fell into a ditch and was drowned. 18 miles. £1 13s 6d.
12 Nov. 1799. Withdean in Patcham. Jane Buckman, spinster: being lunatic, threw herself into a well and was drowned. 7 miles. £1 5s 3d.

14 Nov. 1799. East Grinstead. Isaac Charlwood: being lunatic, hanged himself. 22 miles. £1 16s 6d.
30 Nov. 1799. Brighton. Thomas Lethbridge jun.: accidentally thrown from a horse and killed. 8 miles. £1 6s.
3 Dec. 1799. Brighton. Ann Stiles, infant: died in consequence of being burnt by her clothes accidentally catching fire. 8 miles. £1 6s.
18 Dec. 1799. Newhaven. Thomas Jounham: accidentally fell out of a boat and was drowned. 8 miles. £1 6s.
30 Dec. 1799. Horsted Keynes. William Ottaway: died through the inclemency of the weather. 14 miles. £1 10s 6d.[1]
11 Jan. 1800. Clayton. William Ifold: died of excessive drinking. 10 miles. £1 7s 6d.
Total £14 4s 9d; allowed at Epiphany sessions 1800. [QR/E 682, no 96]

1 Cf. *SCM*, XXX, 32–33.

124 24 Jan. 1800. Ditchling. Richard Bennett: accidentally killed by a wagon going over him. 8 miles. £1 6s.
31 Jan. 1800. Little Horsted. Frances Tippen, widow: accidentally fell into a pond and was drowned. 6 miles. £1 4s 6d.
3 Feb. 1800. Wadhurst. Richard Wickenden, lunatic: hanged himself. 26 miles. £1 19s 6d.
5 Feb. 1800. West Firle. Margaret Samway: fell down in a fit and died suddenly. 5 miles. £1 3s 9d.
16 Mar. 1800. Hailsham. Simon Press, a private in the Suffolk Fencible Cavalry: fell from his horse and was killed. 12 miles. £1 9s.
17 Apr. 1800. Brighton. Henry Oliver: died suddenly. 8 miles. £1 6s.
18 Apr. 1800. New Shoreham. William Miller, master of the barge *Teazer*: accidentally drowned. 14 miles. £1 10s 6d.
Total £9 19s 3d; allowed at Easter sessions 1800. [QR/E 683, no 70]

125 14 May 1800. Lewes House of Correction. Martha Dane, infant. £1.
20 May 1800. East Blatchington Barracks. Rebecca Wright, infant: fell down an area and was killed. 10 miles. £1 7s 6d.
19 June 1800. Frant. George Knight: killed by a wagon loaded with hop-poles turning over and falling on him. 26 miles. £1 19s 6d.
20 June 1800. Balcombe. Hannah wife of John Comber: being lunatic, threw herself into a pond and died in consequence of being thereby exposed to the cold. 16 miles. £1 12s.
20 June 1800. Brighton. Sarah wife of Hards Shepherd: being lunatic, threw herself into a well and was drowned. 8 miles. £1 6s.
22 June 1800. Hangleton. John Bishop: fell down in a fit and died suddenly. 10 miles. £1 7s 6d.
4 July 1800. Brighton. Benjamin Bishop: killed by a boat accidentally falling on one side and pressing him against a wall. 8 miles. £1 6s.[1]
6 July 1800. The Court-house in St John sub Castle, Lewes. Dominic Huggett: shot by a gun which he had in his hand accidentally going off. 3 miles. £1 2s 3d.[1]
12 July 1800. Brighton. Elias Gilbert: went into the sea to bathe and was accidentally drowned. 8 miles. £1 6s.
Total £12 6s 9d; allowed at Midsummer sessions 1800. [QR/E 684, no 87]

1 Cf. *SCM*, XXX, 341.

126 23 July 1800. Clay Hill, Ringmer. William Ashdowne: killed by a wagon going over him. 4 miles. £1 3s.
31 July 1800. Alciston. John Langney: killed by a large quantity of chalk falling on him in Bopeep chalk-pit. 8 miles. £1 6s.
1 Aug. 1800. Newhaven Harbour. William Thompson: fell from the main-yard of a vessel lying in the harbour and was killed. 8 miles. £1 6s.
2 Aug. 1800. Horsted Keynes. William Taylor: threw himself into a pond and was drowned, but the jury could not agree in their verdict and were necessarily adjourned. 14 miles. 10s 6d.
3 Aug. 1800. Horsted Keynes. William Taylor: being lunatic, drowned himself. 14 miles. £1 10s 6d.
11 Aug. 1800. Mayfield Park. James West: went into the park pond to bathe and was accidentally drowned. 17 miles. £1 12s 9d.
16 Aug. 1800. Brighton Race Ground. William Grantham, esq.: killed by his horse falling with him. 8 miles. £1 6s.
3 Sept. 1800. Frant. Joseph Gravett, infant: accidentally fell into a pond and was drowned. 26 miles. £1 19s 6d.
27 Sept. 1800. Brighton. Joseph Maynard, esq.: thrown out of a chaise and killed. 8 miles. £1 6s.
4 Oct. 1800. East Dean. Israel Medhurst: found dead. 15 miles. £1 11s 3d.
Total £13 11s 6d; allowed at Michaelmas sessions 1800. [QR/E 685, no 76]

127 5 Nov. 1800. Ringmer. Mary Sanders, infant: fell down in a fit and died suddenly. 4 miles. £1 3s.
10 Nov. 1800. Brighton. Mary Coupland: accidentally killed by the north wall of the Promenade Grove being blown down in a hurricane and falling upon her. 8 miles. £1 6s.
14 Nov. 1800. Chailey. James Hillman: being riding upon a timber-carriage, was accidentally overturned and killed. 6 miles. £1 4s 6d.
27 Nov. 1800. Ringmer. Michael Starnes: accidentally fell under the wheels of a wagon and was killed. 4 miles. £1 3s.
18 Dec. 1800. Newhaven. Robert Balcombe: accidentally fell into the Ouse and was drowned. 8 miles. £1 6s.
27 Dec. 1800. Ringmer Barracks. Thomas Ridley, a farrier belonging to Captain Blagrave's [Company of the][1] Corps of Captain Commissaries: killed by his horse falling with him. 4 miles. £1 3s.
31 Dec. 1800. Lindfield. James Wille jun.: accidentally fell into the Ouse and was drowned. 12 miles. £1 9s.
Total £8 14s 6d; allowed at Epiphany sessions 1801. [QR/E 686, no 93]

1 Cf. **129**.

128 11 Feb. 1801. Folkington. William Bennett: accidentally killed by a tree falling on him. 12 miles. £1 9s.
23 Feb. 1801. Rotherfield. Unknown man: found drowned in a pond. 18 miles. £1 13s 6d.
28 Feb. 1801. Waldron. William Novis jun.: fell down in a fit and died suddenly in Butler's[1] Wood. 12 miles. £1 9s.
5 Mar. 1801. Brighton. John Bartlett: accidentally killed by a wagon going over him. 8 miles. £1 6s.

7 Mar. 1801. Patcham. Thomas Person: accidentally killed by a wagon going over him. 8 miles. £1 6s.
26 Mar. 1801. Barcombe. Elizabeth Kempton: found drowned in the Ouse. 7 miles. £1 5s 3d.
2 Apr. 1801. Alfriston. Edward Miles: accidentally fell into the Cuckmere and was drowned. 10 miles. £1 7s 6d.
Total £9 16s 3d; allowed at Easter sessions 1801. [QR/E 687, no 93]

1 ?Recte *Butlett's*.

129 6 May 1801. Mayfield. William Weston: accidentally killed by a chimney falling on him. 18 miles. £1 13s 6d.
9 May 1801. Ringmer. William Gorringe: accidentally killed by a piece of timber falling upon him. 4 miles. £1 3s.
[*Date omitted.*] Hove. William Burchill: died suddenly. 10 miles. £1 7s 6d.
13 May 1801. Saddlescombe. John Stevens: accidentally killed by a fall of chalk in Saddlescombe chalk-pit. 12 miles. £1 9s.
14 May 1801. Michelham Mill, Arlington. Robert Child, infant: accidentally strangled by the iron spindle of the machine in the mill catching hold of his clothes. 12 miles. £1 9s.
22 May 1801. Cliffe. Henry Alfrey: fell down in a fit and died suddenly. £1.
30 June 1801. Wellingham in Ringmer. Robert Porteus, a private in Captain Blagrave's Company of the Corps of Captain Commissaries: going into the Ouse to bathe, was accidentally drowned. 2 miles. £1 1s 6d.
6 July 1801. Offham. John Lindfield: accidentally killed by a fall of chalk in Offham chalk-pit. 2 miles. £1 1s 6d.
Total £10 5s; allowed at Midsummer sessions 1801. [QR/E 688, no 107]

130 20 July 1801. Staplefield Common, Cuckfield. Abraham Beckley: being lunatic, threw himself into a pond and was drowned. 18 miles. £1 13s 6d.
[*Date omitted.*] Patcham. Rebecca Carter, widow: being lunatic, threw herself into a well and was drowned. 8 miles. £1 6s.
[*Date omitted.*] Brighton. Thomas Pain: being lunatic, threw himself into the sea and was drowned. 8 miles. £1 6s.
24 July 1801. South Malling. James Lempriere: going into the Ouse to bathe, was accidentally drowned. £1.
7 Aug. 1801. Brighton Barracks. James Kelly: inquest necessarily deferred to give time to procure the necessary witnesses. 7 miles. 5s 3d.[1]
8 Aug. 1801. Brighton Barracks. James Kelly: feloniously killed by John Conolly. 7 miles. £1 5s 3d.[1]
18 Aug. 1801. Ripe. James Strong, infant: accidentally fell down stairs and was killed. 10 miles. £1 7s 6d.
23 Aug. 1801. Clayton. Mary Bignall: being lunatic, hanged herself. 10 miles. £1 7s 6d.
24 Aug. 1801. Ardingly. Cleophas Comber jun.: killed by a fall from his horse. 16 miles. £1 12s.
29 Aug. 1801. East Grinstead. Sarah Mansell, widow: being lunatic, hanged herself. 21 miles. £1 15s 9d.

21 Sept. 1801. Hurstpierpoint. Francis Gander: accidentally fell from a horse and was killed. 12 miles. £1 9s.

7 Oct. 1801. Offham. Thomas Howell: accidentally killed by a fall of rubble in a chalk-pit. 2 miles. £1 1s 6d.

Total £15 9s 3d; allowed at Michaelmas sessions 1801 when 5s was added by order of the court, making £15 14s 3d. [QR/E 689, no 115]

1 Cf. **132**, **366**.

131 30 Nov. 1801. Chelwood Common, Maresfield. Ann Watson: died through the inclemency of the weather on the common. 14 miles. £1 10s 6d.

3 Dec. 1801. Frant. George Rootes: found dead in a barn. 24 miles. £1 18s.

14 Dec. 1801. Uckfield. Catherine Seagrove: found dead in a stable. 8 miles. £1 6s.

22 Dec. 1801. Hailsham. Richard Pierce: accidentally fell into a ditch and was drowned. 13 miles. £1 9s 9d.

28 Dec. 1801. Southwick. Unknown man: found dead on the beach. 13 miles. £1 9s 9d.

[*Date omitted.*] Rotherfield. Elizabeth Waters: being lunatic, cut her throat. 18 miles. £1 13s 6d.

5 Jan. 1802. Bishopstone. Donald McKay, a private in HM's Rifle Corps: died through the inclemency of the weather. 10 miles. £1 7s 6d.

Total £10 15s; allowed at Epiphany sessions 1802. [QR/E 690, no 91]

132 8 Feb. 1802. St Michael's, Lewes. Male infant son of John Emmery, labourer: accidentally overlain and smothered. £1.

23 Mar. 1802. Barcombe. James Skinner: fell down in a fit and died suddenly. 5 miles. £1 3s 9d.

27 Mar. 1802. Paid the clerk of assize his fee on returning the inquest on James Kelly who was feloniously killed by John Conolly 5s.[1]

6 Apr. 1802. Hellingly. William Reed: poisoned by incautiously eating of the root of hemlock dropwort. 12 miles. £1 9s.

12 Apr. 1802. Pease Pottage in Slaugham. John Garlick: being lunatic, hanged himself. 21 miles. £1 15s 9d.

Total £5 13s 6d; allowed at Easter sessions 1802. [QR/E 691, no 68]

1 Cf. **130**, **366**.

133 30 May 1802. West Hoathly. William Killick: found dead. 16 miles. £1 12s.

22 June 1802. Brighton. Mr William Ford: being lunatic, cut his throat. 8 miles. £1 6s.

24 June 1802. Willingdon. Thomas Bridger: killed by the accidental overturning of a wagon. 15 miles. £1 11s 3d.

26 June 1802. Brighton. Robert Marsh: being lunatic, hanged himself. 8 miles. £1 6s.

28 June 1802. [Lewes] House of Correction. Rachel Dennis: natural death. £1.

14 July 1802. Wivelsfield. Elizabeth Tester, widow: being lunatic, hanged herself. 12 miles. £1 9s.

15 July 1802. Lewes. Ann Page: feloniously hanged and murdered herself. £1.

Total £9 4s 3d; allowed at Midsummer sessions 1802. [QR/E 692, no 67]

134 17 July 1802. Cousley Wood Street, Wadhurst. Grace Harding: being lunatic, hanged herself. 26 miles. £1 19s 6d.

28 July 1802. Albourne. Harriet Maskall, infant: accidentally fell into the soil of a privy and was suffocated. 14 miles. £1 10s 6d.
25 Aug. 1802. Mayfield. James Izzard: killed by the accidental overturning of a wagon. 18 miles. £1 13s 6d.
1 Sept. 1802. Lamberhurst. Benjamin Gabriel: being lunatic, cut his throat. 30 miles. £2 2s 6d.
4 Sept. 1802. Handcross in Slaugham. Mr John Edwards: shot by the accidental discharge of a fowling-piece. 20 miles. £1 15s.
1 Oct. 1802. Newick. Thomas Taylor: being lunatic, threw himself into the Ouse and was drowned. 8 miles. £1 6s.
5 Oct. 1802. Brighton Barracks. New-born male child: supposed to have been murdered, but it appeared to have been still-born. 8 miles. £1 6s.
6 Oct. 1802. Boarshead Street, Rotherfield. Mary Crittall, widow: being lunatic, hanged herself. 18 miles. £1 13s 6d.
Total £13 6s 6d; allowed at Michaelmas sessions 1802. [QR/E 693, no 108]

135 11 Oct. 1802. Lewes House of Correction. James, infant child of Mary Waller: natural death. £1.
[*Date omitted.*] Westout in Lewes. Henry Payne: fell down in a fit and died suddenly. £1.
19 Oct. 1802. Brighton. Susannah Mockford, infant: died in consequence of being burnt by her clothes accidentally taking fire. 8 miles. £1 6s.
[*Date omitted.*] Brighton. John Wood: died in consequence of an accidental fall from the top of a house. 8 miles. £1 6s.
11 Nov. 1802. Withyham. Peter Avis: died suddenly in an apoplectic fit. 20 miles. £1 15s.
12 Nov. 1802. Barcombe. William Markwick: accidentally fell into the Ouse and was drowned. 5 miles. £1 3s 9d.
[12 Nov.] 1802. Brighton. Charles Camp: being lunatic, hanged himself. 8 miles. £1 6s.
[12 Nov.] 1802. Brighton. William Pankhurst: being lunatic, hanged himself. 8 miles. £1 6s.
13 Nov. 1802. Magham Down, Hailsham. H Thankful Booth:[1] killed by his horse falling with him. 14 miles. £1 10s 6d.
9 Dec. 1802. Clayton. John Webber jun.: murdered by Robert Bignall jun. 12 miles. £1 9s.[2]
29 Dec. 1802. Kingston by Sea. Auguste Fettinge: accidentally drowned by the oversetting of a boat. 12 miles. £1 9s.
[*Date omitted.*] Kingston by Sea. François Consal: accidentally drowned by the oversetting of a boat. 12 miles. £1 9s.
10 Jan. 1803. Cliffe. John Rogers: accidentally fell out of a boat in the great sewer and was drowned. £1.
11 Jan. 1803. Chiddingly. James Elias Carpenter: accidentally fell into the mud in a road and was suffocated. 10 miles. £1 7s 6d.
12 Jan. 1803. Eastbourne. John Verrall: died through the inclemency of the weather. 18 miles. £1 13s 6d.
Total £20 1s 3d; allowed at Epiphany sessions 1803. [QR/E 694, no 76]

1 *Thankful Booth* in PAR 353/1/1/7. The initial *H* may be a miscopying of *Mr*.
2 Cf. **136**, **367**; *SCM*, XIV, 27–31.

136 17 Jan. 1803. Kingston near Lewes. Edward Martin: died suddenly. 2 miles. £1 1s 6d.
28 Jan. 1803. Alfriston. Ann Goldsmith: died through the inclemency of the weather. 10 miles. £1 7s 6d.
21 Feb. 1803. Hurstpierpoint. John English: fell down in a fit and died suddenly. 12 miles. £1 9s.
22 Feb. 1803. Barcombe. Thomas Muddle: accidentally fell from a towing-path bridge into the Ouse and was drowned. 6 miles. £1 4s 6d.
24 Feb. 1803. Waldron. Edward Sellen: lost his road in the night and died through fatigue and the inclemency of the weather. 12 miles. £1 9s.
25 Feb. 1803. East Grinstead. Sarah McCoomb: being lunatic, wounded herself with a penknife and died. 21 miles. £1 15s 9d.
2 Mar. 1803. Slaugham. John Snashall: fell down in a fit and died suddenly. 20 miles. £1 15s.
8 Mar. 1803. Chailey. John Cott: fell down in a fit and died suddenly. 8 miles. £1 6s.
10 Mar. 1803. Bishopstone. John Ford: going into the sea to swim after a wild duck that had been shot, was accidentally drowned. 8 miles. £1 6s.
12 Mar. 1803. Ringmer. Henry Simmonds, infant: died in consequence of being burnt by his clothes accidentally taking fire. 4 miles. £1 3s.
28 Mar. 1803. Paid the clerk of assize on returning the inquisition taken on view of the body of John Webber jun. 5s.[1]
9 Apr. 1803. Hailsham. New-born male child: appeared to be still-born. 12 miles. £1 9s.
21 Apr. 1803. West Battery, Brighton. Thomas Blaker, a private in the Sussex Militia: died suddenly in a fit on his post as a sentinel. 8 miles. £1 6s.
Total £16 17s 3d; allowed at Easter sessions 1803. [QR/E 695, no 58]

1 Cf. **135**, **367**; *SCM*, XIV, 27–31.

137 25 May 1803. [*Place omitted.*] William Moore: being lunatic, hanged himself. 16 miles. £1 12s.
16 June 1803. East Grinstead. Edward Jenner, infant: his clothes accidentally caught fire and occasioned his death. 21 miles. £1 15s 9d.
22 June 1803. Westout in Lewes. John Bates: accidentally fell under the wheels of a wagon and was killed. £1.
5 July 1803. Westmeston. William Brooker: feloniously killed by Richard Leney. 6 miles. £1 4s 6d.[1]
[*Date omitted.*] Brighton. Sarah Braine: accidentally entangled in a cord and strangled. 8 miles. £1 6s.
7 July 1803. Westout in Lewes. James Free: fell down in a fit and died suddenly. £1.
12 July 1803. Laughton Pound. Richard Bosby, a private in HM's 11th Regiment of Light Dragoons: being delirious from the violence of fever in the smallpox, cut his throat. 6 miles. £1 4s 6d.
Total £9 2s 9d; allowed at Midsummer sessions 1803 when 5s was added by order of the court, making £9 7s 9d. [QR/E 696, no 79]

1 Cf. **138**, **368**.

138 18 July 1803. South Malling. Francesio Pedretti: went into the Ouse to bathe and was accidentally drowned. £1.

24 July 1803. Westout in Lewes. George Cooke, infant: died suddenly in a fit. £1.
25 July 1803. Brighton. James Riley: went into the sea to bathe and was accidentally drowned. 8 miles. £1 6s.
30 July 1803. Frant. William Fairthorne: died of excessive drinking. 26 miles. £1 19s 6d.
31 July 1803. Hove. Edward Sturt: going into the sea to bathe, was accidentally drowned. 10 miles. £1 7s 6d.
5 Aug. 1803. Paid the clerk of assize on returning the inquisition taken on view of the body of William Brooker who was feloniously killed by Richard Leney at Westmeston 5s.[1]
15 Aug. 1803. Pilstye in Cuckfield. Lydia Hall, infant: accidentally killed by being thrown down at play. 18 miles. £1 13s 6d.
19 Aug. 1803. Brighton. Meshach Wharton, a private in the Sussex Militia: going into the sea to bathe, was accidentally drowned. 8 miles. £1 6s.
12 Sept. 1803. Brighton Barracks. Francis Hansman, a private in the 10th[2] Regiment of Light Dragoons: being lunatic, shot himself. 8 miles. £1 6s.
17 Sept. 1803. Southover. Henry Emmery: accidentally fell from a scaffold and was killed. £1.
Total £12 3s 6d; allowed at Michaelmas sessions 1803. [QR/E 697, no 95]

1 Cf. **137**, **368**.
2 *or Prince of Wales's Own*: Swinson, 33.

139 24 Oct. 1803. Eastbourne. Richard Walter: being lunatic, shot himself. 18 miles. £1 13s 6d.
27 Oct. 1803. Mayfield. Sarah Stedman: being lunatic, threw herself into a pond and was drowned. 16 miles. £1 12s.
7 Dec. 1803. Hartfield. William Austen: died suddenly in a fit. 20 miles. £1 15s.
16 Dec. 1803. New Shoreham Harbour. George Gibson: accidentally fell into the harbour and was drowned. 14 miles. £1 10s 6d.
17 Dec. 1803. Little Horsted. Thomas Taylor jun.: died of excessive drinking. 6 miles. £1 4s 6d.
Total £7 15s 6d; allowed at Epiphany sessions 1804. [QR/E 698, no 129]

140 1 Feb. 1804. Portslade. William Scutt: being lunatic, hanged himself. 12 miles. £1 9s.
11 Feb. 1804. Eastbourne. Thomas Hopkins, a private of the 48th[1] Regiment of Foot: accidentally fell into a ditch and was drowned. 20 miles. £1 15s.
29 Feb. 1804. Frant. Thomas Russell: died of excessive drinking. 24 miles. £1 18s.
6 Mar. 1804. Eastbourne. David James, a private of the 48th[1] Regiment of Foot: accidentally ran against the point of a sentinel's bayonet and was killed. 20 miles. £1 15s.
23 Mar. 1804. Ringmer. New-born male child: murdered by its mother, Mary Haselden. 3 miles. £1 2s 3d.[2]
Total £7 19s 3d; allowed at Easter sessions 1804 when 5s was added by order of the court, making £8 4s 3d. [QR/E 699, no 74]

1 *Northamptonshire*: Swinson, 147.
2 Cf. **142**, **369**.

141 13 Apr. 1804. Brighton. James Cleaver: accidentally fell over the cliff and died in consequence of the bruises he received in the fall. 8 miles. £1 6s.
18 Apr. 1804. Rotherfield. William Medhurst: found dead in a wood. 20 miles. £1 15s.
1 May 1804. New Shoreham. Thomas Parker, a private of HM's 91st[1] Regiment of Foot: died suddenly in a fit. 14 miles. £1 10s 6d.
8 May 1804. Portslade. Barbara Baker: died suddenly in a fit. 12 miles. £1 9s.
16 May 1804. Hellingly. William Hall, a private of HM's 23rd[2] Regiment of Foot: accidentally drowned bathing in the river. 12 miles. £1 9s.
21 May 1804. Lewes. Samuel Brown, a gunner of HM's Royal Regiment of Artillery: being lunatic, hanged himself. £1.
25 May 1804. Brighton. Frederick Bell, infant: accidentally fell into a privy and was suffocated in the soil. 8 miles. £1 6s.
29 May 1804. Cuckfield. Peter Leney: being lunatic, shot himself. 14 miles. £1 10s 6d.
7 June 1804. Brighton. Charity Clements: being lunatic, poisoned herself. 8 miles. £1 6s.
11 June 1804. [*Place omitted.*] William Cooper, infant, aged 12: being at play with William Mills, infant, aged 13, casually received a wound on the right side of his head of which he died. 8 miles. £1 6s.
20 June 1804. Mayfield. William Russell: being lunatic, hanged himself. 16 miles. £1 12s.
23 June 1804. Berwick. John Tester: accidentally killed by a large quantity of chalk falling upon him. 9 miles. £1 6s 9d.
23 June 1804. Berwick. Thomas Elliott: killed by a large quantity of chalk falling upon him. 9 miles. £1 6s 9d.
25 June 1804. Brighton. Edward Wood: accidentally fell from the East Groyne into the sea and was drowned. 8 miles. £1 6s.
Total £19 9s 6d; allowed at Midsummer sessions 1804. [QR/E 700, no 100]

1 *Argyllshire Highlanders*: Swinson, 193.
2 *Royal Welch Fusiliers*: Swinson, 115.

142 14 July 1804. Glynde. John Potter: died suddenly in a fit. 3 miles. £1 2s 3d.
16 July 1804. St Michael's, Lewes. New-born female child: died for want of assistance at the delivery. £1.
28 July 1804. Paid the clerk of assize on returning the inquisition on a new-born male child murdered at Ringmer 5s.[1]
3 Aug. 1804. Southwick. Jonathan Langridge: accidentally fell from a wharf down upon the beach at the seaside and was killed. 12 miles. £1 9s.
4 Aug. 1804. South Heighton. William Wood jun.: killed by a wall accidentally falling on him. 8 miles. £1 6s.
10 Aug. 1804. Newhaven. Richard Tiltman: accidentally fell from a ship into the river and was drowned. 8 miles. £1 6s.
3 Sept. 1804. Barcombe. Charles Longhurst, infant: died in consequence of excessive drinking. 6 miles. £1 4s 6d.
15 Sept. 1804. Lewes New Barracks. George Horp, infant: accidentally fell into a tub of water and was drowned. £1.
17 Sept. 1804. Brighton. William Jessop, a private of HM's 6th or Inniskilling Regiment of Dragoons: went into the sea and was accidentally drowned. 8 miles. £1 6s.
18 Sept. 1804. Barcombe. David Brooker: died suddenly. 6 miles. £1 4s 6d.

25 Sept. 1804. Eastbourne. John Jones: accidentally drowned by the oversetting of a sailing-boat. 18 miles. £1 13s 6d.
Total £12 16s 9d; allowed at Michaelmas sessions 1804. [QR/E 701, no 71]

1 Cf. **140, 369**.

143 10 Oct. 1804. Southwick. Unknown boy who belonged to the sloop *Nancy* of Portsmouth, stranded at Southwick:[1] accidentally drowned. 12 miles. £1 9s.
[10 Oct.] 1804. Southwick. John Moorey:[1] accidentally drowned. 12 miles. £1 9s.
11 Oct. 1804. Newhaven. Mary Geere: being lunatic, threw herself into the Ouse and was drowned. 8 miles. £1 6s.
5 Nov. 1804. Magham Down, Hailsham. Samuel Tamkin: being lunatic, hanged himself. 14 miles. £1 10s 6d.
9 Nov. 1804. Edburton. Edward Baker: fell down in a fit and died suddenly. 14 miles. £1 10s 6d.
12 Nov. 1804. Forest Row, East Grinstead. Richard Gower: accidentally fell down and was killed. 17 miles. £1 12s 9d.
15 Nov. 1804. Jevington. James Facer: died of excessive drinking. 14 miles. £1 10s 6d.
1 Dec. 1804. East Blatchington Barracks. Thomas Hogben: accidentally fell into a well and was drowned. 10 miles. £1 7s 6d.
2 Dec. 1804. South Malling. Ann Hopper: accidentally fell into the Ouse and was drowned. £1.
10 Dec. 1804. Maresfield. John Streeter jun.: found dead. 12 miles. £1 9s.
12 Dec. 1804. Westout in Lewes. Susannah Baker: accidentally fell into a well and was drowned. £1.
21 Dec. 1804. Lamberhurst. John Buss: murdered by Richard Russell and another man called Gipsy George alias Black James. 30 miles. £2 2s 6d.[2]
22 Dec. 1804. Jarvis Brook, Rotherfield. Mary wife of Charles Farmer: being lunatic, hanged herself. 16 miles. £1 12s.
[*Date omitted*.] Offham. Mary Howell: accidentally killed by the vanes of a windmill on Spital Hill. 2 miles. £1 1s 6d.
11 Jan. 1805. South Malling. John Berry: accidentally fell into a chalk-pit and was killed. £1.
Total £21 0s 9d; allowed at Epiphany sessions 1805. [QR/E 702, no 141]

1 Presumably the 2 sailor-boys (unnamed) who were wrecked in the *Nancy* of Portsmouth, Charles Germain captain, off the harbour mouth on 8 Oct. and buried at Southwick on 10 Oct.: Par. 180/1/1/4.
2 Cf. **144, 370**.

144 22 Jan. 1805. East Grinstead. Charlotte Thomas: died suddenly in a fit. 20 miles. £1 15s.
28 Jan. 1805. Nutley in Maresfield. Edward Stibs, private soldier: died through the inclemency of the weather. 12 miles. £1 9s.
30 Jan. 1805. Newhaven. John Hemsley: accidentally fell into the river and was drowned. 8 miles. £1 6s.
31 Jan. 1805. Near Beggars Bush, Wadhurst. Sarah Richardson: being sliding on a pond, the ice broke and she was accidentally drowned. 26 miles. £1 19s 6d.
3 Feb. 1805. Jarvis Brook, Rotherfield. Hannah Frost: killed by a turf-stack accidentally falling upon her. 16 miles. £1 12s.

13 Feb. 1805. Eastbourne. William Taylor, a private in the Derby Militia: hanged himself. 18 miles. £1 13s 6d.
21 Feb. 1805. Eastbourne. William Collins: found dead. 18 miles. £1 13s 6d.
27 Feb. 1805. Arlington. William Cooper: found dead. 12 miles. £1 9s.
19 Mar. 1805. Lewes. Abraham Morris jun.: accidentally killed by some deals falling from a wagon upon him. £1.
25 Mar. 1805. Kingston by Sea. William Trupler: being lunatic, hanged himself. 14 miles. £1 10s 6d.
[?25 Mar.] 1805. Paid the clerk of assize on returning the inquisition taken on view of the body of John Buss who was murdered at Wadhurst 5s.[1]
28 Mar. 1805. Lewes Barracks. Mr Robert Marshall: died of excessive drinking. £1.
2 Apr. 1805. Lindfield. James Tomsett: being lunatic, hanged himself. 12 miles. £1 9s.
18 Apr. 1805. Wivelsfield. James Buckman: being lunatic, hanged himself. 12 miles. £1 9s.
Total £19 11s; allowed at Easter sessions 1805. [QR/E 703, no 176]

1 Cf. **143**, **370**.

145 9 May 1805. Brighton. John Paine, infant: accidentally strangled by swallowing a tamarind stone. 8 miles. £1 6s.
12 May 1805. Eastbourne. Unknown man (but supposed to be George Sands, a private of the Derby Militia, drowned at Cuckmere Haven): found dead on the beach at Eastbourne. 18 miles. £1 13s 6d.
25 May 1805. Eastbourne. John Watson, a private of the 10th[1] Regiment of Light Dragoons: being lunatic, hanged himself. 18 miles. £1 13s 6d.
28 May 1805. Lewes House of Correction. Catherine Lewis, vagrant: natural death. £1.
30 May 1805. Lewes. John Jordan: agreeing to fight with Thomas Dykes, was killed by a blow received in the fight. £1.[2]
31 May 1805. Near Old Tye Common, Hartfield. John Thomas: found dead in a field. 22 miles. £1 16s 6d.
19 June 1805. Newhaven. John Browne: found drowned in the Ouse. 8 miles. £1 6s.
29 June 1805. Newhaven Harbour. William Baulkham: going out of the harbour to the sea with others in an open boat, was accidentally drowned by the sinking of the boat. 8 miles. £1 6s.
6 July 1805. [Newhaven Harbour.] James Crips: also accidentally drowned by the sinking of the said boat. 8 miles. £1 6s.
12 July 1805. Albourne. Richard King: died suddenly in a fit. 12 miles. £1 9s.
16 July 1805. Twineham. James White: being lunatic, hanged himself. 14 miles. £1 10s 6d.
17 July 1805. Lindfield. Mary King: being lunatic, hanged herself. 12 miles. £1 9s.
Total £16 16s; allowed at Midsummer sessions 1805. [QR/E 704, no 115]

1 *or Prince of Wales's Own*: Swinson, 33.
2 Cf. **146**, **371**.

146 24 July 1805. Portslade. Samuel Wilson, infant: accidentally fell out of a wagon and was killed by the wheels going over his head. 12 miles. £1 9s.
10 Aug. 1805. Paid the clerk of assize on returning the inquisition on John Jordan who was feloniously killed by Thomas Dykes at Lewes 5s.[1]

4 Sept. 1805. Hurstpierpoint. Sarah Bishop: being lunatic, hanged herself. 14 miles. £1 10s 6d.
9 Sept. 1805. Rottingdean. Unknown man: found drowned. 8 miles. £1 6s.
21 Sept. 1805. Waldron. George Siggs: being lunatic, hanged himself. 12 miles. £1 9s.
2 Oct. 1805. Eastbourne. Henry Wilson: accidentally drowned by the oversetting of a boat. 18 miles. £1 13s 6d.
[2 Oct.] 1805. Eastbourne. Unknown man: the like. 18 miles. £1 13s 6d.
[2 Oct.] 1805. Eastbourne. Unknown woman: the like. 18 miles. £1 13s 6d.
[2 Oct.] 1805. Eastbourne. Unknown man: the like. 18 miles. £1 13s 6d.
[2 Oct.] 1805. Eastbourne. Unknown man: the like. 18 miles. £1 13s 6d.
3 Oct. 1805. East Hoathly. Henry Turner, infant: accidentally killed by a cart running over him. 8 miles. £1 6s.
Total £15 13s; allowed at Michaelmas sessions 1805. [QR/E 705, no 85]

1 Cf. **145, 371**.

147 16 Oct. 1805. Clayton. New-born female bastard child: murdered by its mother, Ann Clarke. 10 miles. £1 7s 6d.[1]
18 Oct. 1805. Piltdown. Joseph Cave: being lunatic, drowned himself. 10 miles. £1 7s 6d.
28 Oct. 1805. Lewes House of Correction. James Bright, infant: being in the House of Correction with his mother for nurture, died a natural death. £1.
11 Nov. 1805. Cliffe. John Chaplin: died suddenly in a fit. £1.
13 Nov. 1805. St Michael's, Lewes. Joseph Drawbridge, infant: poisoned by eating some paste prepared for killing mice. £1.
17 Dec. 1805. Friston, near Birling Gap. John Page: died through the inclemency of the weather on the sea-shore. 14 miles. £1 10s 6d.
27 Dec. 1805. Ringmer. Joseph Moore: died in consequence of having feloniously cut his throat. 3 miles. £1 2s 3d.
31 Dec. 1805. Magham Down, Hailsham. Charles Douch: being lunatic, hanged himself. 14 miles. £1 10s 6d.
7 Jan. 1806. Brighton. George Siggery, infant: killed by his head being accidentally pressed between two beams of a horse-mill for grinding clay. 8 miles. £1 6s.
10 Jan. 1806. Brighton. Gabriel Tattersoll: accidentally fell over the East Groyne into the sea and was drowned. 8 miles. £1 6s.
13 Jan. 1806. Southease. Catherine wife of David Leslie, a private in HM's 21st[2] Regiment of Foot: accidentally fell under the wheels of a baggage-wagon and was killed. £1.
15 Jan. 1806. Falmer. William Wood: died of excessive drinking. 4 miles. £1 3s.
Total £14 13s 3d; allowed at Epiphany sessions 1806. [QR/E 706, no 101]

1 Cf. **148, 372**.
2 *Royal North British*: Swinson, 112.

148 20 Jan. 1806. Newick. New-born male bastard child: still-born. 8 miles. £1 6s.
10 Feb. 1806. Newhaven Harbour. Richard Butler: accidentally fell from the Western Pier into the harbour and was drowned. 8 miles. £1 6s.
11 Feb. 1806. Falmer. Reuben Mockford: accidentally killed by a fall of chalk in a chalk-pit. 4 miles. £1 3s.
13 Feb. 1806. Cuckfield. John Ellis: found dead. 14 miles. £1 10s 6d.

24 Feb. 1806. Portobello Gap, Rottingdean. William Westmar Pope: accidentally drowned in the sea. 8 miles. £1 6s.
14 Mar. 1806. East Aldrington. Mr William Neville: accidentally fell from his horse and was killed. 10 miles. £1 7s 6d.
17 Mar. 1806. Fletching. William Fielder: died through the inclemency of the weather on 12 Mar. 10 miles. £1 7s 6d.
24 Mar. 1806. Paid the clerk of assize on returning the inquisition on Ann Clarke for murder 5s.[1]
5 Apr. 1806. Alfriston. Mr William Stevens: being lunatic, drowned himself. 10 miles. £1 7s 6d.
7 Apr. 1806. Uckfield. Mr W E Eaton:[2] being lunatic, killed himself by swallowing a large dose of laudanum. 8 miles. £1 6s.
14 Apr. 1806. Frant. Emma Hilder: being lunatic, drowned herself. 27 miles. £2 0s 3d.
17 Apr. 1806. Portslade. Lucy Winton: being lunatic, threw herself into a well and was drowned. 12 miles. £1 9s.
Total £15 14s 3d; allowed at Easter sessions 1806. [QR/E 707, no 100]

1 Cf. **147**, **372**.
2 *William Eaton* in PAR 496/1//1/3.

149 23 Apr. 1806. Rottingdean. Unknown man:[1] accidentally fell over the cliffs and was killed. 8 miles. £1 6s.
28 Apr. 1806. Westout in Lewes. Ann Potter, infant: accidentally killed by the wheels of a carriage used for breaking stones going over her head. £1.
7 May 1806. Brighton. Lieutenant John Wemys of the[2] King's Dragoon Guards: accidentally killed by a fall from his horse. 8 miles. £1 6s.
9 May 1806. Portslade. Edward Truseler: accidentally killed by a cart running over him. 12 miles. £1 9s.
10 May 1806. Crawley Down, Worth. William Bish: accidentally killed by the plate of a new erecting cart lodge falling upon him. 22 miles. £1 16s 6d.
20 May 1806. Ringmer. Eleanor Brunsden, infant: accidentally fell into a pond and was drowned. 4 miles. £1 3s.
25 May 1806. Newhaven. Thomas Sanderson: died by excessive drinking. 8 miles. £1 6s.
18 June 1806. Eastbourne. New-born infant child: found buried in the shingle. 20 miles. £1 15s.
5 July 1806. Hailsham. Ann Humphrey, infant: accidentally fell into a pond and was drowned. 13 miles. £1 9s 9d.
Total £12 11s 3d; allowed at Midsummer sessions 1806. [QR/E 708, no 113]

1 Presumably Charles Petty Horton, buried at Rottingdean on 24 Apr., having been found dead on the beach: PAR 466/1/1/4.
2 *1st*: Swinson, 7.

150 2 Aug. 1806. Eastbourne. George Rogers, a collar-maker in the Corps of Royal Artillery Drivers: went into the sea to bathe and was accidentally drowned. 20 miles. £1 15s.
9 Aug. 1806. Brighton. Francis Spratley, infant, aged about 2: died in consequence of drinking boiling water out of a tea-kettle. 8 miles. £1 6s.

11 Aug. 1806. Brighton. Mary wife of James Greenfield: died a natural death, supposed to have been accelerated by the neglect of her husband. 8 miles. £1 6s.
8 Sept. 1806. Ringmer. James Holden, infant: accidentally fell under the wheels of a wagon and was killed. 4 miles. £1 3s.
19 Sept. 1806. Newhaven. Matthew Bulman: being lunatic, hanged himself. 8 miles. £1 6s.
27 Sept. 1806. Kingston near Lewes. Andrew Ringmer: being lunatic, hanged himself. 2 miles. £1 1s 6d.
30 Sept. 1806. Hollington, the coroner for Hastings rape being ill. John Taylor: reported to have been murdered, but died a natural death of a typhus fever. 30 miles. £2 2s 6d.
4 Oct. 1806. North Hall Farm, Cuckfield. Hannah wife of John Croucher: accidentally fell into a pond and was drowned. 17 miles. £1 12s 9d.
7 Oct. 1806. Brighton Barracks. Henry Leggatt: accidentally fell from a scaffold and was killed. 8 miles. £1 6s.
Total £12 18s 9d; allowed at Michaelmas sessions 1806 when 5s was added by order of the court, making £13 3s 9d. [QR/E 709, no 70]

151 8 Nov. 1806. Brighton. Harriet wife of Henry Pocock Fenner: accidentally killed by a fall. 8 miles. £1 6s.
15 Nov. 1806. Brighton. Elizabeth wife of Thomas Guilford: found dead under the cliff. 8 miles. £1 6s.
17 Nov. 1806. Eastbourne. Edward Pankhurst: kicked by a horse and killed. 20 miles. £1 15s.
16 Dec. 1806. Hove. Evan Hughes, a private belonging to the Caernarfon Militia: accidentally drowned. 10 miles. £1 7s 6d.
30 Dec. 1806. Horsted Keynes. John Langridge: found dead in a field. 16 miles. £1 12s.
31 Dec. 1806. Ringmer. George Seal: died of excessive drinking. 3 miles. £1 2s 3d.
Total £8 8s 9d; allowed at Epiphany sessions 1807. [QR/E 710, no 137]

152 21 Jan. 1807. New Shoreham Harbour. Charles Hollingdale: accidentally drowned. 13 miles. £1 9s 9d.
23 Jan. 1807. Brighton. William Hancock: being lunatic, shot himself. 8 miles. £1 6s.
2 and 3 Feb. 1807. Wadhurst. Samuel Noakes: being inebriated, fell into a ditch and was drowned. 24 miles. £1 18s.
4 Feb. 1807. Ripe. James Rippington: being inebriated, fell into a ditch and was drowned. 10 miles. £1 7s 6d.
16 Mar. 1807. Eastbourne. William Cousens: found dead in a stable. 18 miles. £1 13s 6d.
21 Mar. 1807. Brighton. William Leason: accidentally fell from the mast-head of a ship and was killed. 8 miles. £1 6s.
24 Mar. 1807. Unicorn Barracks, North Street, Brighton. William Hawkins, a private of the Royal South Gloucester Militia: died suddenly. 8 miles. £1 6s.
1 Apr. 1807. Hellingly. John Card: found dead. 13 miles. £1 9s 9d.
8 Apr. 1807. Isfield. Elizabeth Newnham, infant: accidentally fell into a ditch and was drowned. 6 miles. £1 4s 6d.
Total £13 1s; allowed at Easter sessions 1807. [QR/E 711, no 138]

153 16 Apr. 1807. Near the West Gate, Lewes. Peter Kind: accidentally fell down a flight of steps and was killed. £1.
20 Apr. 1807. Isfield. Thomas Taylor: accidentally killed by a wagon going over him. 6 miles. £1 4s 6d.
7 May 1807. Ringmer. William Edwards, an Artillery driver at Ringmer: accidentally killed by his horse falling with him. 3 miles. £1 2s 3d.
24 May 1807. Hove. William Foster late of West Chiltington: on his return from the county election was accidentally drowned in the sea. 10 miles. £1 7s 6d.
13 June 1807. Lewes House of Correction. Solomon Lovell, infant: being in the House of Correction with his mother for nurture, died a natural death in convulsion fits. £1.
29 June 1807. Brighton. Margaret Green: found drowned. 8 miles. £1 6s
16 July 1807. Hailsham. Harriet Hoad: accidentally fell into a pond and was drowned. 13 miles. £1 9s 9d.
Total £8 10s; allowed at Midsummer sessions 1807. [QR/E 712, no 85]

154 21 July 1807. Whitesmith. William Davis: accidentally killed by a horse falling with him. 8 miles. £1 6s.
27 July 1807. Brighton. Thomas Gower: accidentally fell from the shafts of a wagon and was killed by the wheels going over him. [8 miles.] £1 6s.
30 July 1807. The hospital of Lewes Infantry Barracks. Peter Hamlett, a private of the Royal Cheshire Militia: being lunatic, cut his throat. £1.
1 Sept. 1807. Framfield. Michael Burt: accidentally fell from a loaded wagon and was killed by one of the wheels pressing upon his head. 8 miles. £1 6s.
8 Sept. 1807. Hurstpierpoint. Elizabeth Backhouse, infant: accidentally fell into a pond and was drowned. 12 miles. £1 9s.
28 Sept. 1807. Near Old Eye, South Malling. Thomas Godley: accidentally fell into the Ouse and was drowned. £1.
3 Oct. 1807. Mayfield. William Hall, infant: accidentally killed by the body of a cart falling on him. 16 miles. £1 12s.
Total £8 19s; allowed at Michaelmas sessions 1807. [QR/E 713, no 89]

155 15 Oct. 1807. Chiddingly. Jesse Guy: accidentally killed by the discharge of a gun. 10 miles. £1 7s 6d.
17 Oct. 1807. Broyle Place, Ringmer. Richard Howell: accidentally killed by one of the wheels of a cart going over his head. 5 miles. £1 3s 9d.
30 Oct. 1807. Brighton. Nathaniel Harman: accidentally drowned by the oversetting of a fishing-boat in a storm on 22 Oct. 8 miles. £1 6s.
31 Oct. 1807. Streat. Mary Izard: accidentally fell into the fire and was burned to death. 8 miles. £1 6s.
3 Nov. 1807. New Shoreham Harbour. Henry Sinclair: accidentally fell into the harbour and was drowned. 14 miles. £1 10s 6d.
7 Nov. 1807. Albourne. Nicholas Burtenshaw: fell down in a fit and died suddenly. 14 miles. £1 10s 6d.
23 Nov. 1807. Brighton. Jonas Corner: accidentally drowned by the oversetting of a fishing-boat in a storm on 21 Nov. 8 miles. £1 6s.
26 Nov. 1807. Hove. Nathan Short: accidentally drowned by the oversetting of a fishing-boat in a storm on 21 Nov. 10 miles. £1 7s 6d.
5 Dec. 1807. Worth. Robert Harris: accidentally killed by a large stone falling upon him whilst at work in a stone quarry. 22 miles. £1 16s 6d.

5 Dec. 1807. Nutley in Maresfield. Thomas Wheeler: being lunatic, threw himself into a well and was drowned. 14 miles. £1 10s 6d.
8 Dec. 1807. Uckfield. Ann Paine: found dead. 8 miles. £1 6s.
1 Jan. 1808. St Michael's, Lewes. Joseph Henry Carr, infant: his clothes having accidentally caught fire, was burned to death. £1.
8 Jan. 1808. Sheffield Bridge, Fletching. Martha Jessop, infant: accidentally fell into the river and was drowned. 10 miles. £1 7s 6d.
Total £17 18s 3d; allowed at Epiphany sessions 1808. [QR/E 714, no 99]

156 16 Jan. 1808. Near New Shoreham Barracks. John Cole, a private in the South Hants Militia: being lunatic, threw himself into a pond. 14 miles. £1 10s 6d.
18 Jan. 1808. Brighton. James Haybiddle: being lunatic, hanged himself. 8 miles. £1 6s.
30 Jan. 1808. Jevington. Mary Howell: died through the inclemency of the weather. 14 miles. £1 10s 6d.
8 Mar. 1808. Lindfield. Faith Constable, infant: strangled by accidentally swallowing a French bean. 12 miles. £1 9s.
19 Mar. 1808. Eastbourne. A man called Robert who looked after the Brighton caravan horses at the Hope and Anchor at Eastbourne: found dead in the stable. 20 miles. £1 15s.
5 Apr. 1808. Isfield. Samuel Gaskin: found dead in a barn. 6 miles. £1 4s 6d.
Total £8 15s 6d; allowed at Easter sessions 1808. [QR/E 715, no 125]

157 30 Apr. 1808. Brighton. Thomas Martin: died by the visitation of God in a natural way in a stable. 8 miles. £1 6s.
11 May 1808. Waldron. Ann Haffenden: being lunatic, threw herself in a rivulet and was drowned. 14 miles. £1 10s 6d.
17 May 1808. Selmeston. John Humphrey: being lunatic, cut his throat. 8 miles. £1 6s.
21 May 1808. Brighton. Thomas Alexander: accidentally fell over the cliff. 8 miles. £1 6s.
7 June 1808. Brighton. John Stent, infant: accidentally fell into a well and was drowned. 8 miles. £1 6s.
[*Date omitted.*] Brighton. Mary Ann Gawen, infant: accidentally scalded to death by boiling coffee falling upon her in consequence of her pulling down the tea-table. 8 miles. £1 6s.
20 June 1808. Hailsham. William Drew, a private of the Royal Berkshire Militia: accidentally fell into the river at Horsebridge in Hellingly and was drowned. 12 miles. £1 9s.
28 and 29 June 1808. Warnham, Mr Johnson[1] being ill. New-born female child: murdered by some person or persons unknown. 28 miles. £2 1s.[2]
13 July 1808. Near Lewes. Richard Dix, a corporal of the 10th Regiment of Light Dragoons:[3] accidentally drowned bathing in the Ouse. £1.
Total £12 10s 6d; allowed at Midsummer sessions 1808. [QR/E 716, no 73]

1 William Johnson, the West Sussex county coroner.
2 Cf. **158**, **373**.
3 By this date it was the 10th or Prince of Wales's Own Hussars: Swinson, 33.

158 30 July 1808. East Chiltington in Westmeston. William Setford: accidentally killed by the overturning of a cart. 6 miles. £1 4s 6d.

4 Aug. 1808. Brighton. Mr Thomas Thong, surgeon of HM's sloop *Port Mahon*: being lunatic, cut his throat. 8 miles. £1 6s.
[*Date omitted*.] Brighton. Unknown man:[1] died suddenly by the visitation of God in a natural way in one of the streets. 8 miles. £1 6s.
8 Aug. 1808. Cliffe. Mary Might: being lunatic, hanged herself. £1.
10 Aug. 1808. Cliffe. John Sumner: died suddenly. £1.
12 Aug. 1808. Brighton Barracks. James Beach: fell down in a fit and died suddenly. 8 miles. £1 6s.
13 Aug. 1808. Paid the clerk of assize on returning the inquisition on a new-born child murdered by some person unknown at Warnham 5s.[2]
16 Aug. 1808. Brighton. Man named Stephens:[3] died suddenly on the steps of the theatre by the visitation of God in a natural way. 8 miles. £1 6s.
[16 Aug.] 1808. Worthing, no coroner being elected in the west. Unknown man: found drowned. 20 miles. £1 15s.
17 Aug. 1808. Storrington. Michael Naish: being lunatic, shot himself. 24 miles. £1 18s.
22 Aug. 1808. Rottingdean. John Stanley: went to bathe and was accidentally drowned. 7 miles. £1 5s 3d.
27 Aug. 1808. West Hoathly. James Wood: accidentally fell from a wheat-stack which he was thatching and was killed. 16 miles. £1 12s.
2 Sept. 1808. Hellingly. Ruth Wenham: being lunatic, threw herself into a well. 12 miles. £1 9s.
8 Sept. 1808. Near Roedean in Rottingdean. James Walker: in riding between Rottingdean and Brighton, accidentally fell with his horse over the cliff and was killed. 7 miles. £1 5s 3d.
14 Sept. 1808. East Grinstead. Ann Gorringe: found dead. 20 miles. £1 15s.
1 Oct. 1808. Brighton. Henry Naldrett: being lunatic, cut his throat. 8 miles. £1 6s.
4 Oct. 1808. West Firle. New-born male child: found buried in the ground. 5 miles. £1 3s 9d.
[4 Oct.] 1808. Turners Hill, Worth. Francis Botting: died suddenly in crossing a stile. 21 miles. £1 15s 9d.
5 Oct. 1808. Brighton. Susannah Hobbs: accidentally fell into a well and was drowned. 8 miles. £1 6s.
Total £25 4s 6d; allowed at Michaelmas sessions 1808. [QR/E 717, no 68]

1 *Richard, surname unknown* in PAR 255/1/1/7.
2 Cf. **157**, **373**.
3 No forename in PAR 255/1/1/7.

159 29 July 1808. Northchapel, there being no coroner elected in the west. James Crafter: accidentally killed by a wagon-wheel going over his head. 40 miles. £2 10s.
17 Aug. 1808. Hardham. Samuel Mann: accidentally fell into the Adur and was drowned. 30 miles. £2 2s 6d.
13 Oct. 1808. Lamberhurst. William Smith: accidentally fell into the river and was drowned. 30 miles. £2 2s 6d.
18 Oct. 1808. East Grinstead. Thomas Diplocke: being lunatic, hanged himself. 20 miles. £1 15s.
24 Oct. 1808. Rotherfield. Lydia Botting, infant: accidentally suffocated by the turning up of a turn-up bed. 20 miles. £1 15s.

29 Oct. 1808. Hurstpierpoint. Stephen Simmons: killed by a roller accidentally falling upon him. 12 miles. £1 9s.
5 Nov. 1808. Brighton. Richard Boon: being intoxicated, accidentally fell down stairs and was killed. 8 miles. £1 6s.
21 Nov. 1808. Horsted Keynes. William Pelling: found dead. 14 miles. £1 10s 6d.
1 Dec. 1808. Brighton. Daniel Marchant: accidentally drowned by the casual oversetting of a sailing-boat. 8 miles. £1 6s.
3 Dec. 1808. Clayton Mill. Thomas Penfold: accidentally killed by being forced between the wheel and the nut of the mill by his clothes getting entangled in the cogs of the wheel. 10 miles. £1 7s 6d.
5 Dec. 1808. Maresfield. Elizabeth Dale: being lunatic, hanged herself. 10 miles. £1 7s 6d.
15 Dec. 1808. New Shoreham Harbour. Thomas Lashmar: accidentally fell out of a boat in the harbour and was drowned. 14 miles. £1 10s 6d.
3 Jan. 1809. Ardingly. James Bennett: being lunatic, threw himself into a fishpond and was drowned. 16 miles. £1 12s.
Total £21 14s; allowed at Epiphany sessions 1809. [QR/E 718, no 164]

160 1 Feb. 1809. Willingdon. John Caplen: being lunatic, threw himself into a pond and was drowned. 16 miles. £1 12s.
1 Apr. 1809. Brighton. Edward Smith: accidentally fell into a cask of beer and was suffocated. 8 miles. £1 6s.
4 Apr. 1809. Worth. Unknown man: accidentally killed by a fall from a horse. 26 miles. £1 19s 6d.
10 Apr. 1809. Clayton. James Bignall: being lunatic, hanged himself. 12 miles. £1 9s.
11 Apr. 1809. Brighton. Edward Hill: being lunatic, hanged himself. 8 miles. £1 6s.
Total £7 12s 6d; allowed at Easter sessions 1809 when 5s was added by order of the court, making £7 17s 6d. [QR/E 719, no 120]

161 17 Apr. 1809. East Grinstead. Charlotte Foster: accidentally killed by the discharge of a gun. 20 miles. £1 15s.
25 Apr. 1809. Plumpton. William Belton: being lunatic, hanged himself. 6 miles. £1 4s 6d.
28 Apr. 1809. Chailey. William Knapp: being lunatic, hanged himself. 8 miles. £1 6s.
6 May 1809. Near Lewes paper-mill. Philip Darwin, a private belonging to HM's 82nd[1] Regiment of Foot: found in the Ouse drowned. £1.
12 May 1809. Maresfield. Ann Batchelor: being lunatic, threw herself into a pond and was drowned. 10 miles. £1 7s 6d.
17 May 1809. South Malling. Richard Morris: went into the Ouse to bathe and was accidentally drowned. £1.
20 May 1809. Bishopstone Mill. John Borchert: killed by lightning. 10 miles. £1 7s 6d.
3 June 1809. New Shoreham Harbour. John Spicer: accidentally drowned by the oversetting of a fishing-boat in a storm on 2 June at the mouth of the harbour. 12 miles. £1 9s.
6 June 1809. Rottingdean. William Priest jun.: accidentally drowned by the oversetting of a fishing-boat on 2 June off Brighton. 7 miles. £1 5s 3d.
14 June 1809. [Brighton.] William Priest sen.:[2] accidentally drowned by the oversetting of a fishing-boat at Brighton on 2 June. 8 miles. £1 6s.

17 June 1809. [Brighton.] John Serjeant:[2] accidentally drowned by the oversetting of a fishing-boat at sea off Brighton on 2 June. 8 miles. £1 6s.
20 June 1809. Tyes Farm, Cuckfield. Unknown travelling man: found hanging in a shaw. 18 miles. £1 13s 6d.
23 June 1809. [Brighton.] William Leach:[2] accidentally drowned by the oversetting of a fishing-boat near Brighton on 2 June. 8 miles. £1 6s.
29 June 1809. West Hoathly. John Brooker: accidentally killed by a wagon going over his head. 18 miles. £1 13s 6d.
30 June 1809. Hellingly. Sergeant Patrick Fox of the 68th[3] Regiment of Foot: accidentally fell under the wheels of a baggage-wagon and was killed. 10 miles. £1 7s 6d.
Total £20 7s 3d; allowed at Midsummer sessions 1809. [QR/E 720, no 108]

1 *Prince of Wales's Volunteers*: Swinson, 183.
2 All 3 buried at Brighton: PAR 255/1/1/7.
3 *Durham*: Swinson, 168.

162 3 Aug. 1809. Lamberhurst. Elizabeth Twort: being lunatic, threw herself into the Medway. 30 miles. £2 2s 6d.
14 Aug. 1809. Cliffe Workhouse. Francis Dunford: being lunatic, hanged himself. £1.
Total £3 2s 6d; allowed at Michaelmas sessions 1809.[1] [QR/E 721, no 59]

1 Payment was made after Wheeler's death to his personal representatives: QO/EW 39.

Bill of John Luttman Ellis

163 [*Date omitted.*] Lewes. William Wheeler, esq.[1] 35 miles. £2 6s 3d.
[*Date omitted.*] Ripe. Thomas Coleman.[2] 46 miles. £2 14s 6d.
[*Date omitted.*] Brighton. John Peto.[3] 28 miles. £2 1s.
[*Date omitted.*] East Hoathly. New-born male infant. 46 miles. £2 14s 6d.
[*Date omitted.*] East Grinstead. Milly Rice.[4] 35 miles. £2 6s 3d.
Total £12 2s 6d; allowed at Michaelmas sessions 1809. [QR/E 721, no 58]

[This bill was for inquests held by Ellis, the county coroner for West Sussex, on account of the death of William Wheeler: QO/EW 39. The journeys were from Petworth but that is not stated in the bill.]

1 Died 16 Aug. and buried at All Saints, Lewes 18 Aug. 1809: *SWA*, 21 Aug. 1809; PAR 410/1/1/5.
2 Buried 5 Sept. 1809: PAR 462/1/1/3.
3 Aged 10 months, buried 15 Sept. 1809: PAR 255/1/1/7.
4 Mildred Rice, buried 20 Sept. 1809: Par. 348/1/1/6.

Bills of Thomas William Wheeler

164 16 Oct. 1809. Lindfield. Ann Durrant: being lunatic, cut her throat. 12 miles. £1 9s.
20 Oct. 1809. Hailsham. New-born bastard child: still-born. 12 miles. £1 9s.
23 Oct. 1809. Brighton. New-born female bastard child: her death was accidentally occasioned by the imprudence of the mother, Ann Jarvis, in her delivery. 8 miles. £1 6s.

30 Oct. 1809. Southover. Unknown man: accidentally fell down a cellar and was killed. £1.
1 Nov. 1809. Ringmer. Rebecca McGee, infant: died in consequence of drinking hot water out of a tea-kettle. 3 miles. £1 2s 3d.
17 Nov. 1809. Ringmer. Samuel Stephens: died by the visitation of God. 3 miles. £1 2s 3d.
8 Dec. 1809. East Blatchington. 7 unknown men: accidentally drowned by shipwreck. 10 miles. £7 7s 6d.
23 Dec. 1809. New Shoreham. William Martin: accidentally fell from the fore-yard of a merchant ship and was killed. 14 miles. £1 10s 6d.
27 Dec. 1809. East Grinstead Poorhouse. Poor man: found dead in his bed. 20 miles. £1 15s.
28 Dec. 1809. Stuckholds in Hurstpierpoint. New-born male bastard child: his death was accidentally occasioned by bad management in the delivery of it. 13 miles. £1 9s 9d.
29 Dec. 1809. Brighton. James Pullen, infant: accidentally burnt to death. 8 miles. £1 6s.
12 Jan. 1810. Westmeston. Ann Burgess: her clothes accidentally caught fire whereby she was burnt to death. 6 miles. £1 4s 6d.
Total £22 1s 9d; allowed at Epiphany sessions 1810. [QR/E 722, no 164]

[Until the second entry of bill **183** all Wheeler's journeys were from Cliffe but that is never stated in his bills.]

165 1 Feb. 1810. East Grinstead. Pietro Gorele, an Italian: being lunatic, lacerated both his arms so horribly that he bled to death. 20 miles. £1 15s.
3 Mar. 1810. Lewes. Henry Fenner, a lad: accidentally fell into the Ouse and was drowned. £1.
10 Mar. 1810. Brighton. Ann Martin, a poor woman: accidentally fell down stairs and was killed. 8 miles. £1 6s.
28 Mar. 1810. Cliffe. Elizabeth Cruttenden: being lunatic, hanged herself. £1.
6 Apr. 1810. New Shoreham. Thomas Pyatt: being lunatic, cut his throat with a penknife. 14 miles. £1 10s 6d.
2 May 1810. Hailsham. George Bettup, infant: accidentally fell into a pond and was drowned. 13 miles. £1 9s 9d.
Total £8 1s 3d; allowed at Easter sessions 1810. [QR/E 723, no 112]

166 5 May 1810. Eastbourne. Ensign Vincent Croxal: being lunatic, drowned himself in the sea. 20 miles. £1 15s.
14 May 1810. Bentley in Cuckfield. Samuel Picknell: accidentally killed by a hurt received by a colt. 16 miles. £1 12s.
16 May 1810. Laughton. New-born female bastard child: accidentally smothered in bed. 6 miles. £1 4s 6d.
31 May 1810. Forest Row, East Grinstead. Thomas Shoosmith: being intoxicated, accidentally fell backwards whilst fighting and was killed. 18 miles. £1 13s 6d.
1 June 1810. Nutley in Maresfield. Henry Carr, infant: accidentally fell into a well and was drowned. 16 miles. £1 12s.
5 June 1810. Maresfield. James Knight, infant: accidentally fell into a hog-cistern and was suffocated. 12 miles. £1 9s.

11 June 1810. Brighton. Henry Lenoard, infant: found drowned in a well. 8 miles. £1 6s.
[*Date omitted.*] Chestham in Henfield. James Sheppard: accidentally killed by the wheel of a water-pipe passing over his body. 16 miles. £1 12s.
13 June 1810. Gardner Street, Herstmonceux, the coroner for Hastings rape being dead. Peter Tanner: being lunatic, hanged himself. 15 miles. £1 11s 3d.
23 June 1810. Ringmer Barracks. Thomas Smith, a bombadier in the Royal Artillery: murdered himself. 4 miles. £1 3s.
25 June 1810. Forest Row, East Grinstead. Ralph Newman: being lunatic, threw himself in a pond and was drowned. 18 miles. £1 13s 6d.
2 July 1810. River's Wood, Lindfield. Elizabeth Wright: being very old and infirm, died by the visitation of God. 14 miles. £1 10s 6d.
5 July 1810. Southwick. Thomas Weston: died by the visitation of God. 12 miles. £1 9s.
Total £19 11s 3d; allowed at Midsummer sessions 1810. [QR/E 724, no 72]

167 24 July 1810. Brighton. Henry Sezeland: accidentally drowned whilst bathing in the sea. 8 miles. £1 6s.
26 July 1810. East Hoathly. Christopher Fielder: died by the visitation of God in a natural way. 8 miles. £1 6s.
30 July 1810. Rottingdean. Unknown man: found drowned on the beach. 6 miles. £1 4s 6d.
20 Aug. 1810. Berwick. Richard Russle: accidentally killed by a quantity of sand falling on him whilst at work in a sand-pit. 9 miles. £1 6s 9d.
21 Aug. 1810. Brighton. Mary Cook: being lunatic, hanged herself. 8 miles. £1 6s.
25 Aug. 1810. Brighton. Thomas Howell: died by the visitation of God in a natural way. 8 miles. £1 6s.
10 Sept. 1810. Brighton. Robert Cole, esq.: died in consequence of bruises which he received by the overturning of a stage-coach. 8 miles. £1 6s.
18 Sept. 1810. Rottingdean. William Holden: accidentally fell out of a cart and was killed. 6 miles. £1 4s 6d.
27 Sept. 1810. Withyham. Hannah Gladman: murdered herself by throwing herself into a pond. 18 miles. £1 13s 6d.
1 Oct. 1810. Fletching Mill. James Decon: accidentally fell into a lock and was drowned. 10 miles. £1 7s 6d.
[1 Oct.] 1810. Henfield. William Penfold: accidentally killed by being thrown out of a cart which the horse had run away with. 16 miles. £1 12s.
2 Oct. 1810. Brighton. Alexander Mattoe: accidentally fell from his horse and was killed. 8 miles. £1 6s.
Total £16 4s 9d; allowed at Michaelmas sessions 1810. [QR/E 725, no 75]

168 11 Oct. 1810. Lewes. John Homar: killed by John Carter who fired a pistol loaded with small pieces of lead at him. £1.[1]
12 Oct. 1810. Hailsham. Matthew Hover: died by the visitation of God. 12 miles. £1 9s.
13 Oct. 1810. Brighton. Elizabeth Boon: accidentally fell off a step-ladder and was killed. 8 miles. £1 6s.
24 Oct. 1810. Rotherfield. Peter Pavey: died by the visitation of God. 20 miles. £1 15s.
25 Oct. 1810. Lewes. Samuel Ridge: being lunatic, shot himself. £1.

29 Nov. 1810. Ringmer. Catherine Lawrence: being lunatic, hanged herself. 3 miles. £1 2s 3d.
24 Dec. 1810. Edburton. Thomas Mitchell: being lunatic, hanged himself. 13 miles. £1 9s 9d.
27 Dec. 1810. Lewes. Ann Parsons, infant: accidentally burnt to death by her clothes taking fire. £1.
14 Jan. 1811. Cuckfield. Elizabeth Brigden: accidentally burnt to death by reason of a cask of spirits taking fire. 14 miles. £1 10s 6d.
Total £11 12s 6d; allowed at Epiphany sessions 1811. [QR/E 726, no 130]

1 Cf. **374**.

169 25 Jan. 1811. Brighton. Hannah Pankhurst: her clothes accidentally caught fire whereby she was burnt to death. 8 miles. £1 6s.
[*Date omitted*.] Brighton. George Harris, infant: his clothes also caught fire whereby he was burnt to death. 8 miles. £1 6s.
29 Jan. 1811. South Malling. William Winter: accidentally killed whilst repairing a well at Mr Marchant's by the coulter of a plough falling into the well on his head. £1.
[*Date omitted*.] Portslade. Ann Waterman: died through the inclemency of the weather. 12 miles. £1 9s.
6 Feb. 1811. Alfriston. John Huggett: died from old age and infirmity. 10 miles. £1 7s 6d.
9 Feb. 1811. Brighton. James Graves: accidentally fell down stairs and was killed. 8 miles. £1 6s.
16 Feb. 1811. Alfriston. Richard Goodwin: died by the visitation of God. 10 miles. £1 7s 6d.
4 Mar. 1811. West Hoathly. Jane Balcomb: being lunatic, threw herself into a well and was drowned. 20 miles. £1 15s.
5 Mar. 1811. Brighton. James Wood: being lunatic, hanged himself. 8 miles. £1 6s.
6 Apr. 1811. East Hoathly. George Stevens: died from excessive drinking. 9 miles. £1 6s 9d.
16 Apr. 1811. New Shoreham. John Hill: died by the visitation of God. 14 miles. £1 10s 6d.
22 Apr. 1811. Buxted. Thomas Mew: died by the visitation of God. 12 miles. £1 9s.
Total £16 9s 3d; allowed at Easter sessions 1811. [QR/E 727, no 129]

170 27 Apr. 1811. Chalvington. John Paris: accidentally killed by a cart running over him. 10 miles. £1 7s 6d.
30 Apr. 1811. South Heighton. William Copper: accidentally killed by a cart running over him. 8 miles. £1 6s.
11 May 1811. Ringmer Barracks. James Avery, a corporal in the Gunner Drivers: died by the visitation of God. 4 miles. £1 3s.
[*Date omitted*.] All Saints, Lewes. James Burshell: being lunatic, hanged himself. £1.
20 May 1811. Maresfield. Phoebe Mott: accidentally fell into a pond and was drowned. 20 miles. £1 15s.
21 May 1811. Cuckfield. Stephen Raustrig: died by the visitation of God. 14 miles. £1 10s 6d.
23 May 1811. Framfield. Thomas Bryant: accidentally fell into a pond and was drowned. 10 miles. £1 7s 6d.

24 May 1811. Withyham. George Marten: accidentally killed by some gravel falling on him whilst at work in a pit. 18 miles. £1 13s 6d.
25 May 1811. Beddingham. James Moore, a boy aged about 11: being lunatic, hanged himself. 4 miles. £1 3s.
10 June 1811. Rotherfield. James Moon: accidentally killed by a wagon overturning on him. 20 miles. £1 15s.
16 July 1811. Cliffe. George Wilbar: died by the visitation of God in a natural way. £1.
18 July 1811. Slaugham. Stephen Wenham: accidentally fell into a well and was drowned. 20 miles. £1 15s.
Total £16 16s; allowed at Midsummer sessions 1811. [QR/E 728]

171 20 July 1811. Ringmer. Charles Beck: accidentally killed by a quantity of chalk falling on him at Glynde. 4 miles. £1 3s.
22 July 1811. Southover. Mr John Fisher: found drowned in the Cockshut sewer. £1.
1 Aug. 1811. Buxted. Richard Gaston jun.: feloniously killed by Esau Parkes whilst fighting. 12 miles. £1 9s.[1]
9 Aug. 1811. Brighton. Daniel Stapleford, esq.: died by the visitation of God in a natural way. 8 miles. £1 6s.
15 Aug. 1811. Chiddingly. Jane Harmer, infant: accidentally killed by a wagon passing over her. 8 miles. £1 6s.
20 Aug. 1811. Fletching. James Wood, infant: accidentally fell into a well-bucket and was drowned. 10 miles. £1 7s 6d.
21 Aug. 1811. Wivelsfield. Mr Thomas William Tanner: being lunatic, cut his throat. 12 miles. £1 9s.
7 Sept. 1811. Piddinghoe. John Baker: accidentally fell into the river and was drowned. 7 miles. £1 5s 3d.
10 Sept. 1811. Lewes. Mary Kennard: died by the visitation of God in a natural way. £1.
11 Sept. 1811. Fletching. Thomas Russell: accidentally killed by a wagon running over him. 10 miles. £1 7s 6d.
24 Sept. 1811. Hailsham. John Jeal: murdered himself by shooting himself with a musket. 12 miles. £1 9s.
27 Sept. 1811. Rottingdean. John Blaze: accidentally drowned by shipwreck. 6 miles. £1 4s 6d.
[27 Sept.] 1811. Rottingdean. 2 unknown men: found drowned. £2.
28 Sept. 1811. Brighton. Rebecca Thorpe: being very ill, took too large a quantity of laudanum for the purpose of relieving her pain which caused her death. 8 miles. £1 6s.
[28 Sept.] 1811. Newhaven. Unknown man: found drowned. 8 miles. £1 6s.
[28 Sept.] 1811. Lewes. John Ventham Grigg: feloniously killed by John Kennard. £1.[2]
5 Oct. 1811. West Dean. Unknown man: found drowned. 13 miles. £1 9s 9d.
[*Date omitted.*] Telscombe. 2 unknown men: found drowned. 6 miles. £2 4s 6d.
Total £24 13s; allowed at Michaelmas sessions 1811. [QR/E 729]

1 Cf. **375**.
2 Cf. **376**.

172 16 Oct. 1811. Brighton. Robert Radford: died by the visitation of God in a natural way. 8 miles. £1 6s.
[*Date omitted.*] Southwick. Unknown man: found drowned. 12 miles. £1 9s.

26 Oct. 1811. Cuckfield. Unknown man: died by the visitation of God in a natural way. 14 miles. £1 10s 6d.
28 Oct. 1811. Mayfield. John Stiles: his death was occasioned by a blow accidentally received on the head. 18 miles. £1 13s 6d.
2 Nov. 1811. Cliffe. John Colwell: died by the visitation of God in a natural way. £1.
4 Nov. 1811. Isfield. William Wood: fell into the Ouse and was accidentally drowned. 7 miles. £1 5s 3d.
28 Nov. 1811. Lewes. Thomas Vockins: his death was accidentally occasioned by his falling on his bayonet. £1.
3 Dec. 1811. Isfield. Thomas Gaston: being lunatic, hanged himself. 7 miles. £1 5s 3d.
24 Dec. 1811. Bolney. Mary Harmer: accidentally killed by the sweeps of a mill striking her. 19 miles. £1 14s 3d.
Total £12 3s 9d; allowed at Epiphany sessions 1812. [QR/E 730]

173 23 Jan. 1812. Hailsham. Samuel Foster: died by the visitation of God in a natural way. 12 miles. £1 9s.
3 Feb. 1812. Brighton. Susannah Hunter: died by the visitation of God in a natural way. 8 miles. £1 6s.
24 Feb. 1812. Brighton. Jane Wood: her clothes accidentally caught fire whereby she was burnt to death. 8 miles. £1 6s.
18 Mar. 1812. Offham. Robert Rossey: accidentally killed by a sudden fall of chalk from the Offham chalk-pits. 3 miles. £1 2s 3d.
21 Mar. 1812. Westout in Lewes. James Herriott: accidentally killed by Mr George Grantham's horse running against him on 9 Mar. at Lewes, near Kingston Laines. £1.
26 Mar. 1812. Glyndebourne. Richard Wood, servant to the Revd Mr Tutty:[1] murdered himself by shooting himself with a gun. 3 miles. £1 2s 3d.
31 Mar. 1812. Henfield. David Botting: found drowned in the Adur. 18 miles. £1 13s 6d.
Total £8 19s; allowed at Easter sessions 1812. [QR/E 731, no 85]

1 Buried at Glynde as the Revd Francis Tutté of Glyndebourne: PAR 347/1/5/1.

174 14 Apr. 1812. Jevington. Mildred Ticehurst: died by the visitation of God in a natural way. 15 miles. £1 11s 3d.
20 May 1812. Pyecombe. William Carter: died by the visitation of God in a natural way. 10 miles. £1 7s 6d.
17 June 1812. Brighton. Ann Morley: accidentally fell down stairs and was killed. 8 miles. £1 6s.
22 June 1812. Chailey. New-born female bastard child: still-born. 7 miles. £1 5s 3d.[1]
4 July 1812. Barcombe. Thomas Trash: accidentally fell into the river and was drowned. 5 miles. £1 3s 9d.
[*Date omitted.*] East Grinstead. John Davis: accidentally fell into a spring and was drowned. 20 miles. £1 15s.
Total £8 8s 9d; allowed at Midsummer sessions 1812. [QR/E 732]

1 Cf. **377**.

175 15 Aug. 1812. Hailsham. Thomas Piper: died by the visitation of God in a natural way. 20 miles. £1 15s.

17 Aug. 1812. South Malling. Sarah Gower: accidentally fell down a precipice and was killed. £1.
[*Date omitted.*] Horsted Keynes. Thomas Brigden: died by the visitation of God in a natural way. 16 miles. £1 12s.
24 Aug. 1812. Brighton. Louisa Maria Goldingham: being lunatic and distracted, cut her throat with a razor. 8 miles. £1 6s.
28 Aug. 1812. Barcombe. Harriet Jenner: being lunatic and distracted, cut her throat with a pair of scissors. 5 miles. £1 3s 9d.
5 Sept. 1812. New Shoreham. James Bennett: accidentally drowned in the harbour. 14 miles. £1 10s 6d.
[*Date omitted.*] New Shoreham. George Moore: accidentally drowned in the harbour. 14 miles. £1 10s 6d.
17 Sept. 1812. Cuckfield. [*blank*] Cornell:[1] died by the visitation of God in a natural way. 14 miles. £1 10s 6d.
2 Oct. 1812. Maresfield. Lucy Ridley: being lunatic and distracted, hung herself. 12 miles. £1 9s.
[*Date omitted.*] Brighton. Joseph Bishop: died by the visitation of God in a natural way. 8 miles. £1 6s.
[*Date omitted.*] Hailsham. New-born female bastard child: supposed to be still-born. 12 miles. £1 9s.
Total £15 12s 3d; allowed at Michaelmas sessions 1812. [QR/E 733]

1 *Cornell, cook at Cuckfield Place, aged 54, found dead in her bed* in Par. 301/1/1/5.

176 17 Oct. 1812. Park Corner, Rotherfield. Sarah Stapely, infant: accidentally fell into a spring and was drowned. 23 miles. £1 17s 3d.
29 Oct. 1812. Piddinghoe. Unknown man: found dead on the sea-shore. 7 miles. £1 5s 3d.
23 Nov. 1812. Arlington. Mary Fox: died by the visitation of God in a natural way. 12 miles. £1 9s.
24 Nov. 1812. East Hoathly. John Page: died by the visitation of God in a natural way. 9 miles. £1 6s 9d.
26 Dec. 1812. Tarring Neville. John Young jun.: died in consequence of drinking boiling water out of a tea-kettle. 7 miles. £1 5s 3d.
Total £7 3s 6d; allowed at Epiphany sessions 1813. [QR/E 734]

177 27 Jan. 1813. Hailsham. John Elphick: died by the visitation of God in a natural way. 12 miles. £1 9s.
29 Jan. 1813. Chailey. John Ford: died by the visitation of God in a natural way. 7 miles. £1 5s 3d.
15 Feb. 1813. Shermanbury. Elizabeth Fairs: being lunatic, hanged herself. 18 miles. £1 13s 6d.
19 Feb. 1813. West Dean. Unknown man:[1] found drowned. 13 miles. £1 9s 9d.
[*Date omitted.*] Friston. Unknown boy: found drowned. 14 miles. £1 10s 6d.
2 Mar. 1813. Boarshead Street, Rotherfield. Philadelphia Porter: accidentally fell into a brook and was drowned. 23 miles. £1 17s 3d.
15 Mar. 1813. Brighton. Sarah Marchant, infant: her clothes accidentally caught fire whereby she was burnt to death. 8 miles. £1 6s.

[*Date omitted.*] Brighton. John Bush: died by the visitation of God in a natural way. 8 miles. £1 6s.
5 Apr. 1813. East Dean. Unknown man: found drowned. 15 miles. £1 11s 3d.
6 Apr. 1813. East Dean. Unknown man: found drowned. 15 miles. £1 11s 3d.
Total £14 19s 9d; allowed at Easter sessions 1813 when 5s was added by order of the court, making £15 4s 9d. [QR/E 735]

1 *A sailor, name unknown, found under Cuckmere Cliffs, aged 30* in PAR 305/1/5/1.

178 16 June 1813. Brighton. Catherine Reeves: died by the visitation of God in a natural way. 8 miles. £1 6s.
19 June 1813. Near the Shingle Barracks, Eastbourne. George Butler, a private of the 50th[1] Regiment of Foot: accidentally drowned while bathing in the sea. 20 miles. £1 15s.
13 July 1813. Newick. William Boots: died by the visitation of God in a natural way. 8 miles. £1 6s.
Total £4 7s; allowed at Midsummer sessions 1813. [QR/E 736]

1 *West Kent*: Swinson, 149.

179 4 Aug. 1813. Hailsham. Elizabeth Foster: died by the visitation of God in a natural way. 14 miles. £1 10s 6d.
14 Aug. 1813. Rotherfield. James Fenner: accidentally killed by a wagon passing over him. 18 miles. £1 13s 6d.
13 Sept. 1813. Lindfield. John Harland jun.: accidentally killed by being thrown from a horse. 12 miles. £1 9s.
18 Sept. 1813. Piddinghoe. Unknown man: found on the sea-shore. 7 miles. £1 5s 3d.
22 Sept. 1813. Lewes House of Correction. George Byfield, infant: natural death. £1.
[*Date omitted.*] Brighton. Daniel Holder: being lunatic, hanged himself. 8 miles. £1 6s.
28 Sept. 1813. Offham. George Ellis: found drowned in the Ouse. 3 miles. £1 2s 3d.
8 Oct. 1813. Brighton. Elizabeth Lucas: died by the visitation of God in a natural way. 8 miles. £1 6s.
Total £10 12s 6d; allowed at Michaelmas sessions 1813. [QR/E 737]

180 14 Nov. 1813. Piddinghoe. 2 unknown men: found dead on the beach. 7 miles. £2 10s 6d.
16 Nov. 1813. Piddinghoe. Unknown man: found dead on the sea-beach. 7 miles. £1 5s 3d.
19 Nov. 1813. Newhaven. Unknown man: found dead on the sea-beach. 8 miles. £1 6s.
3 Dec. 1813. Uckfield. Ann Penticost: her death was accidentally occasioned by taking opium incautiously administered instead of rhubarb. 8 miles. £1 6s.
20 Dec. 1813. Worth. George Millen: died by the visitation of God in a natural way. 22 miles. £1 16s 6d.
1 Jan. 1814. Hove. Charles Henry Fraser, esq.: found dead on the sea-beach, supposed to have died in a fit to which he was subject. 10 miles. £1 7s 6d.
3 Jan. 1814. Rottingdean. Edward Moore: accidentally suffocated from having fallen from his horse into a pond. 6 miles. £1 4s 6d.
11 Jan. 1814. South Malling. Ann Merrylees: died by the visitation of God in a natural way. £1.
Total £11 16s 3d; allowed at Epiphany sessions 1814. [QR/E 738]

181 19 Jan. 1814. Brighton. Louisa Harrington: accidentally fell from an attic window on the pavement and was killed. 8 miles. £1 6s.
[*Date omitted.*] Lewes. Unknown man:[1] found drowned in a piece of water near Mr Chatfield's tan-yard. £1.
28 Feb. 1814. Brighton. William Wigram: being lunatic, cut his throat. 8 miles. £1 6s.
7 Apr. 1814. Southover. Henry Simmonds, infant: accidentally killed by falling under the wheels of a loaded wagon. £1.
16 Apr. 1814. Brighton. Thomas Phipps: being lunatic, drowned himself in the sea. 8 miles. £1 6s.
[*Date omitted.*] Brighton. Nathaniel Gunn: died by the visitation of God. 8 miles. £1 6s.
Total £7 1s; allowed at Easter sessions 1814. [QR/E 739, no 125]

1 Buried at St John sub Castro on 17 Feb. as a poor man, aged 60 or thereabouts, found drowned in the back stream near Mr Chatfield's son's yard: PAR 412/1/5/1.

182 26 Apr. 1814. Copperas Gap. James Thomas: accidentally drowned in the sea. 12 miles. £1 9s.
[*Date omitted.*] Eastbourne. Ann Knight: accidentally killed by a horse and cart running over her. 18 miles. £1 13s 6d.
9 May 1814. Brighton. William Martin: accidentally killed by a wagon going over him. 8 miles. £1 6s.
6 June 1814. Hove. Maria Wadey: died by the visitation of God in a natural way. 10 miles. £1 7s 6d.
3 July 1814. East Grinstead. James Kennard: died by the visitation of God in a natural way. 20 miles. £1 15s.
Total £7 11s; allowed at Midsummer sessions 1814. [QR/E 740]

183 30 July and 2 Aug. 1814. New Shoreham. Elizabeth Redman: being lunatic, swallowed a quantity of arsenic which caused her death. 14 miles. £1 10s 6d.
9 Aug. 1814. Plashett Park, Ringmer. Charles Cook: accidentally killed by a blow from a mare. 13 miles. £1 9s 9d.
17 Aug. 1814. Lindfield. Thomas Willett: suffocated by accidentally falling into a small stream. 15 miles. £1 11s 3d.
20 Aug. 1814. Ringmer. William Novice: accidentally suffocated in a well from the foul vapour arising therefrom. 11 miles. £1 8s 3d.
22 Aug. 1814. New Shoreham. Richard Adams: found drowned in the harbour. 6 miles. £1 4s 6d.
26 Aug. 1814. Tide Mill, Bishopstone. William Martin: accidentally drowned. 11 miles. £1 8s 3d.
22 Sept. 1814. Southbourne. John Rugg: accidentally drowned. 23 miles. £1 17s 3d.
3 Oct. 1814. Hove. Michael Stringer: accidentally drowned in a vessel which foundered there. 2 miles. £1 1s 6d.
[*Date omitted.*] Hove. George Bell: accidentally drowned in a vessel which foundered. 2 miles. £1 1s 6d.
Total £12 12s 9d; allowed at Michaelmas sessions 1814 when an extra 10s 6d (making £13 3s 3d in all) was also allowed for the second journey for the first inquest which, according to a note added by the coroner, had to be adjourned because the case was a

very mysterious one and required more evidence which could not be obtained on the first day. [QR/E 741]

[The journey of 9 Aug. is said to be from Brighton from where all Wheeler's subsequent journeys in this and his following bills were made, although it is never stated again.]

184 7 Nov. 1814. Jarvis Brook, Rotherfield. Henry Weston: died by the visitation of God in a natural way. 30 miles. £2 2s 6d.
26 Nov. 1814. Lewes House of Correction. James Martin, infant: died by the visitation of God in a natural way. £1.
28 Nov. 1814. Southwick. [*blank*] Couespel, foreigner:[1] found drowned. 4 miles. £1 3s.
29 Nov. 1814. Balsdean in Rottingdean. Thomas Highland: died by the visitation of God in a natural way. 5 miles. £1 3s 9d.
14 Dec. 1814. Brighton. Henry Dodd: died by the visitation of God in a natural way. £1.
Total £6 9s 3d; allowed at Epiphany sessions 1815. [QR/E 742]

1 *Couspel, from France, aged 20, drowned at the harbour mouth* in Par. 180/1/5/1.

185 25 Jan. 1815. Preston. William Ward: accidentally killed by a fall from his horse. 4 miles. £1 3s.
1 Mar. 1815. Lindfield. Sarah Lee: feloniously killed by Jane Burnett. 15 miles. £1 11s 3d.[1]
2 Mar. 1815. Lindfield. Sarah Lee. It was necessary to attend this day, as the verdict was not delivered till 2 a.m., in order to get the recognizances to prosecute and the recognizances of the witnesses to appear and give evidence. 15 miles. £1 11s 3d.[1]
[*Date omitted*.] Cliffe. Joseph Punker: accidentally drowned in the Ouse. 8 miles. £1 6s.
9 Mar. 1815. The Buckle, Bishopstone. Unknown man:[2] found drowned. 12 miles. £1 9s.
[9 Mar.] 1815. Seaford. Unknown man:[3] found drowned. 13 miles. £1 9s 9d.
[9 Mar.] 1815. Seaford. Unknown man:[3] found drowned. 13 miles. £1 9s 9d.
9 Mar. 1815. Seaford. Unknown man:[3] found drowned. 13 miles. £1 9s 9d.
31 Mar. 1815. Newhaven. George Stevens otherwise Phillips: accidentally drowned. 9 miles. £1 6s 9d.
3 Apr. 1815. Eastbourne. Mary Kine: being lunatic, hanged herself. 28 miles. £2 1s.
7 Apr. 1815. Ringmer. John Pelham: died in consequence of having taken arsenic by mistake. 12 miles. £1 9s.
Total £16 6s 6d; allowed at Easter sessions 1815. [QR/E 743]

[A note on the bill states that Wheeler was sent for by Mr Chambers, bailiff and coroner of Seaford, to take an inquisition on Solomon Young, who was murdered by Joseph Stephens, and from necessity could not return till very late at night; and when Wheeler met the bailiff and jury, the bailiff desired that all the proceedings might be in his name only, which was complied with, but Wheeler went through the business; it was therefore submitted to the bench whether any remuneration should be allowed Wheeler by the county or not. Nothing was allowed. The inquest survives (with no mention of Wheeler's participation): **468**.]

1 Cf. **378**.
2 *Unknown sailor* in PAR 247/1/5/1.
3 *3 sailors, names unknown, belonging to the* York, *a West Indiaman, wrecked near the Tide Mill, ages and places of residence unknown, buried 12 Mar.* in PAR 480/1/5/1. Other unknown sailors from the same ship were buried at Seaford, 3 on 15 Mar. and one each on 25, 26 and 31 Mar. and 22 Apr.: ibid.

186 26 Apr. 1815. Isfield. Michael Herring: accidentally killed by a kick from a horse. 17 miles. £1 12s 9d.
27 Apr. 1815. Brighton. William Gore: died by the visitation of God in a natural way. £1.
4 May 1815. Brighton. John Mockford: being lunatic, drowned himself. £1.
10 May 1815. Brighton. William Pannett: accidentally drowned off New Shoreham Harbour. £1.
[*Date omitted.*] Hove. James Brown: accidentally drowned off New Shoreham Harbour. 2 miles. £1 1s 6d.
[*Date omitted.*] Portslade. Edward Short: accidentally drowned off New Shoreham. 3 miles. £1 2s 3d.
13 May 1815. Brighton. William Fowler: accidentally drowned off New Shoreham. £1.
[*Date omitted.*] Brighton. Richard Piercy: accidentally drowned off New Shoreham. £1.
[*Date omitted.*] The Rose and Crown, Mayfield. Ann Maria Young:[1] accidentally fell into a spring and was drowned. 29 miles. £2 1s 9d.
[*Date omitted.*] Portslade. William Page: accidentally fell from his horse and was killed. 3 miles. £1 2s 3d.
[*Date omitted.*] Rodmell. Charity Eager:[2] being lunatic, hanged herself. 6 miles. £1 4s 6d.
[*Date omitted.*] Eastbourne. John Morris:[3] accidentally drowned. 28 miles. £2 1s.
7 July 1815. Balcombe. Sarah Comber, infant: accidentally fell into a pond and was drowned. 20 miles. £1 15s.
[*Date omitted.*] Brighton. Daniel Tibble: died by the visitation of God in a natural way. £1.
Total £18 1s; allowed at Midsummer sessions 1815. [QR/E 744]

1 *Ann Young Tompsett, aged 2 years 5 months, buried 22 May* in PAR 422/1/5/1.
2 *Aged 65, buried 4 June* in PAR 464/1/5/1.
3 *Aged 39, buried 28 June* in PAR 309/1/5/1.

187 [*blank*] July 1815. Lewes. Elizabeth Molineux: being lunatic, threw herself into a well and was drowned. 8 miles. £1 6s.
22 July 1815. Danehill in Horsted Keynes. Daniel Davey: being lunatic, hanged himself. 22 miles. £1 16s 6d.
26 July 1815. Brighton. James Mills: accidentally drowned whilst bathing in the sea. £1.
29 July 1815. Eastbourne. Susan Surman: being lunatic, hanged herself. 28 miles. £2 1s.
3 Aug. 1815. Nutley. Mary Barnes: accidentally fell into a cooler of scalding beer and was scalded to death. 19 miles. £1 14s 3d.
[*Date omitted.*] Southover. Rose Edwards: her death was occasioned in consequence of her having incautiously taken hemlock tea. 8 miles. £1 6s.
5 Aug. 1815. Southover. John Townshend: accidentally fell over a high bank and was killed. 8 miles. £1 6s.
14 Aug. 1815. Bopeep in Alciston. Richard Richardson: found dead on the Downs. 15 miles. £1 11s 3d.
18 Aug. 1815. Lewes. William Palmer: died by the visitation of God. 8 miles. £1 6s.
21 Aug. 1815. Brighton. Louisa Ramsey, infant: accidentally run over by a carriage and killed. £1.

24 Aug. 1815. Poynings. James Goddard: accidentally fell from a cart laden with clover upon the fang of a prong and was killed. 6 miles. £1 4s 6d.
1 Sept. 1815. Lewes House of Correction. John Anderson: natural death. 8 miles. £1 6s.
2 Sept. 1815. Southwick. Henry Boxall: found dead under the cliff. 5 miles. £1 3s 9d.
11 Sept. 1815. Preston. Unknown man: died by the visitation of God in a natural way. 2 miles. £1 1s 6d.
19 Sept. 1815. Brighton. George Coldham, esq.: accidentally killed in consequence of being thrown from a gig with which a horse had run away. £1.
20 Sept. 1815. Southbourne. Sarah Hayton: died by the visitation of God in a natural way. 30 miles. £2 2s 6d.
14 Oct. 1815. Ardingly. William Burt: being lunatic, drowned himself. 30 miles. £2 2s 6d.
Total £24 7s 9d; allowed at Michaelmas sessions 1815. [QR/E 745]

188 23 Oct. 1815. Maresfield. George Kingsland, infant: accidentally fell into a ditch and was drowned. 18 miles. £1 13s 6d.
4 Nov. 1815. East Dean. Harriet Mortimer: being lunatic, hanged herself. 24 miles. £1 18s.
15 Nov. 1815. Lewes House of Correction. John Rowe: died by the visitation of God. 8 miles. £1 6s.
23 Nov. 1815. Cuckfield. Sarah Nye: died by the visitation of God. 14 miles. £1 10s 6d.
[23 Nov.] 1815. East Mascalls in Lindfield. John Millar: died by the visitation of God. 17 miles. £1 12s 9d.
24 Nov. 1815. Newhaven. Elizabeth Walters: accidentally killed by a quantity of sand falling upon her. 9 miles. £1 6s 9d.
11 Dec. 1815. Southbourne in Eastbourne. Joseph Beeching: accidentally drowned. 26 miles. £1 19s 6d.
[11 Dec.] 1815. Southbourne in Eastbourne. George Pryor: accidentally drowned. 26 miles. £1 19s 6d.
11 Dec. 1815. Southbourne in Eastbourne. George Sargeant: accidentally drowned. 26 miles. £1 19s 6d.
13 Dec. 1815. Rotherfield. James Turk: accidentally drowned in a pond whilst sliding. 26 miles. £1 19s 6d.
14 Dec. 1815. Maresfield. Walter Dicker: died by the visitation of God. 18 miles. £1 13s 6d.
16 Dec. 1815. Southwick. Unknown man: found drowned. 5 miles. £1 3s 9d.
18 Dec. 1815. West Dean. Unknown man: found drowned in the Cuckmere. 16 miles. £1 12s.
22 Dec. 1815. Chiddingly. Eli Elphick: accidentally killed in consequence of being drawn into the cogs of his father's windmill. 16 miles. £1 12s.
1 Jan. 1816. Brighton. Unknown man: found drowned. £1.
2 Jan. 1816. Barcombe. Thomas Beale: accidentally fell into the river and was drowned. 12 miles. £1 9s.
5 Jan. 1816. Brighton. Nathaniel Greenwood: died by the visitation of God. £1.
8 Jan. 1816. Portslade. William Welling: accidentally killed by the wheels of a wagon passing over him. 4 miles. £1 3s.

Total £27 18s 9d from which 12s 9d was deducted, leaving £27 6s which was allowed at Epiphany sessions 1816. [QR/E 746]

[There are marginal notes against 4 entries. Against that of 4 Nov. is written: *5s 3d; by the coast the nearest way, not more than 9 to Newhaven, 4 to Exceat Bridge, 2 to East Dean, 15.* Against each of the 3 entries of 11 Dec. is *6s, 21.* The sums are much altered and their total is given as 12s 9d.]

189 13 Jan. 1816. Brighton. Unknown man: found drowned. £1.
[*Date omitted.*] Worth. James Goring: being lunatic, drowned himself. 24 miles. £1 18s.
[*Date omitted.*] Lewes House of Correction. Samuel Brookes: died by the visitation of God. 8 miles. £1 6s.
4 Mar. 1816. [*Place omitted.*] Joseph do Mendoza Rios: being lunatic, hanged himself. £1.
25 Mar. 1816. Isfield. John Ringrose: accidentally drowned. 13 miles. £1 9s 9d.
[*Date omitted.*] Isfield. William Blygh: accidentally drowned. 13 miles. £1 9s 9d.
28 Mar. 1816. Alfriston. John Reed: being lunatic, hanged himself. 16 miles. £1 12s.
10 Apr. 1816. Lewes House of Correction. William Longridge: being lunatic, hanged himself. 8 miles. £1 6s.
Total £11 1s 6d; allowed at Easter sessions 1816. [QR/E 747]

190 [*blank*] May 1816. Hartfield. John Killick: died by the visitation of God. 28 miles. £2 1s.
13 May 1816. Maresfield. Ann Wise: being lunatic, hanged herself. 18 miles. £1 13s 6d.
27 May 1816. Hartfield. Edward Card: accidentally killed by a wagon passing over him. 28 miles. £2 1s.
30 May 1816. Eastbourne. [*blank*] Blake:[1] accidentally drowned. 24 miles. £1 18s.
31 May 1816. Chiddingly. Unknown boy: accidentally killed by being struck with the sweeps of a windmill. 15 miles. £1 11s 3d.
8 June 1816. Lewes. John Newton: accidentally killed by a gun-shot. 8 miles. £1 6s.
[*Date omitted.*] Southwick. Thomas Brigden: accidentally drowned. 5 miles. £1 3s 9d.
[*Date omitted.*] Brighton. Oliver Holden: accidentally drowned by the upsetting of a boat. £1.
[*Date omitted.*] Southease. George King: found drowned in the river. 10 miles. £1 7s 9d.[2]
20 June 1816. Newhaven. James Goddard: found drowned in the river. 9 miles. £1 6s 9d.
26 June 1816. Brighton. John Moon: being lunatic, took a quantity of laudanum whereby he poisoned himself. £1.
26 June 1816. Brighton. William Holden: accidentally drowned by the upsetting of a boat. £1.
1 July 1816. Chalvington. William Guy: found dead on the Dicker in Chiddingly. 17 miles. £1 12s 9d.
2 July 1816. Preston. James Hutton: being lunatic, shot himself. 2 miles. £1 1s 6d.
[2 July] 1816. Brighton. James Page: died by the visitation of God. £1.
2 and 3 July 1816. Petworth, in the absence of Mr Ellis.[3] Thomas Muggeridge: killed by Charles Dowden whilst fighting. 30 miles. £2 2s 6d.[4]

5 July 1816. Scotney Castle, Lamberhurst. Edward Hussey, esq.: being lunatic, shot himself. 32 miles. £2 4s.
12 July 1816. Eastbourne. Unknown man: found drowned. 24 miles. £1 18s.
13 July 1816. Hailsham. John Marshall: died by the visitation of God. 21 miles. £1 15s 9d.
Total £29 3s 6d; allowed at Midsummer sessions 1816. [QCC/E2, no 36]

[Wheeler appended a note to the bill stating that in consequence of the distance and difficulty of the inquest of 2 and 3 July he was detained there 2 days and asking the JPs if they would make any addition to the sum charged. They did not. For notes written on the bill see **473**.]

1 *William Blake, aged 37* in PAR 309/1/5/1.
2 Recte *£1 7s 6d*. The extra 3d was included in the bill total and allowed.
3 John Luttman Ellis, the West Sussex county coroner.
4 Cf. **379**.

191 22 July 1816. Rottingdean. John McDonald: accidentally drowned whilst bathing. 4 miles. £1 3s.
[22 July] 1816. Portslade. Maria Goodman:[1] being lunatic, hanged herself. 4 miles. £1 3s.
23[2] July 1816. Brighton. Madame Latour:[3] died by the visitation of God. £1.
7 Aug. 1816. Lindfield. William Wood: died by the visitation of God. 16 miles. £1 12s.
15 Aug. 1816.[4] Newhaven. Unchristened[5] infant: accidentally choked in consequence of a plum-stone sticking in its throat. 9 miles. £1 6s 9d.
17 Aug. 1816. West Firle. Thomas Smith: being lunatic, shot himself. 13 miles. £1 9s 9d.
[*Date omitted*.] Rottingdean. [*blank*]:[6] killed[7] in consequence of the wheel[8] of a wagon passing over him. 4 miles. £1 3s.
31 Aug. 1816. Mayfield. Edward Young: accidentally fell into a pond and was drowned. 30 miles. £2 2s 6d.
[*Date omitted*.][9] Newhaven. Unknown man, supposed to be a Frenchman:[10] accidentally drowned. 9 miles. £1 6s 9d.
[*Date omitted*.][11] Newhaven. [*blank*] Poole:[12] died by the visitation of God. 9 miles. £1 6s 9d.
[*Date omitted*.][13] Brighton. Ann Arnold, infant: accidentally killed in consequence of the neb[14] of a timber-tug falling upon her whilst at play.[15] £1.
16 Sept. 1816. Laughton. Edward Couchman: accidentally fell from a pea-mow and was killed. 14 miles. £1 10s 6d.
21 Sept. 1816. Isfield. Henry Bage:[16] accidentally fell into the Ouse and was drowned. 14[17] miles. £1 9s 9d.
[*Date omitted*.] Cliffe. Elizabeth Short: died by the visitation of God. 8 miles. £1 6s.
24 Sept. 1816. Little Horsted. Francis Crump: being lunatic, hanged himself. 14 miles. £1 10s 6d.
26 Sept. 1816. Rottingdean. Mrs[18] Ann Freeman: being lunatic, hanged herself. 4 miles. £1 3s.
5 Oct. 1816. Newhaven. William Dumbrell: being lunatic, hanged himself. 9 miles. £1 6s 9d.
9 Oct. 1816. Frant. Mary Page: being lunatic, hanged herself. 30 miles. £2 2s 6d.
10 Oct. 1816. Henfield. John Golds: being lunatic, hanged himself. 14 miles. £1 10s 6d.

11 Oct. 1816. West Hoathly. John Goodwin: being lunatic, hanged himself. 22 miles. £1 16s 6d.
[*Date omitted.*] Brighton. John Payne: died by the visitation of God. £1.[19]
Total £29 9s 6d;[20] allowed at Michaelmas sessions 1816. [QCC/E2, no 17]

[There is another version of the bill: QCC/E2, no 62. For notes written on the bills see **474**, **475**.]

1 *Maria Goodman* omitted in no 62; *Ann Pelling* in **482**. Ann Pelling, aged 21, was buried at Portslade on 27 July: Ep. II/16/156B.
2 *22* in no 62.
3 *Margaret Latour of Carlton Row, aged 72* in PAR 255/1/5/2.
4 Date omitted in no 62.
5 *Unchristened* omitted and blank space left for name in no 62.
6 [*blank*] *Muggridge* in no 62; *boy named Charman* in **491**.
7 *accidentally killed* in no 62.
8 *wheels* in no 62.
9 *3 Sept. 1816* in no 62.
10 *Frenchman named Dulervel* in **497**.
11 *4 Sept. 1816* in no 62.
12 *Edward Poole* in no 62 and **497**.
13 *12 Sept. 1816* in no 62.
14 *nab* in no 62.
15 *whilst at play* omitted in no 62.
16 *infant* added in no 62.
17 *13* in no 62 which is correct.
18 *Mrs* omitted in no 62.
19 Whole entry omitted in no 62.
20 *£28 9s 6d* in no 62 where there is nothing about it being allowed.

192 9 Nov. 1816. South Malling. William Piper: died by the visitation of God in a natural way. 8 miles. £1 6s.
14 Nov. 1816. Cuckfield. Daniel Ockenden: died by the visitation of God in a natural way. 14 miles. £1 10s 6d.
15 Nov. 1816. Old Shoreham Bridge. Sarah Reeves, infant: accidentally burnt to death in consequence of her clothes catching fire. 6 miles. £1 4s 6d.
[*Date omitted.*] Hove. Henry Potter, infant: accidentally burnt to death in consequence of his clothes catching fire. 2 miles. £1 1s 6d.
8 Dec. 1816. Lamberhurst. William Bond: being lunatic, shot himself. 38 miles. £2 8s 6d.
10 Dec. 1816. East Grinstead. Sarah Novess: feloniously killed herself by swallowing a quantity of arsenic. 28 miles. £2 1s.
11 Dec. 1816. Wivelsfield. Samuel Denman: being lunatic, hanged himself. 12 miles. £1 9s.
14 Dec. 1816. Brighton. William Reeves, infant: found drowned in a well. £1.
15 Dec. 1816. Brighton. Philadelphia Sherwood: died by the visitation of God. £1.
20 Dec. 1816. Chailey. Thomas Hollingdale: being lunatic, hanged himself. 16 miles. £1 12s.
21 Dec. 1816. Frant. John Sands: died by the visitation of God. 30 miles. £2 2s 6d.
Total £16 15s 6d. [QCC/E2, no 18]

[For notes written on the bill see **476**.]

Bill of John Luttman Ellis

193 8 Mar. 1817. Isfield. Frederick Bruster. 41 miles. £2 10s 9d. Expenses, out all night £1 1s 11d.
9 Apr. 1817. Southwick. James Savage. 25 miles. £1 18s 9d. Expenses 10s 4d.
17 Apr. 1817. Balcombe. Thomas Holman. 27 miles. £2 0s 3d. Expenses, out 1 night £1 6s 6d.
1 May 1817. Hove. Unknown man.[1] 28 miles. £2 1s. Expenses, out 1 night £1 3s 6d.
14 May 1817. Withyham. Thomas Borer. 50 miles. £2 17s 6d. Expenses, out 2 nights £1 17s 5d.
23 May 1817. New Shoreham. Mary Burdur. 22 miles. £1 16s 6d.
25 May 1817. Brighton. John Tree. 29 miles. £2 1s 9d. Expenses, out 1 night £1 19s.
27 May 1817. Hartfield. John Russell. 50 miles. £2 17s 6d. Expenses, out 2 nights £2.
3 June 1817. Preston. Barbara Oram. 30 miles. £2 2s 6d. Expenses, out 1 night 19s 9d.
6 June 1817. Wivelsfield. James Parker. 34 miles. £2 5s 6d. Expenses, out 1 night 16s 4d.
2 July 1817. Newhaven. William Bollin. 39 miles. £2 9s 3d. Expenses, out 1 night £1 17s 9d.
18 July 1817. Henfield. New-born male infant. 24 miles. £1 18s. Expenses, including hire of horse and gig £1 14s 3d.
3 Aug. 1817. Rottingdean. William Watts. 34 miles. £2 5s 6d. Expenses, out 1 night £1 2s 6d.
Expenses £16 9s 3d, inquests and journeys £29 4s 9d, total £45 14s; allowed at Michaelmas sessions 1817. [QR/E 753]

[This bill was for inquests held by Ellis, the county coroner for West Sussex, during the incapacity of Thomas William Wheeler. His journeys were from Petworth but that is not stated in the bill which does, however, contain a note that Ellis travelled 860 miles in taking the inquests and that he was away from home 25 days and 12 nights.]

1 *A man unknown, aged about 60, apparently a foreigner, conjectured to be Swiss, taken from the sea expiring from suffocation and with a wound in his neck as perforated by an instrument* in PAR 386/1/5/1.

Bills of George Gwynne

194 18 Aug. 1817. Cliffe. William Ansell. £1.
23 Aug. 1817. South Malling. Thomas Grover. 2 miles. £1 1s 6d.
28 Aug. 1817. Arlington. George Charriman. 22 miles. £1 16s 6d.
30 Aug. 1817. Brighton. Buckerell Smith. 16 miles. £1 12s.
[30 Aug.] 1817. Brighton. George Pearce. £1.
23 Sept. 1817. Frant. Samuel Seaman. 40 miles. £2 10s.
29 Sept. 1817. Waldron. John Hook. 24 miles. £1 18s.
4 Oct. 1817. Lewes House of Correction. Richard Little. £1.
16 Oct. 1817. Jevington. Thomas Page otherwise Moppette. 26 miles. £1 19s 6d.
3 Nov. 1817. Brighton. Louisa Revill. 16 miles. £1 12s.
7 Nov. 1817. Brighton. Thomas Rowles. 16 miles for 8 several days, being 128 miles. £5 16s.[1]
29 Nov. 1817. Falmer. Robert Henley. 8 miles. £1 6s.
20 Dec. 1817. Rottingdean. Henry Hide. 14 miles. £1 10s 6d.

[20 Dec.] 1817. Rottingdean. William Belton. £1.
22 Dec. 1817. East Grinstead. Richard Edwards. 40 miles. £2 10s.
29 Dec. 1817. Rottingdean. Robert Olliver. 14 miles. £1 10s 6d.
[29 Dec.] 1817. Rottingdean. James Savage. £1.
[29 Dec.] 1817. Lewes. Elizabeth Surgey. £1.
30 Dec. 1817. Brighton. Sarah Baker. 16 miles. £1 12s.
[30 Dec.] 1817. Brighton. Thomas Barrow. £1.
5 Jan. 1818. Worth. William Simmons. 42 miles. £2 11s 6d.
19 Jan. 1818. Preston. Charles Cussmajir Wetherell. 9 miles. £1 13s 6d.[2]
21 Feb. 1818. Eastbourne. Thomas Wilkins. 42 miles. £2 11s 6d.
29 Feb. 1818.[3] Bishopstone. Mary Holloway. 20 miles. £1 15s.
7 Mar. 1818. Cuckfield. Ann Homowood. 28 miles. £2 1s.
18 Mar. 1818. Upper Beeding. James Paskings. 34 miles. £2 5s 6d.
24 Mar. 1818. Ripe. Robert Jenner. 18 miles. £1 13s 6d.
25 Mar. 1818. Rottingdean. John Wright. 17 miles. £1 10s 6d.[4]
28 Mar. 1818. Brighton. William Witmarsh. 16 miles. £1 12s.
30 Mar. 1818. Eastbourne. John Banks. 42 miles. £2 11s 6d.
13 Apr. 1818. Portslade. Unknown man.[5] 24 miles. £1 18s.
21 Apr. 1818. Southover. George Jones. £1.
27 Apr. 1818. Brighton. George Hanks. 16 miles. £1 12s.
28 Apr. 1818. Eastbourne. Henry Baker. 42 miles. £2 11s 6d.
16 May 1818. Eastbourne. Thomas Tutt. 42 miles. £2 11s 6d.
18 May 1818. Newick. William Ware. 16 miles. £1 12s.
30 May 1818. Lewes House of Correction. Francis Foster. £1.
8 June 1818. Lindfield. Samuel Rapley. 24 miles. £1 18s.
19 June 1818. Brighton. John Beatie. 16 miles. £1 12s.
20 June 1818. Uckfield. Ann Dival. 16 miles. £1 12s.
28 June 1818. Eastbourne. Lewis Filder. 42 miles. £2 11s 6d.
1 July 1818. Hartfield. Obadiah Leney. 40 miles. £2 10s.
3 July 1818. Southbourne. John Dyer. 44 miles. £2 13s.
8 July 1818. Brighton. Daniel McFarling. 16 miles. £1 12s.
Total £80 13s 6d; allowed at Midsummer sessions 1818. [QR/E 756]

[All Gwynne's journeys were from Lewes but that is never stated in his bills. The extra 4s 6d resulting from the errors in the claims for the inquests of 19 Jan. and 25 Mar. was included in the bill total and allowed.]

1 Cf. **380**; *SCM*, VI, 741.
2 Recte *£1 6s 9d.*
3 Burial was on 25 Feb.: PAR 247/1/5/1.
4 Recte *£1 12s 9d.*
5 *A poor man, name unknown, who died in a stable at Freemans Court, abode somewhere in Norfolk, aged about 70* in Ep. II/16/156B.

195 17 July 1818. Brighton. John Walker. 8 miles. £1 6s.
25 July 1818. Offham. William West alias Roberts. 2 miles. £1 1s 6d.
[25 July] 1818. Offham. Richard French. £1.
[25 July] 1818. Offham. John Leonard. £1.
27 July 1818. Lamberhurst. Edward Neal. 28 miles. £2 1s.
[27 July] 1818. Lamberhurst. Thomas Neal. £1.
4 Aug. 1818. Cuckfield. John Goddard. 15 miles. £1 11s 3d.

6 Aug. 1818. East Grinstead. Thomas Lambe. 21 miles. £1 15s 9d.
15 Aug. 1818. Brighton. Mrs Porter. 8 miles. £1 6s.
16 Aug. 1818. Lewes. Thomas French. £1.
17 Aug. 1818. Portslade. James Kelley. 12 miles. £1 9s.
19 Aug. 1818. West Hoathly. John Marchant. 18 miles. £1 13s 6d.
20 Aug. 1818. Chiddingly. John Glyd. 10 miles. £1 7s 6d.
26 Aug. 1818. Jevington. William Berry. 14 miles. £1 10s 6d.
27 Aug. 1818. Ringmer. Mary Baker. 4 miles. £1 3s.
30 Aug. 1818. Lewes. Thomas Lindley. £1.
3 Sept. 1818. Southover. Charles Morley. 2 miles, being obliged to adjourn the inquest. £1 1s 6d.
19 Sept. 1818. Twineham. Richard Bachelor. 16 miles. £1 12s.
26 Sept. 1818. Chiddingly. John Barnes. 11 miles. £1 8s 3d.
30 Sept. 1818. Lewes. Ann Neeve. £1.
6 Oct. 1818. Maresfield. Richard Carman. 12 miles. £1 9s.
8 Oct. 1818. Westmeston. John Buckwell. 7 miles. £1 5s 3d.
[8 Oct.] 1818. Westmeston. John Port. £1.
19 Oct. 1818. Rotherfield. Eliza Moon. 20 miles. £1 15s.
20 Oct. 1818. Lewes. Samuel Snashall jun. £1.
15 and 16 Nov. 1818. Tunbridge Wells. Edward Smith. 22 miles, out 2 days. £2 13s.[1]
21 Nov. 1818. Frant. John Harvey. 22 miles. £1 16s 6d.
23 Nov. 1818. Lewes House of Correction. Thomas Shields. £1.
17 Dec. 1818. Bevendean in Falmer. Jane Verrall. 7 miles. £1 5s 3d.
17 Dec. 1818. East Hoathly. John Muggeridge. 8 miles. £1 6s.
17 Dec. 1818. West Firle. George Russell. 5 miles. £1 3s 9d.
22 Dec. 1818. Nutley. Mary Wheeler. 13 miles. £1 9s 9d.
27 Dec. 1818. East Grinstead. William Wood. 21 miles. £1 15s 9d.
Total £45 6s; allowed at Epiphany sessions 1819. [QR/E 758]

1 Cf. **381**.

196 13 Jan. 1819. Lewes. Elizabeth Geere. £1.
19 Jan. 1819. Horsted Keynes. Alex Woolgar. 14 miles. £1 10s 6d.
4 Feb. 1819. Lewes. John Willbar Cook. £1.
6 Feb. 1819. Brighton. William Devonish. 8 miles. £1 6s.
8 Feb. 1819. Rottingdean. Mary Ann Mott. Inquest adjourned. 12 miles. 9s.
9 Feb. 1819. Brighton. John Fairhall. 8 miles. £1 6s.
10 Feb. 1819. Rottingdean. Mary Ann Mott. By adjournment. 12 miles. £1 9s.
[*Date omitted.*] East Grinstead. Mary Mitchell. 22 miles, out all night and adjourned to next day. £2 13s.
13 Feb. 1819. Cuckfield. Henry Bowles. 16 miles. £1 12s.
20 Feb. 1819. The Gas-Light Works, Rottingdean. Richard Gwynett. 10 miles. £1 7s 6d.
27 Feb. 1819. Withyham. Abraham Spencer. 20 miles, out all night and adjourned to next day. £2 10s.
9 Mar. 1819. Brighton. Phoebe Hopkins. 8 miles. £1 6s.
13 Mar. 1819. Lindfield. William Lloyd. 15 miles. £1 11s 3d.
15 Mar. 1819. Ardingly. Elizabeth Ridley. 18 miles. £1 13s 6d.
[*Date omitted.*] Cliffe. Thomas Morris. £1.

[*Date omitted.*] Lewes. Ann Streaton. £1.
17 Mar. 1819. Brighton. Eleanor Luck. 8 miles. £1 6s.
29 Mar. 1819. Hove. Ann Munns. Inquest adjourned. 10 miles. 7s 6d.
30 Mar. 1819. Hove. Ann Munns. By adjournment. 10 miles. £1 7s 6d.
[*Date omitted.*] Brighton. Richard Crunden. 8 miles. £1 6s.
[*Date omitted.*] Lewes. Frances Richardson. £1.
5 Apr. 1819. Eastbourne. Elizabeth Ford. Inquest adjourned. 21 miles. 15s 9d.
6 Apr. 1819. Eastbourne. Elizabeth Ford. By adjournment. 21 miles. £1 15s 9d.
7 Apr. 1819. West Hoathly. John Young. Inquest adjourned. 21 miles. 15s 9d.
8 Apr. 1819. West Hoathly. John Young. By adjournment. 21 miles. £1 15s 9d.
10 Apr. 1819. Brighton. Ann Weaver. 8 miles. £1 6s.
17 Apr. 1819. Westmeston. Thomas Nye. 7 miles. £1 5s 3d.
20 Apr. 1819. Frant. Mary Okyll. Inquest adjourned. 22 miles. 16s 6d.
21 Apr. 1819. Frant. Mary Okyll. By adjournment. 22 miles. £1 16s 6d.
25 Apr. 1819. Brighton. Elizabeth Dymoke. 8 miles. £1 6s.
[25 Apr.] 1819. Piddinghoe. William Noakes. 6 miles. £1 4s 6d.
26 Apr. 1819. Brighton. Adam Taylor. 8 miles. £1 6s.
11 May 1819. Hellingly. Peter Pagden. 12 miles. £1 9s.
14 May 1819. Brighton. Susannah Harvey. 8 miles. £1 6s.
[*Date omitted.*] Brighton. Ann French. 8 miles. £1 6s.
17 May 1819. Lewes House of Correction. Henry Burwood. £1.
19 May 1819. Brighton. Jane Gillam. 8 miles. £1 6s.
19 May 1819. Wivelsfield. Sarah Chatfield. 12 miles. £1 9s.
2 June 1819. Nutley. Sarah Feldwick. 14 miles. £1 11s 6d.[1]
18 June 1819. Cuckfield. Thomas Willet. 16 miles. £1 12s.
21 June 1819. Rottingdean. John Harvey, esq. 7 miles. £1 5s 3d.
30 June 1819. Brighton. William Watson. 8 miles. £1 6s.[2]
5 July 1819. Southbourne. Edward Glazier. Inquest adjourned. 22 miles. 16s 6d.
6 July 1819. Southbourne. Edward Glazier. By adjournment. 22 miles. £1 16s 6d.
[*Date omitted.*] Brighton. Ambrose Powell. 8 miles. £1 6s.
8 July 1819. Southbourne. Stephen Page. By adjournment. 44 miles. £2 13s.
10 July 1819. Hartfield. Joseph Edwards. 18 miles. £1 13s 6d.
11 July 1819. Southbourne. John Cobby. Inquest adjourned. 22 miles. 16s 6d.
12 July 1819. Southbourne. John Cobby. By adjournment. 22 miles. £1 16s 6d.
[*Date omitted.*] Brighton. Joan Russell. 8 miles. £1 6s.
Total £67 19s 9d, from which £7 5s 6d was deducted, leaving £60 14s 3d which was allowed at Midsummer sessions 1819. [QR/E 760]

[The sum of £7 5s 6d was made up of the following amounts noted in the margin against the relevant entries: 8 Feb., 4s 6d; 10 Feb., 4s 6d; the next, undated entry, 16s 6d; 27 Feb., 15s; 30 Mar., 7s 6d; 6 Apr., 15s 9d; 8 Apr., 15s 9d; 21 Apr., 16s 6d; 6 July, 16s 6d; 8 July, 16s 6d; 12 July, 16s 6d. The extra 1s claimed for the inquest of 2 June was included in the bill total and allowed.]

1 Recte *£1 10s 6d.*
2 Cf. **382**.

197 18 July 1819. Ringmer. William Tobitt. 4 miles. £1 3s.
20 July 1819. Rottingdean. John Harman. 7 miles. £1 5s 3d.
28 July 1819. Cuckfield. Thomas Peckham. 16 miles. £1 12s.

31 July 1819. West Dean. Richard Hilton. 12 miles. £1 9s.
2 Aug. 1819. Hamsey. George Ade. 3 miles. £1 2s 3d.
2 Aug. 1819. Hamsey. Richard Ade. 3 miles. £1 2s 3d.
12 Aug. 1819. Cuckfield. Thomas Blake. 16 miles. £1 12s.
17 Aug. 1819. Southbourne. Samuel Pale. It having been supposed deceased had been murdered, adjourned inquest until the next day and attendance there accordingly. 44 miles. £2 13s.
20 Aug. 1819. Kingston by Sea. William McClelon.[1] 13 miles. £1 9s 9d.
21 Aug. 1819. Alfriston. Charles Geering. 10 miles. £1 7s 6d.
28 Aug. 1819. Ardingly. William Francis. 18 miles. £1 13s 6d.
30 Aug. 1819. Newick. Trayton Winton. 8 miles. £1 6s.
2 Sept. 1819. West Hoathly. Joseph Lywood. 21 miles. £1 15s 9d.
4 Sept. 1819. Brighton. John Sawyer. 8 miles. £1 6s.
8 Sept. 1819. Chailey. Thomas Bristow. 9 miles. £1 6s 9d.
8 Sept. 1819. East Grinstead. Unknown person.[2] 22 miles. £1 16s 6d.
22 Sept. 1819. Willingdon. Ruth Clympson. 18 miles. £1 13s 6d.
29 Sept. 1819. Withyham. Mary Dodson. 20 miles. £1 15s.
10 Oct. 1819. Falmer. Thomas Bromley. 4 miles. £1 3s.
25 Oct. 1819. Lindfield. William Broad. 12 miles. £1 9s.
28 Oct. 1819. Southbourne. New-born male bastard child. 22 miles. £1 16s 6d.
30 Oct. 1819. Waldron. Richard Barton. 12 miles. £1 9s.
3 Nov. 1819. Bolney in Cuckfield. John Pitt. 17 miles. £1 12s 9d.
11 Nov. 1819. Newick. Thomas Wood. 8 miles. £1 6s.
12 Nov. 1819. Mayfield. Elizabeth Beal. 18 miles. £1 13s 6d.
14 Nov. 1819. East Langney Point, Willingdon. Thomas Brewer. 23 miles. £1 17s 3d.
17 Nov. 1819. Brighton. Samuel Richardson. 8 miles. £1 6s.
30 Nov. 1819. East Dean. Daniel Fell. 17 miles. £1 12s 9d.
31 Nov.[3] 1819. East Dean. Christian Goodwill. 17 miles. £1 12s 9d.
8 Dec. 1819. Ditchling. Richard Cox. 8 miles. £1 6s.
10 Dec. 1819. Portslade. Daniel Holden. 12 miles. £1 9s.
11 Dec. 1819. New Shoreham. Cornelius Wilkinson. 14 miles. £1 10s 6d.
17 Dec. 1819. Southover. Susannah Bannister. 1 mile. £1 0s 9d.
Total £49 13s 9d; allowed at Epiphany sessions 1820. [QR/E 762]

1 *McCleon* in Ep. II/16/125B.
2 Probably Samuel Pett Broome, found in East Grinstead and buried there on 9 Sept.: Par. 348/1/5/1.
3 ?Recte *30 Nov.* or *1 Dec.*

198 2 Jan. 1820. Brighton. Sarah Greenyer. 8 miles. £1 6s.
8 Jan. 1820. Brighton. James Short. 8 miles. £1 6s.
9 Jan. 1820. Arlington. John Mockford. 10 miles. £1 7s 6d.
19 Jan. 1820. Lewes House of Correction. Henry Grinstead. £1.
28 Jan. 1820. Ringmer. George Divall. 4 miles. £1 3s.
28 Jan. 1820. Cliffe. Sarah Webb. £1.
5 Feb. 1820. Brighton. Henrietta Brown. 8 miles. £1 6s.
12 Feb. 1820. Lewes House of Correction. William Delegate. £1.
20 Feb. 1820. Cuckfield. Samuel Waller. 14 miles. £1 10s 6d.
22 Feb. 1820. Brighton. John Harman. 8 miles. £1 6s.
29 Feb. 1820. East Dean. John Elliott. 16 miles. £1 12s.

6 Mar. 1820. South Malling. Henry Akehurst. 1 mile. £1 0s 9d.
9 Mar. 1820. Lewes. William Tout. £1.
10 Mar. 1820. Mayfield. Elizabeth Seymour. 18 miles. £1 13s 6d.
11 Mar. 1820. Hadlow Down, Buxted. Robert Cottingham. 14 miles. £1 10s 6d.
23 Mar. 1820. Brighton. John Coppard. 8 miles. £1 6s.
27 Mar. 1820. Heathfield. John Lovell. 16 miles. £1 12s.
4 Apr. 1820. Crawley. William Johnson. 24 miles. £1 18s.
6 Apr. 1820. Framfield. Robert Smith. 10 miles. £1 7s 6d.
7 Apr. 1820. Lewes House of Correction. William Brooker. £1.
24 Apr. 1820. Patcham. Stephen Marten. 12 miles. £1 9s.
28 Apr. 1820. Eastbourne. Jane Downing. 22 miles. £1 16s 6d.
28 Apr. 1820. Eastbourne. Louisa Downing. 22 miles. £1 16s 6d.
29 Apr. 1820. Rottingdean. John Kingstone. 8 miles. £1 6s.
1 May 1820. Lewes House of Correction. Eliza Blanch. £1.
12 May 1820. Brighton. Elizabeth Walker. 8 miles. £1 6s.
21 May 1820. Lewes. Maria Webb. £1.
22 May 1820. Waldron. William Bray. 12 miles. £1 9s.
24 May 1820. Southover. William Cheale. £1.
3 June 1820. Laughton. Edward Starnes. 6 miles. £1 4s 6d.
3 June 1820. Hailsham. Catherine Watson. 14 miles. £1 10s 6d.
7 June 1820. Brighton. Gregory Sopp. 8 miles. £1 6s.
14 June 1820. Tarring Neville. Richard Saunders. 8 miles. £1 6s.
25 June 1820. Alfriston. Harriet Warner. 9 miles. £1 6s 9d.
27 June 1820. Streat. Dame Page.[1] 6 miles. £1 4s 6d.
1 July 1820. Brighton. William Jennnings. 8 miles. £1 6s.
4 July 1820. Patcham. William Ballard. 12 miles. £1 9s.
Total £49 1s 6d; allowed at Midsummer sessions 1820. [QR/E 764]

1 *Elizabeth Page, widow* in the Streat parish register: in ESRO microfilm XA/30/174.

199 14 July 1820. Lewes House of Correction. George Williams. £1.
7 Aug. 1820. Worth. William Fuller. 24 miles. £1 18s.
13 Aug. 1820. Wivelsfield. James Renville. 12 miles. £1 9s.
15 Aug. 1820. Hickstead. James Browne. 14 miles. £1 10s 6d.
19 Aug. 1820. Piddinghoe. Robert Carter. 6 miles. £1 4s 6d.
19 Aug. 1820. Piddinghoe. William Hollingdale. 6 miles. £1 4s 6d.
22 Aug. 1820. Brighton. Hannah Baldy. 8 miles. £1 6s.
23 Aug. 1820. ?Hangleton.[1] George Grover. 12 miles. £1 9s.
26 Aug. 1820. Brighton. Frances Polley. 8 miles. £1 6s.
27 Aug. 1820. Brighton. Maria May. 8 miles. £1 6s.
30 Aug. 1820. Waldron. William Wood. 12 miles. £1 9s.
1 Sept. 1820. Ardingly. Stephen Ellzey. 18 miles. £1 13s 6d.
2 Sept. 1820. Brighton. Henrietta Hook. 8 miles. £1 6s.
5 Sept. 1820. Lewes. Elizabeth Knight. £1.
18 Sept. 1820. Brighton. John Bull. 8 miles. £1 6s.
19 Sept. 1820. Lewes. Sarah Herriott. £1.
2 Oct. 1820. Eastbourne. John Ticehurst. 21 miles. £1 15s 9d.
3 Oct. 1820. Hailsham. William Hollands. 14 miles. £1 10s 6d.
28 Oct. 1820. Newick. George Scott. 8 miles. £1 6s.

1 Nov. 1820. Brighton. John Howell. 8 miles. £1 6s.
3 Nov. 1820. Chailey. Allen Anscombe. 7 miles. £1 5s 3d.[2]
7 Nov. 1820. Ringmer. John Tidey. 4 miles. £1 3s.
8 Nov. 1820. Cuckfield. Henrietta Curties. 14 miles. £1 10s 6d.
18 Nov. 1820. Westmeston. Caleb Bax. 6 miles. £1 4s 6d.
20 Nov. 1820. Horsted Keynes. Charity Comber. 14 miles. £1 10s 6d.
21 Nov. 1820. East Grinstead. Edward Turley. 21 miles. £1 15s 9d.
29 Nov. 1820. Ringmer. James Goldsmith. 7 miles. £1 5s 3d.
9 Dec. 1820. Rottingdean. Unknown person. 8 miles. £1 6s.
10 Dec. 1820. Rottingdean. Another unknown person. 8 miles. £1 6s.
13 Dec. 1820. Rodmell. New-born infant male child. 4 miles. £1 3s.
16 Dec. 1820. The extremity of Uckfield. Thomas Richardson. 10 miles. £1 7s 6d.
18 Dec. 1820. Lewes House of Correction. Thomas Hills. £1.
19 Dec. 1820. East Dean. Unknown man.[3] 18 miles. £1 13s 6d.
31 Dec. 1820. East Grinstead. Richard Turley. 21 miles. £1 15s 9d.
Total £46 12s 9d; allowed at Epiphany sessions 1821. [QR/E 766, no 89]

1 MS *Haughton*, possibly a miscopying of *Hanglton*. The journey to Hangleton was 12 miles in **208**.
2 Cf. **383**.
3 *A sailor, found drowned* in PAR 304/1/5/1.

200 4 Jan. 1821. Lewes. Mary Ewens. £1.
4 Jan. 1821. Henfield. Francis Blackamore. 17 miles. £1 12s 9d.
5 Jan. 1821. Plumpton. Henry Peters. 6 miles. £1 4s 6d.
15 Jan. 1821. Ringmer. John Payne. 3 miles. £1 2s 3d.
31 Jan. 1821. Fletching. Joseph Coomber. 10 miles. £1 7s 6d.
1 Feb. 1821. Portslade. James Godley. 12 miles. £1 9s.
7 Feb. 1821. Balcombe. Sarah Tester. 18 miles. £1 13s 6d.
17 Feb. 1821. Lewes House of Correction. William Pillido. £1.
17 Feb. 1821. Brighton. Joseph Dean. 8 miles. £1 6s.
21 Feb. 1821. Plumpton. William Ashdowne. 6 miles. £1 4s 6d.
8 Mar. 1821. Rottingdean. Thomas Prudence. 8 miles. £1 6s.
10 Mar. 1821. Glynde. Thomas Savage. 3 miles. £1 2s 3d.
17 Mar. 1821. Lewes. Thomas Nye. £1.
20 Mar. 1821. Keymer. Elizabeth Tobit. 10 miles. £1 7s 6d.
29 Mar. 1821. East Grinstead. William Ward. 21 miles. £1 15s 9d.
30 Mar. 1821. Hailsham. Caroline Garnham. 14 miles. £1 10s 6d.
2 Apr. 1821. Portslade. New-born infant. 12 miles. £1 9s.
12 Apr. 1821. ?Fulking.[1] Ann Davey. 15 miles. £1 11s 3d.
12 Apr. 1821. ?Fulking.[1] Maria Davey. £1.
23 Apr. 1821. Hove. Samuel Paine. 10 miles. £1 7s 6d.
23 Apr. 1821. Brighton. Amelia Ellis. 8 miles. £1 6s.
24 Apr. 1821. Lewes. George Baker. £1.
28 Apr. 1821. Hailsham. Henry Hollands. 14 miles. £1 10s 6d.
2 May 1821. West Hoathly. Edward Virgoe. 21 miles. £1 15s 9d.
5 May 1821. Brighton. Peter Short. 8 miles. £1 6s.
6 May 1821. Tarring Neville. Elizabeth Ranger. 8 miles. £1 6s.
7 May 1821. Ringmer. William Hassell. 4 miles. £1 3s.
9 May 1821. Eastbourne. John Hunt. 16 miles. £1 12s.

16 May 1821. Thorns Common, Waldron. Stephen Hope. 14 miles. £1 10s 6d.
17 May 1821. Maresfield. John Townsend. 10 miles. £1 7s 6d.
17 May 1821. Hamsey. John Pannett. 2 miles. £1 1s 6d.
18 May 1821. Ringmer. James Spinks. 3 miles. £1 2s 3d.
20 May 1821. Nutley. Thomas Avis. 14 miles. £1 10s 6d.
24 May 1821. Buxted. Catherine Delves. 10 miles. £1 7s 6d.
31 May 1821. Chailey. Thomas Marchant. 7 miles. £1 5s 3d.
31 May 1821. Brighton. Martha Cox. 8 miles. £1 6s.
4 June 1821. Ringmer. Catherine Hoad. 3 miles. £1 2s 3d.
9 June 1821. Worth. Daniel Batchelor. 24 miles. £1 18s.
13 June 1821. Little Horsted. Thomas Wicks. 7 miles. £1 5s 3d.
13 June 1821. Brighton. William Pumphrey. 8 miles. £1 6s.
23 June 1821. Rotherfield. Eliza Bellingham. 18 miles. £1 13s 6d.
25 June 1821. Brighton. Matthew Coombs. 8 miles. £1 6s.
26 June 1821. Brighton. John Gear. 8 miles. £1 6s.
28 June 1821. Brighton. Richard Gillham. 8 miles. £1 6s.
30 June 1821. Brighton. John Gregory. 8 miles. £1 6s.
1 July 1821. Rotherfield. John Morgan. 18 miles. £1 13s 6d.
4 July 1821. Brighton. William Belchambers. 8 miles. £1 6s.
8 July 1821. Beddingham. Samuel Ticehurst. 3 miles. £1 2s 3d.
12 July 1821. Brighton. John O'Ryan. 8 miles. £1 6s.
Total £65 16s 9d; allowed at Midsummer sessions 1821. [QR/E 768]

1 MS *Faulklin*. The journey to Fulking was 15 miles in **201**.

201 16 July 1821. Mayfield. David Balcombe. 18 miles. £1 13s 6d.
17 July 1821. Mayfield. Thomas Page. 18 miles. £1 13s 6d.
25 July 1821. Brighton. Samuel French. 8 miles. £1 6s.
26 July 1821. Eastbourne. Unknown man.[1] 16 miles. £1 12s.
28 July 1821. Slaugham. William Standen. 19 miles. £1 14s 3d.
7 Aug. 1821. Nutley. Unknown man.[2] 14 miles. £1 10s 6d.
8 Aug. 1821. Berwick. Samuel Miller. 8 miles. £1 6s.
8 Aug. 1821. Eastbourne. Richard Lock. 16 miles. £1 12s.
11 Aug. 1821. Lindfield. William Bish. 12 miles. £1 9s.
14 Aug. 1821. Patcham. James Gander. 12 miles. £1 9s.
15 Aug. 1821. Fulking. George Stevens. 15 miles. £1 11s 3d.
17 Aug. 1821. Hailsham. Reuben Reynolds. 14 miles. £1 10s 6d.
18 Aug. 1821. Kingston by Sea. John Hunt. 14 miles. £1 10s 6d.
20 Aug. 1821. Brighton. Mary Sutherland. 8 miles. £1 6s.
23 Aug. 1821. Eastbourne. Edward Wymark. 16 miles. £1 12s.
23 Aug. 1821. Brighton. John Howell. 8 miles. £1 6s.
27 Aug. 1821. Pyecombe. John Groves. 14 miles. £1 10s 6d.
27 Aug. 1821. Lewes House of Correction. John Barry. £1.
28 Aug. 1821. Mayfield. James Turner. 18 miles. £1 13s 6d.
28 Aug. 1821. Hamsey. William Parsons. 3 miles. £1 2s 3d.
3 Sept. 1821. Brighton. [*blank*] Sproule.[3] 8 miles. £1 6s.
21 Sept. 1821. Felbridge in East Grinstead. Nanny Southey. 23 miles. £1 17s 3d.
22 Sept. 1821. Brighton. James Hills. 8 miles. £1 6s.
25 Sept. 1821. Frant. Thomas Martin. 23 miles. £1 17s 3d.

27 Sept. 1821. Rottingdean. Matthew Gibson. 8 miles. £1 6s.
6 Oct. 1821. Arlington. William Child. 12 miles. £1 9s.
20 Oct. 1821. Brighton. Henry Bulbeck. 8 miles. £1 6s.
30 Oct. 1821. East Grinstead. Samuel Webster Shillito. 21 miles. £1 15s 9d.
1 Nov. 1821. East Grinstead. William Thorpe. 21 miles. £1 15s 9d.
7 Nov. 1821. Brighton. George Looms. 8 miles. £1 6s.
23 Nov. 1821. Cuckfield. James Gorringe. 14 miles. £1 10s 6d.
29 Nov. 1821. Chailey. George Flemming. 7 miles. £1 5s 3d.
8 Dec. 1821. Brighton. Henry Haiselgrove. 8 miles. £1 6s.
17 Dec. 1821. Waldron. John Deacon. 12 miles. £1 9s.
18 Dec. 1821. West Hoathly. Richard Pilbeam. 21 miles. £1 15s 9d.
23 Dec. 1821. Hartfield. Mary Piper. 21 miles. £1 15s 9d.
26 Dec. 1821. Eastbourne. Unknown man.[4] 16 miles. £1 12s.
29 Dec. 1821. Brighton. [*blank*] Clayton.[5] 8 miles. £1 6s.
30 Dec. 1821. Hamsey. Walter Wells. 3 miles. £1 2s 3d.
Total £57 15s 9d; allowed at Epiphany sessions 1822. [QR/E 770, no 68]

1 Possibly George Baker, aged 30, buried at Eastbourne 27 July: PAR 309/1/5/1.
2 *Thomas Funnell, a traveller aged 30 or 40, who had come from Canterbury, found dead in a stable at the inn at Nutley and buried at Maresfield 8 Aug.*: PAR 420/1/5/1.
3 *Robert Sproule, aged 52, of Grove Cottage, Little Chelsea, Middlesex* in PAR 255/1/5/2.
4 Possibly George Wood, aged 50, buried at Eastbourne 27 Dec.: PAR 309/1/5/1.
5 *Elizabeth Clayton, aged 50, of Everton Place, Brighton* in PAR 255/1/5/2.

202 2 Feb. 1822. Hailsham. [*blank*] Boon. 14 miles. £1 10s 6d.
2 Feb. 1822. Brighton. Eliza Poulton. 8 miles. £1 6s.
4 Feb. 1822. Langney Point, Eastbourne. Francis Smith. 20 miles. £1 15s.[1]
6 Feb. 1822. Chailey. Henry Teague. 8 miles. £1 6s.
14 Feb. 1822. Brighton. John Sawyers. 8 miles. £1 6s.
14 Feb. 1822. Southwick. George Cheesman. 12 miles. £1 9s.
18 Feb. 1822. Framfield. Louisa Johnson. 10 miles. £1 7s 6d.
19 Feb. 1822. Southwick. Thomas Bartlett. 12 miles. £1 9s.
14 Mar. 1822. Lewes House of Correction. Benjamin Bones. £1.
15 Mar. 1822. Fletching. Richard Allen. 10 miles. £1 7s 6d.
16 Mar. 1822. Slaugham. Henry Pierce. 19 miles. £1 14s 3d.
30 Mar. 1822. Piddinghoe. Henry Copper. 8 miles. £1 6s.
13 Apr. 1822. Rottingdean. Charles Briggs. 8 miles. £1 6s.
13 Apr. 1822. Rottingdean. John Knowles. £1.
17 Apr. 1822. Brighton. Thomas Blamey. 8 miles. £1 6s.
21 Apr. 1822. Hartfield. James Downard. 20 miles. £1 15s.
26 Apr. 1822. Brighton. Thomas Potts. 8 miles. £1 6s.
27 Apr. 1822. East Grinstead. John Dean. 21 miles. £1 15s 9d.
4 May 1822. Brighton. Thomas Lelliott.[2] [8 miles.] £1 6s.[3]
6 May 1822. Eastwood[4] in Buxted. Thomas Hammond. 12 miles. £1 9s.
9 May 1822. Frant. George West. 22 miles. £1 16s 6d.
20 May 1822. Holywell Cliff, Eastbourne. John Brand. 17 miles. £1 12s 9d.
21 May 1822. Brighton. John Harman. 8 miles. £1 6s.
1 June 1822. Brighton. William Jones. 8 miles. £1 6s.
2 June 1822. Southbourne. Joseph Browne. 17 miles. £1 12s 9d.
18 June 1822. Hailsham. David Foster. 14 miles. £1 10s 6d.

19 June 1822. Beddingham. Benjamin Moore. 3 miles. £1 2s 3d.
27 June 1822. Hove. Unknown man.[5] 10 miles. £1 7s 6d.
28 June 1822. Cuckfield. William Cox. 14 miles. £1 10s 6d.
1 July 1822. Lewes. Charles Hackman. £1.
6 July 1822. Bishopstone. Charles Barber. 10 miles. £1 7s 6d.
17 July 1822. Balcombe. George Gatford. 18 miles. £1 13s 6d.
18 July 1822. Cuckfield. Joseph Stocks. 14 miles. £1 10s 6d.
18 July 1822. New Shoreham. John Richards. 14 miles. £1 10s 6d.
Total £48 7s 3d; allowed at Midsummer sessions 1822. [QR/E 772]

1 Cf. *SCM*, X, 578.
2 *Henry Lelliott of Egremont Street, Brighton, aged 22* in PAR 255/1/5/2.
3 Cf. **384**
4 ?Recte *Waste Wood.*
5 *An unknown man, apparently a sailor, found drowned on the beach* in PAR 386/1/5/1.

203 22 July 1822. Frant. James Stockdale. 22 miles. £1 16s 6d.
31 July 1822. Birling Gap, East Dean. Joseph Martin. 19 miles. £1 14s 3d.
2 Aug. 1822. Brighton. Elizabeth Adams. 8 miles. £1 6s.
3 Aug. 1822. Birling Gap. William Williams. 19 miles. £1 14s 3d.
15 Aug. 1822. Brighton. Ann Abrahams. 8 miles. £1 6s.
18 Aug. 1822. Eastbourne. Joseph Morris. 16 miles. £1 12s.
27 Aug. 1822. Brighton. Isaac Steele. 8 miles. £1 6s.
2 Sept. 1822. Brighton. Frances Akehurst. 8 miles. £1 6s.
7 Sept. 1822. Pyecombe. Robert Smithurst. 13 miles. £1 9s 9d.
9 Sept. 1822. South Malling. Joseph Jefferies. 1 mile. £1 0s 9d.
23 Sept. 1822. Brighton. [*blank*] Fauconiere. 8 miles. £1 6s.
26 Sept. 1822. Rottingdean. William Holmes. 8 miles. £1 6s.
3 Oct. 1822. Brighton. Caroline Hedgegrove. 8 miles. £1 6s.
5 Oct. 1822. Patcham. Joseph Cutress. 11 miles. £1 8s 3d.
5 Oct. 1822. Brighton. Thomas Washer. 8 miles. £1 6s.
15 Oct. 1822. Bolney in Cuckfield. Henry Chatfield. 16 miles. £1 12s.
21 Oct. 1822. Chailey. William Brooks. 8 miles. £1 8s.
22 Oct. 1822. Brighton. Robert Crathorne. 8 miles. £1 6s.
31 Oct. 1822. Slaugham. Elizabeth Arnold. 19 miles. £1 14s 3d.
4 Nov. 1822. Rodmell. Hannah Funnell. 3 miles. £1 2s 3d.
7 Nov. 1822. Fletching. Sarah Smith. 12 miles. £1 9s.
8 Nov. 1822. Hove. William Groves. 10 miles. £1 7s 6d.
14 Nov. 1822. Preston. New-born child. 10 miles. £1 7s 6d.
16 Nov. 1822. Newhaven. Richard Bird. 8 miles. £1 6s.
20 Nov. 1822. Brighton. Thomas Henry Hudson. 8 miles. £1 6s.
20 Nov. 1822. Sayers Common, Hurstpierpoint. Sarah Sayers. 14 miles. £1 10s 6d.
21 Nov. 1822. Eastbourne. Thomas Walkins.[1] 16 miles. £1 12s.
26 Nov. 1822. Heathfield. John Miller. 17 miles. £1 12s 9d.
2 Dec. 1822. Hurstpierpoint. Philadelphia Davery.[2] 11 miles. £1 8s 3d.
16 Dec. 1822. Southover. John Carter. 1 mile. £1 0s 9d.
20 Dec. 1822. Horsted Keynes. Ann Isted. 14 miles. £1 10s 6d.
21 Dec. 1822. Nutley. Sarah Ann Yeomans. 14 miles. £1 10s 6d.
24 Dec. 1822. Preston. New-born infant. 10 miles. £1 7s 6d.
26 Dec. 1822. Brighton. Friend Measor. 8 miles. £1 6s.

26 Dec. 1822. Lindfield. Martha Wileman. 12 miles. £1 9s.
27 Dec. 1822. Ripe. John Waters. 8 miles. £1 6s.
28 Dec. 1822. Hove. John King. 10 miles. £1 7s 6d.
28 Dec. 1822. Hove. James King. £1.
Total £53 1s 6d; allowed at Epiphany sessions 1823. [QR/E 774]

1 *Thomas Wilkins, aged 13* in PAR 309/1/5/1.
2 *Philadelphia Davey, aged 30* in Ep. II/16/116B.

204 9 Jan. 1823. Mayfield. William Marchant. 18 miles. £1 13s 6d.
13 Jan. 1823. Cliffe. Ann Pilfold. £1.
13 Jan. 1823. Wivelsfield. Edward Carter. 10 miles. £1 7s 6d.
16 Jan. 1823. Buxted. John Curd. 10 miles. £1 7s 6d.
17 Jan. 1823. Brighton. Charles Archer. 8 miles. £1 6s.
17 Jan. 1823. New Shoreham. William Munn. 14 miles. £1 10s 6d.
18 Jan. 1823. Alciston. Elizabeth Deadman. 8 miles. £1 6s.
28 Jan. 1823. East Grinstead. Sarah Todman. 21 miles. £1 15s 9d.
29 Jan. 1823. Brighton. Thomas Primer. 8 miles. £1 6s.
6 Feb. 1823. Lamberhurst. John Gibbs. 28 miles. £2 1s.
7 Feb. 1823. [Lewes] House of Correction. John Pollard. £1.
8 Feb. 1823. Hurstpierpoint. Elizabeth Bishop. 11 miles. £1 8s 3d.
13 Feb. 1823. Ditchling. Charles Scrase. 7 miles. £1 5s 3d.
17 Feb. 1823. Hamsey. Newly-born male infant. 3 miles. £1 2s 3d.
20 Feb. 1823. Worth. James Gorringe. 24 miles. £1 18s.
21 Feb. 1823. Hartfield. John Patching. 21 miles. £1 15s 9d.
22 Feb. 1823. [Lewes] House of Correction. James Blake. £1.
24 Feb. 1823. Rottingdean. Edward Williams. 8 miles. £1 6s.
28 Feb. 1823. Horsted Keynes. John Taylor. 14 miles. £1 10s 6d.
8 Mar. 1823. [Lewes] House of Correction. John Martin. £1.
10 Mar. 1823. Westmeston. Mary Ann Howell. 7 miles. £1 5s 3d.
12 Mar. 1823. [Lewes] House of Correction. George Ede. £1.
13 Mar. 1823. Bishopstone. Thomas Woollgar. 10 miles. £1 7s 6d.
22 Mar. 1823. Brighton. William Thomas. 8 miles. £1 6s.
23 Mar. 1823. Southbourne. William Hyde. 16 miles. £1 12s.
31 Mar. 1823. Patcham. John Juden. 11 miles. £1 8s 3d.
31 Mar. 1823. Old Tye Common, Hartfield. Elizabeth Awcock. 23 miles. £1 17s 9d.[1]
3 Apr. 1823. Brighton. William Bassett. 8 miles. £1 6s.
7 Apr. 1823. Brighton. James Smith. 8 miles. £1 6s.[2]
14 Apr. 1823. Willingdon. Henry Hall. 13 miles. £1 9s 9d.
16 Apr. 1823. Patcham. Mary Still. 11 miles. £1 8s 3d.
23 Apr. 1823. Brighton. Thomas Hill. 8 miles. £1 6s.
26 Apr. 1823. Hailsham. John Rich. 14 miles. £1 10s 6d.
7 May 1823. Brighton. Samuel Barton. 8 miles. £1 6s.
9 May 1823. Newhaven. Unknown man.[3] 8 miles. £1 6s.
9 May 1823. Lewes. Maria Chapman. £1.
22 May 1823. Hurstpierpoint. John Webber. 11 miles. £1 8s 3d.
29 May 1823. Eastbourne. William Barnard. 15 miles. £1 11s 3d.
31 May 1823. Brighton. Mary Hethersay. 8 miles. £1 6s.
1 June 1823. Uckfield. New-born female infant. 8 miles. £1 6s.

11 June 1823. Bridgwick in South Malling. Ann Gadd. 2 miles. £1 1s 6d.
17 June 1823. Brighton. Martha Richardson. 8 miles. £1 6s.
4 July 1823. Balcombe. Unknown man.[4] 19 miles. £1 14s 3d.
9 July 1823. Newhaven. Charles Geer. 8 miles. £1 6s.
14 July 1823. Lewes House of Correction. James Millar. £1.
15 July 1823. Glynde. Thomas Norman. 4 miles. £1 3s.
15 July 1823. Hartfield. Ann Simmons. 21 miles. £1 15s 9d.
Total £64 13s; allowed at Midsummer sessions 1823. [QR/E 776]

1 Recte *£1 17s 3d.* The extra 6d was included in the bill total and allowed.
2 Cf. **385**.
3 *William Ely of Faversham, Kent, supposed age 21, found drowned and buried 11 May under the coroner's warrant* in PAR 426/1/5/1.
4 *A traveller, name unknown* in Par. 234/1/5/1.

205 [*blank* July] 1823. Brighton. William Ham.[1] 8 miles. £1 6s.
27 [July] 1823. Brighton. William Reeves. 8 miles. £1 6s.
30 [July] 1823. Mayfield. Thomas Gaston. 18 miles. £1 13s 6d.
9 Aug. 1823. Wivelsfield. Samuel Willis. 10 miles. 7s 6d.
16 Aug. 1823. East Grinstead. John Kimber. 21 miles. £1 15s 9d.
25 Aug. 1823. Brighton. John Marshall. 8 miles. £1 6s.
1 Sept. 1823. Rottingdean. John Hollands. 8 miles. £1 6s.
4 Sept. 1823. Brighton. Rose Felix Le Gross. 8 miles. £1 6s.
6 Sept. 1823. Uckfield. Joseph Brooker. 8 miles. £1 6s.
9 Sept. 1823. Brighton. Eleanor Hensford.[2] 8 miles. £1 6s.
13 Sept. 1823. Brighton. John Goddard. 8 miles. £1 6s.
15 Sept. 1823. Brighton. John Edward Tucker. 8 miles. £1 6s.
22 Sept. 1823. Ripe. John Piper. 8 miles. £1 6s.
23 Sept. 1823. Rottingdean. Elizabeth Belton. 8 miles. £1 6s.
25 Sept. 1823. Hamsey. Mary Ann Wilson. 3 miles. £1 2s 3d.
29 Sept. 1823. Hailsham Common. William Dennis. 15 miles. £1 11s 3d.
30 Sept. 1823. Buxted Wood. Ann Hardgrove. 12 miles. £1 9s.
[*Date omitted.*] Brighton. Mary Shaw. 8 miles. £1 6s.
7 Oct. 1823. Newhouse Farm, Hurstpierpoint. Unknown man. 14 miles. £1 10s 6d.
14 Oct. 1823. Frant. Thomas Dibley. 22 miles. £1 16s 6d.
23 Oct. 1823. Bolney in Cuckfield. James Field. 18 miles. £1 13s 6d.
30 Oct. 1823. Hartfield. David Wicks. 20 miles. £1 15s.
31 Oct. 1823. Worth. Margaret Watkins. 24 miles. £1 18s.
17 Nov. 1823. Ditchling Common. Daniel Foord. 10 miles. £1 7s 6d.
1 Dec. 1823. Old Shoreham. Joseph Evans. 14 miles. £1 10s 6d.
3 Dec. 1823. Beachy Head. Unknown man. 17 miles. £1 12s 9d.
5 Dec. 1823. Withyham. William Taylor. 17 miles. £1 12s 9d.
6 Dec. 1823. Brighton. Unknown man.[3] 8 miles. £1 6s.
[*Date omitted.*] Friston. 2 unknown men.[4] 17 miles. £2 12s 9d.
13 Dec. 1823. Friston. Unknown man.[4] 17 miles. £1 12s 9d.
14 Dec. 1823. Birling Gap. 2 unknown men. 19 miles. £2 14s 3d.
18 Dec. 1823. Bishopstone. Thomas Barriss. 10 miles. £1 7s 6d.
20 Dec. 1823. Uckfield. John King. 8 miles. £1 6s.
27 Dec. 1823. Newhaven. James Banks. 8 miles. £1 6s.
28 Dec. 1823. Newhaven. John Medhurst. 8 miles. £1 6s.

30 Dec. 1823. Alciston. William Harvey. 8 miles. £1 6s.
31 Dec. 1823. Birling Gap. Unknown man. 19 miles. £1 14s 3d.
Total £54 19s 9d;[5] allowed at Epiphany sessions 1824. [QR/E 778]

1 *William Ham of Barracks, Church Street, Brighton, aged 36, buried 26 July* in PAR 255/1/5/3.
2 *Maria Eleanor Hensford* in PAR 255/1/5/3.
3 *An unknown man found drowned* in PAR 255/1/5/3.
4 *Sailors found drowned* in PAR 345/1/5/1.
5 Changed from *£55 19s 9d,* presumably when it was realized that only the mileage was charged for the inquest of 9 Aug.

206 3 Jan. 1824. Framfield. Jane Cronck. 10 miles. £1 7s 6d.
12 Jan. 1824. Beachy Head. James How. 17 miles. £1 12s 9d.
15 Jan. 1824. Westup Farm, Cuckfield. John Agate. 17 miles. £1 12s 9d.
19 Jan. 1824. Alciston. New-born infant. 7 miles. £1 5s 3d.
21 Jan. 1824. Laughton. Ann Hyland. 6 miles. £1 4s 6d.
28 Jan. 1824. Mayfield. Henry Tickner. 18 miles. £1 13s 6d.
7 Feb. 1824. Lewes. Archibald Lee. £1.
10 Feb. 1824. Brighton. William Gorringe. 8 miles. £1 6s.
[*Date omitted.*] Brighton. William Smith. 8 miles. £1 6s.
[*Date omitted.*] Brighton. John Jail. 8 miles. £1 6s.
[*Date omitted.*] Brighton. John Maslin. 8 miles. £1 6s.
[*Date omitted.*] Brighton. John Rattey. 8 miles. £1 6s.
16 Feb. 1824. West Dean. Unknown man.[1] 14 miles. £1 10s 6d.
17 Feb. 1824. East Grinstead. Martha Ann Sewell. 21 miles. £1 15s 9d.[2]
23 Feb. 1824. Brighton. John Tuppen. 8 miles. £1 6s.
24 Feb. 1824. Brighton. Thomas Harmer. 8 miles. £1 6s.
10 Mar. 1824. Lewes House of Correction. James Mucklejohn. £1.
18 Mar. 1824. Brighton. Thomas James. 8 miles. £1 6s.
3 Apr. 1824. Isfield. James Cooter Pollard. 8 miles. £1 6s.
8 Apr. 1824. Lewes House of Correction. John Riddles. £1.
17 Apr. 1824. Lewes House of Correction. William Parks. £1.
24 Apr. 1824. Brighton. John Parsons. 8 miles. £1 6s.
[*Date omitted.*] Brighton. Charles Parsons. 8 miles. £1 6s.
[*Date omitted.*] Brighton. Samuel Heather. 8 miles. £1 6s.
1 May 1824. Rottingdean. Thomas Martin. 8 miles. £1 6s.
3 May 1824. Chalvington. Elizabeth Jones. 9 miles. £1 6s 9d.
10 May 1824. Birling Gap. James Powell. 19 miles. £1 14s 3d.
17 May 1824. East Grinstead. John Humphrey. 21 miles. £1 15s 9d.
24 May 1824. Cliffe. Catherine Hughes. 1 mile. £1 0s 9d.
29 May 1824. Lewes House of Correction. John Williams. £1.
29 May 1824. Rottingdean. Thomas Wadham. 8 miles. £1 6s.
29 May 1824. Brighton. William Leggatt. 8 miles. £1 6s.
11 June 1824. Hurstpierpoint. William Daynes. 11 miles. £1 8s 3d.
15 June 1824. Brighton. Grace Gibson. 8 miles. £1 6s.
16 June 1824. Henfield. Jane Thompsett. 16 miles. £1 12s.
20 June 1824. Brighton. George Carter. 8 miles. £1 6s.
20 June 1824. Brighton. Richard Thomas. 8 miles. £1 6s.
21 June 1824. Brighton. Ann Cooper. 8 miles. £1 6s.
Total £50 14s 3d; allowed at Midsummer sessions 1824. [QR/E 780]

1 *An unknown sailor* in PAR 305/1/5/1.
2 Cf. **386**.

207 17 July 1824. Cuckfield. Philip Jenner. 14 miles. £1 10s 6d.
29 July 1824. Brighton. Thomas Shackleford. 8 miles. £1 6s.
5 Aug. 1824. Hove. Thomas King. 9 miles. £1 6s 9d.
12 Aug. 1824. Rottingdean. Unknown man. 8 miles. £1 6s.
20 Aug. 1824. Patcham. William Langridge. 10 miles. £1 7s 6d.[1]
31 Aug. 1824. West Hoathly. William Tester. 20 miles. £1 15s.
1 Sept. 1824. New Shoreham. James Steer. 16 miles. £1 12s.
7 Sept. 1824. South Malling. Ellen Smith. 2 miles. £1 1s 6d.
10 Sept. 1824. Warninglid in Slaugham. John Saunders. 20 miles. £1 15s.
15 Sept. 1824. Brighton. James Blakely. 8 miles. £1 6s.
19 Sept. 1824. Clayton. Thomas Deserell.[2] 12 miles. £1 9s.
23 Sept. 1824. Pounsley Green, Framfield. Frances Gurr. 11 miles. £1 8s 3d.
29 Sept. 1824. The Burlington Arms, Brighton. Frances Herriott. 9 miles. £1 6s 9d.
29 Sept. 1824. Brighton. Ann Martin. 8 miles. £1 6s.
4 Oct. 1824. Birling Gap. Unknown man. 19 miles. £1 14s 3d.
5 Oct. 1824. The Burlington Arms, Brighton. Thomas Dutton. 9 miles. £1 6s 9d.
21 Oct. 1824. East Grinstead. Mary Goodwin. 21 miles. £1 15s 9d.
[*Date omitted.*] East Grinstead. Charles Goodwin. 21 miles. £1 15s 9d.
30 Oct. 1824. South Malling. Richard Brooks. 2 miles. £1 1s 6d.[3]
3 Nov. 1824. St John's Common, Keymer. Thomas Vokes. 12 miles. £1 9s.
4 Nov. 1824. Beddingham. Matthew Bullman. 3 miles. £1 2s 3d.
[*Date omitted.*] Beddingham. William Munt. 3 miles. £1 2s 3d.
[*Date omitted.*] Beddingham. Richard Bartlett. 3 miles. £1 2s 3d.
[*Date omitted.*] Beddingham. John Richardson. 3 miles. £1 2s 3d.
[*Date omitted.*] Beddingham. Robert Wisdom. 3 miles. £1 2s 3d.
9 Nov. 1824. Lewes. William Lloyd. £1.
14 Nov. 1824. East Grinstead. Frances Sturt. 21 miles. £1 15s 9d.
18 Nov. 1824. Brighton. Mary Ann Maldin. 8 miles. £1 6s.
26 Nov. 1824. Brighton. Jane Slaughter. 8 miles. £1 6s.
8 Dec. 1824. Brighton. James Wilson. 8 miles. £1 6s.
9 Dec. 1824. Maresfield. Elizabeth Heasman. 12 miles. £1 9s.
16 Dec. 1824. Brighton. William Petch. 8 miles. £1 6s.
16 Dec. 1824. Brighton. Joseph Reddall. 8 miles. £1 6s.
20 Dec. 1824. Barcombe. Philip Smith. 4 miles. £1 3s.
27 Dec. 1824. Brighton. Joseph Chapman. 8 miles. £1 6s.
Total £47 14s 3d; allowed at Epiphany sessions 1825. [QR/E 782]

1 Cf. **387**.
2 *Thomas Deverell of 91 Oxford Street, St Marylebone, London, aged 33* in Par. 294/1/5/1.
3 Cf. **388**.

208 17 Jan. 1825. Jevington. Thomas Fuller. 14 miles. £1 10s 6d.
19 Jan. 1825. Bishopstone. William Enjon.[1] 10 miles. £1 7s 6d.
27 Jan. 1825. West Hoathly. Thomas Arnold. 21 miles. £1 15s 9d.
28 Jan. 1825. Brighton. Martha Wilkins. 8 miles. £1 6s.
6 Feb. 1825. Worth. John Fuller sen. 24 miles. £1 18s.
12 Feb. 1825. [Lewes] House of Correction. James Gower. £1.

23 Feb. 1825. Framfield. Samuel Willis. 11 miles. £1 8s 3d.
23 Feb. 1825. Brighton. Alice Maxfield. 8 miles. £1 6s.
8 Mar.1825. Bevendean. Joseph Wellfare. 7 miles. £1 5s 3d.
18 Mar. 1825. Brighton. Harriet Husbands. 8 miles. £1 6s.
19 Mar. 1825. Lewes. George Verrall. £1.
28 Mar. 1825. Brighton. Dorothy Matilda Browning. 8 miles. £1 6s.
9 Apr. 1825. Cousley Wood, Wadhurst. George Clifton. 27 miles. £2 0s 3d.
23 Apr. 1825. Plumpton. Jane Ashdowne. 6 miles. £1 4s 6d.
25 Apr. 1825. Brighton. Elizabeth Spicer. 8 miles. £1 6s.
27 Apr. 1825. Old Shoreham. Henry Henderson. 16 miles. £1 12s.
28 Apr. 1825. Brighton. Thomas Dudman. 8 miles. £1 6s.
4 May 1825. Cliffe. George Beech. £1.
6 May 1825. Isfield. John Parker. 7 miles. £1 5s 3d.
7 May 1825. Ardingly. William Rapley. 19 miles. £1 14s 3d.
23 May 1825. Eastbourne. Michael Desmond. 18 miles. £1 13s 6d.
24 May 1825. Riders Well, South Malling. Charles Wheatley. 4 miles. £1 3s.
25 May 1825. Brighton. Mary Tickner. 8 miles. £1 6s.
26 May 1825. Cliffe. Josiah Nicholls. £1.
1 June 1825. West Hoathly. Sarah Sturt. 21 miles. £1 15s 9d.
4 June 1825. Brighton. Drusilla Barrett. 8 miles. £1 6s.
4 June 1825. Brighton. Robert Smith. 8 miles. £1 6s.
5 June 1825. Framfield. Richard Gasston. 11 miles. £1 8s 3d.
6 June 1825. [Lewes] House of Correction. Mary Faulkener. £1.
17 June 1825. Mayfield. Luke Lades. 18 miles. £1 13s 6d.
18 June 1825. Balcombe. William Wood. 19 miles. £1 14s 3d.
30 June 1825. Brighton. Edward Youens. 8 miles. £1 6s.
30 June 1825. Rottingdean. Nathan Rowland. 8 miles. £1 6s.
2 July 1825. Hangleton. Unknown man. 12 miles. £1 9s.
6 July 1825. Maresfield. Thomas Flemming. 12 miles. £1 9s.
8 July 1825. Worth. Thomas Jeal. 25 miles. £1 18s 9d.
Total £50 12s 6d; allowed at Midsummer sessions 1825. An extra 8s was added on the bill, making £51 0s 6d.[2] [QR/E 784]

1 *William Enyon of the Coast Blockade Service, aged 26* in Ep II/16/19B and PAR 247/1/5/1.
2 The £50 12s 6d was paid to Gwynne as coroner and the 8s for his fees on the conviction of a vagrant: QO/EW 47; QAF 2/1/E9, ff 164v–165.

209 19 July 1825. Hove. Edmunds Peters. 10 miles. £1 7 6d.
19 July 1825. Hove. William Tuppen. 10 miles. £1 7s 6d.
19 July 1825. Hove. George Channon. 10 miles. £1 7s 6d.
20 July 1825. Horsted Keynes. Abraham Sherlock. 14 miles. £1 10s 6d.
[20 July] 1825. Horsted Keynes. Henry Wickens. 14 miles. £1 10s 6d.
[20 July] 1825. Horsted Keynes. Thomas Wickens. 14 miles. £1 10s 6d.
[20 July] 1825. Laughton. James Cox. 8 miles. £1 6s.
[20 July] 1825. Brighton. John Richardson. 8 miles. £1 6s.
21 July 1825. Hove. Charles Dyke. 10 miles. £1 7s 6d.
21 July 1825. Brighton. Nicholas Ward. 8 miles. £1 6s.
22 July 1825. Mayfield. Thomas Button. 18 miles. £1 13s 6d.
25 July 1825. Brighton. Unknown man. 8 miles. £1 6s.
27 July 1825. Rottingdean. William Paine. 8 miles. £1 6s.

29 July 1825. Southbourne. New-born male child. 17 miles. £1 12s 9d.
1 Aug. 1825. Lewes. James Riddat. £1.
3 Aug. 1825. Wadhurst. George Ashby. 24 miles. £1 18s.
3 Aug. 1825. Brighton. Mary Tutt. 8 miles. £1 6s.
4 Aug. 1825. West Hoathly. Henry Nicholas. 19 miles. £1 14s 3d.
10 Aug. 1825. Hove. New-born female child. 10 miles. £1 7s 6d.
10 Aug. 1825. Hove. Johanna Doyle. 10 miles. £1 7s 6d.
16 Aug. 1825. Lewes. Thomas Newnham. £1.
18 Aug. 1825. Eastbourne. William Peckham. 16 miles. £1 12s.
22 Aug. 1825. Lewes. Samuel Dorrington. £1.
25 Aug. 1825. Cousley Wood, Wadhurst. George Baldwin. 26 miles. £1 19s 6d.
29 Aug. 1825. Brighton. John Flemming. 8 miles. £1 6s.
5 Sept. 1825. Worth. William Marten. 24 miles. £1 18s.
10 Sept. 1825. East Chiltington. Eleanor Fielder. 8 miles. £1 6s.
12 Sept. 1825. Brighton. Jacob Idle. 8 miles. £1 6s.
13 Sept. 1825. Chalvington. William Button. 9 miles. £1 6s 9d.
13 Sept. 1825. The Burlington Arms, Brighton. William Heasman. 9 miles. £1 6s 9d.
18 Sept. 1825. Piddinghoe. George Langley. 7 miles. £1 5s 3d.
22 Sept. 1825. Framfield. Stephen Westgate. 10 miles. £1 7s 6d.
24 Sept. 1825. Lewes. Ann Davies. £1.
25 Sept. 1825. The Burlington Arms, Brighton. John Beard. 9 miles. £1 6s 9d.
5 Oct. 1825. Lewes House of Correction. Daniel Short. £1.
5 Oct. 1825. Brighton. Thomas Measor. 8 miles. £1 6s.
8 Oct. 1825. Ringmer. William Clark. 4 miles. £1 3s.
17 Oct. 1825. Lewes. Joseph Coventry Lowdell. £1.
28 Oct. 1825. Uckfield. Ann Fleet. 8 miles. £1 6s.
28 Oct. 1825. Uckfield. New-born female child. 8 miles. £1 6s.
9 Nov. 1825. Southbourne. Henry Holter. 17 miles. £1 12s 9d.
11 Nov. 1825. Brighton. Michael Brigden. 8 miles. £1 6s.
12 Nov. 1825. Mayfield. Robert Woodhams. 18 miles. £1 13s 6d.
12 Nov. 1825. Patcham. Catherine Herriott. 12 miles. £1 9s.
16 Nov. 1825. Brighton. William Parkins. 8 miles. £1 6s.
19 Nov. 1825. Wivelsfield. Elizabeth Budd. 12 miles. £1 9s.
24 Nov. 1825. Brighton. John Markwick. 8 miles. £1 6s.
26 Nov. 1825. Horsted Keynes. Hannah Leopard. 14 miles. £1 10s 6d.
30 Nov. 1825. Brighton. Richard Halloway. 8 miles. £1 6s.
30 Nov. 1825. Portslade. James Streeter. 12 miles. £1 9s.
2 Dec. 1825. Eastbourne. Unknown man. 16 miles. £1 12s.
15 Dec. 1825. Brighton. Mary Ann Lashford. 8 miles. £1 6s.
15 Dec. 1825. Brighton. John Wylie. 8 miles. £1 6s.
22 Dec. 1825. Bassett's Farm, Hartfield. Thomas Elliott. 23 miles. £1 17s 3d.
Total £75 1s 6d; allowed at Epiphany sessions 1826. [QR/E 786]

210 8 Jan. 1826. Sayers Common, Hurstpierpoint. Henry Gander. 14 miles. £1 10s 6d.
9 Jan. 1826. Brighton. John Simmonds. 8 miles. £1 6s.
10 Jan. 1826. Denton. Charles Susans. 8 miles. £1 6s.
10 Jan. 1826. Brighton. Thomas Parish. 8 miles. £1 6s.
11 Jan. 1826. Framfield. Charles Wren. 12 miles. £1 9s.
11 Jan. 1826. Kingston by Sea. Thomas Huntress. 15 miles. £1 11s 3d.

14 Jan. 1826. Buxted Common. Ellen Hope. 13 miles. £1 9s 9d.
19 Jan. 1826. Patcham. William Pescodd. 12 miles. £1 9s.
22 Jan. 1826. East Grinstead. Mary Lynn. 21 miles. £1 15s 9d.
31 Jan. 1826. Frant. Elizabeth Reed. 24 miles. £1 18s.
4 Feb. 1826. Brighton. Robert Shrivell. 8 miles. £1 6s.
6 Feb. 1826. Laughton. Henry Inkpen. 8 miles. £1 6s.
8 Feb. 1826. Brighton. John Mockford. 8 miles. £1 6s.
8 Feb. 1826. The Burlington Arms, Brighton. John Austin. 9 miles. £1 6s 9d.
9 Feb. 1826. Isfield. William Heaver. 8 miles. £1 6s.
9 Feb. 1826. Southbourne. Catherine Murphy. 18 miles. £1 13s 6d.
11 Feb. 1826. Henfield. Thomas Sayers. 17 miles. £1 12s 9d.
16 Feb. 1826. Wadhurst. William Sands. 26 miles. £1 19s 6d.
20 Feb. 1826. Lewes. Thomas Harris. £1.
20 Feb. 1826. Brighton. William Ireland. 8 miles. £1 6s.
3 Mar. 1826. Lamberhurst. [*blank*] Smith. 28 miles. £2 1s.
11 Mar. 1826. Streat. Thomas Ewens. 8 miles. £1 6s.
11 Mar. 1826. Barcombe. Henry Evans. 5 miles. £1 3s 9d.
11 Mar. 1826. Rotherfield. Solomon Catt. 18 miles. £1 13s 6d.
11 Mar. 1826. Rotherfield. William Luxford. 22 miles. £1 16s 6d.
13 Mar. 1826. Southwick. Augustus Hobden. 12 miles. £1 9s.
13 Mar. 1826. Southwick. James Browne. 12 miles. £1 9s.
18 Mar. 1826. Patcham. [*blank*] Hunter, infant. 12 miles. £1 9s.
23 Mar. 1826. Pyecombe. David Standing. 12 miles. £1 9s.
4 Apr. 1826. Brighton. John Hopgood. 8 miles. £1 6s.
4 Apr. 1826. Brighton. William Savery. 8 miles. £1 6s.
6 Apr. 1826. Withyham. Mary Avis. 21 miles. £1 15s 9d.
10 Apr. 1826. Stumblewood Common, Maresfield. Mary Nash. 14 miles. £1 10s 6d.
17 Apr. 1826. Horsted Keynes. Richard Butcher. 14 miles. £1 10s 6d.
24 Apr. 1826. Saltdean. William Harford. 10 miles. £1 7s 6d.
9 May 1826. Mayfield. Mary Page. 19 miles. £1 14s 3d.
10 May 1826. Brighton. Naomi Baker. 8 miles. £1 6s.
16 May 1826. Brighton. Mary Casey. 8 miles. £1 6s.
18 May 1826. Dengate in Rotherfield. William Muddle. 19 miles. £1 14s 3d.
22 May 1826. Keymer. Unknown man. 9 miles. £1 6s 9d.
13 June 1826. Horsted Keynes. Sarah Martin. 14 miles. £1 10s 6d.
15 June 1826. Old Shoreham. Unknown man. 15 miles. £1 11s 3d.
20 June 1826. Lindfield. William Billingshurst. 12 miles. £1 9s.
21 June 1826. Lewes House of Correction. Ellen Conner. £1.
22 June 1826. Patcham. Infant. 12 miles. £1 9s.
28 June 1826. Turners Hill, Worth. William Peskett. 24 miles. £1 18s.
1 July 1826. Rottingdean. Josias Evans. 8 miles. £1 6s.
3 July 1826. East Grinstead. William Edwards. 21 miles. £1 15s 9d.
11 July 1826. Newhaven. Maurice Quirk. 8 miles. £1 6s.
Total £72 9s 6d; allowed at Midsummer sessions 1826. [QR/E 788, no 65]

211 14 July 1826. Brighton. Charlotte Ashburnham Brook. 8 miles. £1 6s.
18 July 1826. Brighton. Robert Bedford. 8 miles. £1 6s.
19 July 1826. Chailey. William Heasman. 9 miles. £1 6s 9d.
24 July 1826. Brighton. John Reason. 8 miles. £1 6s.

26 July 1826. Little Horsted. Ann Gaston. 6 miles. £1 4s 6d.
3 Aug. 1826. Rotherfield. Edward Wilmshurst. 18 miles. £1 13s 6d.
4 Aug. 1826. Herstmonceux. Benjamin Hutchinson. 16 miles. £1 12s.
5 Aug. 1826. Cross in Hand, Waldron. John Dearing. 13 miles. £1 9s 9d.
7 Aug. 1826. Brighton. Thomas Tattersall. 8 miles. £1 6s.
9 Aug. 1826. West Hoathly. Elizabeth Marten. 19 miles. £1 14s 3d.
19 Aug. 1826. Southwick. Edward Elyer. 12 miles. £1 9s.
21 Aug. 1826. Brighton. John Trim. 8 miles. £1 6s.
23 Aug. 1826. Brighton. Isaac Burt. 8 miles. £1 6s.[1]
23 Aug. 1826. Lewes House of Correction. Henry Wood. £1.
1 Sept. 1826. Fletching. Spencer Marryon Wilson. 10 miles. £1 15s, the inquest having been necessarily adjourned.
2 Sept. 1826. Southwick. Michael Sweeney. 12 miles. £1 9s.
4 Sept. 1826. Old Shoreham Bridge. John Lindfield. 15 miles. £1 11s 3d.
7 Sept. 1826. Brighton. Richard Cooper. 8 miles. £1 6s.
12 Sept. 1826. Worth. Elizabeth Clifton. 24 miles. £1 18s.
1 Oct. 1826. Southwick. Ellen Hartnell. 12 miles. £1 9s.
2 Oct. 1826. East Blatchington. Andrew Christian. 12 miles. £1 9s.
6 Oct. 1826. High Hurstwood, Buxted. Margaret Dray. 13 miles. £1 9s 9d.
28 Oct. 1826. Brighton. William Ogburn. 8 miles. £1 6s.
28 Oct. 1826. New Shoreham. James How. 14 miles. £1 10s 6d.
8 Nov. 1826. Chailey. Henry Chatfield. 10 miles. £1 7s 6d.
13 Nov. 1826. Brighton. Susannah Valentine. 8 miles. £1 6s.
14 Nov. 1826. Southbourne. William Tutt. 16 miles. £1 12s.
15 Nov. 1826. Brighton. Joseph Goldsmith. 8 miles. £1 6s.
16 Nov. 1826. Southwick. George Short. 12 miles. £1 9s.
20 Nov. 1826. East Grinstead. James Gander. 21 miles. £1 15s 9d.
21 Nov. 1826. Twineham. William Mason. 17 miles. £1 12s 9d.
22 Nov. 1826. Lewes. Sarah Coleman. £1.
24 Nov. 1826. Newhaven. George Sayer. 8 miles. £1 6s.
2 Dec. 1826. Brighton. Mildred Ann Box. 8 miles. £1 6s.
26 Dec. 1826. East Grinstead. Richard Tyman. 21 miles. £1 15s 9d.
27 Dec. 1826. Isfield. Lydia Winder. 6 miles. £1 4s 6d.
30 Dec. 1826. Hartfield. Hannah Heaver. 22 miles. £1 16s 6d.
Total £53 7s; allowed at Epiphany sessions 1827. [QR/E 790]

1 Cf. **389**.

212 1 Jan. 1827. Cuckfield. Richard Hart. 14 miles. £1 10s 6d.
1 Jan. 1827. South Malling. Charles Hillman. 2 miles. £1 1s 6d.
2 Jan. 1827. Wadhurst. Elizabeth Smith. 25 miles. £1 18s 9d.
4 Jan. 1827. Southwick. William Upperton. 12 miles. £1 9s.
6 Jan. 1827. Blackboys Common, Framfield. Sarah Bristow. 11 miles. £1 8s 3d.
8 Jan. 1827. Lewes House of Correction. Enoch Tomsatt. £1.
27 Jan. 1827. Brighton. Elizabeth Browne. 8 miles. £1 6s.
27 Jan. 1827. Brighton. Female bastard child. 8 miles. £1 6s.
31 Jan. 1827. South Malling. New-born male child. 2 miles. £1 1s 6d.[1]
1 Feb. 1827. Lewes House of Correction. William Johnson. £1.
1 Feb. 1827. East Mascalls Farm, Lindfield. James Stevens. 14 miles. £1 10s 6d.

6 Feb. 1827. New Shoreham. Louisa Coomber. 16 miles. £1 12s.
8 Feb. 1827. Blackboys Common, Framfield. New-born male bastard child. 10 miles. £1 7s 6d.
8 Feb. 1827. Patcham. Richard Marten. 12 miles. £1 9s.
14 Feb. 1827. South Malling. James Page. 2 miles. £1 1s 6d.
15 Feb. 1827. The Meads, Eastbourne. Jane Iggulden. 17 miles. £1 12s 9d.
21 Feb. 1827. Lewes. Elizabeth Farncombe. £1.
21 Feb. 1827. Hartfield. Ruth Borer, widow. 22 miles. £1 16s 6d.
26 Feb. 1827. East Blatchington. William Horsecraft. 12 miles. £1 9s.
28 Feb. 1827. Birling in East Dean. Frances Harriett. 19 miles. £1 14s 3d.
8 Mar. 1827. Southbourne. Horatio Finch. 16 miles. £1 12s.[2]
10 Mar. 1827. Southbourne. Horatio Finch. By adjournment. 16 miles. £1 12s.[2]
17 Mar. 1827. Southbourne. Horatio Finch. By further adjournment. 16 miles. £1 12s.[2]
19 Mar. 1827. Chiddingly. Sophia Dallaway. 10 miles. £1 7s 6d.
13 Mar. 1827. The Pier Head, Newhaven. Unknown man. 9 miles. £1 6s 9d.
17 Mar. 1827. Brighton. Amelia Laycock. 8 miles. £1 6s.
24 Mar. 1827. Sayers Common, Hurstpierpoint. Nicholas Burtenshaw. 15 miles. £1 11s 3d.
7 Apr. 1827. The Battery, Newhaven. William Faulkner. 9 miles. £1 6s 9d.
8 Apr. 1827. Rotherfield. Mary Wickens. 18 miles. £1 13s 6d.
9 Apr. 1827. Southbourne. Elizabeth Maynard. 18 miles. £1 13s 6d.
9 Apr. 1827. Keymer. William Pagden. 12 miles. £1 9s.
14 Apr. 1827. Cooksbridge. Benjamin Squires. 3 miles. £1 2s 3d.
14 Apr. 1827. Kemp Town, Brighton. Edmund Henry. 10 miles. £1 7s 6d.
24 Apr. 1827. Hurstpierpoint. Sarah Hider. 12 miles. £1 9s.
28 Apr. 1827. Brighton. Unknown man. 8 miles. £1 6s.
3 May 1827. Blackham Common, Withyham. Edward Mellish. 24 miles. £1 18s.
3 May 1827. Blackham Common, Withyham. John Mellish. 24 miles. £1 18s.
5 May 1827. Southwick. James Young. 12 miles. £1 9s.
9 May 1827. Brighton. William Pumphrey. 8 miles. £1 6s.
12 May 1827. Horsted Keynes. Ann Cook. 14 miles. £1 10s 6d.
17 May 1827. Brighton. John Pocknee. 8 miles. £1 6s.
21 May 1827. Eastbourne. James Downing. 17 miles. £1 12s 9d.
23 May 1827. Waldron. Henry Jarvis. 12 miles. £1 9s.
28 May 1827. Beachy Head. William Hewitt. 19 miles. £1 14s 3d.
29 May 1827. Preston. John Lawrence. 9 miles. £1 6s 9d.
30 May 1827. Mayfield. Male bastard child. 18 miles. £1 13s 6d.
2 June 1827. Piddinghoe. Thomas Camfield. 7 miles. £1 5s 3d.
8 June 1827. Ringmer. Elizabeth Williams. 4 miles. £1 3s.
9 June 1827. Fletching Poorhouse. Peter Bryant. 12 miles. £1 9s.
12 June 1827. Brighton. Elizabeth Johns. 8 miles. £1 6s.
17 June 1827. Brighton. Elizabeth Knell. 8 miles. £1 6s.
19 June 1827. Black Rock, Rottingdean. Unknown man. 10 miles. £1 7s 6d.
25 June 1827. Lewes. Simeon Winch. £1.
2 July 1827. The County Oak, Crawley. William Godsmark. 26 miles. £1 19s 6d.
3 July 1827. West Hoathly. Sarah Johnson. 20 miles. £1 15s.
4 July 1827. Barcombe. John Turner. 4 miles. £1 3s.
4 July 1827. Albourne. James Mills. 12 miles. £1 9s.
8 July 1827. Hove. Emily Tanner. 10 miles. £1 7s 6d.

Total £83 4s; allowed at Midsummer sessions 1827. [QR/E 792]

1 Cf. **390**.
2 Cf. **391**.

213 14 July 1827. Brighton. Thomas Hayler. 8 miles. £1 6s.
15 July 1827. East Langney in Willingdon. Unknown man. 18 miles. £1 13s 6d.
26 July 1827. Dengate in Fletching. John Butler. 13 miles. £1 9s 9d.
30 July 1827. Newhaven. Abraham Wood. 8 miles. £1 6s.
1 Aug. 1827. Brighton. Elizabeth Parham. 8 miles. £1 6s.
2 Aug. 1827. South Malling. Samuel Elliott. 2 miles. £1 1s 6d.
5 Aug. 1827. Eastbourne. Joseph Spiller. 15 miles. £1 11s 3d.
6 Aug. 1827. Plumpton. William Knight. 6 miles. £1 4s 6d.
8 Aug. 1827. [Lewes] House of Correction. William Stapley. £1.
25 Aug. 1827. Hove. John Hills. 10 miles. £1 7s 6d.
28 Aug. 1827. Black Rock. Richard Beard. 10 miles. £1 7s 6d.
3 Sept. 1827. Brighton. Wilhelmina Parr. 8 miles. £1 6s.
15 Sept. 1827. Brighton. Thomas Holden. 8 miles. £1 6s.
7 Oct. 1827. Brighton. Dominic O'Connor. 8 miles. £1 6s.
10 Oct. 1827. Chiddingly. Charlotte Townshend. 8 miles. £1 6s.
15 Oct. 1827. Wadhurst. John Burgess. 24 miles. £1 18s.
15 Oct. 1827. Brighton. James Weston. 8 miles. £1 6s.
18 Oct. 1827. Newhaven. James McKenzie. 8 miles. £1 6s.
18 Oct. 1827. Brighton. James Fleet. 8 miles. £1 6s.
22 Oct. 1827. Turk's Farm, Mayfield. Thomas Wood. 21 miles. £1 15s 9d.
24 Oct. 1827. Portslade. Unknown man. 12 miles. £1 9s.
27 Oct. 1827. Buxted. Lucy Ware. 10 miles. £1 7s 6d.
1 Nov. 1827. East Hoathly. Jane Durrant. 8 miles. £1 6s.
5 Nov. 1827. New *or* Old Shoreham. George Allward. 14 miles. £1 10s 6d.
19 Nov. 1827. Patcham. William Bishop. 12 miles. £1 9s.
20 Nov. 1827. Southbourne. John Pendrill. 16 miles. £1 12s.
10 Dec. 1827. Eastbourne. Sarah Markwicke. 16 miles. £1 12s.
13 Dec. 1827. Black Rock. New-born infant. 10 miles. £1 7s 6d.
14 Dec. 1827. Rotherfield. Lucy Killick. 19 miles. £1 14s 3d.
20 Dec. 1827. Framfield. Unknown man.[1] 9 miles. £1 6s 9d.
26 Dec. 1827. The New Inn, Henfield. George Woollgar. 18 miles. £1 13s 6d.
Total £43 17s 3d; allowed at Epiphany sessions 1828. [QR/E 794]

1 *A travelling man, name unknown, aged about 70* in PAR 343/1/5/1.

214 1 Jan. 1828. Mayfield. Mary Ann Smith. 18 miles. £1 13s 6d.
[*Date omitted.*] Laughton. Richard Hoad. 7 miles. £1 5s 3d.
8 Jan. 1828. Southwick. Edmund Davey. 12 miles. £1 9s.
14 Jan. 1828. Preston. Henry Ayres. 9 miles. £1 6s 9d.
[*Date omitted.*] Henfield. George Matthews. 18 miles. £1 13s 6d.
15 Jan. 1828. Brighton. Infant named White. 8 miles. £1 6s.
17 Jan. 1828. Brighton. Harriet Thurston. 8 miles. £1 6s.
22 Jan. 1828. Brighton. Alice Markwick. 8 miles. £1 6s.
2 Feb. 1828. Chiddingly. Unknown woman.[1] 8 miles. £1 6s.
12 Feb. 1828. Lewes. Sarah Reed. £1.

14 Feb. 1828. Goddard's Green, Hurstpierpoint. John Hamlin. 15 miles. £1 11s 3d.
20 Feb. 1828. Brighton. Sarah Griffin. 8 miles. £1 6s.
25 Feb. 1828. Brighton. Sarah West. 8 miles. £1 6s.
10 Mar. 1828. Cliffe. Thomas King. £1.
14 Mar. 1828. Eastbourne. Mary Ann Stapleton. 16 miles. £1 12s.[2]
15 Mar. 1828. Eastbourne. Mary Ann Stapleton. By adjournment. 16 miles. £1 12s.[2]
18 Mar. 1828. Brighton. Sarah Long. 8 miles. £1 6s.
25 Mar. 1828. Mayfield. Male infant.[3] 19 miles. £1 14s 3d.
25 Mar. 1828. Mayfield. Male infant.[3] 19 miles. £1 14s 3d.
28 Mar. 1828. Waldron. Thomas Piper. 14 miles. £1 10s 6d.
31 Mar. 1828. Brighton. Ann O'Hara. 8 miles. £1 6s.
2 Apr. 1828. Brighton. Richard Payne. 8 miles. £1 6s.
10 Apr. 1828. Brighton. Michael Rowed. 8 miles. £1 6s.
10 Apr. 1828. Brighton. James Palmer. 8 miles. £1 6s.
12 Apr. 1828. Brighton. James Measor. 8 miles. £1 6s.
19 Apr. 1828. Cuckfield. John Brigden. 14 miles. £1 10s 6d.
21 Apr. 1828. Portslade. Thomas Todd. 12 miles. £1 9s.
25 Apr. 1828. Newhaven. Thomas Brown. 8 miles. £1 6s.
25 Apr. 1828. Newhaven. John Morris. 8 miles. £1 6s.
25 Apr. 1828. Newhaven. John Hicks. 8 miles. £1 6s.
26 Apr. 1828. Newtimber. Henry Renvill. 13 miles. £1 9s 9d.
4 May 1828. New Shoreham. Henry Harvey. 14 miles. £1 10s 6d.
4 May 1828. New Shoreham. William Brockett. 14 miles. £1 10s 6d.
5 May 1828. Keymer. William Eager. 12 miles. £1 9s.
17 May 1828. Brighton. Alfred Durell. 8 miles. £1 6s.
29 May 1828. Hailsham. Thomas Harris. 15 miles. £1 11s 3d.
6 June 1828. Rottingdean. Stephen Boys. 8 miles. £1 6s.
14 June 1828. Lindfield. William Marchant. 12 miles. £1 9s.
19 June 1828. Eastbourne. Dr Alexander Brodie. 15 miles. £1 11s 3d.
21 June 1828. Brighton. Joseph Jasper. 8 miles. £1 6s.
4 July 1828. Southerham. William Excell. 2 miles. £1 1s 6d.
5 July 1828. Hove. John Purbrick. 9 miles. £1 6s 9d.
7 July 1828. Rottingdean. Unknown man. 8 miles. £1 6s.
9 July 1828. [Lewes] House of Correction. Charles Philcox. £1.
Total £60 15s 3d; allowed at Midsummer sessions 1828. [QR/E 796]

1 *Elizabeth Avens of Tonbridge, buried at Chiddingly 5 Feb.* in PAR 292/1/5/1 where there is a note in ink that she was found dead in a lane near Mr Aylwin's, farmer, on 31 Jan. and another in pencil that she was found dead in a lane on Frith's Farm.
2 Cf. **392**.
3 *Henry and Samuel Collins, infant twins* in PAR 422/1/5/1.

215 19 July 1828. Lewes House of Correction. Henry White. £1.
28 July 1828. Rottingdean. Mary Moore. 8 miles. £1 6s.
29 July 1828. Withyham. John Maynard. 21 miles. £1 15s 9d.
9 Aug. 1828. Brighton. Mary Ann Ackerson. 8 miles. £1 6s.
11 Aug. 1828. Wadhurst. Herbert Stapley. 23 miles. £1 17s 3d.
14 Aug. 1828. Lewes House of Correction. Theophilus Morgan. £1.
30 Aug. 1828. Cliffe. Thomas M Bennett, esq. £1.
9 Sept. 1828. Brighton. Frederick Andrew Tilt. 8 miles. £1 6s.

20 Sept. 1828. Brighton. Susannah Arnold. 8 miles. £1 6s.
24 Sept. 1828. Brighton. Sarah Bowley. 8 miles. £1 6s.
11 Oct. 1828. New Shoreham. Daniel Connor. 14 miles. £1 10s 6d.
13 Oct. 1828. Brighton. John Patterson. 8 miles. £1 6s.
16 Oct. 1828. Brighton. Mary Ann Brown. 8 miles. £1 6s.
4 Nov. 1828. Cuckfield. James Purser. 14 miles. £1 10s 6d.
8 Nov. 1828. St John sub Castro, Lewes. Ann Tedham. £1.
8 Nov. 1828. Worth. James Tingley. 24 miles. £1 18s.
11 Nov. 1828. East Chiltington. William Cooper. 7 miles. £1 5s 3d.
12 Nov. 1828. Wilmington. Charles Wood. 10 miles. £1 7s 6d.
20 Nov. 1828. Brighton. Stephen Rolleston, esq. 8 miles. £1 6s.
29 Nov. 1828. Ringmer. Henry Washer, infant. 3 miles. £1 2s 3d.
3 Dec. 1828. Lindfield. Elizabeth Woodgate. 12 miles. £1 9s.
8 Dec. 1828. Wadhurst. Thomas Reed. 24 miles. £1 18s.
8 Dec. 1828. Mayfield. George Egles. 19 miles. £1 14s 3d.
9 Dec. 1828. Hartfield. Edward Everest. 21 miles. £1 15s 9d.
22 Dec. 1828. Lewes House of Correction. Adam Perrey. £1.
26 Dec. 1828. Brighton. Elizabeth Crouch. 8 miles. £1 6s.
29 Dec. 1828. Offham in Hamsey. Sarah Smith. 2 miles. £1 1s 6d.
31 Dec. 1828. Brighton. James Dale. 8 miles. £1 6s.
1 Jan. 1829. West Firle. Elizabeth Hughes. 5 miles. £1 3s 9d.
2 Jan. 1829. Brighton. Henry Bevan. 8 miles. £1 6s.
3 Jan. 1829. Lewes House of Correction. Winifred Brown. £1.
6 Jan. 1829. Uckfield. Harriet Hylands. 8 miles. £1 6s.
7 Jan. 1829. Brighton. Samuel Holladay. 8 miles. £1 6s.
8 Jan. 1829. West Hoathly. Sarah Dray. 19 miles. £1 14s 3d.
12 Jan. 1829. Southwick. James Harland. 12 miles. £1 9s.
13 Jan. 1829. Rottingdean. Mary Hunter. 8 miles. £1 6s.
Total £48 16s 6d; allowed at Epiphany sessions 1829. [QR/E 798]

216 17 Jan. 1829. Portslade. Richard Tanner. 12 miles. £1 9s.
28 Jan. 1829. Balcombe. John Steele. 19 miles. £1 14s 3d.
29 Jan. 1829. Cliffe. Sarah Yeomans. £1.
2 Feb. 1829. Laughton. Lucy Funnell. 7 miles. £1 5s 3d.
5 Feb. 1829. Westout in Lewes. Richard Hollingdale. £1.
7 Feb. 1829. South Malling. Mary Ann Shelley. 1 mile. £1 0s 9d.
10 Feb. 1829. East Grinstead. Thomas Silsey.[1] 22 miles. £1 16s 6d.
10 Feb. 1829. Ripe. Caroline Gander, infant. 8 miles. £1 6s.
Total £10 11s 9d; allowed at Midsummer sessions 1829. [QR/E 800]

1 *Thomas Sisley of East Grinstead, aged 30* in Par. 348/1/5/1.

Bills of Francis Harding Gell

217 12 Feb. 1829. Brighton. Emma Beall. 8 miles. £1 6s.
16 Feb. 1829. Barcombe. Ann Constable. 5 miles. £1 3s 9d.
20 Feb. 1829. Brighton. Unknown infant. 8 miles. £1 6s.
23 Feb. 1829. New Shoreham. Joseph Haddon. 14 miles. £1 10s 6d.

25 Feb. 1829. Barcombe. Amelia Morley. 5 miles. £1 3s 9d.
28 Feb. 1829. Preston. Peter Wells. 10 miles. £1 7s 6d.
7 Mar. 1829. Frant. Mary Ann Huggett. 24 miles. £1 18s.
13 Mar. 1829. Brighton. Henry Pink. 8 miles. £1 6s.
21 Mar. 1829. Telscombe. Elizabeth Moore. 6 miles. £1 4s 6d.
21 Mar. 1829. Mayfield. Abigail Hobbs. 16 miles. £1 12s.
21 Mar. 1829. St Michael's, Lewes. Owen Phelan. £1.
10 Apr. 1829. Brighton. Richard Marshall. 8 miles. £1 6s.
16 Apr. 1829. The Sussex County Hospital, Brighton. George Hollands. 9 miles. £1 6s 9d.
23 Apr. 1829. Brighton. Harriet Cox. 8 miles. £1 6s.
25 Apr. 1829. Brighton. William Andrews. 8 miles. £1 6s.
29 Apr. 1829. Uckfield. Jane Markwick. 8 miles. £1 6s.
30 Apr. 1829. Brighton. Gamey Comber. 8 miles. £1 6s.
7 May 1829. Kemp Town, Brighton. Unknown man.[1] 9 miles. £1 6s 9d.
9 May 1829. Kingston near Lewes. John Reed. 2 miles. £1 1s 6d.
9 May 1829. The Sussex County Hospital, Brighton. George Cheesman. 9 miles. £1 6s 9d.
15 May 1829. Lewes House of Correction. John Yates. £1.
25 May 1829. Brighton. Cyrus Burgh. 8 miles. £1 6s.
25 May 1829. Framfield. William John Dugdale. 10 miles. £1 7s 6d.
30 May 1829. Brighton. Mary Barnett. 8 miles. £1 6s.
30 May 1829. Brighton. Sarah Mockford. 8 miles. £1 6s.
1 June 1829. Fletching. Thomas Wood. 10 miles. £1 7s 6d.
3 June 1829. Isfield. Mary Kennard. 6 miles. £1 4s 6d.
2 June 1829. Brighton. Eliza Hill. 8 miles. £1 6s.
3 June 1829. Brighton. Eliza Hill. By adjourment. 16 miles. 12s.
10 June 1829. Wick near Ditchling. Edmund Gatland. 8 miles. £1 6s.
15 June 1829. Brighton. Thomas Burn. 8 miles. £1 6s.
17 June 1829. Brighton. Harriet Skut. 8 miles. £1 6s.
22 June 1829. Little Horsted. Mary Miles. 7 miles. £1 5s 3d.
2 July 1829. Brighton. Georgiana Lower. 8 miles. £1 6s.
7 July 1829. Brighton. Eliza Barham. 8 miles. £1 6s.
8 July 1829. Brighton. John Bearman. 8 miles. £1 6s.
8 July 1829. Brighton. Mary Funnell. 8 miles. £1 6s.
Total £47 6s 6d;[2] allowed at Midsummer sessions 1829. [QR/E 800]

[All Gell's journeys were from Lewes but that is never stated in his bills.]

1 *Unknown man found drowned near Black Rock* in PAR 255/1/5/4.
2 Recte *£47 12s 6d.* The 6s discrepancy must have arisen from the adjournment charge of 3 June: the journey should have been 8 miles and the charge 6s. The 16 miles and 12s appear to have been written later than the rest of the bill. The addition must have been done on another sheet and the 16 miles and 12s added to the bill in error for 8 miles and 6s. Only £47 6s 6d was paid: QO/EW 50; QAF 2/1/E10, ff 138v–139.

218 24 July 1829. Telscombe. Unknown man. 6 miles. £1 4s 6d.
25 July 1829. Brighton. Adam Maiben. 8 miles. £1 6s.
17 Aug. 1829. Bolney. Thomas Pitt. 17 miles. £1 12s 9d.
17 Aug. 1829. Kingston near Lewes. Female infant. 2 miles. £1 1s 6d.
18 Aug. 1829. Kingston by Sea. Richard Randall. 12 miles. £1 9s.

2 Sept. 1829. Mayfield. William Fenner. 17 miles. £1 12s 9d.
4 Sept. 1829. Eastbourne. John Wood. 15 miles. £1 11s 3d.
8 Sept. 1829. Brighton. Elizabeth Ranslee. 8 miles. £1 6s.
18 Sept. 1829. Uckfield. Martha How. 9 miles. £1 6s 9d.
25 Sept. 1829. Maresfield. John Hobbs. 13 miles. £1 9s 9d.
26 Sept. 1829. Mayfield. Sarah Medhurst. 19 miles. £1 14s 3d.
10 Oct. 1829. Lewes House of Correction. Charles Tugwell. £1.
12 Oct. 1829. Brighton. John Woodbridge Hilton. 8 miles. £1 6s.
12 Oct. 1829. 3 miles beyond Cuckfield. Mary Ann Haylor. 17 miles. £1 12s 9d.
13 Oct. 1829. Lewes House of Correction. Robert Knight. £1.
16 Oct. 1829. Brighton. Sarah Ann Marchant. 8 miles. £1 6s.
20 Oct. 1829. Brighton. Edward Clare. 8 miles. £1 6s.
2 Nov. 1829. Brighton. Mary Ann Allcorn. 8 miles. £1 6s.[1]
[*Date omitted.*] Brighton. Mary Ann Allcorn. Adjournment. £1.[1]
9 Nov. 1829. Newhaven. Edward Carpenter. 7 miles. £1 5s 3d.
14 Nov. 1829. East Blatchington. Mary Ann Close. 11 miles. £1 8s 3d.
23 Nov. 1829. East Grinstead. Joseph Holmes. 24 miles. £1 18s.
28 Nov. 1829. Framfield. Elizabeth Banks. 9 miles. £1 6s 9d.
28 Nov. 1829. East Dean. Daniel Sullivan. 16 miles. £1 12s.
7 Dec. 1829. Brighton. William Marchant. 8 miles. £1 6s.
9 Dec. 1829. Kingston by Sea. Unknown boy. 12 miles. £1 9s.
11 Dec. 1829. Battery House, Newhaven. Edward Jones. 8 miles. £1 6s.
26 Dec. 1829. Horney Common, Maresfield. Charles Lambert. 12 miles. £1 9s.
28 Dec. 1829. Lewes. William Brown. £1.
31 Dec. 1829. Buxted. Elizabeth Ann Knight. 10 miles. £1 7s 6d.
Total £40 19s; allowed at Epiphany sessions 1830. [QR/E 802]

1 Cf. **393**.

219 4 Jan. 1830. Rottingdean. Infant. 9 miles. £1 6s 9d.
11 Jan. 1830. West Blatchington. Henry Advad. 11 miles. £1 8s 3d.
14 Jan. 1830. Rodmell. Elijah Ditch. 4 miles. £1 3s.
14 Jan. 1830. Brighton. William Hockham. 8 miles. £1 6s.
16 Jan. 1830. Brighton. Thomas Kent. 8 miles. £1 6s.
20 Jan. 1830. Cacklebury in Hailsham. John Broadhurst. 14 miles. £1 10s 6d.
26 Jan. 1830. Uckfield. Joseph Humphrey. 8 miles. £1 6s.
29 Jan. 1830. The Sussex County Hospital, Brighton. Harriet Sick. 9 miles. £1 6s 9d.
4 Feb. 1830. Brighton. Edward Sales. 8 miles. £1 6s.
6 Feb. 1830. Newhaven Pier. George Morley. 8 miles. £1 6s.
10 Feb. 1830. Brighton. Theodosia Thackeray. 8 miles. £1 6s.
16 Feb. 1830. Brighton. James Packham. 8 miles. £1 6s.
16 Feb. 1830. Lewes House of Correction. Thomas Dunk. £1.
19 Feb. 1830. Uckfield. Edward Gower. 8 miles. £1 6s.
20 Feb. 1830. Brighton. William Jasper. 8 miles. £1 6s.
22 Feb. 1830. Framfield. John Stevens. 10 miles. £1 7s 6d.
22 Feb. 1830. Southover. William Carter. 1 mile. £1 0s 9d.
27 Feb. 1830. Wych Cross. Jasper Wood. 16 miles. £1 12s.
1 Mar. 1830. Brighton. New-born female infant. 8 miles. £1 6s.
5 Mar. 1830. East Grinstead. Flora Clarke. 20 miles. £1 15s.

8 Mar. 1830. Brighton. George Bull. 8 miles. £1 6s.
16 Mar. 1830. Lewes House of Correction. James Scrase. £1.
16 Mar. 1830. Swanborough. Mary Michelborne Verrall. 2 miles. £1 1s 6d.
17 Mar. 1830. Uckfield. James Reed. 9 miles. £1 6s 9d.
18 Mar. 1830. Hove. John Philip Malleson. 10 miles. £1 7s 6d.[1]
[*Date omitted.*] Hove. John Philip Malleson. By adjournment. £1.[1]
19 Mar. 1830. Forest Row. James Johnson. 18 miles. £1 13s 6d.
22 Mar. 1830. Chiddingly. James Elphick. 8 miles. £1 6s.
22 Mar. 1830. Brighton. Thomas Phillips. 8 miles. £1 6s.
29 Mar. 1830. Brighton. Amy Bishop. 8 miles. £1 6s.
1 Apr. 1830. Brighton. Thomas Marchant. 8 miles. £1 6s.
7 Apr. 1830. Buxted. Henry Marchant. 14 miles. £1 10s 6d.
10 Apr. 1830. Brighton. Ann Mason. 8 miles. £1 6s.
12 Apr. 1830. Cuckfield. Mary Hammond. 14 miles. £1 10s 6d.
14 Apr. 1830. The Sussex County Hospital, Brighton. James Harwood. 9 miles. £1 6s 9d.
14 Apr. 1830. Brighton. Female infant. 8 miles. £1.
3 May 1830. Patcham. William Sturt. 10 miles. £1 7s 6d.
5 May 1830. Selmeston. Elizabeth Burgess. 7 miles. £1 5s 3d.
9 May 1830. Frant, near Tunbridge Wells. Male infant. 21 miles. £1 15s 9d.
15 May 1830. South Malling. Catherine Pinion. 1 mile. £1 0s 9d.
17 May 1830. Ditchling. Henry Francis Homewood. 8 miles. £1 6s.
5 June 1830. Piddinghoe. Richard Spearing. 6 miles. £1 4s 9d.[2]
15 June 1830. East Dean. James Mann. 16 miles. £1 12s.
21 June 1830. Lewes House of Correction. John Holland. £1.
22 June 1830. Brighton Poorhouse. Benjamin Benge. 9 miles. £1 6s 9d.
23 June 1830. New Shoreham. Thomas Scarnell. 14 miles. £1 10s 6d.
26 June 1830. Newhaven. William Welch. 7 miles. £1 5s 3d.
[*Date omitted.*] Newhaven. William Welch. By adjournment. £1.
30 June 1830. All Saints, Lewes. Frances Carter. £1.
Total £63 18s; allowed at Midsummer sessions 15 July 1830. [QR/E 804]

1 Cf. **394**.
2 Recte *£1 4s 6d*. The extra 3d was included in the bill total and allowed.

HASTINGS RAPE CORONERS' BILLS

Bills of George Tilden

220 28 Dec. 1753. Burwash. Elizabeth Jarvis: drowned. 9 miles. £1 6s 9d.
4 Mar. 1754. Heathfield. Elizabeth Ellis: drowned. 11 miles. £1 8s 3d.
1 June 1754. Northiam. John [*surname omitted*]:[1] killed by accident. 10 miles. £1 7s 6d.
1 July 1754. Ninfield. Benjamin Fairhall: accidentally killed. 4 miles. £1 3s.
Total £5 5s 6d; allowed at Midsummer sessions 1754 [QR/E 501, no 96]

[All Tilden's journeys were from Battle but that is never stated in his bills.]

1 *John Bates* in PAR 431/1/1/5.

221 15 Oct. 1754. Bexhill. John Weston. 6 miles. £1 4s 6d.
2 Jan. 1755. Ninfield. William Satten. 5 miles. £1 3s 9d.
17 Jan. 1755. Warbleton. Thomas Parks. 10 miles. £1 7s 6d.
5 Feb. 1755. Bexhill. Samuel Newington. 6 miles. £1 4s 6d.
5 Mar. 1755. Peasmarsh. Sarah Dale. 13 miles. £1 9s 9d.
1 Apr. 1755. Peasmarsh. Mary Hartly. 12 miles. £1 9s.
17 Apr. 1755. Ticehurst. Robert Drinker. 12 miles. £1 9s.
8 June 1755. Bexhill. Elizabeth Bartholomew. 7 miles. £1 5s 3d.
Total £10 13s 3d; allowed at Midsummer sessions 1755. [QR/E 505, no 96]

222 2 July 1756. Northiam. John Newman. 12 miles. £1 9s.
6 July 1756. East Guldeford. William Hood. 18 miles. £1 13s 6d.
2 Aug. 1756. Wartling. William Hare. 8 miles. £1 6s.
6 Sept. 1756. Wartling. Thomas Slaughter. 8 miles. £1 6s.
Total £5 14s 6d; allowed at Michaelmas sessions 1756. [QR/E 510, no 137]

223 31 Oct. 1756. Burwash. John Cruttenden. 10 miles. £1 7s 6d.
22 Aug. 1757. Herstmonceux. William Elphick. 11 miles. £1 8s 3d.
3 Oct. 1757. Ticehurst. Stephen Pettitt. 13 miles. £1 9s 9d.
Total £4 5s 6d; allowed at Michaelmas sessions 1757. [QR/E 514, no 117]

224 13 Nov. 1758. Bexhill Down. John Offin. 7 miles. £1 5s 3d.
23 Nov. 1758. Dallington Stream. John Huggett. 7 miles. £1 5s 3d.
15 May 1759. Brightling. William Collins. 6 miles. £1 4s 6d.
9 July 1759. Ewhurst. William Baker. 6 miles. £1 4s 6d.
27 Mar. 1760. Dallington. John Stace. 7 miles. £1 5s 3d.
16 May 1760. Heathfield. William Haselden. 12 miles. £1 9s.
16 July 1760. Ewhurst. Richard Paine. 6 miles. £1 4s 6d.
[Total £8 18s 3d]; allowed at Midsummer sessions 1760. [QR/E 525, no 98]

225 19 Aug. 1760. Beckley. John Clapson. 12 miles. £1 9s.

7 Jan. 1761. Westfield Moor. John Bates. 6 miles. £1 4s 6d.
8 Jan. 1761. Ninfield. Thomas French. 5 miles. £1 3s 9d.
10 June 1761. Crowhurst. John Evernden. 4 miles. £1 3s.
20 June 1761. Salehurst. Stephen Clarke. 6 miles. £1 4s 6d.
Total £6 4s 9d; allowed at Midsummer sessions 1761. [QR/E 529, no 68]

226 28 July 1761. Beckley. Alice Brown. 11 miles. £1 8s 3d.
20 Jan. 1762. Bexhill Down. John Southouse. 7 miles. £1 5s 3d.
26 Jan. 1762. The further end of Heathfield Down. Philip Stoakes. 12 miles. £1 9s.
23 Apr. 1762. Burwash. Martha Funell. 9 miles. £1 6s 9d.
Total £5 9s 3d; allowed at Midsummer sessions 1762. [QR/E 533, no 72]

227 19 July 1762. Hooe. William Keys. 7 miles. £1 5s 3d.
17 Apr. 1763. Salehurst. Jane Goldsmith. 7 miles. £1 5s 3d.
23 Jan. 1764. Burwash. William Constable. 9 miles. £1 6s 9d.
16 Feb. 1764. Burwash. Thomas Sawyer. 9 miles. £1 6s 9d.
2 May 1764. Ticehurst. William Vidler. 14 miles. £1 10s 6d.
19 May 1764. Guestling. Hannah Easton. 9 miles. £1 6s 9d.
29 June 1764. Boreham Street. Thomas Porter. 7 miles. £1 5s 3d.
1 Aug. 1764. Hooe Common. Samuel Beny. 6 miles. £1 4s 6d.
3 Aug. 1764. Sewers Bridge, Hooe. Thomas Wenham. 8 miles. £1 6s.[1]
15 Aug. 1764. Bexhill. Mary Cleaver. 8 miles. £1 6s.
29 Aug. 1764. Breadsell. George Tilby. 2 miles. £1 1s 6d.
Total £14 4s 6d; allowed at Michaelmas sessions 1764. [QR/E 542, no 96]

1 Cf. **420**.

228A 27 Nov. 1764. Catsfield. William Cornwall. 3 miles. £1 2s 3d.
13 Mar. 1765. The farther end of Beckley. John Hyland: found dead. 13 miles. £1 9s 9d. [QR/E 547, no 17]

[This bill was continued after George Tilden's death by John, his son and successor.]

Bills of John Tilden (from 22 Nov. 1797 John Tilden Sampson)

228B 8 July 1765. Wartling. Anthony Avery: kicked by a horse. 7 miles. £1 5s 3d.
27 July 1765. Ninfield. John Husbands: killed by a wagon. 4 miles. £1 3s.
30 Aug. 1765. Beckley. Sarah Pankhurst: drowned. 11 miles. £1 8s 3d.
31 Dec. 1765. Salehurst. William Bishop: drowned. 7 miles. £1 5s 3d.
Total £7 13s 9d; allowed at Epiphany sessions 1766.[1] [QR/E 547, no 17]

[All Tilden's journeys were from Battle but that is never stated in his bills.]

1 Payment of the whole of bill **228** with an additional 5s was made to John Tilden: QM/EW 10; QAF 2/1/E1.

229 10 Mar. 1766. Bexhill. John Bartholomew: found hanging.[1] 7 miles. £1 5s 3d.
28 Apr. 1766. Ticehurst. Joseph Gayler: found dead. 12 miles. £1 9s.
8 Aug. 1766. Wartling. Lydia Marshall, infant: found drowned. 8 miles. £1 6s.
3 Sept. 1766. Mountfield. Elizabeth Card, infant: found drowned. 4 miles. £1 3s.

4 Nov. 1766. Crowhurst. Mark Archer: killed by a wagon. 3 miles. £1 2s 3d.
12 Nov. 1766. Ticehurst. Joseph Mepham: died in a fit. 12 miles. £1 9s.
24 Dec. 1766. Brightling. John Knight: found drowned. 6 miles. £1 4s 6d.
13 Mar. 1767. Brightling. Sarah Fowle: hanged herself. 5 miles. £1 3s 9d.
16 Mar. 1767. Brightling Down. Jonathan Foster: found hanging. 7 miles. £1 5s 3d.
Total £11 8s; allowed at Easter sessions 1767. [QR/E 552, no 68]

[This bill is also in RAF 1/3/1, p 1.]

1 *hanged himself* in RAF 1/3/1.

230 4 June 1767. The farther end of Beckley. James Card: found dead. 15 miles. £1 11s 3d.
16 June 1767. Burwash. Thomas Croft: found drowned. 9 miles. £1 6s 9d.
14 Jan. 1768. Mountfield. Richard Jarman: drowned himself.[1] 4 miles. £1 3s.
26 Jan.1768.[2] Warbleton. Infant:[3] born dead. 10 miles. £1 7s 6d.
29 Feb. 1768. Heathfield. John Clinton: found dead. 12 miles. £1 9s.
9 Mar. 1768. Ticehurst. William Moor: killed by Ann Oxenbridge. 12 miles. £1 9s.[4]
28 Mar. 1768. Ninfield. Unknown person: found hanged. 6 miles. £1 4s 6d.
Total £9 11s; allowed at Easter sessions 1768. [QR/E 556, no 74]

[This bill is also in RAF 1/3/1, p 15.]

1 *in a well* added in RAF 1/3/1.
2 Date omitted in RAF 1/3/1.
3 [blank], *infant, born on the body of* [blank] in RAF 1/3/1.
4 Cf. **421**.

231 21 Apr. 1768. Brightling. Elizabeth Fisher: drowned. 6 miles. £1 4s 6d.
31 July 1768. Ticehurst. Samuel Smith: drowned himself. 12 miles. £1 9s.
19 Aug. 1768. Hurst Green. Elizabeth Boorman: drowned herself. 8 miles. £1 6s.
15 Sept. 1768. Sedlescombe. Male bastard child of Elizabeth Swaine, single woman: born dead. 4 miles. £1 3s.
20 Sept. 1768. Salehurst. Male bastard child of Ann Blackman, single woman: born dead.[1] 7 miles. £1 5s 3d.
24 Mar. 1769. Salehurst. Sarah Cruttenden: drowned herself.[2] 6 miles. £1 4s 6d.
28 Mar. 1769. Hurst Green. John Daw: hanged himself. 8 miles. £1 6s.
30 May 1769. Ninfield. Thomas[3] Dann: found dead. 6 miles. £1 4s 6d.
Total £10 2s 9d; allowed at Midsummer sessions 1769. [QR/E 561, no 92]

[This bill is also in RAF 1/3/1, p 16.]

1 *born dead* omitted in RAF 1/3/1.
2 *was drowned* in RAF 1/3/1.
3 *James* in RAF 1/3/1.

232 9 Nov. 1769. Gardner Street. Joseph Marshall: rode against a wagon and was killed.[1] 9 miles. £1 6s 9d.
13 Nov. 1771. The King's Head, Rye Foreign, the body being removed there. James Barrow: killed by a wagon in Beckley. 17 miles. £1 12s 9d.
5 Dec. 1771. Ninfield. Thomas West: hanged himself in Ninfield churchyard. 5 miles. £1 3s 9d.

10 Dec. 1771. Dallington. Stephen Tendall: killed by a fall from a beam in a barn. 6 miles. £1 4s 6d.
1 Jan. 1772. The Sluice House, Bexhill. Richard Curteis: found dead near the Sluice House. 10 miles. £1 7s 6d.
Total £6 15s 3d; allowed at Epiphany sessions 1772. [QR/E 571, no 26]

[This bill is also in RAF 1/3/1, p 27.]

1 *rode ... killed* omitted in RAF 1/3/1.

233 8 May 1772. Bodle Street Green, Warbleton.[1] Thomas Clapson: killed by the bail of[2] a hop-pole stack. 10 miles. £1 7s 6d.
1 June 1772. Heathfield. Jane Piper, infant: drowned in a saw-pit. 11 miles. £1 8s 3d.
3 July 1772. Catsfield. Ann Tanner, infant: drowned.[3] 3 miles. £1 2s 3d.
14 Oct. 1772. Warbleton. Mary Cornwell: cut her throat. 10 miles. £1 7s 6d.
26 Jan. 1773. Heathfield. Thomas Harmar: found dead. 11 miles. £1 8s 3d.
27 Feb. 1773. Playden. John Rutley: drowned.[4] 17 miles. £1 12s 9d.
Total £8 6s 6d; allowed at Easter sessions 1773. [QR/E 576, no 35]

[This bill is also in RAF 1/3/1, pp 27, 84.]

1 *Warbleton* omitted in RAF 1/3/1.
2 *the bail of* omitted in RAF 1/3/1.
3 *in a pond* added in RAF 1/3/1.
4 *found drowned* in RAF 1/3/1.

234 20 May 1773. Iden. John Godden Farmer, infant: drowned. 18 miles. £1 13s 6d.
13 June 1773. Sedlescombe. John Burt: killed by a wagon. 3 miles. £1 2s 3d.
9 Oct. 1773. The extremity[1] of Mountfield. Thomas Hilder: drowned. 6 miles. £1 4s 6d.
3 Nov. 1773. Gardner Street, Herstmonceux. Richard Hutchinson: killed by a fall from a horse. 10 miles. £1 7s 6d.
22 Dec. 1773. Westfield. Elizabeth Stemp: found dead. 5 miles. £1 3s 9d.
Total £6 11s 6d; allowed at Epiphany sessions 1774. [QR/E 579, no 24]

[This bill is also in RAF 1/3/1, p 84.]

1 *The farther end* in RAF 1/3/1.

235 4 Feb. 1774. Hooe. Elizabeth Ransom, infant: fell down stairs and killed herself.[1] 7 miles. £1 5s 3d.
6 Feb. 1774. Hooe.[2] John Gower, infant: left dead by 2 travelling women.[3] 7 miles. £1 5s 3d.
30 Mar. 1774. Northiam. William Foster: found dead. 9 miles. £1 6s 9d.
4 Apr. 1774. Catsfield. Richard Rue: killed by a fall from his horse. 2 miles. £1 1s 6d.
11 Apr. 1774. East Guldeford. Ann Bailey, infant: drowned. 18 miles. £1 13s 6d.
16 June 1774. Burwash. Elizabeth Weston: hanged herself. 10 miles. £1 7s 6d.
18 Aug. 1774. Salehurst. Thomas Pollard, infant: drowned. 6 miles. £1 4s 6d.
17 Feb. 1775. Burwash Down. Thomas Mercer: killed by Edmund Smith and Edward and Mark Jarvis. 12 miles. £1 9s.[4]
28 Mar. 1775. Wartling. Mary wife of William Sargent: hanged herself. 7 miles. £1 5s 3d.
Total £11 18s 6d; allowed at Easter sessions 1775. [QR/E 584, no 49]

[This bill is also in RAF 1/3/1, pp 84, 112.]

1 *fell down stairs and died* in RAF 1/3/1.
2 *Ninfield* in RAF 1/3/1.
3 *by 2 travelling women* omitted in RAF 1/3/1.
4 Cf. **422**.

236 22 Aug. 1775. Guestling. William Sharpe: fell from his horse in a fit. 9 miles. £1 6s 9d.
14 Mar. 1776. Rye. Unknown person: found dead in a barn. 16 miles. £1 12s.
9[1] May 1776. Brightling. Edward French: died by drinking laudanum. 6 miles. £1 4s 6d.
17 June 1776. The further end of[2] Crowhurst. Edward Metcalfe, infant: drowned. 4 miles. £1 3s.
18 June 1776. Hurst Green. Joseph Mowcoomber: killed by a fall from a wagon. 8 miles. £1 6s.
[22 June] 1776. Brightling. Joseph Cruttenden: killed by his wife Ann.[3] 6 miles. £1 4s 6d.[4]
Total £7 16s 9d; allowed at Midsummer sessions 1776. [QR/E 589, no 54]

[This bill is also in RAF 1/3/1, pp 112–113.]

1 *2* in RAF 1/3/1.
2 *The further end of* omitted in RAF 1/3/1.
3 *killed ... Ann* omitted in RAF 1/3/1.
4 Cf. **423**; *SCM*, XIII, 500.

237 26 July 1776. Seacox Heath,[1] Etchingham. Mary Winch: found dead at Etchingham. 12 miles. £1 9s.
31 Aug. 1776. Peasmarsh. George Mate: dislocated his neck by a fall from his horse. 14 miles. £1 10s 6d.
15 Sept. 1776. Rye. Thomas Fuller: fell from a wagon and was killed. 15 miles. £1 11s 3d.
2 Oct. 1776. Wigsell.[2] Lucy Tyler: drowned herself. 8 miles. £1 6s.
30 Jan. 1777. East Guldeford. John Pledge: found drowned. 18 miles. £1 13s 6d.
13 Feb. 1777. Playden. John Dadd: found dead. 16 miles. £1 12s.
20 Mar. 1777. Westfield. Stephen Crisford: died in a fit.[3] 6 miles. £1 4s 6d.
23[4] Mar. 1777. Warbleton. John Pleydell: cut his throat. 10 miles. £1 7s 6d.
Total £11 14s 3d; allowed at Easter sessions 1777. [QR/E 592, no 23]

[This bill is also in RAF 1/3/1, pp 113–114.]

1 *Seacox Heath* omitted in RAF 1/3/1.
2 *in Salehurst* added in RAF 1/3/1.
3 *at Westfield Weald* added in RAF 1/3/1.
4 *24* in RAF 1/3/1.

238 15[1] Apr. 1777. East Guldeford. Richard Barwick: drowned. 18 miles. £1 13s 6d.
10 May 1777. Ticehurst.[2] Hannah Twopeny: drowned. £1.[3]
[10 May] 1777. Ticehurst. John Twopeny: drowned.[4] 13 miles. £1 9s 9d.
21 June 1777. Playden.[5] Ann Brazeel, infant:[6] killed by a timber-tug. 16 miles. £1 12s.
30 Oct. 1777. Ninfield. Joseph Savage: killed by the overturning[7] of a timber-tug. 5 miles. £1 3s 9d.

6 Nov. 1777. Ticehurst. Thomas Polhill: found dead. 13 miles. £1 9s 9d.
16 Apr. 1778. Ticehurst. James Paine: killed by a cart. 13 miles. £1 9s 9d.
10 May 1778. Ore. Elizabeth wife of John Williams: died from excessive drinking. 6 miles. £1 4s 6d.
10 June 1778. Brightling. Thomas Grant: cut his throat. 6 miles. £1 4s 6d.
13 July 1778. East Guldeford. Thomas Chatterton Robinson: drowned as he was bathing. 18 miles. £1 13s 6d.
Total £14 1s;[8] allowed at Midsummer sessions 1778. [QR/E 596, no 26]

[Part of this bill is also in RAF 1/3/1, p 114 and the rest in RAF 1/3/2, ff 10–11.]

1 Omitted in RAF 1/3/1.
2 *Ticehurst* omitted in RAF 1/3/1.
3 *13 miles, £1 9s 9d* in RAF 1/3/1.
4 *with the above Hannah* added in RAF 1/3/1.
5 *Rye* in RAF 1/3/1.
6 *aged about 13* added in RAF 1/3/1.
7 *fall* in RAF 1/3/1.
8 *Total £14 10s 9d, less 9s 9d (journey to Ticehurst charged twice), leaving £14 1s* in RAF 1/3/2.

239 5 Oct. 1778. Ninfield. Ann King: hanged herself. 5 miles. £1 3s 9d.
15 Oct. 1778. Crowhurst. Thomas Cramp: killed in fighting with Benjamin Beeching.[1] 3 miles. £1 2s 3d.[2]
31 Oct. 1778. Herstmonceux. Daniel Goodwife: hanged himself. 9 miles. £1 6s 9d.
7 Jan. 1779. Mountfield. Christian Warner: burnt to death[3] in a hovel. 5 miles. £1 3s 9d.
10 Feb. 1779. Hurst Green. Robert Furner: hanged himself. 8 miles. £1 6s.
14[4] Apr. 1779. Beckley. Elizabeth Wheeler: drowned herself in a well.[5] 10 miles. £1 7s 6d.
Total £7 10s; allowed at Easter sessions 1779. [QR/E 599, no 26]

[This bill is also in RAF 1/3/2, ff 10–11.]

1 *killed by Benjamin Beeching, fighting* in RAF 1/3/2.
2 Cf. **424**.
3 *to death* omitted in RAF 1/3/2.
4 *15* in RAF 1/3/2.
5 *in a well* omitted in RAF 1/3/2.

240 1 June 1779. Cowbeech in Wartling. William Collins: hanged himself in a wood near Cowbeech.[1] 10 miles. £1 7s 6d.
7 July 1779. Heathfield. William Moon: found dead. 12 miles. £1 9s.
11 Aug. 1779. Heathfield. Joseph Harmer: killed by a fall from a[2] horse. 12 miles. £1 9s.
28 Sept. 1779. Grove Farm,[3] Hooe. John Cooper: found dead. 8 miles. £1 6s.
8 Oct. 1779. Ashburnham. William Newble: killed by a wagon running over him.[4] 3 miles. £1 2s 3d.
24 Oct. 1779. Hooe Common. John Sharpe: died by excessive drinking. 7 miles. £1 5s 3d.
Total £7 19s; allowed at Easter sessions 1780. [QR/E 603, no 11]

[This bill is also in RAF 1/3/2, f 25.]

1 *in a wood near Cowbeech* omitted in RAF 1/3/2.

2 *his* in RAF 1/3/2.
3 *The Grove* in RAF 1/3/2.
4 *fell from a wagon which run over his body and was killed* in RAF 1/3/2.

241 1 Sept. 1780. Burwash Weald. Thomas Wenham, infant:[1] drowned. 10 miles. £1 7s 6d.
[*Date omitted.*] The farther part of Salehurst. Thomas[2] Blackford: hanged himself. 8 miles. £1 6s.
20 Sept. 1780. The farther part of Sedlescombe. Elizabeth Gybbons: died through excessive drinking. 4 miles. £1 3s.
31 Dec. 1780. Mountfield. William Eldridge, infant:[3] killed by firing some gunpowder in the nozzle[4] of a pair of bellows. 5 miles. £1 3s 9d.
7 Jan. 1781. East Guldeford. Unknown man: found dead in a barn. 18 miles. £1 13s 6d.
24 Jan. 1781. Westfield. Elizabeth wife of William Burgess: drowned herself. 7 miles. £1 5s 3d.
10 Feb. 1781. Cade Street, Heathfield. Thomas Drawbridge: shot himself. 10 miles. £1 7s 6d.
26 Mar. 1781. Iden. James Filmer: hanged himself. 18 miles. £1 13s 6d.
7 Apr. 1781. Peasmarsh. Mary Upten: died in a fit. 15 miles. £1 11s 3d.
Total £12 11s 3d; allowed at Easter sessions 1781. [QR/E 607, no 28]

[This bill is also in RAF 1/3/2, ff 25, 56.]

1 *child* in RAF 1/3/2.
2 *John* in RAF 1/3/2; *John Blackford, buried 2 Sept.* in PAR 477/1/1/3.
3 *child* in RAF 1/3/2.
4 *nose* in RAF 1/3/2.

242 2 May 1781. Catsfield. Lawrence Tanner: hanged himself. 3 miles. £1 2s 3d.[1]
2[2] July 1781. Iden. John Ingram, a soldier of the 52 Regiment: hanged himself. 18 miles. £1 13s 6d.
30 July 1781. Bodiam.[3] Benjamin Pope: found dead. 9 miles. £1 6s 9d.
17 Oct. 1781. Catsfield Place. John Philips: killed by a wagon going over his body. 3 miles. £1 2s 3d.
3 Nov. 1781. Ewhurst. Sarah Card, infant: drowned by accident. 6 miles. £1 4s 6d.
24 Nov. 1781. Catsfield. Margaret wife of Thomas Briant: drowned by accident. 3 miles. £1 2s 3d.
27 Jan. 1782. Rye. Henry Wood: found dead. 15 miles. £1 11s 3d.[4]
5 July 1782. The farther part of Herstmonceux. John Matts: drowned by accident. 10 miles. £1 7s 6d.
Total £10 10s 3d;[5] allowed at Michaelmas sessions 1782. [QR/E 613, no 27]

[This bill is also in RAF 1/3/2, ff 56–57.]

1 *2 miles, £1 1s 6d* in RAF 1/3/2.
2 *22* in RAF 1/3/2.
3 *The farther part of Bodiam* in RAF 1/3/2.
4 *16 miles, £1 12s* in RAF 1/3/2.
5 *£10 10s 6d* in RAF 1/3/2. £10 10s 3d was paid with an additional 5s: QO/EW 27; QAF 2/1/E2.

243 15 Nov. 1782. Stunts Green, Wartling. Joseph Pattenden:[1] cut his throat. 10 miles. £1 7s 6d.

8 Dec. 1782. Guestling. Hannah wife of Thomas Foster: drowned herself. 9 miles. £1 6s 9d.
23 Dec. 1782. The farther part of Crowhurst. Edward Metcalfe: hanged himself. 4 miles. £1 3s.
26 Jan. 1783. Salehurst. Rebecca Jarrett: found drowned. 8 miles. £1 6s.
12 July 1783. Herstmonceux. John Baker: killed by a horse. 10 miles. £1 7s 6d.
9 Aug. 1783. Burwash. John Hawkins: found[2] drowned. 10 miles. £1 7s 6d.
15 Aug. 1783. Ewhurst. Henry Kenchley:[3] fell from a wheat-stack and was killed. 8 miles. £1 6s.
Total £9 4s 3d; allowed at Michaelmas sessions 1783. [QR/E 617, no 42]

[This bill is also in RAF 1/3/2, ff 57–59.]

1 *Wattenden* in RAF 1/3/2.
2 *found* omitted in RAF 1/3/2.
3 *Keneley* in RAF 1/3/2; *Kenchly* in PAR 324/1/1/4.

244 21 Nov. 1783. The further part of Fairlight. William Martin: hanged himself. 8 miles. £1 6s.
29 Nov. 1783. Mountfield.[1] Mary Webb: found dead. 3 miles. £1 2s 3d.
13 Sept. 1784. Burwash. Charles Weston: killed by Thomas Adams. 9 miles. £1 6s 9d.[2]
29 Nov. 1784. Iden. John Smith: killed by person or[3] persons unknown. 18 miles. £1 13s 6d.[4]
22 Dec. 1784. Beckley.[5] Henry Peckham: drowned[6] in the Rother. 15 miles. £1 11s 3d.
12 Jan. 1785. Playden.[7] Thomas Piper: shot by accident. 16 miles. £1 12s.
2[8] Mar. 1785. Brightling. Mary French: drowned.[9] £1.
[2 Mar.] 1785.[10] Brightling. Jane Forward:[11] drowned.[12] 5 miles. £1 3s 9d.
Total £10 15s 6d;[13] allowed at Easter sessions 1785. [QR/E 623, no 43]

[This bill is also in RAF 1/3/2, ff 58, 60.]

1 *Vinehall* in RAF 1/3/2.
2 Cf. **425**.
3 *person or* omitted in RAF 1/3/2.
4 Cf. **426**.
5 *The farthest part of Beckley* in RAF 1/3/2.
6 *by accident* added in RAF 1/3/2.
7 *Rye Foreign* in RAF 1/3/2.
8 *10* in RAF 1/3/2.
9 *drowned* omitted in RAF 1/3/2.
10 Date omitted in RAF 1/3/2.
11 *Jane Forwood* in RAF 1/3/2; *Jane daughter of John Forward* in PAR 254/1/1/3.
12 *drowned* omitted in RAF 1/3/2.
13 *£10 15s* in RAF 1/3/2: £6 19s 9d, the correct sum, is said on f 58 to be carried forward, but £6 19s 3d was erroneously brought forward on f 60. £10 15s 6d was paid with an additional 5s: QO/EW 28; QAF 2/1/E2.

245 7 May 1785. Hooe. Richard Peckham: drowned himself. 7 miles. £1 5s 3d.
2 July 1785. Pett. Matthew Newman: found drowned[1] in Pett Level. 12 miles. £1 9s.
9 Sept. 1785. Beckley. Edward Almon: found drowned. 10 miles. £1 7s 6d.
5 Dec. 1785. The farther part of Herstmonceux. Unknown man: found hanging. 12 miles. £1 9s.
18 Feb. 1786. St Mary in the Castle. Robert Young: found dead in a deep waterfall.[2] 6 miles. £1 4s 6d.

23 Feb. 1786. Hollington. Sarah Gower: hanged herself. 5 miles. £1 3s 9d.
25 Feb. 1786. Staplecross in Ewhurst.[3] Stephen Weekes, infant: drowned.[4] 5 miles. £1 3s 9d.
6 Apr. 1786. Playden. Mary Thompsett: drowned herself. 16 miles. £1 12s.
Total £10 14s 9d; allowed at Easter sessions 1786. [QR/E 627, no 78]

[This bill is also in RAF 1/3/2, ff 60, 135.]

1 *accidentally drowned* in RAF 1/3/2.
2 *in a deep waterfall* omitted in RAF 1/3/2.
3 *in Ewhurst* omitted in RAF 1/3/2.
4 *by accident* added in RAF 1/3/2.

246 28 Apr. 1786. Hollington. Thomas Catt: hanged himself. 5 miles. £1 3s 9d.
25 June 1786. Guestling. Ann Oldridge:[1] accidentally shot. 9 miles. £1 6s 9d.
20 Sept. 1786. The further part of Crowhurst. John Button: found dead.[2] 4 miles. £1 3s.
25 Sept. 1786. Mountfield.[3] Ann wife of Joseph Grant: killed by a fall. 4 miles. £1 3s.
20 Oct. 1786. The further part of[4] Ticehurst, next to Wadhurst.[5] Unknown woman: found dead in an oast-house. 15 miles.[6] £1 11s 3d.[7]
30 Oct. 1786. Salehurst. John Pemble: died from taking too large a quantity of laudanum. 6 miles. £1 4s 6d.
19 Nov. 1786. Beckley. William Peckham: run over by the Rye coach.[8] 10 miles. £1 7s 6d.
3 Feb. 1787. Burwash Weald. William Baker: found dead. 10 miles. £1 7s 6d.
6 Mar. 1787. Beauport.[9] Female bastard child of Hannah Rickard: found dead, wrapped up in an apron under the bed. 3 miles. £1 2s 3d.
18 Mar. 1787. Catsfield. William Cramp: killed by a fall from his horse. 2 miles. £1 1s 6d.[10]
28 Mar. 1787. Pett. William Burgess: found dead in a wood. 10 miles. £1 7s 6d.
Total £13 18s 6d;[11] allowed at Easter sessions 1787. [QR/E 631, no 47]

[This bill is also in RAF 1/3/2, ff 135–136.]

1 *Eldridge* in RAF 1/3/2.
2 *fell dead in a fit* in RAF 1/3/2.
3 *John's Cross* in RAF 1/3/2.
4 *The further part of* omitted in RAF 1/3/2.
5 *next to Wadhurst* omitted in RAF 1/3/2.
6 *15 miles* omitted in RAF 1/3/2.
7 *£1 12s* in RAF 1/3/2.
8 *run over by the Rye stage and killed* in RAF 1/3/2.
9 *in Hollington* added in RAF 1/3/2.
10 Whole entry omitted in RAF 1/3/2.
11 *£12 17s 9d* in RAF 1/3/2. £13 18s 6d was paid with an additional 5s: QO/EW 28; QAF 2/1/E2.

247 15 June 1787. Fairlight Poorhouse. Thomas Field:[1] found dead. 8 miles. £1 6s.
12 July 1787. Ashburnham Place. John Wilson: hanged himself. 4 miles.[2] £1 3s.
24 Nov. 1787. Peasmarsh. William Moore: killed by a loaded wagon going over him. 14 miles. £1 10s 6d.
25 Jan. 1788. The farther part of Ticehurst. Elizabeth Farley: being lunatic, poisoned herself. 13 miles. £1 9s 9d.[3]
15 Apr. 1788. Playden. Edward Carswell: killed by his clothes catching and being pulled in between the cog- and trendle-wheels of a mill.[4] 16 miles. £1 12s.[5]

19 Apr. 1788. Rye Foreign. Elizabeth Cloake, infant: poisoned herself eating arsenic. 17 miles. £1 12s 9d.
23 Apr. 1788. Brede. Ann Langford: being lunatic, hanged herself. 7 miles. £1 5s 3d.
20 May 1788. Ticehurst. Thomas French: run over by a wagon and killed. 12 miles. £1 9s.[6]
24 May 1788. Brightling. Thomas Relfe: killed by[7] earth falling on him as he was drawing stone. 5 miles. £1 3s 9d.
24 Nov. 1788. The farther part of Salehurst. William Fowle, infant: killed by a dung-cart falling on him.[8] 9 miles. £1 6s 9d.
3 Feb. 1789. Battle. Charles Morden, esq.: drowned watering his horse. £1.[9]
3 Mar. 1789. Herstmonceux. Elizabeth wife of John Aldridge: being lunatic,[10] hanged herself. 10 miles. £1 7s 6d.
Total £16 6s 3d;[11] allowed at Easter sessions 1789. [QR/E 639, no 39]

[This bill is also in RAF 1/3/2, ff 136, 171–172.]

1 *sen.* added in RAF 1/3/2.
2 *4 miles* omitted in RAF 1/3/2.
3 Cf. *SCM*, XIX, 259, where the date of death, correctly copied from *SWA*, is given in as 28 Jan. Farley was buried by order of the coroner on 27 Jan.: PAR 492/1/1/3; Ep. II/16/188A.
4 *killed by being caught by his clothes and pulled between the cog-wheel and trendle-wheel of a mill and instantly killed* in RAF 1/3/2.
5 Cf. *SCM*, XIII, 739; *SCM*, XX, 51.
6 Cf. *SCM*, XIII, 739; *SCM*, XX, 77.
7 *a quantity of* added in RAF 1/3/2.
8 *falling on him* omitted in RAF 1/3/2.
9 Cf. *SCM*, XXI, 168.
10 *being lunatic* omitted in RAF 1/3/2.
11 *£16 6s 3d; deducted the inquisition taken at Battle which is to be paid to Mr Nairn, £1; leaving £15 6s 3d* in RAF 1/3/2. £16 6s 3d was paid with an additional 5s: QO/EW 29; QAF 2/1/E2. Mr Nairn, who presumably held the inquest, must have been Charles Nairn, the Battle hundred coroner: cf. **300–302**.

248 28 Apr. 1789. Peasmarsh. Samuel Tasker: found dead.[1] 14 miles. £1 10s 6d.
30 Apr. 1789. Udimore. Henry Brissenden: being lunatic, hanged himself. 11 miles. £1 8s 3d.
16 May 1789. Herstmonceux. William Martin: killed by a fall out of a tree in Herstmonceux Park.[2] 10 miles. £1 7s 6d.
24 June 1789. Netherfield. Thomas Barden jun.: hanged himself. 2 miles. £1 1s 6d.
23 July 1789. Wood's Corner, Dallington. Thomas Bates, infant: killed by a fall from a horse. 6 miles. £1 4s 6d.
17 Aug. 1789. Playden. William Simmonds, infant: drowned.[3] 16 miles. £1 12s.
24 Aug. 1789. Warbleton. Catherine Friend: drowned herself.[4] 10 miles. £1 7s 6d.
26 Sept. 1789. Ticehurst. Elizabeth Usherwood: killed by a fall down the cellar stairs.[5] 12 miles. £1 9s.
18 Dec. 1789. Heathfield. Samuel Napp, a child aged 10: accidentally shot by his father. 11 miles. £1 8s 3d.
4 Jan. 1790. Catsfield. James Goldsmith: hanged himself. 2 miles. £1 1s 6d.[6]
6 Jan. 1790. Westfield. Richard Foster, a child:[7] fell into a well and was drowned. 5 miles. £1 3s 9d.
14 Jan. 1790.[8] Ashburnham. John Hook: fell off the mow in a barn and fractured his skull.[9] 5 miles. £1 3s 9d.

Total £15 18s; allowed at Epiphany sessions 1790. [QR/E 642, no 62]

[This bill is also in RAF 1/3/2, ff 172, 218–219.]

1 *supposed to have dropt in a fit* added in RAF 1/3/2.
2 *taking rooks* added in RAF 1/3/2.
3 *by accident* added in RAF 1/3/2.
4 *herself* omitted in RAF 1/3/2.
5 *no person being in the house with her* added in RAF 1/3/2.
6 Cf. *SCM*, XVI, 73, where the date of death, correctly copied from *SWA*, is given as 6 Jan. Goldsmith was buried on 10 Jan.: PAR 288/1/1/3; Ep. II/16/38A.
7 *infant* in RAF 1/3/2.
8 Date omitted in RAF 1/3/2.
9 *fell from a wheat-mow and fractured his skull* in RAF 1/3/2.

249 22 Jan. 1790. Peasmarsh. William Filmer: accidentally drowned. 11 miles. £1 10s 6d.
3 Mar. 1790. Hurst Green. William Peck, a child:[1] accidentally drowned. 8 miles. £1 6s.
10 Mar. 1790. Herstmonceux. John Mitten: being lunatic, hanged himself. 10 miles. £1 7s 6d.
12 May 1790. Beckley. Anthony Husband: killed by a loaded wagon going over him. 11 miles. £1 8s 3d.
18 May 1790. Ewhurst. Elizabeth Leonard alias Ford: found dead and supposed to be[2] killed falling from her chair, she being alone and much intoxicated with liquor.[3] 6 miles. £1 4s 6d.
5 July 1790. Hooe. Mary Bonyface: being lunatic, hanged herself. 6 miles. £1 4s 6d.
9 July 1790. Crowhurst Bridge. John Cramp: being lunatic, hanged himself. 4 miles. £1 3s.
Total £9 4s 3d; allowed at Midsummer sessions 1790. [QR/E 644, no 64]

[This bill is also in RAF 1/3/2, ff 219, 242.]

1 *William Pack, infant* in RAF 1/3/2; buried at Salehurst as William Peck, aged 2: PAR 477/1/1/11.
2 *found ... to be* omitted in RAF 1/3/2.
3 *killed by a fall from her chair, being intoxicated and alone* in RAF 1/3/2.

250 2 Sept. 1790. Udimore. John Butchers, infant: run over by a wagon and killed.[1] 10 miles. £1 7s 6d.
12 Sept. 1790. Guestling. John Swaine: found dead in a ditch. 9 miles. £1 6s 9d.
4 Nov. 1790. The further part of Northiam.[2] Deddecourt Rootes: drowned.[3] 12 miles. £1 9s.
10 Dec. 1790. Ashburnham. Nathaniel Gooding: died through excessive drinking. 4 miles. £1 3s.
5 Jan. 1791. Milkhurst Toll, Heathfield. Hannah wife of John Rabbit: died suddenly on the road.[4] 11 miles. £1 8s 3d.
Total £6 14s 6d; allowed at Epiphany sessions 1791. [QR/E 646, no 68]

[This bill is also in RAF 1/3/2, ff 242–243.]

1 *and killed* omitted in RAF 1/3/2.
2 *next Newenden* added in RAF 1/3/2.
3 *accidentally drowned* in RAF 1/3/2.
4 *on the road* omitted in RAF 1/3/2.

251 19 June 1791. Pett. Samuel Waters: drowned at sea and[1] drove on shore.[2] 12 miles. £1 9s.
30 June 1791. Telham in Battle. Richard Mace: fell in a fit on the road and instantly died. 2 miles. £1 1s 6d.
13 July 1791. The Black Horse, Battle. William Yeilding:[3] killed by the overturn of a wagon.[4] 2 miles. £1 1s 6d.
8 Sept. 1791. Penhurst. Samuel Christian: killed by the falling in of a marl-pit.[5] 3 miles. £1 2s 3d.
21 Dec. 1791. Salehurst. Thomas Gillett: found in a ditch speechless and soon after died. 7 miles. £1 5s 3d.
3 Jan. 1792. Wartling. William Hover: found dead. 8 miles. £1 6s.
11 Jan. 1792. Broadstreet Green,[6] Hooe. William Cramp: found dead.[7] 7 miles. £1 5s 3d.
Total £8 10s 9d; allowed at Epiphany sessions 1792. [QR/E 650, no 99]

[This bill is also in RAF 1/3/2, ff 243–244 and its final entry is in RAF 1/4/1.]

1 *drowned at sea and* omitted in RAF 1/3/2.
2 *was drove on shore on the sea-beach* in RAF 1/3/2.
3 *aged about 12* added in RAF 1/3/2.
4 *killed by a wagon laden with coals overturning upon him* in RAF 1/3/2.
5 *accidentally killed by the falling in of marl as he was digging in a marl-pit* in RAF 1/3/2.
6 *Broadstreet Green* omitted in RAF 1/4/1.
7 *found dead* omitted in RAF 1/4/1.

252 27 Jan. 1792. Standard Hill, Ninfield. Samuel Beeding,[1] a child aged about 13:[2] drowned by accident. 5 miles. £1 3s 9d.
11 Feb. 1792. Brede. Thomas Gaffil:[3] found dead.[4] 7 miles. £1 5s 3d.
[*Date omitted.*] Brede. William Morris: in a violent fit of frenzy cut his throat.[5] 7 miles. £1 5s 3d.
16 Mar. 1792. Wartling. Unknown travelling[6] woman: killed by the sweeps of a windmill. 8 miles. £1 6s.
22 Mar. 1792. Battle.[7] Elizabeth Sargent: hanged herself.[8] 1 mile. £1 0s 9d.[9]
5 June 1792. Playden. Mary wife of William Moon: being intoxicated with liquor, fell with her head against a large stone which occasioned her immediate death. 17 miles. £1 12s 9d.
Total £7 13s 9d; allowed at Midsummer sessions 1792. [QR/E 652, no 92]

[This bill is also in RAF 1/3/3, p 1 and two of its entries are in RAF 1/4/1.]

1 *Samuel Beeching* in RAF 1/3/3; *Samuel son of Charity and Mary Beeching* in PAR 430/1/1/2.
2 *a child ... 13* omitted in RAF 1/3/3.
3 *Gaftil* in RAF 1/3/3; *Gaffel* in PAR 253/1/1/2.
4 *found dead in Westfield; journey to Brede, the body being removed there* in RAF 1/3/3.
5 *died in a fit of frenzy, cut his throat* in RAF 1/3/3.
6 *travelling* omitted in RAF 1/3/3 and RAF 1/4/1. She was probably Elizabeth Clayton, pauper, buried at Wartling 17 Mar.: PAR 503/1/1/2. Cf. *SCM*, XXI, 372, where 26 is an error for 19 Mar. (cf. *SWA*, 19 Mar. 1792).
7 *Battle* omitted in RAF 1/4/1.
8 *being lunatic, hanged herself* in RAF 1/3/3.
9 Annotated: *Mr Nairn* in RAF 1/3/3; *Coroner for Mr Nairn* in RAF 1/4/1. Presumably Charles Nairn held the inquest as Battle hundred coroner: cf. **247**.

253 9 Aug. 1792. Ewhurst. Stephen Nicolls, infant:[1] drowned by accident.[2] 7 miles. £1 5s 3d.
2 Oct. 1792. Catsfield. John Ellis: killed by James Warner in fighting.[3] 2 miles. £1 1s 6d.[4]
27 Dec. 1792. Ewhurst. Ann Edwards: perished through the inclemency of the weather.[5] 7 miles. £1 5s 3d.
12 June 1793. Westfield.[6] Thomas Ransom: found drowned. 7 miles. £1 5s 3d.
7 July 1793. Mountfield.[7] Robert Buss, infant: killed by a dung-cart.[8] 4 miles. £1 3s.
13 Aug. 1793. Bexhill. William Jarratt: accidentally drowned bathing in the sea. 7 miles. £1 5s 3d.
21 Oct. 1793. Ashburnham. Revd Charles Coldcall:[9] being lunatic, threw himself into a well and was drowned.[10] 5 miles. £1 3s 9d.
9 Nov. 1793. Ewhurst. Edward Wybourn: killed by a fall from a haystack. 6 miles. £1 4s 6d.
14 Nov. 1793. Fairlight. Mary wife of Edward[11] Nash: found dead on Fairlight Down. 6 miles. £1 4s 6d.
21 Nov. 1793. Bexhill. Edward Crowhurst: dislocated his neck by a fall from a scaffold. 7 miles. £1 5s 3d.
31 Dec. 1793. Ninfield. Abraham Young: being lunatic, hanged himself. 5 miles. £1 3s 9d.
4 Feb. 1794. Ticehurst. John Eaton: found dead. 13 miles. £1 9s 9d.
18 Mar. 1794. Vinehall. John Rolfe: found drowned. 3 miles. £1 2s 3d.
26 Apr. 1794. Bardown in[12] Ticehurst. Robert Strickland: found dead. 14 miles. £1 10s 6d.
Total £17 9s 9d; allowed at Easter sessions 1794. [QR/E 659, no 41]

[This bill is also in RAF 1/3/3, pp 2–4 and its first two entries are in RAF 1/4/1.]

1 *infant* omitted in RAF 1/4/1.
2 *by accident* omitted in RAF 1/4/1.
3 *in fighting* omitted in RAF 1/3/3 and RAF 1/4/1.
4 Cf. **427**.
5 *and want of sustenance* added in RAF 1/3/3.
6 *The further part of Westfield* in RAF 1/3/3.
7 *Mountfield Park* in RAF 1/3/3.
8 *dung* omitted in RAF 1/3/3.
9 *vicar of this parish* in PAR 233/1/1/3.
10 *being lunatic, threw himself into a well and was there found suffocated and drowned* in RAF 1/3/3.
11 *Samuel* in RAF 1/3/3.
12 *Bardown in* omitted in RAF 1/3/3.

254 28 July 1794. Bexhill.[1] John Osborne: accidentally killed by the throwing of a bowl in a skittle-ground.[2] 6 miles. £1 4s 6d.[3]
16 Aug. 1794. Crowhurst. Robert Fuller: killed by the falling of a wall of Crowhurst church. 3 miles. £1 2s 3d.
3 Sept. 1794. Warbleton. William Elphick: killed by a wagon going over him.[4] 8 miles. £1 6s.
7 Nov. 1794. Hollington.[5] Charlotte Ingall, infant:[6] killed by a baggage-wagon running over her.[7] 4 miles. £1 3s.
16 Jan. 1795. Ore. Humphrey Russell, a private in the Warwick Regiment of Militia: perished through the inclemency of the weather. 6 miles. £1 4s 6d.

11 Apr. 1795. Beechdown in Battle. George Sadd: killed by a fall from a horse. 1 mile. £1 0s 9d.
Total £7 1s; allowed at Easter sessions 1795. [QR/E 663, no 44]

[This bill is also in RAF 1/3/3, pp 4–5 and two of its entries are in RAF 1/4/1.]

1 *Sidley Green in Bexhill* in RAF 1/4/1.
2 *accidentally killed by a bowl* in RAF 1/4/1.
3 Cf. *SCM*, XXIV, 353.
4 *killed by a wagon running over his head* in RAF 1/3/3.
5 *Baldslow* in RAF 1/4/1.
6 *infant* omitted in RAF 1/4/1.
7 *killed by a wagon running over it and killing it on the spot* in RAF 1/3/3; *killed ... over her* omitted in RAF 1/4/1.

255 10 May 1795. Northiam. Thomas Sheather: found dead in a wood. 10 miles. £1 7s 6d.
5 June 1795. Ninfield. William Aldridge: after wrestling with another man in play, soon after[1] fell in a fit and died. 5 miles. £1 3s 9d.
13 June 1795. Burwash Weald. Joseph Leaney: found dead in a barn. 10 miles. £1 7s 6d.
8 July 1795. Beechdown Farm,[2] Battle. James King: killed by a fall from his horse. 2 miles. £1 1s 6d.
4 Feb. 1796. Beckley. John Dale: found dead.[3] 10 miles. £1 7s 6d.
Total £6 7s 9d; allowed at Easter sessions 1796. [QR/E 667, no 52]

[This bill is also in RAF 1/3/3, pp 5–6 and its last entry is in RAF 1/4/1.]

1 *soon after* omitted in RAF 1/3/3.
2 *Beech Farm* in RAF 1/3/3.
3 *died in a fit* in RAF 1/4/1.

256 8 July 1796. Herstmonceux. Jesse Streator:[1] killed by a wagon going over him. 10 miles. £1 7s 6d.
2 Oct. 1796. Kitchenour Farm,[2] Beckley. Thomas Newsham: found dead in a hovel where he had been left the night before very much[3] in liquor. 12 miles. £1 9s.
8 Oct.[4] 1796. Pett. Unknown man: found dead on the sea-shore.[5] 12 miles. £1 9s.
3 Jan. 1797. Brightling. New-born infant: found dead in a hedge. 6 miles. £1 4s 6d.
17 Apr. 1797. The further part of Iden. John Barnes: found dead in the marsh.[6] 18 miles. £1 13s 6d.
24 May 1797. Ashburnham. William Hutchinson: killed by a wagon going over him. 3 miles. £1 2s 3d.
19 June 1797.[7] Warbleton.[8] William Bourne: died through excessive drinking.[9] 10 miles. £1 7s 6d.
Total £9 13s 3d; allowed at Midsummer sessions 1797. [QR/E 672, no 111]

[This bill is also in RAF 1/3/3, pp 6, 281 and three of its entries are in RAF 1/4/1.]

1 *Streater* in RAF 1/3/3.
2 [blank] *Farm* in RAF 1/3/3.
3 *very much* omitted in RAF 1/3/3.
4 *Oct.* erased in RAF 1/3/3.
5 *beach* in RAF 1/3/3 and RAF 1/4/1.
6 *in the marsh* omitted in RAF 1/3/3.
7 Date omitted in RAF 1/4/1.

8 *church* added in RAF 1/4/1.
9 *in Warbleton* added in RAF 1/4/1.

257 18 July 1797. Salehurst. John Soan, infant: drowned. 6 miles. £1 4s 6d.
26 July 1797. Whatlington. Infant: found dead in James Croft's house. 3 miles. £1 2s 3d.
29 July 1797. Heathfield. Samuel Hunt: killed by a fall from a horse. 11 miles. £1 8s 3d.
25 Sept. 1797. Warbleton. Harry Kemp: found dead in a barn. 10 miles. £1 7s 6d.[1]
2 Nov. 1797. Burwash. Richard Winch: died from excessive drinking. 11 miles. £1 8s 3d.
16[2] Nov. 1797. Ticehurst. Mary Wheeler: being lunatic, hanged herself. 12 miles. £1 9s.
29 Jan. 1798. Ninfield. George Piper: being lunatic, hanged himself. 5 miles. £1 3s 9d.
1 Apr. 1798.[3] Battle. Thomas D'Oyley, an Artillery driver:[4] died through excessive drinking. £1.[5]
Total £10 3s 6d; allowed at Easter sessions 1798. [QR/E 675, no 90]

[This bill is also in RAF 1/3/3, pp 281–282 and all its entries except that of 29 Jan. are in RAF 1/4/1.]

1 *9 miles, £1 6s 9d* in RAF 1/4/1.
2 *12* in RAF 1/4/1.
3 Date omitted in RAF 1/3/3.
4 *Thomas Doyle, a driver belonging to the detachment of Royal Artillery station[ed] at Battle* in RAF 1/3/3; *Thomas Doyle, an Artillery driver* in RAF 1/4/1; *Thomas Doyle, artillery* in PAR 236/1/1/5.
5 *£1 0s 6d* in RAF 1/4/1.

258 26 Apr. 1798. Battle Gunpowder Mills.[1] Thomas Lavender: killed by the blowing up of the mills.[1] £1.[2]
[*Date omitted.*] Battle Gunpowder Mills. William Pimm: the like. £1.[2]
[*Date omitted.*] Battle Gunpowder Mills. John Blundell: the like. £1.[2]
17 May 1798.[3] The further part of[4] Ewhurst. George Williamson,[5] a private in the Northamptonshire[6] Regiment of Militia:[7] accidentally drowned.[8] 8 miles. £1 6s.[9]
17 May 1798.[10] Salehurst. Thomas Cowley: killed by a blow given by William Dunk, a private in the East Kent Regiment of Militia.[11] 8 miles. £1 6s.[12]
21 May 1798, the inquest being adjourned to that day.[13] Salehurst.[14] Thomas Cowley. 8 miles. 6s.[12]
23 May 1798. Bexhill. Thomas Cramp: being lunatic,[15] hanged himself. 7 miles. £1 5s 3d.
24 May 1798. Silverhill Barracks.[16] William Quiver, a private in the Northampton Regiment of Militia:[17] stabbed himself with a bayonet.[18] 8 miles. £1 6s.
30 May 1798. Bexhill. Sarah Wenham: being lunatic, hanged herself. 7 miles. £1 5s 3d.
19 June 1798. Bexhill Barracks.[19] Thomas Savage: killed by a loaded wagon running over him.[20] 8 miles. £1 6s.
8 July 1798. The further part of Herstmonceux. Sarah Weekes, infant: found drowned. 12 miles. £1 9s.
Total £12 9s 6d;[21] allowed at Midsummer sessions 1798. [QR/E 676, no 43]

[This bill is also in RAF 1/3/3, pp 282, 353 and every entry except the last is in RAF 1/4/1.]

1 *Works* in RAF 1/4/1.

2 Cf. *SCM*, XXVIII, 192.
3 Date omitted in RAF 1/4/1.
4 *The further part of* omitted in RAF 1/3/3 and RAF 1/4/1.
5 [blank] *Wilkinson* in RAF 1/4/1; *George Williamson, Northampton soldier* in PAR 324/1/1/4.
6 *Northampton* in RAF 1/3/3.
7 *a private ... Militia* omitted in RAF 1/4/1.
8 *found drowned* in RAF 1/4/1.
9 [blank] *miles, £1* in RAF 1/4/1.
10 Date omitted in RAF 1/4/1.
11 *died in consequence of a strike from a soldier of the East Kent Militia in Hastings* in RAF 1/4/1.
12 Cf. **428**.
13 *to finish the inquest* in RAF 1/4/1; *the inquest ... day* omitted.
14 *Hurst Green* in RAF 1/4/1.
15 *being lunatic* omitted in RAF 1/4/1.
16 *Barracks* omitted in RAF 1/4/1.
17 *of Militia* omitted in RAF 1/3/3; *a private ... Militia* omitted in RAF 1/4/1.
18 *in a frenzy* added in RAF 1/4/1.
19 *Barracks* omitted in RAF 1/3/3 and RAF 1/4/1.
20 *killed by a wagon running over his body* in RAF 1/4/1.
21 *£12 9s 3d* in RAF 1/3/3: £8 9s 3d, the correct sum, is said on p 282 to be carried forward, but only £8 9s was brought forward on p 353. £12 9s 6d was paid with an additional 5s: QO/EW 33; QAF 2/1/E3.

259 13 Aug. 1798. Ore. Thomas Barnes: killed by a fall from his horse. 6 miles. £1 4s 6d.
17 Aug. 1798. Silverhill Barracks. Elizabeth Mason: killed by the sweeps of a windmill.[1] 8 miles. £1 6s.
16[2] Nov. 1798. Iden. John Baker: accidentally drowned. 18 miles. £1 13s 6d.
Total £4 4s; allowed at Epiphany sessions 1799.[3] [QR/E 678, no 110]

[This bill is also in RAF 1/3/3, p 353 and all its entries are in RAF 1/4/1.]

1 *mill* in RAF 1/4/1.
2 *10* in RAF 1/3/3 and RAF 1/4/1.
3 Payment was received by Thomas Barton: RAF 1/3/3. Barton was later coroner of Battle, Robertsbridge and Gostrow hundreds and of Hastings rape: cf. **280–290, 307, 308**.

260 21 Jan. 1799. Fairlight church. New-born male bastard[1] child of Elizabeth Lavender. 9 miles. £1 6s 9d.[2]
[25 Mar.] 1799. Paid the clerk of assize fee on returning inquisition of murder 5s.[3]
3 Feb.[4] 1799. Ponts Green, Ashburnham. Edward Jarrett: being in liquor,[5] perished through the inclemency of the weather. 5 miles. £1 3s 9d.
13 Mar. 1799. Battle Park.[6] New-born infant: found dead.[7] £1.[8]
[25 Mar.] 1799. Paid the clerk of assize fee on returning inquisition of murder 5s.[9]
14 Mar. 1799. Warbleton. Samuel York: being lunatic, hanged himself. 11 miles. £1 8s 3d.
26 Apr. 1799. Heathfield. David Mepham: found hanging in a wood.[10] 12 miles. £1 9s.
14 May 1799. The farther part of Wartling. Unknown man: found hanging in a hedge. 12 miles. £1 9s.
Total £8 6s 9d; allowed at Midsummer sessions 1799. [QR/E 680, no 56]

[This bill is also in RAF 1/3/3, p 354 and six of its entries are in RAF 1/4/1.]

1 *bastard* omitted in RAF 1/4/1.
2 *The jury bringing in the verdict of murder against Elizabeth Lavender, fee thereon 13s 4d* in RAF 1/4/1. Cf. **429**.

3 *25 Mar. 1799. East Grinstead assizes. Rex v Lavender. Paid return of inquisition 5s* in RAF 1/4/1. Cf. **429**.
4 *Saturday 2 Feb.* in RAF 1/4/1. 2 Feb. was a Saturday.
5 *being intoxicated* in RAF 1/4/1.
6 *Battle Lawn* in RAF 1/4/1.
7 *found in a pond* in RAF 1/4/1.
8 Cf. **458**.
9 *25 Mar. 1799. East Grinstead assizes. Same of unknown. Paid return of inquisition 5s* in RAF 1/4/1. Cf. **458**.
10 *in a wood* omitted in RAF 1/3/3.

261 13 Aug. 1799. Ashburnham. John Bartlett: killed by a fall of earth in a pit digging for brick-earth.[1] 4 miles. £1 3s.
10 Oct. 1799. Bexhill. John Herbett:[2] died through excessive drinking. 6 miles. £1 4s 6d.
11 Dec. 1799. Burwash. Thomas Pankhurst: accidentally killed by the rope breaking in descending into a limestone-pit. 9 miles. £1 6s 9d.
11 Jan. 1800. Silverhill Barracks. William Arkworth, a gunner in the Royal Artillery: accidentally[3] killed by a gun-carriage going over his body. 8 miles. £1 6s.
22 Jan. 1800. Westfield. Richard Crokett:[4] accidentally drowned. [6 miles.][5] £1 4s 6d.
[*blank*] Apr. 1800. Guestling. Female bastard child of Frances Veness,[6] aged about 6 weeks:[7] died in its mother's arms as she was carrying it over Fairlight Down in a tempestuous rainy night. 9 miles. £1 6s 9d.
Total £7 11s 6d; allowed at Easter sessions 1800. [QR/E 683, no 71]

[This bill is also in RAF 1/3/3, p 467 and three of its entries are in RAF 1/4/1.]

1 *killed by the fall of brick-earth* in RAF 1/3/3; *killed by a fall of brick-earth on him* in RAF 1/4/1.
2 *James Herbet* in RAF 1/3/3; *James Herbert* in RAF 1/4/1; *Isaac Herbert* in PAR 240/1/1/3.
3 *accidentally* omitted in RAF 1/4/1.
4 *Cockett* in RAF 1/3/3.
5 *6 miles* in RAF 1/3/3.
6 *Frances natural daughter of Fanny Venis, buried 16 Apr.* in Ep. II/16/80A.
7 *aged ... weeks* omitted in RAF 1/3/3.

262 22 June 1800. Gardner Street, Herstmonceux. Benjamin Head:[1] found drowned. 10 miles. £1 7s 6d.
17 July 1800. Willard's Hill, Burwash. Henry Beeching: killed by an overturn of a loaded wagon. 9 miles. £1 6s 9d.[2]
20 Dec. 1800. Sedlescombe. John Gibbs: killed by the blowing up[3] of a gunpowder mill. 3 miles. £1 2s 3d.
31 Dec. 1800. Catsfield. Stephen Bennett: perished through the inclemency of the weather. 3 miles. £1 2s 3d.
28[4] Mar. 1801. Battle Gunpowder Mills.[5] John Paine: killed by the blowing up of the drying-house at the gunpowder mills. 1 mile. £1 0s 9d.
Total £5 19s 6d; allowed at Easter sessions 1801. [QR/E 687, no 94]

[This bill is also in RAF 1/3/3, p 468 and four of its entries are in RAF 1/4/1.]

1 *Hoad* in RAF 1/3/3 and PAR 399/1/1/5.
2 *killed by an overturn of a wagon loaded with lime; 8 miles, £1 6s* in RAF 1/4/1. Cf. *SCM*, XXX, 341.
3 *explosion* in RAF 1/3/3.
4 *20* in RAF 1/3/3 and RAF 1/4/1.
5 *Battle Powder-Mills* in RAF 1/3/3; *The Powder-Mills* in RAF 1/4/1.

263 6 July 1801. Gardner Street, Herstmonceux.[1] Thomas Vidler: supposed to have come by[2] his death fighting but it was found he died a natural death. 10 miles. £1 7s 6d.
13 July 1801. Cowbeech in Wartling. Pennington Pettitt: killed by a wagon going over his body.[3] 11 miles. £1 8s 3d.
10[4] Aug. 1801. Bexhill. William Freeman: killed by a fall from his horse.[5] 7 miles. £1 5s 3d.
22 Sept. 1801. Udimore. William Austen: killed by a wagon going over his body.[6] 11 miles. £1 8s 3d.[7]
4 Jan. 1802. Bexhill. Thomas Darby, a soldier in the Westminster[8] Regiment of Militia: found drowned.[9] 7 miles. £1 5s 3d.
13 Jan. 1802. The further part of Brightling Down. John Smith: being lunatic, hanged himself. 7 miles. £1 5s 3d.
Total £7 19s 9d; allowed at Epiphany sessions 1802. [QR/E 690, no 92]

[This bill is also in RAF 1/3/4, p 3 and four of its entries are in RAF 1/4/1.]

1 *Gardner Street* omitted in RAF 1/3/4; *Herstmonceux* omitted in RAF 1/4/1.
2 *got* in RAF 1/4/1; *come by* omitted.
3 *going ... body* omitted in RAF 1/3/4.
4 *18* in RAF 1/3/4 and RAF 1/4/1.
5 *a horse* in RAF 1/3/4.
6 *going ... body* omitted in RAF 1/4/1.
7 *11 (*or *10) miles* omitted; *£1 7s 6d* in RAF 1/4/1.
8 *Middlesex* in RAF 1/3/4.
9 *accidentally drowned* in RAF 1/3/4; *Thomas Darby ... found drowned* omitted (blank space left) in RAF 1/4/1.

264 4[1] Apr. 1802. Battle Barracks. William Blanks, a private in the 9th[2] Regiment of Foot stationed in the barracks:[3] cut his throat. 1 mile. £1 0s 9d.
2 June 1802. Peasmarsh. Thomas Lancaster: found dead in a wood. 14 miles. £1 10s 6d.[4]
26 Aug. 1802. Etchingham. Richard Peck, a child:[5] accidentally drowned. 11 miles. £1 8s 3d.[6]
2 Sept. 1802. Fairlight.[7] John Burton: being lunatic, hanged himself. 9 miles. £1 6s 9d.
27 Sept. 1802. Salehurst. John Burgess: found drowned.[8] 7 miles. £1 5s 3d.
1 Oct. 1802. The Black Horse, Battle. Robert Ballard: killed by a fall from[9] a horse. 2 miles. £1 1s 6d.
4 Oct. 1802. Ponts Green, Ashburnham. Edward Bayley: accidentally[10] killed by a fall from a bridge. 5 miles. £1 3s 9d.
10 Oct. 1802. Burwash. John[11] Burton: suffocated by damp air in a limestone-pit. 9 miles. £1 6s 9d.
24 Oct. 1802.[12] Bexhill. 3 unknown men:[13] their bodies were cast on the sea-coast.[14] 7 miles. £3 5s 3d.
30 Oct. 1802. Battle Barracks. Joseph Heaven, captain of[15] the Royal Artillery stationed in the barracks:[16] being lunatic, cut his throat. 1 mile. £1 0s 9d.
11 Nov. 1802. Fairlight.[17] John Saunders: being lunatic, hanged himself. 9 miles. £1 6s 9d.
18 Nov.[18] 1802. Pett. Jane Coney:[19] found dead in a wagon standing in a hovel.[20] 10 miles. £1 7s 6d.
Total £17 3s 9d; allowed at Epiphany sessions 1803. [QR/E 694, no 77]

[This bill is also in RAF 1/3/4, pp 3–4 and all its entries are in RAF 1/4/1.]

1 *14* in RAF 1/3/4 and RAF 1/4/1.
2 *East Norfolk*: Swinson, 89.
3 *stationed in the barracks* omitted in RAF 1/3/4 and RAF 1/4/1.
4 *13 miles, £1 9s 9d* in RAF 1/4/1.
5 *Richard Peck, an infant* in RAF 1/3/4.
6 *Omitted* written in margin in RAF 1/4/1.
7 *The further end of Fairlight* in RAF 1/4/1.
8 *in Mr Hilder's mill-dam* added in RAF 1/4/1.
9 *of* in RAF 1/3/4.
10 *accidentally* omitted in RAF 1/4/1.
11 *James* in RAF 1/3/4 and RAF 1/4/1.
12 Date omitted in RAF 1/4/1.
13 *unknown* omitted in RAF 1/4/1; *Thomas Hammond, aged 58, and 2 seamen who were drowned* in PAR 310/1/1/3.
14 *whose bodies were cast up by the sea drowned* in RAF 1/3/4; *found drowned and cast up by the sea* in RAF 1/4/1.
15 *in* in RAF 1/3/4.
16 *stationed in the barracks* omitted in RAF 1/3/4 and RAF 1/4/1.
17 *Guestling* in RAF 1/4/1.
18 *Dec.* in RAF 1/4/1. The burial was on 19 Dec.: PAR 442/1/1/2.
19 *Coneyfield* in PAR 442/1/1/2.
20 *found dead in a wagon in a lodge* in RAF 1/3/4; *died by the visitation of God in a wagon* in RAF 1/4/1.

265 7 June 1803. Bexhill.[1] William Campbell, a private in the 91st[2] Regiment of Foot:[3] being lunatic, hanged himself.[4] 7 miles. £1 5s 3d.
12 June 1803. Brede. Thomas Bennett: found dead. 7 miles. £1 5s 3d.
28 July 1803.[5] Bexhill. Felix Roakes: killed by the overturn of a loaded[6] timber-carriage.[7] 7 miles. £1 5s 3d.
6 Sept. 1803. Ore. Henry Gateley: suffocated by a lump of earth falling[8] in a stone-pit. 6 miles.[9] £1 4s 6d.
20 Sept. 1803. Ashburnham. Samuel Honiset: killed[10] by a loaded wagon running over his body.[11] 4 miles. £1 3s.
27 Sept. 1803.[12] North Trade Turnpike Gate, Battle. Thomas Foord, a child:[13] killed by the overturn of[14] a cart. [1 mile.][15] £1 0s 9d.
20 Oct. 1803. Cottenden in Ticehurst. Robert Cane: killed by a fall from a ladder. 13 miles. £1 9s 9d.[16]
31 Oct. 1803. Herstmonceux. James Goble: killed by the sweeps of a windmill. 9 miles. £1 6s 9d.
1 Nov. 1803. Battle Barracks.[17] Mark Kelk and William White, gunners of the Royal Artillery:[18] shot by Andrew Murphey and James Fannan, soldiers belonging to the 70th[19] Regiment of Foot.[20] 1 mile. £2 0s 9d.[21]
Fees to the clerk of assize on returning the inquisitions 10s.[21]
11 Nov. 1803. Battle Barracks. William Bradford:[22] suffocated in the well.[23] 1 mile. £1 0s 9d.
Total £13 12s; allowed at Epiphany sessions 1804. [QR/E 698, no 130]

[This bill is also in RAF 1/3/4, p 120 and all its entries, but not the payment of fees, are in RAF 1/4/1.]

1 *Bexhill Barracks* in RAF 1/4/1.
2 *Argyllshire Highlanders*: Swinson, 193.
3 *of Foot* omitted in RAF 1/4/1.
4 *at Bexhill Barracks* added in RAF 1/3/4.

5 Date omitted in RAF 1/4/1.
6 *loaded* omitted in RAF 1/4/1.
7 *killed by an overturn of a carriage loaded with timber* in RAF 1/3/4.
8 *on him as he was drawing stone* added in RAF 1/3/4 and RAF 1/4/1.
9 *6 miles* omitted in RAF 1/4/1.
10 *accidentally killed* in RAF 1/3/4 and RAF 1/4/1.
11 *running over him* in RAF 1/3/4 and RAF 1/4/1.
12 Date omitted in RAF 1/4/1.
13 *an infant* in RAF 1/3/4 and RAF 1/4/1.
14 *killed by a fall from* in RAF 1/4/1.
15 *1 mile* in RAF 1/3/4.
16 *14 miles, £1 10s 6d* in RAF 1/4/1.
17 *Battle* omitted in RAF 1/4/1.
18 *gunners of the Royal Artillery* omitted in RAF 1/3/4.
19 *Surrey*: Swinson, 170.
20 *soldiers of the 70th* in RAF 1/4/1.
21 Cf. **459**. The assizes began on 19 Mar. 1804, long after this bill was allowed.
22 *Thomas Bradford* in RAF 1/4/1; *Thomas Branford of the 39th Regiment of Infantry* in PAR 236/1/1/5. The 39th was the East Middlesex Regiment of Foot: Swinson, 136.
23 *suffocated in a well by damps at Battle Barracks* in RAF 1/3/4; *accidentally suffocated in a well at Battle Barracks* in RAF 1/4/1.

266 16 Feb. 1804. Ewhurst. John Luck sen.:[1] died by the visitation of God.[2] 7 miles. £1 5s 3d.[3]
27 Feb. 1804. Fairlight. John Whitear, late a corporal in the 40th[4] Regiment of Foot: accidentally drowned in a ditch.[5] 8 miles. £1 6s.
6 Mar. 1804. Silverhill.[6] James Crag, late a private in the 69th[7] Regiment of Foot: died through the inclemency of the weather. 8 miles. £1 6s.
7 Mar. 1804. Bexhill. Robert White, late a private in the 11th Light Dragoons:[8] accidentally[9] drowned in the sea. 7 miles. £1 5s 3d.
11 Apr. 1804. Catsfield. Edward Payne late of Catsfield:[10] accidentally fell down in a fit and died.[11] 3 miles. £1 2s 3d.
18 May[12] 1804. Bexhill. Edward Britt, infant: accidentally drowned.[13] 7 miles.[14] £1 5s 3d.[15]
16 July 1804. Peasmarsh. Robert Johnson: accidentally killed by a cart running against him and striking him on his temple.[16] 14 miles. £1 10s 6d.
2 Sept. 1804. Bexhill.[17] William Immanhausen, a private in[18] the King's German Legion: accidentally drowned[19] in the sea. 7 miles. £1 5s 3d.
2 Sept. 1804.[20] Bexhill. Charles Renseck,[21] a private in the King's German Legion: accidentally drowned[22] in the sea. 7 miles. £1 5s 3d.
10 Sept. 1804. Ewhurst.[23] George Preston: died by excessive drinking. 6 miles. £1 4s 6d.[24]
31 Dec. 1804. Bexhill. Richard Kempe: being lunatic,[25] hanged himself. 7 miles. £1 5s 3d.
3 Jan. 1805. Bexhill. James Marchant: found drowned in a ditch near[26] Cooden in Bexhill. 9 miles. £1 6s 9d.
5 Jan. 1805. Peasmarsh. Thomas Avery: found accidentally[27] drowned in a well. 14 miles. £1 10s 6d.
Total £16 18s;[28] allowed at Epiphany sessions 1805. [QR/E 702, no 142]

[This bill is also in RAF 1/3/4, pp 172–173 and ten of its entries are in RAF 1/4/1.]

1 *sen.* omitted in RAF 1/3/4 and RAF 1/4/1.

2 *found dead* in RAF 1/3/4 and RAF 1/4/1.
3 *6 miles, £1 4s 6d* in RAF 1/4/1.
4 *2nd Somersetshire*: Swinson, 137.
5 *accidentally* and *in a ditch* omitted in RAF 1/3/4 and RAF 1/4/1.
6 *Silverhill Barracks* in RAF 1/3/4 and RAF 1/4/1.
7 *South Lincolnshire*: Swinson, 169.
8 *a private in the 11th Regiment of Dragoons* in RAF 1/3/4 and RAF 1/4/1.
9 *accidentally* omitted in RAF 1/3/4 and RAF 1/4/1.
10 *late of Catsfield* omitted in RAF 1/3/4.
11 *died in a fit* (*accidentally fell down* omitted) in RAF 1/3/4.
12 *10 May* in RAF 1/4/1; *May* omitted in RAF 1/3/4 (the entry being immediately after that of 11 Apr., which was inserted; the previous entry is for March).
13 *drowned at the poorhouse* in RAF 1/3/4; *accidentally drowned at the poorhouse* in RAF 1/4/1.
14 *7 miles* omitted in RAF 1/3/4
15 *8 miles, £1 6s* in RAF 1/4/1.
16 *and striking him on his temple* omitted in RAF 1/3/4; *running ... temple* omitted in RAF 1/4/1.
17 *Hospital* [written above *Sidley* struck through] *in Bexhill* in RAF 1/4/1.
18 *William Immenhausen of* in RAF 1/4/1.
19 *bathing* added in RAF 1/3/4 and RAF 1/4/1.
20 Date omitted in RAF 1/3/4.
21 *John Rensch* in RAF 1/3/4; *Charles Rensch* in RAF 1/4/1; *an Hanoverian soldier* [unnamed] in PAR 240/1/1/3.
22 *bathing* added in RAF 1/3/4 and RAF 1/4/1.
23 *Staplecross in Ewhurst* in RAF 1/3/4 and RAF 1/4/1.
24 *5 miles, £1 3s 9d* in RAF 1/4/1.
25 *being lunatic* omitted in RAF 1/4/1.
26 *the sea at* added in RAF 1/3/4.
27 *accidentally* omitted in RAF 1/3/4.
28 *£16 14s 3d* in RAF 1/3/4. £16 18s is correct and was paid with an additional 5s: QO/EW 36; QAF 2/1/E5, f 108v.

267 24 Jan. 1805. Bexhill Down. William Hammond: being intoxicated with liquor, fell down and was suffocated in the mud. 7 miles. £1 5s 3d.
5 Feb. 1805. Mountfield. William Haiselden: killed by a fall driving a post-chaise. 4 miles. £1 3s.
11 Mar. 1805. Bexhill sea-coast. Joseph Mier, a private in the King's German Legion: being lunatic, drowned himself in the sea. 8 miles. £1 6s.
17 May 1805. Ninfield. Jane Sargeant: being lunatic, drowned herself. 5 miles. £1 3s 9d.
30 June 1805. Bulverhythe. Henry Vine, a private in the King's German Legion: accidentally drowned in a ditch. 8 miles. £1 6s.
3 July 1805. Bexhill. August Ottmer, a private in the King's German Legion: being lunatic, shot himself. 7 miles. £1 5s 3d.
5 July 1805. Cooden. William Man, an Artillery driver: accidentally drowned while bathing in the sea. 9 miles. £1 6s 9d.
27 Aug. 1805. The Royal Oak, Whatlington. John Guy: was accidentally rode over and died from the hurt received thereby. 3 miles. £1 2s 3d.
6 Sept. 1805. Cooden.[1] Bernard Sext,[2] a private in the King's German Legion: found dead in a ditch with his legs tied. 8 miles. £1 6s.[3]
11 Sept. 1805. Cooden. Bernard Sext, the inquest being adjourned for want of evidence. [8 miles.] 6s.[3]
12 Sept. 1805. Bulverhythe. Henry Cutler: died at Bexhill from excessive drinking. 8 miles. £1 6s.

22 Sept. 1805. The further part of Brede. Thomas Griffin, an infant aged about 2: accidentally drowned. 9 miles. £1 6s 9d.
Total £14 3s; allowed at Michaelmas sessions 1805. [QR/E 705, no 86]

[This bill is also in RAF 1/3/4, pp 263–264.]

1 *Cooden Down* in RAF 1/3/4.
2 *Barnard Sexth* in RAF 1/3/4.
3 Cf. **460**.

268 25 Oct. 1805. Herstmonceux. James Griffen: being lunatic, shot himself. 9 miles. £1 6s 9d.
24 Dec. 1805. Warbleton Common. Susannah Clapson: died from a concussion on the brain[1] but whether from a fall or otherwise the jury had no evidence. 10 miles. £1 7s 6d.
8 Jan. 1806. The further part[2] of Bodiam. Richard Fowle: found dead. 10 miles.[3] £1 7s 6d.
5 Mar. 1806. Battle. Mary Inman: found dead in her room. £1.
16 Mar. 1806. The further part of Burwash.[4] Mary Pankhurst: perished in the snow. 13 miles. £1 9s 9d.
16 May 1806. Hurst Green. Amelia Hatton, infant:[5] accidentally killed by a cart.[6] 8 miles. £1 6s.
12 June 1806. Westfield. Thomas Weller: being lunatic, hung himself. 5 miles. £1 3s 9d.
7 July 1806. Wartling. John Farmer: accidentally killed by a fall from his horse. 9 miles. £1 6s 9d.
29 July 1806. Pett. Thomas Porter:[7] accidentally drowned.[8] 12 miles. £1 9s.
14 Aug. 1806. Cooden in Bexhill.[9] George Knight: accidentally[10] killed by a fall from a scaffold.[11] 10 miles. £1 7s 6d.
17 Aug. 1806. Westfield. Thomas Sargent, infant: accidentally[12] drowned. 5 miles. £1 3s 9d.
30 Sept. 1806. Dallington. William Carly: accidentally killed by a wagon. 6 miles. £1 4s 6d.
1 Oct. 1806. Warbleton. Male infant: found dead. 10 miles. £1 7s 6d.
23 Nov. 1806. Salehurst.[13] [*blank*] Allen:[14] found drowned.[15] 7 miles. £1 5s 3d.
20 Dec. 1806. Playden. Elizabeth Baker: found dead.[16] 15 miles. £1 11s 3d.
5[17] Jan. 1807. The further part of[18] Salehurst. Thomas Saxby: found dead. 10 miles. £1 7s 6d.
[*Date omitted.*] Battle.[19] Thomas Barden: accidentally[20] killed in a limestone-pit.[21] 2 miles. £1 1s 6d.[22]
Total £22 5s 9d;[23] allowed at Epiphany sessions 1807. [QR/E 710, no 136]

[This bill is also in RAF 1/3/4, pp 299–300, the final six entries are again in RAF 1/3/5, f 13 and three of the entries are in RAF 1/4/2, where there is also the following entry:
27 Nov. 1806. Inquisition at Robertsbridge Turnpike. £1 4s 6d.]

1 *by a concussion of the brain received by a bruise* in RAF 1/3/4.
2 *The farther end* in RAF 1/3/4.
3 *10 miles* omitted in RAF 1/3/4.
4 *The further part of Burwash Down* in RAF 1/3/4.
5 *aged about 18 months* added in RAF 1/3/4.
6 *accidentally run over by a cart and killed upon the spot* in RAF 1/3/4.
7 *of the Royal Wagon Train* added in RAF 1/3/4.
8 *bathing in the Defence Cut or Canal* added in RAF 1/3/4.

9 *Cooden in* omitted in RAF 1/3/4.
10 *accidentally* omitted in RAF 1/3/4.
11 *at the Martello Tower* added in RAF 1/3/4.
12 *accidentally* omitted in RAF 1/3/4.
13 *Northbridge Street, Salehurst* in RAF 1/3/5.
14 *Infant* in RAF 1/3/5; *William Allen aged 47* in PAR 477/1/1/11.
15 *accidentally drowned* in RAF 1/3/4; *found* omitted in RAF 1/3/5.
16 *found dead* omitted in RAF 1/4/2.
17 *4* in RAF 1/4/2.
18 *The further part of* omitted in RAF 1/4/2.
19 *Battle* omitted in RAF 1/4/2; *Rat Farm, Battle* in RAF 1/3/4.
20 *accidentally* omitted in RAF 1/3/5 and RAF 1/4/2.
21 *lime-pit* in RAF 1/4/2.
22 *2 miles, 1s 6d* struck through in RAF 1/4/2. A 'form of proceeding' based on this inquest states that the jurors were of Battle hundred and the foreman was Thomas Vidler: SHE 2/6/1.
23 After the entry of 17 Aug. RAF 1/3/4 has: *£14 8s 3d; bill made out; received by Mr Barton and paid by him to JTS*; Mr Barton was Thomas Barton, later coroner of Battle, Robertsbridge and Gostrow hundreds and of Hastings rape (cf. **280–290**, **307**, **308**) and JTS was John Tilden Sampson. At the end of the bill it has: *£22 5s 9d; deduct the above bill of JTS £14 8s 3d; carried to Partnership Ledger £7 17s 6d*. The part of the bill in RAF 1/3/5 ends: *Total £7 17s 6d; received at Lewes Jan. 1807; T Barton*. The quarter sessions records list the payment of the whole £22 5s 9d with an additional 5s to Tilden Sampson: QO/EQ 38; QAF 2/1/E6, f 14v.

269 6 Feb. 1807. Battle Barracks. Alexander Irving:[1] accidentally drowned. £1.
22 Feb. 1807. Bexhill. Patrick Reed: wilfully murdered by some person or persons unknown.[2] 7 miles. £1 5s 3d.[3]
[16 Mar.] 1807. Paid the clerk of assize on returning the inquisition 5s.[4]
7 May 1807. The farther part of Mountfield. Female infant: accidentally smothered. 6 miles. £1 4s 6d.
10 June 1807. Vinehall in Mountfield. Joshua Hiscock: died by the visitation of God. 4 miles. £1 3s.
21 May 1807. Brede. Mary Noakes: accidentally drowned. 9 miles. £1 6s 9d.
3 Aug. 1807. Bexhill. Joseph Shoesmith: died by the visitation of God. 7 miles. £1 5s 3d.
8 Sept. 1807. Playden. Maurice Nowland: being lunatic, stabbed himself. 16 miles. £1 12s.
24 Sept. 1807. Bexhill. Benjamin Geering: accidentally killed. 7 miles. £1 5s 3d.
Total £10 7s; allowed at Michaelmas sessions 1807.[5] [QR/E 713, no 88]

[This bill is also in RAF 1/3/5, ff 13–14 and two of its entries are in RAF 1/4/2.]

1 *soldier* added in RAF 1/4/2.
2 *wilfully ... unknown* omitted in RAF 1/4/2.
3 Cf. **461**.
4 *Payment: return inquisition at the assizes 5s* in RAF 1/3/5. Cf. **461**.
5 Payment was received by T Barton: RAF 1/3/5. Thomas Barton was later coroner of Battle, Robertsbridge and Gostrow hundreds and of Hastings rape: cf. **280–290**, **307**, **308**.

270 5[1] Jan. 1808. Playden. John Gilchrist: accidentally drowned.[2] 16 miles. £1 12s.
8 Mar. 1808. Brede. William Sinden: accidentally killed by the blowing up of a powder-mill. £1.
[8 Mar.][3] 1808. Brede. Henry Harrod: accidentally killed by the blowing up of a powder-mill. £1.

[8 Mar.][3] 1808. Brede. William Wenham: accidentally killed by the falling of a house in consequence of the blowing up of the said powder-mill. 5 miles to take the 3 inquests. £1 3s 9d.
10 Mar. 1808. Silverhill, Salehurst. An infant: found dead when it appeared it was[4] still-born. 8 miles. £1 6s.
28 Mar. 1808. Burwash. John Langridge: being lunatic, hanged himself. 12 miles. £1 9s.
10 Apr. 1808. Bexhill. Thomas Crowhurst: accidentally drowned. £1.
[10 Apr.][5] 1808. Bexhill. John Symonds: accidentally drowned. 7 miles to take the 2 inquests. £1 5s 3d.
2 May 1808. Ewhurst. Mary Chrismas: accidentally drowned. 7 miles. £1 5s 3d.
3 June 1808. Fairlight. William Browne: accidentally killed by a cart-wheel passing over his body. 10 miles. £1 7s 6d.
13 Aug. 1808. Hooe. James Foord: accidentally drowned. 6 miles. £1 4s 6d.
20 Sept. 1808. Peasmarsh. Richard Woodland: found dead. 13 miles. £1 9s 9d.
30 Sept. 1808. Battle Barracks.[6] Robert Ellis: died from the effects of mercury taken by him by way of medicine. £1.
12 Nov. 1808. Battle Barracks.[6] James Allen: being lunatic, cut his throat.[7] £1.
17 Nov. 1808. Ewhurst. Richard Eldridge: accidentally shot. 6 miles. £1 4s 6d.
28 Nov. 1808. Bexhill. Frances Foots: supposed to have been poisoned but[8] no evidence appeared from which the cause of her death could be ascertained. 5 miles. £1 3s 9d.
10 Jan. 1809. The further part of Iden. John Keil: accidentally drowned. 20 miles. £1 15s.
Total £21 6s 3d; allowed at Epiphany sessions 1809.[9] [QR/E 718, no 163]

[This bill is also in RAF 1/3/5, ff 14, 68–69 and its first entry is in RAF 1/4/2.]

1 *3* in RAF 1/4/2.
2 *accidentally drowned* omitted in RAF 1/4/2.
3 *8 Mar.* in RAF 1/3/5.
4 *found ... was* omitted in RAF 1/3/5.
5 *10 Apr.* in RAF 1/3/5.
6 *Battle Barracks* omitted in RAF 1/3/5.
7 *killed himself* in RAF 1/3/5.
8 *supposed ... but* omitted in RAF 1/3/5.
9 Payment was received by T Barton: RAF 1/3/5. Thomas Barton was later coroner of Battle, Robertsbridge and Gostrow hundreds and of Hastings rape: cf. **280–290**, **307**, **308**.

271 9 Feb. 1809. Pett. Unknown man: found drowned. 10 miles. £1 7s 6d.
12 Feb. 1809. The further part of Iden. Thomas Parr: accidentally drowned. 20 miles. £1 15s.
12 May 1809. Bexhill. Henry Hesse: died by the visitation of God. 7 miles. £1 5s 3d.
21 May 1809. Icklesham. William Gadd: accidentally killed by falling from a wagon. 12 miles. £1 9s.
24 May 1809. Salehurst. William Webster: found drowned. 7 miles. £1 5s 3d.
28 May 1809. Bexhill.[1] Unknown man: found drowned. 8 miles. £1 6s.
12 June 1809. Bexhill. Caston Meijer: being lunatic, shot himself. 7 miles. £1 5s 3d.
23 June 1809. Ewhurst. Samuel Gunter: accidentally killed by falling from a wagon. 7 miles. £1 5s 3d.
1 July 1809. Crowhurst. Joseph Naylor: fell in a fit and expired. 5 miles. £1 3s 9d.
31 July 1809. Etchingham. Hannah Russell: accidentally drowned. 11 miles. £1 8s 3d.

14 Aug. 1809. Bexhill. Unknown man: cast up by the sea. 6 miles. £1 4s 6d.
4 Sept. 1809. Brede. William Lullham: found dead. 10 miles. £1 7s 6d.
13 Sept. 1809. Icklesham. William Hyland: found dead. 12 miles. £1 9s.
10 Oct. 1809. Bexhill. Unknown man: drowned. 6 miles. £1 4s 6d.
10 Dec. 1809. Bexhill. David Davis: accidentally killed. 6 miles. £1 4s 6d.
20 Dec. 1809. Bexhill. Unknown man: drowned. 6 miles. £1 4s 6d.
3 Jan. 1810. Salehurst. Michael McDonough: found to have died by the visitation of God. 8 miles. £1 6s.[2]
Total £22 11s; allowed at Epiphany sessions 1810.[3] [QR/E 722, no 165]

[This bill is also in RAF 1/3/5, ff 69, 91.]

1 *Little Common in Bexhill* in RAF 1/3/5.
2 Cf. **430**.
3 Payment was received by TB: RAF 1/3/5. TB was Thomas Barton, later coroner of Battle, Robertsbridge and Gostrow hundreds and of Hastings rape: cf. **280–290**, **307**, **308**.

272 27 Mar. 1810. Mountfield. Edward Easton: fell in a fit and expired.[1] 4 miles. £1 4s.
6 Apr. 1810. Bexhill. Edward Woodfine: cut his throat in a delirium. 6 miles. £1 5s 6d.
8 Apr. 1810. Warbleton. Susannah Evenden: being lunatic, hung herself. 12 miles. £1 10s.
19 May 1810. Burwash. Sarah Bishop: being lunatic, threw herself into a well. 12 miles. £1 10s.
Total £5 9s 6d[2] allowed at Midsummer sessions 1810. [QR/E 724, no 71]

[This bill, which is also in RAF 1/3/5, f 96, is unique in that £1 1s was claimed and allowed for each inquest instead of the normal £1.]

1 *immediately* added in RAF 1/3/5.
2 *£5 3s 6d* [in error for *£5 5s 6d*] in RAF 1/3/5 where all the inquest charges are changed from £1 1s to £1. £5 9s 6d was paid, with an additional 5s, after Tilden Sampson's death to his personal representatives: QO/EW 39; QAF 2/1/E6, f 117v.

Bills of William Thorpe

273 19 June 1810. Guestling. Henry Beeching: hung himself; verdict lunacy. 3 miles. £1 2s 3d.
8 July 1810. Robertsbridge. Edmund Dunk: accidentally killed by a wagon. 14 miles. £1 10s 6d.
2 Sept. 1810. Robertsbridge. George Putland: found drowned. 14 miles. £1 10s 6d.
6 Sept. 1810. Penhurst. Thomas Mann: fell in a fit and instantly died. 12 miles. £1 9s.
29 Sept. 1810. Playden. John Biddle: found dead in a stable. 13 miles. £1 9s 9d.
30 Sept. 1810. Bexhill. Johann Zubitzky: found dead. 6 miles. £1 4s 6d.
9 Jan. 1811. Playden. John White: accidentally killed by a wagon. 13 miles. £1 9s 9d.
14 Jan. 1811. Fairlight. William Barnes: killed by the upsetting of a boat at sea in attempting to come on shore. 5 miles. £1 3s 9d.
Total £11; allowed at Epiphany sessions 1811. [QR/E 726, no 129]

[All Thorpe's journeys were from Hastings but that is never stated in his bills. RAF 1/3/5, f 96 has the following entries beneath which there is a cross:
31 Aug. [1810]. Bexhill. John Kryger:[1] being lunatic, hanged himself. 5 miles. £1 3s 9d.

3 Sept. [1810]. Bexhill. Henry Missling:[2] found dead. 6 miles. £1 4s 6d.]

1 *John Cruger, aged 22, buried 1 Sept. 1810* in PAR 240/1/1/3.
2 *Henry Messlin, aged 22, buried 3 Sept. 1810* in PAR 240/1/1/3.

274 10 Apr. 1811. Mountfield. Thomas Slatter: fell in a fit and instantly died. 12 miles. £1 9s.
5 May 1811. Beckley. John Parker: accidentally killed by a wagon. 20 miles. £1 15s.
29 June 1811. Ticehurst. New-born female bastard child: still-born. 20 miles. £1 15s.
17 July 1811. The outbounds of St Mary in the Castle. John Dabner: accidentally killed by a wagon. 3 miles. £1 2s 3d.
10 Aug. 1811. Wartling. Kirby Simmons: accidentally shot. 15 miles. £1 11s 3d.
14 Aug. 1811. Mountfield. John Beng: accidentally burnt to death. 14 miles. £1 10s 6d.
20 Aug. 1811. Bexhill. Child:[1] found dead. 6 miles. £1 4s 6d.
11 Sept. 1811. Bexhill. Frederick Leamann: accidentally killed by a gun-carriage. 6 miles. £1 4s 6d.
11 Oct. 1811. Fairlight. Unknown man: washed on shore. 5 miles. £1 3s 9d.
15 Oct. 1811. Etchingham. Frances Braban: drowned by falling into a saw-pit. 20 miles. £1 15s.
15 Nov. 1811. Heathfield. John Lewes, lunatic: drowned himself. 20 miles. £1 15s.
8 Jan. 1812. Mountfield. Richard Golding: found dead. 14 miles. £1 10s 6d.
25 Feb. 1812. Warbleton. Thomas Haiselden, lunatic: hung himself. 17 miles. £1 12s 9d.
23 Apr. 1812. Peasmarsh. James Selmes: found drowned. 14 miles. £1 10s 6d.
7 Sept. 1812. Flimwell. William Guest: accidentally killed by a wagon. 19 miles. £1 14s 3d.
20 Nov. 1812. Ewhurst. Samuel Ticehurst: fell in a fit and instantly died. 13 miles. £1 9s 9d.
Total £24 3s 6d; allowed at Epiphany sessions 1813. [QR/E 734]

1 Possibly Frederick Dorman, infant, buried at Bexhill 29 Aug.: PAR 240/1/1/3.

275 2 Feb. 1813. Bexhill. Christian Baumgartner: found dead. 6 miles. £1 4s 6d.
2 Mar. 1813. Ashburnham. William Jones: died from excessive drinking. 12 miles. £1 9s.
12 Mar. 1813. Warbleton. Joseph Perry: died by the visitation of God. 17 miles. £1 12s 9d.
29 Mar. 1813. Ewhurst. William Henley, lunatic: drowned himself. 14 miles. £1 10s 6d.
12 Apr. 1813. Bexhill. Christian Fernor: found dead. 6 miles. £1 4s 6d.
12 May 1813. Northiam. George Dunk: found drowned. 20 miles. £1 15s.
15 May 1813. Bexhill. Henry Stellner:[1] found dead. 6 miles. £1 4s 6d.
7 Aug. 1813. Dallington. Ruth Waterman: accidentally killed by a cart. 12 miles. £1 9s.
9 Aug. 1813. Catsfield. Thomas Ballard: accidentally killed by a fall from a horse. 9 miles. £1 6s 9d.
17 Sept. 1813. Dallington. Thomas Dray, lunatic: hung himself. 15 miles. £1 11s 3d.
15 Nov. 1813. Burwash. Jane Hicks: fell into a privy. 18 miles. £1 13s 6d.
25 Dec. 1813. Ashburnham. John Beall: fell into a fit and instantly died. 10 miles. £1 7s 6d.
Total £17 8s 9d; allowed at Epiphany sessions 1814. [QR/E 738, no 100]

1 *Kellner* in PAR 240/1/5/1.

276 6 Sept. 1814. Ashburnham. William Baker: accidentally killed by a fall from a horse. 12 miles. £1 9s.
16 Sept. 1814. Westfield. Benjamin Catt: accidentally killed by a fall from a horse. 6 miles. £1 4s 6d.
28 Sept. 1814. Ashburnham. Benjamin Glyd: died by the visitation of God. 12 miles. £1 9s.
31 Oct. 1814. Herstmonceux. William Kennard: found drowned. 15 miles. £1 11s 3d.
5 Dec. 1814. Guestling. Thomas Fairhall: died from excessive drinking. 3 miles. £1 2s 3d.
[*blank*] Dec. 1814. Pett. William Finch: died from excessive drinking. 5 miles. £1 3s 9d.
12 Jan. 1815. Salehurst. Sarah Friend: suffocated. 15 miles. £1 11s 3d.
21 Feb. 1815. Mountfield. Samuel Heasmer: accidentally killed by the fall of some stone. 12 miles. £1 9s.
31 Mar. 1815. Boreham Street. Maria Davis: found dead. 12 miles. £1 9s.
19 May 1815. Brede. Albert Coleman: accidentally killed by a cart. 10 miles. £1 7s 6d.
11 June 1815. Fairlight. Christopher Thorpe: found drowned. 4 miles. £1 3s.
1 July 1815. Brightling. Joseph Perry, lunatic: hung himself. 15 miles. £1 11s 3d.
Total £16 10s 9d; allowed at Midsummer sessions 1815. [QR/E 744]

277 5 July 1815. Etchingham. Ann King: found drowned. 17 miles. £1 12s 9d.
4 Sept. 1815. Gardner Street. Samuel Wood, lunatic: hung himself. 15 miles. £1 11s 3d.
20 Oct. 1815. Crowhurst. Hannah Lingham, lunatic: hung herself. 6 miles. £1 4s 6d.
13 Nov. 1815. Guestling. John Watson: died from excessive drinking. 4 miles. £1 3s.
29 Nov. 1815. Mountfield. Henry Britt: died by the visitation of God. 14 miles. £1 10s 6d.
5 Dec. 1815. Boreham Street. John Simmonds: died in consequence of a fall from a horse. 12 miles. £1 9s.
17 Dec. 1815. Cliff End, Fairlight. Mary Sinnock: found drowned. 5 miles. £1 3s 9d.
24 Dec. 1815. Cliff End, Fairlight. John Crouch: found drowned. 5 miles. £1 3s 9d.
17 Jan. 1816. Playden. Catherine Lennox: found drowned. 14 miles. £1 10s 6d.
19 Jan. 1816. Hollington. Spencer Maplesden: accidentally killed by a thrashing-machine. 4 miles. £1 3s.
25 Jan. 1816. Catsfield. Unknown child: found dead. 10 miles. £1 7s 6d.
26 Mar. 1816. Peasmarsh. Thomas Jury: died by the visitation of God. 14 miles. £1 10s 6d.
11 May 1816. Warbleton. Richard Apps, lunatic: hung himself. 18 miles. £1 13s 6d.
27 May 1816. Burwash. James Napp: died by the visitation of God. 17 miles. £1 12s 9d.
12 July 1816. Ninfield. John Cox: accidentally killed by a horse. 10 miles. £1 7s 6d.
24 Aug. 1816. Wartling. William Punnett: found drowned. 14 miles. £1 10s 6d.
18 Nov. 1816. Playden. William Couchman: found drowned. 14 miles. £1 10s 6d.
21 Dec. 1816. Fairlight. Henry Hogsflesh: accidentally killed by a fall from his horse. 4 miles. £1 3s.
26 Dec. 1816. Ewhurst. John Brown: died by the visitation of God. 15 miles. £1 11s 3d.

Total £26 19s; allowed at Epiphany sessions 1817. [QR/E 750]

278 13 Feb. 1817. Fairlight. Charles Paine: died from excessive drinking. 5 miles. £1 3s 9d.
24 Apr. 1817. Beckley. Thomas Fulman: accidentally killed by a cart. 15 miles. £1 11s 3d.
28 June 1817. Playden. Sarah Drawbridge: died by the visitation of God. 13 miles. £1 9s 9d.
10 July 1817. Catsfield. Thomas Wenham: died by the visitation of God. 12 miles. £1 9s.
20 Aug. 1817. Witherenden. Ann Gibbs, lunatic: cut her throat. 20 miles. £1 15s.
1 Sept. 1817. Hollington. Thomas Soane: died by the visitation of God. 5 miles. £1 3s 9d.
20 Oct. 1817. Hooe. Sarah Gibson, lunatic: hung herself. 10 miles. £1 7s 6d.
7 Nov. 1817. Fairlight. Unknown man:[1] died by the visitation of God. 3 miles. £1 2s 3d.
3 Dec. 1817. Heathfield. Samuel Hunt: died by the visitation of God. 20 miles. £1 15s.
1 Mar. 1818. Ashburnham. John Phillips, lunatic: hung himself. 13 miles. £1 9s 9d.
14 Apr. 1818. Heathfield. Levi Luck: accidentally drowned. 19 miles. £1 14s 3d.
16 May 1818. Netherfield. Richard Moon: accidentally killed by the fall of some stone. 12 miles. £1 9s.
2 June 1818. Hollington. William Ashdown, lunatic: hung himself. 5 miles. £1 3s 9d.
13 June 1818. Ashburnham. John Kennard: accidentally killed by a water-barrel. 15 miles. £1 11s 3d.
2 July 1818. Ashburnham. Arthur West: killed by a kick from a horse. 13 miles. £1 9s 9d.
8 July 1818. Ewhurst. James Iggens: died in consequence of taking too large a quantity of medicine called Black Drops. 12 miles. £1 9s.
Total £23 4s; allowed at Midsummer sessions 1818. [QR/E 756]

[Attached to the bill is a note of the sum of £7 4s to which was added 5s, making £7 9s. Thorpe was paid the £23 4s with an additional 5s in July and the £7 9s, for inquisitions (no detailed bill of which survives), in Aug: QAF 2/1/E8, ff 41v–42, 46v–47.]

1 *John, surname and abode unknown, aged about 30* in PAR 325/1/5/1.

279 23 July 1818. Bexhill. George Ockenden: found drowned. 6 miles. £1 4s 6d.
11 Dec. 1818. Guestling. John Gurr, lunatic: hung himself. 3 miles. £1 2s 3d.
12 Dec. 1818. Etchingham. Wakeham Sutton: accidentally killed. 20 miles. £1 15s.
31 Dec. 1818. Burwash. John Weston: died by the visitation of God. 20 miles. £1 15s.
21 Jan. 1819. Heathfield. Jane Crowhurst: died from taking poison. 20 miles. £1 15s.
Total £7 11s 9d; allowed at Midsummer sessions 1819. [QR/E 760]

Bills of Thomas Barton

280 16 July 1819. Fairlight. Charles Field: accidentally drowned. 9 miles. £1 6s 9d.
5 Aug. 1819. Brede. Sophia Weller: killed by her brother, a lunatic.[1] 10 miles. £1 7s 6d.[2]
[*Date omitted.*] Rye. William Stone: found dead in Rye Foreign.[3] 15 miles. £1 11s 3d.

11 Aug. 1819. Bodiam. Sarah Ann Richardson:[4] died in consequence of taking laudanum administered medicinally.[5] 8 miles. £1 6s.
3 Sept. 1819. Dallington. John Starr: accidentally drowned.[6] 7 miles. £1 5s 3d.
30 Sept. 1819. Burwash.[7] John Haylor:[8] died by the visitation of God. 12 miles. £1 9s.
1 Nov. 1819. Guestling. Stephen Pont: shot at Pett. 9 miles. £1 6s 9d.
2 Nov. 1819. Guestling. Stephen Pont, it being necessary to adjourn. [9 miles.] 6s 9d.
29 Jan. 1820. Herstmonceux. Joseph Johnson: accidentally burned to death. 10 miles. £1 7s 6d.
27 Mar. 1820. Burwash. John Pilbeam: accidentally killed. 12 miles. £1 9s.
29 Apr. 1820. Heathfield. New-born male infant:[9] found dead.[10] 12 miles. £1 9s.
23 May 1820. Pett. Hammond Fairbrother, lunatic: shot himself.[11] 10 miles. £1 7s 6d.[12]
30 May 1820. Bexhill. Edmund Daw: accidentally killed. 7 miles. £1 5s 3d.
29 June 1820. Iden. Edward Martin: accidentally drowned. 14 miles. £1 10s 6d.
26 Sept. 1820. Battle. Francis Parker: died by the visitation of God. £1.
14 Oct. 1820. Salehurst. James Gillett: accidentally burned to death. 9 miles. £1 6s 9d.
15 Oct. 1820. Beckley. Catherine Santer: accidentally killed. 10 miles. £1 7s 6d.
Total £22 2s 3d; allowed at Michaelmas sessions 1820. [QR/E 765]

[All Barton's journeys were from Battle but that is never stated in his bills. Seven of the entries of this bill are also in RAF 1/4/2. Earlier inquests taken by Barton as Hastings rape coroner are in **308**.]

1 *killed ... lunatic* omitted in RAF 1/4/2.
2 *9 miles, £1 6s 9d* in RAF 1/4/2.
3 *found ...Foreign* omitted in RAF 1/4/2.
4 *Sophia Richardson* in RAF 1/4/2. She had been baptized on 10 Aug. as Sarah Ann daughter of Martha Richardson: PAR 250/1/2/1.
5 *died ...medicinally* omitted in RAF 1/4/2.
6 *accidentally drowned* omitted in RAF 1/4/2.
7 *Burwash Weald* in RAF 1/4/2.
8 *John Haylor* omitted (blank space left) in RAF 1/4/2.
9 *New-born child* in RAF 1/4/2.
10 *dead* omitted in RAF 1/4/2.
11 *lunatic, shot himself* omitted in RAF 1/4/2.
12 *12 miles, £1 9s* in RAF 1/4/2.

281 15 Dec. 1820. Catsfield. Mary Jeffery: being lunatic, hung[1] herself. 4 miles. £1 3s.[2]
25 Dec. 1820. Burwash. Henry Langridge: accidentally killed. 12 miles. £1 9s.
5[3] Feb. 1821. Mountfield. John Ashdown: died by the visitation of God.[4] 4 miles. £1 3s.[5]
16 Feb. 1821. Ninfield. Charles Cox: accidentally shot himself.[6] 6[7] miles. £1 4s 6d.[8]
22 Feb. 1821. Brightling. William Dunk: died by the visitation of God.[9] 5[10] miles. £1 3s 9d.[11]
20 Mar. 1821. Brede. Hannah Apps: accidentally burnt to death. 9 miles. £1 6s 9d.
6 Apr. 1821. Ewhurst. George Baker: died by the visitation of God. 8 miles. £1 6s.
11 Apr. 1821. Dallington. William Wilmshurst: accidentally drowned. 7 miles. £1 5s 3d.
1 May 1821. Battle. Unknown man: found dead. 2 miles. £1 1s 6d.
7 May 1821. Crowhurst. William Hammond: accidentally drowned. 4 miles. £1 3s.
14 May 1821. Salehurst. Thomas Page: accidentally killed. 8 miles. £1 6s.

13 June 1821. Peasmarsh.[12] George Masters: accidentally killed at Burwash.[13] 12 miles. £1 9s.
19 June 1821.[14] Battle. Joseph Goodman: accidentally killed.[15] £1.
[19 June][16] 1821. Mountfield. Mark Jarvis: found hanging.[17] 4 miles. £1 3s.[18]
23 June 1821. Fairlight. New-born male[19] infant: found.[20] 8 miles. £1 6s.
30 June 1821. Guestling. William Piper: died by the visitation of God.[21] 9 miles. £1 6s 9d.[22]
16 July 1821. Bodiam. John Smith: found drowned. 8 miles. £1 6s.
24 Aug. 1821. Battle. Edward Barnes: accidentally drowned.[23] £1.
26[24] Aug. 1821. Warbleton. William Catt: accidentally killed.[25] 12 miles. £1 9s.[26]
1 Oct. 1821. Northiam. Mary Booth: accidentally killed. 9 miles. £1 6s 9d.
8 Oct. 1821. Etchingham. James Hicks: accidentally burnt to death. 10 miles. £1 7s 6d.
15 Oct. 1821. Beckley. William Carter: died by the visitation of God. 11 miles. £1 8s 3d.
6 Nov. 1821. Ewhurst. New-born male child:[27] found dead. 8 miles. £1 6s.[28]
10 Dec. 1821. Sedlescombe. Female bastard child: found dead. 3 miles. £1 2s 3d.
12 Dec. 1821. Guestling. William Stace: died by the visitation of God. 9 miles. £1 6s 9d.
27 Dec. 1821. Udimore. Richard Tap: accidentally killed. 13 miles. £1 9s 9d.
Total £32 18s 9d;[29] allowed at Epiphany sessions 1822. [QR/E 770, no 66]

[This bill is also in RAF 1/3/7, ff 25–26 and twelve of its entries are in RAF 1/4/2.]

1 *destroyed* in RAF 1/4/2.
2 [*3 miles* omitted], *£1 2s 3d* in RAF 1/4/2.
3 *9* in RAF 1/4/2.
4 *died ... God* omitted in RAF 1/4/2.
5 *£1 3s* omitted in RAF 1/4/2.
6 *accidentally shot himself* omitted in RAF 1/4/2.
7 *5* in RAF 1/4/2.
8 *£1 3s 9d* omitted in RAF 1/4/2.
9 *died ... God* omitted in RAF 1/4/2.
10 *4* in RAF 1/4/2.
11 *£1 3s* omitted in RAF 1/4/2.
12 *Peasmarsh* written over *Beckley* which is struck through in RAF 1/4/2.
13 *Burwash* altered to *Peasmarsh* in RAF 1/3/7; *George ... Burwash* omitted in RAF 1/4/2.
14 Date omitted in RAF 1/4/2 where this entry follows the next.
15 *by a fall from his horse* added in RAF 1/4/2.
16 *19 June* in RAF 1/4/2 where this entry precedes the one before.
17 *found dead* in RAF 1/4/2.
18 Cf. **432**.
19 *female* in RAF 1/4/2.
20 *found* omitted in RAF 1/4/2.
21 *died in a fit* in RAF 1/4/2.
22 *8 miles, £1 6s* in RAF 1/4/2.
23 *accidentally drowned* omitted in RAF 1/4/2.
24 *27* in RAF 1/4/2.
25 *accidentally killed* omitted in RAF 1/4/2.
26 *10 miles, £1 7s 6d* in RAF 1/4/2.
27 *New-born male infant* in RAF 1/4/2.
28 *found dead* omitted; *7 miles, £1 5s 3d* in RAF 1/4/2.
29 *£33 3s 9d* in RAF 1/3/7 (i.e. £32 18s 9d with an additional 5s) which was paid: QO/EW 45; QAF 2/1/E9, ff 10v–11.

282 15 Jan. 1822. Ninfield. Richard Cramp: died by the visitation of God. 5 miles. £1 3s 9d.
5 Feb. 1822. Bexhill. Unknown man: found drowned. £1.[1]
[5 Feb.] 1822. [Bexhill.][2] Another unknown man: found drowned. 7 miles. £1 5s 3d.[3]
6 Feb. 1822. Brightling. Thomas Hawkins: died by the visitation of God. 6 miles. £1 4s 6d.
9 Feb. 1822. Ashburnham. Mary Crouch: accidentally killed.[4] 6 miles. £1 4s 6d.[5]
5 Mar. 1822. Pett. John Meryon: accidentally killed.[6] 10 miles. £1 7s 6d.
8 Mar. 1822. Northiam. James Rootes: accidentally killed. 10 miles. £1 7s 6d.
2 May 1822. Herstmonceux. Henry Brook: accidentally drowned. 10 miles. £1 7s 6d.
6 May 1822. Crowhurst. John Peacham: accidentally killed. 4 miles. £1 3s.
13 June 1822. Beckley. Elizabeth Gilbert: accidentally drowned. 11 miles. £1 8s 3d.
15 July 1822. Burwash. William Thomson: died by the visitation of God. 12 miles. £1 9s.
27 July 1822. Ewhurst. James Osborne: accidentally drowned. 8 miles. £1 6s.
14 Aug. 1822. Hooe. Elizabeth Chapman: died by the visitation of God. 7 miles. £1 5s 3d.
18 Sept. 1822. Battle. James Baker: being lunatic, hung himself. £1.
1 Oct. 1822. Robertsbridge. Elizabeth Dropshort:[7] died by the visitation of God. 6 miles. £1 4s 6d.
11 Oct. 1822. Heathfield. Elizabeth Holmes: accidentally killed. 12 miles. £1 9s.
17 Oct. 1822. Ninfield. James Page: accidentally killed. 6 miles. £1 4s 6d.
28 Nov. 1822. Heathfield. Edward Brooker: accidentally killed. 12 miles. £1 9s.[8]
5 Dec. 1822. Herstmonceux. New-born female infant. 10 miles. £1 7s 6d.
26 Dec. 1822. Salehurst. Ann Cheesman: died by the visitation of God. 7 miles. £1 5s 3d.
28 Dec. 1822. Battle. Edwin Metcalf: accidentally drowned. £1.
4 Sept. 1822. Ewhurst. James Noakes: accidentally killed. 8 miles. £1 6s.[9]
13 Jan. 1823. Rye. Thomas Barden: found drowned. 14 miles. £1 10s 6d.
19 Feb. 1823. Northiam. John Carter: accidentally burnt to death. 10 miles. £1 7s 6d.
Total £30 15s 9d; allowed at Easter sessions 1823. [QR/E 775]

[This bill is also in RAF 1/3/7, ff 26–27 and four of its entries are in RAF 1/4/2.]

1 *Man found drowned on 3 Feb.* (*Bexhill, unknown* and *£1* omitted) in RAF 1/4/2.
2 *Bexhill* in RAF 1/3/7.
3 *Man found drowned on 4 Feb.* (*Bexhill, another unknown* and *7 miles, £1 5s 3d* omitted) in RAF 1/4/2.
4 *by a mill* added in RAF 1/4/2.
5 *4 miles, £1 3s* in RAF 1/4/2.
6 *accidentally killed* omitted in RAF 1/4/2.
7 *Elizabeth Dropshort alias Sargeant, aged 44, who died in the* [sc. Salehurst] *workhouse* in PAR 477/1/5/2.
8 Cf. **433**.
9 This entry is in its correct chronological position in RAF 1/3/7.

283 30 Apr. 1823. Bodiam. James Davis: accidentally drowned. 9 miles. £1 6s 9d.
18 June 1823. Fairlight. Female bastard child: died by the visitation of God. 9 miles. £1 6s 9d.
1 July 1823. Northiam. Anthony Fuller: died by the visitation of God. 10 miles. £1 7s 6d.
9 July 1823. Silverhill, Salehurst.[1] William Bayley: accidentally killed. 8 miles. £1 6s.

15 Aug. 1823. Ticehurst. Edmund Cooper: being lunatic,[2] hung himself. 12 miles. £1 9s.
1 Sept. 1823. Battle Powder-Mills. Benjamin Beeching: accidentally killed. £1.
[1 Sept.] 1823. Battle Powder-Mills. William Bovis: accidentally killed. 2 miles. £1 1s 6d.
29 Sept. 1823. Salehurst. Daniel Oyler: accidentally scalded to death. 9 miles. £1 6s 9d.
18 Oct. 1823. Bexhill. Mary Fuller: being lunatic, drowned herself. 7 miles. £1 5s 3d.
22 Oct. 1823. Guestling. Francis Mead: found dead. 10 miles. £1 7s 6d.
27 Jan. 1824. Battle. John Gell: found drowned. £1.
2 Feb. 1824. Westfield. New-born female infant:[3] found dead. 5 miles. £1 3s 9d.
5 Feb. 1824. Burwash. Mary Buss: accidentally[4] burnt to death. 12 miles. £1 9s.
2 Mar. 1824. Rye.[5] Edward Skinner:[6] accidentally killed. 15 miles. £1 11s 3d.
16 Apr. 1824. Brede. William Bryant: found drowned. 8 miles. £1 6s.
19 Apr. 1824. Heathfield. Sophia Harmer: died by the visitation of God. 12 miles. £1 9s.
27 Apr. 1824. Warbleton. Richard Evenden: accidentally killed. 10 miles. £1 7s 6d.
28 Apr. 1824. Sedlescombe. Sarah Hewett: died by the visitation of God. 4 miles. £1 3s.
29 June 1824. Mountfield. Harriet[7] Luck: accidentally killed. 4 miles. £1 3s.
9 July 1824. Bodiam. Mary Stedman: accidentally drowned.[8] 9 miles. £1 6s 9d.
14 July 1824. Ticehurst. [*blank*] Bartlett: accidentally killed. 11 miles. £1 8s 3d.
Total £27 4s 6d; allowed at Midsummer sessions 1824.[9] [QR/E 780]

[This bill is also in RAF 1/3/8, ff 46–47 and all its entries are in RAF 1/4/3.]

1 *Salehurst* omitted in RAF 1/4/3.
2 *being lunatic* omitted in RAF 1/4/3.
3 *Infant child* (*new-born female* omitted) in RAF 1/4/3.
4 *accidentally* omitted in RAF 1/4/3.
5 *Playden* in RAF 1/4/3.
6 *Edward Skinner* omitted (blank space left) in RAF 1/4/3.
7 *Harriet* omitted (blank space left) in RAF 1/4/3.
8 *accidentally killed* in RAF 1/4/3.
9 Payment was received by Thomas Charles Bellingham, Barton's successor: RAF 1/3/8.

284 21 July 1824. Burwash. Thomas Head: died by the visitation of God. 10 miles. £1 7s 6d.
26 July 1824. Pett. William Martin: shot. £1.
[26 July] 1824. Pett. James Gladwish: accidentally drowned. £1.
[26 July] 1824. Pett. William Page: accidentally drowned. £1.
[26 July] 1824. Pett. Samuel Page: accidentally drowned. £1.
[26 July] 1824. Pett. Isaac Brann: accidentally drowned. £1.
[26 July] 1824. Pett. William Foster: accidentally drowned. 11 miles. £1 8s 3d.
28 July 1824. Pett. Spencer Cruttenden: accidentally drowned. 11 miles. £1 8s 3d.
6 Aug. 1824. Peasmarsh. Henry Brissenden: died by the visitation of God. 12 miles. £1 9s.
27 Aug. 1824. Netherfield. Mary[1] Chapman: accidentally killed. 3 miles. £1 2s 3d.
25 Sept. 1824. Bexhill. William Welsh: found drowned. 10 miles. £1 7s 6d.
14 Oct. 1824. Bexhill. William Barden: being lunatic, hung himself. 7 miles. £1 5s 3d.
24 Nov. 1824. Iden. John Woodhouse: accidentally killed. 16 miles. £1 12s.
6 Dec. 1824. Brightling. Still-born bastard child. 7 miles. £1 5s 3d.

30 Dec. 1824. Bexhill. Thomas Sawyer: murdered. 6 miles. £1 4s 6d.[2]
31 Dec. 1824. Bexhill. Thomas Sawyer. It being necessary to adjourn the inquest, a second journey. 6 miles. 4s 6d.[2]
18 Mar. 1825. Fairlight. James Gray: died of apoplexy. 9 miles. £1 6s 9d.
22 Mar. 1825. Ninfield. Bastard child: died by the visitation of God. 6 miles. £1 4s 6d.
28 Apr. 1825. Bexhill. Henry Eastwood: died by the visitation of God. 7 miles. £1 5s 3d.
10 May 1825. Iden. Thomas Hezekiah Milgate: accidentally drowned. 16 miles. £1 12s.
16 May 1825. Heathfield. George Thomson: died from excessive drinking. 12 miles. £1 9s.
14 July 1825. Icklesham. New-born infant. 14 miles. £1 10s 6d.
27 July 1825. Heathfield. Samuel Langford: died by the visitation of God. 13 miles. £1 9s 9d.
29 July 1825. [*Place omitted.*] James Weymark: died from poison administered by mistake. £1.
10 Sept. 1825. Dallington. Ann Burgess: died by the visitation of God. 7 miles. £1 5s 3d.
11 Sept. 1825. Burwash. Stephen Dunk: accidentally killed. 10 miles. £1 7s 6d.
1 Oct. 1825. Rye. John Dyatt: being lunatic, hung himself. 16 miles. £1 12s.
12 Oct. 1825. Bexhill. Thomas Bevis: killed by foul air in a well. £1.
[12 Oct.] 1825. Bexhill. George Barker: killed by foul air in a well. 6 miles. £1 4s 6d.
17 Oct. 1825. Battle. Aaron Cruttenden: being lunatic, hung himself. £1.
Total £37 1s 3d; allowed at Michaelmas sessions 1825.[3] [QR/E 785]

[This bill is also in RAF 1/3/8, ff 47–48 and all except the last entry are in RAF 1/4/3.]

1 *Sarah* in RAF 1/3/8 and RAF 1/4/3.
2 Cf. **467**.
3 Payment was received by Thomas Charles Bellingham, Barton's successor: RAF 1/3/8.

285 19 Oct. 1825. Ninfield. David Crouch: accidentally killed. 6 miles. £1 4s 6d.
22 Oct. 1825. Battle. James Baker: being lunatic, hung himself. £1.
24 Nov. 1825. Bexhill. Unknown man: found dead. 7 miles. £1 5s 3d.
1 Dec. 1825. Iden. William Verrall: being lunatic, hung himself. 15 miles. £1 11s 3d.
8 Dec. 1825. Salehurst. William Page: accidentally killed. 6 miles. £1 4s 6d.
23 Jan. 1826. Westfield. John Noakes: found dead. 5 miles. £1 3s 9d.
4 Apr. 1826. Fairlight. Samuel Kennard: died by the visitation of God. 8 miles. £1 6s.
10 Apr. 1826. Westfield. Maria Noakes: being lunatic, poisoned herself. 6 miles. £1 4s 6d.
15 Apr. 1826. Bexhill. James Forristal: accidentally killed. 6 miles. £1 4s 6d.
17 Apr. 1826. Guestling. Mary Standen: accidentally killed. 8 miles. £1 6s.
25 Apr. 1826. Bexhill. Charlotte Dunk: died by the visitation of God. 6 miles. £1 4s 6d.
10 May 1826. Burwash. Benjamin Russell: found dead. 9 miles. £1 6s 9d.[1]
11 May 1826. Burwash. Benjamin Russell. It being necessary to adjourn the inquest, a second journey was made. 9 miles. 6s 9d.[1]
[*Date omitted.*] Ticehurst. Henry Hicks: accidentally drowned. 12 miles. £1 9s.
28 June 1826. Icklesham. Edward Creasy: died by the visitation of God. 12 miles. £1 9s.
19 July 1826. Salehurst. William Card: being lunatic, hung himself. 7 miles. £1 5s 3d.

3 Sept. 1826. Bexhill. Francis Chrismas: accidentally shot himself. 8 miles. £1 6s.
22 Sept. 1826. Mountfield. George Hayward: accidentally killed. 5 miles. £1 3s 9d.
12 Oct. 1826. Mountfield. Thomas Crouch: died by the visitation of God. 5 miles. £1 3s 9d.
Total £23 5s; allowed at Michaelmas sessions 1826.[2] [QR/E 789, no 95]

[This bill is also in RAF 1/3/8, ff 48–49.]

1 Cf. **434**; *SCM*, XI, 118–122.
2 Payment was received by Thomas Charles Bellingham, Barton's successor: RAF 1/3/8.

286 30 Oct. 1826. Dallington. Robert Elliott: died in a falling fit. 6 miles. £1 4s 6d.
31 Oct. 1826. Ore. Thomas Chapman: died by the visitation of God. 7 miles. £1 5s 3d.
3 Nov. 1826. Etchingham. Mary Gillett: found drowned in a well. 9 miles. £1 6s 9d.
9 Nov. 1826. Peasmarsh. Thomas Butler: accidentally killed. 13 miles. £1 9s 9d.
23 Dec. 1826. Mountfield. James Simes: found drowned. 4 miles. £1 3s.
19 Feb. 1827. Mountfield.[1] Mary Clarke: died by the visitation of God. 4 miles. £1 3s.
[22 Feb.] 1827.[2] Icklesham. Unknown woman:[3] found dead.[4] 11 miles. £1 8s 3d.
12 Mar. 1827. Salehurst. William Carley: being lunatic, hung himself. 8 miles. £1 6s.
29 Mar. 1827. Burwash. Henry Adams: died from excessive drinking. 9 miles. £1 6s 9d.
16 Apr. 1827. Fairlight. Henry Ashdown: shot.[5] 9 miles. £1 6s 9d.
29 Apr. 1827. Battle. Joseph Allen: accidentally killed. £1.
2 May 1827. Beckley. Thomas Bryant: accidentally killed. 13 miles. £1 9s 9d.
23 May 1827. Etchingham. Alfred Sawyer: accidentally killed by a wagon. 9 miles. £1 6s 9d.
13 June 1827. Ewhurst. William King: found drowned. 6 miles. £1 4s 6d.
30 June 1827. Northiam. Samuel Monk: found drowned. 9 miles. £1 6s 9d.
4 July 1827. Peasmarsh. Mary Jane Butler: being lunatic, cut her throat. 14 miles. £1 10s 6d.
3 Aug. 1827. Burwash. John Relf: accidentally killed. 10 miles. £1 7s 6d.
8 Aug. 1827. Playden. Samuel Watson: found drowned. 16 miles. £1 12s.
18 Aug. 1827. Crowhurst Powder-Mills. Reuben Morris: accidentally killed. £1.
[18 Aug.] 1827. Crowhurst Powder-Mills. James Hounsell: accidentally killed. 4 miles. £1 3s.
13[6] Sept. 1827. Ashburnham. Mary Wilson: died by the visitation of God.[7] 6 miles. £1 4s 6d.[8]
26 Sept. 1827. Heathfield. William Brushett: shot himself. 12 miles. £1 9s.
2 Oct. 1827. Peasmarsh. Isaac Butler: being lunatic, hung himself. 14 miles. £1 10s 6d.
5 Oct. 1827. Brede. George Butler. 8 miles. £1 6s.
15 Oct. 1827. Sedlescombe. Ann Miller: died by the visitation of God.[9] 4 miles. £1 3s.[10]
Total £32 13s 9d; allowed at Michaelmas sessions 1827.[11] [QR/E 793]

[This bill is also in RAF 1/3/8, ff 49–50 and summaries of four of the inquests are in SHE 2/2/5 and SHE 2/2/8.]

1 *Ashburnham* in RAF 1/3/8.
2 *22 Feb. 1827* in SHE 2/2/8.
3 *a stranger* added in SHE 2/2/8; *aged woman, found dead, buried 23 Feb.* in PAR 401/1/5/1.
4 *died from the inclemency of the weather* added in SHE 2/2/8.
5 *smuggling* added in SHE 2/2/5.

6 *23* in SHE 2/2/8.
7 *Mary Wilson, aged 55, a travelling woman, taken with illness and died in an outbuilding* in SHE 2/2/8.
8 *Inquest held by T C Bellingham, coroner* in SHE 2/2/8.
9 *Ann Miller, a stranger, fell in a fit and died in an outbuilding* in SHE 2/2/8.
10 *Inquest held by T C Bellingham, coroner* in SHE 2/2/8.
11 Payment was received by Thomas Charles Bellingham, Barton's successor: RAF 1/3/8.

287 24 Oct. 1827. Guestling. Samuel Phillips: being lunatic, hung himself. 10 miles. £1 7s 6d.
2 Nov. 1827. Iden. Unknown woman: died by the visitation of God.[1] £1.[2]
[2 Nov.] 1827. Iden. Harriet Phipps: accidentally burnt to death. 16 miles. £1 12s.
24 Nov. 1827. Ore. William Chapman: accidentally killed. 7 miles. £1 5s 3d.
5 Jan. 1828. Bexhill. Unknown man:[3] shot.[4] £1.
[5 Jan.] 1828. Bexhill. Another unknown man:[5] also shot.[4] £1.
[5 Jan.] 1828. Bexhill. Charles Collins: murdered by some person unknown. 7 miles. £1 5s 3d.
16 Feb. 1828. Ticehurst. John Hamilton: being lunatic, hung himself. 15 miles. £1 11s 3d.
8 Mar. 1828. Bexhill. Patrick Brown: accidentally killed. 8 miles. £1 6s.
15 Mar. 1828. Brede. James Selmes alias Eastwood: accidentally drowned. 7 miles. £1 5s 3d.
2 May 1828. Beckley. Benjamin Brett: hung himself. 12 miles. £1 9s.
3 May 1828. East Guldeford. Henry Pope: accidentally drowned. 18 miles. £1 13s 6d.
25 May 1828. Sedlescombe. Alfred Eldridge: accidentally drowned. 4 miles. £1 3s.
27 May 1828. Peasmarsh. John[6] Swyer jun.: accidentally drowned. 12 miles. £1 9s.
21 June 1828. Guestling. Charity Morris: died by the visitation of God. 8 miles. £1 6s.
4 July 1828. Peasmarsh. Eliza Swyer: accidentally killed. 14 miles. £1 10s 6d.
10 July 1828. Northiam. Edward Lord: accidentally drowned. 10 miles. £1 7s 6d.
Total £22 11s; allowed at Midsummer sessions 1828.[7] [QR/E 796]

[This bill is also in RAF 1/3/8, ff 50, 68 and summaries of four of the inquests are in SHE 2/2/5 and SHE 2/2/8.]

1 *Was ill at Iden a fortnight before she died and was well attended to* added in SHE 2/2/8.
2 *Inquest held by D Manser, coroner* in SHE 2/2/8.
3 *S Waddle, aged 23, abode unknown* in PAR 240/1/5/1.
4 *smuggling* added in SHE 2/2/5.
5 *A male person unknown* in PAR 240/1/5/1.
6 *James* in RAF 1/3/8 and PAR 440/1/5/1.
7 Payment was received by Thomas Charles Bellingham, Barton's successor: RAF 1/3/8.

288 4 Oct. 1828. Warbleton. John Tookey: found dead. 10 miles. £1 7s 6d.
11 Oct. 1828. Bexhill. Sarah Edmonds: being lunatic, cut her throat. 6 miles. £1 4s 6d.
1 Nov. 1828. Northiam. Eleanor Yorke: accidentally burnt to death. 9 miles. £1 6s 9d.
26 Nov. 1828. Hurst Green. Thomas Reed: died from excessive drinking. 8 miles. £1 6s.
2 Feb. 1829. Ticehurst. Louisa Baldwin: accidentally burnt to death. 13 miles. £1 9s 9d.
4 Feb. 1829. Burwash. Benjamin Lado:[1] accidentally burnt to death. 14 miles. £1 10s 6d.
26 Feb. 1829. Guestling. John Watt: died by the visitation of God. 10 miles. £1 7s 6d.

17 Mar. 1829. Northiam. Sarah Ann Betts: being lunatic, drowned herself. 10 miles. £1 7s 6d.
Total £11; allowed at Easter sessions 1829.[2] [QR/E 799]

[This bill is also in RAF 1/3/8, ff 68, 86.]

1 *Lade* in RAF 1/3/8 and PAR 284/1/5/1.
2 Payment was received by Thomas Charles Bellingham, Barton's successor: RAF 1/3/8.

289 30 Apr. 1829. Ewhurst. Jane Edmonds: died by the visitation of God. 8 miles. £1 6s.
2 June 1829. Playden. James Smith: accidentally killed by a windmill. 17 miles. £1 12s 9d.
26 Aug. 1829. Beckley. William Pain: being lunatic, hung himself. 12 miles. £1 9s.[1]
14 Sept. 1829. Heathfield. Mary Akehurst: accidentally drowned. 12 miles. £1 9s.
25 Sept. 1829. Hooe. Hannah Hoad: found drowned. 8 miles. £1 6s.
17 Oct. 1829. Bexhill. John Sayers: accidentally killed. 6 miles. £1 4s 6d.
12 Nov. 1829. Whatlington. Philadelphia Ashdown: died by the visitation of God. 3 miles. £1 2s 3d.
19 Nov. 1829. Burwash. Francis[2] Parsons: accidentally burnt to death. 14 miles. £1 10s 6d.
5 Dec. 1829. Pett. William Sargent: shot.[3] 14 miles. £1 10s 6d.
[*Date omitted.*] Etchingham. Harriet Hyland: being lunatic, drowned herself. 11 miles. £1 8s 3d.
2 Jan. 1830. Catsfield. Louisa Thompson: accidentally burnt to death. 3 miles. £1 2s 3d.
21 Jan. 1830. Ewhurst. George Baker: died from taking[4] opium. 7 miles. £1 5s 3d.
5 Feb. 1830. Etchingham. Male infant: died from the inclemency of the weather. 12 miles. £1 9s.
25 Mar. 1830. Bexhill. Unknown man: found drowned. 6 miles. £1 4s 6d.
Total £18 19s 9d; allowed at Easter sessions 1830.[5] [QR/E 803]

[Part of this bill is also in RAF 1/3/8, f 86 and the rest in RAF 1/3/9, p 222 and a summary of one of the inquests is in SHE 2/2/5.]

1 Cf. **435**.
2 *Frances* in RAF 1/3/8.
3 *smuggling* added in SHE 2/2/5.
4 *too great a dose of* added in RAF 1/3/9.
5 Payment was received by Thomas Charles Bellingham, Barton's successor: RAF 1/3/9.

290 21 Apr. 1830. Etchingham. Thomas Leney: died by the visitation of God. 12 miles. £1 9s.
28 Apr. 1830. Bexhill. Thomas Tupp: accidentally killed. 6 miles. £1 4s 6d.
10 May 1830. Battle. Thomas Hyland: found drowned. £1.
13 May 1830. Burwash. Maria Funnell: died by the visitation of God. 10 miles. £1 7s 6d.
7 June 1830. Wartling. John Clapson: died by the visitation of God. 8 miles. £1 6s.
18 Sept. 1830. Battle. Jane Turner: accidentally drowned. £1.
13 Oct. 1830. Salehurst. William Bayley: being lunatic, hung himself. 9 miles. £1 6s 9d.
19 Oct. 1830. Westfield. William Hutchinson: accidentally killed. 6 miles. £1 4s 6d.

24 Dec. 1830. Crowhurst. Mary Ransom: accidentally burnt to death. 3 miles. £1 2s 3d.[1]
Total £9 18s 3d; allowed at Easter sessions 1831.[2] [RAF 1/3/9, p 222]

[By Easter 1831 Barton was dead and payment was made to his representatives: QO/EW 51; QAF 2/1/E11, ff 27v–28.]

1 Entry struck through.
2 Payment was received by Thomas Charles Bellingham, Barton's successor: RAF 1/3/9.

Bills of Thomas Charles Bellingham

291 24 Dec. 1830. Crowhurst. Mary Ransom: accidentally burnt to death. 4 miles. £1 3s.
6 Jan. 1831. Fairlight. William Cruttenden: shot engaged on smuggling. £1.
[6 Jan.] 1831. Fairlight. George Harrod: shot engaged on smuggling. 8 miles. £1 6s.
14 Jan. 1831. Ticehurst. Elizabeth Kemp: died by the visitation of God. 12 miles. £1 9s.
21 Feb. 1831. Ninfield. Margaret Slaughter: died by the visitation of God. 4 miles. £1 3s.
21 Mar. 1831. Salehurst. Mary Standen: died by the visitation of God. 6 miles. £1 4s 6d.
12 May 1831. Guestling. William Cruttenden: died by the visitation of God. 9 miles. £1 6s 9d.
21 June 1831. Catsfield. Sarah Whiting: hung herself. 3 miles. £1 2s 3d.
11 July 1831. Brightling. William Croft: accidentally drowned. 6 miles. £1 4s 6d.
5 Aug. 1831. Battle. William Joseph Sadler: accidentally killed. £1.
6 Aug. 1831. Heathfield. Elizabeth Howell: died by the visitation of God. 9 miles. £1 6s 9d.
11 Aug. 1831. Northiam. Sarah Collins: being lunatic, poisoned herself. 10 miles. £1 7s 6d.
1 Sept. 1831. Mayfield. George Clarke: accidentally killed. 12 miles. £1 9s.
17 Sept. 1831. Mayfield. Henry Durrant: died by the visitation of God. 12 miles. £1 9s.
24 Sept. 1831. Battle. George Mepham: accidentally killed. £1.
5 Oct. 1831. Herstmonceux. Unknown man: found dead. 9 miles. £1 6s 9d.
12 Oct. 1831. Ticehurst. Thomas Dann: died by the visitation of God. 14 miles. £1 10s 6d.
Total £21 8s 6d; allowed at Michaelmas sessions 1831. [RAF 1/3/10, pp 14–15]

[All Bellingham's journeys were from Battle but that is never stated in his bills. There are summaries of two of the inquests of this bill in SHE 2/2/5.]

292 24 Oct. 1831. Battle. William Collins: died by the visitation of God. £1.
4 Nov. 1831. Salehurst. William Harris: accidentally killed. 6 miles. £1 4s 6d.
30 Nov. 1831. Wartling. Elizabeth Stubberfield: being lunatic, hung herself. 9 miles. £1 6s 9d.
1 Dec. 1831. St Leonards. Charles Head: shot engaged in smuggling. 6 miles. £1 4s 6d.
3 Jan. 1832. Icklesham. William Stone jun.: died from a gun-shot wound.[1] 11 miles. £1 8s 3d.

17 Jan. 1832. Ticehurst. Richard Morris: being lunatic, shot himself. 13 miles. £1 9s 9d.
11 Feb. 1832. Catsfield. Hannah Quaife: accidentally killed. 3 miles. £1 2s 3d.
20 Feb. 1832. Heathfield. John Smith: died by the visitation of God. 10 miles. £1 7s 6d.
21 Mar. 1832. Mountfield.[2] Thomas Simmonds.[3] 5 miles. 3s 9d.[4]
22 Mar. 1832. Northiam. Clara Jarman:[5] died by the visitation of God. £1.
[22 Mar.] 1832. Northiam. Female bastard child not baptized:[6] died by the visitation of God. 9 miles. £1 6s 9d.
23 Mar. 1832. Mountfield.[2] Thomas Simmonds:[3] found dead.[7] Journey to conclude proceedings, inquest having been adjourned from 21st.[8] [5 miles.] £1 3s 9d.[4]
28 Apr. 1832. Salehurst. Edward Catt: being lunatic, hung himself. 7 miles. £1 5s 3d.
15 May 1832. Heathfield. Rhoda Elizabeth Reed:[9] died by the visitation of God. 11 miles. £1 8s 3d.
19 May 1832. East Guldeford. Henry Clarke: accidentally drowned. 18 miles. £1 13s 6d.
28 May 1832. Ashburnham. Edward Quaife: accidentally drowned. 6 miles. £1 4s 6d.
16 June 1832. Crowhurst. Hannah Taylor: being lunatic, poisoned herself. 5 miles. £1 3s 9d.
29 June 1832. Ore. Spencer Catt: died by the visitation of God. 7 miles. £1 5s 3d.
20 July 1832. Icklesham. Henry Roberts: accidentally killed. 12 miles. £1 9s.
24 July 1832. Heathfield. Sarah Balcomb: died by the visitation of God. 11 miles. £1 8s 3d.
13 Aug. 1832. Battle. Edward Saxby: died by the visitation of God. £1.
18 Aug. 1832. Battle. Mary Kenward: accidentally drowned. 2 miles. £1 1s 6d.
5 Sept. 1832. Herstmonceux. John Atherall: accidentally killed. 9 miles. £1 6s 9d.
10 Sept. 1832. Salehurst. William Hilder: being lunatic, shot himself. 7 miles. £1 5s 3d.
27 Sept. 1832. Battle. Thomas Balcomb: accidentally killed. £1.
Total £30 9s; allowed at Michaelmas sessions 1832. [RAF 1/3/10, pp 15–16]

[There are summaries of six of the inquests in SHE 2/2/5, SHE 2/2/6, SHE 2/2/8 and SHE 2/2/9.]

1 *shot smuggling* in SHE 2/2/5.
2 *Mountfield Poorhouse* in SHE 2/2/8.
3 *James Simmonds, aged 70* in SHE 2/2/8 and PAR 424/1/5/1.
4 Cf. **436**.
5 *aged 5 months* added in SHE 2/2/9.
6 *aged 3 weeks* added in SHE 2/2/9.
7 *in a wood* added in SHE 2/2/8.
8 The adjournment is not mentioned in SHE 2/2/8.
9 *aged 4 months* added in SHE 2/2/9.

293 10 Oct. 1832. Icklesham. William Foord: accidentally killed. 10 miles. £1 7s 6d.
23 Oct. 1832. Ninfield. James Rogers: murdered. 5 miles. £1 3s 9d.[1]
14 Nov. 1832. Pett. William Kennard: being lunatic, hung himself. 11 miles. £1 8s 3d.
30 Nov. 1832. Bodiam. Walter Wenban: accidentally killed. 9 miles. £1 6s 9d.
17 Dec. 1832. Dallington. John Blunden: died by the visitation of God. 7 miles. £1 5s 3d.
30 Jan. 1833. East Guldeford. Mary Crowhurst: being lunatic, hung herself. 18 miles. £1 13s 6d.
15 Feb. 1833. Salehurst. Jesse Jarvis: died by the visitation of God. 7 miles. £1 5s 3d.
27 Mar. 1833. Salehurst. Edmund Terry: found drowned. £1.

[27 Mar.] 1833. Burwash. Eleanor Kemp: accidentally burnt to death. 14 miles. £1 10s 6d.
30 Apr. 1833. Sedlescombe. Martha Sargent: accidentally drowned. £1.
[30 Apr.] 1833. Sedlescombe. William Sargent: accidentally drowned. 4 miles. £1 3s.
16 May 1833. Crowhurst. James Britt: found drowned. 4 miles. £1 3s.
21 May 1833. Warbleton. Elizabeth Hawkins: being lunatic, drowned herself. 9 miles. £1 6s 9d.
28 May 1833. Peasmarsh. Thomas Stemp: accidentally killed. 15 miles. £1 11s 3d.
31 May 1833. Fairlight. James Terry: hung himself. 8 miles. £1 6s.
24 June 1833. Dallington. John Piper: found drowned. 6 miles. £1 4s 6d.
27 June 1833. East Guldeford. George Skeere: found drowned. 18 miles. £1 13s 6d.
4 July 1833. Penhurst. Henry Spears: accidentally killed. 4 miles. £1 3s.
23 Aug. 1833. Ticehurst. James Malyon: accidentally killed. 14 miles. £1 10s 6d.
21 Oct. 1833. Battle. George Cockett: being lunatic, cut his throat. £1.
19 Nov. 1833. Ninfield. Henry Page: shot at Pevensey engaged in smuggling and died at Ninfield. 6 miles. £1 4s 6d.
11 Dec. 1833. Salehurst. Sarah Lusted: found drowned. 8 miles. £1 6s.
19 Dec. 1833. Battle. Stephen Spilsted: died by the visitation of God. £1.
20 Apr. 1834. Northiam. Mahalah Longley: accidentally drowned. 10 miles. £1 7s 6d.
30 Apr. 1834. Mountfield. Harriet Waters: accidentally drowned. 4 miles. £1 3s.
1 June 1834. Brede. Sarah Ann Selmes:[2] accidentally burnt to death. 6 miles. £1 4s 6d.
21 June 1834. Salehurst. Jonathan Page: being insane, poisoned himself. 8 miles. £1 6s.
29 July 1834. Bexhill. Susannah Haines: being insane, drowned herself. 7 miles. £1 5s 3d.
1 Aug. 1834. Burwash. Caesar Bennett: died of concussion of the brain. 9 miles. £1 6s 9d.[3]
2 Aug. 1834. Warbleton. Eleanor Buckland: died by the visitation of God. 7 miles. £1 5s 3d.[4]
18 Aug. 1834. Ticehurst. Elias Tompsett: accidentally killed. 11 miles. £1 8s 3d.
3 Sept. 1834. Ninfield. Denis Ibberson:[5] died by the visitation of God. 5 miles. £1 3s 9d.
4 Sept. 1834. Burwash. Michael Nagle: accidentally drowned. 10 miles. £1 7s 6d.
10 Sept. 1834. Heathfield. Thomas Fuller: accidentally killed. 13 miles. £1 9s 9d.
12 Sept. 1834. Northiam. George Cruse: died by the visitation of God. 10 miles. £1 7s 6d.
6 Oct. 1834. Bodiam. Eliza Lane: accidentally burnt to death. 9 miles. £1 6s 9d.
Total £46 14s 6d; allowed at Michaelmas sessions 1834. [RAF 1/3/10, pp 17, 191–192]

[There are summaries four of the inquests in SHE 2/2/5, SHE 2/2/8 and SHE 2/2/9.]

1 Cf. **437**.
2 *aged 7 weeks* added in SHE 2/2/9.
3 Cf. **438**.
4 Cf. **439**.
5 *a travelling man, a stranger, taken to the workhouse* added in SHE 2/2/8.

294 3 Nov. 1834. Heathfield. Mary Beaching: died by the visitation of God. 11 miles. £1 8s 3d.
11 Dec. 1834. Udimore. Jeremiah Goodsell: accidentally shot himself. 5 miles. £1 3s 9d.

[*Date omitted.*] Catsfield. Thomas White: died by the visitation of God. 3 miles. £1 2s 3d.
26 Dec. 1834. Sedlescombe. Martha Sellens: accidentally burnt to death. 4 miles. £1 3s.
9 Jan. 1835. Ewhurst. Stephen Goodsell jun.: accidentally burnt to death. 8 miles. £1 6s.
24 Jan. 1835. Iden. Mrs Watt:[1] accidentally drowned. 16 miles. £1 12s.
9 Feb. 1835. Ore. Tryphenia Austin: being insane, cut her throat. 6 miles. £1 4s 6d.
23 Mar. 1835. Burwash. John Head: died by the visitation of God. 10 miles. £1 7s 6d.
28 Mar. 1835. Hooe. Stephen Page: died by the visitation of God. 6 miles. £1 4s 6d.
[*Date omitted.*] Playden. William Longley: accidentally drowned. 16 miles. £1 12s.
6 Apr. 1835. Iden. Caroline Smith: being insane, hung herself. 16 miles. £1 12s.
23 Apr. 1835. Ore. James Ginner: died of inanition. 6 miles. £1 4s 6d.
29 Apr. 1835. Salehurst. John Bailey: accidentally killed. 2 miles. £1 1s 6d.
25 May 1835. Salehurst. William Kemp: accidentally drowned. 8 miles. £1 6s.
29 May 1835. Salehurst. William Woodgate: being insane, hung himself. 8 miles. £1 6s.
22 July 1835. Battle. John Adams jun.: accidentally killed. £1.
25 July 1835. Salehurst. William Goldsmith: accidentally killed. 7 miles. £1 5s 3d.
4 Aug. 1835. Heathfield. Ezekiel Collins: died by the visitation of God. 10 miles. £1 7s 6d.
3 Sept. 1835. Bexhill. Benjamin Thomas Dallaway: accidentally drowned. 7 miles. £1 5s 3d.
6 Sept. 1835. Bexhill. Stephen Holland: being lunatic, hung himself. 5 miles. £1 3s 9d.
9 Sept. 1835. Salehurst. Frances Eliza Kemp: being lunatic, hung herself. 8 miles. £1 6s.
24 Sept. 1835. Ashburnham. Benjamin Talbot: accidentally killed. 5 miles. £1 3s 9d.
2 Oct. 1835. Beckley. Harriet Mills: accidentally burnt to death. 11 miles. £1 8s 3d.
3 Oct. 1835. Salehurst. Emma Lusted: being lunatic, hung herself. 8 miles. £1 6s.
Total £30 19s 6d; allowed at Michaelmas sessions 1835. [RAF 1/3/10, pp 192–193, 394]

1 *Mrs Watt of Rye Foreign, Christian name unknown, aged about 65* in PAR 402/1/5/1.

295 28 Dec. 1835. Wartling. Charles Edmonds: died by the visitation of God. 8 miles. £1 6s.
5 Jan. 1836. Heathfield. Jane Harmer: accidentally burnt to death. 12 miles. £1 9s.
6 Jan. 1836. Udimore. Edgar Coleman: accidentally burnt to death. 11 miles. £1 8s 3d.
9 Jan. 1836. Iden. Thomas Dee: found drowned. 17 miles. £1 12s 9d.
6 Feb. 1836. Rye. Unknown man:[1] died a natural death. 14 miles. £1 10s 6d.
5 Mar. 1836. Hastings. Mark Phillips: accidentally drowned. 8 miles. £1 6s.
23 Mar. 1836. Bexhill. Margaret Wilson: died by the visitation of God. 7 miles. £1 5s 3d.[2]
20 Apr. 1836. Westfield. Ebenezer Bishop: died by the visitation of God. 6 miles. 8£1 4s 6d.
29 Apr. 1836. Battle. Mary Wekeford: died of concussion of the brain. £1.
17 May 1836. Heathfield. Jonathan Humfrey:[3] died by the visitation of God. 12 miles. £1 9s.
1 June 1836. Ticehurst. William Pope: killed by John Snatt in self defence. 12 miles. £1 9s.

4 June 1836. Hastings. James Gallop: being insane, hung himself. 8 miles. £1 6s.
11 June 1836. Ore. Henry Joseph Spears: accidentally killed. £1.
Total £17 6s 3d; allowed at Midsummer sessions 1836. [RAF 1/3/10, pp 394–395]

[There are summaries of three of the inquests in SHE 2/2/5, SHE 2/2/8 and SHE 2/2/9.

1 *a stranger, traveller* added in SHE 2/2/8.
2 Cf. **440**.
3 *aged 6 months* added in SHE 2/2/9.

296 27 June 1836. Ewhurst. Thomas Osborne: accidentally killed. 5 miles. £1 3s 9d.
29 June 1836. Etchingham. Benjamin Hayler jun.: died by the visitation of God. 10 miles. £1 7s 6d.
12 July 1836. Bexhill. William Simmonds: died by the visitation of God. 6 miles. £1 4s 6d.
16 July 1836. Rye. Frederick Weeks: accidentally killed. 14 miles. £1 10s 6d.
23 July 1836. Hastings. Unknown female infant:[1] found dead.[2] 8 miles. £1 6s.
19 Aug. 1836. Catsfield. George Chapman: died by the visitation of God. 3 miles. £1 2s 3d.
12 Sept. 1836. Ewhurst. John Carcey: died by the visitation of God. 8 miles. £1 6s.
8 Oct. 1836. Salehurst. Henry Challen: being insane, drowned himself. 6 miles. £1 4s 6d.
22 Oct. 1836. Bodiam. Daniel Ranger: accidentally killed at Salehurst and died at Bodiam. 8 miles. £1 6s.
31 Oct. 1836. Playden. James Burt: accidentally drowned. 16 miles. £1 12s.
5 Dec. 1836. Ewhurst. John Luxford: died from laudanum administered to him by mistake. 8 miles. £1 6s.
10 Nov. 1836. Ninfield. Stephen Fox: accidentally killed. 5 miles. £1 3s 9d.
15 Dec. 1836. Rye. John Holt: being insane, killed himself. 15 miles. £1 11s 3d.[3]
28 Dec. 1836. Battle. Sarah Miles:[4] died from exposure to the weather.[5] 3 miles. £1 2s 3d.
5 Jan. 1837. Rye Foreign. William Yeo: died from exposure to the weather. 15 miles. £1 11s 3d.
7 Jan. 1837. Battle. William Etherden: accidentally killed. 2 miles. £1 1s 6d.
19 Jan. 1837. Salehurst. William Pitt:[6] died by the visitation of God. 7 miles. £1 5s 3d.
25 Feb. 1837. Westfield. Mary Lucas: being insane, drowned herself. 6 miles. £1 4s 6d.
28 Feb. 1837. Salehurst. Keziah Honeysett: died from a fall in a fit. 9 miles. £1 6s 9d.
1 Mar. 1837. Northiam. Serena Lillburn: accidentally burnt to death. 10 miles. £1 7s 6d.
6 Mar. 1837. Ashburnham. George Tutt: died by the visitation of God. 5 miles. £1 3s 9d.
7 Mar. 1837. Wartling. Samuel Fuller: died from loss of blood from an accidental wound in his leg. 8 miles. £1 6s.
1 Apr. 1837. Salehurst. Mary Bridger: died by the visitation of God. 12 miles. £1 9s.
17 Apr. 1837. Brede. Thomas Barnes: accidentally burnt to death. 8 miles. £1 6s.
[*Date omitted.*] Beckley. John Larkins: died by the visitation of God. 11 miles. £1 8s 3d.
2 May 1837. Westfield. Edwin Cruttenden: accidentally killed. 6 miles. £1 4s 6d.
9 May 1837. Bexhill. Thamer[7] Talbot:[8] died by the visitation of God.[9] 7 miles. £1 5s 3d.

13 May 1837. Crowhurst. Jane Button: being insane, poisoned herself. 4 miles. £1 3s.
17 May 1837. Bodiam. Eliza Relf: accidentally burnt to death. 9 miles. £1 6s 9d.
31 May 1837. Brede. Alfred Furner:[10] died by the visitation of God.[11] 8 miles. £1 6s.[12]
10 June 1837. Crowhurst. Thomas Collins: being insane, hung himself. 3 miles. £1 2s 3d.[13]
29 June 1837. Salehurst. [*blank*] Weatherbourn:[14] died by the visitation of God. 8 miles. £1 6s.
18 July 1837. Ore. Sarah Homewood: accidentally drowned. 7 miles. £1 11s 11d.
5 Aug. 1837. Salehurst. Sarah Smith: died by the visitation of God. 8 miles. £1 12s 8d.
8 Aug. 1837. Herstmonceux. Sarah Cornford: accidentally suffocated. 10 miles. £1 14s 2d.
9 Aug. 1837. Battle. George Dengate: died by the visitation of God. 2 miles. £1 8s 2d.
[9 Aug.] 1837. Westfield. John Easton: died by the visitation of God. 7 miles. £1 11s 11d.[15]
21 Aug. 1837. Northiam. William Cook: accidentally suffocated. 10 miles. £1 14s 2d.
9 Sept. 1837. Wartling. Jephthah Fordich: accidentally drowned. 9 miles. £1 13s 5d.
15 Sept. 1837. Northiam. James Watson: accidentally drowned. 10 miles. £1 14s 2d.
22 Sept. 1837. Icklesham. Henry Sargent: killed. 11 miles. £1 14s 11d.
23 Sept. 1837. Burwash. John Still: died by the visitation of God. 10 miles. £1 14s 2d.
2 Oct. 1837. Hooe. Aaron William Winborne: accidentally drowned. 7 miles. £1 11s 11d.
[*Date omitted.*] Ewhurst. Sarah Newton: died by the visitation of God. 7 miles. £1 11s 11d.
Paid expenses at inquests as per account £17 6s.
Total £78 9s 3d; allowed at Michaelmas sessions 1837.

[RAF 1/3/10, pp 395, 397, 466–467]

[The entries to 10 June 1837 were totalled and the sum, £40 3s 9d, was included in the final total as 'former bill'. The expenses claimed at the end of the bill were detailed in an attachment to RAF 1/3/10, p 482 as follows::

Sarah Homewood: constable 5s; 12 jurymen 12s; 2 witnesses 2s; total 19s.
Sarah Smith: constable 5s; 13 jurymen 13s; 1 witness 1s; surgeon £1 1s; total £2.
Sarah Cornford: constable 5s; 14 jurymen 14s; 2 witnesses 2s; surgeon £1 1s; total £2 2s.
George Dengate: constable 5s; 13 jurymen 13s; surgeon £1 1s; total £1 19s.
John Easton: constable 5s; 14 jurymen 14s; 2 witnesses 2s; total £1 1s.
William Cooke: constable 5s; 14 jurymen 14s; 2 witnesses 2s; total £1 1s.
Jephthah Forsdich: constable 5s; 15 jurymen 15s; total £1.
James Watson: constable 5s; 13 jurymen 13s; 2 witnesses 2s; surgeon £1 1s; total £2 1s.
Henry Sargent: constable 5s; 13 jurymen 13s; 3 witnesses 3s; total £1 1s.
John Still: constable 5s; 13 jurymen 13s; 2 witnesses 2s; surgeon £1 1s; total £2 1s.
Sarah Newton: constable 5s; 13 jurymen 13s; 2 witnesses 2s; total £1.
Aaron William Winborne: constable 5s; 13 jurymen 13s; 3 witnesses 3s; total £1 1s.
Total £17 6s.

There are summaries of five of the inquests of this bill in SHE 2/2/6, SHE 2/2/8 and SHE 2/2/9.]

1 *aged under a year* added in SHE 2/2/9.
2 *under a hedge wrapped up in a cloth* added in SHE 2/2/8.
3 Cf. **441**.
4 *a travelling woman* added in SHE 2/2/8.
5 *died in an outbuilding from exposure to the cold* in SHE 2/2/8.
6 *a stranger, travelling man, aged 80, taken into the poorhouse* added in SHE 2/2/8.
7 *Thomas* in SHE 2/2/9; *Thamer* in SHE 2/2/8.

8 *aged 5 months* added in SHE 2/2/8; *aged 14 weeks* added in SHE 2/2/9.
9 *died in the union workhouse from the effects of a bowel complaint* in SHE 2/2/8. Before the new Battle Union workhouse was opened in 1840 children were sent to Bexhill: P M Corbett, *Crime and Criminals of Battle in the middle of the nineteenth century* (Wealden Press, 1998), 24.
10 *Turner* in SHE 2/2/8; *Furner* in PAR 253/1/5/1.
11 *an inmate of the workhouse, subject to fits, found dead in his bed* in SHE 2/2/8.
12 Cf. **442**.
13 Cf. **443**.
14 [blank] *Weatherbourn, a traveller, at Hurst Green, from Newcastle upon Tyne, aged 42* in PAR 477/1/5/2.
15 Cf. **444**.

297 13 Nov. 1837. Ashburnham. William Morrison: died of concussion of the brain. 4 miles. £1 9s 8d. Expenses (witness etc.) £3 1s 6d.
15 Nov. 1837. Warbleton. James Butchers: accidentally burnt to death. 9 miles. £1 13s 5d. Expenses (witness etc.) £1 4s 6d.
25 Nov. 1837. Ewhurst. Thomas Eldridge: accidentally shot. 8 miles. £1 12s 8d. Expenses (witness etc.) £2 2s 6d.
27 Dec. 1837. Brightling. George Miller: accidentally shot. 6 miles. £1 11s 2d. Expenses £2 13s 6d.
Total £15 11s 11d; allowed at Epiphany sessions 1838. [RAF 1/3/10, p 467]

298 4 Jan. 1838. Ashburnham. William Beney: died by the visitation of God. 4 miles. £1 9s 8d. Expenses £2 2s 6d.
13 Jan. 1838. Crowhurst. Edward Taylor: being temporarily deranged, hung himself. 4 miles. £1 9s 8d. Paid constable etc. £1 3s 6d.
16 Jan. 1838. Peasmarsh. Mary Elizabeth Hicks: accidentally burnt. 13 miles. £1 16s 5d. Paid constable etc. £1 8s.
26 Jan. 1838. Fairlight. Thomas Sivyer: accidentally burnt. 10 miles. £1 14s 2d. Paid constable etc. £1 5s.
[*blank*] Feb. 1838. Penhurst. Thomas French: being lunatic, hung himself. 5 miles. £1 10s 5d. Paid constable etc. £1 3s 6d.
22 Feb. 1838. Hucksteep Wood, Mountfield.[1] New-born female child: found dead. 3 miles. £1 8s 11d. Expenses £2 6s 6d.
9 Mar. 1838. Bexhill. New-born male child of Jane Prior, single woman.[2] 7 miles. £1 11s 11d. Paid constable etc. £2 6s 6d.
14 Mar. 1838. Ticehurst. Benjamin Leney: being insane, hung himself. 12 miles. £1 15s 8d. Expenses £1 8s.
19 Mar. 1838. Brightling. Henry Beddes Pound: being insane, drowned himself. 7 miles. £1 11s 11d. Expenses £2 1s.
Total £29 13s 3d; allowed at Easter sessions 1838.[3] [RAF 1/3/10, p 482]

[There are summaries of two of the inquests in SHE 2/2/6 and SHE 2/2/9.]

1 *Battle* in SHE 2/2/9; *Hucksteep Wood, Mountfield* in SHE 2/2/6.
2 *New-born male bastard child; not known whether born alive or not* in SHE 2/2/6. *Jane Prior of Bexhill, single woman, brought forth the male child on 6 Mar. but there was no evidence took on whether the child was brought forth alive or not* in SHE 2/2/9.
3 Annotated: *9 May 1838. Received CA.* CA was presumably Charles Arnold, a witness to Bellingham's will: PROB 11/1896, f 204v (manuscript foliation).

299 28 Mar. 1838. Beckley. Peter Gill:[1] died by the visitation of God. 12 miles. £1 15s 8d. Paid constable etc. £3 7s.
3 Apr. 1838. Mountfield. James Lawrence Daws: died by the visitation of God. 5 miles. £1 10s 5d. Paid constable etc. £1 8s 6d.
Total £8 1s 7d; allowed at Midsummer sessions 1838.[2] [AMS 5622/1/4, p 39]

[There is a summary of one of the inquests in SHE 2/2/9.]

1 *aged 11 months* added in SHE 2/2/9.
2 By Midsummer 1838 Bellingham was dead and payment was ordered to be made to his executors: QO/EW 55; QAF 2/1/E12, ff 215v–216. The bill has a note: *Received 5 July 1838 CA*. CA was presumably Charles Arnold, a witness to Bellingham's will: PROB 11/1896, f 204v (manuscript foliation).

HUNDRED CORONERS' BILLS

Bills of Charles Nairn (Battle and Robertsbridge Hundreds)

300 4 Aug. 1766. Robertsbridge. John Summers: hanged himself. 6 miles. £1 4s 6d.
2 Oct. 1766. Whatlington. Ann Watson: died in a fit. 2 miles. £1 1s 6d.
29 July 1768. [*Place omitted.*] William Slatter: died of a fall. £1.[1]
Total £3 6s; allowed at Michaelmas sessions 1768.[2] [QR/E 558, no 142]

[All Nairn's journeys were from Battle but that is never stated in his bills.]

1 Repeated in **301** and paid for twice.
2 Payment was received by Mr Farnes: QAF 2/1/E1. He was probably Thomas Farnes, a Lewes solicitor, who was dealing with matters on the Kent–Sussex border in that year: FRE 6031; FRE 6061.

301 29 July 1768. [*Place omitted.*] William Slatter: died by a fall. £1.[1]
7 June 1769. Whatlington. George Goldsmith: drowned. 3 miles. £1 2s 3d.[2]
23 May 1770. Westfield. Joseph Johnson: drowned. 4 miles. £1 3s.[2]
Total £3 5s 3d; allowed at Epiphany sessions 1771. [QR/E 567, no 15]

1 Also in **300** and paid for twice.
2 Repeated in **302** and paid for twice.

302 7 June 1769. [Whatlington], Battle hundred. George Goldsmith: drowned. £1.[1]
23 May 1770. Sedlescombe, Robertsbridge hundred. Joseph Johnson: found drowned. 3 miles. £1 2s 3d.[1]
30 Nov. 1770. [Battle], Battle hundred. George Jones: killed by fighting. £1.[2]
13 July 1771. [*Place omitted*], Battle hundred. Richard Vidler: drowned. £1.
30 Apr. 1774. [*Place omitted*], Battle hundred. James Tasker: killed by a cart going over him. £1.
15 June 1775. Robertsbridge, Robertsbridge hundred. Susannah Simmons: died suddenly. 6 miles. £1 4s 6d.
10 Aug. 1776. [*Place omitted*], Battle hundred. William Dobell: killed by a cart falling on him. £1.
14 Jan. 1777. [*Place omitted*], Battle hundred. William Hyland: died by a fall from a horse. £1.
30 Aug. 1777. Whatlington, Battle hundred. Thomas Price: killed by a fall from a horse. 2 miles. £1 1s 6d.
[*blank*] 1779. [*Place omitted*], Battle hundred. John Jeffery: found dead. 2 miles. £1 1s 6d.
3 May 1780. [*Place omitted*], Battle hundred. John Coleman: killed by a wagon going over him. £1.
Total £11 9s 9d; allowed at Michaelmas sessions 1780.[3] [QR/E 605, no 45]

1 Also in **301** and paid for twice.
2 Cf. **456**.
3 Payment was received by Stephen Swatland: QAF 2/1/E2. Swatland was Robertsbridge hundred deputy coroner in 1782: **463**.

Bills of Joseph Acton (Gostrow and Bexhill hundreds)

303 11 Aug. 1768. Udimore. Isaac Cloake: killed by a fall from his horse. 10 miles. £1 7s 6d.[1]
[19 Apr. 1770.] Brede. Elizabeth Frankwell: found dead in a barn. 8 miles. £1 6s.[2]
9 Sept. 1772. Brede. Mary Creasy: hanged herself. [8 miles.] £1 6s.
Total £3 19s 6d; allowed at Michaelmas sessions 1772. [QR/E 574, no 23]

[All Acton's journeys were from Hastings but that is stated only in the first entry of this bill, which is for Gostrow hundred only, and in none of his other bills.]

1 Cf. **455**.
2 Cf. **457**.

304 23 Sept. 1773. Brede. William Coleman: drowned in a well in his garden. 7 miles. £1 5s 3d.[1]
19 June 1774.[2] [Brede.] Thomas Freeman: killed by a timber-tug. 8 miles. £1 6s.[3]
Total £2 11s 3d; allowed at Michaelmas sessions 1777.[4] [QR/E 593, no 35]

[This bill is for Gostrow hundred only.]

1 Repeated in **305** and paid for twice. Cf. **453**.
2 Recte *1775*. Thomas Freeman jun. was buried 20 June 1775: PAR 253/1/1/2.
3 Repeated in **305** and paid for twice. Cf. **454**.
4 Payment was received by Mr Jackson: QAF 2/1/E1. He was almost certainly Henry Jackson who held lands in Brede and Udimore and was son-in-law of John Collier, a former Hastings rape coroner: *E Sx Land Tax*, 27, 205; Baines, 377; **415**.

305 23 Sept. 1773. Brede. William Coleman: found dead in a pond in his garden. 7 miles. £1 5s 3d.[1]
19 June 1775. Brede. Thomas Freeman: killed by a fall from a timber-tug. 8 miles. £1 6s.[2]
17 Oct. 1775. Bexhill. John Smith: found dead. 6 miles. £1 4s 6d.
3 Feb. 1779. Brede. Charles Creswell, private soldier: found dead in a sewer. [8 miles.] £1 6s.[3]
Total £5 1s 9d; allowed at Midsummer sessions 1779.[4] [QR/E 600, no 64]

[This bill is for Gostrow and Bexhill hundreds.]

1 Also in **304** and paid for twice. Cf. **453**.
2 Also in **304** and paid for twice. Cf. **454**.
3 Cf. **462**.
4 Payment was received by Charles Bristow: QAF 2/1/E2. Bristow held the last inquest as Gostrow hundred coroner for that turn: **462**.

306 18 Jan. 1781. [*Place omitted.*] Mary Wyburn: found dead and reported to have been murthered. 6 miles. £1 4s 6d.
3 Sept. 1781. [*Place omitted.*] James Lord: drowned. [6 miles.] £1 4s 6d.
26 Jan. 1782. [Bexhill.] John Merrit: found dead in the High Road. [6 miles.] £1 4s 6d.
21 Mar. 1782. [*Place omitted.*] John Cruttenden: found drowned in a marsh ditch. [6 miles.] £1 4s 6d.
2 Apr. 1782. [*Place omitted.*] William Smith: found dead in a brook. [6 miles.] £1 4s 6d.
Total £6 2s 6d; allowed at Midsummer sessions 1782. [QR/E 612, no 49]

[This bill is for Bexhill hundred only.]

Bills of Thomas Barton (Battle, Robertsbridge and Gostrow hundreds)

307 23 July 1811. Brede. Thomas Ninvell:[1] accidentally killed. 9 miles. £1 6s 9d.
1 June 1812. Battle. Edward Higgins: died by the visitation of God. £1.
16 June 1812. Robertsbridge. Leonard Fryman: accidentally killed. 6 miles. £1 4s 6d.
8 May 1813. Brede. Ann Barnes: found drowned. 9 miles. £1 6s 9d.
8 June 1813. Battle. Stephen Fuller: accidentally drowned. £1.
22 May 1814. Brede. William Noakes: found drowned. 9 miles. £1 6s 9d.
19 July 1814. Battle. John Sindon, John Eldridge and Philip Mann: accidentally killed. £1.
17 Jan. 1815. Westfield, Robertsbridge hundred. John Webb: being lunatic, hanged himself. 5 miles. £1 3s 9d.
9 May 1815. Battle. Ann Ives: accidentally killed. £1.
26 May 1815. Battle. Stephen Middlemas: accidentally killed. £1.
Total £11 8s 6d; allowed at Epiphany sessions 1816. [QR/E 746]

[All Barton's journeys were from Battle but that is never stated in his bills.]

1 *Linvill* in PAR 253/1/1/2.

308 7 May 1816. Brede. Thomas Kennard: accidentally killed. 9 miles. £1 6s 9d.
22 May 1816. Robertsbridge. Thomas Tassell: died by the visitation of God. 6 miles. £1 4s 6d.
16 Oct. 1816. Robertsbridge. Hannah Clout: died by the visitation of God. 6 miles. £1 4s 6d.
16 Nov. 1816. Battle. Mary Inskipp: being lunatic, destroyed herself. £1.
19 Feb. 1817. Brede. William Baseby and Henry Reed: accidentally killed. 6 miles. £1 4s 6d.
2 July 1817. Battle. Hannah Coomber: died by the visitation of God. £1.
5 Aug. 1817. Battle. Thomas Sturt: found drowned. £1.
8 Nov. 1817. Battle.[1] Cornelius Foord: found drowned.[2] £1.
18 Mar. 1819. Wartling. John Apps: shot. 9 miles. £1 6s 9d.[3]
19 Mar. 1819, it being necessary to adjourn. Wartling. John Apps. [9 miles.] 6s 9d.[3]
12 Apr. 1819. Northiam. Samuel Hanson: died by the visitation of God. 10 miles. £1 7s 6d.
21 May 1819. Battle. Thomas Page: being lunatic, hanged himself. £1.
1 June 1819. Burwash. Eleanor Kemp: burned to death. 10 miles. £1 7s 6d.
Total £14 8s 9d; allowed at Midsummer sessions 1819. [QR/E 760]

[Barton took the last four inquests as Hastings rape coroner. One of the other entries is also in RAF 1/4/2.]

1 *Battle* omitted in RAF 1/4/2.
2 *found drowned* omitted in RAF 1/4/2.
3 Cf. **431**.

COUNTY CORONERS' INQUESTS

Inquests of Alexander Luxford

309 7 June 1689. [*Place erased.*] Jurors: Nathaniel Welch, George Kempe, John English, Thomas Hoult, Francis Cheeman, Thomas Smith, William Munns, John Stempe, William Reynoldes, Thomas Batchelor, Edward Swift, Edward English, Thomas Newington, David Batchelor, Nathaniel Newington. Witnesses: Elizabeth Temple, Mary Baldwin, Lydia Stone, Hester Jacob, George Kempe. On 28 May Catherine Murrin late of New Shoreham, 'spinster', gave birth at New Shoreham to a live female child which by the laws of the kingdom 'was a bastard' and on the same day murdered her at Kingston by Sea, taking her in her hands, throwing her naked and alive into 'a hedge' belonging 'to the farme' of Edward Blaker, gent., and leaving her there in the bitter cold without sustenance with the intention that she should die for lack of sustenance, which she did on the same day. Murrin had no goods or chattels, lands or tenements in Sussex or elsewhere at the time of the murder or ever after to the jurors' knowledge.

[ASSI 94/4, m 7]

[Delivered to Horsham assizes on 20 July when the grand jury, to which the same 5 witnesses gave evidence, presented 2 indictments identical to the inquest verdict but omitting the final sentence; and one of them, for which the coroner also gave evidence, added that after committing the murder Murrin concealed the child in order that it might not be known whether or not she had been born alive. Murrin pleaded not guilty and was acquitted; she had not fled. ASSI 94/4, mm 5, 7–9.]

310 24 Apr. 1690. Eastbourne. Jurors: Samuel Parker, John Collier, James Machin, Simon Banckes, Henry Head, Edward Vincent, John Read, Thomas Earle, R... Tutt, John Rigden, Ambrose Smith, Thomas Hunden, Thomas Price, Thomas Earle, Thomas Smith, Thomas Copper, John Vernon. Witnesses: Elizabeth Webb, Mary Turle, Mary Godfrey, Mary Smith. On 17 Apr. Catherine Bunce late of Eastbourne, 'spinster', gave birth at Eastbourne to a live male child which by the laws of the kingdom 'was a bastard' and immediately murdered him: she 'thrust' him with both hands into 'a chest' and suffocated him in it, whereby he immediately died. Bunce had no goods or chattels, lands or tenements in Sussex or elsewhere at that time or ever after to the jurors' knowledge.

[ASSI 94/16, m 12]

[Delivered to Horsham assizes on 11 Sept. when a bill of indictment was preferred identical to the inquest verdict but omitting the last sentence. The grand jury, to which the same 4 witnesses gave evidence, rejected the bill. Bunce pleaded not guilty to the inquest and was acquitted; she had not fled and so was discharged. ASSI 94/16, mm 6, 12; ASSI 94/18, m 4; PRO 30/26/104, f 61.]

311 7 June 1690. Hartfield. Jurors: Richard Jones, James Everist, William Marten, William Griggs, John Humfry, William Gilberd, Robert Burges, Robert Pope, William Lettermarke, Richard Stannard, Thomas Gye, Jeremiah Marten sen., Robert Hards, Robert Humfry. About 11 p.m. on 2 June, when Lewis Andrewes was walking alone in Ashdown Forest near 'le old bay' in Hartfield, by misadventure and against his will he suddenly fell into a deep ditch, whereby he received 'one mortall bruise' on the right side of his head of which he immediately died in the ditch.

[KB 11/14, Mich. 2 William and Mary]

[Delivered to King's Bench in Michaelmas, probably by the coroner. At the Horsham assizes of 11 Sept. a bill of indictment was preferred which charged Thomas Hobbs, Denham Baker and Edward May, all late of Hartfield, labourers, and Hobbs's wife Jane with murdering Andrewes at Hartfield on 2 June: Thomas Hobbs striking him on the right side of his head with a wooden staff of no value which he held in both hands and giving him a bruise of which he immediately died; and the 3 others being feloniously present aiding and abetting him. The grand jury, to which Isaac Snelling, Joan Burgis and John Bartholomewe gave evidence, rejected the bill. ASSI 94/18, m 1; KB 29/349, m 82d.]

312 12 Aug. 1691. Chalvington. Jurors: Edward Newington, John Reynolds, William Acton, Richard Waterhouse, Edward Shadwell, Thomas Newington, Lawrence Avery, Thomas Wade, Thomas James, James Markwick, William Grover, Thomas Plumer, 'Forister' Withered, Thomas Shadwell, William Plumer. About 6 a.m. on 7 Aug., when Richard Faulconer late of Chalvington, gent., was in 'an empty wagon', driving it on the common highway leading from his dwelling-house in Chalvington to that of John Dulake there, 'one gelding' which belonged to Faulconer drawing the wagon, 'the offward wheels' of the wagon suddenly, by misadventure and against Faulconer's will fell into 'a deep hole' in the highway, whereby Faulconer was thrown violently from the wagon to the ground, receiving a wound on the back of his head 1 inch wide and 1 inch deep of which he languished at Chalvington until 10 Aug. and then died. The gelding, worth 13s 4d, and the wagon, worth 6s 8d, were moving to his death and remained with Daniel Mills of Hellingly, 'yeoman'. [KB 11/15, Mich. 4 William and Mary]

[Delivered to King's Bench in Michaelmas 1692, probably by the coroner. Mills was summoned to King's Bench to answer for the deodands; he was later outlawed. KB 29/351, m 64.]

313 19 Sept. 1691. Litlington. Jurors: Robert Andrewes, James Newman, Richard Hamlen, Samuel Collingham, Nicholas Heyward, Thomas ?Saere, John Exeter, Thomas Bevis, John Dorridge, Isaac Colvill, William Waymarke, William Wood, John Harrison, Edward Bartholomew, Richard Surgion. About 5 p.m. on 16 Sept., when John Finch late of Litlington, 'shepard', was alone in the close of Henry Beane of Litlington, 'yeoman', at Litlington, he took a piece of rope worth 1d in both hands and fixed one end of it around 'a bough' of 'an ash tree' which was growing there and tied the other round his neck, threw himself from the branch and so hanged and murdered himself. At that time he possessed 'one iron porridge pott' worth 3s, 2 'bedsteds' worth 5s, 2 'chests' worth 4s, 6 'pewter dishes' worth 7s 6d, 2 'pewter porringers' worth 6d, 'a feather bedd' worth 15s, 'a coverlet' worth 2s, 'one woolen blanket' worth 2s and 'ten sheepe' worth 20s, all of which came to the hands of Henry Beane, 'yeoman', Longbridge hundred constable, and remained with him; and no other goods or chattels to the jurors' knowledge.

[KB 11/15, Mich. 4 William and Mary]

[Delivered with **312**. The constable was summoned to King's Bench to answer for the goods and chattels, worth 59s; he was later outlawed. KB 29/351, m 64.]

314 16 Dec. 1691. Nutley in Maresfield. Jurors: John ..., Martin Hoath, William Pryor, John Norman, Edward ?Fenn, William Heasman, ?John ..., Oliver Knight, ... Knight, ?William ?Harmer, John Smith, Stephen Smith, William Smith, John ?Lockyer, ..., Stephen ?Foster, ... Norman. About 9 a.m. on 14 Dec. William Dobson late of

Maresfield, ?'laborer', murdered William Morris late of Nutley, 'laborer', at Maresfield with 'a hoe' worth 4d which he held in both hands, giving him a wound 'on the top of the head' 1 inch wide and 1 inch deep of which he languished at Maresfield until 5 p.m. and then died. Dobson had no goods or chattels, lands or tenements in Sussex or elsewhere at the time of the murder or ever after to the jurors' knowledge. [*Damaged.*]

[ASSI 94/37, m 1]

[Delivered to Horsham assizes on 18 Mar. 1692 when the grand jury, to which Francis Croft, Thomas Hemsly, John Norman, Richard Relph and the coroner gave evidence, presented an indictment identical to the inquest verdict except for the omission of the last sentence and that Morris was not described as of Nutley, labourer. Dobson was remanded without bail. At the East Grinstead assizes of 14 July he pleaded not guilty and was acquitted of murder but convicted of manslaughter; he had no chattels. He then successfully pleaded benefit of clergy and was branded on the hand and discharged, paying his fees. ASSI 94/37, mm 1, 2, 15d; ASSI 94/41, mm 2, 17d.]

315 7 Jan. 1692. Horsham. Jurors: James Pilfold, Richard Honywood, William Hunt, John Waterton, Richard Clarke, Samuel Bythwood, Robert Hurst, William Waller, Alexander Wilfold, Giles Huish, William Satcher, William Chambers, Robert Lutman, Thomas Groombridge, Alexander Hibson, Henry Groombridge, William Hunt. On 4 Jan., when Thomas Dumbrell of Horsham, 'laborer', aged 14 and not more, apprentice of John Clarke of Horsham, blacksmith, was in Clarke's dwelling-house at Horsham, trying to mend the iron 'cock' of 'a pistoll' which was 'out of order and rusty', having been left to do it by William Kewell, servant of Thomas White, gent., in Clarke's absence; not knowing that the pistol was 'charged with gunpowder and a leaden bullet', Dumbrell moved 'the cocke' with the fingers of his right hand 'up and downe' with the intention of inspecting the 'fault' and mending it; but the gunpowder 'being fired' by Dumbrell's moving the cock, the pistol 'did discharge and shoot off', giving John Clarke, an infant aged 6, the blacksmith's son, who was standing in his father's house, a wound in the left part of his body a little under the left breast 1 inch wide and 8 inches deep of which he languished at Horsham until the next day and then died. So Dumbrell killed him suddenly, by chance and misfortune and against his will. Dumbrell had no goods or chattels in Sussex or elsewhere at the time of the homicide or ever after to the jurors' knowledge. [ASSI 94/37, m 9]

[Delivered with **314**. At the assizes the grand jury, to which John Clarke, Robert Hurst, Mary Miller and Joseph Chasmor gave evidence, presented an indictment which charged Dumbrell with murdering Clarke, aged 6, at Horsham on 4 Jan. with a pistol worth 2s charged with gunpowder and a lead bullet which he held in his right hand and which he discharged (details of wound and death as in inquest). Dumbrell pleaded not guilty and was acquitted; he had not fled and so was discharged, paying his fees. ASSI 94/37, mm 9, 10, 15d.]

316 26 Apr. 1705. Framfield. Jurors: Edward Chatfeild, John Colgate, Thomas Olliffe, John Wacklyn, Edward Devonish, William Miles, Andrew Read, Edward Page, Thomas Attree, William Wood, John Comber, Francis Chatfeild, John Knight, Thomas Morphew, Edward Harling, John Alchorne, Henry Wardraper, Henry Day, Henry Thompsett, Stephen Rothwell. About 3 p.m. on 24 Apr. John Pupp late of Framfield, 'laborer', murdered Edward Gilham at Framfield with 'a naked penknife' of iron and steel worth 4d which he held in his right hand: he 'did strike and thrust' him in the chest near the left breast, giving him 'one mortall wound' ½ inch wide and 3 inches deep of which he languished at Framfield until 10 p.m. and then died. Pupp had no goods or chattels, lands or tenements in Sussex or elsewhere at the time of the murder or ever after to the jurors' knowledge. [ASSI 94/214, m 6]

[Delivered to Horsham assizes on 16 July when the grand jury, to which Edward and Susan Sisley gave evidence, presented an indictment identical to the inquest verdict except for the omission of the last sentence. Pupp pleaded not guilty and was acquitted on the indictment; he had not fled. On the inquest he was acquitted of murder but convicted of manslaughter; he had no chattels. He then successfully pleaded benefit of clergy and was branded on the hand and discharged, paying his fees. ASSI 94/214, mm 5–7, 13d.]

317 29 Mar. 1706. Cuckfield. Jurors: Robert Norden, Thomas Ives, Richard Burt, Henry Burtenshaw, James Mitchell, Thomas Vivins, Richard Virgoe, William Heasman, William Fuljames, Thomas Newman, Thomas Mather, Samuel Ither, Stephen Gates, 'Gibeon' Mather, John Holford, Henry Sharpe, Samuel Savage. Witnesses: Robert Cave, John Jenning, Barbara Jenner, Edward Chatfeild, Jane Weekes, Mary Juniper. On 25 Mar. Hugh Vincent late of Cuckfield, 'laborer', feloniously killed Francis Juniper at Cuckfield with his hands, arms, legs and feet, violently throwing him to the ground and beating and kicking him on the head, chest, stomach and sides, of which he languished at Cuckfield until 27 Mar. and then died. Vincent had no goods or chattels, lands or tenements in Sussex or elsewhere at the time of the felony or ever after to the jurors' knowledge. [ASSI 94/227, m 3]

[Delivered to Horsham assizes on 2 Sept. when 2 bills of indictment were preferred. One was similar to the inquest verdict except that Juniper was called Jenifer, the charge was murder and the last sentence was omitted. The grand jury, to which Samuel and Mary Jenifer, Jane Wicks, Thomas Cannon, Edward Chatfeild, Edward Miles, Francis Nye and Barbara Jenner gave evidence, rejected the bill. Vincent pleaded not guilty to the inquest and was acquitted, the trial jury finding that Juniper had died a natural death; Vincent had not fled and so was discharged, paying his fees. The other bill charged Francis Greene late of East Grinstead, gent., with unlawfully assuming and exercising the office of county coroner at Cuckfield on 29 Mar. by viewing the body of Francis Jenifer and holding an inquest on it, Jenifer having been found lying dead at Cuckfield on that day, supposed to have been killed by Hugh Vincent. The grand jury, to which Samuel Jenifer gave evidence, rejected it. ASSI 94/227, mm 2, 3, 11d (where convicted is an error for acquitted); ASSI 94/232.]

Inquests of John Michell

318 25 Aug. 1711. Ringmer. Jurors: Samuel White, William Bean, Thomas Forster, John French, William Mathews, Stephen Rusbridge, Isaac Ollive, John Ford, John Gosden, John Weller, John Blacklock, John Kennard, Thomas Payne, Isaac Baldy, Thomas Coules, Thomas Dumbrell, Henry Goodwyn. On 24 Aug. Mary wife of John Martin killed their son Thomas, an infant aged 12 months, at Ringmer, she then being non compos mentis and 'phrantique', lunatic and 'disturbed' in her mind and senses: she took him in both hands, threw him into a well full of water near her husband's dwelling-house and 'did choake and drowne' him, whereby he immediately died. [ASSI 94/292, m 11]

[Delivered to East Grinstead assizes on 17 Mar. 1712 when the grand jury, to which John Martin, Elizabeth Standley, John Mantle, Nicholas Roberts and Elizabeth Winchester gave evidence, presented an indictment similar to the inquest verdict except that the charge was murder, there being no mention of Mary Martin's insanity, and John Martin was called late of Ringmer, yeoman.

Mary pleaded not guilty and was acquitted; she had not fled and so was discharged, paying her fees. ASSI 94/292, mm 5, 12, 16d.]

319 13 July 1713. Ringmer. Jurors: Thomas Wood, Joseph ?Mee [*or* Lee], John Weller, James Bryan, Benjamin Beale, Richard Wakerill, Edward Murrell, John Nicholls, Thomas Winchester, John Pighurst, Thomas Carter, John Moore, William Nicholls. About 6 p.m. on 13 July Mary wife of John Martyn late of Ringmer, 'agricole', being non compos mentis and 'frantique', lunatic and 'distracted' in her mind and senses, took their son Robert, an infant aged 6, in both hands, threw him into the water of 'a pond' near her husband's dwelling-house at Ringmer and drowned him, whereby he immediately died. [ASSI 94/309, m 2]

[Delivered to Lewes assizes on 17 July when the grand jury, to which John Ford, William Dudeney and Elizabeth Gallop gave evidence, presented an indictment similar to the inquest verdict except that the charge was murder, there being no mention of Mary Martyn's insanity, and John Martyn was styled yeoman. Mary pleaded not guilty and was acquitted; she had not fled and so was discharged, paying her fees. ASSI 94/309, mm 5, 6, 18d.]

320 25 Mar. 1714. New Shoreham. Jurors: John Alexander, William Bridger, Shadrach Seager, Thomas Dunton, Thomas Jeffery, Thomas Towner, Thomas Snooke, John Tweedall, John Pelham, James Glazpoole, John Robinson, John Chantler, Henry Light, William Forster, Lawrence Mathewes, Thomas French, Thomas Moorey, Adam Daniell. On 22 Mar., when Thomas Howell late of New Shoreham, servant of Thomas Brigden, had 'a pistoll' of Brigden's in his right hand to clean, not knowing it to be 'charged with gunpowder and leaden bulletts', 'the cocke', which was attached to the gun with flint, being 'halfe bent', suddenly, by chance and without the knowledge and against the will of Howell set fire to the gunpowder by the force of which the bullets were discharged and penetrated the right part of the forehead of Ann Goldsmith, 'spinster', who was near Howell, giving her a wound 1 inch wide and 2 inches deep of which she languished at New Shoreham until the next day and then died. So Howell killed her suddenly, by chance, without his knowledge and against his will. What goods or chattels he had at the time of her death or ever after the jurors did not know. [ASSI 94/320]

[Delivered to Horsham assizes on 5 July when the grand jury, to which John Innett, Thomas Brigden and the coroner gave evidence, presented an indictment similar to the inquest verdict except that Howell, styled labourer, fired the pistol, worth 2s, at Goldsmith knowing that it was charged, the indictment was for murder and the last sentence was omitted. Howell pleaded not guilty and was acquitted; he had not fled. ASSI 94/320.]

321 4 Sept. 1716. Worth. Jurors: George Virgo, John Jeale, Thomas Davis, John Penfold, Roger Potter, Richard Potter, William Flint, John Snelling, James Ridge, Richard Willett, John Jeale jun., Edward West, William Titchenor, Edward Scott, William Williams, John Humphery, John Butcher. On 2 Sept. Brian Scrase late of Worth, 'laborer', murdered Ann Jeale, 'spinster', at Worth with 'an handkercheif' and 'the hemm of an handkercheife' worth 2d which he held in both hands, fastening them round her neck and strangling her, whereby she immediately died. What goods or chattels, lands or tenements Scrase had at that time or ever after the jurors did not know. [ASSI 94/353]

[Delivered to East Grinstead assizes on 25 Mar. 1717 when the grand jury, to which William Hampton, James and Sarah Jeale, John Hills, William Bell and the coroner gave evidence, presented an indictment identical to the inquest verdict except for the omission of the last sentence.

Scrase pleaded not guilty but was convicted and sentenced to be hanged; he had no chattels. ASSI 94/353.]

322 9 Aug. 1717. Framfield. Jurors: William Mesken, Henry …, Richard Newton, John Taylor, John Cottington, James Taylor, William Chene, John Ford, Richard ?Hemsell, Nicholas Read, John King, James Longley, Henry Calchin. About 1 a.m. on 8 Aug. Richard Skinner, with several others unknown, illegally broke and entered 'the parke' of Henry Gage at Framfield commonly called Bentley Park, which was then and long before used and kept for the care and nurture of deer, with the intention of killing Gage's deer there and assaulted William Sheppard, Gage's servant guarding the deer in the park, violently struck him on the head with a large wooden staff and 'followed after' him striking him. To protect himself and save his life, since he could not otherwise avoid Skinner's violence, Sheppard shot at him with 'a gunn charged with gunpowder and a leaden bullett', giving him a wound in the left part of the head 1 inch wide and 3 inches deep of which he immediately died. Sheppard had no goods or chattels, lands or tenements in Sussex or elsewhere at that time or ever after to the jurors' knowledge. [*Damaged.*] [ASSI 94/361]

[Delivered to Lewes summer assizes when the grand jury, to which Richard Hanson, Joseph Treader and Francis Davis gave evidence, presented an indictment which charged Sheppard, late of Framfield, labourer, with murdering Skinner at Framfield on 8 Aug. with a gun worth 2s which he held in both hands (details of gun, wound and death as in inquest). Sheppard pleaded not guilty and was acquitted; he had not fled and so was discharged, paying his fees. ASSI 94/361.]

323 … Jan. 1718. Cuckfield. Jurors: …, John Stone, Henry Sharp, Stephen Agate, John Smith, William Best, John Heasman, Michael …, …, John Hurst, John Wood sen., John Wood jun., Thomas Jenner, Thomas …, Edward Curteis, John …, Nicholas Hunt, William Heasman. On 8 Jan. Elizabeth Coats late of Cuckfield, 'spinster', gave birth at Cuckfield to a live female infant which by the laws of the kingdom 'was a bastard' and immediately murdered her: she took her in both hands and 'did putt and thrust' her into 'a close stoole' in which she suffocated her, whereby she immediately died. What goods or chattels, lands or tenements Coats had at that time or ever after the jurors did not know. [*Damaged.*] [ASSI 94/369, m 10]

[Delivered to East Grinstead assizes on 24 Mar. when the grand jury, to which Richard Falconer, Richard Simonds and Elizabeth Dennett gave evidence, presented an indictment identical to the inquest verdict except for the omission of the last sentence. Coats pleaded not guilty and was acquitted; she had not fled and so was discharged, paying her fees. ASSI 94/369, mm 2d, 7, 10.]

324 20 May 1719. Glynde. Jurors: John Grover, Henry Arnatt, Henry Burges, John Care, Richard Jarvis, William Bodle, Thomas Carter, Daniel Skinner, Stephen Simpson, George Winkles, Thomas Howell, Thomas Chapman, John Trangmore, Richard Cheale, Simon Grover. On 18 May Mary Forster late of Glynde, 'spinster', gave birth at Glynde to a live female infant which by the laws of the kingdom 'was a bastard' and immediately murdered her: she took her in both hands and 'did hold and gripe' her by the neck and strangled her, whereby she immediately died. What goods or chattels, lands or tenements Forster had at that time or ever after the jurors did not know. [ASSI 94/386]

[Delivered to Lewes assizes on 16 July when the grand jury, to which Alice Young and Elizabeth Inskipp gave evidence, presented an indictment identical to the inquest verdict except for the omission of the last sentence. Forster pleaded not guilty and was acquitted; she had not fled and so was discharged, paying her fees. ASSI 94/386.]

325 12 Mar. 1723. Bolney. Jurors: Henry Bull, Michael Harmes jun., James Mathew, Henry Ockenden, William King, Edward West, Thomas Woolven, Charles Mathew, Thomas Reeve, Richard Blaker, John Lintott, John Hills, John Dolton, William Marten, Thomas West, John Murrell, William Murrell. About 9 a.m. on 8 Feb. Sarah Blink late of Bolney, 'widow', murdered Ann, the infant daughter of Thomas Jupp, at Bolney. She put a poison called 'white arsenicke' into a drink called 'wort', prepared in a wooden dish for Ann to drink, knowing that the arsenic was a deadly poison. She then gave it to Ann to drink as good and wholesome wort and she drank it, believing it to be good and wholesome, by reason of which she languished at Bolney until 8 p.m. and then died. What goods or chattels, lands or tenements Blink had at the time of the murder or ever after the jurors did not know. [ASSI 94/426]

[Delivered to East Grinstead assizes on 1 Apr. when the grand jury, to which Francis Chasmore and Thomas Jupp gave evidence, presented an indictment similar to the inquest verdict except for the omission of Ann being Jupp's infant daughter and of the last sentence, and that Blink was styled labourer, not widow. Blink pleaded not guilty but was convicted; she had no chattels and was sentenced to be hanged. ASSI 94/426.]

326 23 Oct. 1730. Withyham. Jurors: Alexander Pococke, John Mills, William Baker, Solomon Neve, John Russell, William Pilbeam, Thomas Neve, Thomas Inkpen, Robert Pawley, Edward Peckham, Edward Jenner, Robert Sparrow, John Grombridge sen., John Grombridge jun., John Bennett. On 13 July John Nash late of Withyham, 'laborer', murdered Richard Game, then high constable of Hartfield hundred, at Withyham, while he was duly performing the duties of his office, with 'a knife' worth 2d which he held in his right hand, giving him a wound on the right hand 3 inches long and ½ inch deep of which he languished at Withyham until 17 Oct. and then died. What goods or chattels, lands or tenements Nash had at the time of the murder or ever after the jurors did not know. [ASSI 94/521]

[Delivered to East Grinstead assizes on 22 Mar. 1731 when the grand jury, to which Thomas Townsend, Mary Game, widow, Jane and Sarah Bennett, [William Relfe *struck through*], John Knightley, Thomas Mepham, John Wickes and John Board, esq., gave evidence, presented an indictment identical to the inquest verdict except that the knife was of iron and steel and the last sentence was omitted. Nash pleaded not guilty and was acquitted, the trial jury finding that Game had died a natural death; Nash had not fled and so was discharged, paying his fees. ASSI 94/521.]

327 30 May 1734. Ditchling. Jurors of Ditchling and 4 neighbouring townships: Henry Cheale, Thomas Harris, Edward Moor, Thomas Butcher, John Parsons, Edward Townsett, William Phillery, Edward Carter, Edward Geer, James Potter, Giles Browne, William Mills, John Seaman. On 26 May James alias Jacob Hirsh alias Harris late of Ditchling, labourer, murdered Richard Miles at Ditchling with a knife of iron and steel worth 2d which he held in his right hand, giving him 2 mortal wounds on the throat, each 5 inches long and 2 inches deep, of which he languished at Ditchling until 30 May and then died. What goods or chattels, lands or tenements Hirsh had at the time of the murder the jurors did not know. [ASSI 94/572]

[Delivered to Horsham assizes on 12 Aug. when the grand jury presented 2 indictments. One, for which Henry Cheale, James and Edward Geer and John Parsons gave evidence, was identical to the inquest verdict except for the omission of the last sentence. The other, for which the same 4 witnesses and also John Oliver, John Harling and Richard Keckett gave evidence, charged Hirsh alias Harris with breaking and entering Miles's dwelling-house at Ditchling at about 7 p.m. on 26 May, putting Miles's wife Dorothy, who was in the house, in fear of her life and stealing and carrying away a riding-coat worth 10s of Miles's goods and chattels found in the house. Hirsh pleaded not guilty and was acquitted of housebreaking but convicted of murder and sentenced to be hanged; he had no chattels. ASSI 94/572. Cf. *SCM*, VIII, 137, 272.]

Inquests of Thomas Attree

328 29 Apr. 1736. Buxted. Jurors of Buxted and 4 neighbouring townships: John Olive, gent., William Nutt, gent., Richard Foster, gent., William Pettitt, gent., Charles Inkledon, gent., Henry Hall, John Smith, John Hamblin, William Devonish, Thomas Solomon, John Cooke, Richard Alchern, John Curless, Thomas Fitness. On 11 Apr. William Chainey late of Buxted, gent., murdered James Storer [*once called* Story][1] at Buxted with a gun worth 5s charged with gunpowder and a lead bullet which he held in both hands and discharged against Storer, giving him a wound on the left side of the back of the neck 2 inches deep and ½ inch wide of which he immediately died. [ASSI 94/604]

[Delivered to Horsham assizes on 9 Aug. when a bill of indictment was preferred identical to the inquest verdict except that Storer was so named throughout and William Hardwick late of Buxted, gent., was charged with murder by being feloniously present aiding and abetting Chainey. The grand jury, to which Richard Turner and Thomas Morris gave evidence, rejected the bill. There were no proceedings on the inquest. ASSI 94/604.]

1 He was buried on 13 Apr. as James Story: Ep. V/10/1A; PAR 286/1/1/2.

329 21 May 1739. William Hillman's house, South Malling. Jurors of South Malling and 3 neighbouring townships: John Whitfeld, Henry Tapsfield, John Woodgate, Andrew Tasker, Thomas Smith, Edward Comber jun., Thomas Awcock, John Heaver, John Lambert, Thomas Baldy, William Tooth, Thomas Harbin, John Ansell, William English, Daniel Kenward, Edward Hood, William Attree, William Hill, Edward Clarke, John Day, Edward Bland, John Everenden, Samuel Betting. On 12 May Sarah wife of Joseph Goldsmith late of South Malling feloniously killed Elizabeth wife of William Hillman at South Malling, throwing her with both hands to the ground and, while she was lying there, striking her with both hands on the head, breast, stomach, back and sides and thereby giving her one mortal bruise on the right side of the head and another on the stomach, both 2 inches long and 1 inch wide, of which she languished at South Malling until the next day and then died. Sarah Goldsmith had no goods or chattels, lands or tenements at the time of the felony to the jurors' knowledge. [ASSI 94/647]

[Delivered to Lewes assizes on 18 Aug. when the grand jury, to which William Hillman, John Diplock, Robert Bayley, James, Thomas, Ann, Elizabeth and Mary Hillman, Jane Green, Mary Young, Elizabeth Russell and Elizabeth Ball gave evidence, presented an indictment similar to the inquest verdict except that Joseph Goldsmith was styled labourer, Sarah threw Elizabeth Hillman to the ground with both hands and feet and struck and kicked her with both hands and feet, the charge was murder and the last sentence was omitted. Sarah, who had been committed to gaol by the coroner on the day of the inquest as wife of Joseph Goldsmith of South Malling, blacksmith, pleaded not guilty and was acquitted of murder but convicted of manslaughter, burnt on the hand and then discharged. ASSI 94/647.]

330 6 Mar. 1741. East Grinstead. Jurors of East Grinstead and 4 neighbouring townships: William Kent, gent., David Dudley, James Dane, George Brown, Robert Goodwin, John Jordan, Thomas Malyan, Henry Farley, John Shewen, Richard Marten,

Christopher Ashdown, Francis Hamlin, Robert Dane, John Mason, William Bradbourn, Edward Jorden. On 25 Feb., as Walter Smith and John Finch, both of East Grinstead, labourers, were walking together in a wood at East Grinstead, each having a gun or fowling-piece in his right hand charged with powder and shot with which they intended to kill wild fowl, Finch's gun, worth 1s, was discharged by the accidental striking of a bough on its cock, which was then 'on the half-bent', giving Smith a wound in the right thigh 1 inch wide and 5 inches deep of which he languished at East Grinstead until 1 Mar. and then died. So Finch killed him by misfortune and accident. [ASSI 94/671]

[Delivered to East Grinstead assizes on 16 Mar. when a bill of indictment was preferred which charged Finch with feloniously killing Smith at East Grinstead on 25 Feb. with a gun worth 2s charged with gunpowder and lead shot which he held in one hand, discharging it at him (details of wound and death as in inquest). The grand jury, to which William Osman, William Kent, Francis Murrell, Robert Pope and Richard Martin gave evidence, rejected the bill. ASSI 94/671.]

331 27 Mar. 1741. Lindfield. Jurors of Lindfield and 4 neighbouring townships: Thomas Comber, John Batchelor, John Osborn, George Neale, Richard Heaver, Stephen Jenner, Thomas Wickens, Henry Wickens, Edmund Muddle, John Tabb, William Topset, Robert Rothwell, Thomas Neale, William Batchelor, Thomas Durrant. Between 5 and 6 p.m. on 2 Mar. James Wellar late of Lindfield, labourer, Martha his wife and Ann wife of William Davy late of Lindfield, labourer, murdered Elizabeth wife of James Matthew of Lindfield, labourer, at Lindfield: they threw her down upon the ground in James Matthew's dwelling-house, struck her with their hands and drew her on the ground and over the sill of the house door, thereby giving her a bruise across the small of the back 6 inches long and 4 inches wide of which she languished at Lindfield until 13 Mar. and then died. [ASSI 94/678]

[Delivered to Lewes assizes on 18 July when a bill of indictment was preferred which charged the same 3 with murdering Elizabeth wife of James Matthew at Lindfield on 2 Mar. by throwing her to the ground and, as she lay there, striking her with their hands and fists on the head, stomach, back and sides, thereby giving her a bruise on the lower part of the back (dimensions and details of death as in inquest). The grand jury, to which James Matthew, Elizabeth Bannister, Elizabeth Cox, Judith Martin, Frances Homan, Mary Pelling, Mary Smith and Mary Smead gave evidence, rejected the bill. James and Martha Wellar and Ann Davy had been committed to gaol on 26 Mar. by John Board, JP, charged on the oath of James Matthew on suspicion of killing his wife. The Wellars had both died before the assizes, at which Ann Davy pleaded not guilty to the inquest and was acquitted and discharged. ASSI 94/678.]

332 3 Dec. 1744. Maresfield. Jurors of Maresfield and 4 neighbouring townships: Martin Hoath sen., Thomas Hoath, Edward Page, William Mulford, John Banister jun., James Standing, Martin Hoath jun., Thomas Pelling, Walter Comber, Richard Verrall, William Feldwick, Edward Jarrett, Henry Foord, Joseph Colchin. On 2 Dec., when William Feldwick of Maresfield and William Symonds of Buxted, labourers, were walking together in 'a piece of hop-ground' of Thomas Sevenoaks in Maresfield, each with a gun or fowling-piece charged with powder and shot in his right hand, intending to kill fieldfares and other wild fowl, Symonds set the butt end of his gun, worth 1s, on one of the hop-hills in the hop-ground, still holding it in his right hand. Feldwick, seeing a parcel of fieldfares, came up to Symonds and, in a great hurry, with his right hand caught hold of Symonds's gun, the cock of which was on the half-bent, causing it to discharge and thereby to give him a wound in his right temple 2 inches wide and 6 inches deep of which he immediately died. So Symonds killed Feldwick by misfortune and accident. [ASSI 94/722]

[Delivered to East Grinstead assizes on 18 Mar. 1745 when a bill of indictment was preferred which charged Symonds late of Maresfield, labourer, with murdering Feldwick at Maresfield on 2 Dec. with a gun worth 5s charged with gunpowder and lead shot which he held in one hand, giving him a wound in the right side of the head 3 inches wide and 7 inches deep of which he immediately died. The grand jury, to which Robert Meads and John Isted gave evidence, rejected the bill. ASSI 94/722.]

333 17 Sept. 1746. Rottingdean. Jurors of Rottingdean and 4 neighbouring townships: Richard Collier, John Beeding, John Triggs, Richard Legat, Humphrey Payne, Joseph Duckwell Payne, Thomas Saunders, William Friend, Richard Humphery, John Mayle, William Bradford, Thomas Bradford, Richard Smith, Henry Beach, William Gold. Before or about 8 a.m. on 17 Aug., when William Mills and Stephen Boys, both of Rottingdean, labourers, were together in John Matthews's dwelling-house in Rottingdean, on a sudden, but by what provocation the jurors could not learn, an affray occurred between them in which Boys threw Mills onto the floor and there kneed him on the body with both knees, thereby giving him a shock or contusion upon his brain of which he languished at Rottingdean until 13 Sept. and then died. So Boys killed him. [ASSI 94/746]

[Delivered to East Grinstead assizes on 6 Apr. 1747. At the Lewes assizes of 15 Aug. 1747 the grand jury, to which John Greenaway, John Bean, John Snashal, Nicholas Willard, John Martin, Martha West, Elizabeth Deadman, Elizabeth Palmar and Samuel Snatt gave evidence, presented an indictment which charged Boys with murdering Mills at Rottingdean on 17 Aug. by striking him violently with his hands and fists on the head, face, back, belly, loins and shoulders and throwing him to the ground, thereby giving him several bruises of which he languished at Rottingdean until 13 Sept. and then died. Boys pleaded not guilty and was acquitted of murder but convicted of manslaughter. He then pleaded for a pardon under the recent statute[1] and because the offence was committed before 15 June 1747 he was discharged. ASSI 94/746; ASSI 94/752.]

1 20 George II c 52.

334 2 Jan. 1747. Fletching. Jurors of Fletching and 4 neighbouring townships: William Hardwick, Hugh Dowglas, Richard Holman, James Skinner, Henry Cooper, John Lashmer, Francis Heasman, Charles Clarke, John Botting sen., Richard Tester, John Botting jun., William Creasy, Thomas Vinall, Thomas Brown. Between 6 and 7 p.m. on 27 Dec. 1746, when John Towner and Caleb Fuller, both of Fletching, labourers, were fighting together in the king's highway in Fletching, Fuller killed Towner with a staff about 5 feet long and worth 1d which he held in both hands, giving him a wound on the left side of the head 1 inch long and half a quarter of an inch deep of which he languished at Fletching until 30 Dec. and then died. [ASSI 94/746]

[Delivered with **333**. At the assizes a bill of indictment was preferred which charged Fuller with murdering Towner at Fletching on 27 Dec. with a staff worth 1d which he held in both hands, giving him a wound on the left side of the head 1 inch long and half a quarter of an inch wide (details of death as in inquest). The grand jury, to which Francis Heasman, Elizabeth and Susannah Harman and John Franks gave evidence, rejected the bill. Fuller pleaded not guilty to the inquest and was acquitted; he had not fled and so was discharged. ASSI 94/746.]

335 2 Dec. 1748. Cliffe. Jurors of Cliffe and 3 neighbouring townships: Andrew Tasker, George Verrall, Thomas Tasker, Herbert Stiles, John Verrall, Daniel Kenward,

Edward Hood, John Heaver jun., Benjamin Mott, Thomas Harben, Simon Grover, Samuel Botting, John Gasson, William Gasson, Henry Godman, John Mercer. Between 11 p.m. and midnight on 28 Nov. Hugh MacCollum late of Cliffe, labourer, one of HM's foot-soldiers, murdered Richard Hull late of Cliffe, labourer, at Cliffe with a handgun or musket, worth 10s, charged with gunpowder and a lead bullet which he held in both hands and discharged at Hull, striking him on the right arm just below the point of the shoulder and in the body, giving him a wound on the right arm 1 inch wide and 6 inches deep of which he languished at Cliffe until 30 Nov. and then died. MacCollum had no goods or chattels, lands or tenements in Sussex at the time of the murder to the jurors' knowledge. [ASSI 94/772]

[Delivered to East Grinstead assizes on 13 Mar. 1749 when the grand jury, to which George Bunting, Richard Valler, Elizabeth Boor and Thomas Davey gave evidence, presented an indictment similar to the inquest verdict except for the omission of the point of the shoulder, the striking in the body and the last sentence. MacCollum, who had been committed to gaol on 29 Nov. by John Bridger, JP, charged with shooting a man at the King and Queen in Cliffe and wounding him so that his life was in great danger and later charged with a warrant of detainer of the coroner on his inquest for murdering Hull, pleaded not guilty but was convicted and sentenced to be hanged; he had no chattels. ASSI 94/772.]

336 3 Dec. 1748. Slaugham. Jurors of Slaugham and 3 neighbouring townships: Francis Taylor, William Hards, John Johnson, Thomas Isted, William Page, John Gatford, William Gibson, John Feast, Richard Feast, James Brooker, Jeremy Pryer, John Nigh, William Gatford, John Rice. Between 8 and 9 p.m. on 30 Nov., when John Russon late of Slaugham, labourer, was at Slaugham, lodging at a faggot-stack of John Gatford of Slaugham, yeoman, there came James Miers late of Oxted in Surrey, labourer, James Lewis late of Slaugham, labourer, and another man unknown called John, each having a handgun worth 5s in his hands charged, as the 3 apprehended, with gunpowder only, without any shot or bullet, with the intent to discharge the guns at Russon's place of residence at the faggot-stack which he then inhabited against the will of Gatford, the owner, to frighten Russon from it, but not intending to do him any bodily harm. The 3 then discharged their guns at Russon, whereby one or more of them struck him on the right side of the neck just below the ear with a shot or bullet which by accident and unknown to them happened to be in one of the guns, giving him a wound ¼ inch long and 5 inches deep of which he immediately died. So the 3 feloniously killed him. [ASSI 94/772]

[Delivered with **335**. At the assizes a bill of indictment was preferred which charged Miers, Lewis and John Fraiser, all late of Slaugham, labourers, with murdering Russon at Slaugham on 30 Nov., each having in his hands a gun worth 5s charged with gunpowder and lead bullets, which they all shot at him, giving him a wound on the right side of the neck a little below the left ear (dimensions of wound and death as in inquest). The grand jury, to which John Linkfield, Henry Hall and John Graveley gave evidence, rejected the bill. Miers, Lewis and Fraiser had been committed to gaol on 1 Dec. by John Wicker, JP, charged on an information of John Gatford of Slaugham, warrener, that Russon, broom-maker, was killed at Slaugham on 30 Nov. and there was a strong reason to believe that one or more of them had killed him. Miers and Lewis pleaded not guilty to the inquest and were acquitted, the trial jury finding that Russon had come to his death by chance medley; they had not fled and so were discharged. Fraiser was discharged by proclamation. ASSI 94/772.]

337 9 Nov. 1750. The White Hart, Cuckfield, John Steel's house. Jurors of 4 townships neighbouring Cuckfield: John Hamlyn, gent., Richard Gunter, Edward Hubbard, Walter

identical to the inquest verdict except that the charge was murder and the last sentence was omitted. Greentree, who had been committed to gaol by the coroner on 1 Apr., pleaded not guilty and was acquitted; he had not fled and so was discharged. ASSI 94/862. Cf. **5**.]

342 30 May 1759. Brighton. Jurors of Brighton and 4 neighbouring townships: Richard Harman, Matthew Bourne, Francis Carter, John Palmer, Richard Hemsley, Edward Cheesman, John Noble, James Ridge, John Lashmer, John Double, Thomas Kent, Samuel Dean, William Chapman, Hugh Sanders, John Brooker, William Lucas. Between 5 and 6 p.m. on 24 May John May late of Brighton, labourer, feloniously killed Robert Howell at Brighton, violently kicking him with his right foot and giving him a bruise on the belly and private parts of which he languished at Brighton until 27 May and then died. What goods or chattels, lands or tenements May had at the time of the manslaughter or ever after the jurors did not know. [ASSI 94/913]

[Delivered to Lewes assizes on 4 Aug. when the grand jury, to which [Thomas Hurst *struck through*] Ann Howell gave evidence, presented an indictment identical to the inquest verdict except that the charge was murder and the hours and the last sentence were omitted. May, who had been committed to gaol by the coroner on the day of the inquest, pleaded not guilty and was acquitted; he had not fled and so was discharged. ASSI 94/913. Cf. **11**.]

343 1 Aug. 1759. East Grinstead. Jurors of Hartfield and 4 neighbouring townships: Charles Woodman, James Hall, Henry Isted, John Wood, Nathaniel Pryer, Richard Roods, John Kember of Stone, Richard Fairhall, Edward Alteyning,[1] Edward Banister, Nicholas Harman, George Langridge, Benjamin Heaver, Abraham Huggett. At 1 a.m. on 29 July William Mayor late of Hartfield, warrener, murdered Richard Finch at Hartfield with a pistol worth 5s charged with gunpowder and lead shot which he held in both hands, giving him a wound in the upper and posterior part of the left thigh 5 inches wide and 10 inches deep of which he languished at Hartfield and East Grinstead until the next day and then died at East Grinstead. [ASSI 94/913]

[Delivered with **342**. At the assizes the grand jury, to which John Finch, farmer, Richard Turley, John Finch, blacksmith, John Strickland, Thomas May, James Lucas and Thomas Weaire gave evidence, presented an indictment identical to the inquest verdict except that Mayor was styled labourer and the murder was said to have been committed in the night, not at 1 a.m. Mayor pleaded not guilty and was acquitted; he had not fled and so was discharged. ASSI 94/913. Cf. **11**.]

1 ?Recte *Steyning*.

344 4 June 1763. Eastbourne. Jurors of Eastbourne and 4 neighbouring townships: Benjamin Dutton, John Grace, Richard Hart, William Breeden, Samuel Beckett, James Tutt, William Streeton, Henry How, John Akehurst, Stephen Jones, Joseph Bellimore, Thomas Hart, Friend Dyer, Thomas Breach. On 30 May Benjamin Hooper late of Eastbourne, labourer, killed Mary Smith late of Eastbourne, spinster, at Eastbourne with a wooden ninepin bowl worth 6d which he held in his right hand, throwing it at her and giving her 2 mortal wounds on the left side of the head, one 1 inch long and ¼ inch deep and the other ¾ inch long and ¼ inch deep, of which she languished at Eastbourne until 2 June and then died. Hooper had no goods or chattels, lands or tenements in Sussex at the time of the killing or ever after to the jurors' knowledge.
Marginal note: Homicide per infortunium. [ASSI 94/975]

[Delivered to Lewes assizes on 23 July when the grand jury, to which George Payn, Charles Ballard, George Chapman and John Latter gave evidence, presented an indictment identical to the inquest verdict except that the charge was murder and the last sentence was omitted. Hooper pleaded not guilty and was acquitted; he had not fled and so was discharged. ASSI 94/975. Cf. **17**.]

345 11 July 1763. Cliffe. Jurors of Cliffe and 4 neighbouring townships: Andrew Tasker, Edward Stanford, George Verrall, William Rathbone, Herbert Stiles, Thomas Hall, Joseph Attree, Thomas Harben, Thomas Ansell, Brian Berks, James Lambert, Edward Green, William English, Hugh Talbert, George Beard, Edward Tooth, William Hearnden, Richard Marshall, William Hill, William Eager, Thomas Michell. On 9 July Sarah Young late of Cliffe, single woman, gave birth at Cliffe to a live male child which by the laws of the kingdom was a bastard and on the same day murdered him there with a knife of iron and steel worth 1d which she held in her right hand, giving him a wound on the throat 2 inches wide and ½ inch deep of which he immediately died. Young had no goods or chattels, lands or tenements in Sussex at that time or ever after to the jurors' knowledge. [ASSI 94/975]

[Delivered with **344**. At the assizes the grand jury, to which [Elizabeth Rickman *struck through*], Thomas Davey, surgeon, William Rathbone, Grace Wilson and Elizabeth Verrall gave evidence, presented an indictment identical to the inquest verdict except that the last sentence was omitted. Young could not be tried because of illness and it was ordered that she remain in the Lewes House of Correction until fit to be removed and then be conveyed to the county gaol until the next assizes. She was committed to the gaol on 8 Aug. by Luke Spence, JP, having confessed to the murder. At the East Grinstead assizes of 26 Mar. 1764 she pleaded not guilty but was convicted and sentenced to be hanged and then dissected and anatomized. ASSI 94/975; ASSI 94/982. Cf. **17**.]

Inquests of Francis Wheeler

346 16 Aug. 1764. Hurstpierpoint. Jurors: William Marchant, Thomas Butcher, Philip Card, John Parsons, Thomas Hamper, William King, Michael Longmer, Richard Wood, John Walker, Abraham Muzzall, Joseph Greenaway, Henry Fowler, Stephen Cave. On 15 Aug. Hannah Davey of Hurstpierpoint, widow, traitorously murdered her husband John Davey late of Hurstpierpoint, farmer, at Hurstpierpoint with a piece of wood like a cricket bat of no value which she held in both hands, giving him a wound on the head 1½ inches long and ½ inch deep of which he immediately died. Hannah had no goods or chattels, lands or tenements in Sussex or elsewhere at that time or ever after to the jurors' knowledge. [ASSI 94/988]

[Delivered to Horsham assizes on 20 Aug. when the grand jury, to which Henry Davey and Thomas Mitchell gave evidence, presented an indictment similar to the inquest verdict except that John Davey was styled yeoman, the weapon was a piece of wood called a cricket bat, the wound was on the top of the head and the last sentence was omitted. Hannah Davey, who had been committed to gaol by the coroner on the day of the inquest, pleaded not guilty and was acquitted; she had not fled, but because it appeared by evidence that she was a lunatic it was ordered that she remain in gaol to be taken care of and removed by order of 2 JPs to her last legal settlement, there to be kept as a lunatic. ASSI 94/988. Cf. **19**.]

347 24 Apr. 1766. Playden. Jurors of 4 townships neighbouring Playden: John Turk, Henry French, Stephen Williamshurst, John Thompson, John Pain, John Carman, John Millam, Benjamin Apps, William Hull, Richard Woodhams, George Quested, James Edmonds, Thomas Fisher, John Watson, Jeremiah Smith. On 21 Apr. Ann Kersby late of

Playden, single woman, alone and secretly gave birth at Playden to a live female child which by the laws of the kingdom was a bastard and immediately murdered her, strangling her with both hands whereby she immediately died. Kersby had no goods or chattels, lands or tenements in Sussex or elsewhere at that time or ever after to the jurors' knowledge. [ASSI 94/1015]

[Delivered to Horsham assizes on 28 July when the grand jury, to which Daniel Cook, Thomas and Elizabeth Pelham and Mary Batchelor gave evidence, presented an indictment identical to the inquest verdict but omitting the last sentence. Kersby, who had been committed to gaol by the coroner on the day of the inquest, pleaded not guilty and was acquitted; she had not fled and so was discharged. ASSI 94/1015. Cf. **22**.]

348 13 May 1769. Newhaven. Jurors of Newhaven and 4 neighbouring townships: Thomas Geere, Charles Tasker, John Arlewood, William Knight, Henry Clark, James Carter, John Terry, William Holloway, William Stevens, John Adams, John Haine, William Arlwood, Thomas Hollands, Thomas Holloway. Between midnight and 1 a.m. on 13 May, when HMS *Speedwell* was stationed off the coast of Sussex to look out for and capture smugglers and Nathaniel Storey, her master, was with William Ternmen, Thomas Thomas, Joseph Hardy, John Tomlinson, John Williams and Thomas Henmore, sailors or common men of the ship, in the *Speedwell*'s gig or long-boat at sea off Portobello Gap in Telscombe looking out for smugglers, a boat called the *Welcome* of Hastings [?appeared][1] with prohibited goods on board, viz 92 half-ankers of brandy and 50 lb of tea, and with John Phillips, John Smith, William Batchelor, Richard Duke and another John Phillips, all of Hastings, mariners. Storey, having command of the gig, ordered his men to row after the *Welcome*, but, being unable to catch up with her, he took a musket belonging to the king which was charged with powder and a lead bullet and fired it by way of a signal for the *Welcome* to strike or bring to according to the usage of HM's Custom House boats, and the bullet gave the first-named John Phillips a wound on the right side of the head 2 inches wide and 3 inches deep of which he immediately died. Thus Storey killed him by chance and misfortune and against his will. What goods or chattels Storey had at that time the jurors did not know. [ASSI 94/1054]

[Delivered to Lewes assizes on 24 July when Storey was discharged by proclamation. ASSI 94/1054. Cf. **27**.]

1 A verb is omitted.

349 7 Mar. 1774. Fletching. Jurors of Fletching and 4 neighbouring townships: William Wood, James Ware, William Thorp, John Wheeler, Thomas Wood, John Gander, Vince Carr, Thomas Colchin, Anthony Wheeler, John Langridge, Joseph Goord, Francis Devall, William Devall, John Awcock. On 4 Mar. Thomas Yates, a common man in General Carpenter's Regiment of Dragoons[1] who was quartered at Uckfield, murdered John Crowhurst late of Keymer at Fletching with a pistol worth 4s charged with gunpowder and a lead bullet which he held in his right hand, giving him a wound in the belly and bowels ½ inch wide and 2 inches deep of which he languished until the next day and then died. Yates did not flee because of the murder. He had no goods or chattels, lands or tenements in Sussex or elsewhere at the time of the murder to the jurors' knowledge. [ASSI 94/1113]

[Delivered to East Grinstead assizes on 21 Mar. when a bill of indictment was preferred similar to the inquest verdict except that Yates was described as late of Fletching, labourer, the wound was in the belly on the left side of the navel, Crowhurst languished and died at Fletching and the last

2 sentences were omitted. The grand jury, to which Thomas Young, Thomas Histed, Thomas Budd and Susannah Pollington gave evidence, rejected the bill. Yates, who had been committed to gaol on 9 Mar. by the coroner, pleaded not guilty to the inquest and was acquitted; he had not fled and so was discharged. ASSI 94/1113. Cf. **35**.]

1 General Benjamin Carpenter was colonel of the 4th Dragoons: N B Leslie, *The Succession of Colonels of the British Army from 1660 to the Present Day* (Society for Army Historical Research, Special Publication XI, 1974), 19; Swinson, 23.

350 31 Jan. 1778. Worth. Jurors of Worth and 4 neighbouring townships: William Tidy, William Vallance, John Savage, John Tidy, Edward Collins, John Bashford, William Potter, Mark Brooker, Richard Taylor, Elias Eason, John Illman, George King, James Newman. On 27 Jan. John Saunders died a natural death at Worth and not from any violence. [ASSI 94/1164]

[Delivered to East Grinstead assizes on 16 Mar. Cf. **40**.]

351 6 Apr. 1781. Wilmington. Jurors of Wilmington and 4 neighbouring townships: Stephen Wood, John Bodle, Edward Bodle, Thomas Crowhurst, Thomas Stephens, Thomas Parris, William Howell, Thomas Hilton, John Overing, John Bonniface, Richard Hilton, Henry Walker, William Brook, Henry Harman. On 31 Mar. Robert Hitchcock late of Warbleton murdered Thomas Holloway at Arlington with a hanger of iron and steel worth 1s which he held in one hand, giving him a wound on the left side of the head near the temple 4 inches long through the skull to the brain of which he languished at Arlington and Wilmington until 4 Apr. and then died at Wilmington. Hitchcock had no goods or chattels, lands or tenements in Sussex or elsewhere at the time of the murder or ever after to the jurors' knowledge. [ASSI 94/1215]

[Delivered to Lewes assizes on 10 Aug. when the grand jury, to which Richard Huggett, Edward Bryant, William Miles, James Hoope and David Bayford gave evidence, presented an indictment similar to the inquest verdict except that Hitchcock was called late of Arlington, labourer, the hanger was held in his right hand, the wound was 4 inches long and 1 inch deep, and 'near the temple' and the last sentence were omitted. At the East Grinstead assizes of 18 Mar. 1782 Hitchcock, who had been committed to gaol by the coroner on 5 Sept., pleaded not guilty but was convicted and sentenced to be hanged on 21 Mar. and then dissected and anatomized. ASSI 94/1215; ASSI 94/1223. Cf. **48**, **50**.]

352 28 Sept. 1782. Slaugham. Jurors of Slaugham and 4 neighbouring townships: Richard Edwards, Edward Titchenor, Henry Booker, Matthew Hards, William Jupp, Henry Bishop, James Wells, James Harland, Richard Ewen, James Hobden, John Knight, William Bechely, John Fist. On 25 Sept. Thomas Rogers late of Slaugham, a private in HM's 10th Regiment of Dragoons, murdered Jonathan Godfrey at Slaugham with a pistol worth 1s charged with gunpowder and a lead bullet which he held in his right hand, giving him a wound with the bullet which penetrated his breast and went through his body of which he languished at Slaugham until the next day and then died. At the time of the murder John Fisher late of Slaugham, excise officer, was present aiding and abetting Rogers. Rogers and Fisher had no goods or chattels, lands or tenements in Sussex or elsewhere at that time or ever after to the jurors' knowledge. [ASSI 94/1235]

[Delivered to East Grinstead assizes on 17 Mar. 1783 when a bill of indictment was preferred similar to the inquest verdict except that both Rogers and Fisher were expressly charged with the murder, the pistol was worth 10s, the wound was 5 inches deep and ½ inch wide, Godfrey died immediately and the last sentence was omitted. The grand jury, to which James Weaver, Jenny

Johnson, William Rich and Charles Jones gave evidence, affirmed the charge against Rogers but rejected that against Fisher. Rogers pleaded not guilty but was convicted and sentenced to be hanged on 20 Mar. and then dissected and anatomized; he had no chattels. He was reprieved before execution and recommended for a free pardon. Fisher pleaded not guilty to the inquest and was acquitted; he had not fled and so was discharged. ASSI 94/1235. Cf. **54**, **56**; *SCM*, XI, 370.]

353 23 May 1783. Rottingdean. Jurors of Rottingdean and 4 neighbouring townships: James Ingram, John Farncombe, William Knight, Samuel Ridge, Henry Harwood, Thomas Rowland, James Vallance, Thomas Newington, William Richardson, Henry Packham, John Balcomb, William Barnett, John Butler. At 2 a.m. on 23 May a person unknown murdered Thomas Noakes at Rottingdean with a pistol charged with gunpowder and a lead bullet which he held in his right hand, giving him a wound in the left thigh which penetrated the groin of which he languished until 3 p.m. on the same day and then died. [ASSI 94/1241]

[Delivered to Lewes assizes on 15 Aug. Cf. **57**, **58**.]

Inquests of William Wheeler

354 18 June 1787. Preston. Jurors of Preston and 4 neighbouring townships: John Smith, Philip Vallance, John Vallance, Jonas Corner, Bartholomew Smithers, John Moor, Henry Bound, James Hunter, John Leffen, Thomas Ward, Richard Moorey, John Barnett. On 7 June Philip Jenden late of Horsham, a supernumerary in the excise, murdered Henry Bonner at Aldrington with a drawn sword of iron and steel worth 5s which he held in his right hand, giving him a wound on the back of the head 5 inches long and ½ inch deep of which he languished at Aldrington, Hove and Preston until 16 June and then died. Jenden had no goods or chattels, lands or tenements in Sussex or elsewhere at the time of the murder or ever after to the jurors' knowledge. [ASSI 94/1290]

[Delivered to Lewes assizes on 4 Aug. when the grand jury, to which William Greenaway, Philip Sawyers, John Bonny, Henry Strivens, Ann Bonner, Richard Morley, John Comber, Richard Moorey, John Newington, Jeremiah Bonner and Richard Tillstone gave evidence, presented an indictment similar to the inquest verdict except that Jenden was called late of Aldrington, labourer, the weapon was called a hanger, Hove was not mentioned, the death was at Preston and the last sentence was omitted. Jenden, who had been committed to gaol by the coroner on 19 June but released on bail by King's Bench, pleaded not guilty but was convicted and sentenced to be hanged on 9 Aug. and then dissected and anatomized; he had no chattels. The sentence was respited. ASSI 94/1290. Cf. **73**, **74**; *SCM*, XVIII, 22, 54–55.]

355 8 Dec. 1787. West Firle. Jurors of West Firle and 4 neighbouring townships: Richard Ellman, William Marten, William Fennall, George Geere, John Ansell, John Collingham, James Burt, Jethro Farrant, Samuel Swift, Richard Kennard, William Tompsett, John Vinall. On 6 Dec. George Stephens of West Firle, labourer, feloniously killed his wife Mary at West Firle, striking her on the right side with both hands and giving her several bruises of which she immediately died. [ASSI 94/1301]

[Delivered to East Grinstead assizes on 24 Mar. 1788 when the grand jury, to which Thomas Davy, Mary Geer, Ann Fennill, Elizabeth Baker, Mary Turner and Edward Barber gave evidence, presented an indictment similar to the inquest verdict except that the charge was murder and the bruises were on the right side and other parts of the body. George Stephens, who had been committed to gaol by the coroner on 9 Dec., pleaded not guilty and was acquitted; he had not fled and so was discharged. ASSI 94/1301. Cf. **75**, **76**.]

356 25 Feb. 1788. Bramber. Jurors of Bramber and 4 neighbouring townships: Edward Young, Richard Hollands, Thomas Howell, William Campion, Henry Newington, Edward Hall, Richard Jenner, John Marchant, Thomas Soane, James Michaux, John Kidd, Thomas Carter. On 18 Feb. Elizabeth Davy late of Bramber, single woman, alone and secretly gave birth at Bramber to a live female child which by the laws and customs of the kingdom was a bastard and on the same day murdered her there with scissors of iron and steel worth 6d which she held in her right hand, cutting her throat or gullet and giving her a wound 3 inches long and 1 inch deep of which she immediately died. Davy had no goods or chattels, lands or tenements in Sussex or elsewhere at that time or ever after to the jurors' knowledge. [ASSI 94/1301]

[Delivered with **355**. At the assizes a bill of indictment was preferred identical to the inquest verdict except that the last sentence was omitted. The grand jury, to which [William Davy alias Tester *struck through*], John Ingram and John Penfold gave evidence, rejected the bill, the inquest was quashed and Davy, who had been committed to gaol by the coroner on the day of the inquest, was discharged by proclamation. ASSI 94/1301. Cf. **110**.]

357 7 Aug. 1788. Brighton. Jurors of Brighton and 4 neighbouring townships: Richard Gorringe, Thomas Best, Charles Lind, John Stone, Thomas Whales, James Saunders, Richard Cole, John Smart, James Leach, Barak Wingham, Richard Pain, William Tuppen. On 6 Aug. Thomas Tine late of Brighton, labourer, feloniously killed Richard Earle late of Woodstock Street in St Marylebone, Middlesex, cordwainer, who was standing on a wooden stage erected at Brighton, throwing him to the floor of the stage with both hands and giving him a bruise on the back of the head of which he immediately died. Tine fled after and on account of the manslaughter. He had no goods or chattels, lands or tenements in Sussex or elsewhere at that time or ever after to the jurors' knowledge. [ASSI 94/1313]

[Delivered to East Grinstead assizes on 23 Mar. 1789 when a bill of indictment was preferred similar to the inquest verdict except that the charge was murder and the last 2 sentences were omitted. The grand jury, to which Banastre Tarleton, esq., John Butcher and John Cristall, surgeon, gave evidence, rejected the bill. Tine pleaded not guilty to the inquest but was convicted; he had no goods and was fined 1s and to remain in gaol until he paid. He was later discharged. ASSI 94/1313. Cf. **78**, **80**.]

358 17 June 1791. Wivelsfield. Jurors of Wivelsfield and 4 neighbouring townships: William Russell, John Langham, William Bean, Thomas Knight, John Leaney, Thomas Ockenden, Richard Cook, William Knight, John Whiting, Allen Atheroll, John Copperd, John Broad. On 15 June Stephen Thompson late of Wivelsfield, labourer, feloniously killed Henry Farncomb at Wivelsfield, striking him with both hands and giving him a bruise on the right side of which he immediately died. Thompson fled after and on account of the manslaughter. He had no goods or chattels, lands or tenements at that time or ever after to the jurors' knowledge. [ASSI 94/1351]

[Delivered to Lewes assizes on 13 Aug. when the grand jury, to which William Hawkes and William Bean gave evidence, presented an indictment similar to the inquest verdict except that the bruise was caused by Thompson striking Farncomb several times on the head, stomach, back, belly and sides and by throwing him to the ground, the charge was murder and the last 2 sentences were omitted. Thompson pleaded not guilty and was acquitted; he had not fled and was discharged by proclamation. ASSI 94/1351. Cf. **89**, **90**; *SCM*, XVII, 143.]

359 8 Nov. 1791. Buxted. Jurors of Buxted and 4 neighbouring townships: Thomas Coe, Henry Weller, George Hollands, John Hobbs, Richard Young, John Field, Edward Willett, Joseph Richard Moore, John Arnold, Thomas Weare, John Piper, John Skinner. On 7 Nov. some person unknown murdered a new-born female child at Buxted, striking her on the head with both hands and giving her a bruise on the right side of the head of which she immediately died. [ASSI 94/1364]

[Delivered to East Grinstead assizes on 19 Mar. 1792. Cf. **91**, **92**.]

360 30 Dec. 1793. New Shoreham. Jurors of New Shoreham and 4 neighbouring townships: John Boyce, John Butler sen., Caleb Burrows, John Roberts Hawkins, John Butler jun., Joseph Deadman, Richard Osboldeston, Samuel Egden, George Lewis Wilson, Thomas Pelham, Simon Clement, Henry West. On 23 Dec., when HMS *Swallow* was stationed on the Sussex coast to look out for and take uncustomed goods liable to pay duties which had never been paid or secured, Samuel Clark, deputed mariner, and Matthew Cox, John Page, William and Richard Lashmer, Nicholas Bartlett, Richard Hollands, Joseph Humphreys, William Kimbers, William Stock and Richard Blair, mariners, all belonging to the *Swallow*, went in the *Swallow*'s galley about ½ league from Shoreham Harbour in New Shoreham to look out for such goods. The galley came near to a cutter, name unknown, and some persons unknown on board the cutter murdered Blair with a gun charged with gunpowder and an iron bullet, giving him a wound in the left side in and through his body of which he languished upon the sea and at New Shoreham until 29 Dec. and then died at New Shoreham. [ASSI 94/1391]

[Delivered to East Grinstead assizes on 24 Mar. 1794. Cf. **99**, **100**.]

361 17 Oct. 1795. Southwick. Jurors of Southwick and 4 neighbouring townships: Caleb Burrows, John Hooper, Thomas Amos, John Boyce jun., Benjamin Reynolds Hay, John Tree Amos, Rice Jones, William Westover, George Kent, Daniel Young, James Turner, John Smith jun. On 15 Oct. some person unknown murdered John Bridger Norton, esq., at Southwick, striking him with both hands on the back of the head and giving him a bruise of which he languished at Southwick until the next day and then died. After committing the murder he fled on that account. [ASSI 94/1415]

[Delivered to East Grinstead assizes on 14 Mar. 1796 when George Bradley and John Young, who had been committed to gaol on the day of the inquest by John Norton, JP, charged on a strong suspicion of feloniously stealing a cotton handkerchief, a knife and several keys from the person of John Bridger Norton in Southwick and giving him wounds of which he died within a few hours, were remanded in gaol charged with murder because a material witness for the prosecution was unable to attend to give evidence against them — Young until the next assizes and Bradley also unless, with the consent of Mr Knowlys, counsel for the prosecution, he should in the meantime enter into a recognizance before a JP in £50, with sureties in £25 each, for his appearance at the next assizes to answer the charge, giving Mr Marshall of Steyning, solicitor for the prosecution,[1] 48 hours' notice of the names and addresses of the proposed sureties before entering the recognizance. At the Horsham assizes of 22 July 1796 a bill of indictment was preferred which charged Young and Bradley, both of Southwick, labourers, with assaulting John Bridger Norton on the king's highway at Southwick on 15 Oct. 1795 and feloniously stealing from his person and carrying away a cotton handkerchief worth 2s, 4 iron keys worth 2s, a clasp-knife worth 5s, a comb worth 6d, a steel corkscrew worth 1s and 4 copper halfpennies worth 2d belonging to Norton. The grand jury, to which Susannah Norton, Elizabeth Hall, Abraham Trahar, Richard Patrick, John Rogers, John Blatcher, Thomas Edwards, Richard Kent, John Comber and Benjamin Reynolds Hay gave evidence, affirmed the charge against Young but rejected that against Bradley. Young pleaded not guilty to highway robbery and was convicted of stealing but not violently from the person; he had no goods and was sentenced to transportation for 7 years. ASSI 94/1415; ASSI 94/1416. Cf. **108**.]

1 Charles Marshall, attorney at law and master in Chancery: *The Universal British Directory 1793–1798* (facsimile text edn, King's Lynn, 1993), IV, 450.

362 19 May 1796. Brighton. Jurors of Brighton and 4 neighbouring townships: Edward Thunder, Thomas Westgate, Thomas Tugwell, John Hughes, Edward Streeter, Richard Smith, Thomas Pocock, Thomas Harmer, George Nye, Thomas Bayley, Richard Chapman, Adam Maiben. On 25 Apr. some person unknown murdered Elizabeth Hedgeley at Brighton, violently throwing her with both hands into a well in a yard of stables at the upper end of North Street commonly called the New Inn stables whereby she was drowned, dying immediately. After committing the murder he fled on that account. [ASSI 94/1416]

[Delivered to Horsham assizes on 22 July. Cf. **109**, **110**; *SCM*, XXVI, 237.]

363 7 Nov. 1796. Falmer. Jurors of Falmer and 4 neighbouring townships: James Ingram, Richard Chrismas sen., Richard Chrismas jun., Edward Dowlen, John Sutton, Henry Hubbard, Henry Boys, Edward Freeman, John Botting, John Hunter, Thomas Brown, John Randalls. On 6 Nov. Joseph Sayers late of Falmer, labourer, feloniously killed Richard Criss at Falmer, striking him and throwing him to the ground with both hands and thereby giving him several bruises in and on the head, breast, stomach, belly and sides of which he immediately died. [ASSI 94/1432]

[Delivered to East Grinstead assizes on 13 Mar. 1797 when a bill of indictment was preferred similar to the inquest verdict except that the charge was murder and the injury to the sides was omitted. The grand jury, to which John Walls and John Walker gave evidence, rejected the bill. Sayers, who had been committed to gaol by the coroner on 17 Nov., pleaded not guilty to the inquest but was convicted; he had no goods and was fined 1s and to remain in gaol until he paid. ASSI 94/1432. Cf. **111**, **112**.]

364 19 Nov. 1796. Patcham. Jurors of Patcham and 4 neighbouring townships: William Drew, Thomas Scrase, Richard Berry, William Stedman, Edward Brunsdon, John Catt, Edward Sayers, Charles Cuttridge, John Fennell, Samuel Baker, John Bishop, Charles Murrell. On 17 Nov. William Leach late of Patcham, mariner, feloniously killed Daniel Scales at Patcham with a pistol worth 5s charged with gunpowder and a leaden bullet which he held in his right hand, giving him a wound in and through the head of which he immediately died. [ASSI 94/1432]

[Delivered with **363**. At the assizes a bill of indictment was preferred similar to the inquest verdict except that Leach was styled labourer, the wound was in the left eye and through the head, 1 inch wide and 8 inches deep, and the charge was murder. The grand jury, to which Thomas Bartley and William Harding gave evidence, reduced the charge to manslaughter. Leach, who had been committed to gaol by the coroner on 23 Nov., pleaded not guilty but was convicted; he had no goods and was fined 1s and to remain in gaol until he paid. ASSI 94/1432. Cf. **111**, **112**; *SCM*, XXI, 226.]

365 22 Sept. 1798. Newhaven. Jurors of Newhaven and 4 neighbouring townships: Philip Collins, Thomas Howell, John Greathead, Henry Arlword, Albert Goodright, Thomas Lee, William Waters, Benjamin Harris, John Inskip, William Diggins, William Brooker, Matthew Bulman. On 17 Sept. John Hanning late of Newhaven, labourer, murdered William Pope at Newhaven with a knife of iron and steel worth 6d which he held in his right hand, giving him a wound in the left side of the belly 3 inches wide and 3 inches deep of which he languished at Newhaven until 21 Sept. and then died. Hanning had no goods or chattels, lands or tenements at the time of the murder or ever after to the jurors' knowledge. [ASSI 94/1478]

[Delivered to East Grinstead assizes on 25 Mar. 1799. Cf. **118**, **120**.]

366 8 Aug. 1801. Preston. Jurors of Preston and 4 neighbouring townships: William Bradford, Daniel Stableford, Mark Fricker, Richard Spearing, James White, John Dumbrell, John Wood, Nicholas Johnson, Richard Venner, Charles Robinson, John Last, William Wood. On 6 Aug. John Conolly late of Preston, labourer, feloniously killed James Kelly who was at the top of some stone stairs in a building in Preston called the Officers' Barracks, kicking him with his right foot from the stairs onto the stone pavement at the bottom of them and thereby giving him a bruise on the back of the head of which he languished at Preston until the next day and then died. [ASSI 94/1538]

[Delivered to Horsham assizes on 27 Mar. 1802 when the grand jury, to which Thomas Grout, James Campbell, John Burgess and Matthew Parker, surgeon, gave evidence, presented an indictment similar to the inquest verdict except that it did not state with which foot Conolly kicked Kelly or name the building, but said that Kelly received a fracture of the skull and the charge was murder. Conolly, who had been committed to gaol by the coroner on the day of the inquest but had been allowed bail, pleaded not guilty and was acquitted of murder but convicted of manslaughter; he was fined 1s and to remain in gaol until he paid. ASSI 94/1538. Cf. **130**, **132**.]

367 9 Dec. 1802. Clayton. Jurors of Clayton and 4 neighbouring townships: John Bull jun., Thomas Dominic Whiteman, Stephen Croskey, Thomas English, William Jenner, William Ockenden, George Bishop, James Gander, John Burten, Nathan Holford, John Broomfield, John Randall. On 30 Nov. Robert Bignall jun. late of Clayton, labourer, murdered John Webber jun. at Clayton with a pistol worth 5s charged with gunpowder and a lead bullet which he held in his right hand, giving him a wound in the left side of the belly near the navel and through the body of which he languished at Clayton until 8 Dec. and then died. Bignall had no goods or chattels, lands or tenements in Sussex or elsewhere at the time of the murder or ever after to the jurors' knowledge. [ASSI 94/1551]

[Delivered to Horsham assizes on 28 Mar. 1803 when the grand jury, to which Nathan Holford, Richard Oram, Richard Pratt, John White, Anthony Hole, William Davey, John Bignall, Mary Davey, Edward and Mary Warner, Richard Weekes, Thomas Pelham, John Perrin and Thomas Stephens gave evidence, presented an indictment similar to the inquest verdict except that the pistol was valued at 1s and the last sentence was omitted. Bignall, who had been committed to gaol by the coroner on the day of the inquest, pleaded not guilty and was acquitted; he had not fled and so was discharged. ASSI 94/1551. Cf. **135**, **136**; *SCM*, XIV, 27–31.]

368 5 July 1803. Westmeston. Jurors of Westmeston and 4 neighbouring townships: Anthony William Hodson, William Faulconer, George Mott, Michael Tulley, Francis Homewood, Richard Cox jun., John Stapley, John Kent, James Hemsley, Thomas Herriott, John Dench, James Redman. On 2 July Richard Leney late of Westmeston, labourer, feloniously killed William Brooker at Westmeston, striking him with both hands on the stomach, breast and belly and giving him several bruises of which he languished at Westmeston until the next day and then died. [ASSI 94/1552]

[Delivered to Lewes assizes on 5 Aug. when the grand jury, to which Thomas Brooker, George Miles and Hampton Weeks, surgeon, gave evidence, presented an indictment similar to the inquest verdict except that the blows and bruises were on the breast, stomach, belly, sides, back and shoulders, death was immediate and the charge was murder. Leney pleaded not guilty but was convicted of manslaughter and fined 1s and to remain in gaol for a year and until he paid the fine; he had no goods. He was in gaol at the assizes of 19 Mar. and 28 July 1804. ASSI 94/1552; ASSI 94/1564; ASSI 94/1565. Cf. **137**, **138**.]

369 23 Mar. 1804. Ringmer. Jurors of Ringmer and 4 neighbouring townships: James Smart, William Hillman, Henry Jones, John Hassell, James Costin, James Packham, Harry Payne, Richard Greenfield, Peter Edwards, Daniel Harris, Stephen Swaysland, Samuel Dabson. On 22 Mar. Mary Hasleden late of Ringmer, single woman, alone and secretly gave birth to a live male child at Ringmer which by the laws of the kingdom was a bastard and immediately murdered him, striking him with both hands and giving him several bruises on the head, stomach, belly, back and sides of which he immediately died. Hasleden had no goods or chattels, lands or tenements in Sussex or elsewhere at that time or ever after to the jurors' knowledge. [ASSI 94/1565]

[Delivered to Lewes assizes on 28 July when the grand jury, to which Sarah, Charles and Mary Stanford, Ann Sexton, midwife, and James Moore, surgeon, gave evidence, presented an indictment which charged Hasleden on 2 counts of giving birth to the male bastard alone and secretly at Ringmer on 2 Mar. and on the same day murdering him there: the first that she threw him with both hands into a large quantity of human excrement and other filth in a necessary, whereby he was suffocated and immediately died; and the second that she threw him with both hands against the sides of a privy, thereby giving him a wound on the left side of the head 2 inches long and 1 inch wide of which he immediately died. Hasleden, aged 17, who had been committed to gaol by the coroner on 19 Apr., pleaded not guilty and was acquitted; she had not fled and so was discharged. ASSI 94/1565. Cf. **140**, **142**.]

370 21 Dec. 1804. Wadhurst. Jurors of Wadhurst and 4 neighbouring townships: Thomas Bull, William Barton, Robert Smith jun., cordwainer, George Siggs, Thomas Wallis, Edward Dadswell, Thomas Cooper, Jesse Stevens, Benjamin Newark, Thomas Brazier, Robert Smith, blacksmith, John David. At 11 a.m. on 17 Dec. Richard Russell late of Lamberhurst, labourer, and Gipsy George of Lamberhurst, labourer, alias Black James murdered John Buss at Lamberhurst: Russell giving him several bruises on the head, stomach, back, thighs, legs, arms and sides with a large stick of no value which he held in his right hand, of which Buss languished at Lamberhurst and Wadhurst until 4 p.m. on the same day and then died at Wadhurst; and George being feloniously present aiding and abetting him. Russell and George had no goods or chattels, lands or tenements in Sussex or elsewhere at the time of the murder or ever after to the jurors' knowledge. [ASSI 94/1577]

[Delivered to Horsham assizes on 25 Mar. 1805 when the grand jury, to which Thomas Swift, John Godden, John Bailey Brooks, Samuel Mitchel and John Pomfret Blackman gave evidence, presented an indictment which charged Russell and George alias James, both late of Wadhurst, labourers, with murdering Buss at Wadhurst on 17 Dec. with a stick worth 1d, giving him several wounds and bruises on the head, shoulders, back, sides, belly, arms and legs of which he immediately died. Neither Russell nor George was in gaol at the time of the assizes. ASSI 94/1577. Cf. **143, 144**.]

371 30 May 1805. Cliffe. Jurors of Cliffe and 4 neighbouring townships: Gabriel Egles, Joseph Simes, Nathaniel Polhill, John Farnes, Christopher Elliott, Richard Goodyer, Joseph Attree, Robert Tugwell, Richard Porter, Thomas Mockford, John Smith, William Mesley. On 29 May Thomas Dykes late of St John sub Castro, Lewes, labourer, feloniously killed John Jordan at St John sub Castro, striking him with both hands on the head, stomach, breast and sides and giving him several bruises of which he immediately died. Dykes had no goods or chattels, lands or tenements in Sussex or elsewhere at that time or ever after to the jurors' knowledge. [ASSI 94/1578]

[Delivered to Lewes assizes on 10 Aug. when the grand jury, to which William Farmer, Thomas Hart, Elizabeth Sale, John Taylor and James Moore, surgeon, gave evidence, presented an indictment similar to the inquest verdict except that Dykes also threw Jordan to the ground, the blows and bruises were to the head, stomach, sides and belly, the charge was murder and the last sentence was omitted. Dykes, who had been committed to gaol by the coroner on the day of the inquest, pleaded not guilty and was acquitted of murder but convicted of manslaughter; he was fined 1s and to remain in gaol until he paid. ASSI 94/1578. Cf. **145, 146**.]

372 16 Oct. 1805. Clayton. Jurors of Clayton and 4 neighbouring townships: Thomas Blackman, Herbert Brooker, Richard Orrom, Thomas Pennifold, Henry Potter, John Corney sen., Thomas Woolvin, John Corney jun., Richard Gander, George Holms, Richard Tulley, Thomas Jeffery. On 15 Oct. Ann Clarke late of Clayton, single woman, alone and secretly gave birth to a live female child at Clayton which by the laws of the kingdom was a bastard and immediately murdered her with a penknife of iron and steel worth 6d which she held in her right hand, giving her a wound in the throat and gullet 3 inches long and 1 inch deep of which she immediately died. Clarke had no goods or chattels, lands or tenements in Sussex or elsewhere at that time or ever after to the jurors' knowledge. [ASSI 94/1590]

[Delivered to Horsham assizes on 24 Mar. 1806 when, or at the Lewes assizes of 2 Aug. 1806, the grand jury, to which Thomas Hitchener, Elizabeth Morgan and Richard Weekes jun. gave evidence, presented an indictment (now in the Lewes indictments file but perhaps originally in the Horsham file since both have loose membranes) similar to the inquest verdict except that the knife was not called a penknife or said to be of iron and steel and was given no value, the wound was in the neck and throat 5 inches long and 3 inches deep and the last sentence was omitted. ASSI 94/1591. Cf. **147, 148**.]

373 29 June 1808. Warnham. Jurors of Warnham and 4 neighbouring townships: William Joanes, James Tamplin, John Cave, Edward Potter, Daniel Ven, Edward Child, Richard Redford, Charles Child, Michael Cave, John Caffyn, William Honeywood, Francis Craig. On 26 June some person unknown murdered a new-born female child at Warnham, gripping her about the neck with both hands and strangling her whereby she immediately died. After committing the murder he fled on that account. [ASSI 94/1615]

[Delivered to Lewes assizes on 13 Aug. Cf. **157, 158**.]

Inquests of Thomas William Wheeler

374 11 Oct. 1810. Westout in Lewes. Jurors of Westout and 4 neighbouring townships:

Thomas Read, Frederick Willard, Richard Lambe, Charles Verrall, Thomas Figg, William Stuard, John Wilmshurst, John Baxter, Thomas Whiteman, George Chassereau, Jeremiah Dodson, Samuel Brierly. On 9 Oct. John and Richard Carter, Thomas Sergeant, William Oakshed, Allen Ruel, William Tompsett and Thomas Morley, all of St John sub Castro, Lewes, labourers, servants in husbandry employed in the service of Thomas Tourle of St John sub Castro, esq., by order of Thomas Tuppen, Tourle's bailiff and the superintendent of his farming concerns there, assembled on a piece of ground there planted with potatoes, the property of Tourle, to guard it from depredation, John Carter having a pistol worth 5s charged with gunpowder and 5 small pieces of lead. Seeing John Homar, Francis White and Edward Thomas, the last 2 late of Westout and all 3 privates in HM's 37th[1] Regiment of Foot, on Tourle's land and thinking that they were there to steal some of the potatoes, John Carter pursued and tried to overtake and apprehend Homar. During the pursuit Carter frequently ordered Homar in a loud and audible voice to stop and surrender, stating that if he refused he would fire at him, but Homar disregarded him and continued to run away in order to escape. Then Carter discharged the pistol, which he held in his right hand, solely to alarm and thereby to stop and apprehend Homar, but by misfortune and against his will and intention killed him with one or more of the pieces of lead, giving him a mortal wound in the back and another in the loins, both 1 inch wide and 4 inches deep, of which he languished at St John sub Castro and in the military hospital in Westout until the next day and then died in the hospital. What goods or chattels Carter had at the time of the killing or ever after the jurors did not know.
[ASSI 94/1662]

[Delivered to Horsham assizes on 25 Mar. 1811 when a bill of indictment was preferred which charged John Carter with murdering Homar at St John sub Castro on 9 Oct. with a pistol worth 2s charged with gunpowder and lead slugs, giving him a wound in the back ½ inch wide and 6 inches deep of which he languished at St John sub Castro and Westout until the next day and then died at Westout. The grand jury, to which Thomas Tourle, esq., and Thomas Tuppen [Francis White, John Costisey, John ?Vaughan, … ?Thompsett *struck through*] gave evidence, rejected the bill. Carter, who had been committed to gaol by the coroner on 13 Oct. charged with manslaughter, was discharged by proclamation. ASSI 94/1662. Cf. **168**.]

1 *North Hampshire*: Swinson, 134.

375 1 Aug. 1811. Buxted. Jurors of Buxted and 4 neighbouring townships: John Gorringe, William Brunden, John Gibbs, George Britt, Thomas Cooter, George Hollands, George Eastwood, James Best, Thomas Ware, John Curd, John Newnham, John Olive Turner [*but signature is* Tanner], John Jarrett. Witnesses: Thomas Wood, Philip Bannister, Samuel Ware, Charles Prince. On 1 Aug. Esau Parks late of Buxted, cordwainer, feloniously killed Richard Gaston jun. at Buxted, throwing him to the ground with his right hand and thereby giving him a bruise on the lower part of the belly of which he immediately died. Parks had no goods or chattels, lands or tenements in Sussex or elsewhere at that time or ever after to the jurors' knowledge. [ASSI 94/1663]

[Delivered to Lewes assizes on 17 Aug. when a bill of indictment was preferred which charged Parks, labourer, with murdering Gaston at Buxted on 1 Aug. by beating him with both hands and giving him several bruises on the stomach, back, belly and sides of which he immediately died. The grand jury, to which the same 4 witnesses (Prince called surgeon) and Thomas Wren gave evidence, rejected the bill. Parks pleaded not guilty to the inquest and was acquitted; he had not fled and so was discharged. ASSI 94/1663. Cf. **171**.]

376 28 Sept. 1811. Westout in Lewes. Jurors of Westout and 4 neighbouring townships: Cater Rand, William Elphick, Richard Tugwell, William Miles, Simon Grover, Robert Neale, William Verrall, William Figg, John Baxter, Thomas Figg, Alexander Cheale, William Stuard, Henry Pawsons, John Bartlett, George Chassereau. On 21 Sept. John Kennard late of Westout, miller, feloniously killed John Ventham Grigg there, throwing him to the ground with his right hand and thereby giving him a bruise on the skull of which he languished at Westout until 28 Sept. and then died. Kennard had no goods or chattels, lands or tenements in Sussex or elsewhere at the time of the manslaughter or ever after to the jurors' knowledge. [ASSI 94/1676]

[Delivered to Horsham assizes on 23 Mar. 1812 when a bill of indictment was preferred which charged Kennard, labourer, with murdering Grigg at Westout on 21 Sept. by beating him on the head with both hands and giving him several bruises of which he languished there until 28 Sept. and then died. The grand jury, to which William Farmer, Sarah Baker, Samuel Booth, William Oakshut, George Smith, Henry Novis, Thomas Blair, Thomas Hodson, Benjamin Bailey and Charles Carter gave evidence, rejected the bill. Kennard pleaded not guilty to the inquest and was acquitted; he had not fled and so was discharged. ASSI 94/1676. Cf. **171**.]

377 22 June 1812. Chailey. Jurors of Chailey and 4 neighbouring townships: Thomas Roots Beard, Stephen Garnham, John Ayres, Gabriel Best, John Blackstone, John Peckham, John Allen, James Corney, Henry Smith, Thomas Peckham, Henry Snatt, Richard Cruse. On 12 June Mary Tester late of Chailey, single woman, alone and secretly gave birth at Chailey to a female child which by the laws and custom of the kingdom was a bastard and on or about the same day assaulted her there and buried and concealed her with both hands. On 22 June the child was found in an orchard covered with mould or dirt and in such a putrid state that it was impossible for the surgeon to perform an experiment on the lungs to ascertain whether she was born alive or not, but on that day Tester twice confessed in the surgeon's presence that she delivered herself of the child on 12 June, put her in a box and afterwards buried it in the garden or orchard. She declared that the child was not born alive and did not cry. The jurors' verdict was that Tester buried the stillborn child as above. [ASSI 94/1677]

[Delivered to Lewes assizes on 1 Aug. when the grand jury, to which John Wicker, Sarah Page, Lydia Brasier, Henry Verrall and Edward Stenning gave evidence, presented an indictment which charged Tester, spinster, with giving birth as above and on the same day murdering the child at Chailey by burying her in the earth with both hands and thereby suffocating her so that she immediately died. Tester, aged 21, who had been committed to gaol on 27 June by Thomas Partington, JP, pleaded not guilty and was acquitted of murder and had not fled, but was convicted of secretly burying the child (which if born alive would have been a bastard) in an attempt to conceal the birth; she was sentenced to a fine of 1s and a year's imprisonment with hard labour in the Lewes House of Correction. ASSI 94/1677. Cf. **174**.]

378 1 Mar. 1815. Lindfield. Jurors of Lindfield and 4 neighbouring townships: Edward Colbran, Richard Buckley Stone, Robert Wood, Abel Brown, John Shirley, Francis Barnett, John Wicking, John Pilfold, Charles Comber, Thomas Gower jun., John Gower, Francis Blaker, Thomas Murrell. On 1 Jan. Jane wife of John Burnett of Scaynes Hill in Lindfield, victualler, several times struck Sarah Lee at Lindfield on the head, shoulders, back, breast, arms, legs and thighs with a stick of no value which she held in her right hand; and on various days before and after 1 Jan. she several times struck her at Lindfield on the same parts of the body with both hands and also with a hempen rope, a hand whip, a leather boot, a [*blank*][1] sticks, all of no value, which she held in her right hand; giving her several bruises of which she languished at Scaynes Hill and in Lindfield poorhouse from 1 Jan. until 27 Feb. and then died in the poorhouse. So Jane Burnett feloniously killed her. [ASSI 94/1721]

[Delivered to Horsham assizes on 20 Mar. when the grand jury, to which John Everest, James Shelley, Charles Cox, William Potter, Charles Watford, Hannah Standen, [Charles Setford *struck through*], Elizabeth Wickens, [Ann Smith *struck through*], Richard Stapley Tuppen, surgeon, and Robert Martin gave evidence, presented an indictment which charged Jane Burnett with murdering Sarah Lee, spinster, by cruelly and excessively kicking, whipping and beating her on the head, shoulders, stomach, sides, back, arms, legs and feet with sticks, whips and ropes of no value at Lindfield on 1 Nov. 1814 and on various other days between then and 6 Feb. 1815, thereby giving her various grievous bruises, wounds and sores, and at the same time, during which Lee was John Burnett's servant, omitting to provide her with sufficient sustenance and food, as she ought to have done; from which assaults and neglect Lee became greatly emaciated in body and limbs and mortally sick and debilitated, whereof she languished at Lindfield from 6 until 27 Feb. and then miserably died. Jane Burnett, aged 39, who had been committed to gaol on 13 Mar. by Robert Hurst, JP, pleaded not guilty and was acquitted; she had not fled and so was discharged. ASSI 94/1721. Cf. **185**.]

1 ?*and* omitted.

379 3 July 1816. Petworth. Jurors of Petworth and 4 neighbouring townships: Robert Upperton, William Ludby, John Greenfield, Matthew Halliday, John Upton, Thomas Colebrook, Edward Tooth Petar, Charles Eade, James Embling, William Southerton, James Row, Edward Butt, Thomas Chrippes. On 29 June Charles Dowden late of Petworth, labourer, feloniously killed Thomas Muggeridge at Petworth, striking him on the head with both hands and giving him a bruise of which he languished at Petworth until 1 July and then died. Dowden had no goods or chattels, lands or tenements in Sussex or elsewhere at the time of the manslaughter or ever after to the jurors' knowledge. [ASSI 94/1742]

[Delivered to Lewes assizes on 10 Aug. when a bill of indictment was preferred similar to the inquest verdict except that there were several mortal bruises, the charge was murder and the last sentence was omitted. The grand jury, to which John James Blagden, Henry Herrington, Robert Eade, Charles Herrington and George Stedman gave evidence, rejected the bill. Dowden, aged 28, who had been committed to gaol by the coroner on the day of the inquest, pleaded not guilty to the inquest but was convicted; he had no goods and was sentenced to one calendar month in gaol. ASSI 94/1742. Cf. **190**.]

Inquests of George Gwynne

380 7 Nov. 1817. Brighton. Jurors of Brighton: John Mills, Thomas West, William Williams, John Jackson, James Tweedale, Richard Humber, William Isted, Henry Martin, Richard Whichelo, William Blacklock, Richard Locke, John Slee. On 5 Nov. James Day, a private in the 21st Regiment of Royal Scotch Fusiliers stationed at Brighton, John Williams late of Brighton, coal-merchant, Whalesbone hundred constable, and James White late of Brighton, stationer, murdered Thomas Rowles at Brighton: Day stabbing him through the body near the middle of the back with a bayonet of iron and steel worth 3s which he held in both hands, of which he languished at Brighton until the next day and then died; and Williams and White being feloniously present aiding and abetting him. After committing the murder all 3 severally fled on that account. None of them had any goods or chattels, lands or tenements in Sussex or elsewhere at the time of the murder or ever after. [ASSI 94/1780]

[Delivered to Horsham assizes on 16 Mar. 1818 when a bill of indictment was preferred similar to the inquest verdict except that Day and Williams were both called late of Brighton, labourers, the bayonet was worth 5s and held in Day's right hand, the wound was 2 inches wide and 9 inches deep, Williams and White were charged with counselling and procuring Day to commit the murder earlier on 5 Nov. as well as aiding and abetting him and the last 2 sentences were omitted. The grand jury, to which James Gregory, Thomas Saunders, Eastman Barnard, Richard Chapman, George Chittenden, William Maiben, [William South, John Martin *struck through*], Abraham Mathews, Peter Crambie, John Yeates, [John Wise *struck through*], James Ireland, [Robert Coomber *struck through*], John Murray, George Richardson, Edward Blaker, George Battcock, George Hemsley, Joseph Allen, Benjamin Hunt, [Thomas Harman *struck through*], Alexander James Ross, Richard Rankin, [John Murray, William Catling *struck through*], John Cheesman, Thomas Beaty, Thomas Laurence, Nicholas Lawson and [*blank*] Darrah gave evidence, rejected the bill. A writ of 21 Nov. 1817 had summoned the inquest and any depositions and examinations into King's Bench and it is endorsed as executed, with the coroner's signature and seal, dated at Lewes on 24 Nov., but the writ and the attached inquest remain on the assizes file and no proceedings in King's Bench have been found. At the assizes Day, Williams and White pleaded not guilty to the inquest and were acquitted; they had not fled. ASSI 94/1780. Cf. **194**; *SCM*, VI, 741.]

381 15 Nov. 1818. Frant. Jurors of Frant: James Cranborne Strode, esq., Charles Strode, esq., William Budgen, Charles Budgen, Adam Jacob, Thomas Nuttall, Richard George Morgan, Robert Field, John Taylor, John Jones, William Smith, Edward Vaux. On 13 Nov. John Douch late of Speldhurst in Kent, labourer, feloniously killed Edward Smith at Speldhurst, striking him several times on the head, breast and stomach and violently throwing him to the ground with both hands whereby a blood vessel in his head was burst open, of which he languished at Speldhurst, at Tonbridge in Kent and at Frant until the next day and then died at Frant. [ASSI 94/1798]

[Delivered to Horsham assizes on 24 Mar. 1819 when a bill of indictment was preferred which charged Douch with murdering Smith at Speldhurst on 13 Nov. by striking him on the head, neck and stomach and throwing him to the ground with both hands, thereby giving him several bruises on the head of which he languished at Speldhurst and Frant for one hour and then died at Frant on the same day. The grand jury, to which David Fry, Richard Young, John Wiggins, Jeremiah Hart, Thomas Longley, William Gilbert, Richard Hickmott, George Hollamby, James Jeffery and James Cornwall [Isaac Cox *struck through*] gave evidence, reduced the charge from murder to manslaughter. Douch, aged 22, who had been committed to gaol by the coroner on 16 Nov. for the manslaughter of Smith, late of Frant, pleaded not guilty and was acquitted; he had not fled and so was discharged. ASSI 94/1798. Cf. **195**.]

382 30 June 1819. Brighton. Jurors of Brighton: Henry Bates, esq., Joseph Allen, William Chapman, Edward Blaker, William Williams, Richard Ewens, Thomas Tilt, Richard Chandler, John Donaldson, Thomas Newington, George Wood, Joseph Chittenden. On 29 June Edward Broadbent late of Brighton, labourer, murdered William Watson at Brighton with a gun worth 10s charged with gunpowder and a lead bullet which he held in both hands, giving him a wound in the body of which he immediately died. Broadbent had no goods or chattels, lands or tenements in Sussex or elsewhere at that time or ever after to the jurors' knowledge. [ASSI 94/1799]

[Delivered to Lewes assizes on 7 Aug. when the grand jury, to which John Thomas, William Hunter, [William Lang *struck through*], John Shannon, David Pilmer, Thomas Vizer, James McCabe and Isaac Sillcock, surgeon, gave evidence, presented an indictment similar to the inquest verdict except that the wound was in the back near the right shoulder-blade 1 inch wide and 10 inches deep and the last sentence was omitted. Broadbent, aged 29, who had been committed to gaol by the coroner on the day of the inquest for the murder of Watson, a sergeant in the 90th[1] Regiment of Foot stationed at Brighton, pleaded not guilty but was convicted and sentenced to be hanged on 13 Aug. and then dissected and anatomized; he had no goods. ASSI 94/1799. Cf. **196**.]

1 *Perthshire Light Infantry*: Swinson, 192.

383 3 Nov. 1820. Chailey. Jurors of Chailey: Benjamin Beal, George Beard, John Alcorn, Thomas Jeffery, Christopher Pointing, James Corney, Richard Norman, John Johnson, Edward Stenning, William Hunt, Henry Snatt, William Vinall. On 21 Oct. William Stevens and James Ashdowne, both late of Chailey, labourers, feloniously killed Allen Anscombe at Chailey: they struck him several times on the head, temples, breast and stomach with both their hands, violently threw him to the ground and, while he was lying there, again struck him several times on the head, temples, breast and stomach with both hands, thereby giving him several bruises of which he languished at Chailey until 2 Nov. and then died. Stevens and Ashdowne had no goods or chattels, lands or tenements in Sussex or elsewhere at the time of the manslaughter or ever after to the jurors' knowledge. [ASSI 94/1832]

[Delivered to Horsham assizes on 26 Mar. 1821 when the grand jury, to which William Lupton, Phyllis Ridley, Mary Smith, George Jeffery, Thomas Hemsley, Henry Chambers Verrall and Thomas Hodson gave evidence, presented an indictment similar to the inquest verdict except that the charge was murder and the throwing to the ground and the last sentence were omitted. Stevens, aged 21, and Ashdowne, aged 30, who had been committed to gaol by the coroner on the day of the inquest for the manslaughter of Anscombe late of Chailey, husbandman, pleaded not guilty. Stevens was acquitted of murder but convicted of manslaughter; he had no goods and was sentenced to imprisonment in the common gaol for 8 calendar months. Ashdowne was acquitted; he had not fled. ASSI 94/1832. Cf. **199**.]

384 4 May 1822. Brighton. Jurors of Brighton: George Chassereau, John Baker, James Elmes, John Fabian, John Collins, Francis Hendy, Richard Ranger, John Barnes, John Daniels, Mark Wingfield, Thomas Furner, John Pritchard. On 20 Apr. James Wiggins late of Brighton, labourer, feloniously killed Henry Lelliott at Brighton, striking him with both hands on the head, temples, breast, stomach, loins and hips, violently throwing him to the ground and, while he was lying on the ground, kicking and trampling on his head, temples, breast, stomach, loins and hips, thereby giving him several bruises of which he languished at Brighton until 2 May and then died. Wiggins had no goods or chattels, lands or tenements in Sussex or elsewhere at the time of the manslaughter or ever after to the jurors' knowledge. [ASSI 94/1855]

[Delivered to Lewes assizes on 3 Aug. when the grand jury, to which William Piper, Henry Hall, William Butler, William Manktellow, Susannah Lelliott, Ann Butler, Thomas Lelliott, Harry Blaker, Thomas Baldey, William Caudle[1] and George Chassereau gave evidence, presented an indictment which charged Wiggins with murdering Lelliott at Brighton on 20 Apr. by striking him on the head, breast and stomach with both hands, throwing him to the ground and, while he was on the ground, kicking him with both feet on the loins, hips and thighs, thereby giving him several bruises on the loins, hips and thighs of which he languished at Brighton until 2 May and then died. Wiggins, aged 21, who had been committed to gaol by the coroner on the day of the inquest charged with the manslaughter of Lelliott, late of Brighton, pleaded not guilty and was acquitted of murder but convicted of manslaughter; he had no goods and was sentenced to remain in gaol for 6 calendar months. ASSI 94/1855. Cf. **202**.]

1 *Not present* is written in pencil against Caudle although he is ticked in the same way as the others and all 11 are said to have been sworn in court.

385 7 Apr. 1823. Brighton. Jurors of Brighton: John Smith, Thomas Pocock, William Field, Henry Mitchener, William Pocock, James Lugsdin, James Griffiths, Phineas Jupp, Joseph Chittenden, Thomas Pelham, John Pitt, Joseph Field. On 4 Apr. Daniel Watts late of Brighton, labourer, feloniously killed James Smith at Ovingdean, striking him with both hands on the head, temples, breast and stomach and giving him several bruises of which he languished at Ovingdean and Brighton until the next day and then died at Brighton. [ASSI 94/1879]

[Delivered to Lewes assizes on 26 July when a bill of indictment was preferred similar to the inquest verdict except that the charge was murder, Watts was said to be late of Ovingdean and the blows were to the head, temples, neck and stomach. The grand jury, to which George Chassereau, George Hope, Abraham Smith, John Chowne, James Alfred Tabois and Harry Blaker gave evidence, rejected the bill. Watts, aged 24, who had been committed to gaol by the coroner on the day of the inquest, pleaded not guilty to the inquest and was acquitted and discharged. ASSI 94/1879. Cf. **204**.]

386 17 Feb. 1824. East Grinstead. Jurors of East Grinstead: Thomas Stevens Burt, Benjamin Martin, Thomas Wakeham Collins, John Finch, James Sanderson, Martin Walls, Richard Best, George Monk, Thomas Finch, Thomas Soper, Christopher Middleton, James Wells. On 14 Feb. Esther Gorringe late of East Grinstead, single woman, murdered Martha Ann Sewell at East Grinstead, taking her in both hands and violently throwing her into a copper filled with water in a wash-house, whereby she drowned and immediately died. [ASSI 94/1905]

[Delivered to Horsham assizes on 22 Mar. when a bill of indictment was preferred similar to the inquest verdict except that Gorringe, spinster, forced Sewell under the water with both hands. The grand jury, to which John and Lucy Sewell, William and John Histed, Thomas Waghorne, John Collins and George Butcher [John Holland *struck through*] gave evidence, rejected the bill. Gorringe, aged 15, who had been committed to gaol by the coroner on the day of the inquest, pleaded not guilty to the inquest and was acquitted; she had not fled and so was discharged. ASSI 94/1905. Cf. **206**.]

387 20 Aug. 1824. Patcham. Jurors of Patcham: John Bull, William Tanner jun., George Blaker, Henry Ridge, Joseph Harland, John Streeter, Bartholomew Smithers, Page Dick, Charles Page, Henry Herriott, John Ayling, Thomas Scrase. On 16 Aug. Robert Snow late of Patcham, ?yeoman, justifiably and of inevitable necessity killed William Langridge at Patcham. He justifiably struck the foremost of 4 horses, worth £10 each, on its head and back with a whip of leather, whalebone and wood worth 1s which he held in his right hand, the horses then drawing a carriage called a timber-tug worth £10, loaded with timber worth £10. By reason of the beating the foremost horse became restive and unmanageable and threw Langridge to the ground whereby the near hind wheel of the carriage went over his left leg and thigh, the weight of the loaded carriage giving him several bruises of which he languished at Patcham until 18 Aug. and then died. [ASSI 94/1906]

[Delivered to Lewes assizes on 14 Aug. Cf. **207**.]

388 30 Oct. 1824. South Malling. Jurors: Thomas Hooper, Thomas Berry, John Morley, John Inskip, William Phillips, William Simmonds, William Hall, John Mitchell,

Caleb Nutley, Richard Barnden, John Peirce, James Wisdom. On 24 Aug. Thomas Stacey late of South Malling, labourer, murdered Richard Brooks at South Malling with a large knife of iron and steel worth 6d which he held in his right hand, giving him a wound in the right side of the belly 2 inches wide and 3 inches deep of which he languished at South Malling until 29 Oct. and then died. [ASSI 94/1907]

[Delivered to Lewes special assizes on 20 Dec. when the grand jury presented 3 indictments for all of which Thomas Pettit, Benjamin Price, [Maria Funnell *struck through*], Rhoda Price, [James Dyke *struck through*], Ambrose Istead, George Hicks, Edward Hopley, Henry Verral and James Dyke gave evidence. One indictment was similar to the inquest verdict except for omitting that the knife was of iron and steel. The second had charged Solomon Stevens and Stacey, both of South Malling, labourers, with assaulting Benjamin Price at South Malling on 24 Aug. on 2 counts: assault with intent to murder and common assault. The grand jury endorsed the charge against Stevens but rejected that against Stacey. The third indictment charged Stevens with cutting Price on the left leg with a sharp instrument at South Malling on 24 Aug. on 3 counts: intent to murder, intent to disable and intent to do grievous bodily harm. Stacey, aged 35, mariner, who had been committed to gaol on 9 Sept. by T[homas][1] Partington, JP, charged on the oath of Brooks with having stabbed him with a knife at South Malling on 24 Aug. with intent to murder him or do him grievous bodily harm and later detained also on the coroner's warrant charged with his murder, pleaded not guilty to both the first indictment and the inquest and was acquitted of murder but convicted of manslaughter; he had no goods and was sentenced to a fine of 1s and imprisonment with hard labour in the Lewes House of Correction for one year. Stevens, aged 45, who had been committed on the same day by the same JP charged on the oath of Price with having stabbed him at South Malling on 24 Aug. with intent to murder him or do him grievous bodily harm, pleaded not guilty to the second and third indictments. He was acquitted on the third and had not fled. On the second he was acquitted of assault with intent but convicted of common assault and sentenced to remain in gaol for 9 calendar months. ASSI 94/1907. Cf. **207**.]

1 Cf. **377**.

389 23 Aug. 1826. Brighton. Jurors: William Williams, Samuel Shepherd Folker, George Dancaster, Edmund Savage, Edward Parker Durrant, Richard Shephard, William Nye, William Fisk, Samuel Francis, Thomas Mockford, George Suggers, Abraham Johnson Lamprell. On 22 Aug. William Burt late of Brighton, labourer, murdered Isaac Burt at Brighton with a large knife of iron and steel worth 2d which he held in his right hand, giving him 2 mortal wounds in the left side of the belly of which he immediately died. [ASSI 94/1962]

[Delivered to Lewes special assizes on 3 Jan. 1827 when the grand jury, to which Ann Young, William Harfield, George Beard, Ann Loveridge, Henry Rawley, William Catling, William Caudle and Thomas Baldey gave evidence, presented an indictment charging William Burt on 2 counts of murdering Isaac Burt at Brighton on 22 Aug. with a knife worth 6d: the first, that he stabbed him in the belly, thighs, knees and other parts of his body, giving him several mortal wounds in the belly, thighs and knees of which he immediately died; and the second, that he stabbed him in the belly, giving him 2 mortal wounds each 1 inch long and 2 inches deep of which he immediately died. William Burt, aged 28, cordwainer, who had been committed to gaol by the coroner on the day of the inquest, pleaded not guilty but was convicted; he had no goods and was sentenced to be hanged on 8 Jan. and then dissected and anatomized. ASSI 94/1962. Cf. **211**.]

390 31 Jan. 1827. South Malling.

[The inquest does not survive, but at the Horsham assizes of 26 Mar. a bill of indictment was preferred which probably relates to it. It charged Ann and Sarah Starnes late of Cliffe, single women, on 4 counts of murdering a bastard male child at Cliffe on 3 Dec. 1826, Ann having given birth to him alone and secretly at Cliffe earlier on that day: the first, that Ann had squeezed his neck and throat with both hands, thereby strangling him, of which he immediately died; the second was similar except that Ann had strangled the child with a cotton shawl worth 1d which she tied round his neck, throat and face; the third charged her with throwing the child with both hands into a privy belonging to Stephen Starnes and containing a great quantity of water, human excrement and other filth in which he was suffocated and drowned, dying immediately; and the fourth charged her with throwing the child into the Ouse in which he was drowned, dying immediately. All 4 counts charged Sarah with being feloniously present aiding and abetting her. The grand jury, to which Elizabeth and William Moon, Elizabeth Verrall, Sarah Knight, Mary Browne, Thomas Gibson, Edward Gwyther, Robert Pinion, Edward Hopley, Harriet Wells, Caleb Nutley and Stephen and Jane Starnes gave evidence, rejected the bill. Ann Starnes, aged 20, and Sarah, aged 14, had been committed to gaol by John Hoper, JP, on 20 Feb. ASSI 94/1991. Cf. **212**.]

391 8 Mar. 1827. Eastbourne. Jurors: Richard Buckley Stone, Joseph Fielder, Thomas White, Charles William Lewis, Spencer Weston, Samuel Weller, John Mann, Richard Mockett, John Rason, William Sutton, William Dyer, Richard Smith. On 6 Mar. a person unknown murdered Horatio Finch at Eastbourne, taking him in both hands and violently throwing him into a tub partly filled with water in a dwelling-house in the occupation of John Finch whereby he was drowned, dying immediately. [ASSI 94/1991]

[Delivered to Horsham assizes on 26 Mar. with 10 depositions which had been taken at Eastbourne by the coroner, from Sophia Burrows and Maria Pankhurst who had deposed on 8 Mar., from Mary Vine, Ann Miller, John Head, George Phillips, Susannah Banks and George Sinnock on 9 Mar., and from Ann Finch and Sarah Sutton on 17 Mar.:

Sophia Burrows of Eastbourne, widow: About 8.30 p.m. on 6 Mar. Ann wife of John Finch, waiter at the New Inn, Eastbourne, came and knocked at the front door of her house which adjoined that at which the Finches lived. The door was locked and on Burrows opening it Ann Finch and her servant-girl, Ann Miller, were there. Burrows, having previously heard their screaming, asked them if the house was on fire. Finch replied: 'No, my child is lost.' Burrows asked her if the child was gone off in a fit and she replied: 'No, someone had stolen it.' Burrows then observed that her husband must have been at home and taken it away and then said to the girl: 'Have you been asleep, Ann, or have you been out?' She replied: 'Neither' and that no one had been in the house during the time her mistress had left it. Finch was crying and screaming much during this time and Miller was similarly affected. All 3 then left the house and Finch went on forward to the New Inn to ask her husband if he had taken away the child and Burrows followed her. Before Burrows got there she met the Finches coming back to the house with John Head and they had heard nothing of the child. They all went back to the house together and searched about for the child, but the Finches got there first and when Burrows arrived she observed them going upstairs with Susannah Banks, single woman, cook at the New Inn, and they had a candle with them. The door of the staircase opened into the kitchen where the body of the child was afterwards found. They all came downstairs in about 2 minutes and John Finch said to those present: 'I wish you would take a candle and look about the back part of the premises by the privy.' But Burrows said the wind was too high and that it could not be done without a lanthorn. John Finch then turned round and said: 'Oh, here is my boy, here is my boy' and took the body from a tub which was placed on a form in the kitchen. The top of the tub was about a yard high from the floor and it was rather more than half filled with water. The body was then given by John Finch to George Phillips, a fellow servant at the New Inn who acted there in the capacity of what is generally called boots. Ann Finch was present when her husband took the body from the water and they were both violently affected by the circumstance. Burrows did not at this time observe Miller there. The body was placed on the floor in the parlour and the clothes was taken off the body which was afterwards put into warm water by Banks. Less than ½ hour later Mr Sinnock, a surgeon, arrived and attempted to restore the child to life, but it was unavailing. Burrows had known Ann Finch about 2 years and had lived next door to her nearly 1¼ years. They used to see and converse with each other daily. About 2 months earlier she first thought that there was something strange in Ann Finch's manners as she then cried very much and expressed fears that she should come to poverty and appeared violently depressed. Mrs Vine, who lived in the same house as Burrows, thought the same: that Ann Finch's mind was not right. One day about this time John Finch called Burrows and Vine where he and his wife were and she was then raving and throwing her hands about and crying much and assigned no reason for so doing. She continued in this melancholy state for the greatest part of the day and the husband wished Burrows and Vine to look a little to her. The next day Mrs Pankhurst was procured by John Finch to take care of her. She was with her about a week when Ann Finch became more composed and quiet in mind. About a fortnight before the inquest Ann Finch appeared again to be getting into the same melancholy state of mind, but the disorder passed off apparently with less violence and no one was employed to look after her as before. Burrows saw her about 11 a.m. of 6 Mar. and she then appeared in good spirits and in that state of mind in which she usually was when not depressed by melancholy. Miller had the chief care of the child and she as well as Ann Finch appeared to be very fond of it.

Maria wife of Thomas Pankhurst of Eastbourne, fisherman: About the beginning of January John Finch applied to her to take charge of his wife, alleging that she was in a low state of mind and that if she was with her he thought she would get better. Pankhurst agreed and continued with her on the first day from about 11 a.m. till 8 p.m. when she went to bed and Pankhurst carried to her her child. Pankhurst clearly perceived that she did not possess her usual consistency of conduct or the same quietude of mind as previously. She cried much when Pankhurst first came to her and though she was afterwards more composed in her mind yet she was during the whole day much depressed in spirits and in a sullen mood. Pankhurst continued with her from day to day about a week. On one evening during the week, while Ann Finch was reading a newspaper — but whether or no she had seen therein any account of a person being drowned Pankhurst did not know — she said: 'If ever I make off with myself I shall drown myself.' Pankhurst instantly expressed her disapprobation at such a thought and asked her what she thought in that case would become of her baby which was then lying in the cradle before her and she made no reply. On another occasion during the week Finch appeared particularly depressed and went upstairs and there cried bitterly. On Pankhurst's inquiring the cause, she assigned none but expressed a wish that her husband should be sent for. He came and went upstairs to her and they shortly afterwards came downstairs together and she was then a little more composed but did not make known the cause of her grief. Miller, who had the care of the child, was particularly fond of it and appeared always to bestow care and concern for it; and the child appeared equally fond of her.

Mary Vine of Eastbourne, widow: About 2 months earlier, in consequence of Miller having come to her at the house where she was living and requested her presence at Ann Finch's house, she went and found her with her husband upstairs. She appeared in great distress and was wringing her hands and throwing them about in a distracted manner. After about ½ hour John Finch left Vine and his wife together and Vine urged her, as she had done before, to make known to her the cause of her grief. At length she caught Vine by the arm and said: 'Oh, Mrs Vine, Mrs Vine, I thought I must have made off with myself. I thought something said that I must make off with myself.' She assigned no reason for her grief. The next day, as Vine believed, she was put under the care of Mrs Pankhurst and a few days later she returned to her accustomed state of cheerfulness. Vine was not in the habit of having but little intercourse or conversation with her, though living at the next house, but had seen her on the day of the child's death and on her passing the door of the house where Vine lived she made some commonplace observation on the weather and said, as Vine believed: 'It continues to be very wet.' She spoke very cheerfully and did not appear to be in a troubled state of mind. The Finches were both particularly fond of the child.

Ann Miller of Eastbourne, spinster: She had lived with the Finches about 3 months and her chief employment had been to take care of the child. Ann Finch had during that time occasionally been much depressed. On 1 Mar. Finch said while she was washing the child's hands: 'Bless you, my darling boy. I wish you was in heaven and out of this wicked world' and instantly cried a little. She had been low spirited the whole of the day. On 5 and 6 Mar. she appeared to be as cheerful as she usually was and Miller observed nothing in particular in her conduct. They both drank tea together on the evening of the child's death, which was over and the tea-things put by at about 6.45 p.m. After they had drunk tea the child was undressed by Finch and by her put into the cradle which was standing on the side of the parlour opposite the window and as you turned your back on the window the cradle was on the right-hand side of the room which was not its usual place but on the left-hand side, though Miller had seen it so placed several times. It was about 7.30 p.m. when the child was placed in the cradle and Finch, after putting it there, placed over the head of the cradle a shawl, but for what purpose Miller did not know, but she thought at the time that it was to keep off the glare of the candle on the table from the child's eyes for it had that effect. About 10 minutes later Finch gave Miller 1s 6d and desired her to go to Mr Turner's and get 1lb cheese, 1lb candles (rushlights) and a ball of cotton and that she was to run up there and be quick back. Miller was certain that she had not left the room after the child had been placed in the cradle until she went to Mr Turner's shop. She returned in about 20 minutes and opened the outer or street door which had a thumb-latch and was in the act of shutting it when Finch came from the parlour and desired her to take off her things, meaning her bonnet and shawl, and then to come into the parlour. At the same time she took from her hands the cheese and candles and if she had not have done so Miller would have hung up the candles in their place, which was on a nail by the side of the kitchen window and close by the tub in which the child's body was found, but the cheese she would have taken into the parlour and put into the cupboard, its usual place. Finch then desired her to sit down and take some needlework which she pointed out to her and to do it as quick as she could because she wanted it done. Finch then went upstairs to put on her bonnet and shawl and came back into the parlour and said that she should not be gone long and then left the house, but for what purpose Miller did not know. She returned in a little less than ½ hour and instantly came into the parlour and asked Miller if the child had lain still and she answered: 'Yes.' She then took away the candle and went upstairs and took off her bonnet and shawl. On her return she put the candle on the table and went to the cradle and threw back the shawl as if to look at the child. Miller then thought it was for the purpose of seeing if the child's hands were covered which she was in the habit of doing. She took up the clothes from the cradle and said: 'Jane, where is the child?' and appeared much alarmed. Miller said: 'Is it not there, mam?' She then said: 'What have you done with it?' Miller told her that she had not been from the room and had done nothing with it. Finch then screamed out: 'The baby is gone, the baby is gone' and went out of the house and knocked and kicked at the door of Mrs Burrows's house, which was the next house, and made her loss known to her. Shortly afterwards several persons came to the house and while Miller was in the parlour she heard someone say: 'Here is the child in the tub.' Finch had neither cheese or rush-candles in the house at the time she sent Miller for some. The tub was on a form in the kitchen in its usual place, but it was generally empty and laid with its bottom uppermost. On the day the child was found dead, by the desire of Finch, who had observed a tub at the corner of the house to catch the water was running over, Miller took 2 buckets of water therefrom and placed it in the tub in the kitchen and left one bucket full. Miller had on a former occasion done the like by Finch's desire. Finch was always very fond of the child and Miller knew of no facts to induce her to believe that she put it into the tub water.

John Head of Eastbourne, fisherman: His premises adjoined those occupied by John Finch whom he had known as a waiter at the New Inn for some time. Between 8 and 9 p.m. on 6 Mar., as he was sitting by the fireside with his wife and family, he heard a noise in the street which appeared to him to be the screaming of some woman. He instantly went into the street and there saw Ann Finch who was running to and fro and appeared to be in much distress and anguish of mind. As soon as she saw him she ran towards him and took hold of his hands and stated that she had lost her child and that somebody had taken it away, which she repeated several times. He begged of her to calm herself and accompanied her to the New Inn. As soon as they arrived there she ran into the bar and called for her husband, of whom she enquired if he had got her child, which she continued to repeat so that no answer to the husband's enquiries could be obtained from her. Head and the Finches returned together to John Finch's house and were followed by the cook at the New Inn. On the whole road there Ann Finch continued in the same distracted state of mind. As soon as they arrived at the house the Finches and Head went into the parlour and John Finch enquired of his wife where his boy was. She answered that she had left him asleep in the cradle and told Miller, who was living with them as a servant, that if it awoke she was to rock the cradle and she gave her some work and told her that she should be gone only a few minutes and she was absent from home only ½ hour. John Finch and Head instantly searched the parlour for the child but it could not be found there. John Finch then took a candle and hastened upstairs. After he had been gone about 2 minutes he called out to Head to look about the privy. Before Head had opened the door John Finch came downstairs into the kitchen and was in the act of directly crossing it and put his hand on the cellar door, but did not go into the cellar but went up to a tub which stood on the table not 2 yards from the cellar door and exclaimed: 'Here is my child.' After pausing a while he took the child from the tub which was more than half full of water and the child was apparently dead. The child's feet and the bottom part of its clothes hung over the side of the tub and merely the head and a portion of the body was immersed in the water. As soon as the child had been taken from the water the cook at the New Inn took it from John Finch, who seemed completely paralysed, and placed it before the parlour fire, in which room was his wife, but whether she saw the child after it was taken from the water Head did not know for she was hurried from the room upstairs. Head went for Mr Sinnock who afterwards arrived at Finch's house and attempted to restore animation in the child which he did not succeed in doing. Head was not personally acquainted with Ann Finch but had several times been informed that her mind was occasionally deranged.

George Phillips of Eastbourne, servant at the New Inn: About 9 p.m. on 6 Mar. Ann Finch came to the New Inn and enquired in much anguish of mind for her husband. On his appearing to her she enquired of him if he had been home and he replied: 'No.' On that she said: 'I have lost my baby.' John Finch took hold of her and accompanied her home and Phillips and the cook at the inn followed them. When they arrived at Finch's house a search was made in the parlour for the child but it could not be found and John Finch asked Miller where she had been. She answered: 'Nowhere' and that no one had been in the house. She also stated to a question that she had not been asleep. John Finch then went upstairs to make search for the child but it was not found there. On his coming downstairs to go out to the privy to make search for the child he crossed the kitchen and went up to a washing-tub which stood on a table or form and exclaimed: 'Oh, my God, here is my baby' and which he took out of the water. Phillips took the child from him and carried it into the parlour before the fire but it was then dead. When the child was taken from the tub Ann Finch was near her husband and a scream escaped from either her or Miller but from which Phillips did not recollect as there was much confusion at the time, but Ann Finch seemed to be in a very wild and agitated state of mind. Phillips instantly after left the house and went to the New Inn and procured some hot water in which the child was placed but life could not be restored. Phillips was not personally acquainted with Ann Finch, not having lived in Eastbourne more than 4 months, and could not speak of the state of her mind but had heard that she had at times been deranged.

Susannah Banks of Eastbourne, cook at the New Inn: About the middle of January she went to see Ann Finch who was stated to be in a deranged state of mind. On going to the house she was directed to go upstairs which she did and there saw her standing in the room by the side of her husband who was endeavouring to compose her. On Banks's enquiring of her what was the matter she replied: 'I must go' and 'I will go' and 'Pray let me go' and attempted to get away from her husband. She altogether acted like one bereft of reason. Banks continued with her for about ½ hour during the whole of which period she continued to make use of many incoherent expressions, such as 'She would do it' and 'She must do it for she had long determined to do it' but yet she alluded to no particular subject and while Banks continued with her she did not know her although she had been some time acquainted with her. Banks called again in the evening of the same day and she was then more composed and knew her and did not make use of any of the incoherent expressions which she had done earlier. She gradually grew better and had lately appeared much improved in health. On the evening of 6 Mar. Banks was at John Finch's house when the child was found by him in the tub and Ann Finch appeared to her to be in no greater anguish than any other mother would be by the loss of her child.

George Sinnock of Eastbourne, surgeon: On 11 Jan. he was requested by John Finch to visit his wife who, as he expressed himself, had during the preceding night conducted herself in such a strange and extraordinary manner as to occasion much anxiety and alarm in his mind. Soon after on that day Sinnock called upon her and was desired to walk upstairs where she and her husband were sitting at the foot of the bed. The husband had his arm round her waist, apparently using restraint towards her, and she was extending and throwing her arms about and evidently endeavouring to escape from him to the window, but occasionally lapsing into a more quiet state with her eyes directed upwards and her hands clasped firmly together. She was for a few minutes in apparent silent supplication, then muttered some incoherent and unintelligible expressions. On Sinnock asking John Finch how long he had noticed any indication of this state of mind in her and if he could trace it to any cause, he replied he had perceived nothing of the kind anterior to the preceding evening and that he was not aware of any circumstance which could probably produce such an effect. Sinnock then asked Ann Finch a few questions with a view to ascertain if she was conscious of his presence and who he was, but she made no reply neither did she take any notice of him. John Finch then addressed her and said: 'Well, my dear, we will now go downstairs and Mr Sinnock will stay and chat a few moments with you.' He arose from the bed and took her hand for the purpose of leading her downstairs. When they were preparing to descend the stairs he let go her hand and, instead of following him, she made a turn and endeavoured to rush into another room close to the head of the stairs, which John Finch, perceiving her, turned round and caught hold of part of her dress and said: 'Come, come, my dear, this is the way downstairs' on which she appeared to be following him downstairs, but instead of descending the stairs step by step she extended her arms and stepped off the stairs and would have fallen to the bottom had not John Finch been in front of her and the narrowing of the stairs prevented her passing by him. After they had got into the parlour below stairs Sinnock asked John Finch if he had heard her complain of any bodily indisposition and he replied that she had a day or two before stated that her appetite was not so good as usual, with some trifling complaint of languor and headache. Sinnock then said: 'If that is the case, it may be prudent to administer some little medicine with the view of increasing the energy of the stomach and moderately exciting the bowels' but confessed he considered it a case in which, when she became a little tranquil, moral arguments and reasoning would have more avail than medicine for he conceived it a case of strong delusion of the mind for she was continually harassed with the idea that she should come to poverty, although they were in very comfortable circumstances of life, and also with regard to her future state, for she also continually exclaimed: 'I am lost, I am lost, what shall I do?' Sinnock then advised John Finch to have someone with her who would calm and soothe her mind and shortly after left her. He called again the next day and found her sitting at dinner with Mrs Pankhurst. On addressing her and enquiring of her who[1] she found herself, she in a very feeble voice said she was a little better. She appeared calm, but evidently dejected and desponding. Sinnock then requested of her not to allow her mind to be depressed from causes which had no real existence and after some further consolatory remarks left her. He called again on the third day when she appeared better and expressed herself to be considerably so and expressed her wish to decline any further medical assistance, from which time he had seen nothing of her but had occasionally enquired of John Finch how she was and his reply was that she was going on comfortably.

Ann wife of John Finch, waiter at the New Inn: She arose from her bed about 8 a.m. on 6 Mar. and felt quite well. She and the servant-girl, Ann Miller, took their breakfast together, as usual, about 9 a.m. After breakfast Miller nursed the child and Finch might for a short time have taken it from her, yet Miller had the principal care of it till 11.30 a.m. when Finch put it asleep in the cradle and pinned a shawl over the head of the cradle, but so as not in any way to conceal the child's face. The child slept then till 1.30 p.m. When she first put it to sleep she desired Miller to put some of the water from the tub at the corner of the house, which had caught the rain-water, into the tub in the kitchen, but did not make any mention of any particular quantity. Miller went accordingly and was gone about 5 minutes and did not make any remark as to the quantity she had put in the tub, neither did Finch make any inquiry on that head. Finch then set Miller on needlework and Miller did not appear in the least to be out of temper. The child awoke about 1.30 p.m. and just before Finch and Miller were going to sit down to take their dinner. Finch took it from the cradle and nursed it herself while she and Miller were eating their dinner. When dinner was over she gave the child to Miller who nursed it for about an hour and, having cried to come to Finch, she took it and set Miller again on needlework. The child was at [that] time a little fractious, but Finch quieted it by nursing. She and Miller so continued to nurse it, each taking for a short time as it became dissatisfied and noisy, until tea-time. Between dinner and tea, while Miller was leading the child across the parlour, he dropped something from his hands and Miller desired it not throw it down again but to hold it in its hands. Finch, thinking she spoke rather cross to the child, desired her not do so and she made no answer but did not do the like again. Finch and Miller sat down to take their tea in the parlour, the place they were accustomed to take it in, about 6.15 p.m. and Finch nursed the child in her lap and he was quiet and very good. It was nearly 7 p.m. before tea was over. Miller washed up the tea-things and put them in their place and then went into the cellar to chop and split some wood for lighting the fires as she was accustomed to do. While she was in the cellar Finch undressed the child and put it into the cradle and put over the head of the cradle the same shawl that she had laid over it in the morning and set so as not in any manner to conceal its countenance. Miller brought into the parlour the wood she had chopped in about 10 minutes and placed some under the grate. Finch at this time was rocking the cradle and the child was quiet. The head of the cradle was near the sideboard and the foot of it nearer the cupboard than the head of it. This was the position in which it always stood. The head of the cradle was never placed nearer the cupboard than the foot of it, but the foot was always nearest. After having placed the chopped wood under the grate, Miller went into the kitchen to wash her hands and returned in a few minutes. John Finch had rushed in to kiss the child as he had not been there the whole day since he had left about 7.30 a.m. He was in the room when Miller brought in the wood. He did not remain more than 5 minutes and went out of the parlour just as Miller was coming in after washing her hands. Miller was then sitting down in a chair when Ann Finch took up the candle from the table and went upstairs to get her some money to be laid out at the shop. She returned in less than 2 minutes and found Miller in the chair as she had left her. She then gave her 18d and desired her to go to Mr Turner's and fetch 1 lb Derby cheese, 1 lb rushlights and a ball of cotton and made no remark as to her being quick back and not hurrying herself. While Miller was gone Finch was the whole of the time employed in needlework and in the letting in an oblong piece of linen cloth into an article of dress and she had sewn and completed one of the short sides and about ¼ of one of the long sides on Miller's return. She had been gone between 10 minutes and ¼ hour. Finch thought it was about 8 p.m. when she returned. She heard her open the street door into the kitchen and the parlour door was on the jar. After she had shut the street door she wiped her shoes on the mat lying close to the parlour door on the kitchen side. Finch said to her: 'Jane, bring the things to me' and she came into the parlour with her bonnet and shawl on and gave into Finch's hands the cheese, candle and cotton. Finch arose from her chair to receive the articles over or from across the table. She put the ball of cotton into her work-box standing on the table and the cheese in the cupboard in the parlour, its proper place, and then went into the kitchen and hung up the rushlights on a nail by the side of the kitchen window, their proper place, and returned into the parlour. As soon as she had taken the articles from Miller, Miller went into the kitchen and hung up her bonnet and shawl on a nail between the ?fore door and the staircase door and as Finch was hanging up the candles Miller was hanging up her bonnet. Finch returned into the parlour just before Miller. If the child had been in the tub of water at this time Finch was sure she must have seen it. She then gave Miller the article of dress on which she had been working while Miller had been to the shop and said: 'Jane, take this work and when you have finished sewing this piece on turn it on the other side and run it 2 or 3 times across and clam it down. I am going up street and shall not be gone long.' She then took the candle from the table and went upstairs and put on her bonnet and shawl and came down with it on in 3 minutes and placed the candle on the table, Miller being at this time in the chair in which she had left her, and then went out of doors. She did not at this time make any look at the cradle so as to take any particular notice, but was sure that if the shawl had been put over the head of the cradle so as to shut out all light of the child's face she should have observed it. She went to the house of John Sutton, a shoemaker, for the purpose of borrowing an infant's frock for a pattern to make another by and she procured it and brought it home. She had before spoken to Mrs Sutton about it and had a few days before asked Mrs Vine what quantity of nankeen would be required to make 2 frocks. She was, as she believed, absent from her house about ½ hour. On her return she opened the street door and went in. On her passing into the parlour she observed Miller in the same chair she had left her with the needlework she had given her in her hands. She then observed nothing to raise the slightest suspicion that her child was no more. She said: 'Jane, has the baby been quiet?' and she replied she had. Finch then took the candle from the table and went upstairs and took off her bonnet and shawl and came down again in a few minutes. Miller was still with her needlework in her hands. Finch then went up to the cradle and the shawl was still over the head of the cradle as she had put it after her tea. Not seeing the child therein she exclaimed: 'Jane, where is the baby? What have you done with it?' She said: 'I have done nothing with it.' 'Have you been away anywhere?' She replied she had not. 'Had anyone been there?' She said: 'No.' Finch then ran and called Mrs Burrows who shortly after returned with her, and Burrows asked Miller: 'What have you done with the baby? Have you been asleep?' She answered: 'No.' Finch asked her if her master had been home and she replied: 'No.' Finch then ran across to the New Inn to John Finch and enquired of him if he had been across to the house and taken the baby and if not someone had stolen it. He replied that he had not and returned to his house with Ann Finch. They, Burrows, Susannah Banks and John Head all went into the kitchen together and the candle was in the parlour on the table. John Finch then took the candle and said possibly someone may have taken it to the privy and was in the act of going out of doors to search when Burrows observed to him that the wind was too high. John Finch then said: 'Let us go upstairs' and he went and Ann Finch and Banks followed. They all searched about the bed and room and then went into the adjoining unfurnished room. Not making any discovery of the child, they all went downstairs, John Finch first, Ann Finch next and Banks following them. John Finch then proposed to go down in the cellar and had his hand on the door but did not go down as he at that instant discovered the child lying in the tub of water. Ann Finch was at this moment in the kitchen, resting on Banks's arm. On her return with John Finch and the others she observed Miller standing before the table in the parlour crying. John Finch asked Miller if she had been away from the house or had been asleep and she replied: 'Neither.' Miller always appeared to be very fond of the child and the child to be fond of her.

Sarah wife of John Sutton of Eastbourne, shoemaker: About 8 p.m. of 6 Mar. Ann Finch came to her and asked for the pattern of a frock as she wanted to make a frock for the child and which she gave her. At the same time she enquired after the child and Finch replied that it was quite well and that she left it asleep in the cradle. Finch continued with her for nearly ½ hour and in the course of conversation she enquired of her how she found her general health and she replied that she was quite well and that her head was quite well. During the whole of the time Finch was with her she appeared to be very well and quite cool and collected and seemed to have the complete possession of her mental faculties. Soon after 8 p.m. Finch left her house and about 10 p.m. the same evening she heard of the child's death. ASSI 36/1. Cf. **212**.]

1 Recte *how*.

392 14 Mar. 1828. Eastbourne. Jurors: James Pagden, John Starr, Samuel Rason, William Morris, William Sutton, Thomas Noakes, Thomas Luck, William Hyland, Thomas White, John Colman, Richard Buckley Stone, William Luxford. On 17 Feb. Mary Ann Stapleton late of Eastbourne, single woman, alone and secretly gave birth at Eastbourne to a live female child which by the laws and customs of the kingdom was a bastard and on the same day murdered her there, taking her in both hands and violently throwing her into a privy whereby she was suffocated in the soil and filth which it contained and immediately died. [ASSI 94/2018]

[Delivered to Horsham assizes on 24 Mar. with depositions taken by the coroner at the inquest on 14 Mar. from 8 witnesses:

Harriet Luxford, nursemaid in the service of Robert Booth of Eastbourne, clerk: On 12 Mar., having occasion to go to the privy of Booth's dwelling-house to which all the servants of the house go and looking down one of its holes, she discovered the back of an infant floating in the privy. She procured a stick and moved it. Having satisfied herself that it was a human body, she immediately told Sarah Michell, single woman, a cook in Booth's service, and they both went to the privy. Michell touched the body with a stick and while they were there John Goodwin, a footman and groom in the same service, was called in as he was passing by and he also looked down the hole and agreed that it was a human body. All 3 assisted in taking it from the privy and it was placed on the floor. Luxford then went into the house and told Booth that Goodwin wanted to see him and Booth instantly went to him. About 5 minutes later Goodwin came to Luxford and told her that Booth wished her not to mention the circumstance to her mistress or to Mrs Stone, the nurse, who was in the same service. About ¼ hour after Goodwin had been in Booth came into the house from the privy, went into the drawing-room and called Luxford there to him. After interrogating her whether she knew any circumstance relative to the birth of the child or how the body came in the privy, he desired her not to mention the circumstance to her mistress or to Mrs Stone or the people in the village, and Luxford promised him that she would not. Luxford entered Booth's service on 28 Nov. 1827 and about 3 weeks later she first believed from appearance that Mary Ann Stapleton, a nurse in Booth's service, was pregnant. She grew larger and Luxford became more confirmed in that opinion. About 7 a.m. on 17 Feb. Luxford went into the bedroom where Stapleton and 4 of Mr and Mrs Booth's children slept. Stapleton was dressed and was by the side of a hand-basin in which there was some water the colour of which Luxford did not observe. Stapleton asked her as soon as she came in whether she smelt anything and Luxford said that she did not. She then told Luxford that she had had a stomach ache very bad and had used the pot and said that she would take down the slop-pail which Luxford had not observed but believed it was in the closet in the same room, its usual place. Luxford then swept up the fireside and saw the bed-foot carpet placed on a screen before the fire in the same bedroom and asked Stapleton how it came wet. She told her that one of the children had thrown the pot over it and she had washed it out. Luxford also observed that the floor at the foot of the bed was also wet and Stapleton said it was occasioned by the pot falling over and she had washed it over, and while Luxford was there she again washed it. She went downstairs with the pail while Luxford was sweeping up the fireside. After her return, in less than ¼ hour, she desired Luxford not to tell Mrs Stone, the new nurse who was about to take Stapleton's place, that she had lighted the fire or that she had been up so long and Luxford promised that she would not. Luxford was always accustomed to light the fire in the bedroom and also to empty the slop-pail. Stapleton had never emptied the slop-pail before and had not, or on few occasions, lighted the fire as it was Luxford's business so to do. Nothing further passed between them at this time. Luxford thought that Stapleton looked very poorly the whole of the day and manifested reluctance in going out in the air with Mrs Booth's infant child which she was in the daily habit of doing. On the same day Luxford thought that Stapleton was in her waist grown less and so told Michell. Stapleton left Booth's service on 20 Feb., 3 days after the day on which Luxford suspected that she had delivered herself of a child, and went off by the coach going to London.

Sarah Michell, a cook in the service of Mr and Mrs Booth: She had been in their service about 13 months and Stapleton was then in the same service as a nurse. On 12 Mar. Luxford came from the privy to Michell who was in the yard near thereto and told her that there was a child in the privy. Michell went there with her and, on looking down one of the holes, saw the body of an infant floating in the water. She was present when it was taken out. About 4 months earlier she and the rest of the servants all thought that Stapleton was big with child and Michell was certain that up to 17 Feb. she was increasing in size by reason of being pregnant, but no one to her knowledge ever charged or taxed her with it. About 7 a.m. on 17 Feb. Stapleton was washing the slop-pail at the pump and Michell observed to her that it was a strange thing to see her wash a slop-pail. She replied it was and that she had been very ill in her inside all night. She afterwards was standing in the kitchen while Michell was lighting the fire there and said that she had been very poorly all night and that she then had a pain in her stomach. She then left the kitchen and Michell never saw her afterwards. Booth desired her not to mention the circumstance to her mistress or Mrs Stone or to any people of the village, but about ½ hour after the child was found he sent Goodwin to a magistrate to make the circumstance known.

John Goodwin, footman and groom in the service of Mr and Mrs Booth: He had been in Booth's service about 10 months and Stapleton was at that time in the same service as a nurse. For about 4 months prior to 17 Feb. he always violently suspected that she was with child by reason of an increase in her waist and the rest of the servants thought the same. He was so confirmed in his opinion that at the end of January he thought proper to and did make known his suspicions to James Michell, the parish beadle, and requested him to inform the parish officers of the circumstance. He was induced to do so lest Stapleton should be secretly delivered in Booth's house. About an hour after the child's body had been found Booth desired him to go to the nearest magistrate and inform him of the occurrence and he went to the house of John Willard, JP, who came from home. Goodwin then made the circumstance known to Thomas Baker, an inhabitant of Eastbourne, and they together informed Henry Lemon, one of the parish overseers.

Elizabeth Hall, housemaid in the service of Mr and Mrs Booth: She had lived in such service for about 2 months and Stapleton was living with the Booths when Hall first entered such service. When she first saw her she believed her to be big with child and had stated her opinion to Luxford and Sarah Michell. About 10 or 11 a.m. on 17 Feb. she went into the bedroom where Stapleton and 4 of the Booths' children (the eldest of whom was between 10 and 11) slept and Stapleton was sitting taking her breakfast and looking very pale and ill. She informed Hall that she had a pain in her back and a very bad headache. Hall had seen her about 7 a.m. that morning when she came to Hall, who was in the drawing-room, and requested her to button her frock behind, which she did. She had never before seen her in a frock, though she was in the daily habit of seeing her. Stapleton said it was a fine morning for a walk and observed that she could have called Hall as she had been about for hours. Between 3 and 4 p.m. of the same day Hall saw Stapleton sitting by the fire in the nursery with an additional handkerchief tied outside her dress over her neck. She complained of a violent pain in her back and she looked pale and ill and was shivering and stated that she had been walking out with the Booths' infant which had fatigued her much. Stapleton left the Booths' service on 20 Feb. and appeared much dejected and to be unwell until that day and she cried in Hall's presence. On 19 Feb. Hall went into the bedroom where Mrs Stone, the new nurse, slept and Stapleton was there crying. She told Hall, in much agony, that she had been taken ill on 16 Feb. and that Mrs Akehurst, a washerwoman, had been with Mrs Booth on that day and told her that Stapleton's linen was in a very bad state and that she was not in a fit state to travel to town but that she was determined to go though her mistress wished her not to. On 18 Feb. Hall thought that Stapleton appeared to be less in size in her waist than she had been since Hall knew her and she told her fellow servants so and they said that they were of the same opinion.

Elizabeth Stone, a nurse in the service of Mr and Mrs Booth: On 12 Feb., in consequence of a request by Mrs Booth, she came to her house to stay a few days. On the same day Mrs Booth expressed her wish that she should make the necessary inquiries whether or not Stapleton was pregnant. The next day Stone spoke to Stapleton upon the subject and she told Stone that she did not care what anyone said about it and that she was not with child. Stone made her denial known to Mrs Booth who desired Stone to send Stapleton to her, which she did. Stone had a knowledge of Stapleton before making this inquiry and from her appearances was perfectly satisfied that she was pregnant. On 18 Feb., the day after the supposed delivery, Stone went into the bedroom where Stapleton slept with the children, which was also the nursery, and observed her scouring the floor at the foot of the bed with soap and a brush and Stone told her that Mrs Booth would be very angry if she knew it. She said that she was accustomed to do so every Monday morning, but that if Mrs Booth was to know it she would be very angry.

Sarah wife of Samuel Akehurst of Eastbourne, carpenter: She washed for Mr and Mrs Booth, their children and for the nurse and under-nurse and had done so for the previous 5 months. She had always washed for Stapleton as the nurse and took away or sent for the linen every Monday morning. On Monday 18 Feb. Mary wife of William Tutt of Eastbourne, labourer, and Ann wife of William Breach of Eastbourne, labourer, the women she generally employed to wash for her, by her desire fetched away the linen and that belonging to Stapleton was put into a separate parcel, which she never observed before. She examined Stapleton's linen so sent to her to be washed and it consisted of the shift, 2 petticoats (one flannel and one linen) and a napkin, the whole of which was much stained with blood and in a state in which she had never before seen it. She had never before observed a napkin amongst Stapleton's linen and none of her linen had before been stained with blood since she had washed for her. She had often observed that the bosoms of Stapleton's shifts which she had to wash had been washed out and were more stiff than the other parts of the shift and she verily believed that the bosoms had been wetted by the flow of milk from Stapleton's breasts. Akehurst made known to Mrs Booth what she had discovered on Stapleton's linen and she wished Akehurst to speak to Stapleton on the subject and she did so in Mrs Booth's bedroom. Akehurst told her that she had observed the state of her linen and that she could not be in a fit state to travel, but Stapleton said that she was and should go the next morning.

Ann wife of William Breach of Eastbourne, labourer: On the morning of 18 Feb. she went to the Booths' house to bring away the dirty linen to be washed and the linen belonging to Stapleton was packed up by itself, put into a handkerchief and tied up, which had never been the case before. When she arrived at the house of Samuel Akehurst, whose wife washed for the Booth family, she opened the handkerchief and the contents were 2 shifts, 2 petticoats (one flannel and one linen), 2 pairs of stays, 2 night-caps, a napkin, a day-cap and 2 handkerchiefs. One of the shifts, both petticoats, one pair of stays and the napkin was stained by blood. She had never before observed any part of Stapleton's linen to be stained with blood, though she had assisted in washing her clothes for the previous 5 months. The bosoms of her shifts were stiffer than the other parts and had the appearance of being wetted by the flow of the milk from her breasts.

John Ranking of Eastbourne, surgeon: Understanding that a new-born female child had been found in the privy belonging to Booth's dwelling-house, he attended in the presence of William Dyer, constable of Eastbourne hundred, and Samuel Rason, one of the parish overseers of the poor, to inspect the body which was lying in the coach-house belonging to the dwelling-house. The body was in an advanced stage of putrefaction and in his opinion had been born more than 2 weeks. It was impossible to form any opinion whether the child was born alive or not, but it appeared to have been born perfect and the mother to have gone her full time.

At the assizes a bill of indictment was preferred which charged Stapleton on 2 counts of murdering a live female child on 17 Feb. at Eastbourne, she having earlier on that day given birth to her alone and secretly there, which child by the laws of the kingdom was a bastard: first, that she threw her into a privy belonging to Robert Booth, clerk, and containing a great quantity of human excrement and other filth by which she was suffocated and immediately died; and second, that she threw her into a pail containing a great quantity of water and filth in which she was drowned, dying immediately. The grand jury, to which the same witnesses gave evidence, rejected the bill. Stapleton, aged 22, who had been committed to gaol by the coroner on 19 Mar., pleaded not guilty to the inquest and was acquitted. ASSI 36/1; ASSI 94/2018. Cf. **214**.]

Inquests of Francis Harding Gell

393 2 Nov. 1829. The Golden Fleece, Brighton, the house of Frances Frost, widow. Jurors: Lewis Slight, Christopher Vick, William Towner, Abraham Johnson Lamprell, Richard Ranger, John Fabian, John Good, John William March, Francis Harling, Richard Marchant Lashmar, Thomas Feldwick, Henry Ratty. On 2 Nov. Edward Richardson late of Brighton, labourer, feloniously killed Mary Ann Allcorn at Brighton, striking her with his right hand on the head and face and giving her a bruise on the back of the head of which she immediately died. [ASSI 94/2047]

[Delivered to Lewes special assizes on 19 Dec. when the grand jury, to which William Larkin, Jane Hutchins, John Fellingham, Thomas Baldey, surgeon, and John Moody gave evidence, presented an indictment which charged Richardson with feloniously killing Allcorn at Brighton on 2 Nov. by striking her several times with both hands on her head, face and neck and throwing her with both hands against an iron railing and then onto the ground, thereby giving her several mortal bruises on the head, face and neck and a dislocation of the neck of which she immediately died. Richardson, aged 26, who had been committed to gaol by the coroner on the day of the inquest, pleaded not guilty but was convicted and sentenced to be transported for 7 years. ASSI 94/2047. Cf. **218**.]

394 18 Mar. 1830. Hove. Jurors: John Vallance, James Harvey Nickoll, Charles Berridge, Alexander Tate, John Bartlett, George Webb, Charles Augustine Busby, James Bartlett, Henry Downard, Henry Sargant, Richard Sturt, Thomas Kingswood. On 13 Mar. Edward Port and Thomas Hole late of Hove, labourers, feloniously killed John Philip Malleson jun. at Hove. Port, who was riding on a horse worth £10, forced the horse upon Malleson thereby throwing him to the ground and the horse with its fore-feet kicked him on the back of the head, giving him a fracture and contusion of which he languished at Hove until 15 Mar. and then died; and Hole was feloniously present aiding and abetting him. [ASSI 94/2071]

[Delivered to Horsham assizes on 22 Mar. with depositions taken by the coroner at the inquest, held at The Ship, Hove, Richard Sturt's dwelling-house, from 11 witnesses:

Thomas Watson of Brighton, coachman: He was in the service of Charles Elliott, esq., then residing at Brighton. On 13 Mar. he was driving his mistress and on returning to Brighton about 11.30 a.m. saw a person riding on horseback at full speed in the turnpike road at Hove. A woman and 2 children were in the road and endeavoured to get out of his way. They pulled off towards a gap. The horse struck one of the children down with his fore-feet and drove the woman and other child down the gap into a little garden. His mistress ordered him to get down and assist them, which he did. Whilst he was getting off, another person on horseback came up, riding slowly. Several other persons then came up and took the children away. His mistress then desired him to go to the house into which the children were carried to inquire whether a surgeon should be sent and he was requested to send one. He requested Mr Lawrence, a surgeon of North Street, Brighton,[1] to attend. When Watson first saw the woman she had one of the children in her arms. The horse fell over the bank. Watson could not tell whether the rider had any control over it. There was room for the horse to pass between the woman and his carriage. Watson pulled off to let the horse pass. The rider fell with the horse into the garden. Watson took the child which was struck up in his arms and it was immediately taken from him by some person. The horse did not appear to be hurt by the fall. The second horse was coming in a direction from Brighton. Watson believed that the child which was struck was a boy. He was nearly opposite the child when it was struck. He did not observe whether the rider used any efforts to stop the horse as his attention was directed to the children. The rider appeared much frightened when he got up. Watson was not certain whether he should know him again. He saw him for about 50 yards before the occurrence took place. He appeared to be riding after the rate of 15 m.p.h. He had since seen 2 men named Edward Port and Thomas Hole but could not identify either of them.

John Weller of Brighton, labourer: About 11.30 a.m. on 13 Mar., as he was returning from ?New Shoreham to Brighton with a load of coals, he saw 2 persons on horseback riding at full speed. They passed him nearly opposite Revd Mr Malleson's house and he gave way for them. Just after they had passed him he looked back and saw one of the horses with his rider fall over a bank into a garden. He stopped his horses and went back, when he saw William Paskins with a child in his arms. It was apparently a boy. The blood was gushing out of his nose. Weller got over into the garden and picked up a woman who was lying there. Her nose bled very much. Another person then came to his assistance and they took her to a small cottage close by, where Weller left her. He did not know the names of the persons who were riding but knew their persons. Before they came to him they appeared to him to be urging on their horses and also when they passed him. He did not observe the woman and children in the road as he passed by the garden. When one horse fell over the bank he observed the other horse near the spot. It was then standing still with his rider on its back. They appeared to him to be racing when they passed him. He did not notice whether the riders had any whips and believed they did not wear spurs. The horses had saddles and bridles upon them. He saw Mr Howell stop the riders after the affair had taken place. He asked them for their names. The rider of the horse which fell over the bank refused to give his name. He appeared to be much agitated. Weller did not hear whether anything was said by the other rider. If the riders had attempted to stop their horses as they passed him he must have noticed it. They appeared to him to be cheering them on. The child which was hurt was dressed in a blue frock. Weller had just[2] seen Edward Port. The child was struck by the horse which he rode.

William Paskins of Brighton, labourer: He was in Mr Colborne's service. On the morning of 13 Mar., as he was returning from ?New Shoreham to Brighton with a timber-carriage, he saw 2 men on horseback riding very fast along the turnpike road at Hove as if coming from Brighton. They passed his carriage and, looking back, he saw one of the horses strike a child near the road and immediately afterwards go over a bank with its rider. The child was standing at the time rather on the inside of a post close to the road. He went to the spot and took the child from Thomas Watson. The child was lying close to the post when Paskins went up. He delivered the child to a person who came up. It groaned and immediately afterwards blood came from its mouth and nose. Paskins saw a woman led into a cottage near the spot by 2 men. She seemed to be hurt and could scarcely walk. John Weller told him that 2 horses were coming very fast and Paskins pulled off to get out of the way. He could not tell whether they were racing or not. There was plenty of room for the horses to pass. He afterwards saw the other rider who had dismounted and was standing close by Paskins's timber-carriage. Paskins could not tell whether the second horse stopped immediately or not. He did not see whether the riders had whips or spurs. He had just[2] seen Edward Port. The child was struck by the horse he rode. He could swear positively to him.

Mary Ann Sibbet of Hove, single woman, aged under 21: She was nursery-maid to Revd Mr Malleson. Soon after 11 a.m. on 13 Mar. she left his house with 3 of his children and Master Peter Esdaile to cross over to the playground which was on the opposite side of the road. She had no recollection of what happened afterwards. She did not see any horse as far as she remembered. She had since been very ill in consequence of something which then occurred. When she first came to her recollection she found herself in the kitchen of Malleson's house. This was about noon on the same day.

Peter Esdaile of Hove, aged about 15: He was a pupil of Revd John Philip Malleson. In the morning of 13 Mar. he was walking with Malleson's nursemaid and 3 of his children near some rails nearly in front of Malleson's house when he saw a person on horseback riding towards them at full speed. He gave the alarm to the nurse. She looked round and ran with the children towards a gap to get out of the way. As she was going down the bank she was knocked down by the horse which fell on its side to the bottom of the bank. Directly afterwards he saw John Philip Malleson in the road. His nose was covered with blood. Mr Malleson came out and took him into the house. Esdaile did not see any other horse.

Charles Howell of Hove, esq.: In the morning of 13 Mar. he was riding from Brighton to Hove near some houses called Mills's Terrace when 2 men passed him on horseback riding at their greatest speed and urging on their horses. In consequence of some coal-carts being in the road he lost sight of them, but soon after met them returning to Brighton. One of them was then on horseback and the other leading his horse. Howell stopped them to inquire their names. The one who was mounted passed on, but Howell stopped the other by laying hold of the bridle of his horse. He refused to give his name. Howell then led him part of the way back towards Hove. There was a sack under the saddle on which he perceived the name of Goodman in red letters. He then rode back towards Brighton for the other rider. There was a sack under the saddle of his horse which had likewise the name of Goodman upon it. Neither of them told him their names. He saw one of Malleson's children carried into his house, upon which he went to inquire what had happened and in consequence of information received by him from Malleson he went off immediately for Mr Lawrence, a surgeon. He had since seen the 2 riders before the magistrates at Brighton and was informed that their names were Edward Port and Thomas Hole. The led horse was covered with dirt as if it had had a fall. On laying hold of the bridle he observed that its mouth was bloody. He had no hesitation in saying that the men were racing when they passed him. One was about 10 yards behind the other. He had that morning[3] again seen the 2 riders and the man who called himself Edward Port was the man who was leading the horse.

Revd Edward Everard of Hove, clerk: He was a clergyman residing at Wick in Hove. Between 11 a.m. and noon on 13 Mar. he was passing near Regency Square in Brighton when he observed 2 men who appeared to be horse-keepers pass him along the high road on horseback towards Hove at full speed. He saw them afterwards for the distance of 200 or 300 yards. The horses appeared to be stage-coach horses. They had cloths on them with letters marked on the cloths. The men appeared to him to be racing. They were laughing at the time. The prisoner Thomas Hole then[2] present was dressed precisely similar to one of the men who passed him on horseback.

Joseph Wisden of Hove, gent.: Soon after 11 a.m. on 13 Mar., as he was sitting with Mr Meads and Mr Sarjeant on the esplanade near the Bedford Hotel in Brighton, he saw 2 men riding furiously along the high road. He observed the name of Goodman upon one of the saddle-cloths and remarked to Meads that the riders deserved to be sent to the treadmill and that he should take an opportunity of seeing Mr Goodman to inform him in what manner his horses were treated. The dress of the men corresponded with that of the prisoners Port and Hole. In his opinion they endeavoured to make the horses go as fast as they could.

Michael Saunders, a private seaman in the Blockade Service stationed at Hove: In the morning of 13 Mar., as he was on duty at the Watch House, he saw a man on horseback riding very fast along the turnpike road. He wore, as Saunders believed, a white cloth coat. When he came opposite the Watch House he pulled up his horse suddenly and dismounted and returned to a place on the road opposite Mr Howell's where a number of persons was assembled. Saunders did not particularly notice his coat.

Harriet Bastide of Hove, single woman: She was present at the child's death. He was 3 years old and died about 8.15 p.m. on 15 Mar.

Brewster Seabrook of Brighton, surgeon: He saw the deceased on 15 Mar. and was with him from 10 a.m. until 1.30 p.m. He was dangerously ill, apparently owing to a concussion of the brain. There was no appearance of any external bruise on his head. He had a bruise on his shoulder and another on his hip. On 16 Mar., since his death, he opened his head. The skull at the back part of the head was extensively fractured. Two small pieces of the bone were detached from the other part of the skull. In his opinion the fracture was the cause of death together with the concussion of the brain. He thought the fracture was caused by a blow from the horse, not by a fall.

All the witnesses entered recognizances in £20 each to appear at the assizes with the exception of Sibbet and Esdaile, for whom Howell entered recognizances in the same sum, and Howell himself. At the assizes a bill of indictment was preferred similar to the inquest verdict except that Malleson received several mortal bruises on the head, a mortal contusion of the brain and a mortal fracture of the skull and the value of the horse was omitted. The grand jury, to which the same witnesses, with the exception of Sibbet, and also William Richardson gave evidence [William King, surgeon *struck through*], seems at first to have decided to reject the charge against Hole but it ultimately affirmed the whole bill. Port, aged 19, and Hole, 18, who had been committed to gaol by the coroner on the day of the inquest, pleaded not guilty. Port was convicted and sentenced to 12 months hard labour in the Lewes House of Correction. Hole was acquitted. ASSI 36/1; ASSI 94/2071. Cf. **219**.]

1 Probably John Lawrence who in 1839 was a surgeon to the Sussex County Hospital and living at 2 Pavilion Colonnade: *Pigot's Directory*, 237.
2 sc. *at the inquest.*
3 sc. *of 18 Mar.*

395 9 Oct. 1830. The Bridge Inn, Newhaven, Henry Smith's house. Jurors: William Cole, William Stone, George Smith, William Stevens, Thomas Eagles, Edward Brian Parkhurst, Henry Smith, Henry Dean Stone, Robert Brooke, Thomas Stone, Thomas Tasker, Charles William Towner. On 8 Oct. Harry Winter late of Newhaven, mariner, murdered Ann Winter at Newhaven with an iron poker which he held in his right hand, striking her several times on the head, face, sides and other parts of her body and thereby giving her several mortal bruises and wounds on the head, face, sides and other parts, a mortal fracture of the skull and mortal fractures of 3 of her left ribs of which she immediately died. [ASSI 94/2073]

[Delivered to Lewes special assizes on 18 Dec. when the grand jury, to which Sarah Lower, Elizabeth and Albert Goodright, William Michael Mantell, Martha Lower, William Ellis, William King, Ann Dyer, Elizabeth Head, Charles Verral, surgeon, and John Bissett, surgeon, gave evidence, presented an indictment similar to the inquest verdict except that the weapon was a piece of iron worth 1s and the blows were to Ann Winter's head, stomach, back and sides whereby she received several mortal bruises, fractures and wounds. Harry Winter, aged 58, who had been committed to gaol by the coroner on the day of the inquest, pleaded not guilty and was acquitted of murder but convicted of manslaughter and sentenced to transportation for life. ASSI 94/2073.]

396 28 Mar. 1831. The Union, Brighton, Richard Shoosmith's dwelling-house. Jurors: James Lloyd, James Dench, Philip Wymark, James Dunk, John Nye, William Butcher, John Ellis, John Pennifold, John Rose, John Knight, William Brigden, William King. On 27 Mar. William Ockenden late of Patcham, labourer, murdered James Crosweller at Patcham with a large stick of no value which he held in both hands, giving him a bruise on the right side of the head near the temple of which he languished at Patcham and Brighton for about 9 hours and then died at Brighton on the same day. [ASSI 94/2103]

[Delivered to Lewes assizes on 30 July when the grand jury, to which Solomon Stone, George Boxall, Thomas Peters, Benjamin Grinsted, John Comber, Thomas Bartlett, William Long, surgeon, and John Caudle, surgeon, gave evidence, presented an indictment which charged Ockenden with murdering Crosweller at Patcham on 27 Mar. by striking him on the head with a piece of wood which he held in both hands and giving him a bruise, a fracture of the skull and a contusion of the brain of all of which he immediately died. Ockenden pleaded not guilty and was acquitted of murder but convicted of manslaughter and sentenced to 9 months in gaol. ASSI 94/2103.]

397 16 July 1831. The Globe, Brighton, the house of Elizabeth Wright, widow. Jurors: William Paul, James Feldwicke, William Tankard, Richard Butcher, John Smith, Richard Howell, Denis Breach, James French, Benjamin Tully, John Higdon, Richard Reed, Michael Botting. On 14 July Patrick Tincey late of Brighton, labourer, feloniously killed Hannah Tincey at Brighton, striking her on the head and left temple with his right hand and giving her a bruise on the left temple of which she immediately died. [ASSI 94/2103]

[Delivered with **396**. At the assizes the grand jury, to which Catherine Callaghan, Mary Gorman, William Long, surgeon, William and Ann Foley and Lucy Hills gave evidence, presented an indictment which charged Patrick Tincey with feloniously killing Hannah Tincey at Brighton on 14 July by striking her on the head and temples with his fists and giving her several bruises and wounds on the head and temples and several ruptures of blood vessels of the brain of all of which she immediately died. Patrick Tincey, tinman, aged 39, who had been committed to gaol by the coroner on the day of the inquest, pleaded not guilty and was acquitted. ASSI 94/2103.]

Inquests of John Luttman Ellis

398 12 Aug. 1831. John Balcombe's house, Heathfield. Jurors: Samuel Baker, John Baker, John Waters, John Geer, Thomas Knight sen., Thomas Knight jun., Thomas Roades, George Ellis, James Haffenden, Henry Winchester, John Covell, Benjamin Bryant. On 1 Aug. Thomas White late of Heathfield, labourer, murdered Thomas Pilbeam at Heathfield with a large wooden weapon or bludgeon of no value which he held in both hands, striking him on the head and giving him a fracture 10 inches long of which he languished at Heathfield until 9 Aug. and then died. [ASSI 94/2104]

[Delivered to Lewes special assizes on 10 Dec. when the grand jury, to which Mary Pilbeam, Sarah and Lily White, Thomas Barton, George Haffenden, William Stone, surgeon, Robert Colgate, surgeon, [Thomas Rhoades *struck through*] and Boyd Silvester gave evidence, presented an indictment similar to the inquest verdict except that the weapon was a piece of wood worth 1d and White struck Pilbeam several times, giving him a mortal bruise on the head and a mortal fracture of the skull. White, aged 36, who had been committed to gaol by the coroner on the day of the inquest, pleaded not guilty and was acquitted of murder but convicted of manslaughter and sentenced to transportation for life. ASSI 94/2104.]

399 14 Aug. 1831. The Crown and Anchor, Preston, Elizabeth Ayres's house. Jurors: Thomas Scrase, George Blaker, William Tanner, Charles Newman, William Botting, William Butcher, John Hammond, George Downs, George Over, Joshua Rowland, John Bartlett, Charles Augustine Busby. On 14 July John Holloway late of Brighton, labourer, murdered Celia Holloway at Preston with a sharp instrument worth 6d, cutting her on the neck and throat and thereby severing her head from her body of which she immediately died. [ASSI 94/2104]

[Delivered with **398**. At the assizes the grand jury, to which David Maskell, Gabriel Gillam, William Elphick, Samuel Duly, William Mewett, William Pilbeam, John Hargraves, Daniel Richardson, Somers Clarke, Charles Chatfield, William Hely, Charles Orchard, George Alfred Gainwood, George Nye, James Thoburn, Solomon Nathan Berncastle, Isaac Tester, Frances Hawkins, James, Amelia and Frances Symonds, Catherine Bishop, Ruth Bashford, Lydia Symonds, Ann Dawes, [Sarah Tunnell *struck through*][1], Frances Taylor, Mary and James Marchant, Elizabeth Humphry, Mary Allcorn, Daniel Manthorp Folkard, Ann Leaver, Ann Brown, Matilda Johnson, William Gawan, William Johnson, Mary Gawan, Elizabeth Mathews, William Gale, Mary Golds, Charlotte Thomas, Robert Salvage, Robert Harvey, George Mathews, [Harriet Holloway *struck through but ticked*], and Joseph Allcorn [William Stendman *struck through but ticked*] gave evidence, presented an indictment which charged John William Holloway, labourer, and Ann Kennett, spinster, both late of Brighton, on 3 counts of murdering Celia Holloway on 14 July at Brighton: the first, that both fastened a cord worth 1d round her neck and throat and strangled her whereby she immediately died; the second, that Holloway strangled her as above and that Kennett was feloniously present aiding and abetting him; and the third, that Holloway cut her on the neck and throat with a knife worth 6d which he held in his right hand, giving her a wound 5 inches long and 3 inches deep of which she immediately died, and that Kennett was feloniously present aiding and abetting him. John Holloway, mariner, aged 25, who had been committed to gaol by the coroner on the day of the inquest charged at the inquest with the murder of his wife Celia at Brighton, and Kennett, aged 23, committed by David Scott, bt, JP, on 1 Sept. charged with feloniously receiving and harbouring John Holloway alias Goldsmith knowing that he had murdered his wife, pleaded not guilty. Holloway was convicted and sentenced to be hanged on 16 Dec. and then dissected and anatomized. Kennett was acquitted but ordered to remain in gaol until the assizes of 19 Mar. 1832. ASSI 94/2104; ASSI 94/2135. Cf. *SCM*, V, 723–733.]

1 In pencil against her name: *to be called upon her recognizance.*

Inquests of Francis Harding Gell

400 31 Aug. 1831. The White Horse, Rottingdean, Samuel Sutton's house. Jurors: James Ingram, John Farncombe, Henry Kennedy, Charles Beard, John Cornford, Thomas Richardson, John Miller, Henry Hide, John Hide, James Champion, Samuel Sutton, William Dumbrell. On 28 Aug. William Hemsley and Henry Brooker late of Rottingdean, labourers, feloniously killed Mary Dunn at Rottingdean, striking her on the head and right temple with both their hands and giving her a bruise on the right temple of which she immediately died. [ASSI 94/2104]

[Delivered with **398**. At the assizes the grand jury, to which Elizabeth Kelly, Harry Bishop, William Simon Clarke, James Jupp, John Rich, James Newman, Thomas March, William Gibson, Henry Crunden, Thomas Patching, Thomas Walls, William Peirce and Thomas Jupp gave evidence, presented an indictment which charged Hemsley and Brooker on 5 counts of the manslaughter of Dunn on 28 Aug. at Rottingdean: the first, that with both hands Hemsley struck her on the head and right side and threw her to the ground and, while she was on the ground, struck and kicked her on the head, neck, breast, belly, sides and back with both his hands, legs and feet, thereby breaking 2 of her ribs and forcing one rib into her lungs and giving her 3 wounds — 2 on the right side of the head, each 7 inches wide and 4 inches deep, and the other on the right side 6 inches wide and 6 inches deep — of which she immediately died; the second, that he struck her on the head and body with his fists, giving her a wound on the right side of the head 7 inches wide and 4 inches deep of which she immediately died; the third, that with his hands and arms he threw her over a high and dangerous cliff near the sea onto the sea-shore below, thereby giving her 2 bruises and wounds — one on the right side of the head 7 inches wide and 6 inches deep and the other on the right side whereby 2 of her ribs were broken — of which she immediately died; the fourth, that, knowing that she was near the edge of a high and dangerous cliff near the sea-shore and that if she were pursued and frightened there was great and immediate danger of her falling over the cliff, he pursued and threatened to beat her and frightened her so that she fell over the edge of the cliff and with great force onto the ground below and thereby received 2 wounds — one on the right side of the head 7 inches wide and 4 inches deep and the other on the right side 7 inches wide and 6 inches deep — of which she immediately died; and the fifth, that he threw her with both hands into the sea whereby she was drowned, dying immediately. All counts charged Brooker with being feloniously present aiding and abetting Hemsley. Hemsley, aged 21, and Brooker, 20, who had been committed to gaol by the coroner on the day of the inquest, were discharged on entering into recognizances in £40 each, each with 2 sureties in £20 each, to appear and answer when called upon to do so. That was probably at the Lewes assizes of 19 Mar. 1832 with whose records the indictment is filed. ASSI 94/2104; ASSI 94/2135.]

401 24 Apr. 1832. The White Horse, Brighton, Stephen Tutt Hodd's house. Jurors: Thomas Rowell, William Tozer, William Whitfield Hemsley, James French, David Ramsay Kerr Cooke, William Bowdidge, Thomas Marchant, John Smith, Francis Moone, William Spears, Jonathan Cheesman, Thomas Killick. The inquest was adjourned.
6 p.m. on 26 Apr. Brighton. On 23 Apr. James Gale late of Brighton, cabinet-maker, feloniously killed James Launder at Brighton, striking him on the head and the right side of the forehead and giving him a bruise of which he immediately died. [ASSI 94/2136]

[Delivered to Lewes assizes on 4 Aug. when the grand jury, to which George Launder, James Richardson, Joseph Hayselden, William Blackwell, David Wilkins, William Nash, Henry Solomon, William St George Davis, surgeon, [Sarah Beeching *struck through*] and Henry Nye gave evidence, presented an indictment which charged Gale, labourer, with feloniously killing Launder at Brighton on 23 Apr. by striking him with both fists on the head, face, chest and various parts of the body, thereby throwing him to the ground and giving him ruptures of several blood vessels in the head of which he immediately died. Gale, aged 23, who had been committed to gaol on 6[1] Apr. by the coroner and bailed on 14 May, pleaded not guilty but was convicted and sentenced to one month in gaol. ASSI 94/2136.]

1 Recte *26*.

402 22 May 1832. The Castle, Brighton, George Shiers's house. Jurors: Lewis Slight, Edward Blaker, John Poune, Benjamin Wood, John Yearsley, Uriah Lane, John Thomas, John Holford, George Chassereau, William Jolly, Robert Perry, William Weston. On

18 May Edward Heath late of Brighton, journeyman chemist, being employed at Brighton to make up a prescription for George Burdett, wilfully, negligently and unlawfully sent him, instead of the medicine directed by the prescription, a large quantity, viz 10 drachms, of a noxious liquid called oil of tar to drink; and Burdett, not knowing it was oil of tar but believing it to be the medicine directed to be prepared by the prescription, on 19 May drank it at Brighton and thereupon became sick and distempered in his body of which he languished at Brighton until the next day and then died. So Heath feloniously killed him. [ASSI 94/2136]

[Delivered with **401**. At the assizes the grand jury, to which [John Head Burdett *struck through*], Ann Wells, James Brady, Frances Ann Denham, John Dill, surgeon, Thomas Yates, surgeon, and James Matthews gave evidence, presented an indictment similar to the inquest verdict except that Heath, labourer, gave the oil of tar to Burdett on 19 May. Heath, chemist, aged 22, who had been committed to gaol on 25 May by W[illiam], Seymour, JP, charged on the inquest and had been bailed on 9 June, surrendered, pleaded not guilty and was acquitted. ASSI 94/2136.]

403 27 July 1832. The Bull, Ditchling, William Hubbard's house. Jurors: James Browne, John Tanner, Stephen Rowland, Peter Rowland, Thomas Homewood, Thomas Tester, John Howell, John Tamplin Parsons, James Edwards, Thomas Sinnock, Thomas Goldsmith, Thomas Hallett. On 25 July James Collins late of Keymer, labourer, feloniously killed Moses Morgan at Ditchling, striking him with his right hand on the head and under the left ear and thereby giving him a bruise on the left ear of which he immediately died. [ASSI 94/2136]

[Delivered with **401**. At the assizes the grand jury, to which Thomas Miller, Jonathan Stevens, Patrick Hunt, Thomas Walter and Robert Boddington, surgeon, gave evidence, presented an indictment which charged Collins late of Ditchling, labourer, with feloniously killing Morgan at Ditchling on 25 July by striking him with his fists on the head, neck, stomach, shoulders and other parts of the body and throwing him to the ground, thereby giving him several bruises on the head and left side of the neck and ruptures of several blood vessels in the head of all of which he immediately died. Collins, aged 23, who had been committed to gaol by the coroner on the day of the inquest, pleaded not guilty and was acquitted. ASSI 94/2136.]

404 31 May 1833. Brighton Poorhouse. Jurors: Robert Loder, John Coventry, Joseph Wilmshurst, Robert Williams, James Bromley, James Taylor, Thomas Lulham, James Legg, William Spears, John Martin, Alexander Lowe, Edward Chatfield. The inquest was adjourned.

9 a.m. on 1 June. Brighton Town Hall. On 29 May William Gould late of Brighton, labourer, feloniously killed George Walker at Brighton, striking him with both hands on the head and the right and left temples and giving him several bruises of which he languished at Brighton until the next day and then died. [ASSI 94/2169]

[Delivered to Lewes assizes on 27 July with 16 depositions and Gould's examination, all taken by the coroner at the inquest, the first 10 depositions at the poorhouse on 31 May, the final 6 and the examination at the Town Hall on 1 June:

Charles Sayers: He was a boat-maker and lived at 27 Upper Russell Street, Brighton. A little before 8 p.m. on 29 May he went into the tap-room of the Running Horse public house in King Street, Brighton, and remained there until a little before 11 p.m. Walker came into the room about ½ hour before Sayers went away, leaving him in the house. Whilst he was in the tap-room he wished to drink some of Sayers's beer but he refused to let him. He appeared to be tipsy but not very bad. Sayers never saw him before. Gould, the soldier then[1] in custody, and a sergeant were the only persons present. Sayers did not see Walker have any liquor. He was standing at the bar when Sayers went away. Sayers saw no blow or marks upon him whilst he was there. Sayers told the sergeant that Walker was tipsy and he should not give him any beer. Walker told the sergeant that he had been abroad. He went out of the tap-room to the bar of his own accord. The soldiers did not appear to know him. They were there before Sayers went. They were quartered there. All were sober except Walker. The soldiers and Sayers had 2 pots of beer between them. Sayers paid for one pot. Walker was talking to the landlord whilst he was at the bar.

John Peters: He was a servant out of place and lodged at the Running Horse. About 11 p.m. on 29 May he went to the tap-room. Sayers, Gould, Sgt James Taylor and Walker were there. Walker was talking to the soldiers about being abroad. There appeared to be no angry feeling between them. Sayers left the room about 10 minutes after Peters went in. Walker appeared to be in liquor but was not what they call drunk. He was not quarrelsome. Whilst Sayers was there Walker attempted to take some of his beer. Sayers told him he should not have any. The landlord, James Stokes, came in just after 11 p.m. and told the party it was past 11 p.m. and time for them to go. He addressed this to Sayers and Walker. Walker got up and went to the bar and had a glass of gin there. Peters had followed him into the bar. After he had drunk the gin, Stokes said: 'Now, my friend, you had better go out.' Some conversation passed between them as to the payment for the gin. Walker hesitated at first about paying, but paid for it very soon after. Stokes again requested him to go out. Whilst this was going on Gould came along the passage leading from the tap-room towards the front door, took Walker by the arm and told him he must go out — it was time. Peters believed it was his left arm. A moment or two after, Peters heard the noise of a person falling in the street. He then ran out into the street where he found Walker lying on his back straight across the road. He was not quite certain whether Walker had cleared the kerb-stone of the pavement or not. There are 2 steps from the house into the street. Gould was standing in the passage at the time and went out to assist Walker. Two men came along and helped them to take him into a fly-shed close by. They laid him down there, considering him intoxicated, and then left him. Peters passed Gould in the passage as he went to assist Walker. Whilst they were raising him, Gould said that Walker had fallen down from the steps. Peters saw no blood where he fell. Two of them carried him into the shed. Gould took hold of his arm gently and Walker looked round at him, but made no resistance. As far as Peters could recollect, Gould took hold of the arm which was next to the street. When Peters went downstairs about 8.30 a.m. on 30 May he was informed that Walker was lying in a dangerous state, upon which he went to the shed where he found him lying on his back — one of his knees was bent upwards — as near as possible where he left him overnight. He was unable to speak. His eyes were much swollen and his nose clotted with congealed blood. Mr Caudle, a surgeon,[2] was sent for. He examined Walker's head; the back part was bruised. According to the best of Peters's recollection and belief Walker was lying on his back when he went to pick him up with his feet towards the door of the house.

Henry Dine: He was a fisherman and lived at 17 Orange Row, Brighton. He knew Walker. A few minutes after 11 p.m. on 29 May Dine was coming up King Street when he observed some persons standing nearly opposite the door of the Running Horse. He went to the spot and saw a man lying on the ground upon his back with his feet towards the door. There might be 5 or 6 persons round him. His feet were lying on the pavement. Dine enquired what was the matter with him and some of the party said he was drunk. Gould and Peters were stooping down endeavouring to raise him. Gould spoke to Walker about getting him home but received no answer. Dine recommended taking him to a stable and assisted in taking him to the fly-shed. Some of Walker's blood — he believed from his head — fell upon Dine's frock. He did not observe any bruise on him. Four persons assisted in carrying him to the shed. Dine did not recollect Walker that night. He left Gould in the shed with several others. Dine had worked with Walker. He would sometimes get drunk. The street door of the Running Horse was shut whilst he was lying in the street.

James Taylor: He was a sergeant in the 52nd[3] Regiment of Foot and was quartered at the Running Horse. He and Gould were together in the tap-room from 8 p.m. until about 11.10 p.m. on 29 May. Sayers came into the tap-room about 8 p.m. and sat down with them. Walker came into the room about 10.40 or 10.45. He was somewhat in liquor but able to take care of himself. He seated himself by them and in the course of conversation told Taylor he had been a soldier and had been abroad, but did not tell him in what regiment or where. Gould, Sayers and Taylor had 2 pots of beer in the course of the evening. Walker came in whilst they were drinking their first pot. He took hold of the pot but whether he drank any beer Taylor could not say. Sayers refused to let him have any beer upon which he left the room. Taylor did not see him again until the next morning. Gould went out of the tap-room 2 or 3 minutes after Walker. Taylor remained there until about 11.20. Gould was gone only a few minutes and then came back to the tap-room. He said nothing to Taylor about Walker. Whilst Taylor was in bed the next morning Gould came to him between 7 and 8 a.m. and told him that Walker, who was in liquor overnight, was lying in the shed, that he had had a fall and was bruised and had black eyes and that he had helped to carry him into the shed. Peters was in the tap-room in the course of the evening. If any high words had passed at the bar Taylor might have heard them in the tap-room. The tap-room door was not shut when Gould went out nor when Walker went out.

James Stokes: He was the landlord of the Running Horse. He saw Walker in his tap-room about 10.55 p.m. on 29 May but did not know when he came in. He was sitting down with Taylor, Gould, Sayers and Peters. Stokes went into the tap-room in consequence of hearing some loud talking. Walker was talking about being abroad and said he knew more about being abroad than all the soldiers together. Taylor requested him to speak lower and not to make such a noise. Stokes then shut up the house, leaving the street door ajar, and went again into the tap-room. He said to the soldiers: 'Now it's time to go to bed' and told Walker he was keeping him up and requested him to go. He waited a few seconds and Walker followed. Stokes stepped into the bar in order to leave the passage clear for him. Instead of going out Walker stepped into a little recess and requested Stokes to give him a glass of gin which he did. Walker made a slight resistance about paying, but soon after did so. Stokes requested him again to go out. Gould then came out of the tap-room along the passage and took Walker gently by the left arm and said: 'Now, old man, you had better go; it is time you were gone.' Gould then turned him round in the passage, but as Walker slightly resisted him Gould put his hand to his back as if to keep him from coming back. Stokes could not see Walker go out of the street door. He was within 2 or 3 feet of the door when Gould put up his hand. Immediately after Stokes found Walker was out of the door he stepped forward to close it to prevent him from coming in again. He then saw Walker on the ground on his back in the street. Gould was in the house and Stokes requested him and Peters to go out to put the old man on his feet. Stokes heard the sound of a fall when he left the house. Taylor was in the tap-room. When Gould and Peters went out to assist Walker, Stokes shut the door and afterwards let them in. He did not think they said anything about Walker on their return. Stokes never saw Walker before that evening to his knowledge. He saw him the next morning. His eyes were much puffed up. If he had not known that he had had a fall he should have supposed the blackness about his eyes to have been occasioned by a blow. He thought he requested Gould to go out to see Walker in the morning. He had been informed by Mr Jupp's man of the state in which he was lying in the fly-shed. In Stokes's opinion Gould was not drunk.

Thomas Swann: He was a flyman and lived in King Street. About 5.30 a.m. on 30 May he found Walker lying upon his face in Swann's fly-shed, close by a fly. It was an open shed. The gates of the yard in which it was situated did not lock but were kept shut by a latch. Walker was lying on the boulders. Swann spoke to him twice but he returned him no answer.

Eleanor Bowley: She was a widow and lived at 40 King Street, exactly opposite the Running Horse. A little after 11 p.m. on 29 May, as she was washing in the lower part of her house, she heard the noise of a person falling violently either on the pavement or against a door. She immediately went upstairs, when she saw a man lying on the ground surrounded by 2 or 3 persons. One of them said: 'I don't know who he is; he says he has been an old soldier. Help me to lift him into the stable.' She had heard no quarrelling before and if there had been a noise at the door of the Running Horse she must have heard it. It appeared to her that the man was lying on or near a trap-door in front of the house. The persons had begun to lift him up before she looked out.

George Jupp: He was a flyman at Brighton. His fly stood in King Street. About 7.30 a.m. on 30 May he went to the shed in which his fly was kept and saw a man lying on the ground upon his face. He supposed him to be in liquor. He fed his horse and then went back to the shed with a person named Knight. They endeavoured to get the man to speak but without effect. They turned him over on his back. His eyes were very black indeed. He had bled at the nose but there were no marks of blood at the spot. Knight went for a policeman and a surgeon.

Levi Stead: He was a whitesmith and lived at 9 Frederick Street, Brighton. About 11 p.m. or soon after on 29 May Thomas Allcorn and he were talking at the top of King Street about 60 yards from the Running Horse when he heard a great rush and 3 or 4 persons came out of the Running Horse. One of them fell very heavily, apparently as if on a trap-door. One of the party said: 'Damn you, be off or we'll make you.' Allcorn and Stead went towards the Running Horse. Stead saw a man lying on his face upon the trap-door and his feet upon the pavement. Two of the persons who came out of the house walked down King Street and 2 returned into the house. Allcorn and Stead were discussing together whether the man was dead or drunk and, whilst doing so, a soldier came out of the Running Horse and said: 'Damn you, you will remember drinking a man's beer or calling a soldier.' Two men followed him out of the house. One of them wore a coat and the other a striped jacket. Several persons gathered round and the soldier told them the man had been abusive in the house and had told them he had been an old soldier himself. As the man did not stir, Stead loosened his handkerchief and the soldier assisted him in turning him over on his back. The soldier and another man then took him into the stable-yard and Stead saw no more of him. When he first went up to the man his face was doubled towards his breast. Stead could not say whether the soldier then[1] in custody was the one who came out of the house. Stead and Allcorn were the first persons who went up to the man.

Thomas Allcorn: He was a shoemaker and lived at 43 Bread Street, Brighton. About 11.15 p.m. on 29 May he and Levi Stead were talking at the top of King Street. They had been there about 10 or 15 minutes when he saw 3 or 4 men come out of the Running Horse. One of them fell very heavy as if he had fallen upon a trap-door. Allcorn heard someone say once or twice: 'Damn you, go away.' Two of the persons then went down the street and the others returned into the house. Stead and Allcorn then went to the spot, where they found a man lying upon his face between the window of the Running Horse and the street door. His head was on the trap-door and the rest of his body on the bricks. His head was doubled on his breast and his arms straight by his body. Stead and Allcorn were going to move him when 2 persons came out of the Running Horse. The first had a dark frock-coat and white trousers but no hat. The second wore a short red jacket trimmed with lace and a foraging-cap and appeared to be a soldier. He said: 'He's only drunk' and began to move him on his back. Stead loosened his neckerchief. The soldier said the man had been in there calling him and his comrade anything but a soldier and wanted to force himself into their company and to drink their beer, that he had no money to pay for it and that he fell out of doors. Henry Dine then came by. The soldier called to him, saying: 'Henry, help me to get this man up.' Stokes looked out and wished to know what was the matter but did not come into the street. Allcorn thought the man was drunk.

Richard Vinall: He was footboy to Mr Blaker of Brighton, surgeon. He was returning home through King Street about 11.15 p.m. on 29 May when he saw a man lying on his face in front of the Running Horse. His head was on the trap-door of the house. A soldier and 2 or 3 other persons were standing round him. He should not know the soldier again. He was a foot-soldier. His jacket was unbuttoned. He heard the soldier say he was not so drunk as he pretended to be. A person named Dine then came up the street. Dine and the soldier took hold of the man by the arms and some other person by the legs and carried him towards the fly shed. Vinall knew Dine before. Vinall was there about 10 minutes. The door of the Running Horse was partly open. *Annotated*: Not bound over.

Henry Potter: He lived with Mr Bromley of North Street, Brighton. He was with Vinall about 11.10 or 11.15 p.m. on 29 May and went with him into King Street where he saw a man lying upon his face in front of the Running Horse. His head and the upper part of his body was lying on a trap-door and the lower part on the pavement. The soldier then[4] present and in custody with 2 or 3 other persons were standing by looking at him. The soldier said he did not think the man was so drunk as he made out to be. Dine was one of the persons present. He said: 'Let's take him away to the fly-shed.' The soldier said to Dine: 'I know you, Harry, don't I?' The soldier said: 'The man came in and said he had been a soldier.' The soldier and Dine lifted the man up but he fell down again on the boards of the trap-door, apparently lifeless.

Henry Nye: He was a policeman at Brighton. About 9 a.m. on 30 May he was on duty in North Street and, being informed that a man was lying in a dangerous state in the Running Horse yard, he went to the spot and found him lying on his back in the fly-shed. He lifted him up and sent for Mr Caudle, a surgeon.[2] The man could not move and was completely insensible. Caudle arrived in a few minutes. In the meantime Nye sent for some water and a sponge. The man breathed with great difficulty, his nose being stopped up with congealed blood. There was blood about his mouth which appeared to have proceeded from his nose. When Caudle came he examined the head and felt the pulse. Nye observed a wound near the back of his head. There was blood round it. Caudle said the man was dangerous and ought to be removed immediately. In consequence of this Nye procured a fly and took him to the poorhouse. Nye understood he was sent for by the landlord of the Running Horse. The landlord, the soldier in custody and the sergeant came into the yard and assisted in placing the man in the fly. Nye enquired of the landlord how it happened. He told him the man came to his house about 11 p.m. and went through into the tap-room; that he was upstairs when the man came in and when he went down, hearing a strange voice rather loud, he went into the tap-room to see what was the matter; that the man was disputing with the soldiers something about his having been abroad and having seen more places than they had; it was a mere wrangle and did not amount to a quarrel; that he was obliged to shut up his house and requested the soldiers to go to bed and the man to leave the house; that the man then left the tap-room and went to the bar and requested him to let him have a glass of gin; that whilst the man was talking to him at the bar, wishing him to leave, the soldier came and said: 'Come, old boy' or something of that sort, 'you had better go out of the house' and at the same time took him by the arm and put him towards the door and he believed he saw the soldier's hand against his back and that he knew no more until the man fell in the street; he then desired the soldier and another young man to go out and pick him up and put him on his legs; he did not go out himself.

William Long: He was a surgeon and resided at Brighton. He saw the deceased at the poorhouse about 10 a.m. on 30 May. He was insensible and apparently suffering from pressure on the brain. Long had his head shaved for the purpose of examining it. He found a small contused wound on the upper part of the right side of the head. He then bled him and called in Mr Blaker. He and Blaker saw him together between noon and 1 p.m. and decided that Long should trepan him, which he did. He found a fracture immediately under the wound extending for about 3 inches, a very slight depression of the bone; the edges of the bone at the fracture were separated. Long removed a large piece of coagulated blood under the part of the bone he took away; also several fragments of bone. The man appeared relieved by the operation but did not regain his senses. Long saw him again between 9 and 10 p.m. He was then dying. He died about an hour afterwards. His body was much bruised on the left side of the chest. The arm from the elbow-joint to the shoulder was much swollen. There was a severe bruise on the left temple and both eyes, the left more particularly, were much swollen, as were the eyelids. Long examined the body on the evening of 31 May after it had been viewed by the jury. He opened the head. Under the scalp there was a good deal of extravasated blood, more particularly on the back part of the left side and on the left temple. There was a fracture extending from the back part of the right ear towards the right temple for about 4 inches or a little more. Long then removed the skull-cap and found a great quantity of extravasated blood between the dura mater and the bone. He found a considerable lesion of the brain on the left side; a great deal of extravasated blood in the substance of the brain. Within the upper part of the orbit of the left eye there was a fracture with a great quantity of extravasated blood opposite to it. Long thought his life could not have been saved by immediate medical aid. His opinion was that the mischief to the head was the cause of death, that it could not have been produced by one blow, that the fracture within the orbit of the left eye must have been produced by some blunt instrument being forced against it. He thought it would not have been occasioned by a blow from a fist because the portion of the bone fractured was pushed upwards towards the brain. It might have been caused by falling upon some blunt projecting substance. The bruise on the upper part of the back temple might have been produced by the same fall or blow. The wound on the upper part of the right side of the head with the fracture immediately under it could not have been occasioned by the same fall or blow because the lower part of the bone was pushed in. Either of the fractures on the right or left side of the head would have produced death. The left arm appeared to have been bruised in wrestling, as if by a strong grasp. The bruise on the left side of the chest appeared to have arisen from a struggle, but it might have happened from a fall.

William Marner: He was a labourer in the service of Mr Richardson of Spring Gardens, Brighton, coal-merchant. He and Henry Tutt went about the same time into the yard near the Running Horse about 5.30 a.m. on 30 May. They found the deceased lying in the shed with his face downwards, partly on his side. He was alive. Marner observed to Tutt that he thought he was drunk enough. They did not examine him particularly, but, thinking he was drunk, went about their business. They called out to him and he made some noise like fetching his breath hard.

Peter Knight: He was a stableman at Brighton and used a stable in the yard close to the Running Horse. He went to his stable about 7.30 a.m. on 30 May and on looking into the fly-shed saw a man lying flat on his face with his head upon his left hand. His right hand was under the spokes of the near wheel of the fly. Knight tried to wake him up but without success, upon which with the assistance of his master he turned him upon his back. Finding him to be in a dreadful state, he went into the Running Horse and told the landlord of it. He requested Knight to go for a policeman, which he did, and by the desire of the policeman he went for a surgeon.

William Gould: The deceased came into the house about 10.45 or 10.50 p.m. and began to talk to the sergeant about being an older soldier than he was. He took hold of the beer and drank twice and was then refused by Sayers. He then went out to the bar. Gould believed he had a glass of gin. Gould was going out of the door and, seeing the man there, took hold of his arm. He turned round and looked at Gould and went out of door. The landlord was going to shut the door and told Gould the man had fallen down in the middle of the road and asked him to go out and pick him up. He picked him up and carried him under the shed.

At the assizes a bill of indictment was preferred which charged Gould with feloniously killing Walker at Brighton on 29 May by striking him with his fists on the head and face and with both hands and arms violently throwing him onto the ground and a stone pavement and against a wooden trap-door, thereby giving him several bruises and wounds on the head and face and 2 fractures of the skull of all of which he languished at Brighton until the next day and then died. The grand jury, to which all the deponents of 31 May and 1 June except Vinall gave evidence, rejected the bill. Gould, aged 29, who had been committed to gaol by the coroner on 1 June, pleaded not guilty to the inquest and was acquitted. ASSI 36/2; ASSI 94/2169.]

1 sc. *on 31 May.*
2 John Caudle: cf. **396**.
3 *Oxfordshire Light Infantry*: Swinson, 151.
4 sc. *on 1 June.*

405 28 Nov. 1835. The Maiden's Head, Uckfield, Henry Cloake's house. Jurors: Samuel Lidbetter, Thomas Shephard, John Jenner, Edward Kenward, Nicholas Kenward, George Rouse Rake, Thomas Merricks, William Fowle, Thomas Pentecost, George King, Henry Cloake, William How. On 27 Nov. Ann Chatfield late of Uckfield, single woman, alone and secretly gave birth at Uckfield to a live male child which by the laws and customs of the kingdom was a bastard and on the same day murdered him there, clasping him round the neck with both hands and strangling him, of which he immediately died.
[ASSI 94/2206]

[Delivered to Lewes assizes on 21 Mar. 1836 when a bill of indictment was preferred identical to the inquest verdict except for the omission of the child's bastardy. The grand jury, to which Mary Mannington, Jane Wheatley, Elizabeth Markwick, William Henry Covey, surgeon, and Henry Holman, surgeon, gave evidence, rejected the bill. Chatfield, aged 20 and able to read imperfectly, who had been committed to the Lewes House of Correction by the coroner on 22 Dec., seems not to have stood trial on the inquest. ASSI 94/2206.]

406 19 May 1836. The Five Bells, Chailey, Thomas Hurst's house. Jurors: George Beard, William Lupton, John Beard, Joseph Walls, Henry Brooke, Thomas Hurst, James Corney, William Hobden, Richard Russell, Gabriel Best, William Terry, Benjamin Ford. On 30 Apr. John Latter late of St John sub Castro, Lewes, labourer, feloniously killed William Allen at Newick, striking him with his right hand on the head and under the left ear and giving him a bruise on the head and left ear of which he languished at Newick and Chailey until 17 May and then died at Chailey. [ASSI 94/2207]

[Delivered to Lewes assizes on 23 July when a bill of indictment was preferred which charged Latter, late of Newick, labourer, with murdering Allen at Newick on 30 Apr. by striking him several times with both fists on the head, neck, face, breast, sides and other parts of his body and throwing him to the ground, thereby giving him a contusion and inflammation of the brain of which he languished at Newick and Chailey until 17 May and then died at Chailey. The grand jury, to which William Gatland, William Turner, Robert Bassett, Thomas Martin, Henry Pitt, William Peacock, Edmund Cause, surgeon, and Henry Chambers Verrall, surgeon, gave evidence, rejected the bill. Latter, aged 23 and able to read well, who had been committed to the Lewes House of Correction by the coroner on the day of the inquest, pleaded not guilty to the inquest and was acquitted. ASSI 94/2207.]

407 5 July 1836. The King's Arms, St John sub Castro, Lewes, James Bish's dwelling-house. Jurors: Nathan Hammond, John Elliott, Peter Broad, Durrant Ade, George Bailey, Selven Martin, Edward Everest, William Smart, Stephen Rusbridge, Thomas Birch, Edward Boore, William Bridger. The inquest was adjourned.
9 p.m. on 6 July. The Crown, All Saints, Lewes, George Bailey's dwelling-house. On 21 June Charles Buckman late of Southover, labourer, feloniously killed Robert Brand at Southover with a chalk stone of no value which he held in his right hand, throwing it onto the right side of Brand's head and giving him a wound 2 inches long and 1 inch deep of which he languished at Southover and St John sub Castro until 3 July and then died at St John sub Castro. [ASSI 94/2207]

[Delivered with **406**. At the assizes a bill of indictment was preferred similar to the inquest verdict except that the chalk was not said to be of no value and the wound was 1½ inches long and a third of an inch deep. The grand jury, to which Thomas Hollman, William Emery, Ann Allchin, Edwin Blaber and John Sheldon Armstrong, surgeon, gave evidence, rejected the bill. Buckman, aged 12 and able to read and write well, who had been committed to the Lewes House of Correction by the coroner on 6 July, pleaded not guilty to the inquest and was acquitted. ASSI 94/2207.]

408 6 Aug. 1836. The Sussex County Hospital, Brighton. Jurors: Charles Dumbrell, Thomas Mockford, John Smith, Philip Davey, George Kirkham, Denis Breach, John Corney, James Potter, Samuel Clark, George Boxall, Thomas Gooder, Samuel Taylor. On 5 Aug. William Phillips late of Brighton, labourer, feloniously killed George Thomas Daniel at Ovingdean, striking him on the head and neck with both hands and giving him a bruise of which he languished for an hour at Ovingdean and at the hospital and then died at the hospital on the same day. Christopher Lee late of Brighton, labourer, was feloniously present aiding and abetting him. [ASSI 94/2232]

[Delivered to Lewes assizes on 20 Mar. 1837 when the grand jury, to which James Morris and Edmund Joseph Furner, surgeon, gave evidence [Charles Goldring, John Bannister and William Holt were called on their recognizances but did not appear], presented an indictment which charged

Phillips and Lee late of Ovingdean, labourers, with feloniously killing Daniel at Ovingdean on 5 Aug.: Phillips striking him several times with his fists on the head, face, neck, throat, chest, sides and other parts of his body and several times throwing him to the ground, thereby giving him several bruises on the head, face, neck, throat, chest, sides and other parts and several ruptures of blood vessels in the head of all of which he languished at Ovingdean and Brighton and died at Brighton on the same day; and Lee being feloniously present aiding and abetting him. Phillips, baker, aged 19 and able to read imperfectly, who had been committed to the Lewes House of Correction by R[obert] Pedder, JP, on 8 Aug. charged with feloniously killing Daniel at Brighton, pleaded not guilty and was acquitted. Lee did not stand trial. ASSI 94/2232.]

409 17 May 1837. The Bull, Ditchling, William Hubbard's house. Jurors: Thomas Friend Bull, John Packett, Francis Scrase, Thomas Muddle, George Verrall, Nehemiah Dancey, Thomas Sinnock, Charles Wood, George French, James Edwards, Thomas Grinyer, John Butcher. The inquest was adjourned.
6 p.m. on 18 May. On 16 May George Pollard late of Westmeston, labourer, feloniously killed Amos Hemsley at Plumpton, striking him with his right hand on the head and left ear and giving him a bruise of which he languished for 12 hours at Plumpton and Ditchling and then died at Ditchling on the same day. Edward Fuller late of Streat and James Brooker late of Westmeston, labourers, were feloniously present aiding and abetting him. [ASSI 94/2233]

[Delivered to Lewes assizes on 29 July when the grand jury, to which William Hemsley, George Welfare, William White, Henry Bristow, Robert Harland Whiteman, surgeon, Thomas Walder and Thomas Brown gave evidence [John Howell was called on his recognizance but did not appear], presented an indictment which charged Pollard, Fuller and Brooker, all late of Plumpton, labourers, with feloniously killing Hemsley at Plumpton on 15 May: Pollard striking him several times with his fists on the head, face, neck, chest, sides and other parts of his body and several times violently throwing him to the ground, thereby giving him several bruises on the head, face, neck, chest, sides and other parts, several ruptures of blood vessels in the head and concussion of the brain, of all of which he languished at Plumpton and Ditchling until the next day and then died at Ditchling; and Fuller and Brooker being feloniously present aiding and abetting him. Pollard, labourer, aged 23 and able to read, Fuller, labourer, 27 and unable to read or write, and Brooker, carpenter, 25 and able to read and write imperfectly, who had been committed to the Lewes House of Correction by the coroner on 18 May, pleaded not guilty but were convicted. Pollard was fined 1s and to be imprisoned until he paid; the others were sentenced to imprisonment with hard labour in the House of Correction, Fuller for 3 calendar months and Brooker for 6 months. ASSI 94/2233.]

HASTINGS RAPE CORONERS' INQUESTS

Inquest of John Purfeild

410 22 Jan. 1689. Westfield. Jurors of the rape: John Winter, gent., John Blackman, John Fuller, William Wimble, James Wimble, Henry Weekes, gent., George Hudson, Robert Boorman, George Aston, John Boddy, William Barly, John Polhill, William Boorman, John Shaw, Francis Balcombe, William Beale, John Ford, William Clarkeson, Simon Freind, Richard Cooper, John ?Bonner, Abraham Fuller, Thomas Sivier. On 19 Jan. William Theobald late of Brede, 'carpenter', feloniously killed Ann Duplock, 'spinster', at Westfield with 'an handgunne' worth 5s 'charged' with 'gunpowder and haileshott' which he held in both hands. He 'did shoote of and discharge' it at her, striking her on the left side of the chest with the lead shot and giving her 'one mortall wound' 1 inch wide and 6 inches deep of which she immediately died. Theobald had no goods or chattels, lands or tenements in Sussex or elsewhere at that time or ever after to the jurors' knowledge. [*Damaged.*] [ASSI 94/4, m 2]

[Delivered to Horsham assizes on 20 July with another inquest into Theobald's death in gaol before the assizes. The latter, whose verdict was that Theobald had died a natural death, was delivered into King's Bench in Michaelmas but no longer survives as the indictments file is missing. ASSI 94/4, m 2; KB 29/348, m 27d.]

Inquest of George Purfeild

411 23 Jan. 1697. Westfield. Jurors of the rape: Adrian Spray, Michael Mihill, Francis Godfrey, John Body, John Smith, Richard Cooper, Richard Henley, John Baker jun., Thomas Darby sen., Richard Grayling, Thomas Brooke, Ralph Langford, Michael Punnett, Thomas Martin, John Tassell. On 21 Jan. Mary Crampe late of Westfield, 'spinster', gave birth at Westfield to a live female infant which by the laws of the kingdom 'was a bastard' and immediately murdered her, taking her in both hands, gripping her by the neck and throat and strangling her whereby she immediately died. Crampe had no goods or chattels, lands or tenements in the rape or elsewhere at that time or ever after to the jurors' knowledge. [ASSI 94/110, m 5]

[Delivered to Horsham assizes on 22 Mar. when the grand jury, to which Susannah Darby and Mary Harvey gave evidence, presented an indictment identical to the inquest verdict but omitting the last sentence. Crampe pleaded not guilty and was acquitted; she had not fled and so was discharged, paying her fees. ASSI 94/110, mm 2, 5, 6, 17d.]

Inquest of Samuel Brewer

412 31 Dec. 1707. Beckley. Jurors of the rape: Richard Martin, John Holt, Henry Steevens, Thomas Carman, Thomas Scrimas, Edward Piper, Richard Catt, John Vann, George Fryman, John Russell, Thomas Marter, John Suiters, Thomas Furminger, William Newball, Daniel Catt, Thomas Goaller. On 28 Dec. William Steevens late of Beckley, 'laborer', then being non compos mentis and 'franticke' and 'distracted' in his mind and senses, killed his daughter Mary, an infant aged 5, with a knife of iron and steel worth 1d which he held in his right hand. He 'did strike and thrust' her in the right part of the abdomen, giving her a wound 2 inches wide and 4 inches deep of which she immediately died. [ASSI 94/239, m 5]

[Delivered to East Grinstead assizes on 8 Mar. 1708 when the grand jury, to which Adam Murrells, Thomas Walker and Richard Luckins gave evidence, presented an indictment similar to the inquest verdict except that the charge was murder, no mention being made of Steevens's insanity, and the killing was about 4 p.m. on 28 Dec. Steevens pleaded not guilty and was acquitted of murder, the trial jury finding that he had killed Mary while non compos mentis; he was discharged, paying his fees. ASSI 94/239, mm 2, 6, 11d.]

Inquests of Anthony Trumble

413 24 May 1715. Battle. Jurors of the rape: Nicholas Maynard, Thomas Martin, 2Henry Cradocke, John Stunt, John Cruden, Tobias Daw, Richard Poynett, John Wells, Thomas Ager, Thomas Evernden, William Baker, Richard Cox, William Borman, William Venner, William Eldridge, Francis Sexton. On 22 May Richard Carswell and other of the king's officers duly appointed to detain and seize 'brandy' imported from overseas in vessels each containing at least 6 'gallons', being notified that certain persons unknown were assembled at Battle in order to carry off several casks or 'halfe anchors' of brandy which had recently been brought ashore near Bulverhythe, were at Battle with persons who were assisting them and met William Beeching and 2 others unknown who had in their keeping several casks of brandy recently imported and ordered them to stand and deliver to Carswell and the other officers. Beeching and the 2 others resolutely refused and Beeching, who had 'a pistoll' in his right hand 'charged with gunpowder and leaden bulletts', threatened to discharge it at James Smith, Carswell's servant, who was assisting Carswell and the other officers, whereupon Smith, who had in both hands 'a gunn' worth 4s 'charged with gunpowder and haile shott', discharged it at Beeching, giving him a wound in the left part of the body near the left breast 4 inches deep and 1 inch wide of which he immediately died. So Smith killed him in self defence to save his life. Smith had no goods or chattels, lands or tenements at that time or ever after to the jurors' knowledge. [*Damaged.*] [ASSI 94/334]

[This inquest, which is in Latin, on parchment and signed only by the coroner, was delivered to East Grinstead assizes on 4 Aug. There is another version, in English, on paper and with the signatures or marks of the coroner and jurors, as follows:

8 June, adjourned from [*blank*] May. The White Hart, Breadsell Green, Baldslow hundred. Same coroner, lawfully constituted by Thomas Holles, earl of Clare. Jurors of the hundred: [*as above*]. Witnesses: Solomon Duke, John Norrington, Richard Caswell, Thomas Butler, Thomas Martin, Thomas Foster, Robert Felle, John Wilson, Thomas Sere, James Smith, who deposed that on 22 May they, being HM's riding officers riding on the sea-coast near Hastings and having information that some smugglers were to carry away from the sea-coast several half-ankers of brandy, met together at Telham in Battle and at about 3 a.m. there came up William Beeching late of Hollington and several others unknown who had loaded 14 half-ankers of brandy on 4 horses, at which time the deponents charged them in the king's name to stand and deliver, which they accordingly did, and the deponents seized the brandy and carried it into Bartholomew Walker's house where it was secured; and shortly afterwards the deponents, watching the road, heard the trampling of horses coming up the same way and charged the persons on the horses, who had more

brandy, to stand and deliver their goods which they refused to do and, upon their resistance, Beeching rode up to Smith and threatened him that if he did not deliver a burthen-[1] or fowling-piece which Smith had a little before taken from one of the smugglers he would shoot him dead and, drawing out a pistol from under his coat, presented it to Smith's body; whereupon Smith levelled the burthen-piece at Beeching, Smith not knowing that it was charged with small shot, and it went off, shooting Beeching through the body under the left breast, of which wound he died about 7 p.m. on the same day. The jury found that Beeching came to his death by such misfortune and that Smith shot him in self defence.

At the assizes the grand jury, to which John Naughington, Thomas Butler and Solomon Luke[2] gave evidence, presented an indictment which charged James Smith late of Battle, labourer, with murdering Beeching at about 4 a.m. on 22 May with a gun worth 4s charged with gunpowder and hail-shot which he held in both hands, giving him a wound in the left part of the body near the left breast 4 inches deep and 1 inch wide of which he languished at Battle until 6 p.m. on the same day and then died. Smith pleaded not guilty and was acquitted; he had not fled and so was discharged, paying his fees. ASSI 94/334; SAY 330.]

1 sc. *birding*.
2 Recte *Duke*, a common Battle surname: PAR 236/1/1/2.

414 15 Jan. 1717. Mayfield. Jurors of the rape: John Harvey, Samuel Mott, Samuel …, John Brooker, John Mabb, John Stephens, John Diplock, Joseph Mepham, James ?Westeion, John Sands, John …, … Mowgridge, John Fleming. On 7 Jan. Thomas Parsons, John Keys and William Munck, all late of Heathfield, 'laborers', murdered Richard Seymer at Heathfield: Parsons violently throwing him to the ground with 'an axe' of iron and steel worth 6d which he held in both hands and violently striking him with the axe on the head, chest, stomach, sides, back, arms and hands of which he languished at Heathfield and Mayfield until 14 Jan. and then died at Mayfield; and Keys and Munck being feloniously present at the time of the murder aiding and abetting him. What goods or chattels, lands or tenements the 3 had at that time or ever after the jurors did not know. [*Damaged*.] [ASSI 94/353]

[Delivered to East Grinstead assizes on 25 Mar. when the grand jury, to which Thomas Sands, John Beale jun., John Sands, Thomas Moon, John Beale sen., John Langham and William Sands gave evidence, presented an indictment identical to the inquest verdict except for the omission of the blows to the back and the last sentence. Parsons, Keys and Munck pleaded not guilty. Parsons was acquitted of murder but convicted of manslaughter; he had no chattels. He then pleaded benefit of clergy and was branded on the hand and discharged, paying his fees. Keys and Munck were acquitted; they had not fled and so were discharged, paying their fees. ASSI 94/353.]

Inquest of John Collier

415 16 Mar. 1716. Fairlight. Jurors: James Baker, Richard Brattle, Thomas Easton, Samuel Messengs, Thomas Smith, Richard Blackman, Thomas Nabbs, Thomas Richardson, Thomas Avann, Edward Burden, John Butler, John Stoneham, Michael Morris. On 14 Mar. Elizabeth Stephens gave birth at Fairlight to a live female infant, which 'was a bastard', 6 weeks prematurely. On the same day the infant died a natural death at Fairlight and not from any other cause or violence. [SAS/SM 14]

[Delivered to East Grinstead assizes on 19 Mar. when a bill of indictment was preferred which charged Stephens, late of Fairlight, spinster, with giving birth to the live female bastard at Fairlight on 14 Jan. and immediately murdering her by taking her in both hands and gripping her neck and throat, thereby strangling her, of which she immediately died. The grand jury, to which Susannah Morris, Stephen Nabbs and Thomas and Elizabeth Brooke gave evidence, rejected the bill. SAS/SM 13.]

Inquest of Robert Chambers

416 26 Oct. 1735. Hollington. Jurors of the 2 townships nearest to Hollington: Richard Sevenoakes, Peter Delvey, Richard Bridger, Henry Bine, Nicholas Fry, Richard ..., Abraham Stace, John Stunt, Tobias Daw, Robert Peters, John Glazier, John Hoadly, Benjamin Bran. On 24 Oct. 2 persons unknown feloniously killed Thomas Peene at Hollington with muskets worth 16s charged with gunpowder and lead bullets which they held and discharged against Peene, giving him several wounds on the back of the head of which he immediately died. [ASSI 94/595]

[Delivered to East Grinstead assizes on 22 Mar. 1736 when a bill of indictment was preferred which charged John Elgood late of Hollington, labourer, with murdering Peene at Hollington on 24 Oct. with a gun worth 8s charged with gunpowder and a lead bullet which he held and discharged against Peene, giving him a wound on the back of the head 2 inches wide and 1 inch deep of which he immediately died. The grand jury, to which Elizabeth Peene, John Angel, William Bourne, John Hyde and Thomas Carswell gave evidence, rejected the bill. ASSI 94/597.]

Inquests of George Tilden

417 3 Jan. 1741. Salehurst. Jurors of Salehurst and 4 neighbouring townships: Richard Weller, John Pook, Bartholomew Walker, Thomas Weston, William White, William Avery, Richard Waghorne, Stephen Taylor, Thomas Campany, Thomas Burgess, Thomas Hilder, Thomas Woodgate, Edward Rhodes. On 26 Dec. 1740 a person unknown with 20 or more others assaulted Thomas Carswell at Salehurst and the unknown person murdered him there with a gun worth 2s charged with gunpowder and a lead bullet which he held in one hand, giving him a wound in the right side of the head a little sbove the ear 3 inches deep and 1 inch wide of which he immediately died. The person had no goods or chattels, lands or tenements in Sussex or elsewhere at that time or ever after to the jurors' knowledge. [ASSI 94/671]

[This inquest, which is on parchment, without corrections and unsigned and calls Tilden county coroner, was delivered to East Grinstead assizes on 16 Mar. with another version, on paper, with several corrections, signed by the coroner and jurors and calling Tilden Hastings rape coroner, as follows:

27 Dec. 1740. The Bull, Hurst Green, Salehurst, Robert Adds's house. The inquest was adjourned. 3 Jan. 1741. The Five Bells near Salehurst church, Thomas Tyrrell's house. Jurors of Henhurst hundred: [*as above*]. About 10 a.m. on 26 Dec., when Thomas Carswell, one of the Custom House officers of the port of Hastings, was with 5 other men in Salehurst in the king's highway leading from Silverhill to Hurst Green, 20 or more men armed with fire-arms came up to him and fired several shots at him, wounding him in 3 parts of the head, of one of which wounds he immediately died. So he was murdered by some person or persons unknown.

At the same assizes the grand jury, to which James Finlater, James Crabtree, Christopher Cleghorn, John Brackenridge, Bartholomew Cross, Robert Adds, William Dunk and Thomas Woodgate gave evidence, presented an indictment which charged George Kingsmere, Daniel and Richard Wenham, John Amos, Henry Grant, Arthur Grey, John Boxhill, John Macdonald, George Chapman, James

Stanford, Thomas Cooke, John Apps, William Drewry, Joseph Nobody, William Hutchins, Richard Smith and Thomas Fryman, all late of Salehurst, labourers, with murdering Carswell at Salehurst on 26 Dec.: Kingsmere shooting at him with a gun worth 2s charged with gunpowder and a lead bullet which he held in one hand and giving him a wound in the right side of the head a little above the ear 3 inches deep and 1 inch wide of which he immediately died; and all the others being feloniously present aiding and abetting him. Bartholomew Cross, who had been committed to gaol on 17 Jan. by John Board and William Poole, JPs, charged with aiding and abetting the murder of Carswell, one of the officers of HM's Customs in the port of Rye, was discharged by proclamation. Thomas Fryman, who had been removed from Hastings gaol to the county gaol by a habeas corpus on 18 Jan. charged with being in the company of a large gang of smugglers at Hurst Green and suspected of being concerned in the murder of Carswell, one of the officers of HM's Customs in the port of Rye, pleaded not guilty and was acquitted; he had not fled and so was discharged. At the Lewes assizes of 18 July 1741 Arthur Grey, who had been committed to gaol on 12 July by John Board but had neither been arraigned nor pleaded to the indictment, was bailed to appear at the next assizes. His name is on the calendar of prisoners for the East Grinstead assizes of 22 Mar. 1742 but there is no record of proceedings against him. At the East Grinstead assizes of 18 Mar. 1745 John Macdonald, who had been committed to gaol by Richard Hay, JP, on 2 Aug. 1744 on a warrant from William Lee, kt, Lord Chief Justice, having been indicted in 1741 for Carswell's murder but having neither been arraigned nor pleaded to the indictment, was bailed to appear at the next assizes. He surrendered at the East Grinstead assizes of 10 Aug. 1745, pleaded not guilty and was acquitted and discharged. At the Lewes assizes of 29 July 1749 the grand jury, to which John Hayward, William Gery, Edward Oxenbridge, George Slater, Thomas and Elizabeth Cruttenden, William Burchett, William Dunk, Susan Adds, Thomas Drury, John Boxall, William and Edward Drury, John Crisford, William Thorp and Thomas Carswell gave evidence, presented an indictment which charged George Kingsmere, George Chapman, John Ford and Richard Double, commonly called or known by the name of Ensign, all late of Salehurst, labourers, with murdering Thomas Carswell at Salehurst on 26 Dec. 1740: Kingsmere shooting him with a gun worth 2s charged with gunpowder and a lead bullet which he held in one hand, giving a wound him on the right side of the head a little above the ear 3 inches deep and 1 inch wide of which he immediately died; and the 3 others being feloniously present aiding and abetting him. Chapman, who had been removed with John Boxall by a habeas corpus from Maidstone on 19 July charged with being concerned with others in Carswell's murder and in rescuing and carrying away from him and William Gery, officers of HM's Customs, over 80 bags of tea containing about 2000 weight which the 2 officers had seized, pleaded not guilty but was convicted; he had no chattels and was sentenced to be hanged at Horsham on 19 Aug. Boxall was discharged by proclamation. Double, who had been committed to gaol on 10 Apr. 1749 by Edward Tredcroft, JP, charged on the oath of Richard Smith with the same offences as Chapman, pleaded not guilty but was convicted; he had no chattels and was sentenced to be hanged at Horsham on 19 Aug. but was reprieved and was still in gaol at the East Grinstead assizes of 26 Mar. 1750. Ford, who had been committed to gaol on 17 June 1749 by John Wicker, JP, charged with the same offences as Chapman and Double, pleaded not guilty and was acquitted; he had not fled and so was discharged. Kingsmere was still at large and so a capias was issued for his arrest and appearance at the assizes of 26 Mar. 1750 when the sheriff returned that he had not been found in his bailiwick. At that assizes the grand jury, to which William Gery, John Hayward, John Boxhill, John Crisford, Edward and Thomas Drury, William Dunk and James Baily gave evidence, presented an indictment which charged Thomas Carey, commonly called or known by the name of Lame Jockey, and George Chapman, both late of Salehurst, labourers, with murdering Thomas Carswell at Salehurst on 26 Dec. 1740: Carey shooting him with a gun worth 2s charged with gunpowder and a lead bullet which he held in one hand, giving him a wound on the right side of the head a little above the ear 3 inches deep and 1 inch wide of which he immediately died; and Chapman being feloniously present aiding and abetting him; and which also charged James Stanford late of Salehurst, labourer, with commanding, hiring and counselling Carey and Chapman at Salehurst on 26 Dec. to commit the murder. Carey, who had been committed to gaol on 20 Aug. 1749 by John Fuller, JP, charged with being assembled with others with fire-arms at Silverhill on 26 Dec. 1740 and assisting in retaking some goods in the course of which Carswell was shot dead and because he was seen about 2 hours after the murder with others loaded with part of the retaken tea, pleaded not guilty but was convicted; he had no chattels and was sentenced to be hanged. Stanford pleaded not guilty and was acquitted; he had not fled and so was discharged. ASSI 94/671; ASSI 94/678; ASSI 94/685; ASSI 94/722; ASSI 94/728; ASSI 94/778; ASSI 94/784.]

418 29 June 1747. The house of William Beeny sen., Northiam. Jurors of Staple hundred: Thomas Beall, Edmund Chittenden, David Davy, Thomas Apps, Henry King, Daniel Fryer, John Ashenden, Robert Stone, John Hovenden, John Weeks, Thomas Cook, William Susans. On 26 June William Beeny jun. late of Northiam, labourer, murdered Mary Davis, a travelling woman, at Northiam, striking her with both hands close shut upon both sides of her body under the short ribs and giving her 2 mortal contusions, each 4 inches long and 3 inches wide, of which she languished for about 1½ hours and then died. What goods and chattels Beeny had at the time of the murder the jurors did not know. [ASSI 94/752]

[Delivered to Lewes assizes on 15 Aug. At the East Grinstead assizes of 28 Mar. 1748 the grand jury, to which Stephen Boyd and John Hussey gave evidence, presented an indictment similar to the inquest verdict except that Davis was styled spinster, the contusions were called wounds and bruises, she died immediately and the last sentence was omitted. Beeny was at large at the time of the East Grinstead assizes. ASSI 94/760.]

419 26 Apr. 1750. The Huntsman and Hound, Brightling, Netherfield hundred, William Wood's house. Jurors of Brightling and 4 neighbouring townships: Stephen Fuller, esq., John Atkins, gent., James Stevens, Anthony Eyles, Stephen Tendall, William Wickham, Thomas Freeman of Hollingrove, Thomas Freeman, weaver, Stephen Smith, John Stace, Thomas Venice, Robert Nash, John Fowle, Peter Sanders. On 25 Apr. Thomas Markwick of Brightling, labourer, Joseph Ditchfield, a corporal in the regiment called the Old Buffs[1] then quartered at Salehurst, and Richard Holman of Brightling, carpenter, feloniously killed Thomas Boden at Brightling, all 3 striking, beating and bruising him on the head and other parts of his body and afterwards violently throwing his body upon the ground, thereby giving him several bruises of which he languished at Brightling for about 4 hours and then died. Markwick, Ditchfield and Holman had no goods or chattels, lands or tenements at the time of the felony or ever after to the jurors' knowledge. [ASSI 94/790]

[Delivered to Horsham assizes on 6 Aug. when a bill of indictment was preferred which charged Markwick, Ditchfield and Holman, all late of Brightling, labourers, with murdering Boden at Brightling on 25 Apr.: Markwick with both his hands and feet throwing him to the ground and striking, bruising, beating and kicking him on the head, breast, stomach, back and sides, thereby giving him several bruises of which he immediately died; and Ditchfield and Holman being feloniously present aiding and abetting him. The grand jury, to which James Little, William Wood, William Weston, Charles Jenkins, Francis Hutchins, [*2 illegible names struck through*] and Paul Castleman gave evidence, rejected the bill. Markwick, Ditchfield and Holman, who had been committed to gaol on 4 May by John Nicoll and James Markewicke, JPs, charged with Boden's murder, pleaded not guilty to the inquest and were acquitted; they had not fled and so were discharged. ASSI 94/790.]

1 In 1751 the Buffs became the 3rd Regiment of Foot: Swinson, 77.

420 3 Aug. 1764. Hooe. Jurors of 4 townships neighbouring Hooe: Richard Sampson, John Buckshall, John King, Robert Burt, John Dunk, William Mercer, John Cutberd, Edward Bristow, William Wickham, John West, James Russell, John Russell, Robert

Grant, Thomas Bruttle, 'Dioness' Geer. On 26 July some person or persons unknown murdered Thomas Wenham at Bexhill, one of them shooting him with a pistol worth 2s charged with gunpowder and a lead ball and giving him a wound on the right cheek, lower jaw-bone and neck 3 inches deep and ½ inch wide of which he languished at Bexhill and Hooe until 2 Aug. and then died at Hooe. [ASSI 94/988]

[Delivered to Horsham assizes on 20 Aug. Cf. **227**.]

Inquests of John Tilden (from 22 Nov. 1797 John Tilden Sampson)

421 9 Mar. 1768. Ticehurst. Jurors of Shoyswell hundred: Richard Austen, John Clifton, Robert Fuller, John Bonnick, Thomas Waghorne, Edward Paine, John Bushnell, William Austen, Richard Tandy, John Brisenden, John Lowles, Samuel Smith. On 25 Feb. Ann Oxenbridge late of Ticehurst, widow, feloniously killed William Moor at Ticehurst, throwing him to the ground with both hands and thereby giving him a bruise on the right groin of which he languished at Ticehurst until 6 Mar. and then died. Oxenbridge had no goods or chattels, lands or tenements in Sussex or elsewhere at the time of the manslaughter or ever after to the jurors' knowledge. [ASSI 94/1034]

[Delivered to East Grinstead assizes on 21 Mar. when a bill of indictment was preferred similar to the inquest verdict except that the bruise was given by Oxenbridge striking Moor on the right groin with both hands while he was lying on the ground, the charge was murder and the last sentence was omitted. The grand jury, to which John Polhill, Samuel Newington and Daniel Waghorne gave evidence, rejected the bill. Oxenbridge, who had been committed to gaol by the coroner on the day of the inquest charged on the inquest with the murder of Moor late of Ticehurst, pleaded not guilty to the inquest and was acquitted; she had not fled and so was discharged. ASSI 94/1034. Cf. **230**.]

422 17 Feb. 1775. Burwash. Jurors of 4 townships neighbouring Burwash: Joseph Jarvis, Hab Hood, Richard Mepham, John Holman, John Gibbs, John Croft, John Harmer, John Cruttenden, John Bowles, Thomas Balcomb, Richard Leadbetter, James Cornford, John Dadswell, William Skinner, William Woodsell. On 14 Feb. Edmund Smith and Edward and Mark Jarvis, all late of Burwash, labourers, feloniously killed Thomas Mercer sen. at Burwash: Smith beating him on the top of the head with the butt end of a whip worth 12d which he held in his right hand and giving him a bruise of which he languished at Burwash until 16 Feb. and then died; and the Jarvises being feloniously present aiding and abetting him. None of the 3 had any goods or chattels, lands or tenements in Sussex or elsewhere at the time of the felony or ever after to the jurors' knowledge. [ASSI 94/1126]

[Delivered to East Grinstead assizes on 27 Mar. when the grand jury, to which Thomas Mercer, Thomas Baldock and William Giles gave evidence, presented an indictment similar to the inquest verdict except that the charge was murder and the last sentence was omitted. Smith and the Jarvises were at large at the time of the assizes. At the Lewes assizes of 14 Aug. a capias issued to the sheriff ordering him to have them at the next assizes; it was returned at East Grinstead on 18 Mar. 1776 endorsed that they had not been found in the sheriff's bailiwick. A further capias therefore issued which was returned at the Horsham assizes of 5 Aug. 1776 endorsed that Edward Jarvis had been arrested but the others were still not found. On 5 Aug. Edward Jarvis, who had been committed to gaol on 31 July, pleaded not guilty and was acquitted; he had not fled and so was discharged. ASSI 94/1126; ASSI 94/1140; ASSI 94/1146. Cf. **235**.]

423 22 June 1776. Brightling in Netherfield hundred. Jurors of 4 townships neighbouring Brightling: William Gregson, James Little, John Croft, Thomas Croft, Edward Batchellor, William Hoyle, Thomas Marchant, John Croft jun., John Devonish, Isaac Veness, William Honysett, David Honysett. On 15 June Ann Cruttenden of Brightling, widow, traitorously murdered her husband Joseph at Brightling with a knife worth 2d which she held in her right hand, giving him a wound in the right side of the neck 2 inches wide and ½ inch deep of which he immediately died. Ann had no goods or chattels, lands or tenements in Sussex or elsewhere at that time or ever after to the jurors' knowledge. [ASSI 94/1146]

[Delivered to Horsham assizes on 5 Aug. when the grand jury, to which Sarah Skinner, Susannah Perry, Francis Batchellor and Richard Smith gave evidence, presented an indictment similar to the inquest verdict except that Joseph Cruttenden was late of Brightling, butcher, and the last sentence was omitted. Ann Cruttenden, who had been committed to gaol by the coroner on the day of the inquest, pleaded not guilty but was convicted; she had no chattels. She was sentenced to be drawn on a hurdle to the place of execution on 8 Aug. and there burnt to death. ASSI 94/1146. Cf. **236**; *SCM*, XIII, 500.]

424 15 Oct. 1778. Crowhurst.

[The inquest does not survive but at the East Grinstead assizes of 15 Mar. 1779 the grand jury, to which Thomas Mathis, Thomas Sargent and Solomon Dukes gave evidence, presented an indictment which charged Benjamin Beeching late of Crowhurst, labourer, with murdering Thomas Cramp at Crowhurst on 14 Oct. by striking him with both hands on the left ear and left side of the head and throwing him to the ground, thereby giving him a bruise on the left ear and left side of the head of which he immediately died. Beeching, who had been committed to gaol by the coroner on the day of the inquest charged by the inquest with the accidental manslaughter of Cramp, pleaded not guilty and was acquitted of murder but convicted of manslaughter; he was sentenced to be branded on the hand and to remain in gaol for 3 months and then be discharged. ASSI 94/1179. Cf. **239**.]

425 13 Sept. 1784. The Crown, Burwash, William Masters's house. Jurors of Hawksborough hundred: Joseph Jarvis, Joseph Newington, William Taylor, John Gibbs, Henry Constable, Thomas Balcombe, John Kennard, William Jennings, James Bayley, John Flemmings,[1] Thomas Wood, Richard Barnard. On 12 Sept. Thomas Adams late of Burwash, blacksmith, feloniously killed Charles Weston at Burwash, striking him with his fist and throwing him to the ground, thereby giving him a bruise on the side of the head of which he immediately died. Adams immediately fled on account of the manslaughter. He had no goods or chattels, lands or tenements in Sussex or elsewhere at that time or ever after to the jurors' knowledge. [ASSI 94/1260]

[Delivered to East Grinstead assizes on 21 Mar. 1785 when the grand jury, to which John Leany and Richard Johnson gave evidence, presented an indictment which charged Adams late of Burwash, labourer, with the murder of Weston on 12 Sept. at Burwash by striking him with his right hand on the right side of the head and giving him a bruise of which he immediately died. Adams, who had been committed to gaol by George Courthope, JP, on 15 Sept., pleaded not guilty and was acquitted of murder but convicted of manslaughter; he had no chattels and was burnt on the hand and discharged. ASSI 94/1260. Cf. **244**.]

1 He signed the inquest *John Fleming*.

426 29 Nov. 1784. The Bell, Iden, John Varrier's house. Jurors of Goldspur hundred: Joseph Tuersley, James Bray, William Bannister, Benjamin Wood, Thomas Underdown,

James Tasker, Edward Bannister, John Watson, William Neaves, Richard Woodhams, Thomas Attey, Moses Clive, Fairhall Bates. It appeared that on 13 Nov., when John Smith was coming along the sea-shore in Winchelsea with his wagon, he was met by several persons unknown and an affray arose between them. The unknown persons feloniously killed Smith, some or one of them throwing him to the ground and thereby giving him one or more bruises on the head and body of which he languished at Winchelsea and Iden until 25 Nov. and then died at Iden. [ASSI 94/1260]

[Delivered with **425**. Cf. **244**.]

427 2 Oct. 1792. Catsfield. Jurors: John Hunt, John Hayward, William Woodiwiss, James Spray, John Fowle, Samuel Usher, John Farmer, Thomas Hepden, George Goldsmith, John Garner, James Crouch, John Carter, Richard Hobden. Witnesses: John Creasy, Mary wife of James Crouch. On 1 Oct. James Warner late of Catsfield, bricklayer, feloniously killed John Ellis at Catsfield, throwing him to the ground with both hands and violently with one hand pulling a handkerchief which was tied round Ellis's neck whereby he was strangled and immediately died. [ASSI 94/1378]

[Delivered to East Grinstead assizes on 18 Mar. 1793 when the grand jury, to which John Creasey, Mary Cresye and Samuel Ellis gave evidence, presented an indictment [now filed with those of the Lewes assizes of 19 July 1793] similar to the inquest verdict except that Warner was called labourer, the handkerchief was worth 6d and was pulled, twisted and tied by Warner with both hands, and the charge was murder. Warner, who had been committed to gaol by the coroner on the day of the inquest, pleaded not guilty and was acquitted of murder but convicted of manslaughter; he had no goods and was ordered to pay a fine of 1s and to remain in gaol until he had paid and then be discharged. ASSI 94/1378; ASSI 94/1379. Cf. **253**.]

428 17 May 1798. Salehurst. Jurors: Thomas Tyrrell, Robert Overy, William Hilder, Thomas Boots, Henry Huntly, John Heathfield, James King, George French, Robert Willsher, Richard Page, Samuel Harmer, Robert Day. On 13 May William Dunk late of St Clement's, Hastings, soldier, feloniously killed Thomas Cowley at St Clement's, striking him on the head with his right hand whereby he was thrown upon the ground and received a bruise on the head of which he languished at St Clement's, Ore and Salehurst until 16 May and then died at Salehurst. After committing the felony Dunk fled on that account. He had no goods or chattels, lands or tenements in Sussex or elsewhere at the time of the felony or ever after to the jurors' knowledge. [ASSI 94/1455]

[Delivered to Horsham assizes on 27 July when a bill of indictment was preferred similar to the inquest verdict except that Dunk, labourer, struck Cowley with one of his hands whereby he was knocked against a wooden bench and then to the ground and received a bruise on the left side of the head, the charge was murder and the last 2 sentences were omitted. The grand jury, to which Thomas Eyles, Stephen Gomme, John Shibbing, William Satterley and John Colvill gave evidence, rejected the bill. Dunk, who had been committed to gaol by the coroner on 22 May, pleaded not guilty to the inquest and was acquitted; he had not fled and so was discharged. ASSI 94/1455. Cf. **258**.]

429 21 Jan. 1799. Fairlight. Jurors of the rape: John Thorpe, Henry Gorham, Thomas Collins, Richard Butler, Robert Russell, Moses Cloke, John Standen, William Blackman, Christopher Hoad, George King, Thomas Overy, Thomas Russell, John Reed. On the night of 19 or the morning of 20 Jan. Elizabeth Lavender late of Fairlight, single woman, alone and secretly gave birth at Fairlight to a live male infant which by the laws and customs of the kingdom was a bastard and afterwards, on one of those days, murdered him there with a knife of iron and steel which she held in one hand, stabbing him in the throat or gullet whereby he immediately died. Lavender had no goods or chattels, lands or tenements in Sussex or elsewhere at the time of the murder or ever after to the jurors' knowledge. [ASSI 94/1478]

[Delivered to East Grinstead assizes on 25 Mar. when the grand jury, to which John Thorpe, Thomas Hedgcock and Charles Steevens Crouch gave evidence, presented an indictment similar to the inquest verdict except that Lavender was called spinster, the birth and murder were on 20 Jan., the knife was worth 1d and held in Lavender's right hand, the wound was in the neck and throat 5 inches long and 3 inches deep and the last sentence was omitted. Lavender, who had been committed to gaol by the coroner on the day of the inquest, was remanded in gaol until the next assizes because Elizabeth Hedgecock, a material witness for the prosecution, was unable to attend the March assizes through illness, being so advanced in pregnancy as to make it unsafe for her to travel. At the Lewes assizes of 19 July Lavender pleaded not guilty but was convicted; she had no goods and was sentenced to be hanged on 22 July and then dissected and anatomized. ASSI 94/1478; ASSI 94/1479; RAF 1/4/1. Cf. **260**.]

430 3 Jan. 1810. Salehurst.

[The inquest does not survive but there is an outline warrant of [*blank*] Jan. issued by the coroner to the constables and headboroughs of Henhurst hundred to convey [*blank*], late a private in the 50th[1] Regiment of Foot stationed at Silverhill Barracks, Salehurst, to Horsham gaol in consequence of the inquest on Michael McDonough with whose death he was charged. SHE 2/6/2. Cf. **271**.]

1 *West Kent*: Swinson, 149.

Inquests of Thomas Barton

431 19 Mar. 1819. Wartling. Jurors of Foxearle hundred: John Scrase, Thomas Arkcoll, Henry Dorsett, James Lingham, James Everest, Nicholas Wratten, Abel Attwood, Richard Pocock, Ned Barnard, Joseph Dawes, Henry Delves, James Brook, Thomas Fuller. On 15 Mar. some person unknown murdered John Apps at Pevensey in the liberty of Pevensey with a pistol or gun charged with gunpowder and a lead bullet which he held in one hand, giving him a wound in the back, the bullet penetrating the intestines and passing out below the ribs, of which he languished at Pevensey and Wartling until the next day and then died at Wartling. [ASSI 94/1798]

[Delivered to Horsham assizes on 24 Mar. Cf. **308**.]

432 19 June 1821. Tilden Smith's house, Mountfield. Jurors of the rape: [*blank*]. Witnesses: [*blank*]. On 18 June Mark Jarvis murdered himself at Mountfield, fastening one end of a silk handkerchief worth [*blank*] onto [*blank*] and the other about his neck and therewith hanging himself of which he immediately died. At that time he had no goods or chattels, lands or tenements in the rape or elsewhere to the jurors' knowledge. [SHE 2/6/6]

[A warrant of the same date from the coroner to the churchwardens and constables of Mountfield and of Netherfield hundred required them to cause Jarvis's body to be buried in some public highway and to certify him of the place. SHE 2/6/6. Cf. **281**.]

433 28 Nov. 1822. Heathfield.

[The inquest does not survive but on 27 Nov. the coroner issued a warrant to the constables and headboroughs of Hawksborough hundred to summon 24 men of the hundred to Heathfield poorhouse at noon on 28 Nov. to be a jury to inquire concerning [Edward] Brooker's death. *Footnote*: 12 would be sufficient. SHE 2/6/7. Cf. **282**.]

434 10 and 11 May 1826. Burwash.

[The inquest does not survive but at the Lewes assizes of 26 July the grand jury, to which William Russell, Thomas Hawkins, John Woodsell, John Sheather, Samuel Cruttenden, Thomas Abel Evans, Robert Crowhurst, Lydia and William Collins, Joseph Oliver, Robert Bowles, Elizabeth Elliott, Hananiah Hilder, Francis and James Russell, Ann Hicks, Thomas Relf, Thomas Luck, James French, Mark Blackford and Robert Ellis gave evidence, presented an indictment which charged Hannah Russell late of Brightling, widow, and Daniel Leney late of Brightling, labourer, with murdering Benjamin Russell late of Brightling, labourer, then Hannah's husband, at Brightling on 8 May; Hannah administering to him a large quantity, viz 4 drachms, of white arsenic, well knowing it to be a deadly poison, which he swallowed down into his body whereby he became sick and immediately died; and Leney being feloniously present aiding and abetting her to commit the treason and murder. Hannah, aged 32, and Leney, 19, who had been committed to gaol on 16 May by John Cobb, JP, charged on the oath of William Russell and others with murdering Benjamin at Burwash on 8 May, pleaded not guilty but were convicted. Hannah, who had no goods, was sentenced to be drawn to the place of execution and both were to be hanged there on 31 July and then dissected and anatomized. Both sentences were respited, Hannah's until further order and Leney's until 3 Aug. Hannah was still in gaol at the assizes of 3 Jan. 1827. ASSI 94/1961; ASSI 94/1962. Cf. **285**; *SCM*, XI, 118–122.]

435 26 Aug. 1829. Beckley.

[The inquest does not survive but on 26 Aug. the coroner issued a warrant to the churchwardens and constables of Beckley to cause the body of William Pain jun., who was found at the inquest to have murdered himself, to be privately buried in the churchyard or other burial place of Beckley, without any stake being driven through his body, between 9 p.m. and midnight on 26 Aug. SHE 2/6/12. Cf. **289**.]

Inquests of Thomas Charles Bellingham

436 21 Mar. 1832. Mountfield.

[The inquest does not survive but there is an outline warrant of [*blank*] Mar. issued by the coroner for the conveyance of [*blank*] late of [*blank*], labourer, to Horsham gaol, he having been charged at the inquest with [Thomas] Simmonds's murder. SHE 2/6/14. Cf. **292**.]

437 23 Oct. 1832. Ninfield. Jurors of the rape: George Davey, Samuel Skinner, Walter Wrenn, Thomas Morris, John Farmer, Jonathan Parrish, John Sheather, John Atwood, John Reeves, Frederick Willard, William Bridger, Hugh Colman, Peter Carey. On 22 Oct. Timothy Harrington late of Ninfield, labourer, murdered James Rogers at Ninfield with a pistol worth 5s charged with gunpowder and a lead bullet which he held in his right hand, giving him a wound in the left breast 1 inch wide and 9 inches deep of which he immediately died. [ASSI 94/1237]

[Delivered to Lewes special assizes on 15 Dec. when the grand jury, to which James Willby, Ann and Alexander Coleman and William Blackman, surgeon, gave evidence, presented an indictment similar to the inquest verdict except that the pistol was not valued and the wound was in the left side of the chest 6 inches deep and 1 inch wide. Harrington, aged 30, who had been committed to gaol by the coroner on the day of the inquest, pleaded not guilty but was convicted and sentenced to be hanged. He was later reprieved and sentenced to transportation for life. ASSI 94/1237. Cf. **293**.]

438 1 Aug. 1834. Burwash. Jurors of the rape: [*blank*]. On 28 July [*blank*] late of Burwash, labourer, feloniously killed Caesar Bennett at Burwash, assaulting him and [*blank*] and thereby giving him [*blank*] of which he languished at Burwash until 31 July and then died. [SHE 2/6/15]

[Cf. **293**.]

439 2 Aug. 1834. Warbleton. Jurors of the rape: [*blank*]. On [*blank*] 1834 at Warbleton [Eleanor] Buckland mixed a quantity of white arsenic and a quantity of tea infused in warm water and afterwards, on the same day, well knowing the arsenic to be a deadly poison, feloniously drank a great quantity of the tea and arsenic, by means [*blank*]. [SHE 2/6/16]

[Cf. **293**.]

440 23 Mar. 1836. Bexhill.

[The inquest does not survive but on 24 Mar. Thomas Breton[1] wrote to the coroner from Bexhill about information that had come to light since the inquest on Margaret Wilson. Stewart White, a mounted guardsman, was in her house on 21 Mar., the evening of her death, and her husband found a paper containing arsenic which he gave to White who opened and examined the paper on which was written 'poison, arsenic'. He showed the paper to William Ford who said it was his writing. In his deposition Wilson denied having anyone in the house, but it now appeared that he knew of the arsenic being found. Breton thought it right to leave any further investigation to the coroner's judgment and would the next morning examine the body in the presence of a medical friend. Bellingham replied to Breton on the same day approving of his plan to examine the body and stating that he could do nothing more as coroner, a verdict having been returned, but that the matter was still open to investigation before the magistrates. After Wilson's examination, and his deposition had been signed, he was asked if he had any arsenic for killing rats or for any other purpose and he said he had not and did not know of any having been got. Bellingham asked to be informed of the result of the examination of the body and advised Breton to tell the parish officers what had occurred. On 26 Mar. Breton wrote again to the coroner about the previous day's examination. He had found the left hemisphere of the brain much gorged with blood and the vessels much distended but sound. In the right hemisphere the veins were much gorged and there was an effusion of about 3 tablespoonfuls of blood in the ventricles. The stomach was perfectly natural and contained about ¼ pint of bilious fluid only. The intestines were quite sound and free from any marks of poison. Lungs, mouth, liver, etc. were perfectly healthy. He had submitted the liquid found in the stomach to various tests and could say it was free from any notable poison. The quantity of blood found in the ventricles of the brain was such as to cause immediate death. SHE 2/6/17. Cf. **295**.]

1 Breton was a Bexhill surgeon: cf. **467**.

441 15 Dec. 1836. Rye.

[The inquest does not survive but there is an undated outline order from the coroner to [*blank*] to appear at the inquest at [*blank*] at [*blank*] o'clock on [*blank*] to give evidence on the cause of the death of [John Holt *struck through*] and to make or assist in making a post-mortem examination of the body with an analysis of the contents of the stomach or intestines and report them to the inquest. SHE 2/6/18. Cf. **296**.]

442 31 May 1837. Brede.

[The inquest does not survive but on 20 May George Bourne, constable, wrote to the coroner from Brede stating that Alfred Furner, a young man, had been found dead in his bed about 4 p.m. on 19 May and asking what time would be convenient to come on the next day. SHE 2/6/22. Cf. **296**.]

443 10 June 1837. Crowhurst.

[The inquest does not survive, but on 18 June James Young, vicar of Heathfield, wrote to the coroner that the body of a man named Collins had been brought from Crowhurst to Heathfield and buried there on 14 June with only one person, his son, attending. As Collins had formerly lived in Heathfield and had buried some relations there — Young thought a wife or wives — there was nothing extraordinary in the application for leave to be buried there. After the interment the son told 2 persons that his father had hanged himself. One was Mr Upfield, a particular friend (and known to the coroner), who had seen Young about muffling the bell as Collins had formerly been a ringer there. The clerk did not hear of that until noon on 15 June and came and told Young, who had been out all day until nearly 6 p.m., after Young had dined. Young immediately sent for Upfield who acknowledged having been told the fact. Young told him to send immediately to the son and get the coroner's certificate to confirm that an inquest had been taken; and also to see the churchwarden. He promised to do so early the next morning, but after morning service on 18 June the clerk told Young that Bellingham had not yet been consulted and the churchwarden, Mr Huggett, was to see him the next day at ?Thorn Hill. No certificate having yet been seen, Young feared that there had been no inquest. SHE 2/6/23. Cf. **296**.]

444 9 Aug. 1837. John Easton's house, Westfield.

[The inquest does not survive but on 9 Aug. the coroner issued a warrant to the constables and headboroughs of Baldslow hundred to summon 24 men of the hundred to Easton's house at 3 p.m. on that day to be a jury to inquire concerning Easton's death. It has a footnote that 13 would be sufficient and is endorsed with the constables' return of the names of the men summoned: John Mowle, foreman, Stephen Crisford sen., Stephen Crisford jun., Stephen Watson, Thomas Baker, Samuel Tyhurst, Stephen Catt, John Tyhurst, Thomas Stunt jun., James Crisford, Stephen Easton, John Catt, Robert Noakes sen, Robert Noakes jun. SHE 2/6/21. Cf. **296**.]

HUNDRED CORONERS' INQUESTS

Inquests of Richard Taylor (Rotherfield Hundred)

445 25 May 1696. Frant. Jurors of the hundred: Thomas Maynard, Edward Budgen, John Coe, David Clifton, William Russell, John Barber, William Willett, Samuel Walter, Thomas Ovenden, John Turke, John Weston, James Ovenden, Thomas Weller, John Hosemer, John Hovenden, Thomas Pullen, Richard Carde. On 1 May Christian Crocker late of Frant, 'spinster', gave birth at Frant to a live male infant which by the laws of the kingdom 'was a bastard' and immediately murdered him, taking him in both hands and with her hands round his neck and throat strangled him whereby he immediately died. Crocker had no goods or chattels, lands or tenements in the hundred or elsewhere at that time or ever after to the jurors' knowledge. [ASSI 94/99, m 11]

[Delivered to Horsham assizes on 27 July when the grand jury, to which Mary Osbourne and Mary Tredcraft gave evidence, presented an indictment identical to the inquest verdict but omitting the last sentence. Crocker pleaded not guilty and was acquitted; she had not fled and so was discharged, paying her fees. ASSI 94/99, mm 4, 11, 12, 18d.]

446 13 May 1712. Rotherfield. Jurors of the hundred: John Weston, William Luck, John Cheesman, William Slaughterford, John Stapley, Edward Homesby, David Clifton, Thomas Stevens, Anthony Cole, William Cornford, James Mugridge, Thomas Hodely, Thomas Boakes, Nicholas Filtness, Stephen Sawyer, John Wickens, William Lambert, Robert Guilbert, Robert Swift, John Gallett, Thomas Latter, Adam Catt. On 15 Mar. John Taylor late of Rotherfield, 'laborer', murdered John Waters at Rotherfield with 'a wooden sticke' of no value which he held in his right hand, giving him '[o]ne mortall bruise' on the left part of his head near the left ear of which he languished at Rotherfield until 9 May and then died. What goods or chattels, lands or tenements Taylor had at the time of the murder or ever after the jurors did not know. [ASSI 94/295, m 4]

[Delivered to Horsham assizes on 28 July when the grand jury, to which Thomas Maynard, William Waters, Abraham Heasman, Alexander Pocock, Robert Guilbert, Frances Blunt and Denise Catt gave evidence, presented an indictment identical to the inquest verdict except for the omission of the last sentence. At the assizes of 16 Mar. 1730 Taylor pleaded not guilty and was acquitted, the trial jury finding that Waters had died a natural death. Taylor had not fled. ASSI 94/295, mm 4, 5.]

447 11 Feb. 1721. Rotherfield. Jurors of the hundred: Thomas Latter, Thomas Butcher, Thomas Ovenden, William Banister, John Turner, Samuel Farnes, James Mugridge, John Mugridge, William Damper, William Cheeseman, William Downard, John Ovenden, John Taylor, John Smith, John Perfitt, John Jenkins, Thomas Simons. On 10 Feb. Thomas Woolgar late of Rotherfield, 'laborer', feloniously killed Richard Jillett, an infant aged 5, at Rotherfield with 'a gunn' worth 2s 'charged with gunpowder and small shott' which he held in both hands and 'did shoot off and discharge' at him, the lead shot giving him 'one mortall wound' in the chest 1 inch deep and 2 inches wide of which he immediately died. What goods or chattels, lands or tenements Woolgar had at that time or ever after the jurors did not know. [ASSI 94/406]

[Delivered to East Grinstead assizes on 20 Mar. when the grand jury, to which Elizabeth and Avis Smith and Dorothy Hard gave evidence, presented an indictment similar to the inquest verdict except that the weapon was a small gun, the charge was murder and Jillett's age and the last sentence were omitted. Woolgar pleaded not guilty and was acquitted of felonious homicide but convicted of accidental homicide; having given security to appear at the next assizes, he was discharged, paying his fees. ASSI 94/406.]

Inquests of Anthony Trumble (Dill and Guestling hundreds)

448 2 Jan. 1714. Hailsham in Dill hundred, Pevensey rape. Jurors: John Miller, Edward Luxford, William Clarke, William Tendall, John Lenham, William Smith, George Pupp, John Woods, John Hodge, Thomas Clifford, Benjamin Dutton, Richard Glover. On 25 Dec. 1713 John Woods late of Hailsham, 'yeoman', having in his right hand at Hailsham 'a gunn' worth 3s 'charged with gunpowder and small shott', 'the cock', which was attached to the gun with flint, being 'half bent' and Samuel Elliott being near Woods, 'the cocke' suddenly, by chance and without the knowledge and against the will of Woods set fire to the gunpowder by the force of which the shot was discharged from the gun and penetrated 'the right legg' of Elliott, giving him a wound ½ inch wide and 4 inches deep of which he languished at Hailsham until 1 Jan. and then died. So Woods accidentally killed him. What goods or chattels, lands or tenements Woods had at the time of Elliott's death or ever after the jurors did not know. [ASSI 94/316]

[Delivered to East Grinstead assizes on 15 Mar. when the grand jury, to which John Elliott and John Mackley gave evidence, presented an indictment similar to the inquest verdict except that Woods, labourer, held the gun in both hands and shot Elliott knowing that it was charged, the indictment was for murder and the last sentence was omitted. Woods pleaded not guilty and was acquitted; he had not fled and so was discharged, paying his fees. ASSI 94/316.]

449 9 Feb. 1723. Guestling. Jurors of Guestling hundred and Hastings rape: Thomas Carman, Thomas Easton, John Wilmshurst, Peter Carsingham, Samuel Message, Robert Fuller, Joseph Roades, John Roofe, Henry Obell, Thomas Smith, William Burgess, Thomas Forster, Thomas Crunden, Samuel Hendley, John Bovis. On 6 Feb. John Beney late of Guestling, 'laborer', feloniously killed John Morrice at [Guestling] with 'a prong' which he held in both hands, giving him a contusion on the right part of the head of which he languished until the next day and then died at [Guestling]. What goods or chattels, lands or tenements Beney had at the time of the homicide or ever after the jurors did not know. [ASSI 94/426]

[Delivered to East Grinstead assizes on 1 Apr. when the grand jury presented an indictment identical to the inquest verdict except that the charge was murder and the last sentence was omitted. Beney pleaded not guilty and was acquitted; he had not fled and so was discharged, paying his fees. ASSI 94/426.]

Inquest of Robert Lovelace Chambers (Gostrow hundred)

450 27 Oct. 1743. Widow Tassell's house in Brede, near the furnace. Jurors of the hundred: Henry Brook, William Jerman, Samson Barns, Samuel Furminger, John Fuller, Edward Brown, William Terrey, James Bonden[1], Benjamin Gain, Thomas Black, William Coleman, Thomas Taylor, John West, John Barber, Thomas Fale, John Corns,

William Gain, Thomas Rummens, Stephen Reeve, William Booth. Witnesses: William Tassell jun., Thomas Chambers. It appeared that about 11 a.m. on 24 Oct., when William Tassell was digging sand in a sand-pit with his brother William and filling a court,[2] the cope, or earth, fell in upon him and bruised him very much across the small of his back which bruised the bones and hurt or burst the vessel of his back which hindered or obstructed the circulation of his blood. He lay until about 6 p.m. on the same day and then died. His death was entirely accidental. [ACC 7022/1]

[Chambers held this inquest as Gostrow hundred deputy coroner for this turn only. Two depositions were taken at the inquest:

William Tassell of Brede jun., aged over 19: He was at work with his brother William in a sand quarry at Brede about 11 a.m. on 24 Oct. a filling a court with sand and, the bank being undermined, the cope, or earth, fell in upon him. He did not see it fall but heard his brother cry out: 'Lord have mercy upon me; brother, I am killed' or words to that effect. He and Thomas Rummens put him into the court and brought him to Widow Tassell's, his mother, and he complained of the small of his back and said he should die. He lay in very great agonies from the time he was brought home, about noon, till about 6 p.m. and then died.

Thomas Chambers of Battle, aged about 18: He together with his master, Robert Young of Battle, surgeon, came over and viewed the body and, upon examining of it, it appeared to them that he had had a great blow cross the small of his back which bruised the bones and hurt or bruised the vessel of his back which hindered or obstructed the circulation of his blood. Young tried to bleed him twice but could not make him bleed which was occasioned by the circulation of his blood being obstructed and which Chambers apprehended was the occasion of his death. ACC 7022/1.]

1 He signed *James Benden*.
2 *sc.* a cart for carrying stones, bricks, lime, sand, etc.

Inquest of George Worge (Gostrow hundred)

451 25 Nov. 1751. John Woodhams's house, Udimore.

[The inquest does not survive, but there is a jury summons issued to Thomas Freebody, Gostrow hundred constable, by the coroner on 25 Nov., ordering him to have 24 good and lawful men of the hundred before Worge himself or his deputy, Henry Dodson, at Woodhams's house at 3 p.m. on that day for an inquest on Edward Henly who was lying dead there; and also to summon everyone who could give any account of the death. The summons is endorsed: Thomas Swain, William Wicks, John Honis, Henry Dearing, sworn; Thomas Crittenden, Alexander Reeve, John Longford, John Sloman, sworn; Caleb Stredwick, Charles Skinner, sworn; William Woodhams, sworn; John and Thomas Whiteman, sworn; John Liddens, Thomas Woodgate, sworn; Joseph Philmer, John Potten, Richard Noakes, John Wilshire, Edward Apes; Richard Hillier, John Randall, Joseph Selden, Sarah Marten, witnesses sworn and examined. ACC 7022/2.]

Inquests of Joseph Acton (Goldspur and Gostrow Hundreds)

452 24 May 1763. The house of John Woodhams jun., Goldspur hundred. Jurors of the said hundred of Gostrow: Robert Maynard, Stephen Wilmshurst, Isaac Weymark, John Watson, Fairhall Bates, Gershom Humphry, John Petter, William Blackman, Richard Wilding, James Filmer, James Tasker, William Marks, Richard Woodhams, John Woodhams jun., John Stone. Witnesses: Mary Wilding, John Sutehurst, William Philpot.

On 23 May, when William Kennett was coming along the very high and steep wall of a ditch in Tillingham Level, he was suddenly taken in a fit, which he was very subject to, and, being deprived of his sense and motion, tumbled down into the ditch with his head almost all under water and was there drowned. The jury believed the death was entirely accidental. [ACC 7022/11]

[Acton held this inquest as Goldspur hundred deputy coroner for this turn. He took 3 depositions on 23[1] May:

Mary Wilding, single woman, aged about 25, and John Sutehurst, aged about 16, both of Peasmarsh, examined jointly and severally: About 5 or 6 p.m. on 23 May, being coming from Rye, they saw a person lie with his head in a ditch in Tillingham Level, upon which they went up nearer to it and saw twas Kennett quite dead, as they believed, his head being in the water of the ditch which they believed to be about 12 inches deep. They had often heard that he was very subject to falling fits which often seized him suddenly and deprived him of his sense and motion. Coming along the wall of the ditch, which is very high and steep, he was suddenly seized with a fit and fell into the ditch and was drowned. They believed same was entirely accidental.

William Philpot of Peasmarsh, labourer, aged about 50: About 6 p.m. on 23 May Mary Wilding came to him and told him that there was somebody lay dead in a ditch in Tillingham Level, upon which he immediately went to the place directed to by her and found Kennett with his head lying in the water of the ditch, quite dead. He then went and told John Woodhams sen. what had happened and they both went back to the place again and saw Kennett lie as before but did not meddle with him. Philpot had often seen him taken in fits which suddenly deprived him of his senses and motion and that he immediately tumbled down where e'er he was taken. He believed that Kennett, being coming along the wall of the ditch, was suddenly taken in a fit and fell down into the ditch and was there drowned, and same was entirely accidental. ACC 7022/11.]

1 Recte *24*.

453 23 Sept. 1773. The house of Mary Coleman, widow, Brede. Jurors of Gostrow hundred: Henry Richardson sen., Henry Richardson jun., William Gad, Robert Black, Joseph Benden, Stephen Stemp, Richard Skinner, [Thomas Brissenden *struck through*], John Buss, Newland Martin, Samuel Elphick, Samuel Jarrett, William Buss, Thomas Bourne. Witnesses: Thomas Black, Nathaniel Furner, Richard Coleman, Joseph Benden. It appeared that between 5 and 6 p.m. on 22 Sept., when William Coleman was going to fetch water in a tea-kettle from a very deep pit in his garden from which water for the service of the house was usually taken, he accidentally fell into the pit from the steps leading down to it and was drowned, there being no one near to assist him. His death was entirely accidental, no person or persons being accessory to it. [ACC 7022/5]

[There is a note on the inquest that the journey was 7 miles and the total fee £1 5s 3d. Cf. **304**, **305**.]

454 19 June 1775. Thomas Freeman's house, Brede. Jurors of Gostrow hundred: Richard Barnes, Francis Bourne, Joseph Benden, Thomas Noakes, William Buss, Samuel Jarrett, Stephen Stemp, Daniel Philcox, John Barnes, John Smith, William Gad, Samuel Harris, Ephraim Hemmings. Witnesses: Stephen Ades, Samuel Standen, John Stace, William Hasselden, Daniel Dawson. On 17 June, when Thomas Freeman jun. was going to unload a timber-tug in a field in Brede belonging to Stephen Ades and was getting on the timber on it in order to strike off part of the timber and standing across the upper piece, the butt end of that piece gave way and the little end of it caught him between his legs and tossed him a considerable height. He fell to the ground on his head and the same piece of timber fell across his loins and another piece fell on that whereby he was so hurt and bruised that he languished until between 7 and 8 p.m. of the same day and then died by misadventure. The piece of timber which threw him up and fell on him chiefly caused his death, was worth about 4s and was lying in the field. [ACC 7022/6]

[A second copy of the inquest has William Hasselden among the jurors, between John Smith and William Gad, but struck through. ACC 7022/6. Cf. **304**, **305**.]

Inquests of Charles Nairn (Gostrow and Battle Hundreds)

455 11 Aug. 1768. Jane Cloke's house, Brede. Jurors of Gostrow hundred: William Woodhams, Francis Pooke, Peter Waters, John Woodhams, Thomas Woodhams, Alexander Reeve, Thomas Swaine, Thomas Whiteman, George Sloeman, Thomas Gowland, Thomas Ransom, Joseph Felmer. Witnesses: Stephen and Edward Adds. It appeared that between 11 p.m. and midnight on 8 Aug., when Stephen and Edward Adds and Isaac Cloke were riding together on the road, Cloke's horse accidentally fell with him and flung him with great violence to the ground whereby he received a violent stroke on the left side of the head of which he languished until between 10 and 11 p.m. on 11 Aug.[1] and then died. [ACC 7022/3]

[Nairn held this inquest as Gostrow hundred deputy coroner for this turn only. There is a note on the inquest that the journey was 10 miles and the total fee £1 7s 6d; it is initialled by Joseph Acton on his receiving that sum in 1772. Nairn had issued a summons on 11 Aug. to the constable of Gostrow hundred for a jury of 24 to appear before him at Jane Cloke's house at 4 p.m. on that day. It is endorsed with the jurors named above. ACC 7022/3. Cf. **303**.]

1 ?Recte *10 and 11 a.m.* or *10 Aug.*

456 30 Nov. 1770. Battle. Jurors of 4 townships neighbouring Battle: John Cheesman, Stephen Katte, William Weston, Charles Laurence, Robert Sargent, William Palmer, John Griffen, Thomas Alderton, John Hayward, William Badcock, David Pugh, William Martin, Joseph Lidwell, John Pearson, George Philcox, John Mills, Francis Pearson, John Vidler, George Clare, Edward Jarrett, John Ashby. On 27 Nov. Nicholas Reed late of Battle, labourer, feloniously killed George Jones at Battle, violently pushing him with both hands against the edge of a brick wall and thereby giving him a bruise and fracture on the right side of the head a little above the ear of which he languished at Battle until the next day and then died. Reed had no goods or chattels, lands or tenements in Sussex or elsewhere at the time of the felony or ever after to the jurors' knowledge. [ASSI 94/1073]

[This inquest, which Nairn held as Battle hundred coroner, was delivered to East Grinstead assizes on 18 Mar. 1771 when the grand jury, to which Mary Jones, Thomas Venes, John Skeath, John Jenner, Joseph Fuller and John Hammond gave evidence, presented an indictment similar to the inquest verdict except that the charge was murder and the last sentence was omitted. Reed, who had been committed to gaol on 1 Dec. by Edward Frewen, JP, for beating and bruising George Jones of Battle whereby he later died, pleaded not guilty and was acquitted of murder but convicted of manslaughter; he had no chattels and was branded on the hand and discharged. ASSI 94/1073. Cf. **302**.]

Inquests of John Tilden (Gostrow, Battle and Bexhill Hundreds)

457 19 Apr. 1770. The Maypole, Brede, William Coleman's house. Jurors of Gostrow hundred: Henry Richardson jun., Francis Bourne, Joseph Manser, James Duke, John Stace, Thomas Gain, William Colman sen., John Barnes, Thomas Fuller, William Colman jun., Edward Colman, William Gadd, John Colman, Robert Thomas, Thomas Thompsett. Witnesses: Thomas Bull, Mary Taylor, Mary Sargent. On 17 Apr. Elizabeth Frankwell was found dead in a lodge at Brede belonging to Mr Francis Bourne. She had been very ailing and infirm for some time, had no marks of violence on her body and died a natural death and not by any violent means to the jurors' knowledge. [ACC 7022/4]

[Tilden held this inquest as deputy for this turn only to Joseph Acton, Gostrow hundred coroner. There is a note on the inquest that the journey was 8 miles and the total fee £1 6s. Cf. **303**.]

458 13 Mar. 1799. Battle. Jurors of Battle hundred: Thomas Vidler, William Wickham, James Blackman, William Gillmore Croft, John Hayward, Nicholas Slatter, Thomas Sinden, James Gower, John Fox, Richard Phillips, John Longley, William Walker, John Gausden. On 12 Mar. a new-born infant was found dead in a pond on the lawn belonging to Battle Abbey in Battle. It was so mutilated that its sex could not be discovered and there were marks of violence on its body and limbs. Some woman unknown was delivered of the child near the pond and either she or others unknown murdered it at Battle on the same day, violently throwing it into the pond whereby, or by some other means unknown, it was suffocated and drowned. [ASSI 94/1478]

[Delivered to East Grinstead assizes on 25 Mar. Cf. **260**.]

459 2 Nov. 1803. Battle. Jurors of Battle hundred: Thomas Vidler, John Austin, James Gower, Nicholas Slatter, John Shaw, William Cruttenden, John Newington, William Badcock, William Ticehurst, William Birch, Richard Ashby, George Horton, John Alderton. On 2 Nov. Andrew Murphy late of Battle, a private in HM's 70th[1] Regiment of Foot, and James Fannan late of Battle, a corporal in the same regiment, murdered Mark Kelk and William White at Battle with 2 guns or muskets, each worth 20s and loaded with gunpowder and a lead bullet, which they held in both hands, giving them wounds which penetrated their bodies and of which they immediately died. Murphy and Fannan had no goods or chattels, lands or tenements in the hundred or in Sussex or elsewhere at that time or ever after to the jurors' knowledge. [ASSI 94/1564]

[Delivered to Horsham assizes on 19 Mar. 1804 when it was quashed and the grand jury, to which Thomas Stonham, George Austen, John Forbes, Bell Rowe, James McDermott, John Watts, surgeon, Thomas Sinclair, Thomas Brooks, William Bosworth, John Fox and John Smith gave evidence, presented 2 indictments, both of which called Murphy and Fannan late of Battle, labourers. One charged them both with murdering White on 2 Nov. at Battle with a gun worth 5s loaded with gunpowder and a lead ball, giving him a wound in the left side 1 inch wide and 12 inches deep of which he immediately died; and on a second count charged Murphy with shooting White and giving him the above wound and Fannan with aiding and abetting him. The other was identical for the murder of Kelk except that the wound was in the breast 1 inch wide and 12 inches deep and the second count was that Fannan was his assassin and Murphy the accessory. Murphy, aged 21, and Fannan, 36, who had been committed to gaol by the coroner on the day of the inquest, pleaded not guilty and were acquitted; they had not fled and so were discharged. ASSI 94/1564. Cf. **265**.]

1 *Surrey*: Swinson, 170.

460 6 Sept. 1805. Bexhill. Jurors of Bexhill hundred: John Wood, William Lansdell, Christopher Heyott, Thomas Gillham, Thomas Eastwood, John Maplesden, William Weston, Henry Rich, Benjamin Stevens, Samuel Bishop jun., Richard Chandler, Joseph Savage, Samuel Bishop sen. Witnesses: Thomas Mould and Edward Langton, privates in the Derby Regiment of Militia, Ludowick Tanton, a private in the 2nd Battalion of the Light Infantry of the King's German Legion stationed at Bexhill, John Plumb. On 14 July Bernhard Sixt was seen in the barrack yard at Bexhill but the jurors saw no evidence of his having been seen or heard of again until 5 Sept. when his dead body was found lying in a ditch on Cooden Down in Bexhill with his face downwards, his legs tied together with a linen handkerchief and his body covered with fern. It was so putrefied that no marks of violence or wound could be discovered. Therefore some person or persons unknown murdered Sixt at Bexhill on 14 July. [ASSI 94/1590]

[Delivered to Horsham assizes on 24 Mar. 1806. Cf. **267**.]

461 22 Feb. 1807. The Bell, Bexhill, John Vincett's house. Jurors of Bexhill hundred: William Russell, Stephen Brook, William Duke, Thomas Pumphry, Benjamin Stevens, Henry Mate, John Crowhurst, Thomas Mugilston, Levet Osborn, Henry Rich, Joseph Mitten, William Curtis, Thomas Christian. Witnesses: Theady Shehan, Peter Cahill, John Walker. On 27 Jan. some person or persons unknown murdered Patrick Reed at Bexhill with guns, pistols or other fire-arms loaded with gunpowder and a lead bullet, shooting him in the body and giving him a wound which penetrated his knee and of which he languished at Bexhill until 20 Feb. and then died. [ASSI 94/1603]

[Delivered to Horsham assizes on 16 Mar. Cf. **269**.]

Inquest of Charles Bristow (Gostrow hundred)

462 3 Feb. 1779. The Maypole, Brede, William Coleman's house. Jurors of Gostrow hundred: Stephen Ades, Robert Thomas, Thomas Noakes, Robert Blake, Stephen Stemp, Ephraim Hemmings sen., Ephraim Hemmings jun., Thomas Blake, Thomas Henley, John Buss, Samuel Elphick, William Coleman, [Thomas Friend *struck through*], William Gadd. Witnesses: Daniel Fraser, Charles Gott, John Tranter, Thomas Friend. When Charles Creswell was spearing for eels alongside a pool in Bridge Marsh, it was supposed that, not knowing the depth of the pool which contained more than 9 feet of water, he followed the stroke of his spear, fell into the pool and accidentally died, there being no one near to help him. [ACC 7022/7]

[Bristow held this inquest as Gostrow hundred coroner for this turn only. Cf. **305**.]

Inquest of Stephen Swatland (Robertsbridge hundred)

463 2 Apr. 1782. John Mills's house, Salehurst.

[The inquest does not survive but there is a jury summons issued on 2 Apr. to the constable of Robertsbridge hundred by Swatland as deputy coroner for this turn only, ordering him to have 24 men of the hundred at John Mills's house at 9 a.m. on that day to be a jury to inquire concerning Richard Mills's death. The summons is endorsed: Mr Richards, Mr Weston, Mr Keutenius [*or*

Kentenius], Mr Turrell, Mr Daw, William Waghorn, A Standing, Mr Piper, Mr Alderton, Mr Martin, Mr Vigar, Mr Vine, Mr Jones, [Mr Lawrence *struck through*]. ACC 6077/3/1, no 27.]

Inquests of Walter Acton (Gostrow hundred)

464 15 Dec. 1794. The late Thomas Jarrett's house, Brede. Jurors of the hundred: Henry Richardson jun., Thomas Austin, William Colman, John Bourne, John Richardson, David Smith, Ephraim Hemings, Robert Blake, Thomas Noakes, James Colman, Joseph Butcher, Richard Cruttenden, Henry Campbell, William Morris, Humphrey Davis, Samuel Barnes, Richard Padgham, James Fuller, William Furner Ditch, Samuel Standen, Henry Henly, Joseph Croft, James Stace. Witnesses: Lucy Bumstead, James and Edward Jarrett, James Fuller. On 13 Dec. Thomas Jarrett, being lunatic, came alone to an oak tree in Brake's Wood in Brede and hanged himself. [ACC 7022/8]

[On 13 Dec. John Tilden, Hastings rape coroner, had issued a summons to the constables and headboroughs of the hundred for a jury of 24 to appear before him at Jarrett's house at 11 a.m. on 15 Dec. Three depositions were taken before Acton on 15 Dec.:

Lucy Bumstead of Brede, widow, aged about 63: She had lived with Jarrett upwards of 10 years, during which time he generally appeared perfectly sane and of sound mind and memory till within about 8 or 10 days of his death during which period he appeared very much depressed in spirits and several times cried and said to her he thought the world was all against him and made use of several expressions that seemed to indicate an unhappy and deranged mind. About 8 a.m. on 13 Dec. he left her at his usual dwelling-house and went, as she supposed, to his daily labour, but about 11 a.m. Sarah wife of Richard Cruttenden told her that he had hanged himself.

James Jarrett of Brede, labourer, aged about 11: Being at work with his father Edward on 13 Dec. in a field called the Highfield, his father desired him to go into a wood adjoining to the field, commonly called Brake's Coppice, to get some binders or whifs[1] for faggots and, having walked about 8 rods into the wood, he saw Thomas Jarrett hanging by a limb of an oak tree there and he called to his father who immediately came and cut him down.

Edward Jarrett of Brede, labourer, aged about 39: Being at work in the Highfield on 13 Dec. with his son James, about 11 a.m. he sent him into Brake's Wood for some whifs or binders for faggots. His son soon after called to him, saying: 'Father, father, pray come to me for here is a man hanging in a tree.' He immediately went into the wood and found Thomas Jarrett hanging by the limb of an oak tree with a cord about his neck and he cut him down and with the assistance of others brought him to the place where he then[2] lay. ACC 7022/8.]

1 sc. *wisps*.
2 sc. *on 15 Dec.*

465 4[1] Mar. 1796. The late Richard Noakes's house, Brede. Jurors of the hundred: [Robert Blake *struck through*], Thomas Blake, John Philcox, John Gibbs, John Eldridge, Stephen Stemp, John Rumens, Robert Tilby, Thomas Noakes, Joseph Manser, Samuel Reed, James Smith, John Apps, Edward Gayen. It appeared that in the afternoon of 4 Mar., when Richard Noakes was in a barn belonging to Henry Richardson of Brede, he was taken in a fit, fell down and died a natural death almost instantly, as no marks of violence appeared on any part of his body. [ACC 7022/9]

[On 5 Mar. the coroner had issued a summons to the constables and headboroughs of the hundred for a jury of 24 to appear before him at Noakes's house at 3 p.m. on that day. The following 2 depositions were taken by the coroner on the same day:

Thomas Sinden of Brede, labourer, aged about 13: About 3 p.m. on 4 Mar. he went into a barn in Brede belonging to Henry Richardson where he found Noakes laying on some straw, apparently asleep; but, on attempting to wake him, he found he was dead, upon which he went to William Colman and informed him of the circumstance.

William Colman of Brede, labourer, aged about 31: Between 3 and 4 p.m. on 4 Mar., being at work on Richardson's land, Sinden came to him and told him that Noakes was dead, whereupon he went to the barn and found him in the situation described by Sinden. ACC 7022/9.]

1 Recte *5*.

466 23 Aug. 1796. Daniel Philcox's house, Brede. Jurors of the hundred: John Bourne, Robert Blake, John Apps, John Merricks, Samuel Reed, William Crouch, Thomas Furner, Thomas Gowen, Thomas Markwick, John Watson, Abraham Marten, John Rumens, William Colman, [John ?Bourne *struck through*]. Witnesses: Josias Polhill, Thomas Rumens, [George Richardson *struck through*]. It appeared that about 5 p.m. on 18 Aug., when William Philcox was in a field in the occupation of Mr John Richardson with a wagon and 4 oxen and tried to remove the oxen from the wagon, they suddenly moved on and knocked him down and the wagon went over him, broke his collar-bone and hip-bone and injured him internally, of which he languished until about midnight the next day and then died. The jurors believed that the oxen and wagon moved to his death, were worth 2s 6d and remained with John Richardson of Brede, yeoman. [ACC 7022/10]

Inquest of Thomas Barton (Bexhill Hundred)

467 30 Dec. 1824. The Bell Inn, Bexhill. Jurors of the hundred: Stephen Brook, James Turner, Everenden Cruttenden, James Russell, John Crowhurst, Henry Reeves, William Russell, Henry Rich, John Griffith, Arthur Brook, Levet Osborne, John Manley, Joseph Mitten, John Ockenden. On 29 Dec. some person or persons unknown murdered Thomas Sawyer at Bexhill, striking and beating him and thereby giving him a bruise on the left side of the head of which he immediately died. [ASSI 94/1929]

[Delivered to Horsham assizes on 23 Mar. 1825 with 2 sets of depositions. The first set was taken by the coroner at the inquest from the following 13 witnesses:

Richard Delves of Bexhill, labourer: He knew Thomas Sawyer, a shepherd. About 5 p.m. on 28 Dec. he saw him in Gate Field on Bragg's Farm, about ¼ mile from where the body was found, going towards that place which was also the direction towards his own house. Delves immediately went to his own house. Edward Daw, who lodged there, was in the house when Delves went in, but left shortly after and was out for some time. When he returned he went to bed and Delves soon followed him. They slept together. They were half-brothers. Daw remained in bed all night. When Daw came home the next evening he said that he had been at the place where the body was found, that perhaps people would say that he had done it and that if he was taken up Delves could be a witness to prove that he was at home all the previous night.

Edward Sawyer of Bexhill, labourer: The deceased was his son. He saw him about 7 a.m. on 28 Dec. when he left home to go to work. He saw him take his watch with a seal from the head of his bed; they were those then[1] produced. About 1 p.m. on 29 Dec. another son told him that the deceased was in the pond in Chinting Field in Bexhill. He went there and took him out of the water. He was quite dead. His head was under water and his coat was covered over his head. His shepherd's crook was in the pond a few feet from the body. The ground on the edge of the pond was very much trodden down. One of the deceased's dogs came home about 7 or 8 p.m. on 28 Dec.

which led Edward Sawyer to fear that some accident had befallen his son and he immediately set about a search. On the morning of 29 Dec. Edward Daw of Bexhill, labourer, came to him and asked if he had lost his son, saying that he supposed he might be murdered in the Parson's Wood where there were many rough persons about and that he would go and look for him if anyone would go with him. Daw also said that he was sure it was not him as he had a witness that he was at home all night.

John Prior of Bexhill, shoemaker: About 11 a.m. on 29 Dec. he saw a dog lying near the side of a pond in Chinting Field and soon afterwards heard that Thomas Sawyer could not be found which induced him to tell Sawyer's brother where he had seen the dog. He later assisted in taking the deceased from the pond.

John Lamb of Bexhill, labourer: Between 5 and 6 p.m. on 28 Dec. he met George Daw on Bexhill Down coming towards Bexhill Street and spoke to him. At the same time he saw a man go across the Down towards a gate which leads into a field of Mr Brook's on Collington Farm called the Hop Garden Field, but did not know who he was. At that moment Daw said: 'I'll be damned if I must not be off' and immediately proceeded towards Bexhill Street. The gate mentioned leads to a road through the land to Chinting Field on which the deceased was found. At the time Lamb met Daw it was growing rather dark.

George Gates of Bexhill, labourer: On 28 Dec. he saw Thomas Sawyer with George Daw at Little Common in Bexhill, near the public house. He saw Sawyer go away on the road towards Bexhill and go into Mr Stride's shop at Little Common, but did not see which way Daw went. He also saw Sawyer come out of the shop alone and go on the road towards Bexhill.

Jane Mitten of Bexhill, spinster: About 5 p.m. on 28 Dec. she was coming from Bexhill Street when she met George Daw on the road near Kewhurst and Little Common. On proceeding a very short way on her road she met Thomas Sawyer. She spoke to both of them and was quite sure of their persons. She lived with her father in the same house with Daw, who came into the house between 6 and 7 p.m. and remained there until she went to bed at 9 p.m. Daw had on a round frock over a waistcoat with sleeves; it was the waistcoat then[1] produced.

Abel Winborn of Bexhill, labourer: About 5.30 p.m. on 28 Dec. he met George Daw on Bexhill Down coming towards Bexhill Street. When he was about 12 rods further on the road he met Thomas Sawyer who had 2 dogs with him. He spoke to both men and was quite certain of their persons.

Thomas Wyborn of Bexhill, labourer: Between 5 and 6 p.m. on 28 Dec. he was overtaken on Bexhill Down by George Daw coming towards Bexhill Street. He came with Daw about 20 rods when Daw turned off the road on the right towards his brother Henry Daw's house which was only a few rods from the road and about 40 or 50 rods nearer to Bexhill Street than the gate of the Hop Garden Field. There was a roadway leading past the house and Wyborn was uncertain whether Daw went into the house or past it.

Mary Sawyer of Bexhill, spinster: She knew Edward Daw. Some time the previous summer they came together on the road from Hastings towards Bexhill. Daw said that if he could get an opportunity slyly he would do for her brother Thomas. She heard her brother say that Daw once met him near her father's house and said: 'It is very well I met you here for if I had met you anywhere else death would have been your doom.' She always considered that Daw had animosity towards her brother in consequence of his having given information against him for killing game. Her brother often expressed himself afraid that Daw would do him some injury.

Thomas Thwaites, a Bexhill hundred headborough: He searched George Daw and found on his person the seal then[1] produced.

Thomas Dallaway, Bexhill [hundred] constable: Last July he sold the silver watch to Thomas Sawyer and also sold him the seal, both then[1] produced. He found the watch on the day of the inquest in the custody of Mr Lemmon, watchmaker, at Battle.

Orange Lemmon of Battle, watchmaker: On 29 Dec. George Daw came to his shop in Battle and wished to sell him the watch then[1] produced. He refused to purchase it but, on Daw stating that he was in great distress, agreed to lend him £1. Daw left the watch in his possession and was told that he might have it again on repaying the £1.

Thomas Breton of Bexhill, surgeon: He examined the body with another surgeon and found a fracture of the skull on the left side immediately above the ear and, on further examination, a considerable extravasation between the scalp and cranium. On removing the cranium, extravasation was also discovered on the brain immediately under the fracture. He was of the oponion that the deceased came by his death from a blow by either a fist or a hard instrument. No other marks of violence were discovered. He did not think that death was by drowning after the blow, the blow being sufficient to cause immediate death.

The second set of depositions was taken by Francis P Bedingfield, JP, at Battle on 6 Jan. 1825 from the following 18 witnesses and one of the accused:

Thomas Thwaites, a Bexhill hundred headborough: On 30 Dec. the prisoner George Daw was given into his custody. On searching him he found a seal and part of a steel watch-chain in one pocket of his trousers and in the other a paper of tobacco, which articles Thwaites then[2] produced. On 31 Dec. he received 2 waistcoats which he understood belonged to Daw, likewise produced. He also found a box with some tobacco in it on Daw, also produced.

Thomas Dallaway, Bexhill hundred constable: The previous July he sold a watch to Thomas Sawyer of Bexhill, labourer, and afterwards sold a seal to him. On 30 Dec. he received the watch from Orange Lemmon, then[2] produced. The seal, likewise produced by Thomas Thwaites, was the one he sold to Sawyer. On 30 Dec., when George Daw was in custody at the Queen's Head in Bexhill, he positively denied having been at Battle on the preceding day.

Orange Lemmon of Battle, watchmaker: On 29 Dec. George Daw came to his shop in Battle and offered to sell a watch to him. Lemmon declined purchasing it but, on Daw stating that he was in great distress, consented to let him have 20s. Daw said he was going into Kent for a few days to see friends. Lemmon told him he might have the watch again at any time if he paid the 20s, as he had more watches than he knew what to do with. On the morning of 30 Dec. the watch was delivered by Lemmon to Thomas Dallaway and was the one then[2] produced by him. It did not appear to have been recently wet when Lemmon received it.

Arthur Brook of Bexhill, yeoman: About 11 a.m. on 29 Dec. he met the prisoner Edward Daw at Cooden Down in Bexhill and asked him where he was going in such a hurry. He said he had just seen Old Master Sawyer who told him Tom was lost and wished him to come to Cooden to look after him. Brook told Daw it was no use for him to look after him there for Brook had been up to Little Common and seen Weston and Stride and they had told him that Sawyer went away from there about 5 p.m. towards Bexhill and the boy he thought was nearer Bexhill. Daw said: 'You may depend upon it he is murdered in Kewhurst Wood for there are so many rough fellows about they would not mind murdering him for his watch.' Brook replied: 'Ned, you make me shudder. Surely nobody would murder such a poor, harmless boy as that?' Daw said: 'Yes they would, they would do anything for 1s.' He added that he could clear himself as he was in at Easton's at 7 p.m. Daw then said he would go and look for him in Kewhurst Wood but would not go there alone because if he found the body they would say he murdered him and he would get the 2 Easton boys to go with him which Brook requested he would. Brook did not recollect the precise words used but the foregoing was the substance of the conversation.

Seby wife of Stephen Christian of Bexhill, labourer: She resided in Bexhill at a house in Collington Lane a short distance from the house at which Edward Daw lodged. On 29 Dec. about noon she was informed by her husband that Daw had told him young Sawyer was lost. About 2 p.m. she saw Daw and they had some conversation about it. She enquired whether Sawyer was found and he said he was not. He thought some person must have made a hand of him for the sake of his watch. He said he should go and look but he should not like to find him alone because it might be said he had made a hand of him and he had told Mr Brook so. She enquired which Mr Brook and thought he said Mr Arthur Brook. He also said Mr Brook had said he thought he must be drowned, but he had told him that he could not as there was no water out anywhere. She could not recollect the exact words which passed but the foregoing was the substance of the conversation. She did not to her recollection see Daw on 28 Dec.

Edward Sawyer jun. of Bexhill, labourer: He was the brother of Thomas Sawyer late of Bexhill who was found in Chinting Pond on 29 Dec. The previous summer he was at work with George Daw at Mr Deudeney's lime-kiln in Bexhill and Daw flogged him for some cause. His brother spoke to Daw about it and they quarrelled about it and Daw told his brother he would leather him if he did not look out. After Thomas Sawyer was gone away Daw said to Edward Sawyer that he would do for his brother Tom before it was long and appeared very angry. He remembered Edward Daw having been in prison some years since and when he returned he heard him say he would do for his brother. He also heard George Daw and their father about the same time speak in the same manner of his brother.

Harriet West of Bexhill: On 26 Dec. Edward Daw came into the house where she resided in Bexhill and after some conversation Thomas Sawyer's name was mentioned in consequence of something being said about shooting when Daw said that he was the person — using offensive expressions — who got Daw sent to gaol and that he owed him a good hiding for it and it would not be long before he should drop in with him and then he would give him a bloody good hiding.

Mary Sawyer of Bexhill, spinster: Same deposition as at the inquest.

Richard Delves of Bexhill, labourer: He resided in Bexhill with his father-in-law at Collington House and Edward Daw lived there also, his father having married Delves's mother. Delves usually slept with Daw. On 28 Dec. he was at work at Bragg's Farm and on leaving his work a little after 5 p.m. he saw Thomas Sawyer a short distance from the farm-house going towards his own home by a path which passed through Chinting Field. He had one dog with him but Delves did not know if he had another. He knew Sawyer very well and was quite certain it was him. He immediately went home to Collington House through the fields, leaving the Hop Garden Field on his right. On arriving he found Daw sitting in the corner. Daw remained there some time and then went out and remained away until he returned to bed a little after 8 p.m. He went to bed a short time before Delves. Delves got up soon after 5 a.m. the next morning and left him in bed. After Delves had breakfasted he went to work about 6 a.m. About noon he heard that Thomas Sawyer was lost. He went home from work about 5 p.m., having previously heard that Sawyer was found dead in Chinting Pond. Soon after he returned home Daw also returned and said he had been at the place where the body was found, that perhaps people would say he did it and if he was taken up Delves could be a witness for him to prove that he was at home all the previous night.

Thomas Wyborn of Bexhill, labourer: Between 5 and 6 p.m. on 28 Dec. he was in conversation with John Lamb when George Daw came up to them in a direction from Duke's Lane and spoke to them. Lamb and Daw had some conversation but Wyborn did not notice what passed. Daw very soon passed on in a direction towards Bexhill Street and Wyborn followed close after him. After he had gone a short distance Daw turned off to the right towards a house occupied by his brother Henry Daw which is only a few rods from the road and is nearer to Bexhill Street than the Hop Garden Field. There is a track which passes by Henry Daw's house and leads through the land to Chinting Field, but Wyborn did not see whether George Daw went to his brother's house or past it.

John Lamb of Bexhill, labourer: Between 5 and 6 p.m. on 28 Dec. he was in conversation with Thomas Wyborn in a lane or road on Bexhill Down called Duke's Lane near the entrance to Collington Lane when George Daw came up and spoke to them. Immediately afterwards he saw some person go across the Down towards a gate which leads into a field on Collington Farm called the Hop Garden Field, but he was not near enough to distinguish who it was. Daw was standing with his face in the same direction as Lamb's, but they both at the same time turned their heads towards Collington Lane. Daw said: 'I'll be damned if I must not be off' and immediately proceeded towards Bexhill Street and Wyborn followed him. Lamb turned into Collington Lane and went home. He knew Chinting Field in which Thomas Sawyer's body was found and that the gate towards which he saw some person go led to a road through the land to Chinting Field.

Abel Winborn of Bexhill, labourer: About 5.30 p.m. on 28 Dec. he met George Daw on Bexhill Down in Duke's Lane near the entrance to Collington Lane going in a direction towards Bexhill

Street. When he had passed Daw about 12 rods in Duke's Lane he met Thomas Sawyer who had 2 dogs with him. Both Daw and Sawyer spoke to him, wishing him good night. He had known them both for some years and was quite certain as to their persons.

Jane Mitten of Bexhill, spinster: On the evening of 28 Dec., having been to Bexhill Street, she was on her return home to Little Common when about 5 p.m. she met George Daw near a road leading to Kewhurst and had some conversation with him. It was dusk when she met him but he had lodged at her father's for about 3 weeks and, having had conversation with him, she could not be mistaken as to his person. She went directly home to her father's and Daw came home between 6 and 7 p.m. — she thought nearly 7 p.m. — and went to bed about 9 p.m. He had on a round frock and waistcoat with sleeves. The waistcoat was afterwards delivered to Thomas Thwaites. Daw got up about 7 a.m. the next morning and had his breakfast and went away between 7 and 8 a.m., but she did not know where he went. A very short time after she met Daw near Kewhurst Road, she met Thomas Sawyer going in the same direction as Daw had gone and he spoke to her. She was quite certain of his person and that he had 2 dogs with him.

Robert Stride of Bexhill, shopkeeper: He kept a shop at Little Common. About dusk on 28 Dec. Thomas Sawyer came to his shop and purchased 1½ oz tobacco and ½d worth of bulls' eyes. He had 2 dogs with him. Stride had examined the paper and tobacco then[2] produced by Thomas Thwaites and they were exactly similar to those he sold to Sawyer. George Daw had occasionally purchased tobacco at his shop but never more than ½ oz at a time. He had examined the tobacco in a box likewise produced by Thwaites which appeared to be of a different quality from that purchased by Sawyer. At the time Sawyer was at his shop he was quite sober and appeared to be quite well.

George Gates of Bexhill, labourer: On the evening of 28 Dec. he was at a place in Little Common called Cooden Gate when Thomas Sawyer and George Daw overtook him, Daw on a pony and Sawyer walking beside him. Gates walked behind them as far as the blacksmith's shop belonging to one Weston at Little Common and saw Sawyer go into a shop belonging to Mr Stride but did not observe which way Daw went. He afterwards saw Sawyer come out of Mr Stride's shop alone and go on the road leading towards Bexhill Street.

William Sawyer of Bexhill: He assisted in looking for his brother Thomas who was missed on 28 Dec. The next day, in consequence of John Prior's telling him there was a dog near Chinting Pond, he went to the place and saw his brother in the pond and one of his dogs on the bank beside the pond. He immediately went to his father and informed him of it and the dog followed him. His father returned with him to the pond where they met Prior and the body was taken out.

John Prior of Bexhill, shoemaker: About 11 a.m. on 29 Dec. he saw a shepherd's dog lying near a pond in Chinting Field. A short time afterwards he met a boy named William Sawyer who enquired if he had seen his brother Tom as they had not seen him since the previous day. Prior told him he had not but that he had seen a shepherd's dog lying near the pond in Chinting Field and recommended him to go that way. Some time afterwards Prior went back and in consequence of the enquiry which Sawyer had made he went back by Chinting Field and, on getting near the pond, saw some person was in it and he immediately went for assistance and returned to the place in a few minutes. Edward Sawyer arrived there at the same time. On taking the body out of the water it was found to be Thomas Sawyer. He was quite dead. Edward Sawyer searched his pockets and said that his watch was gone. There was a mark under one of his ears which appeared to have been occasioned by a blow.

Edward Sawyer of Bexhill, labourer: He was in the employ of Mr Arthur Brook of Bexhill and resided at Marine Cottage, about ½ mile from Bexhill Street. On 28 Dec. his son Thomas left home to go to his work about 7 a.m., at which time he had with him his watch, chain and seal which he saw him take from the head of his bed when he got up. His son was employed by Brook as a shepherd and was nearly 19. He generally took his dinner with him, his employment being about 3 miles from home, and usually returned about 6 p.m. He took his dinner with him as usual on 28 Dec. He did not return at his usual time that evening which surprised him as he was very regular, but between 7 and 8 p.m. one of his dogs returned which led him to fear some accident had befallen him or that he might have been murdered. In consequence he immediately set about a search. When his son left home in the morning he had 2 dogs with [him] but only one returned that night. About 5 years since, an information was laid against Edward Daw for an offence against the game laws and he was convicted on the evidence of his son Thomas and imprisoned. His son had frequently since that time said that he was afraid to be out after dark as Daw had threatened to kill him. Edward Sawyer himself had some dispute with Daw in which he accused Daw of having threatened to kill his son and he said in reply: 'And so I will.' It was these circumstances which led him to fear his son might have been murdered. Soon after the dog returned he commenced his search for his son and continued it until about 1 a.m. but without effect. About noon on 29 Dec. he saw Daw who asked him if he had not lost his son and said he supposed he might be murdered and thrown into the Parson's Wood where there were so many rough persons about. He replied: 'God knows where he is, but I am sure there is something the matter.' Daw said he would go and look for him if anybody would go with him, but he should not like to go alone. He also said he was sure it was not him as he was at home before daylight shut in and had a witness that he was at home all night and did not get up until 11 a.m. when his mother called him and told him Tom Sawyer was lost or words to that effect. Daw then went away in a direction towards Cooden. Between 1 and 2 p.m. on the same day another of Edward Sawyer's sons named William informed him that Thomas was in the pond in Chinting Field. He immediately went to the place and met Prior there who arrived at the same time. When his son William came to him the dog which had not returned the preceding evening was with him and went back with Edward Sawyer to the pond. He found his son Thomas in the pond with his head under water, his coat covered over his head and his crook in the pond a few feet from his body. The pond was very small and had only about 2 feet of water in it. On taking him out he was found to be quite dead. Edward Sawyer, on examining his pockets, found that his watch, chain and seal were gone and a mark under one of his ears which appeared to him to have been occasioned by a blow but he did not at that time discover any other marks of violence on him. The grass and ground on the edge of the pond near which he found the body was very much trodden down.[3] The watch then[2] produced by Thomas Dallaway and the seal likewise produced by Thomas Thwaites were the same which his son had in his possession on 28 Dec. when he left home.

George Daw, in custody on the charge of having murdered Thomas Sawyer and cautioned by Bedingfield that if in making his defence or any other statement on the subject he said anything which might criminate himself it would be taken in writing and given in evidence against him on his trial: On 28 Dec. he was taking up a hare which he found in a wire in Gillham Wood and Thomas Sawyer came along. He asked Sawyer not to tell his master of it, but he said he would. Daw told him if he did he would box his ears for him. Daw hid it up in the hedge because he would not carry it home and that he might see him again and see what he said. He fell in with him again at night as Daw came along Cooden Down and Daw asked him about it. Sawyer said he would then and Daw told him if he did he would box his ears and that was all that passed just then. Then they went to the blacksmith's shop with the horse and stood there about ¼ hour talking and then Sawyer went away towards Stride's and Daw went away up the road down to his brother's and never saw him any more afterwards till he stood talking with Wyborn and Lamb and then he cut away across the road through Mr Brook's Hop Garden Field towards Bragg's Farm. Then Daw cut away across by his brother's and away up the track and there he fell in with him in a meadow and fetched him a rap on the side of his head with his fist and snatched his watch away as he was falling down. Then Daw went away and when he got about 6 or 7 rod away he looked round and saw Sawyer was going along the track and that's all he knew about it. His brother Edward was not with him. If any person had anything to say about the waistcoat Daw could talk with them about it. He said there was a print of a hand upon the waistcoat and this was the way it came. On the night of 26 Dec. Ben Catt and Daw had a few words and Catt knocked Daw down on the road and his hand was all dirty and he catched hold of Daw by the arm and pulled him up again and that's how it came dirty.

At the assizes the grand jury, to which all the witnesses of 30 Dec. and 6 Jan., except Richard Delves, and also James Russell, William Duke, Edward Cossum, Edward Veness, John Charles Brook and Thomas Charles Bellingham gave evidence, presented an indictment which charged

George and Edward Daw late of Bexhill, labourers, with murdering Thomas Sawyer at Bexhill on 28 Dec. There were 3 counts: that they struck him on the left side of the head with their right fists, thereby giving him a fracture on the left side of the skull 3 inches long, ½ inch wide and ½ inch deep of which he immediately died; that they struck him on the left side of the head each with a bludgeon worth 3d which they held in their right hands, thereby giving him a fracture as above of which he immediately died; and that they threw and pushed him into a pond which contained a great quantity of water whereby he was drowned, dying immediately. George Daw, aged 21, and Edward Daw, 30, who had been committed to gaol by Bedingfield on 6 Jan., pleaded not guilty. George was convicted and sentenced to be hanged on 28 Mar. and then dissected and anatomized; he had no goods. Edward was acquitted; he had not fled and so was discharged. ASSI 36/1; ASSI 94/1929. Cf. **284**.]

1 sc. *on 30 Dec.*
2 sc. *on 6 Jan.*
3 *Query footmarks* in pencil in the margin.

SEAFORD CORONERS' INQUESTS

Inquest of Thomas Chambers

468 20 Mar. 1815. Seaford. Jurors of Seaford and 4 neighbouring townships: James Brooker, Edward Shoosmith, James Chambers, John Gorring, Thomas Allwork, James Simmons, John Banks, John Simmons, John Haine, James Pierce, John Wood, William Pitcher, Edward Simmons. On 15 Mar. Joseph Stevens late of Seaford, labourer, murdered Solomon Young at Seaford with a clasp-knife of iron and steel worth 3d which he held in his right hand, giving him a wound in the left side of the breast 1 inch long and 2 inches deep of which he languished at Seaford until 18 Mar. and then died. Stevens had no goods or chattels, lands or tenements in Sussex or elsewhere at the time of the murder to the jurors' knowledge. [ASSI 94/1721]

[This inquest, which Chambers held as Seaford bailiff and coroner for the time being, was delivered to Horsham assizes on 20 Mar. when the grand jury, to which Henry Wood, Jane Shingleton, Jane Jenner, Charles Verrall, surgeon, and Richard Ade gave evidence, presented an indictment similar to the inquest verdict except that the weapon was a knife worth 2d, the wound was in the left side of the body 3 inches deep and 2 inches wide and the last sentence was omitted. Stevens, aged 63, who had been committed to gaol by Charles Harison, JP, on 16 Mar. charged on the oath of Jane Shingleton and others with having stabbed Young in the left side with a knife at Seaford on 15 Mar. with the intention of murdering him, pleaded not guilty and was acquitted of murder but convicted of manslaughter; he had no goods and was sentenced to pay a fine of 1s and to a year in Horsham gaol and until he paid the fine. He was in gaol at and after the assizes of 22 July. ASSI 94/1721; ASSI 94/1722. Cf. **185**.]

EARLY INQUESTS NOT PREVIOUSLY PUBLISHED

469 26 Apr. 1398. [Hellingly], Dill hundred. Thomas Preston, county coroner. Jurors: John Wysel, William Hendenne, Thomas Bothel, John Belsaunt, Robert atte Melle, John atte Welle, Thomas Fonel, Simon Holte, William Chylly, Richard Courtevyle, Nicholas atte Gate, Thomas Wyltonesherst. On 26 Apr. Richard Baron of Mayfield broke William Fyssh's house in the tithing of Hellingly and feloniously killed William Mabbe of Hellingly there with a dagger worth 1d. Baron fled from the neighbourhood on that account. The finders were William Fyssh and Richard Wayte who were attached; their sureties were Thomas Fonel and William Hendenne. The nearest neighbours were Richard Wayte and William Chylly. [AMS 5592/114]

470 [*Date, place and coroner omitted.*] Jurors: William Batenor, Richard Markewyk, Thomas Levyng, [William Batenore *struck through*], Simon Galope, Peter Tayllour, Robert [*written above* John *struck through*] Shypherd, Robert a Burrowe, Richard Dunston, Roger Melleward, John Nevell, John Christofer, [Richard Lucas *struck through*], Gilbert Turk. Richard Jamys late of Lewes, 'laborer', was in a small boat on a large river and by misadventure a pole called 'a quante' broke whereby he fell into the water and drowned. [SC 2/206/34, f 45v]

[Entered after the proceedings of a court held at Uckfield on 25 May 1506.]

471 [*Date, place and coroner omitted.*] Jurors: [Andrew Elis *struck through*], John a Gate, William Repe sen., John Selwyn, Richard Dunston, ..., John Lane, Thomas Wrenbury, William Repe jun., Thomas Walcot, Gilbert Turke, John Nevill, ..., Cuthbert Hostyll, Peter Valantyne. Andrew Denys of Cliffe, 'hu[?sbandman'], was drowned in ... of a 'pyn' called 'a dolpyn'[1] of no value on a small boat and so from carelessness fell into a stream and died in the tithing of Southerham in South Malling on 15 Dec. 1506. [*Damaged.*] [SC 2/206/34, f 204]

1 sc. *dowel-pin.*

472 21 Jan. 1507. Wellingham in Ringmer. William Staple, coroner of the archbishop of Canterbury's bailiwick of South Malling. Jurors: William Lydyng, John Webbe, Robert Breden, Robert a Borough, Robert Shepherd, John Adcok, John a Wode of Wellingham, John Galop, Simon Galop, Thomas Broderton [*written above* John Sharpe *struck through*], John Borne, John Puppe. About 1 a.m. on 19 Jan., when a female stranger came to Wellingham, feloniously broke and entered Thomas Levyng's house there to rob him and took 1½ measures of salt worth 12d and a ... worth 9d of his goods and chattels found there, John Levyng of Ringmer, 'laborer', and Robert Shepherd were lying in wait ... So John Levyng and Shepherd, in self defence and to arrest the woman in the house, by misadventure struck her on the head with 'a hegbill', giving her a wound of which she immediately died. [*Damaged.*] [SC 2/206/34, f 204v]

APPENDIX

DOCUMENTS CONCERNING REX v THOMAS WILLIAM WHEELER

473 Wheeler's bill **190**. The entries are lettered from A to T (with the omission of I) for ease of reference to and from **495–501** and **505**. A pencilled note above the undated Southease entry says that the inquest was taken at Itford in Beddingham.[1] Another pencilled note at the end of the bill reads: 'Beddingham — Write to officers about King, stated to have been drowned at Southease.' That is preceded by a list of the following inquest venues: Hartfield 2, Maresfield 1, Eastbourne 2, Chiddingly 1, Southwick 1, Brighton 4, Southease 1, Newhaven 1, Chalvington 1, Preston 1, Hailsham 1.

[QCC/E2, no 36]

1 George King was buried at Beddingham on 14 June, aged 53: PAR 238/1/5/1.

474 Wheeler's bill **191**. The entries are numbered in pencil from 1 to 21 for ease of reference to and from **479**, **481**, **482**, **484–489**, **491**, **493**, **494**, **497** and **506**. There is a small pencilled circle against those of 7 and 31 Aug. and 26 Sept. and a pencilled cross against that of 15 Aug.

[*blank*] Oct. 1816. Covering letter from Wheeler, 43 Russell Street, Brighton, to Mr Sacre[1] at Mr Langridge's office, Lewes.[2] He had requested Mr Hodd to call on Sacre with his bill which he would like him to get allowed, giving Sacre authority to give Hodd the order upon Mr Hoper[3] and asking that that be done the next day, before the Brighton coach set out.

[QCC/E2, no 17]

1 Thomas Sacre: cf. **527**.
2 William Balcombe Langridge was clerk of the peace for Sussex from 1806 until 1832: Brent, 66. In subsequent letters he was usually addressed as either solicitor or clerk of the peace and his address was usually given as Lewes but occasionally as the Record Room, County Hall (**487**, **498**, **535**) and once (**540**) as the Court-house, Lewes. In the following entries he is referred to merely as Langridge and the Lewes addresses are omitted.
3 John Hoper was county treasurer for the eastern division of Sussex from 1801 to 1821: Brent, 67.

475 The second version of Wheeler's bill **191**. It has a pencilled note: 'Of no use.'

[QCC/E2, no 62]

476 Wheeler's bill **192**. There are 3 separate pencilled notes on it: 'Did you hold the whole of these inquests? If not, have the goodness to mark them by whom the same respectively were taken.' 'Have the goodness to write the name of the party taking the inquests against them respectively in the margin.' 'I do not know by whom those were taken which are not marked. I presume they were taken by Wheeler himself. Sometimes a Mr Hargraves has gone for Wheeler and at others a man of the name of Brown.' Mr Barrow is written against the entry of 10 Dec. and Mr Billingham against the last 4 entries.

[QCC/E2, no 18]

477 17 Oct. 1816. Letter from James Cranbourne Strode, Thornfield Park, Frant, to Langridge, asking what the coroner was entitled to for his expenses and journey from Brighton to Frant, 32 miles. He had come the previous week and charged £4 3s, which was paid by the poor woman's family who sent for him, and his expenses of tea etc. — more than the 1s a mile and guinea for the body which Strode understood he was allowed. [QCC/E2, no 7]

478 31 Oct. 1816. Draft reply to **477**. Langridge had presented to the quarter sessions at the White Hart, Lewes, Strode's letter and Wheeler's bill in which he had charged the county the full amount allowed by statute for the inquest. He was severely censured and his bill was disallowed. Langridge was ordered to inquire about his conduct in all the inquests taken since the Midsummer sessions, particularly whether by him personally or by deputy. Wheeler's justification for taking £4 3s from the deceased's family was that he told the messenger (probably the constable) that if they required an unusually speedy inquest they must pay for a post-chaise, to which they agreed, and he received from them no more than his actual expenses. Strode, as a magistrate, was requested to investigate the facts. [QCC/E2, no 7]

479 20 Nov. 1816. Examination of deponents before James Cranbourne Strode, JP, at Frant concerning the inquest on Mary wife of George Page of Frant, butcher, sent to Langridge on 6 Dec.

Robert Rogers, constable of Frant: On 8 Oct. he went to Brighton and asked Wheeler to come as quickly as possible to Frant to view the body, but nothing was said about the expenses of a post-chaise. He recommended Wheeler to come on horseback, the roads being bad. Wheeler told him to summon a jury for noon the next day and that he would be there about then, but he did not arrive until about 5 p.m. when he issued a warrant to Rogers, dated 4 p.m., to summon a jury which had been waiting ever since noon. Wheeler asked Rogers for the deceased's husband and said he should look to Rogers for his expenses.

William Homewood of Frant, innkeeper: Wheeler arrived at his house in a post-chaise with a pair of horses about 5 p.m. on 9 Oct. with 2 ladies and a child. After the inquest Wheeler ordered refreshments and told Homewood to charge it to the deceased's relatives, as was customary. The cost was 6s which the deceased's brother had since paid.

Edward Page of Wadhurst, butcher, the deceased's son-in-law: The inquest was adjourned from the Bull Inn to his father's house to view the body. In the kitchen Wheeler asked him who was going to pay the £4 3s expenses. He agreed to pay and followed the jury back to the Bull Inn and heard evidence and the verdict of insanity. Wheeler objected to receiving the £4 3s in the jury's presence but told him to bring it upstairs where he paid him and Wheeler delivered the burial warrant. [QCC/E2, no 8]

480 31 Oct. 1816. Draft letter from Langridge to the overseers of the poor of [*blank*] parish, by order of the quarter sessions, concerning inquests taken by Wheeler between the Midsummer and Michaelmas sessions. In the coroner's bill presented at the last sessions it was stated that an inquest was taken in your parish on [*blank*] on view of the body of [*blank*] who [*blank*]. Langridge was directed to inquire whether such an inquest was taken by Wheeler in person or by deputy; if by the latter, his name; whether any gratuity by way of fee or otherwise was demanded and taken, by Wheeler or his deputy, of the deceased's relatives or any other person on account of attending such inquest or under any other representation; and whether any deodand was assessed on the inanimate thing occasioning the death, to what amount, whether it was paid and to and by whom. [QCC/E2, no 22]

481 3 Nov. 1816. Reply of W Wisden, overseer of Henfield, to **480**. Wheeler himself attended the inquest on John Golds on 10 Oct. Wisden had been informed on 3 Nov. by John Golds sen., the deceased's son, that Wheeler had demanded £5 which he paid him on the day of the inquest. [QCC/E2, no 27]

482 4[1] Nov.1816. Reply of John Borrer, overseer of Portslade, to **480**. The only inquest in Portslade was on Ann Pelling, an unfortunate girl who hanged herself. He could not discover that the coroner, who attended in person, demanded or received any gratuity from anyone for attending. [QCC/E2, no 26]

1 Altered from *2*.

483 Note: Mr Borrer could state no more about the inquest at Portslade than already communicated.[1] [QCC/E2, no 30]

1 sc. in **482**.

484 4 Nov. 1816. Reply of James Damper, vestry clerk of Mayfield, to **480** for the parish officers. Wheeler personally took the inquest on 31 Aug. on Edward Young who accidentally fell into a pond and was drowned. After returning with the jury to the Star Inn he told Joel Beeching, the governor of the workhouse, that if Young's relatives were unable to pay the expenses of the inquest the charge must fall on the parish. He then made out the enclosed bill for £5 11s and receipted it, but the governor paid him only £5. He also paid 14s expenses at the inn which Wheeler told him was customary. Wheeler then paid 12s expenses on the jury out of the £5.

Enclosed bill: Sums of 10s, 1s, 1s, £2, £2, 4s 6d, £1 and 2s 6d, total £5 11s.[1] Received of Joseph Beeching the above sum of £5 11s: T W Wheeler. [QCC/E2, no 9]

1 Altered from *£5 19s*.

485 4 Nov. 1816. Reply of Joseph Als, overseer of Little Horsted, to **480**. The inquest on Francis Crump, who hanged himself on 23 Sept., was held on 24 Sept. and attended by Wheeler himself. A verdict of lunancy was returned. Nothing was paid to Wheeler, but he demanded 40s of Als for his fees, telling him it was always paid by the overseers when the deceased's relatives could not pay it. Als told Wheeler that he was unacquainted with the business, but he could depend upon having whatever was right. Wheeler then went away and Als had not heard from him since. [QCC/E2, no 19]

486 4 Nov. 1816. Reply of Thomas King, overseer of Cliffe, to **480**. Wheeler took the inquest on Elizabeth Short himself. No fee was demanded. [QCC/E2, no 23]

487 4 Nov. 1816. Reply of W H Barrow, East Grinstead, to **480** which the churchwardens and overseers of West Hoathly had just delivered to him. Barrow himself had taken the inquest on John Goodwin, a lunatic, as Wheeler's deputy at his request. He had been in the habit of acting in that neighbourhood for many years for both Wheeler and his great uncle.[1] No gratuity by way of fee or otherwise was demanded or taken in that or any other instance in which he had acted as Wheeler's deputy. Goodwin was a pauper of the parish with no relatives to Barrow's knowledge. [QCC/E2, no 24]

1 Recte *uncle*. Thomas William Wheeler's father was Charles, a son of Francis Wheeler, and William Wheeler was another son of Francis: PAR 414/1/1/3; PAR 410/1/1/5.

488 6 Nov. 1816. Reply of John Shoosmith, Laughton, to **480**. On 14 Sept. Edward Couchman fell from a ladder getting down from a pea-mow about 8 or 9 feet high in Shoosmith's barn and died within 24 hours. Shoosmith sent for Wheeler and it was proved by a witness, George Rowe, who held the ladder, that Couchman was clear from the mow and about 3 steps down the ladder when he fell, thought to be taken in a fit. The top of the ladder was 2 or 3 feet above the mow and the jury found that there was no fault on Shoosmith's part from either the mow or the ladder. Nevertheless Wheeler fined him and laid the fine of 40s on the mow, which Shoosmith paid him in the presence of the jury. He considered it an imposition and that the fine should have been laid on the ladder which was worth no more than 5s. He hoped that something could be done. [QCC/E2, no 21]

489 6 Nov. 1816. Reply of Ambrose Bray, overseer of Lindfield, to **480**. By inquiry he found that Wheeler attended the inquest on William Wood on 7 Aug. in person and made a charge of £2 for advice on Mr Beard, Wood's friend, which was paid to Wheeler by Thomas Fairhall of the Red Lion Inn where the inquest was taken.

Evidence of Thomas Fairhall, Red Lion, Lindfield: The inquest on Wood was at his house on 7 Aug. William Beard, Wood's reputed father, sent him a message wishing him to pay all reasonable expenses attending the funeral etc. At the same time Wheeler asked Fairhall where Wood's friends were and who was to pay him his fees. Fairhall asked what fees. Fairhall replied: 40s besides his expenses. Fairhall paid him that and was repaid it with Wheeler's expenses at his house by George Hackman. [QCC/E2, no 15]

490 19 Mar. 1817. Letter from Thomas Fairhall, Lindfield, to Langridge. He was mistaken about Hackman paying him Wheeler's bill.[1] He was paid by John Harland, shopkeeper undertaker, by order of Hackman. He had got Wheeler's bill, and the receipt in his own handwriting, and would bring it to Langridge at Horsham. [QCC/E2, no 49]

1 Cf. **489**.

491 9 Nov. 1816. Reply of Thomas Beard, Rottingdean, to **480**. Wheeler himself attended the inquests at Rottingdean on John McDonald, a boy named Charman and Ann Freeman. On the first he received 20s or more from McDonald's friends. On the second no fee was paid but a deodand was set on the wagon and horses which had occasioned the death; it was paid to Wheeler by Beard at the time and had since been repaid to Beard by Mr Alexander, the proprietor of the wagon and horses. On the third £1 3s was demanded by Wheeler and paid by the husband.

Note: 20s and upward as fees; deodand £5; 23s and upward as fees. All paid. [QCC/E2, no 13]

492 Evidence of Ann wife of Thomas Chapman of Rottingdean: She was present at the inquest on Mrs Freeman on 26 Sept. 1816. After the inquest Wheeler called her aside and asked whether her uncle Edward Freeman, the deceased's husband, was able to pay him his demand, saying that if he was not he must apply to the parish for it. She asked what his demand was and was told £1 3s. She then went downstairs to her uncle and told him of it. He gave her £1 3s which she paid to Wheeler. [QCC/E2, no 12]

493 9 Nov. 1816. Reply of George Richardson, high constable of Brighton, to **480** for the overseers, as it was his duty to attend on the coroner and summon the juries. The inquest on Madam Latour[1] was perfectly correct. So was that on Ann Arnold, an infant, but the jury fined Daniel Haylar, the owner of the timber-tug, 10s as a deodand for its being left in the street instead of being kept in a cart-house. As to John Paine, there must be some mistake as no inquest was held on him. He certainly died rather suddenly, Richardson believed in a fit. His son-in-law told him at the time of his death that his friends and relations thought an inquest quite unnecessary and so none was held. The 2 inquests were both taken by Wheeler himself and Richardson was sure that no gratuity was taken from the friends of either deceased or from any other person. Richardson had since asked Haylar whether he had paid the 10s and he said he had not.

Enclosed: 9 Nov. 1816. Note from Richardson that he had inquired of Mr Williams about an inquest taken the previous year on a child[2] run over by a gentleman's carriage. Williams did not attend the coroner himself, but Mr Mandy, the headborough, did and said that the inquest was held at the White Swan, High Street, Brighton, and that the jury awarded £50 on the carriage and horses as a deodand, but he did not know if it was paid. [QCC/E2, no 25]

1 *Margaret Latour of Carlton Row, aged 72* in PAR 255/1/5/2.
2 *Louisa Ramsey*: cf. **187**, **501**.

494 15 Nov. 1816. Reply of William Knight, West Firle, to **480**. Wheeler made no other demand at the inquest on Thomas Smith than his bill of about 6s at the Ram Inn where he took the inquest. He carried away the fowling-piece with which it appeared Smith shot himself. [QCC/E2, no 20]

495 16 Nov. 1816. Reply of Thomas Guy, Chalvington, to a letter similar to **496**. Wheeler himself was at the inquest on his brother and demanded £2 which he paid him. Death was not thought to be occasioned by the horse, but the deceased dropped in a fit as he had twice before. [QCC/E2, no 31]

496 19 Nov. 1816. Letter from Langridge to the overseers of Preston, asking whether an inquest on 2 July on James Hutton, who shot himself in a fit of lunacy, was taken by Wheeler in person or by deputy; if by the latter, his name; and whether any gratuity by way of fee or otherwise was demanded and taken, by Wheeler or his deputy, of Hutton's relatives or any other person on account of attending such inquest or under any other representation.

Subscribed: Wheeler attended in person and received no fee: B Smithers, churchwarden, Preston. [QCC/E2, no 33]

497 20 Nov. 1816. Reply of William Elphick, Newhaven, to a letter similar to **496**. The first inquest was on James Goddard, a child found drowned in the river on 20 June. Wheeler did not attend personally but by a substitute, whose name Elphick believed was Whichelo. The second was on a Frenchman named Dulervel who was accidentally drowned on 3 Sept. Wheeler attended personally; Elphick was foreman of the jury. The third was on Edward Poole who died by the visitation of God on 4 Sept. Wheeler attended personally; Elphick was foreman of the jury. The fourth was on William Dumbrill who hanged himself on 4 Oct. Wheeler was sent for on 5 Oct. but did not attend until 6 Oct.; he attended personally. Elphick was not on the jury. As to the inquest said by Wheeler to have been held on 15 Aug. on an unchristened infant, the child was 5 or 6 years old, named Ockenden, the son of a boat officer,[1] and was baptized at Seaford and buried there. Wheeler was sent for but did not attend himself or by substitute. He said there was no occasion as the doctor was with the child when it choked with the plum-stone. Elphick had called at County Hall on the previous 2 Saturdays to see Langridge but found he was in London. He could see him at any time to give him more information. [QCC/E2, no 11]

1 *Joseph Ockenden*: cf. **527**.

498 21 Nov. 1816. Reply of W H Barrow, East Grinstead, to a letter similar to **496**. He took the inquests on John Killick and Edward Card at Hartfield in May as Wheeler's deputy. [QCC/E2, no 37]

499 22 Nov. 1816. Reply of Samuel Attree, Maresfield, to a letter similar to **496** for the overseers. The inquest on Ann Wise was taken by Mr Barrow of East Grinstead, Wheeler's deputy, who told the jury that he officiated for Wheeler occasionally. No fee was demanded of Wise's relatives except 1s for each of the 12 jurymen and 2s 6d for the headborough which Barrow said was the customary allowance on such occasions. Those sums and 1s more given to James (the driver of the London coach from Lewes to Brighton) to take a note to Wheeler desiring his attendance were all that had been paid. Attree had sent for Wise's brother who gave him the above information. No deodand was assessed on the wagon. Attree did not know if Barrow had a right to claim anything further, but knew that when Wheeler had attended at Maresfield after a child[1] had drowned itself in a ditch, he charged the headborough 20s because its parents were unable to pay through poverty. [QCC/E2, no 38]

1 *George Kingsland*: cf. **188**, **505**.

500 23 Nov. 1816. Reply of John Parris, Hellingly, to a letter similar to **496** for the officers of Hailsham. Concerning the inquest on Marshall[1] on 13 July, as he was a pauper of Hellingly J P, one of the constables of the hundred,[2] was immediately applied to on Marshall's being found. J P wrote to Wheeler who attended in person and on view of the body appeared particular in desiring the attendance of the doctor, Mr Long, who had previously attended Marshall in his illness. No fee was demanded or paid by anyone nor any gratuity other than some refreshment which the parish desired J P to offer him at Horsebridge. [QCC/E2, no 34]

1 *John Marshall*: cf. **190**.
2 sc. Dill hundred.

501 23 Nov. 1816. Reply of George Richardson, high constable, Brighton, to a letter similar to **496**. An inquest was held on 8 June at the Lord Nelson's Arms, Russell Street, on Oliver Holden, unfortunately drowned with his brother William by the upsetting of their boat off Brighton. As Richardson could not find Wheeler, Mr Billingham came to Richardson with the proper documents and said that he was deputed by Wheeler to take the inquest in his absence which he accordingly did. Nothing was demanded or taken by him as a fee or remuneration. Some time later Captain Bales and Mr Ingram, high sheriff,[1] called upon Richardson and seemed much displeased at the inquest being taken by deputy and insisted that in future he should seek out Wheeler or send to Petworth for the coroner there. Since then Wheeler had attended at Brighton inquests. On 26 June William Holden was picked up on shore and Wheeler held an inquest on him at the Packet in Brighton. Nothing was demanded by him of the father or any of their relations by way of fee or remuneration. The parish allows 12s on each inquest, i.e. 1s to each juryman, but where the friends and relations are able they are generally asked to pay it instead of the expenses falling on the parish. In the above cases the father of the 2 youths paid the jurors' expenses, viz £1 4s, which the coroner had nothing to do with.

Also on 26 June Wheeler took an inquest at the King's Arms, George Street, on John Moon who had taken a quantity of laudanum which caused his death. No fee or remuneration was either taken or demanded of Moon's friends or relations.

On 2 July Wheeler held an inquest on James Page, a hairdresser, who suddenly died a natural death. The expense, viz 12s, was placed to the account of the parish, but no fee or remuneration was taken or demanded by him of Page's relations or friends.

These are all the particulars, with the others already sent,[2] that had occurred during his time of office since 16 Apr.

As to the death of Louisa Ramsey, Mr Mandy, who summoned the jury and attended the inquest, was not at home nor would be for some time, but Richardson obtained all the particulars from him that he knew and sent them to Langridge in his last letter.[2] Since then Richardson had found out Ramsey's parents living at 16 Thomas's Street, Brighton, who said that no fee or remuneration was demanded by Wheeler of them on account of the inquest. He also inquired of Nathaniel Bradford, the foreman of the jury, who said that the jury fined £50 as deodand on the carriage and horses of Mr Newland, their owner, who then lived at Mr Alderton's, the cabinet-maker, 16 St James's Street, Brighton, but Alderton could not tell if Newland paid the £50. He said he left Brighton soon after and Bradford, the foreman, of Church Street, could not tell if the deodand was paid.

Richardson hoped and trusted that, whatever the result of the inquiries, it would look with pity and mercy on Wheeler and his infant family. [QCC/E2, no 32]

1 sc. James Ingram of Rottingdean: *List of Sheriffs for England and Wales* (PRO Lists and Indexes, IX, 1898), 143.
2 In **493**.

502 24 Jan. 1817. Reply of James Turner, Southwick, to Langridge's letter of 23 Jan. Wheeler held an inquest on Henry Boxall on 2 Sept. 1815 at the Schooner, the house of Samuel Adams jun., in Southwick. Adams came to Turner as churchwarden, in the absence of the overseers, and asked him to come to his house as Wheeler had demanded £2, saying that the body could not be buried until it was paid. Turner went to his house and found the jury sitting. He asked Wheeler if it was customary to pay the £2. Wheeler said that it was and that it must be paid before Boxall could be buried. Turner then paid him the £2 and Wheeler told him that he (Turner) was to be repaid out of the county rate. [QCC/E2, no 10]

503 8 Mar. 1817. Letter from William Furner, Brighton, to Langridge. At Langridge's request Furner went to Shoreham to inquire of any acts of extortion or malpractice committed by Wheeler as coroner in Shoreham or its neighbourhood and found one at Old Shoreham which appeared to be of a most flagrant nature, the man on whom it was practised being a poor labourer in the employ of Mr Parsons of Old Shoreham, farmer. The man's examination was enclosed together with a letter afterwards written by Wheeler to him proposing to return the money extorted from him,[1] which was never done. After the man had paid the 10s 6d he was informed that Wheeler's demand was illegal and he accordingly came to Brighton to get him to refund the money, but without success. His wife's sister, who resided as a servant with Mr Lamb of Brighton, several times afterwards called on Wheeler for the same purpose, but with no better success. At length Lamb, thinking it a very hard case on the poor man and a most glaring imposition by the coroner, personally interfered with Wheeler on the subject who in consequence wrote the letter mentioned above. So the matter ended, Wheeler never having returned the money and the man thinking it useless to make further inquiries about it.

There was another case of extortion practised by Wheeler on Mr Turner of Southwick whom Furner had called on the previous day and who informed him that he had sent the particulars to Langridge recently in reply to a request from him.[2]

PS. Since writing the above Furner had seen Lamb who informed him that after repeated applications to Wheeler he had received from him the enclosed note telling him that he had given instructions for the money to be repaid to Reeves.[1] [QCC/E2, no 55]

1 **504**.
2 **502**.

504 7 Mar. 1817. Evidence of William Reeves of Old Shoreham, husbandman. On 15 Nov. 1816 Wheeler attended at his house at Old Shoreham to take an inquest on his daughter Sarah who was accidentally burnt. After the inquest was over and the jury had gone away Wheeler told him that his charge on him was a guinea, but as he understood that he was very poor he would accept ½ guinea which he must pay immediately. Reeves, having lately received his wages from his master to enable him to pay for the child's funeral, happened to have 10s 6d which he immediately paid to Wheeler. Having later understood that Wheeler's demand was illegal, he went to Brighton to try to get the money back. He could not see Wheeler and accordingly asked Mr Lamb of Brighton to try to get the money for him as he was much in want of it. Shortly after Lamb had made an application to Wheeler, Reeves received a letter from Wheeler stating that he had directed a person in his employ to leave with him the 10s 6d which Lamb had interfered about, but [no] such sum nor any part thereof was ever paid to him.

Attached. Letter from Wheeler to Reeves, near the Gate, Old Shoreham. His employee would leave him the 10s 6d which Lamb had interfered about. He thought it better to send it to him. He would receive it in a day or two.

Letter from Wheeler, Russell House, to G Lamb, Ship Street. He had given instructions for the money to be paid to Reeves. [QCC/E2, no 14]

505 Schedule of inquests in **190** with extracts from **496–501**. The extract from **495** adds that the £2 was assessed as a deodand on the horse from which Guy was supposed to have fallen; that from **498** adds that no gratuity was demanded or taken at either inquest; and that from **499** gives further information about the former inquest, viz about 12 months before, when Wheeler took an inquest on Thomas Kingsland's child who was drowned, he demanded of the headborough 20s, the parents being too poor to pay, and it was paid to him by John Bright. There is an extract from one letter which does not survive. It states that the undated Southease inquest was taken by Frederick Lee, printer, Wheeler's brother-in-law, but no fee was demanded or taken. [QCC/E2, no 35]

506 Schedule of inquests in **191** with extracts from **477**, **479**, **481**, **482**, **484–489**, **491**, **493**, **494** and **497**. The extract from **485** wrongly calls Joseph Als overseer of Isfield instead of Little Horsted; and that from **493** adds that it was not ascertained if the deodand of 10s had been paid. There is an extract from one letter which does not survive. It states that the inquest of 21 Sept. was taken by Wheeler who went with the jury to the public house and spent 12s which was left for the overseer of Isfield to pay. [QCC/E2, no 16]

507 Another version of **506**, with less detail and a few unimportant variations and stating that the deodand of 10s in **493** had not been paid. [QCC/E2, no 28]

508 11 Jan. 1817. Serjeant S Shepherd's[1] opinion on the travelling expenses of coroners. In some counties, such as Middlesex and Kent, they were allowed 9d a mile for travelling to and from inquests while in others the payment was for the outward journeys only. Shepherd's opinion was that the true construction of 25 George II c 29 was that 9d a mile should be paid for the outward and home journeys. [QCC/E2, no 66]

1 Sir Samuel Shepherd, king's serjeant, solicitor-general: *ODNB*.

509 17 Jan. 1817. Order of Lewes quarter sessions for the clerk of the peace to take the attorney-general's opinion as to how to proceed against Wheeler for misdemeanour in his office, viz acts of extortion, and how provision might be made for the performance of his duties while he is unable to execute them; for the clerk to proceed against him as he should be advised; and for the suspension of the payment of the bills then presented by Wheeler's agent and of those produced by Wheeler at the last sessions. [QO/EW 42]

510 Draft case against Wheeler. Sussex has only 2 coroners elected by the freeholders, one for the western part who resides at Petworth in Arundel rape and the other for the eastern part usually residing at Lewes or Brighton in Lewes rape. The former's district is the 3 western rapes of Chichester, Arundel and Bramber, or as nearly so as may be, and that of the latter Lewes and Pevensey rapes, each district running through the county from the sea to its northern boundary. For the other eastern rape, Hastings, another coroner is elected, not by the freeholders of the county but by the earl of Chichester who has the appointment, except for a small portion over which another coroner is appointed by the lord of the hundreds comprising that portion or district. Of the last 2 coroners the former lives at Hastings and the latter at Battle. The distance between the usual residences of the 2 county coroners, at Petworth and Brighton, is about 30 miles and that between Brighton and Battle over 30 miles. Since the election of the present eastern coroner, Wheeler, on the death of the former one, and until about a month ago he had lived at Brighton, but since then he has been confined as a debtor in Horsham gaol. On the day of the last Michaelmas quarter sessions at Lewes a letter was delivered to the clerk of the peace from a magistrate not attending, asking what the coroner was entitled to for attending an inquest at Frant on a female who had hanged herself, Wheeler having made a charge of £4 3s on her family which was paid to him. The clerk laid the letter before the bench, which requested Wheeler's attendance. His answer to the charge not proving satisfactory and his demeanour induced the court to suspend an order for payment of his bill then presented and to direct the clerk to write to the overseers of the parishes in which inquests had lately been taken for information whether they had been taken by the coroner in person or by deputy and whether any gratuity by way of fee or otherwise was demanded or taken by the coroner or his deputy of the relatives of the deceased or of anyone for attending such inquest or under any other representation. Those letters produced answers that the coroner personally had demanded and taken of the deceased's relatives and also of the parish officers considerable sums, viz from £2 to £5, as allowed for fees and expenses on attending such inquests as coroner, despite his having charged in his bill on the county the amount allowed for them by 25 George II c 29. Also in more than one instance in the last 9 months he charged the county with inquests which from the overseers' returns appear never to have been taken. During the last month, while Wheeler was in gaol, several inquests were taken by a person deputed by him, which was often the case before his confinement, and, although presumably illegal, it appears in the existing circumstances indispensable, the other county coroner living at a great distance and having a large extent of country to superintend.

From the present coroner's conduct in extorting money from individuals and parish officers for performing his duties and from his general habit, demeanour and conduct — disgraceful in an individual but more especially in a person entrusted with the execution of public duties of so high an import — the magistrates felt imperatively called upon to cause his conduct to be publicly and legally investigated, that in the event of such charges being substantiated he might be removed and another appointed; and considering the extreme difficulty under which the county laboured, and would labour, for want of a legal appointed officer during such investigation, they asked, through the clerk, for an opinion on:

1 Whether such deputations by the coroner to execute the office at his pleasure or in his absence are legal and authorized.

2 If illegal, what steps are to be pursued to obtain the appointment of a proper person (other than the other county coroner who, on account of the duty he has to perform, is incapable of performing it) pro tempore and during such investigation to perform the duties as they ought to be done.

3 Whether a more summary investigation is to be obtained than by indictment or presentment at quarter sessions or assizes.

4 If the opinion should be that the only mode of obtaining an investigation is by indictment or presentment, would the coroner not be entitled to his traverse and, if so, would it not expedite the investigation to indict or present him at the next quarter sessions immediately after receiving it into King's Bench in order to obtain his plea in Trinity term? Or what other mode could be pursued for the more expeditious investigation of the charges intended to be preferred and for what offence beyond extortion is it necessary to exhibit him as in the event of his conviction to ensure his removal? [QCC/E2, no 65]

511 Revised draft of **510**. In Sussex there are 2 coroners elected by the freeholders, one being resident in and ordinarily acting for that part west of the Shoreham river[1] and containing Chichester, Arundel and Bramber rapes and a small part of Lewes rape, the other acting for the rest of Lewes rape and Pevensey rape. Hastings rape is under the jurisdiction of a coroner appointed by the earl of Chichester as lord of the honor of Hastings, with the exception of some hundreds for which the lords exercise a similar authority as possessed of a particular franchise; but the coroners of those as well as those appointed by the freeholders are paid out of the county stock. In consequence of a complaint laid before the JPs at the last Michaelmas quarter sessions in the eastern division that Wheeler, the coroner elected by the freeholders and acting in that division, had improperly exacted money from the relative of a female upon whom he had held an inquest as fees due to him, to which he gave no satisfactory answer, and because they believed that that was not an isolated case, the court ordered the clerk of the peace to inquire into his conduct by applying to the officers of the parishes in which inquests had been taken for some time back and in the meantime suspended the allowance of Wheeler's charges on the county. An inquiry was accordingly made and information sent to the clerk of the peace, by which it appeared that Wheeler made a frequent practice, on taking inquests, of demanding from the deceased's relatives or (on their inability to pay) from the parish officers sums of from £2 to £5 or more as and for fees and expenses on attending such inquests as coroner and for which attendance he regularly charged the county under 25 George II c 29. Such demands were sometimes complied with and at other times refused. He had also charged the county with some inquests which had never been taken and in many instances he had authorized others to take them, charging the county as if they were taken by him and with travelling expenses according to the distance from his ordinary place of residence. After those sessions and about a month before the last ones Wheeler was arrested and had ever since been in Horsham gaol. At the last sessions a bill was presented on Wheeler's behalf by a person calling himself his agent or deputy. It contained charges for inquests taken by the agent as under Wheeler's authority during his confinement and the court suspended its allowance pending further consideration. The JPs, wishing to protect the public from impositions by a county officer and to remove the inconvenience arising from the eastern division's having no legal or authorized officer at hand, requested opinion on the following questions:

1 Is the coroner in any respect justifiable in taking or demanding money of individuals or parishes as above or is not every such instance an act of extortion?

2 Are the facts reported by the clerk of the peace sufficient to institute proceedings and to effect the removal of such coroner from office; and what would be the most proper and expeditious method of proceeding for that purpose?

3 Can the quarter sessions legally, and ought it as a matter of propriety, order any prosecution for that purpose to be carried on at the county's expense?

4 During the continuance of the present coroner in office and his inability to execute his office in person, how can the deficit be supplied? Can he legally authorize anyone to take inquests for him? Or is there any power, and in whom, of appointing an extra coroner or a coroner pro tempore? Or, lastly, is it absolutely necessary in every case arising in the district to apply to the western coroner from places perhaps 50 or 60 miles from his residence? It is presumed that the Hastings rape coroner cannot act outside his franchise.

5 *Deleted.*

Upon further consideration the last query might as well be omitted as it might, by going into minutiae, take attention away from the main points. [QCC/E2, no 6]

1 sc. the Adur.

512 Statement of facts referred to in the second question of **511**. Summaries of the extortions and other misdeeds practised by Wheeler at the inquests (or concerning the alleged inquests) of 26 Sept., 7, 15, 17 and 31 Aug., 16 and 24 Sept. and 9 and

10 Oct. 1816, the undated inquest on John Payne and the inquest of 2 Sept. 1815, based on **477**, **479**, **481**, **484**, **485**, **488**, **489**, **491–494**, **497** and **502**. [QCC/E2, no 61]

513 Case for the opinion of the attorney-general sent by Messrs Palmer and France, Bedford Row, for the clerk of the peace for Sussex, identical to **511**, with the following opinions added by W Gasson, Lincoln's Inn, on 4 Feb. 1817 after the relevant questions:

1 The coroner is not justified in demanding or receiving, from either individuals or parish officers, any sum beyond his legal fees, but every such demand and receipt is an act of extortion.

2 The facts reported by the clerk of the peace are sufficient to warrant the instituting of proceedings by indictment against the coroner for malversation in his office and if he should be found guilty the judgment on such conviction would be sufficient ground for removing him from his office.

3 An order by quarter sessions for payment of the expenses of such prosecution out of the county rate could not by law be enforced.

4 He understood that the coroner appointed for Hastings rape alone cannot legally act as coroner for the county at large or beyond the limits of his own jurisdiction. The coroner for the eastern division of the county cannot legally appoint anyone as his deputy or authorize anyone to execute the duties of his office. No power exists in any person or body of men to appoint an extra coroner or a coroner pro tempore while the present coroner remains in office, although incapable of executing its duties. The only course, however expensive and inconvenient, is to apply to the county coroner usually acting, where he resides, in the western division.

There follows the statement of facts referred to in question 2, as in **512** except that the inquest of 26 Sept. is in its correct chronological position and there are more details on that of 9 Oct. derived from **479**. [QCC/E2, no 67]

514 21 Feb. 1817. Reply of J Stafford, Bow Street, to Langridge. The cases of extortion from individuals were clear enough. There was only one case of a charge made against the county for taking an inquest which was not taken. If there were any other such cases, whether or not the money was paid, he would like copies of the relevant bills, or the heads, conclusions and relevant charges if the bills were long. It would not be proper to have in the same bill extortion from individuals and obtaining or attempting to obtain by false charges the money of the county. Circuit subpoenas issued by Mr Knapp, deputy clerk of assize, should be sufficient to compel the witnesses' attendance.

[QCC/E2, no 52]

515 3 Mar. 1817. Letter from J Stafford, Bow Street, to Langridge. The suspension of the Habeas Corpus Act[1] was only partial and confined to those committed for high treason or treasonable practices and would not prevent him obtaining one to bring Wheeler into court to plead. [QCC/E2, no 54]

1 sc. 43 George III c 140.

516 9 Mar. 1817. Letter from J Stafford, Bow Street, to Langridge, sending drafts of 2 indictments[1] for correction and any necessary comments. When the bills were found the assize judge might, as a judge of Common Pleas, grant a writ of habeas corpus on the principle in 43 George III c 140[2] — no doubt if it was to bring the defendant to trial, less certain if only to plead to an indictment.

PS. Langridge might direct his agent (Lord Ellenborough[3] being in town) to inquire at the Crown Office in the Temple if they would issue a habeas corpus to bring a prisoner for debt in the county gaol into court at the assizes to plead to an indictment expected to be found against him for a misdemeanour. If he were not charged in execution the gaoler would not run much risk in bringing him into court without a writ. [QCC/E2, no 53]

1 **517, 518.**
2 An Act to enable judges of the central courts of record to award writs of habeas corpus for bringing persons in gaol before commissioners etc. for trial.
3 Chief Justice of King's Bench: *ODNB*.

517 Draft indictment (with corrections) of Thomas William Wheeler late of Brighton, who at the time of committing the following offences was one of the county coroners. There follow details of his extortions at the inquests of 2 Sept. 1815 and 7 and 31 Aug., 26 Sept., 9 and 10 Oct. and 15 Nov. 1816 based on **477**, **479**, **481**, **484**, **489**, **491**, **502** and **503**, none of the sums demanded and received being due to him from those who paid. [QCC/E2, no 2]

518 Draft indictment (with corrections) of Thomas William Wheeler late of Brighton, who on 18 Oct. 1816 and long before was one of the Sussex county coroners and as such was allowed to charge certain sums of money for executing his office by virtue of the statute, viz 20s for every inquest not taken on view of a body dying in gaol and for every mile which he should be compelled to travel from his usual place of abode to take such inquest the further sum of 9d over and above the said 20s out of the monies arising from the county rates, of which allowances and charges Wheeler as coroner quarterly during the time he was such coroner made out an account and presented the same to the JPs in their quarter sessions at Lewes to be paid by order of the JPs out of the monies arisng from the rates; and it was Wheeler's duty as coroner quarterly during the time he was coroner to make out and deliver to the JPs a just and true account of all such charges and allowances in order that the same should be ordered to be paid as directed by the statute, viz at Lewes. Wheeler, well knowing the premises and being an evil disposed person and devising, contriving and intending as much as in him lay wickedly, fraudulently and unjustly to obtain and acquire to himself divers sums of money out of the county rates by imposing upon and deceiving the JPs by making false charges for taking inquests and for travelling to take the same when in truth no such inquests had been taken, viz for the alleged inquest of 15 Aug. 1816 and the undated inquest allegedly on John Payne (with relevant extracts from **191**). [QCC/E2, no 1]

519 10 Mar. 1817. Letter from George Palmer, Bedford Row, to Langridge. His clerk in court said, and Mr Platt, Lord Ellenborough's clerk, agreed, that Langridge was not entitled to a habeas corpus to bring the defendant to plead to an indictment for a misdemeanour until the assizes after the finding of the bill, he being not bound to appear and plead until then. But if he chose to appear and plead at the forthcoming assizes, which was unlikely, Langridge would probably be able to get Mr Knapp[1] to attend at the gaol and take the plea, first mentioning it to the judge. [QCC/E2, no 58]

1 Deputy clerk of assize: cf. **514**.

520 16 Mar. 1817. Letter from J Stafford, London, to Langridge. He thought it sufficient for the indictment for extortion to prove that Wheeler acted as coroner at the times when he took the pretended fees and that in the other case he presented the bill or that it was in his handwriting and contained the false charges alleged. It might be worth considering if other evidence might not be necessary at the trial. [QCC/E2, no 48]

521 17 Mar. 1817. Letter from George Palmer, Bedford Row, to Langridge. He had no doubt that the grand jury would find the bill if those who proved the extortions should prove that at the time he demanded the money he acted as county coroner in taking the inquests and demanded and received the money for taking them. There would be no need to produce the return. Palmer would be at the assizes. He attended Wheeler's election as under-sheriff and returned the writ of election and would prove it before the grand jury if necessary, but not in order to prove the bill. [QCC/E2, no 47]

522 12 Feb. 1817. Draft writ to Martha Paine, Joseph Ockenden, Ann Chapman and [*blank*] to be at Horsham assizes on 24 Mar. to testify before the grand jury against Wheeler for misdemeanours, under penalty of £100. [QCC/E2, no 44]

523 12 Feb. 1817. Draft writ, similar to **522**, to Robert Rogers, Edward Page and Joel Beeching. [QCC/E2, no 46]

524 12 Feb. 1817. Draft writ, similar to **522**, but omitting addressees.

Endorsed by W B Langridge, solicitor for the prosecution, Lewes, 13 Mar.: You are required to meet me at the King's Head Inn at Horsham on 24 Mar. at 10 a.m. at farthest — enquire for me at the bar of the inn immediately upon your arrival there.

Attached. In pencil: Mr Edward Freeman, carpenter, Mr William Freeman, cordwainer, near the Burrells Arms, West Grinstead; Mrs Chapman, Rottingdean. *In ink*: 26 Sept. 1816 inquisition on Ann Freeman of Rottingdean, 23s paid by the husband; 15 Aug. 1816 at Newhaven on the child of Ockenden, a boat officer; 11 Oct. 1816 on John Payne of Brighton. [QCC/E2, no 45]

525 Very brief abstract of **517** with the following witnesses wanted for the inquests of: 2 Sept. 1815, James Turner of Southwick; 7 Aug. 1816, [*blank*][1] Beard and Thomas Fairhall of Lindfield; 31 Aug. 1816, Joel Beeching of Mayfield; 26 Sept. 1816, [*blank*][2] Freeman of Rottingdean; 9 Oct. 1816, Edward Page and Robert Rogers of Frant; 10 Oct. 1816, John Golds of Henfield; 15 Nov. 1816, William Reeves of Old Shoreham. Similar abstract of **518** concerning inquests on an infant choked and John Payne.

Note: To prove the bill of charges by [*blank*]; that no inquests were held by [*blank*]; to ascertain the pretence for which the charge of £1 3s demanded of Freeman of Rottingdean was made.

Endorsed: Minutes on indictments and evidence before grand jury. Turner 1; Beard and Fairhall 1; Beeching and Page 1; Golds and Freeman 1; Reeves and Newhaven man 1; Newhaven woman 1; Sampson 1. [QCC/E2, no 59]

1 *William*: cf. **489**.
2 *Edward*: cf. **492**.

526 Abstract of **517** with the following witnesses for the inquests of: 2 Sept. 1815, James Turner; 7 Aug. 1816, Thomas Fairhall; 31 Aug. 1816, Joel Beeching;[1] 26 Sept. 1816, Ann Chapman; 9 Oct. 1816, Robert Rogers and Edward Page; 10 Oct. 1816, John Golds; 15 Nov. 1816, William Reeves. [QCC/E2, no 56]

1 The deceased is named as William Wood in error for Edward Young.

527 Abstract of **518** with the following witnesses for the inquests on: a child choked with a plum-stone, Joseph Ockenden, the father; John Payne, his daughter Martha Payne. Thomas Sacre would produce Wheeler's bill and prove the handwriting. [QCC/E2, no 57]

528 26 Feb. 1817. Letter from ?W Lamb, vestry clerk, Frant, to Langridge. The churchwardens and overseers of Frant would hold themselves liable to pay £20 towards the expenses of the prosecution of Wheeler for illicit conduct in the execution of his office. [QCC/E2, no 29]

529 23 Mar. [1817]. Note of various payments made in Rex v Wheeler, including £11 4s to Stafford, £1 to Ockenden, 9s to Reeves and £20 to Sacre. [QCC/E2, no 60]

530 24 Mar. 1817. At Horsham assizes the grand jury, to which James Turner, Thomas Fairhall, Joel Beeching, Ann Chapman, Robert Rogers, Edward Page, John Golds and William Reeves gave evidence, presented an indictment virtually identical to **517**. Wheeler pleaded not guilty and traversed the indictment and was remanded in gaol until the next assizes unless in the meantime he entered into a recognizance in £100 with 2 sureties in £50 each to enter and try his traverse at the next assizes. He was also detained in custody on a writ of capias ad satisfaciendum at the suit of Edward Cobby Sharpin for £31 13s 4d and on an attachment for contempt of court for non-payment of £1859 11s 5d upon an award pursuant to a rule of court with the costs of attachment. [ASSI 94/1755]

531 24 Mar. 1817. At Horsham assizes the grand jury, to which Thomas Sacre, Joseph Ockenden and Martha Payne gave evidence, presented an indictment virtually identical to **518**. Plea, traverse, remand and detention as in **530**. [ASSI 94/1755]

532 William T Roe, W Roe and Co., to Langridge. To move that Wheeler, a county coroner charged in 2 indictments with malversation in office and a debtor confined in Horsham gaol, might be brought into court to plead.

Note: Mr Roe's fee paid at Easter sessions,[1] £1 3s 6d. [QCC/E2, no 43]

1 sc. *18 Apr. 1817*

533 Letter from Lord Egremont, Petworth, to the earl of Chichester[1] concerning the current difficulties in the eastern division, with the coroner imprisoned for debt and the western coroner being so distant, and the need for an easier method for removing improper and incapable coroners and for providing lawful substitutes in cases of temporary incapacity, e.g. sickness. [SAS/A 748]

1 Joint Postmaster General and formerly a Sussex MP: *ODNB*.

534 17 Apr. 1817. Letter from Wheeler, Horsham, to G Shiffner, MP, begging him to intercede for him with the court to allow his bills as coroner, or such part of them as should be considered due, to relieve his wife, 2 small children and mother from some degree of their distress and misery resulting from his long imprisonment, over 4 months. He had no relations able to render any assistance. [QCC/E2, no 51]

535 [24] Apr. 1817. Draft letter from Langridge to Sir Godfrey Webster, bt, and Walter Burrell, esq. There were 2 coroners elected by the freeholders of Sussex, one for the western and the other for the eastern division. In the latter Wheeler had for several months been incapable of executing his office, being confined for debt in the sheriff's gaol, in addition to which an indictment was pending against him for malversation in his office, to be tried at the ensuing assizes. By law no one but one of the elected coroners could take an inquest, no deputy being allowed, so that inquests in the eastern division had then to be taken by the western coroner who lived at least 50 miles from many parts of the east. It was presumed that, as a result, many cases were not being investigated, and if the western coroner could not attend from illness or accident the whole county would have no investigating officer. The JPs had therefore instructed Langridge to suggest to Webster and Burrell, as Sussex MPs, a conference with the attorney-general to consider the propriety of applying to Parliament for a change in the law. [QCC/E2, no 50]

536 1 May 1817. Walter Burrell's reply to **535**. He had conferred with the attorney-general who was opposed to drawing up a bill to amend the law on coroners, saying that the chancellor had the power to remove a coroner for malversation, which in Wheeler's case had to be proved by following up the indictment against him, and that he would never agree to power being given to JPs in quarter sessions to remove coroners for malversation or incapacity. It would be hopeless to try to pass such a bill through Parliament without the law officers' approval. [QCC/E2, no 40]

537 1 and 2 May 1817. Letters from Lord Middleton to the earl of Chichester concerning possible methods of removing coroners and defraying the expense. [SAS/A 748]

538 Copy of documents relating to a Somerset case:

13 Jan. 1817. Petition of the JPs at Somerset quarter sessions for a writ de coronatore exonerando to discharge from office Richard Phillips of Queen Camel who had neglected to discharge his duties as county coroner since June 1816 and had been absent from home since then and whose estates, goods and chattels had been seized into the king's hands and sold for debt in Oct.; and for a writ de coronatore eligendo.

31 Jan. 1817. Affidavit by the clerk of the peace that he would give due notice of the time and place for the execution of the second writ. On 8 Jan. he went to the coroner's house and found it shut up and unoccupied as it had been since June. His estate and effects had been seized and sold for debt and he had left the county and was unlikely to return.

11 Feb. 1817. Order of the Lord Chancellor to the cursitor of Somerset to make out a writ de coronatore amovendo.

12 Feb. 1817. Similar order for the issue of a de coronatore eligendo. [QCC/E2, no 39]

539 9 June 1817. Reply of the earl of Chichester, Stratton Street, to a letter from Langridge which had enclosed a copy of a letter from Wheeler. JPs out of sessions cannot stop the proceedings already entered, but he would agree to the withdrawing of the prosecution if Wheeler resigned, as he understood that a criminal prosecution was resorted to as the only means then thought competent to remove him. [QCC/E2, no 41]

540 14 June 1817. Reply of James ?Bird, Cuckfield, to Langridge's letter of 11 June which had enclosed a copy of a letter from Wheeler. The parish of Frant and ?Bird would approve whatever Langridge recommended. [QCC/E2, no 42]

541 19 July 1817. Letter from Wheeler, Horsham gaol, to Langridge. He had sent his affidavit, about the inquests taken by him, by post on 17 July for Langridge to lay before the JPs on 18 July. What were their observations on them and what did they decide about the indictments pending against him? [QCC/E2, no 4]

542 22 July 1817. Letter from Wheeler, Horsham gaol, to Langridge, enclosing a petition Langridge had asked for. A similar petition had been sent to Wheeler's agent, Mr Hilditch of 12 Sidmouth Street, Gray's Inn Road. He hoped there was no difficulty in accepting his resignation. He was grateful to the JPs for allowing his bill, regretted his offence to them and hoped they would accept his apology instead of continuing to prosecute the indictments, which would ruin him, his wife and his innocent children.

PS. He regretted that he could not show any preference to Mr Hodd and had written to him about it. He sent him 10s for the receipt stamp as Langridge had filled it up. He asked Langridge to get it and send it to Wheeler or, if he could not, send Wheeler the receipt form. [QCC/E2, no 3]

543 2 Aug. 1817. Writ to the sheriff of Sussex to remove Wheeler from office, he having held it ever since his election as county coroner on 16 Oct. 1809 but was currently confined to Horsham gaol charged in execution for debt and wholly unable to satisfy it, there being no prospect of his discharge from gaol, and otherwise much embarrassed in his pecuniary circumstances, having no means of relieving himself, and therefore no longer able to execute the duties of his office.

Endorsed by James Cranbourne Strode, sheriff, that he had removed him from office. [C 202/205/20]

544 4 Aug. 1817. Writ to the sheriff of Sussex for the election of a coroner in place of Wheeler who could not perform the duty of county coroner and whom the king had removed from office.

Endorsed by James Cranbourne Strode, sheriff, that George Gwynne had been elected and sworn in place of Wheeler. [C 202/205/20]

545 9 Aug. 1817. At Lewes assizes Wheeler, aged 29, who had been charged at the Horsham assizes of 24 Mar. and pleaded, traversed, was remanded and detained as in **530** and **531**, was acquitted and discharged. [ASSI 94/1756]

546 18 Aug. 1817. Letter from Messrs Palmer and France, solicitors, Bedford Row, London, to Langridge, enclosing rough copies of:

1 Wheeler's petition to Lord Eldon, Lord Chancellor, that he was elected a Sussex county coroner on 16 Oct. 1809 and had held the office ever since, but being in Horsham gaol for debt and unable to satisfy it and there being no prospect of his discharge from gaol and being otherwise much embarrassed in his pecuniary circumstances and unable to execute the duties of his office, desired to resign it. Witness to Wheeler's signature Thomas Charles Medwin, master extraordinary in Chancery.

2 Wheeler's affidavit repeating the above facts.

3 Langridge's affidavit that Wheeler's annexed petition was delivered to him by Wheeler on 13 July; that he well knew Wheeler as coroner, having been present at his election, knew his handwriting and believed his name subscribed to the petition to be his handwriting; and that he also knew the handwriting of Medwin of Horsham, attorney-at-law, and believed the name subscribed to the petition as witness was his handwriting.

4 Certificate of the JPs at the quarter sessions of 18 July that Wheeler's petition was presented to them in open court by Langridge and they accepted his resignation.

On the above proceedings the Lord Chancellor made an order for a writ de coronatore amovendo, which issued.

5 Petition of the freeholders of Sussex to the Lord Chancellor for a writ de coronatore eligendo for a new coroner in place of Wheeler to be made out without delay, they having learned that he had petitioned, or was about to, for permission to resign and the county having already experienced considerable inconvenience from his having been prevented from attending his duties.

6 Undertaking of 28 July by Thomas France, Bedford Row, a solicitor of Chancery, that due notice should be given in all the market towns of Sussex of the time and place of the writ de coronatore eligendo 6 days before its execution.

Thereon the Lord Chancellor made an order for a writ de coronatore eligendo, which issued. [QCC/E2, no 5]

547 Wheeler's petition to the JPs at the Lewes quarter sessions of 18 July 1817 to be allowed to resign as county coroner (details as in **546**, item 1). Witness to his signature Thomas Charles Medwin, master extraordinary in Chancery.

Certificate of the JPs as in **546**, item 4, but ending: they accepted his resignation so far as it pertained to them.

Langridge's affidavit as in **546**, item 3, sworn at Lewes on 24 July before Thomas Cooper, master extraordinary in Chancery.

Wheeler's petition to the Lord Chancellor as in **546**, item 1.

Wheeler's affidavit as in **546**, item 2, sworn and signed.

Petition of freeholders as in **546**, item 5.

France's undertaking as in **546**, item 6. [QCC/E2, no 64]

548 26 Sept. 1817. Epitome of proceedings against Wheeler. At Horsham spring assizes 2 indictments were preferred for malversation in his office which the grand jury returned as true bills, whereupon a habeas corpus was immediately obtained from the judge under which Wheeler (then a prisoner in Horsham gaol for debt) was brought up to plead and pleaded guilty to both indictments. They were then traversed to trial at the next summer assizes and Wheeler was remanded for want of bail. On 5 June the clerk of the peace received from Wheeler by post a letter of the same date saying that he intended to forward a resignation from his office and asking that his intentions be communicated to the JPs. Later, and a few days before the quarter sessions, a petition was delivered to the clerk addressed to the JPs praying that he might be permitted to resign. The clerk presented the petition and the letter of 5 June to the JPs at the quarter sessions who, considering the situation of Wheeler and his family (his wife and several small children), ordered that further proceedings on the indictments should be stayed and, in the event of his resignation being accepted by the chancellor or a writ de coronatore amovendo being otherwise granted by him, abandoned.

The epitome, with extracts of the charges in the indictments and Wheeler's letter to the JPs, was for delivery to George Shiffner, esq., and forwarding to the earl of Egremont. [QCC/E2, no 63]

549 3 Apr. 1818. Order by quarter sessions for the payment of Langridge's bill of £125 18s 7d for prosecuting Wheeler. [QO/EW 43]

INDEX OF PERSONS

Arabic numbers refer to entries, small roman numbers to pages.

Every number following a forename with an asterisk refers to a different person of that name; where there is no asterisk the numbers all refer to the same person.

The following abbreviations are used for the most frequently occurring forenames:

Alex	Alexander	Fran	Francis	Mic	Michael
And	Andrew	Fred	Frederick	Nat	Nathaniel
Ant	Anthony	Geo	George	Nic	Nicholas
Bart	Bartholomew	Hen	Henry	Phil	Philip
Ben	Benjamin	Hum	Humphrey	Ric	Richard
Cath	Catherine	Jas	James	Rob	Robert
Chas	Charles	Jn	John	Rog	Roger
Chris	Christopher	Jos	Joseph	Sam	Samuel
Dan	Daniel	Lawr	Lawrence	Ste	Stephen
Edm	Edmund	Margt	Margaret	Thos	Thomas
Edw	Edward	Mat	Matthew	Wal	Walter
Eliz	Elizabeth			Wm	William

INDEX OF PLACES

Places are in Sussex unless otherwise stated.

INDEX OF SUBJECTS

Most subjects are arranged in groups under the following main headings: Army buildings; Army personnel; Army regiments and corps; Boats and ships; Building material; Buildings; Clothing; Containers; Criminal and other offences; Farm equipment and other tools; Farm produce; Food and drink; Household articles; Land; Livestock and other fauna; Occupations; Officials; Punishment; Records; Roads and paths; Sports and pastimes; Vehicles; Weapons and ammunition.